Perelman's Pocket Cyclopedia of Cigars

1998 edition

Compiled by
Richard B. Perelman

Published by
**PERELMAN
PIONEER &
COMPANY**

Los Angeles, California

$ 9.95 U.S.

ISBN 0-9649258-5-0

Published in Los Angeles, California, USA. First printing 1997. Printed by Pace Lithographers, Inc. of Industry, California. Cover photography by Long Photography, Inc. of Los Angeles, California.

Please address inquiries to:

PERELMAN PIONEER & COMPANY

POST OFFICE BOX 67B99
CENTURY CITY STATION
LOS ANGELES, CALIFORNIA 90067 USA

Things will never be
the same again.

HERDMAN Distributors inc.

Introducing our new family.
The Adventure continues...

Premium Honduran Cigars

Limited Reserve

CHIEF

TEEPEE

TOMAHAWK

BOXER

CHIEF

Indian Tabac Cigar Co.

Perelman's Pocket Cyclopedia of Cigars

1998 edition

TABLE OF CONTENTS

TABLE OF CONTENTS

Please send comments, inquiries, questions and suggestions to the author at:

PERELMAN, PIONEER & COMPANY
POST OFFICE BOX 67B99
CENTURY CITY STATION
LOS ANGELES, CALIFORNIA 90067 USA

Telephone: (213) 965-4905
Facsimile: (213) 965-4919

subscribe to

S M O K E

cigars, pipes and life's other burning desires

fashion, cars,
technology,
music, books,
and the best
damn cigars
in the world.

CALL
1-800-766-2633

or look for us on the Internet at
http://www.smokemag.com

INTRODUCTION

"I'm tired."

> — Madeline Kahn as Lili von Shtupp
> in *Blazing Saddles* (1974)

That's about how I feel as our fourth edition of the *Perelman's Pocket Cyclopedia of Cigars* goes to press. The wild ride that is the cigar industry in the United States seemed to career out of control as new brands were introduced at the rate of more than one a day!

In handmade cigars — the focus of most of the industry — the number of brands in national distribution reached 961 by our count. This is an increase of **95 percent** from our 1997 edition, mirroring the 97.1 percent increase in imports of large cigars for the 12 months ended July 1997, according to the Cigar Association of America. And, of course, our tally does not count the roughly 50-100 locally-distributed house brands of cigar lounges and smokeshops across the nation.

All of this activity is even more amazing in the face of continued pressure on tobacco at the legislative and regulatory levels. Now that this year's book is completed, maybe I can have a cigar and think about this contradiction.

As always, our goal is to try to bring some discipline to the classification to the 1,138 brands on the U.S. market today in this, our fourth annual compilation.

Here are a few tips to help users of this book, to make your exploration and research efforts more fun:

INTRODUCTION

About this book:

We have provided critical details on a lot of cigars. A total of 1,138 brands are profiled, comprising more than 7,000 different models. When considering the growth of the cigar trade in the U.S., compare that total to the 659 brands we profiled in the 1997 edition, the 457 brands in the 1996 edition or 370 brands in our first edition in 1995.

We note that our listing represents virtually every brand marketed nationally. Readers will find some brands which are not listed here, but which are available at his or her local smokeshop. These brands are very likely:

▸ Private label, unbranded cigars offered in bundles by major manufacturers, on which store names are placed for local sale;

▸ House brands produced for individual cigar lounges or retailers, which are not generally available through wholesalers for national distribution to tobacco stores;

▸ Cigars produced in limited quantities by small, local factories and marketed regionally;

▸ New lines introduced after this book was completed;

▸ Close-outs or discontinued brands which are no longer available from manufacturers.

This should not dissuade readers from trying or enjoying these cigars. We actively encourage everyone to try new cigars and refrain from the kind of "cigar snobbery" which is so easy for premium cigar smokers to fall into. *The best cigar you will ever smoke might be the next one you try.*

That's how I have discovered many of my favorite brands; I try to keep up with new products by buying one or two cigars of a new brand and note my reaction to it on a small index card. After a while, some of these "new" cigars become favorites that are integrated into the rotation of brands that I already like – an experience that would have been missed if the opportunity to try new brands was dismissed.

About the brands:
Another contradiction comes in the area of supply. Even though there are shortages of many brands as demand has outstripped supply, hundreds of new brands are being introduced! As regards our listings, this situation has had an important impact in many ways:

▸ We have tried to list, for each handmade brand, the country of origin of the wrapper, filler and binder. While we have received wonderful cooperation from the manufacturers and distributors, more than one executive has told us something like, "This is what we would like to use, but if we can't get it, we will blend in something else."

In most cases, this should *not* be of great concern. After all, most consumers buy specific cigars based on an expectation of taste and draw, not on the ingredients. Recent history shows that master blenders have little difficulty re-configuring brands with different tobaccos to achieve the same taste and quality of construction. But . . .

There are also brands from smaller factories which have limited access to the quality and type of tobacco that they would like to use. Their blends may change considerably, as will the taste of their brands. *Buyer beware* is the watchword for some brands, which may change considerably as they go through the seasons. We can say that the information we present here is an accurate "snapshot" of these brands in the fall of 1997.

About the shapes:
The cigar boom has changed the style and type of cigars preferred by smokers. Three obvious trends have emerged during the last year:

‣ Cigars with larger and larger ring gauges. Where lonsdales were considered large cigars in years past, we now see robustos, churchills and double coronas as standard smokes for many. As the desire for more and more complex flavors grows, we will continue to see this trend expand.

‣ More and more smokers are attracted to shaped cigars, such as perfectos, torpedoes and pyramids. These are hard to make and carry a premium price, but continue to grow in popularity. Hard to find just 3-4 years ago, there are now hundreds of brands which include these shapes in their line.

‣ Wild mutations in size, color and flavor are on the rise. Consider the "barber pole" or "candy cane" cigar which features a double wrapper for a striped effect. Or the number of lines which offer cigars of more than 9 inches and ring gauges of 60 or more. Or the explosion of flavored cigars in every imaginable style!

A list of the brands which feature these extra large, extra long or striped-wrapper cigars is listed in section 2.04, along with a list of brands which are artificially flavored.

Cuban cigars:
Because of our concentration on cigars available in the U.S., listings of cigars produced in Cuba are not included. In response to many requests for this information, however. we have produced a companion volume, *Perelman's Pocket Cyclopedia of Havana Cigars,* available through your local tobacconist or by writing to us directly.

The future:
The "smart set" in the cigar industry has predicted the demise of hundreds of brands in 1998 as consumers become more sophisticated and begin to attach themselves to specific brands. However, there is always room for another quality cigar and 1998 will bring hundreds of new brands, perhaps to replace many others which will perish for lack of interest, sales or supply of tobacco. For better or worse, these will be cataloged in our 1999 edition.

With our thanks:
This book could not have been produced without a tremendous amount of help from many people in and around the cigar industry. Representatives of most every manufacturer and distributor in the country endured many telephone calls

INTRODUCTION

requesting information, and virtually everyone we contacted was not only forthcoming, but enthusiastic about the project.

I would like to express special thanks to individuals whose efforts went far beyond the norm; without them, this book would not have been produced: Jules Abbosh, Fernando Alvarez, Oscar Boruchin, Reagan Brewer, Sam Clark, Alan Edwards, Mark Estrin, Dickson Farrington, Carol Jean Llaneza, Dr. Steve Nathan, Ph.C., Brad Part, Janelle Rosenfeld, Amy Townsend, Eric Workman and Arthur Zaretsky. And the help of our editorial staff: assistant editors Bruce Dworshak and Bruce Tenen and associate editor Mitchel Sloan, without whom this work could not have been completed.

I hope that our readers will enjoy our work; if you have suggestions on how to make this book better, we would be pleased to hear from you; our address follows the Table of Contents.

We will also be pleased to meet our readers, either in person at our LE CIGAR NOIR festivals which we produce around the nation in cooperation with our friends at *Smoke* magazine, or on-line at the CigarCafe site on America Online (keyword: CigarCafe). I hope to see you in a smoke-filled room soon!

RICHARD B. PERELMAN
Los Angeles, California
November 1997

Profesor Sila

Superior Quality Hand Made Cigar Producers
-1934-

HECHO TOTALMENTE A MANO

Mild Flavor

1.
CIGAR BASICS

1.01 ABOUT CIGARS

The joy of smoking rolled tobacco leaves began in the Americas hundreds of years ago and was introduced to Europeans after Christopher Columbus' return from his first voyage in 1492.

In the ensuing years, the popularity and sophistication of tobacco products has grown and the 1990s has brought a significant increase in the popularity of cigars in the United States. Despite much controversy, the status of cigars as a luxury product in American culture is secure.

The important technical elements to be appreciated in cigars include their construction and the many shapes and sizes.

1.02 CONSTRUCTION

What goes into cigars? The answer to this question is the key to assessing the quality of a specific cigar. All but the thinnest cigars include three elements: (1) the filler tobacco at the center, (2) a binder leaf which holds the filler together and (3) the outer wrapper, which is rolled around the binder.

Cigars which are made by hand use "long filler" tobacco: leaves which run the length of a cigar. In a handmade, the filler, binder and wrapper are combined manually to create a cigar.

Machine-made cigars utilize high-speed machinery to combine "short filler" tobacco - usually scraps or pieces of tobacco -

with a binder and wrapper. Because of the tension placed on the tobacco by the machines, the binders and wrappers are often made of a homogenized tobacco product which is stronger than natural leaves and can be produced in a variety of flavors, strengths and textures.

A few brands combine machine-bunching (using long-filler tobacco) with hand-rolled wrappers; this practice has been very properly dubbed "hand-rolled" as opposed to handmade by cigar expert Rick Hacker in *The Ultimate Cigar Book*. And some larger cigars use "mixed" or "combination" filler of long-filler and short-filler tobaccos.

The most obvious characteristic of most cigars is the color of the exterior wrapper. While not the only factor in the taste of a cigar, it is an important element and a key in many people's purchase of specific cigars. Although manufacturers have identified more than 100 different wrapper shades, six major color classifications are used herein, as noted below:

Color	Abbrev.	Description
Double Claro	*"DC"*	Also known as "American Market Selection" [AMS] or "Candela," this is a green wrapper. Once popular, it is rarely found today.
Claro	*"Cl"*	This is a very light tan color, almost beige in shade; usually from Connecticut.
Colorado Claro	*"CC"*	A medium brown found on many cigars, this category covers many descriptions. The most popular are "Natural" or "English Market Selection" [EMS]. Tobaccos in this shade are grown in many countries.

CIGAR BASICS

Color	Abbrev.	Description
Colorado	*"Co"*	This shade is instantly recognizable by the obvious reddish tint.
Colorado Maduro	*"CM"*	Darker than Colorado Claro in shade, this color is often associated with African tobacco, such as wrappers from Cameroon, or with Havana Seed tobacco grown in Honduras.
Maduro	*"Ma"*	Very dark brown or black; this category also includes the deep black "Oscuro" shade. Tobacco for Maduro wrappers is grown in Connecticut, Mexico, Nicaragua and Brazil.

The listing of cigar brands in this book assumes that, unless otherwise noted, handmade cigars utilize long-filler tobacco and machine-made cigars use short-filler.

1.03   SHAPES AND SIZES

There are cigars of every shape and every size for every occasion. From tiny, cigarette-like cigarillos to giant monsters resembling pool cues, there is a wide variety to choose from.

Certain sizes and shapes which have gained popularity over the years and have become widely recognized, even by non-smokers. Cigar shape names such as "corona" or "panatela" have specific meanings to the cigar industry, although there is no formally agreed-to standard for any given size.

The following table lists 19 well-known shapes, and is adapted from Paul Garmirian's explanation of sizes in *The Gourmet Guide to Cigars*. The "classical" measurements for which this shape is known are given, along with a size and girth range for each size for classification purposes:

Shape	*Classical Lngth. x Ring*	*Length range*	*Ring range*
Giant	9 x 52	8 & up	50 & up
Double Corona	7¾ x 49	6¾-7¾	49-54
Churchill	7 x 47	6¾-7⅞	46-48
Pyramid	7 x 36⇒54	all	flared
Torpedo	6½ x 52	all	tapered
Toro	6 x 50	5⅝-6⅝	48-54
Robusto	5 x 50	4½-5½	48-54
Grand Corona	6½ x 46	5⅝-6⅝	45-47
Corona Extra	5½ x 46	4½-5½	45-47
Giant Corona	7½ x 44	7½ & up	42-45
Lonsdale	6½ x 42	6½-7¼	40-44
Long Corona	6 x 42	5⅞-6⅜	40-44
Corona	5½ x 42	5¼-5¾	40-44
Petit Corona	5 x 42	4-5	40-44
Long Panatela	7½ x 38	7 & up	35-39
Panatela	6 x 38	5½-6⅞	35-39
Short Panatela	5 x 38	4-5⅜	35-39
Slim Panatela	6 x 34	5 & up	30-34
Small Panatela	5 x 33	4-5	30-34
Cigarillos	4 x 26	6 & less	29 & less

For the purposes of classification, the cigar models of the 1,138 brands profiled have been separated into these 19 major groups. Other shapes worth noting include:

- Culebras, which is made up of three small cigars twisted

together. Davidoff is now the only brand offering this shape on the U.S. market today.

▸ Perfecto, which has two tapered ends. Until recently, there were just a few cigars which offered Perfecto "tips" on the foot, but true Perfectos are making a comeback. For the bold, take a look at the Puros Indios Gran Victoria (10 inches long by 60 ring) to see a true "pot-bellied" cigar.

▸ Torpedo, which was traditionally a fat cigar with two fully closed, pointed ends, but has now come to mean a cigar with an open foot and a straight body which tapers to a closed, pointed head. This "new" torpedo was popularized by the Montecristo (Havana) No. 2.

The Torpedo differs from "Pyramid"-shaped cigars, which flare continuously from the head to the foot, essentially forming a triangle.

Like the Torpedo, whose meaning has changed over time, the Royal Corona or Rothschild title is seen less and less on cigars now known as "Robustos." This change has been rapid over the past 4-5 years, but some manufacturers still label their shorter, thicker cigars as Rothschilds or even as a "Rothchild" (an incorrect spelling of the famous German banking family name). A few manufacturers use both and label their 5-5½-inch, 50-ring models as "Robustos" and reserve the "Rothschild" name for shorter, but still 50-ring, cigars of 4-4½ inches!

Many other shape names are used by manufacturers; some cigars even have multiple names. For the sake of convenience,

Big cigars:
Double Coronas and Giants

These are very large cigars, in fact, some of the largest available. The dimensions of these shapes include:

- Double Corona   6¾-7¾ inches long; 49-54 ring.
- Giant   8 inches and more; 50 ring and more.

Pictured opposite are:

‣ **ESPANOLA RED LABEL** *Fabuloso*		*(shape)*
(Dominican Republic)	8 x 52	Giant
‣ **ST. GEORGE** *Dragonslayer*		
(Dominican Republic)	8 x 50	Giant
‣ **COSSACK** *Tsar*		
(Nicaragua)	8 x 54	Giant
‣ **JUAN CLEMENTE** *Gargantua*		
(Dominican Republic)	13 x 50	Giant
‣ **DON TOMAS** *Gigantes*		
(Honduras)	8½ x 52	Giant
‣ **KING DOMINICAN** *No. 9*		
(Dominican Republic)	10 x 66	Giant

Worth noting: the King Dominican No. 9's ring gauge of 66 is one of the largest you can buy in a regular-production, straight-sided cigar which is available in the United States. The record? The Hannibal Emperador has a ring gauge of 125!

the many types of small, very thin cigars are grouped under the "Cigarillo" title rather than distributed over a long list of names such as "Belvederes," "Demi-Tasse" and others.

1.04 ENJOYING CIGARS

The enjoyment of cigars is a personal pleasure, which is as varied as the 1,138 brands profiled. However, there are certain matters which should be considered carefully by all smokers and which require attention.

- ▸ Foremost among these is storage and the usefulness of a humidor in proper working condition cannot be underestimated. The death of a quality cigar due to a lack of care is a sad occurrence indeed.

- ▸ For those carrying cigars on the go, travel humidors or leather cigar cases are important items to keep your cigars safe and in good smoking condition.

- ▸ Finally, the proper tools for cutting and lighting your cigar are necessary accessories for full enjoyment.

Other authors have written extensively on these topics and references to leading books on cigars are listed in section 9. Each offers many suggestions on how to enjoy and store cigars and many details about the history and manufacture of cigars.

In addition, ***an often under-utilized resource for the smoker is your local smokeshop.*** Most are experienced, knowledgeable and have access to experts, manufacturers and the Retail Tobacco Dealers of America trade association. Use their expertise to help you!

2.
THE CIGAR ALMANAC

Here are facts, figures and a little fun about the 1,138 brands (961 handmades, 124 mass-market and 53 small cigars) profiled in this year's edition:

2.01 BIRTHS AND DEATHS

The cigar renaissance has led to an explosion of 514 new handmade brands introduced since our 1997 edition, contrasted with 170 in the 1997 edition and the 56 new handmades listed in the 1997 Cyclopedia:

Handmade (514):

A.T. Cofino
Absoluto
Acapa Sweets
Alamo
Alpha Candela Cubana
Amoroso
Anacaona
Ancla y Cazador
Andros
Andulleros
Anillo de Plata
Antillas Toro Bravo
Antonio y Cleopatra Private Reserve
Aperitif
Aqua D'T
Armenter Reservas
Aromella
Artus
Aruba
Ashé
Azteca Dominican Maduro
Bagatelle
Bahia Gold
Bahia Maduro

Bahia Trinidad
Bali Hai
Bandera
Bandoleros
Bellero
Belmondo
Ben Miguel
Biarritz
Big Chief
Bijao
Bijao Classico
Blair Silver Label
Blue Chip
Bogar
Bohio (Honduras)
Bohio (Dom. Rep.)
Bolivar
Boom Boom El Campeon
Boss
Boyero
Boyero Primero
Bravos (Canary Islands)
Bravos (Mexico)
Breton Legend

Briones
Bufido
Bulldog
Burma
Caleyes
Cammano
Camorra Limited Reserve
  Dominican Vintage
Campeones
Caoba Gold
Caoba Platinum
Capricho Cubano
Carabana
Carlos Oliva
Carlos Toraño (Nicaragua)
Carmen Platinum Label
Carmen White Label
Carnival Havana
Carnival Havana Supreme
Casa de Gonzalez
Casa de Klafter
Cascada
Castaño
Cavana
Cecil Brooks III
Cedar Joe Dulce
Chacaro Black Stallion
Charles Fairmorn Connshade
Chessman Royal Reserve
Christiano Leoné Director's Selection
Churchill
Cibao
Cielo Umo
Cigar Compadres
The Cigar Connection
Cigarros Cibao
Cimarron
Cimero
Cinco Vegas
Cinco Vegas Vintage
Cisso

Cisso Premium Loma
Clipper Gold Reserve
Classico de Continental
Club Sweets
Columbus
Commandante
Confedacion Suiza
Connoisseur's Choice
Conquistador
Copa Havana
Cossack
Coticas
Credo Ligas
Cremosa Cubanos
Creston
Creston "Los Montes"
Cristal de Venezuela
Crown Achievement
Crown Classics
Cruz Real Special Edition
Cruzado Reserva Especial
Cruzado Reserva Grande
Cu-Avana
Cuban Sandwich
Cubana Royale
Cupido
Cusano Estate Reserve
Cusano Selection
Dalaly Diamantes
D. Marshall Artist Reserve
D. Marshall Signature (Dom. Rep.)
Da Vinci (Nicaragua)
Dante
De Cossio
De Ortega
DeBerto & Martinez
Del Sol
Del Valle
Diamante
Diego de Ocampo
Diego Silang

ALMANAC

Dignity
Dominican Delicias
Dominican Elites
Dominican Maduro Special
Dominican Selection
Don Antonio
Don Armando (Dom. Rep.)
Don Augusto
Don Bartolo
Don Bienve
Don Carlos (Dom. Rep.)
Don Carlos (Honduras)
Don Cisso
Don Corleone
Don Dominguez
Don Elegante
Don Ernesto
Don Fausto
Don Francisco
Don Francisco Reserve
Don Guillermo
Don Jivan Classico
Don Juan Platinum
Don Julian
Don Lima
Don Lino Oro
Don Norberto
Don Otilio
Don Patricio
Don Priamo
Don Pupo
Don Quixote
Don Rafael
Don Rene Vintage
Don Rex
Don Ricardo
Don Salvador
Don Salvatore
Don Sixto
Don Suerte
Dos Reinas

Dos Rios
Duarte 1884
Dulce Diamante
Dulce Maria
Duo
888
1861
1876
Edgar
Edgar Private Reserve
El Campeon Suave
El Cid
El Diablo
El Diamante
El Dorado Gold
El Emperador
El Fidel
El Esencial
El Esencial White Label
El Faro
El Gato
El Gaucho
El Murazo
El Noble
El Rey de Florez
El Sig Ropes
El Sol
El Tigre (Nicaragua)
El Trofeo Habano
El Trofeo HabanoVintage
El Turquito
El Valle Dorado
Entre Rios
Entrepreneur
Escudo Cubano
Espanola Green
Espanola Red
Esponisa Classico
Espinosa Gold
Estevan Rey Cabinet Selection
Estevan Rey Premium Selection

ALMANAC

Estrada y Argueta
Estrella
Estrella Blanca
Evita
Express Imports
Famous Private Selection
Fantastic Flavor
Felipe II
Fittipaldi
Flamenco Puro
Flor de Amor
Flor de Dios
Flor de Florez Miami Blend
Flor de Los Reyes
Flor de Oro
Flor de Selva
Flor del Todo
Fonticiella
Francisco Hernandez
Fuego Cubano
Fuego Cubano Gold
Fuego Cubano Platinum
Galante Chase
Gallardo
Gargoyle
Garmeister
Garo Maduro
Garo Verde
Gato
Geoffrey Red
Gilfranco Dominican
Gilfranco Vanilla Bombers
Gitano
Gloria Palmera
Gran Habano
Gran Reserve Suarez
Grand Cruz
Gurkha
H M
Hamiltons House
Habanos Hatuey

Hannibal
Havana 7
Havana Blends
Havana Clase
Havana King (Dom. Rep.)
Havana King (Dom. Rep.)
Havana Royale
Havana Select
Havana Verde
Heaven
Heavenly Vanilla
Hecho a Mano
Henry George
Hermosa Flor
Hidalgos
Hobo
Hoja Cubana
Hoja Real
Hombre de Oro
Hoyo de Cortez Corto
Hoyo de Cortez Escogido
Hoyo de Cortez Premera Calidad
Hugo Cassar (Mexico)
Hugo Cassar Private Collection
 (Indonesia)
Hugo Gold
Hugo Signature Series (Dom. Rep.)
Hurricanos
Il Fiore d'Oro
Indian Anniversary Reserve A
Indian Princess
Indigo
Insurgentes
International
Isabella
Islands
J.L. Ferrer 1891
Jimenez
John Hay
José Girbés
Jose L. Piedra

ALMANAC

Jose R. Oliva
Joya del Cibao
Juan Dolio
Juan Guillermo de Robles
Justino
Kennedy
Key West Havana Gold Label
King Cobra
King Richard
Kings Club
L'Attitude 18
La Avida
La Bamba
La Cobra Cubana
La Concha
La Cosecha
La Damita
La Estrella Cubana
La Favorita (Canary Islands)
La Flor de Navarette
La Hoja del Sabor
La Hoja Rica (Dom. Rep.)
La Hoja Rica (Nicaragua)
La Lunda de la Habana
La Lunda
La Lunda de Santa Maria
La Nubia
La Palma de Oro
La Paloma
La Pantera Emerald Collection
La Perla
La Perla Habana
La Prueba
La Regenta
La Tradicion Cabinet (Nicaragua)
La Veleza
La Vieja Habana
Lady Jane
Lancelot
Largo y Zorro
Lars Tetens Phat Cigars

Lazarus
Legion
Leyenda
Licey
Little Havana Cigar Factory
Lone Wolf
Los Nicas
Luna Azul
Macarena
Madame Marshall
Maestro Cubano
Maestro de La Palma
Maker's Mark
Manifiesto
Manuel Casals
Marquez Mendoza
Marsh 1840
Master Bradley's Premium
Matador
Match Play Series Medallista
Maxim's
Mayorga
Memphis Blue
Mendez y Lopez
Mercedes
Mi Flor
Miguelon
Millenium
Monte Real
Monte Rio
Montebello
Montenegro
Montes de Oro
Moran
Morel
Motta
Mulato
Mursuli's
Napa
Napoleon's Dream
Nativo

Navarro
nextGeneration
Nicaragua Supremo
Nicaro
Nicole Miller
Niño Vazquez
Nivelacuso Private Reserve
Nostalgia
O&B Dominican Reserve
Octavio Tavares
Old Fashioned
Old Trinidad XVIII Century
Olor Vintage
One Plus
100 Fuegos
Orama
Oro Dominicano
Oro 750
Paisanos
Palmarejo
Panabano
Panama Jones
Panorea
Pantera de Oro
Paseana
Pecado
Penguin
Pera
Philippine Cigar
Pirata
Plasencia
Pleiades Reserve Privee
Presidente
Presidente Caceres
Prestigio Cubano
Prize Pointer
Profesor Sila Baba
Profesor Sila Navegador
Profesor Sila Santa Maria
Providencia
Pueblo Dominicano

Puerto Rico
Puro Placer
Purofino Blue
Purofino Gold
Puros Don Abreau
Puros Nirvana
Puros Polanco
Puros Tejera
Pyramid
Quetzal (Dom.Rep.)
Quetzal (Honduras)
Quintin Q-Oro
Quirantes
Rambling River
Real Veracruz
Red Lion
Reina Dominicana
Remedios
Reserva del Patron
Rey de Zaba
Rey del Mar
RG Santiago Dominican
Robusto de Casa
Roly
Romano's Connoisseur
Ronaldo Somma
Rosa Blanca Reserva
Rosario
Rosato
Rough Rider
Rovanoff
Royale Gold
Royale Saludo
Royce
Rum Raider
Rum Royale
Sabor
Sabor Habano Dominican Reserve
St. Christobal
St. George
San Angelo

Santiago Silk
Santo Diego
Sebastian Reserva
Selecto Puro Dominicano
Sevilla
Smok-A-Cuba
Socorro
Soleares
Soleares Limited Reserve
Soleares Special Reserve
SP Maduro
Speakeasy
Spirit Valley
Strelsky
T.J.
Tabacon Vintage Selection
Taino (Dom. Rep.)
Taino (Puerto Rico)
Tamayo y Pareto
Tamboril Cordova Collection
Tamboril Fore
Tampa Tropics
Tatou
Tenorio
Terri Welles Signature
Tesoro
Third Millenium
Thomas Hinds Cabinet Selection
Thomas Hinds Vintage I

Tipo
Torcedor
Toro Bravo
Torquino
12 Stars
Ultimate Dominican
Universo
V Centennial 500
V.M. Santana/Sumatra
Valle del Sol
Van Winkle
Vanilla Delight
Vanilla Sweets
Vega del Rey
Vegas Cubano
Ventura
Victor Sinclair Grande Reserve
Victor Sinclair Vintage Select
Villa
VIP Club Collection
VSOP Vintage Reserve
Wall Street Portfolio
Wild Javanos
Xclusivo
Xilado
Xotica
Xquisito
Yulerdi
Zelo de Cuba

Machine-made (15):
Casino Club
Cazadores
El Gozo
Emanuela
George Burns Vintage
Governor
John Hay
Le Petit Chateau

Lucky Lady
Mocha Lights
P & K Cigarren
Royal Hawaiian
Sweet-Nut
Wuhrmann
X-Rated

(A few brands which are new to this book are not listed as new in this list, since they were previously in regional or occasional distribution and not actually a "new" brand.)

The following brands have either been discontinued or are not currently in production for national sale:

Handmade (48):

Adante	Honduran Gold
Babalu	Jose Marti Vitola Series
Calle Ocho Perez Family Selection	La Bala
Casanova	La Herencia Cubana
Caveat Emptor	Los Reyes
Costa Dorada	Milano Santana
Charles Fairmorn Vintage	Morro Castle
Chavelo	Off Colors
Cleopatra	Papayo
Coloniales	Primo del Rey Club Selection
Connisseur Gold Label	Primo del Rey Gift Pack
Cuba Aliados	Private Selection
Dominican Lords	Republica Dominicana
Don Asa	Riata
Don Tonioli Epicure Selection	Sabana
Don Vito	San Luis
Doña Elba	Sillem's Las Terenas
El Triunfo	Solo Aroma
El Valle	Tabaquero
Estrella Fina	Tabantillas
Flor de A. Allones	Tulas
Franco	Vintage Honduran
Gilfranco Aztec Collection	W&D
Harriel's Dream	Yago

Machine-made (7):

B-H	Rio Hondo
Clubmaster	San Vicente
Ideal	Santa Fe
Jon Piedro	

Small cigars(3):
Hamlet Slims
Manikin
The Tobacconist Choice

A handful of brands listed in the 1997 edition and not listed in this year's work are still in production, but are now house brands of their manufacturers and no longer available at wholesale.

2.02 BRAND FACTS
Here are some entertaining facts about cigar brands and where they are produced:

Ancient brands:
Some brands have been with us since the early part of the 19th Century, originating primarily in Cuba. Some of the older brand names still being produced for the U.S. market, with their original country of origin, include:

1810 Cabanas (Cuba)	1881 Calixto Lopez (Cuba)
1834 Por Larranaga (Cuba)	1882 Garcia y Vega (USA)
1837 Ramon Allones (Cuba)	1884 Cuesta-Rey (USA)
1840 Bances (Cuba)	1884 Judge's Cave (USA)
1840 Marsh Wheeling (USA)	1887 White Owl (USA)
1840 Punch (Cuba)	1888 Villiger (Germany)
1844 H. Upmann (Cuba)	1891 Fonseca (Cuba)
1845 La Corona (Cuba)	1896 Topper (USA)
1845 Partagas (Cuba)	1901 Bolivar (Cuba)
1848 El Rey del Mundo (Cuba)	1903 Leon Jimenes (Dom. Rep.)
1850 Romeo y Julieta (Cuba)	1903 Topstone (USA)
1867 Hoyo de Monterrey (Cuba)	1905 Bering (USA)
1868 Bauza (Cuba)	1912 Arturo Fuente (USA)
1868 Macanudo (Jamaica)	1912 Muniemaker (USA)
1871 Baccarat (USA)	1916 El Producto (USA)
1873 Dannemann (Brazil)	1928 Rafael Gonzalez (Cuba)
1876 Temple Hall (Jamaica)	1935 Montecristo (Cuba)

1946 Davidoff Chateau series
    of Hoyo de Monterrey
    (Cuba)

1959 Montecruz (Canary Islands)
1964 Don Diego (Canary Islands)

Bands on brands:
It is well established that in 1850, Gustave Bock of the
Netherlands put bands on cigars for the first time, as a method
of distinguishing his firm's Cuban-made cigars.

Brand production:
The Dominican Republic and Honduras still dominate the
production origin statistics of the 961 handmade brands
profiled, but production is up everywhere.

Some 43.6 percent of the handmade brands now come from the
Dominican Republic, with another 20.9 percent from
Honduras. But compare the brand increases against the 1996-
edition totals: Dominican-produced brands increased from 419
from 166, a unimaginable 252% increase! Mexican brands
increased 280% (to 63 brands from 22½), Nicaraguan
production increased 250% (to $107^1/_5$ from $42^5/_6$) and
Honduran brands increased 155⅔ to 201 (up 29%).

Production increased in the U.S. to 61 brands from 44½, but
fell to fifth place in handmades behind the Dominican
Republic, Honduras, Nicaragua and Mexico. The U.S. was
third in the overall total with 184½ brands of all kinds.

In classifying the origin of each brand, fractional attributions
were made for cigars that are produced in more than one
country (example: Padron cigars are made in both Honduras
and Nicaragua). The statistics by group and country:

ALMANAC

Country	Handmade Cigars	Machine Made	Small Cigars	Total
Barbados	1			1
Belgium		2	4	6
Brazil	5		2	7
Costa Rica	11½			11½
Denmark			1½	1½
Dominican Republic	419	2		421
France			3	3
Germany	3	4	6	13
Guatemala	2			2
Honduras	201			201
Indonesia	12		1	13
Ireland			2	2
Jamaica	16½			16½
Mexico	63			63
Myanmar	1			1
Netherlands		6½	4½	11
Nicaragua	$107^{1}/_{5}$			$107^{1}/_{5}$
Panama	6⅓			6⅓
Philippines	14			14
Spain: . Canary Islands	24½	1	1 1	1 26½
Switzerland		1½	2	3½
United States . Puerto Rico	61 9	101 12	22½ 2½	184½ 23½
Venezuela	5			5

Distributed by SJI Wholesale

PIRATA CIGARS

JOHN HA

TORPÉDO COLLEZIÓNE

CAMÓRRA

DOMINICAN   VINTAGE

IMPORTED LIMITED RESERVE

1942

SANTIAGO
R

FINEST QUALITY HANDMADE DOMINICAN CIGARS

RARE
AGED   PRIVATE
                        RESERVE

SOLD ONLY BY PRIV

SELLO GARANTIA

SJI
TOBACCO

CAP DAME MARIE

Jérémie
Anse-d' Hainault
NAVASSA I.
(U.S.)

Coteaux
Les C

POINTE À

Edgar

The Only Thing Your Cigar Will **Ever** Need.

Introducing the

A Revolutionary New Kind of Tobacco Preservation System.

The first **all natural** alternative to traditional humidors, the **Humi-Pouch**™ is inexpensive, reclosable, portable and never requires water. Any true cigar connoseiur knows the fragile nature of fine premium cigars and the importance of keeping them humidified. **Humi-Pouch**™ preserves your premium cigars and pipe tobacco for up to 60 days by utilizing water, not chemicals. So whether you're traveling, boating or on the golf course, the quality of your cigars is always naturally preserved.

2.03   CIGARS: LARGE AND SMALL

Length:

The longest cigars? Here are the longest shapes:

19 inches	(x 60 ring)	Santa Clara Magnum
18	(x 60)	Puros Indios Chief
15	(x 125)	Hannibal Emperador
14¼	(x 60)	Tabacalera Gigantes
13¾	(x 49)	Mexican Emperador
13	(x 50)	Juan Clemente Gargantua
10 inches		Cigars of this length are offered by Carbonell, Casa Blanca, Cerdan, Dominican Original, King Dominican, Mendez y Lopez, Puros Indios and Royal Jamaica.

The shortest? Cigarillos of just under three inches in length are offered by:

2¾	Al-Capone	2⅞	Dannemann
2¾	Schimmelpennick	2⅞	Henri Winterman
2¾	Villiger	2⅞	Panter
2⅞	Agio	2⅞	Schimmelpennick
2⅞	Candlelight		

Ring gauge:

The fattest of the fat? Remembering that ring gauge is measured in 64ths of the inch, there are 21 in-production cigars of an inch (64/64) or more in diameter:

125 ring	(x 15 inches)	Hannibal Emperador
68	(x 8)	Carbonell Piramide Gigante
68	(x 8)	Mendez y Lopez Piramide Gigante
66	(x 18)	Puros Indios Chief
66	(x 10)	Casa Blanca Jeroboam
66	(x 10)	Dominican Original Fat Tub
66	(x 10)	King Dominican No. 9
66	(x 7¼)	Don Tito Piramides

66	(x 7)	Lars Tetens Tesshu Torac Fusako
66	(x 5)	Casa Blanca Half Jeroboam
66	(x 5)	Dominican Original Gorilla
66	(x 5)	King Dominican No. 13
64	(x 9½)	Ornelas 250 mm
64	(x 9)	Royal Jamaica Goliath
64	(x 7½)	Carbonell Piramide
64	(x 7½)	Cedar Joe Mega Torpedo
64	(x 7½)	Charles Fairmorn Belmore Piramide
64	(x 7½)	Don Carlos Super Pyramid
64	(x 7½)	Mendez y Lopez Piramide
64	(x 7½)	Regalos Especial
64	(x 7¼)	Moore & Bode Full Brass

The thinnest? There are a number of brands of small cigars which match the ring gauge of cigarettes, at 20 ring.

Shapes:
The leading brands by the number of shapes offered under one brand name:

47 Nat Sherman	23 Don Alberto
32 Lars Tetens Phat Cigars	23 Macanudo
30 La Plata	23 Ornelas
28 Honduras Cuban Tobaccos	22 Ashton
28 Partagas	21 Davidoff
28 Punch	21 El Rey del Mundo
27 Flor de Nicaragua	21 H. Upmann
27 Rosalones	21 Indian Head
25 Te-Amo	21 Quintin Q-Oro
23 Arturo Fuente	

Honoranle mention goes to the 76 models in the 16 different series of Hugo Cassar cigars.

2.04   CIGARS: SPECIAL MODELS

Two new fashions in cigars today are flavored cigars and

special double-wrapped cigars which emulate barber poles. A census of these brands:

Handmade brands with one or more flavored shapes:	*Flavor(s)*
Acapa Sweets	Amaretto, cognac, Irish Creme, mocha, vanilla
Arango Statesman	Vanilla
Aromella	Anisette, rum, vanilla
Baccarat Havana	Sugar cap
Boom Boom El Campeon	Amaretto, cafe, chocolate, cognac, vanilla
Camorra Limited Reserve	Sweet cap
Cedar Joe Dulce	Sweet
Chateau Amaretto	Amaretto
Christiano Leoné	Vanilla
Club Sweets	Mocha, vanilla
Cojimar	Vanilla
Conquistador	Vanilla
Creston	Sugar cap
Creston Prestige Cuvee	Sugar cap
Cubana Royale	Sweet, vanilla
Don Armando	Sweet vanilla
Don Pablo Cigar Co.	Brandy, cognac, rum or sweet
888	Cappuccino, chocolate, Guarapo, rum, vanilla
El Incomparable	Scotch
El Sublimado	Cognac
Famous Rum Runner	Rum
Fantastic Flavor	Amaretto, cherry, rum, vanilla
Flamenco Puro	Rum, vanilla
Gilfranco Vanillas	Vanilla
Heavenly Vanillas	Vanilla
Hobo	Almond brandy, chocolate, cognac, rum, sweet, vanilla
Island Amaretto	Amaretto
John T's	Amaretto, Brown Gold, Cafe Ole, Cappuccino, Cherry Cream
La Cobra Cubana	Amaretto, rum, sweet
La Diva	Cognac
La Hoja del Sabor	Sweet
La Favorita	Vanilla
La Prueba	Cherry, chocolate, coffee, rum, tequila, vanilla
La Tradicion Cubana	Rum, vanilla
Las Vegas Cigar Co.	Rum or sweet
Lew's Smokers	Sugar cap

ALMANAC

Maker's Mark	Bourbon
Monte Rio	Amaretto, cognac, mango, scotch, strawberry, vanilla
Mursuli's	Sweet
Napoleon's Dream	Cognac, rum, Southern Comfort
Nicole Miller	Vanilla
Ornelas	Cognac, vanilla
Profesor Sila Baba	Amaretto, bourbon, coffee, cognac, rum, vanilla
Puros Polanco	Amaretto, rum, vanilla
Rosato	Cognac
Rum Raider	Rum
Rum Royale	Rum
Sabor	Vanilla
Suerdieck	Cherry, clove
Tamboril Cordova Collection	Cocoa
Tatou	Amaretto, Coconut, rum, vanilla
Tradicionales	Vanilla
Vanilla Delight	Vanilla
Vanilla Sweets	Vanilla
VIP Club Collection	Anisette, vanilla
West Indies Vanilla	Vanilla
Xotica	Amaretto, black cherry, caffe con leche, chocolate, coconut, mango, menthol, piña colada, rum, tequila and vanilla

Machine-made brands with at one least flavored shape:	*Flavor(s):*
Al-Capone	Sweet
Arango Sportsman	Vanilla
Avanti	Anisette
Blackstone	Sweet Cherry
Cima	Vanilla
Dannemann	Sweet
Dutch Masters	Vanilla
Garcia y Vega Whiffs	Pipe tobacco
Hav-A-Tampa	Pipe Tobacco, sweet
Indiana Slims	Rum
King Edward	Sweet Cherry, Sweet Vanilla
Lucky Lady	Cherry
Mocha Lights	Mocha
Muriel	Cherry, menthol, pipe tobacco, sweet
Nat Cicco	Almond Liquer, Cuban Cafe
Phillies	Sweet
Ramrod	Bourbon

Rivalo	Chocolate, rum
Royal Hawaiian	Kona Coffee
Ruy Lopez	Vanilla
Schimmelpennick	Mango
Sierra Sweets	Vanilla
Swisher Sweets	Sweet
Tampa Nugget	Sweet
Tampa Resagos	Sweet
Villazon Deluxe Aromatics	Vanilla
White Owl	Sweet
William Penn	Sweet
Wolf Bros.	Rom, sweet, vanilla
X-Rated	Honey

Three brands - Black & Mild, Cherry Blend and Gold & Mild - are dedicated to the use of pipe tobacco fillers.

Please note that many brands of small cigars have one or more models which have flavoring of one type or another:

Agio	Indiana Slims
Alamo	Omega
Al-Capone	Pedroni
Alternativos	Phillies Little Cigars
Avanti	Prince Albert
Backwoods	Rustlers
Blackstone	St. Regis
Captain Black	Schimmelpennick
Charles Fairmorn Piper's	Super Value
Dannemann	Supre Sweets
Dutch Treats	Tijuana Smalls
Erik	Tiparillo
Hav-A-Tampa Little Cigars	Winchester Little Cigars

Brands with "barber pole"-wrapped models include:

Brand	Model
Anillo de Oro	5 models
AZ	Bolero

Cojimar	Cortaditos
Dominican Elites	Lonsdale
Don Alberto Royal Series	4 models
Hugo Cassar Diamond Dominican Mystique	4 models
Hugo Cassar Diamond Honduran Mystique Classic	4 models
Oliveros	Mulato
Penguin	6 models
Santa Clara	Fiesta

2.05   OUR FAVORITE BRANDS

Here are some of our favorite brands, primarily from the perspective of interesting names of brands and shapes.

Themed brands:

The production of cigars is a serious business, but some manufacturers take a light-hearted - or at least a themed - approach to naming their shapes:

Brand	*Theme*
Alamo	6 defenders of the Alamo
Black Label	9 Mexican cities
Boom Boom El Campeon	2 boxing weight classes
Cacique	7 American Indian tribes
Camorra Limited Reserve	7 Italian cities
Charles the Great	6 Spanish cities
Chessman Royal Reserve	8 chess pieces and moves
Chevere	5 Jamaican cities
Double Happiness	6 states of high happiness
El Fidel	3 kinds of political status
Famous Rum Runner	3 pirate characters
Garo Maduro	4 types of singers
Jamaica Gold	8 court characters
La Fontana	8 Italian artists and scientists
Las Cabrillas	9 New World explorers
Match Play	6 famous golf courses
Nat Sherman Landmarks	5 famous New York landmarks
Nat Sherman Manhattan	5 famous New York neighborhoods
Nat Sherman VIPs	5 famous New Yorkers

ALMANAC

New York, New York	6 famous New York streets/sites
Pleiades	12 constellations and planets
Pyramid	6 Egyptian pyramid names
Romanticos	5 great lovers and love-gods
Royal Honduras	8 royal court characters
Tiburon	3 types of sharks

Fun shape names:

Check out these names in the brand listings, compiled alphabetically for your amusement by our Assistant Editor, Bruce Tenen:

Shape name	Brand
Baguette	Dulce Diamante
Black Tie	Nicole Miller
Bolero	AZ
Buccaneers	Mario Palomino
Cha-Cha Cherry	Fantastic Flavor Cigars
Charlemagne	La Gloria Cubana
Chocolate Sensation	Little Havana Cigar Factory
Collector's Tin	Gurkha
Ecstacy	Double Happiness
El Jefe	Big Butt
El Mambi	Don Tuto Habanos
Farouk Gigante	Creston Prestige Cuvee
Fancytale	Special Jamaicans
Fat Tub	Dominican Original
Filly	Chacaro Black Stallion
Gallapagos	Penguin
Goliath	Royal Jamaica
Insurrectos	La Flor Dominicana
Jeroboam	Casa Blanca
John McKay Super Rothschilds	Bustillo
King Kong	Dominican Original
Lunchour	La Tradicion Cubana
Machine Guns	Speakeasy
Monalisa	Da Vinci
Momotomito	Flor de Farach
No. 10 Downing Street	Royal Jamaica

Pandukas	Don Mariano
Pop's Choice	Lew's Smokers
Pythagoras	Credo
Rat Tail	Crown Achievement
Rough Rider	Rico Havana
Scarface	Heaven
Smokin' Lulu	Fighting Cock
Snorkys	Scarface
Sun Tzu	Heaven
Teepee	Indian
Texas Red	Fighting Cock
Tiger Shark	Tiburon
Victor No. 1	La Plata
Wakizashi	Lars Tetens Phat Cigars
Yumbo	Tesoros de Copan
Zorro	Hamiltons Reserve

2.06   THE CIGAR BOWL

Of course there was a college football bowl game named for cigars! The Cigar Bowl was played in the hotbed of U.S. cigar-making: Tampa, Florida, from 1947-54, between college-division teams. The scores:

I	1947	(Jan. 1)	Delaware 21, Rollins 7	(attendance 7,500)
II	1948	(Jan. 1)	Missouri Valley 26, West Chester 7	(10,000)
III	1949	(Jan. 1)	Missouri Valley 13, St. Thomas (Mn), 13	(11,000)
IV	1950	(Jan. 1)	Florida State 19, Wofford 6	(14,000)
V	1951	(Jan. 1)	Wisconsin-La Crosse 47, Valparaiso 14	(12,000)
VI	1951	(Dec. 29)	Brooke Army Medical 20, Camp LeJeune Marines 0	(7,500)
VII	1952	(Dec. 13)	Tampa 21, Lenoir-Rhyne 12	(7,500)
VIII	1954	(Jan. 1)	Missouri Valley 12, Wisconsin-LaCrosse 12	(5,000)
IX	1954	(Dec.)	Tampa 21, Morris Harvey 0	(unknown)

How about a bowl game in Havana? Absolutely! On January 1, 1937, Auburn and Villanova played to a 7-7 tie in the first and only "Bacardi Bowl," held before 12,000 spectators as a part of the Cuban National Sports Festival.

Married...

Carlos Toraño
*Dominican
Selection*

Carlos Toraño
*Nicaragua
Selection*

RAND NICA · NOSTALGIA · *Virtuoso* · ST. CHARL

CASA TORAÑO

With Children

rand Nica
orano
Nicaragua

Nostalgia
Casa Toraño
Honduras

Virtuoso
Toraño
Honduras

St. Charles
Dominican
Republic

CARLOS
TORAÑO

Since 1916

Toraño Cigars. Good Taste Runs In the Family.

Cigar Legends: Carlos Toraño

"It is in our hands, really," says a thoughtful Carlos Toraño. "We have an obligation to make a good cigar . . . at a fair price . . . or we will lose them."

Making good cigars at fair prices has been the life's work of Toraño, who was born in Cuba and worked on his family's farm until he left in August 1959. But he left his tobacco heritage to earn a degree in business at the University of Miami in 1964. But he left a growing success in business to help his cousins, who needed marketing help with the tobacco they were growing in Nicaragua.

But the internal strife inside Nicaragua forced Carlos and his relations to move their growing efforts to the Dominican Republic in 1979. There, operating on a former General Cigar farm, they grew Connecticut-seed wrapper leaf – years before it became the rage.

Soon, there were farms in Costa Rica, Ecuador and later in Nicaragua when the situation improved. Next, the farms needed help with marketing and the factories they sold to needed distribution assistance with their finished cigars. In stepped Toraño, who now sells 20 million of these cigars a year through his Central American Tobacco Corp.

But he gave in to pressure and started his own brands in 1991. Starting in 1994, his respected Carlos Toraño, Virtuoso Toraño and Grand Nica brands have enjoyed great success. In 1997, he introduced "Nostalgia" as a tribute to his homeland. Now *you* have an obligation to try them . . . to see if Carlos has lived up to *his* obligations.

3.
HANDMADE CIGARS:
INDEX

Here are 961 handmade brands in a compact index to country of origin, body and shapes.

For each brand, a two-letter code denotes the country of manufacture and a one-digit code indicates the strength of the brand:

Country of Origin

Ba Barbados
Be Belgium
Br Brazil
CI Canary Islands
CR Costa Rica
DR Dominican Republic
Ge Germany
Gu Guatemala
Ho Honduras
In Indonesia
Ja Jamaica
Mx Mexico
My Myanmar
Ni Nicaragua
Pa Panama
Ph Philippines
US United States
Ve Venezuela

Strength

1 Mild
2 Mild to medium
3 Medium
4 Medium to full
5 Full

New listings (and name changes) for 1998 are marked by a "+" symbol.

In addition, each line lists the shape "groups" in which the brand is produced. The 19 standard shapes listed in section 1.03 are broken into ten groups, including:

HANDMADE CIGARS: INDEX

The widest range? Only five brands had models in *all* ten shape groups:

- Davidoff (Dominican Republic)
- El Rey del Mundo (Honduras)
- La Gloria Cubana (United States)
- Macanudo (Jamaica & Dominican Republic)
- Punch (Honduras)

Additional, detailed information about each of these brands is available in the following section, offering brand listings.

HANDMADE CIGARS: INDEX

Brand	Made in	Strength	Cigarillo	Panatela	Corona	Lonsdale	Grand Corona	Figurado	Robusto-Toro	Churchill	Double Corona	Giant
A.T. Cofino +	DR	4			●	●			●	●	●	
Absoluto +	DR	3					●		●		●	
Acapa Sweets +	DR	3	●	●	●							
Aguila	DR	2			●	●	●		●		●	
Al-Capone	Ni	3				●			●			
Alamo +	Ho	3				●			●	●	●	●
Alhambra	Ph	1			●	●			●			●
Alpha Candela Cubana +	US	3		●		●	●	●	●	●	●	
Alvaro	CI	1		●	●							
Amoroso +	Ho	1				●			●		●	●
Anacaona +	DR	1-2				●		●	●	●		
Ancla y Cazador +	Ni	4			●			●	●		●	
Andros +	DR	3		●	●		●		●	●		●
Andujar	DR	5	●	●		●			●		●	●
Andulleros +	DR	3					●		●		●	●
Anillo de Oro	DR	1	●	●	●	●	●		●			●
Anillo de Plata +	Ho	2				●		●		●	●	●
Antelo	US	1-5	●	●	●	●	●			●	●	
Antillas Toro Bravo +	DR	4			●	●	●		●	●	●	
Antonio y Cleopatra Private Reserve +	DR	2			●			●	●		●	

HANDMADE CIGARS: INDEX

Brand	Made in	Strength	Cigarillo	Panatela	Corona	Lonsdale	Grand Corona	Figurado	Robusto-Toro	Churchill	Double Corona	Giant
Aperitif +	DR	4		●								
Aqua D'T +	Ho	2			●	●			●		●	
Arango Statesman	Ho	3			●					●		
Armenter Reservas +	CI	1		●	●	●		●	●	●	●	
Aromas de San Andres	Mx	3			●	●	●		●		●	
Aromella +	Mx	2		●	●							
Arturo Fuente	DR	3-5		●	●	●	●		●	●	●	●
Artus +	Mx	1			●	●			●		●	
Aruba +	DR	1			●	●			●			
Ashé +	DR	1			●	●	●		●			●
Ashton	DR	2		●	●	●		●	●	●	●	
Astral	Ho	3				●			●	●	●	
Avo	DR	1		●	●	●	●	●	●	●	●	
AZ	Mx	5		●	●				●		●	
Azteca Dominican Maduro +	Mx	4						●				
Baccarat Havana	Ho	1		●	●	●		●	●		●	
Bagatelle +	Ho	3				●			●	●		●
Bahia	CR	5			●			●	●		●	●
Bahia Gold +	CR	5			●			●	●	●		
Bahia Maduro +	CR	5						●	●		●	

HANDMADE CIGARS: INDEX

Brand	Made in	Strength	Cigarillo	Panatela	Corona	Lonsdale	Grand Corona	Figurado	Robusto-Toro	Churchill	Double Corona	Giant
Bahia Trinidad +	CR	1				●		●	●		●	●
Balboa	Pa	5	●	●	●					●		●
Bali Hai +	In	2			●			●	●	●		
Ballena Suprema	Ho	2				●		●	●	●		●
	Mx	4				●			●	●	●	
Bances	Ho	4		●	●	●				●		●
Bandera +	DR	3			●		●	●	●		●	
Bandoleros +	DR	5										
Bauza	DR	4		●	●	●			●	●	●	
Belinda	Ho	4	●	●	●		●		●	●	●	
Bellero +	Ni	2		●	●				●	●	●	
Belmondo +	Mx	3			●				●		●	●
Ben Miguel +	DR	2		●		●			●	●	●	
Bering	Ho	5		●	●	●	●	●	●			●
Beverly Hills-VIP	Ho	1		●	●				●		●	
Biarritz +	DR	3			●				●		●	
Big Butt	Ni	4							●		●	
Big Chief +	Ho	5			●			●	●		●	●
Bijao +	DR	4							●		●	
Bijao Classico +	DR	3							●		●	
Black Label	Mx	3		●	●		●		●		●	●
Blair Gold Label	Ho	4				●			●	●		●
Blair Silver Label +	CI	1							●	●		

HANDMADE CIGARS: INDEX

Brand	Made in	Strength	Cigarillo	Panatela	Corona	Lonsdale	Grand Corona	Figurado	Robusto-Toro	Churchill	Double Corona	Giant
Blue Chip +	US	3							●			
Blue Label	Ho	2		●	●	●			●	●	●	●
Bogar +	Ho	5			●		●		●		●	
Bohio +	DR	2			●			●	●	●	●	
Bohio +	DR	2		●		●			●		●	
Bolivar +	DR	2		●		●	●					
Boom Boom El Campeon +	US	1		●	●							
Boquilla	US	4		●	●	●		●	●	●	●	●
Boss +	DR	3				●			●	●		
Boyero +	DR	1			●				●		●	
Boyero Primero +	DR	3			●				●		●	
Bravos +	Mx	4			●							
Bravos +	CI	3				●			●		●	
Breton Legend +	DR	5		●	●		●	●			●	●
Briones +	Ho	2				●		●	●	●	●	
Bufido +	Mx	3			●				●		●	
Bulldog +	DR	3			●				●		●	
Burma +	My	5			●							
Bustillo	US	3,5							●			
Butera Royal Vint.	DR	3		●	●	●			●	●		
C.A.O.	Ho	3			●	●		●	●			●
C.A.O. Gold	Ni	2			●				●	●	●	

HANDMADE CIGARS: INDEX

Brand	Made in	Strength	Cigarillo	Panatela	Corona	Lonsdale	Grand Corona	Figurado	Robusto-Toro	Churchill	Double Corona	Giant
C.C.I. Royal Satin	Ho	3			●			●	●	●	●	
Caballeros	DR	2			●				●	●	●	
Cabañas	DR	1			●	●	●		●			
Cacique	DR	1		●	●	●		●	●	●	●	
Caleyes +	DR	1		●	●			●	●	●	●	
Calixto Lopez	Ph	1		●	●	●	●		●			●
Calle Ocho	DR	1				●		●	●		●	
Camacho	Ho	5		●	●	●			●	●	●	●
Cammano +	DR	2		●				●	●		●	
Cammarata	US	3,5			●		●	●	●	●		
Camorra Imported Limited Reserve	Ho	3		●	●	●		●	●	●		
Camorra Lim.Res. Dominican Vint. +	DR	4						●	●			●
Campeones +	DR	3				●		●	●		●	●
Canaria d'Oro	DR	4		●	●	●			●			
Canonero	Br	1-3		●	●	●			●	●	●	
Caoba	DR	2	●	●	●		●	●	●	●	●	●
Caoba Gold +	DR	1		●	●			●	●	●	●	
Caona Platinum +	DR	2		●	●			●	●	●	●	
Caonabo	DR	2		●	●			●	●		●	
Capote	CI	2		●		●			●		●	
Capricho Cubano +	DR	4			●		●		●		●	

HANDMADE CIGARS: INDEX

Brand	Made in	Strength	Cigarillo	Panatela	Corona	Lonsdale	Grand Corona	Figurado	Robusto-Toro	Churchill	Double Corona	Giant
Cara Mia	CI	3			●	●		●	●		●	
Carabana +	Ho	2			●	●			●			
Carbonell	DR	1	●	●	●	●		●	●	●	●	●
Carlin	DR	5			●				●	●		●
Carlos Oliva +	Ni	4					●	●	●		●	●
Carlos Toraño	DR	1		●	●	●	●		●	●	●	
Carlos Toraño +	Ni	3			●			●	●	●	●	
Carmen Gold	Ho	2			●				●	●	●	
Carmen Platinum +	US	1			●		●		●	●	●	●
Carmen White +	DR	1		●	●				●	●	●	●
Carnival Havana +	Ni	3		●	●			●	●	●	●	
Carnival Havana Supreme +	Ni	1			●			●	●	●	●	●
Carrington	DR	2		●	●			●	●	●	●	
Casa Blanca	DR	1		●	●	●			●		●	●
Casa Blanca Reserve	DR	1			●	●			●		●	
Casa Buena	CI	1			●				●		●	
Casa de Gonzalez +	Ho	2	●	●	●			●	●		●	
Casa de Klafter +	US	1-5		●		●			●	●	●	
Casa de Nicaragua	Ni	1			●	●			●		●	●
Casa Martin	CI	2			●	●			●	●		

HANDMADE CIGARS: INDEX

Brand	Made in	Strength	Cigarillo	Panatela	Corona	Lonsdale	Grand Corona	Figurado	Robusto-Toro	Churchill	Double Corona	Giant
Cascada +	Mx	4			●				●		●	
Casillas	US	4	●	●			●	●	●	●	●	●
Castaño +	Ho	5		●			●		●	●	●	
Cavana +	US	1,5	●	●	●	●			●		●	●
Cecil Brooks III +	US								●		●	
Cedar Joe	Ho	2			●			●	●		●	
Cedar Joe Dulce +	Ho	1			●				●	●	●	
Cedros	DR	1		●					●	●		
Celestino Vega	In	5			●			●	●		●	
Cerdan	DR	2	●	●	●	●			●	●	●	●
Cervantes	Ho	3			●	●	●					
Chacaro Black Stallion +	Ho	4			●				●			
Chairman's Choice	Ho	3			●			●	●	●	●	
Charles Fairmorn	Ho	4	●	●							●	
Charles Fairmorn Belmore	DR	3	●			●		●	●	●	●	
Charles Fairmorn Connshade +	Ge	1	●	●								
Charles the Great	Ho	3			●		●		●		●	
Chateau Amaretto+	DR	3			●							
Chessman Royal Reserve +	US	3			●	●		●	●	●		
Chevere	Ja	2			●	●	●				●	●

HANDMADE CIGARS: INDEX

Brand	Made in	Strength	Cigarillo	Panatela	Corona	Lonsdale	Grand Corona	Figurado	Robusto-Toro	Churchill	Double Corona	Giant
Christiano Leoné Director's Selection +	DR	3		●	●		●	●	●		●	●
Churchill +	Ni	3			●				●		●	●
Cibao +	DR	1		●	●			●	●	●	●	
Cielo Umo +	In	4		●		●			●			
Cifuentes	Ja	2				●		●	●		●	
Cigar Compadres +	DR	2,4			●		●	●	●		●	●
The Cigar Connection +	Ni	2							●	●		
Cigarros Cibao +	DR	1		●	●				●		●	
Cimarron +	DR	2			●				●	●		
Cimero +	DR	2			●				●	●	●	
Cinco Vegas +	Ni	2		●	●			●	●		●	
Cinco Vegas Vintage +	Ni	1		●	●			●	●		●	
Cisso +	DR	2		●	●		●	●	●		●	
Cisso Premium Loma +	DR	3			●				●			
Clipper Gold Reserve +	DR	4				●			●	●	●	
Classico de Continental +	DR Ho	4 3			●		● ●		● ●	●		
Clementine	Ho	5			●	●			●		●	●
Club Sweets +	Mx	1			●							

HANDMADE CIGARS: INDEX

Brand	Made in	Strength	Cigarilo	Panatela	Corona	Lonsdale	Grand Corona	Figurado	Robusto-Toro	Churchill	Double Corona	Giant
Cohiba	DR	4			●	●	●	●	●		●	
Cojimar	DR	1	●				●	●	●			●
Colorado	DR	3		●	●			●	●		●	●
Columbus +	DR	3			●		●		●		●	
Commandante +	DR	3			●		●		●			●
Condal	CI	1	●	●	●				●	●	●	
Confederacion Suiza +	Ho	3			●							
Connoisseur's Choice +	DR	2			●	●			●		●	
Conquistador +	Mx	3,4	●	●	●	●	●	●	●	●		●
Conucos	DR	1			●				●			
Copa Havana +	Ho	3-5			●		●	●	●	●		
Cossack +	Ni	3				●		●	●	●		●
Coticas +	DR	3			●	●			●	●	●	
Credo	DR	3		●	●				●	●	●	
Credo Ligas +	Ho	4		●	●				●			●
Cremosa Cubanos +	DR	3			●	●		●	●		●	
Creston +	Ho	5			●				●		●	●
Creston "Los Montes" +	Ho	5			●	●						
Creston Prestige Cuvèe	Ho	3,4		●	●	●			●	●	●		●

HANDMADE CIGARS: INDEX

Brand	Made in	Strength	Cigarillo	Panatela	Corona	Lonsdale	Grand Corona	Figurado	Robusto-Toro	Churchill	Double Corona	Giant
Cusano Selection +	DR	4						•	•			
Dalaly Diamantes +	Ni	2				•			•		•	•
D. Marshall Artist Reserve +	DR	4			•				•	•		
D. Marshall Signature	DR	4			•				•	•		
D. Marshall Signature	Ho	4			•				•		•	
D. Marshall Signature +	DR	3			•				•	•		
Danlys	Ho	4		•	•		•		•		•	
Davidoff	DR	1,3	•	•	•	•	•	•	•	•	•	•
Da Vinci +	Ho	2			•			•	•	•		•
	Ni	3			•			•	•	•		•
Dante +	DR	4		•	•				•		•	
De Cossio +	Ho	3			•	•			•		•	
De Ortega +	DR	1,3		•			•	•	•	•		
DeBerto & Martinez +	Ho US	3					•		•		•	
Defiant	Ho	3			•			•	•		•	
Del Sol +	DR	3							•		•	
Del Valle +	Ho	4			•			•	•		•	•
Diamante +	DR	1			•	•			•	•	•	
Diamond Crown	DR	1							•		•	•

HANDMADE CIGARS: INDEX

Brand	Made in	Strength	Cigarillo	Panatela	Corona	Lonsdale	Grand Corona	Figurado	Robusto-Toro	Churchill	Double Corona	Giant
Diana Silvius	DR	3				●			●	●	●	
Diego de Ocampo+	DR	3			●	●			●		●	
Diego Silang +	Ph	2		●	●	●				●	●	
Dignity +	DR	3			●				●		●	
Domingold	DR	3			●				●		●	
Dominican Delicias +	DR	2			●	●			●		●	
Dominican Elites +	DR	3				●		●	●	●	●	
Dominican Estates	DR	1			●	●			●		●	
Dominican Maduro Special +	DR	5							●		●	
Dominican Original	DR	1		●	●	●		●	●	●	●	●
Dominican Selection +	DR	3		●	●	●			●		●	●
Dominican Specials	DR	1			●	●			●		●	
Dominicana Superba	DR	1			●	●			●		●	●
Dominico	DR	2			●	●		●	●	●		●
Dominique	DR	1			●	●	●		●		●	●
Domino Park	DR	4				●		●	●		●	
Don Alberto	DR	1-3		●		●	●	●	●			●
Don Antonio +	Ge	1		●		●	●	●			●	
	Ge	2	●	●								

- 55 -

HANDMADE CIGARS: INDEX

Brand	Made in	Strength	Cigarillo	Panatela	Corona	Lonsdale	Grand Corona	Figurado	Robusto-Toro	Churchill	Double Corona	Giant
Don Armando +	DR	2		●	●	●	●		●		●	
Don Armando	Ho	1		●	●		●		●		●	●
Don Augusto +	DR	2			●	●	●		●		●	●
Don Barco	DR	3							●	●	●	
Don Bartolo +	Ph	2			●				●	●	●	
Don Bienve +	PR	1			●							
Don Carlos +	DR	3			●				●			
Don Carlos +	Ho	1			●			●	●		●	
Don Cisso +	DR	2			●				●			
Don Corleone +	Ho	1			●			●	●		●	●
Don Diego	DR	1	●	●	●	●●			●	●		
Don Dominguez +	DR	5			●		●		●		●	
Don Elegante +	US	1-3					●	●	●	●	●	
Don Ernesto +	DR	3							●			
Don Esteban	DR	3			●	●			●		●	●
Don Fausto +	DR	3		●	●				●	●		
Don Fife	Ho	2		●	●	●			●	●		
Don Francisco +	Mx	5				●			●		●	
Don Francisco Reserve +	Ho	3				●			●		●	
Don Guillermo +	DR	3			●				●	●		●
Don Jivan Classico +	DR	3			●				●	●	●	

HANDMADE CIGARS: INDEX

Brand	Made in	Strength	Cigarillo	Panatela	Corona	Lonsdale	Grand Corona	Figurado	Robusto-Toro	Churchill	Double Corona	Giant
Don Jose	Ho	3			●				●		●	●
Don Juan	Ni	3	●	●	●				●		●	●
Don Juan Platinum +	DR	3		●	●	●		●	●		●	●
Don Julian +	Ni	2		●					●	●	●	
Don Julio	DR	1			●	●			●			●
Don Leo	DR	2		●	●	●		●	●	●	●	●
Don Lima +	Ho	2		●	●				●	●		
Don Lino	Ho	1		●		●	●		●		●	
Don Lino Oro +	DR	5		●	●				●	●		
Don Manolo Coll.	DR	2-4		●	●		●	●	●		●	
Don Marcos	DR	2		●	●	●		●	●	●		
Don Mariano	DR	3		●	●	●			●	●	●	
Don Mateo	Ho	3		●	●	●			●	●	●	●
Don Melo	Ho	4			●		●		●		●	●
Don Melo Centenario	Ho	3			●				●		●	
Don Norberto +	Ni	2		●	●				●	●	●	
Don Otilio +	DR	2			●			●	●	●		●
Don Pablo	US	2	●	●	●			●	●	●	●	●
Don Patricio +	Ni	1			●	●			●		●	
Don Pepe	Br	1	●	●					●	●	●	
Don Priamo +	DR	1			●		●	●	●		●	●

HANDMADE CIGARS: INDEX

Brand	Made in	Strength	Cigarillo	Panatela	Corona	Lonsdale	Grand Corona	Figurado	Robusto-Toro	Churchill	Double Corona	Giant
Don Pupo +	DR	2		●	●			●	●		●	
Don Quijote	Ve	3		●	●		●					
Don Quixote +	Ho	4		●		●			●		●	
Don Rafael +	DR	3			●		●		●		●	
Don Rene de Cuba	US	3		●	●	●	●	●	●		●	
Don Rene Vintage +	DR	2			●				●		●	
Don Rex +	Ho	4			●	●					●	
Don Ricardo +	Mx	4							●			
Don Salvador	Ni	4		●	●				●		●	●
Don Salvador +	Ni	2				●		●	●		●	●
Don Salvatore +	Ho	4			●				●		●	●
Don Sixto +	Ho	3		●	●			●	●		●	
Don Suerte +	DR	2		●	●		●	●	●		●	
Don Tito	US	5		●		●	●	●	●		●	
Don Tomas	Ho	4		●	●	●	●	●	●		●	
Don Tomas Int'l	Ho	5			●	●			●			
Don Tomas Special Edition	Ho	3		●		●	●		●		●	
Don Tuto Habanos	CR	4			●	●		●	●		●	
Don Xavier	CI	1	●	●	●	●	●	●	●	●	●	
Don Yanes	Ve	5		●	●				●		●	
Dos Reinas +	Ni	4			●			●	●	●		

HANDMADE CIGARS: INDEX

Brand	Made in	Strength	Cigarilo	Panatela	Corona	Lonsdale	Grand Corona	Figurado	Robusto-Toro	Churchill	Double Corona	Giant
Dos Rios +	Ni	5			●		●	●	●		●	
Double Happiness	Ph	1			●			●	●	●		
Duarte 1884 +	DR	3			●				●	●	●	
Dulce Diamante +	Ho	1,3		●	●				●		●	
Dulce Maria +	DR	2			●	●			●	●		
Dunhill	Cl	2		●	●	●			●			
Dunhill	DR	2		●	●	●		●	●	●	●	●
Duo +	DR	2				●					●	
888 +	Mx	2			●				●			
898 Collection	Ja	1			●	●			●		●	
1861 +	DR	2			●	●			●		●	●
1876 +	DR	2		●	●			●	●	●	●	
1881	Ph	3			●	●			●			●
Edgar +	DR	3			●		●		●		●	
Edgar Private Reserve +	In	3			●	●	●		●		●	
El Campeon Suave +	DR	5			●				●	●		
El Canelo	US	2		●	●	●			●	●		●
El Cid +	Br	4				●				●	●	
El Credito	US	3		●	●	●	●		●	●	●	●
El Diablo +	DR	4					●	●	●			
El Diamante +	Ni	1-5			●	●		●	●		●	

HANDMADE CIGARS: INDEX

Brand	Made in	Strength	Cigarillo	Panatela	Corona	Lonsdale	Grand Corona	Figurado	Robusto-Toro	Churchill	Double Corona	Giant
El Dorado Gold +	Ho	5				●			●	●		●
El Emperador +	DR	3							●	●	●	
El Fidel +	DR	1		●					●		●	
Elegante	Ho	3		●	●	●			●	●		
El Esencial +	DR	5			●				●	●	●	
El Esencial White Label +	DR	4			●				●	●	●	
El Faro +	DR	5			●		●	●	●		●	●
El Gato +	Ve	3			●		●		●		●	
El Gaucho +	Ho	5			●				●	●	●	●
El Incomparable	Ho	5			●			●	●	●		
El Murazo +	DR	1							●	●	●	
El Noble +	DR	1				●			●	●		
El Paraiso	Ho	3		●				●	●	●	●	●
El Rey del Mundo	Ho	1,4	●	●	●	●	●	●	●	●	●	●
El Rey de Florez +	DR	5			●	●	●	●	●		●	
El Rico Habano	US	5		●	●		●		●	●	●	
El Sabinar	DR	3			●		●		●	●		
El Sig Ropes +	CR	4				●			●	●		
El Sol +	DR US	1			●	●	●		●		●	
El Sublimado	Ho	2			●			●	●			●
El Tigre	Ho	4			●			●	●		●	●

HANDMADE CIGARS: INDEX

Brand	Made in	Strength	Cigarillo	Panatela	Corona	Lonsdale	Grand Corona	Figurado	Robusto-Toro	Churchill	Double Corona	Giant
El Tigre +	Ni	1			•				•			•
El Trofeo Habano +	DR	1		•	•	•			•		•	
El Trofeo Habano Vintage +	DR	1			•	•			•		•	
El Turquito +	Ho	3			•				•		•	•
El Unicornio	Gu	5				•			•			•
El Valle Dorado +	Ni	2			•				•	•	•	
Encanto	Ho	4		•	•	•			•		•	•
Entre Rios +	DR	3			•				•			
Entrepreneur +	DR	2			•	•			•	•	•	
Escudo Cubano +	DR	2		•		•	•	•	•		•	
Escudo Cubano	Ni	1		•		•			•		•	•
Espada de Oro	Ho	3		•	•				•	•		•
Espanola Gold	DR	1		•	•	•			•	•	•	•
Espanola Green +	DR	3		•	•	•			•	•	•	•
Espanola Red +	DR	5		•	•	•			•	•	•	•
Espinosa Classico +	Ho	3			•				•		•	
Espinosa Gold +	DR	4			•	•			•	•		
Estevan Rey Cabinet Sel. +	DR	3			•				•	•		
Estevan Rey Premium Sel. +	DR	2			•				•	•		
Estrada y Argueta+	Ni	5		•	•			•	•	•	•	•

HANDMADE CIGARS: INDEX

Brand	Made in	Strength	Cigarillo	Panatela	Corona	Lonsdale	Grand Corona	Figurado	Robusto-Toro	Churchill	Double Corona	Giant
Estrella +	Mx	1			●				●		●	
Estrella Blanca +	Mx	1			●				●			
Evelio	Ho	5			●	●		●	●	●		
Evita +	DR	2		●	●		●	●	●	●	●	●
Excalibur	Ho	4	●	●	●		●		●	●	●	
Excelsior	Mx	3			●	●			●	●		●
Express Imports +	Ho	3	●	●	●			●	●	●	●	●
F.D. Grave	Ho	5			●				●		●	
Famous Private Selection +	DR	1			●		●	●	●		●	
Famous Rum Runner	In	1	●	●	●	●						
Fantastic Flavor +	US	2			●							
Fat Cat	DR	5			●			●	●		●	●
Felipe Gregorio	Ho	5			●			●	●	●	●	
Felipe II +	Ho	4			●			●	●	●	●	
Fighting Cock	Ph	3			●			●	●	●		
First Priming	Ho	3									●	●
Fittipaldi +	DR	2	●		●	●		●	●	●		●
Flamenco Puro +	US	1			●			●	●			
Flor Cubana	Ho	2		●	●	●			●	●	●	
Flor de Amor +	Ni	1						●	●	●		
Flor de Consuegra	Ho	5		●	●	●	●		●	●		●

HANDMADE CIGARS: INDEX

Brand	Made in	Strength	Cigarillo	Panatela	Corona	Lonsdale	Grand Corona	Figurado	Robusto-Toro	Churchill	Double Corona	Giant
Flor de Dios +	Ni	3							•		•	
Flor de Farach	Ni	4	•	•				•	•	•	•	
Flor de Filipinas	Ph	3	•	•	•			•		•		
Flor de Florez	Ho	2		•	•				•		•	
Flor de Florez Cabinet Selection	Ni	4		•			•	•	•	•	•	
Flor de Florez Miami Blend +	US	4	•	•	•			•			•	•
Flor de Honduras	Ho	1			•			•	•		•	•
Flor de Jalapa	Ni	2		•					•	•		•
Flor de Los Reyes +	DR	3		•			•		•		•	•
Flor de Manila	Ph	2	•	•	•			•		•		
Flor de Mexico	Mx	5	•	•		•			•		•	
Flor de Nicaragua	Ni	1	•	•	•	•			•	•	•	•
Flor de Oro +	Ni	2			•			•	•		•	•
Flor de Palicio	Ho	3		•	•					•		
Flor de Selva +	Ho	3	•	•					•	•		
Flor del Caribe	Ho	4		•						•	•	
Flor del Todo +	Ni	5	•	•					•		•	
Fonseca	DR	3			•		•	•	•		•	
Fonticiella +	DR	3		•		•		•	•	•	•	
Francisco Hernandez +	DR	3			•				•	•		

HANDMADE CIGARS: INDEX

Brand	Made in	Strength	Cigarillo	Panatela	Corona	Lonsdale	Grand Corona	Figurado	Robusto-Toro	Churchill	Double Corona	Giant
Free Cuba	DR	4			●			●	●		●	
Fuego Cubano +	US	3		●	●	●	●	●	●		●	●
Fuego Cubano Gold +	US	3		●	●	●	●	●	●		●	●
Fuego Cubano Platinum +	US	4		●	●	●	●	●	●		●	●
Fundadores Jamaica	Ja	1			●	●			●		●	
Galante Chase +	Ho	2		●	●				●		●	●
Galiano	DR	2		●	●	●			●	●	●	
Gallardo +	Ho	3		●	●				●		●	●
Gargoyle +	Ph	1			●				●		●	
Garmeister +	US	1						●	●		●	
Garo	DR	2		●	●	●			●	●	●	
Garo Maduro +	DR	5						●	●			
Garo Verde +	DR	4			●				●		●	
Garcia y Vega	Ja	3		●		●				●		
Gato +	DR	3			●				●		●	
Geoffrey Red +	DR	1			●				●		●	
Gilberto Oliva	Ni	3				●		●	●		●	
Gilfranco Dominican +	DR	3					●		●		●	
Gilfranco Vanilla Bombers +	PR	3						●				

HANDMADE CIGARS: INDEX

Brand	Made in	Strength	Cigarillo	Panatela	Corona	Lonsdale	Grand Corona	Figurado	Robusto-Toro	Churchill	Double Corona	Giant
Gioconda	Ho	3			●				●	●	●	
Gispert	Ho	2				●			●		●	
Gitano +	DR	3		●	●		●		●	●		●
Gloria Palmera +	CI	1				●			●		●	
Gran Habano +	DR	4			●				●		●	
Gran Reserve Suarez +	DR	3		●			●	●	●		●	
Grand Cruz +	DR	4			●	●	●		●			●
Grand Nica	Ni	4				●		●	●		●	●
The Griffin's	DR	2		●	●	●			●			●
Guaranteed Jamaica	Ja	2			●		●		●			
Gurkha +	DR	2			●	●	●	●	●		●	
H M +	Ph	1			●	●			●	●	●	
H. Upmann	DR	3	●	●	●	●	●		●	●		
H. Upmann Cabinet Selection	DR	3							●			●
H. Upmann Chairman's Reserve	DR	3		●				●	●	●	●	
Habana Gold	Ho	3			●				●	●	●	●
Habana Gold Sterling Vintage	Ho	5			●				●	●	●	●
Habanica	Ni	3		●			●	●	●	●		

HANDMADE CIGARS: INDEX

Brand	Made in	Strength	Cigarillo	Panatela	Corona	Lonsdale	Grand Corona	Figurado	Robusto-Toro	Churchill	Double Corona	Giant
Hamiltons	DR	4	●	●	●	●		●	●	●		
Hamiltons Reserve	DR	3	●	●	●			●	●	●	●	●
Hamiltons House +	DR	3			●			●	●		●	
Habanos Hatuey +	DR	3			●	●			●	●		
Hannibal +	In	3-4	●	●	●	●		●	●	●	●	●
Hasa Rey	Ho	5		●	●		●		●			
Havana	US	4		●	●	●		●	●	●	●	●
Havana 7 +	US	4			●	●	●	●	●	●	●	
Havana Blends +	DR	2		●	●		●		●			●
Havana Clase +	Ho	3			●	●			●		●	
Havana Classico	DR	5				●		●	●		●	
Havana Cool	Ni	4		●	●				●	●		
Havana King +	DR	1			●			●	●	●	●	
Havana King +	DR	4		●	●			●	●	●	●	
Havana Reserve	Ho	3		●		●	●		●		●	
Havana Royale +	DR	2			●			●	●	●		●
Havana Select +	Ni	5			●			●	●		●	●
Havana Sunrise	US	4	●	●	●			●	●	●	●	●
Havana Verde +	Ho	4					●		●			
Heaven +	DR	3,4			●			●	●		●	
Heavenly Vanilla +	DR	1		●								
Hecho a Mano +	DR	2			●		●		●		●	

HANDMADE CIGARS: INDEX

Brand	Made in	Strength	Cigarillo	Panatela	Corona	Lonsdale	Grand Corona	Figurado	Robusto-Toro	Churchill	Double Corona	Giant
Henry Clay	DR	3			●		●			●		
Henry George +	DR	4				●			●		●	
Hermosa Flor +	Ni	3				●			●		●	
Hidalgo	Pa	3		●	●					●		●
Hidalgos +	Mx	2							●		●	
Hobo +	DR	1	●		●		●		●		●	
Hoja Cubana +	Ni	3			●			●	●		●	
Hoja de Honduras	Ho	4	●		●	●			●		●	●
Hoja de Mexicali	Mx	5			●	●			●		●	●
Hoja de Nicaragua	Ni	3	●		●	●			●		●	●
Hoja de Oro	Mx	3				●	●		●		●	
Hoja Real +	Mx	3			●				●		●	
Hombre de Oro +	DR	1			●	●			●	●	●	
Honduran Cuban Tobaccos	Ho	1-5		●	●	●		●	●	●	●	●
Honduras Special	Ho	3		●	●	●	●		●		●	●
Hoyo de Cortez Corto +	DR	3			●				●	●	●	
Hoyo de Cortez Escogido +	DR	3				●		●	●	●	●	
Hoyo de Cortez Premera Cal. +	DR	3						●	●	●	●	
Hoyo de Honduras	Ho	5		●	●		●		●	●		
Hoyo de Monterrey	Ho	4	●	●	●		●		●	●	●	●

HANDMADE CIGARS: INDEX

Brand	Made in	Strength	Cigarillo	Panatela	Corona	Lonsdale	Grand Corona	Figurado	Robusto-Toro	Churchill	Double Corona	Giant
Hugo Cassar	Ho	3				●	●		●	●	●	●
Hugo Cassar +	Mx	5			●				●			●
Hugo Cassar	Mx	3	●	●					●		●	●
Hugo Cassar Diamond Dominican	DR	2			●	●	●		●			●
Hugo Cassar Diamond Mystique	DR	3				●		●	●			●
Hugo Cassar Diamond Honduran	Ho	4			●		●	●	●		●	
Hugo Cassar Mystique Classic	Ho	4			●			●	●	●		
Hugo Cassar Private Collection	DR	1			●			●	●		●	
Hugo Cassar Private Collection	Ho	5			●	●			●		●	
Hugo Cassar Private Collection +	In	3	●	●					●	●		
Hugo Cassar Private Collection	Mx	5			●				●		●	
Hugo Gold +	Ni	3			●				●	●		●
Hugo Signature Series +	DR	3				●			●	●		●
Hugo Signature Series	Ni	3			●	●			●	●		●

HANDMADE CIGARS: INDEX

Brand	Made in	Strength	Cigarillo	Panatela	Corona	Lonsdale	Grand Corona	Figurado	Robusto-Toro	Churchill	Double Corona	Giant
Hurricanos +	Ho	3			●	●			●		●	
Ideal	PR	3			●					●		
Il Fiore d'Oro +	Ho	5			●				●	●		●
Imperio Cubano	US	3			●	●		●	●	●		
Indian Anniv. Reserve Series A +	Ho	5							●	●	●	
Indian Classic	Ho	2		●	●				●	●		●
Indian Head	Ho	2		●	●	●			●	●	●	●
Indian Princess +	Ho	3			●		●		●	●	●	●
Indigo +	DR	3			●	●	●	●	●	●		
Infiesta	US	1-3		●	●	●			●	●		●
Insurgentes +	Mx	3			●							
International +	US	3			●			●	●		●	
Iracema	Br	3	●		●	●						
Isabella +	DR	1			●	●			●		●	
Island Amaretto	In	5	●	●	●	●						
Islands +	In	1			●			●	●	●		
J. Cortes	DR	1		●	●				●			
J.L. Ferrer 1891 +	DR	3			●	●		●	●			
Jamaica Bay	Ja	1		●	●	●			●		●	
Jamaica Gem	Ja	4		●	●	●	●				●	●
Jamaica Gold	Ja	2		●	●	●		●	●		●	
Jamaica Heritage	Ja	1			●	●	●		●		●	●

HANDMADE CIGARS: INDEX

Brand	Made in	Strength	Cigarillo	Panatela	Corona	Lonsdale	Grand Corona	Figurado	Robusto-Toro	Churchill	Double Corona	Giant
Jimenez +	US	3	●		●	●		●	●	●	●	
John Aylesbury	Ho	3		●	●	●			●			
John Aylesbury Premium	DR	1		●	●	●			●	●		
John Hay +	DR	3				●			●		●	●
John T's	DR	1		●								
Jose Benito	DR	3	●	●	●	●			●		●	●
José Girbés +	DR	3	●		●	●			●		●	
Jose L. Piedra +	Ni	5							●	●	●	
Jose Llopis	Pa	3		●	●	●			●	●	●	●
Jose Llopis Gold	Pa	1		●	●	●			●	●		●
Jose Marti	DR	1		●	●	●			●	●		
Jose Marti	Ni	5		●	●	●		●			●	●
Jose R. Oliva +	Ni	2			●			●	●		●	●
Joya de Honduras	Ho	2		●	●			●	●		●	●
Joya del Rey	Ho	3		●	●				●		●	●
Joya de Nicaragua	Ni	1,5		●	●	●			●	●	●	●
Joya del Cibao +	DR	5			●	●			●		●	
J-R Ultimate	Ho	5	●	●	●	●	●		●	●	●	●
Juan Clemente	DR	3	●	●	●	●	●	●	●	●		●
Juan Dolio +	DR	3			●	●			●		●	
Juan Guillermo de Robles +	Ge	1		●					●		●	

HANDMADE CIGARS: INDEX

Brand	Made in	Strength	Cigarillo	Panatela	Corona	Lonsdale	Grand Corona	Figurado	Robusto-Toro	Churchill	Double Corona	Giant
Juan Lopez	Ho	4			●	●			●		●	●
Juan y Ramon	DR	3	●	●				●	●		●	
Justino +	DR	1		●				●	●	●		
Kennedy +	DR	3		●					●	●	●	
Key West Havana Gold Label +	DR	2	●	●				●	●		●	
King Cobra +	DR	5					●		●		●	
King Dominican	DR	1	●	●	●				●		●	●
King Richard +	US	2-5	●		●			●	●	●	●	
Kings Club +	Ho	3			●			●	●	●		●
Kingston	Mx	5	●	●	●				●		●	●
Kiskeya	DR	3		●	●				●	●	●	
L'Attitude 18 +	DR	3		●					●			
La Aurora	DR	3	●	●				●	●		●	
La Avida +	US	3		●					●	●	●	
La Bamba +	DR	1				●			●		●	●
La Cobra Cubana +	Mx	2	●	●				●	●	●	●	●
La Concha +	DR	2		●				●	●	●	●	
La Cosecha +	Ni	1		●					●		●	
La Damita +	PR	1	●									
La Diligencia	Ho	2		●					●	●		●
La Diva	DR	3		●				●	●			●
La Eminencia	Ho	2	●	●			●		●	●		●

HANDMADE CIGARS: INDEX

Brand	Made in	Strength	Cigarillo	Panatela	Corona	Lonsdale	Grand Corona	Figurado	Robusto-Toro	Churchill	Double Corona	Giant
La Estrella Cubana +	Ni	5		●	●				●		●	
La Fabuloso	Ho	2		●	●		●		●		●	
La Fama	CI	1		●	●		●				●	
La Favorita +	CI	1				●			●		●	
La Favorita	Ho	1		●	●							
La Finca	Ni	5			●		●	●	●	●		●
La Flor de Armando Mendez	US	3							●			
La Flor de Cuba	PR	4					●			●	●	
La Flor de Navarette +	DR	3			●				●		●	
La Flor Dominicana	DR	2,4		●	●	●		●	●	●	●	
La Fontana Vintage	Ho	1		●	●	●		●	●	●	●	
La Gianna Havana	Ho	1,3			●			●	●		●	
La Gloria Cubana	US DR	3	●	●	●	●	●	●	●	●	●	●
La Habanera	DR	2		●	●	●			●	●	●	
La Hoja del Sabor+	DR	3,4		●	●			●	●		●	
La Hoja Rica +	DR	4					●		●	●		
La Hoja Rica +	Ni	3			●		●		●			●
La Hoja Selecta	US	1		●	●	●			●	●	●	

HANDMADE CIGARS: INDEX

Brand	Made in	Strength	Cigarillo	Panatela	Corona	Lonsdale	Grand Corona	Figurado	Robusto-Toro	Churchill	Double Corona	Giant
La Isla	PR	5					•					
La Isla	US	4		•	•	•			•	•		•
La Luna de la Habana +	US	2-5			•				•		•	
La Lunda +	Mx	3		•	•	•	•	•	•	•	•	
La Lunda de Santa Maria +	Pa	3							•			
La Maximiliana	Ho	3			•	•			•		•	
La Native	Ho	3		•	•				•	•		•
La Nubia +	CI	1		•	•	•			•		•	
La Palma de Oro +	CI	1		•	•				•	•	•	
La Paloma +	DR	3			•	•			•		•	•
La Pantera Diamond Coll.	Ho	2		•	•			•	•		•	•
La Pantera Emerald Coll. +	Ni	5					•	•	•		•	
La Pantera Sapphire Coll.	Ho	4		•	•			•	•		•	•
La Perla +	Ni	2				•			•	•		
La Perla Habana +	DR	3			•	•		•	•		•	
La Plata	US Ho DR	1-5		•	• •	•	•	•	• •	•	• •	•
La Primadora	Ho	1		•	•	•			•			•
La Primera	DR	3			•	•			•		•	•

- 73 -

HANDMADE CIGARS: INDEX

Brand	Made in	Strength	Cigarillo	Panatela	Corona	Lonsdale	Grand Corona	Figurado	Robusto-Toro	Churchill	Double Corona	Giant
La Prueba +	Mx	2			●							
La Real	Ni	5							●		●	
La Regenta +	CI	1			●	●		●		●	●	●
La Regional	CI	5	●		●	●			●	●	●	
La Restina	PR	4			●						●	
La Tradicion Cabinet Sel. +	US Ni	4		●	●			●	●		●	
La Tradicion Cubana	US	4		●	●			●	●		●	
La Unica	DR	1			●	●			●		●	●
La Veleza +	DR	2			●			●	●	●	●	
La Venga	Ho	4			●		●		●	●	●	●
La Vieja Habana +	DR	5			●	●		●	●		●	
Lady Jane +	Ho	1			●							
Lambs Club	DR	3			●				●		●	
Lancelot +	Mx	1			●	●			●		●	●
Largo y Zorro +	DR Ni	3,5 1						●	● ●	● ●		●
Lars Tetens Phat Cigars +	US	2-5	●	●	●	●	●	●	●	●	●	●
Las Cabrillas	Ho	3	●	●	●				●	●	●	●
Las Vegas Cigar	US	1-5	●	●	●			●	●	●	●	●
Lazarus +	Mx	1		●	●				●	●		●
Legacy	Ho	3			●	●			●	●	●	●

HANDMADE CIGARS: INDEX

Brand	Made in	Strength	Cigarillo	Panatela	Corona	Lonsdale	Grand Corona	Figurado	Robusto-Toro	Churchill	Double Corona	Giant
Legend•Ario	Ho	3			●	●			●	●		
Legion +	Ni	3			●	●			●	●	●	●
Lempira	Ho	3		●	●	●			●	●	●	
Leon	US	3		●		●			●	●	●	●
Leon	DR	2				●		●	●	●		●
Leon Jimenes	DR	5		●	●	●		●	●	●	●	
Lew's Smokers	Ho	3			●					●		
Leyenda +	DR	1			●			●	●		●	
Licenciados	DR	3		●	●	●			●	●		●	●
Licey +	DR	1			●		●	●	●			●
Little Havana Cigar Factory +	US	3		●	●		●	●	●		●	
Lone Wolf +	DR	2-3		●	●	●		●	●	●	●	
Los Nicas +	Ni	3			●				●		●	
Luza Azul +	DR	3			●	●	●		●	●	●	
Macabi	DR	3			●	●		●	●		●	
Macanudo	Ja DR	2	●	●	●	●	●	●	●	●	● ●	●
Macarena +	CI	1				●			●		●	
Madame Marshall+	DR	3		●								
Madrigal Habana	Mx	1			●	●			●		●	●
Maestro	US	5					●	●	●			
Maestro Cubano +	Ho	3			●			●	●		●	

HANDMADE CIGARS: INDEX

Brand	Made in	Strength	Cigarillo	Panatela	Corona	Lonsdale	Grand Corona	Figurado	Robusto-Toro	Churchill	Double Corona	Giant
Maestro de La Palma +	Cl	1					●		●		●	
Maker's Mark +	DR	4							●			
Manifiesto +	DR	3		●	●	●		●	●	●	●	●
Manuel Casals +	Mx	3			●		●		●		●	
Maria Mancini	Ho	5		●	●	●			●		●	
Mario Palomino	Ja	5		●	●	●	●				●	●
Marquez Mendoza +	DR	1		●					●		●	
Marsh 1840 +	Ho	2				●						
Master Bradley's Premium +	DR	2		●					●	●		
Matacan	Mx	3		●	●	●			●		●	●
Matador +	Ho	3			●	●		●	●	●		
MATASA Seconds	DR	1		●	●	●	●				●	●
Match Play	DR	3			●			●	●	●	●	
Match Play Serie Medallista +	DR	4						●				
Maxim's +	DR	3		●	●	●			●	●	●	
Maxius	DR	2,4		●	●	●			●	●	●	
Maya	Ho	2		●	●	●		●	●	●	●	●
Mayorga +	Ni	3			●			●	●	●		
Medal of Honor	Ho	3				●					●	●
Memphis Blue +	Mx	3			●				●		●	

HANDMADE CIGARS: INDEX

Brand	Made in	Strength	Cigarillo	Panatela	Corona	Lonsdale	Grand Corona	Figurado	Robusto-Toro	Churchill	Double Corona	Giant
Mendez y Lopez +	DR	1	●	●	●	●		●	●	●	●	●
Mercedes +	DR	3,4		●	●			●	●		●	
Mexican Emperador	Mx	3										●
Mi Flor +	Ho	2			●				●	●	●	
MiCubano	Ni	5			●	●			●	●		●
Miguelon +	Ph	3			●				●			
Millenium +	DR	4			●				●			
Mocambo	Mx	5	●		●	●			●	●	●	●
Montague	In	3			●	●	●		●		●	
Monte Canario	CI	1	●		●	●		●	●		●	
Monte Real +	DR	1			●	●			●	●	●	
Monte Rio +	DR	3			●		●	●	●	●		●
Montebello +	Mx	5	●		●	●			●		●	●
Montecassino	Ho	2		●		●						●
Montecristo	DR	4			●	●	●	●	●	●		
Montecruz	DR	2,4	●	●	●	●			●	●		●
Montenegro +	Mx	1				●					●	
Montero	DR	3			●			●	●	●	●	
Montes de Oca	CR	5			●				●	●		
Montes de Oro +	CR	3			●					●		
Montesino	DR	3			●	●				●		
Montoya	Ho	1			●	●			●		●	●

HANDMADE CIGARS: INDEX

Brand		Made in	Strength	Cigarillo	Panatela	Corona	Lonsdale	Grand Corona	Figurado	Robusto-Toro	Churchill	Double Corona	Giant
Moore & Bode		US	2,4		●	●	●	●	●	●		●	
Moran	+	DR	2		●	●	●		●	●	●	●	
Morel	+	DR	2		●					●			
Moreno Maduro		DR	2		●	●	●			●	●	●	●
Motta	+	Mx	2		●					●		●	
Mulato	+	DR	4		●								
Mursuli's	+	US	4		●			●	●	●	●	●	●
Napa	+	DR	3		●	●				●	●		
		Ni	1			●				●	●		
Napa Reserve		CI	4			●	●		●	●		●	
		DR	4			●	●		●	●		●	
Napoleon's Dream	+	Ho	2			●							
National Brand		Ho	2		●	●				●	●		●
Nat Sherman		DR	1-4	●	●	●	●	●	●	●		●	
		Ho	3		●	●	●	●	●	●		●	
Nativo	+	PR	2				●	●	●	●	●		
Navarro	+	Ni	3				●			●		●	●
Nestor 747		Ho	5								●		
Nester 747 Series II		Ho	5							●	●		
New York, New York		Mx	3		●	●	●			●	●		
nextGeneration	+	DR	1,3		●				●	●	●		

HANDMADE CIGARS: INDEX

Brand	Made in	Strength	Cigarillo	Panatela	Corona	Lonsdale	Grand Corona	Figurado	Robusto-Toro	Churchill	Double Corona	Giant
Nicaragua Especial	Ni	3		●	●				●		●	●
Nicaragua Supremo +	Ni	2			●				●		●	●
Nicaro +	Ni	4			●				●		●	●
Nicole Miller +	DR	2-4			●	●			●			●
Niño Vasquez +	DR	3			●			●	●		●	●
Nivelacuso Private Reserve +	DR	3				●	●		●			●
Nording	DR	3			●	●			●		●	
Nostalgia +	Ho	5			●			●	●	●	●	
O&B Dominican Reserve +	DR	1			●			●	●		●	●
Ocho Rios	Ja	1			●	●			●		●	●
Octavio Tavares +	DR	1-5							●	●	●	
Oh Que Bueno	CI	3			●	●						
Old Fashioned +	DR	4		●	●	●			●		●	
	Ja	2	●	●						●		
Old Trinidad XVIII Century +	CI	2			●				●	●	●	
Oliveros	DR	2,4		●	●	●		●	●		●	●
Olor	DR	3		●	●	●			●	●	●	
Olor Vintage +	DR	3			●			●	●		●	
One Plus +	DR	2			●				●	●		

HANDMADE CIGARS: INDEX

Brand	Made in	Strength	Cigarillo	Panatela	Corona	Lonsdale	Grand Corona	Figurado	Robusto-Toro	Churchill	Double Corona	Giant
100 Fuegos +	Mx	4			•			•	•		•	
Onyx	DR	1		•			•		•		•	•
Opus X	DR	5	•	•	•	•			•	•	•	•
Orama +	US	1					•	•	•	•		•
Orient Express	Ho	1	•	•	•				•		•	
Ornelas	Mx	1-2	•	•	•		•		•		•	•
Oro Dominicano +	DR	2			•				•			
Oro 750 +	DR	3			•	•			•	•		
Orosi	Ni	3			•				•		•	
Oscar	DR	4	•	•	•	•		•				•
Padron	Ho Ni	4		•	•	•	•	•	•	•	•	•
Paisanos +	DR	3			•				•	•	•	•
Palmarejo +	DR	3			•				•		•	
Panabano +	Pa	1						•	•		•	
Panama Jones +	DR 3 Mx 3 Pa 2				•	•			•	•		
Panorea +	DR	4			•	•		•	•		•	
Pantera	DR	1	•		•		•		•			
Pantera de Oro +	Ni	1			•				•		•	
Partagas	DR	4	•	•	•	•	•	•			•	
Particulares	DR	3		•	•	•			•	•	•	•

HANDMADE CIGARS: INDEX

Brand	Made in	Strength	Cigarillo	Panatela	Corona	Lonsdale	Grand Corona	Figurado	Robusto-Toro	Churchill	Double Corona	Giant
Paseana +	Ho	3			●			●	●	●		●
Paul Garmirian	DR	4		●	●	●	●	●	●	●	●	●
Pecado +	DR	3			●			●	●	●		
Penguin +	DR	3				●			●		●	●
Pera +	Ni	3			●			●	●	●	●	
Peterson Hallmark	DR	2		●	●				●	●	●	
Peter Stokkebye	DR	1		●	●						●	
Petrus	Ho	2		●	●		●	●	●		●	
Petrus Etiquette Rouge	Ho	3			●			●	●	●		
Petrus Oro Negro +	Ho	3			●		●	●	●		●	
Pheasant	Ho	1				●			●		●	
Philippine Cigar +	Ph	3		●	●	●	●	●	●	●	●	
Phillips & King Guardsmen	DR	1		●	●				●	●	●	●
Pinnacle	DR	3							●	●		
Pirata +	DR	3						●	●	●		●
Plasencia +	Ni	3			●			●	●		●	
Playboy	DR	3				●	●		●	●	●	
Pleiades	DR	1-5	●	●	●				●	●		●
Pleiades Reserve Privee +	DR	1							●	●		
Porfirio	DR	1			●	●			●		●	●

HANDMADE CIGARS: INDEX

Brand	Made in	Strength	Cigarillo	Panatela	Corona	Lonsdale	Grand Corona	Figurado	Robusto-Toro	Churchill	Double Corona	Giant
Por Larrañaga	DR	1		●	●	●		●	●		●	
Por Matt Amore	DR	3			●				●		●	
Porto Bello	DR	1		●	●	●		●	●	●	●	●
Presidente +	US	3		●	●			●	●		●	●
Presidente Caceres +	DR	2							●	●		
Prestigio Cubano +	Ho	4				●		●	●	●		●
Pride of Copan	Ho	4	●	●	●						●	
Pride of Jamaica	Ja	1			●	●	●		●		●	
Primera de Nicaragua	Ni	2			●				●		●	●
Primo del Cristo	Ho	4		●	●				●			●
Primo del Rey	DR	1	●	●	●	●						
Private Stock	DR	2	●	●	●		●		●		●	
Prize Pointer +	DR	5			●	●			●		●	
Profesor Sila	DR	2		●			●	●	●		●	●
Prof. Sila Baba +	DR	1				●						
Prof. Sila Navegador +	DR	3		●			●		●		●	
Prof. Sila Santa Maria +	DR	5		●	●	●	●		●		●	
Providencia +	DR	3			●		●		●			●
Pueblo Dominicano +	DR	4		●	●		●		●	●		●

HANDMADE CIGARS: INDEX

Brand	Made in	Strength	Cigarillo	Panatela	Corona	Lonsdale	Grand Corona	Figurado	Robusto-Toro	Churchill	Double Corona	Giant
Puerto Rico +	PR	3			●					●		
Punch	Ho	4	●	●	●	●	●	●	●	●	●	●
Puro Nicaragua	Ni	5		●	●	●			●		●	●
Puro Placer +	Ni	3			●				●		●	
Purofino Blue +	Ho	4				●		●	●		●	
Purofino Gold +	Ho	5				●		●	●		●	
Puros Don Abreu +	DR	3		●	●	●	●	●	●	●	●	●
Puros Indios	Ho	3		●	●	●	●	●	●	●	●	●
Puros Nirvana +	Ni	3			●				●		●	
Puros Polanco +	Mx	3				●						
Puros Tejera +	DR	2			●	●			●		●	
Pyramid +	DR	3			●	●		●	●		●	
Quetzal +	DR	1		●	●	●			●	●		●
Quetzal +	Ho	1			●	●			●	●	●	●
Quintero Blue Ribbon +	Ni	3			●	●			●		●	
Quintin Q-Oro +	DR	3			●			●	●		●	
	Ho	1				●			●		●	
	Mx	3							●		●	
	Ni	3				●			●		●	
	US	5			●			●	●		●	
Quirantes +	DR	5	●	●	●	●			●	●	●	●
Ramar	US	2		●	●	●	●	●	●	●	●	●
Rambling River +	Mx	3		●	●	●	●		●		●	●

HANDMADE CIGARS: INDEX

Brand	Made in	Strength	Cigarillo	Panatela	Corona	Lonsdale	Grand Corona	Figurado	Robusto-Toro	Churchill	Double Corona	Giant
Ramon Allones	DR	4		●	●	●			●		●	
Real Veracruz +	Mx	4			●		●		●		●	
Red Lion +	DR	4					●		●		●	
Regalos	Ho	4			●			●	●			●
Reina Dominicana +	DR	1		●		●	●		●			●
Remedios +	Ni	4					●				●	
Repeater	Ho	3			●	●					●	
Reserva del Patron +	Mx	3			●		●			●		
Rey de Zaba +	DR	4			●	●			●			
Rey del Mar +	DR	4			●				●	●		
RG Santiago Dominican +	DR	3	●		●	●		●	●		●	
Rico Havana	Ho	3			●	●			●	●		●
Ricos Dominicanos	DR	2			●	●			●		●	
Rigoletto	DR	3				●			●	●		
Robali	CR	2			●	●			●	●		●
Robusto de Casa +	Mx	3							●			
Rodriguez & Menendez	US	3		●		●	●		●	●	●	
Rolando	DR	2			●				●	●		
Roller's Choice	DR	1			●	●	●	●	●		●	

HANDMADE CIGARS: INDEX

Brand	Made in	Strength	Cigarillo	Panatela	Corona	Lonsdale	Grand Corona	Figurado	Robusto-Toro	Churchill	Double Corona	Giant
Roly +	DR Ho	3		●	●	●	●		●	●	●	
Romano's Connoisseur +	DR	3		●					●	●	●	
Romanticos	DR	2			●			●	●		●	●
Romeo y Julieta	DR	3		●	●	●		●	●		●	●
Romeo y Julieta Vintage	DR	1			●		●	●	●	●	●	
Ronaldo Somma +	DR	2				●		●	●		●	●
Rosa Blanca Reserva +	Ni	2			●			●	●	●		
Rosa Cuba	Ni	4		●	●	●	●		●	●	●	●
Rosalones	Ni	1		●	●	●	●		●	●	●	●
Rosario +	Mx	3			●	●			●		●	
Rosato +	Ni	5		●	●				●	●		●
Rough Rider +	DR	3							●			
Rovanoff +	Ni	3		●	●				●	●	●	●
Royal Barbados	Ba	1		●	●		●					
Royal Court	Ho	1		●	●						●	●
Royal Dominicana	DR	2		●	●	●	●				●	
Royale Gold +	DR	4		●	●			●	●		●	
Royale Saludo +	DR	1			●		●	●	●			●
Royales	DR	1		●	●	●			●		●	●
Royal Honduras	Ho	2			●	●		●	●	●		●

HANDMADE CIGARS: INDEX

Brand	Made in	Strength	Cigarillo	Panatela	Corona	Lonsdale	Grand Corona	Figurado	Robusto-Toro	Churchill	Double Corona	Giant
Royal Jamaica	DR Ja	3		●	●	●	●		●			●
Royal Manna	Ho	3		●	●	●			●		●	
Royal Nicaraguan	Ni	3			●				●		●	●
Royce +	Ho	4			●				●		●	
Rubirosa	DR	1			●			●	●	●	●	●
Rum Raider +	DR	3						●				
Rum Royale +	DR	3			●							
Sabor +	DR	1		●	●							
Sabor Habano	Ni	3			●				●		●	●
Sabor Habano Dom. Reserve +	DR	3			●				●		●	
Sabroso	Ni	5			●				●	●		●
St. Christobal +	DR	4			●				●		●	
St. George +	DR	2			●		●	●	●	●		●
Saint Luis Rey	Ho	5				●		●	●		●	
St. Tropez	Ho	1		●	●							
San Angelo +	DR	1			●				●			
San Fernando	Ho	5			●				●	●		
San Marcos	Ho	5			●				●	●		●
San Vicente 50	Ni	3		●	●	●			●	●	●	●
Santa Clara 1830	Mx	3	●	●	●	●			●		●	●
Santa Damiana	DR	3				●	●		●	●	●	

HANDMADE CIGARS: INDEX

Brand	Made in	Strength	Cigarillo	Panatela	Corona	Lonsdale	Grand Corona	Figurado	Robusto-Toro	Churchill	Double Corona	Giant
Santa Rosa	Ho	1		●	●	●	●	●	●		●	●
Santiago	DR	1		●	●		●			●		
Santiago Silk +	DR	3			●			●	●	●		●
Santo Diego +	Mx	1			●	●			●		●	
Savinelli ELR	DR	3			●		●		●	●		
Sebastian Reserva +	Ni	3							●	●	●	
Segovia	Ni	5			●		●		●		●	
Selecto Puro Dominicano +	DR	3		●			●	●	●	●		●
Sevilla +	Ho	1			●			●	●	●		
Siglo 21	DR	3				●		●	●	●		●
Signature Collection	US	3				●		●	●		●	
Signet	DR	1			●				●	●		
660 Red	US	5							●			
Smok-A-Cuba +	DR US	3		●	●	●			●	●		●
Socorro +	DR	3							●		●	
Sol y Mar	Ho	3			●			●	●		●	
Soleares +	CR	3			●	●	●		●	●		●
Solearas Limited Reserve +	CR	3							●	●		●

HANDMADE CIGARS: INDEX

Brand	Made in	Strength	Cigarillo	Panatela	Corona	Lonsdale	Grand Corona	Figurado	Robusto-Toro	Churchill	Double Corona	Giant
Soleares Special Reserve +	CR	3				●			●	●		●
Sosa	DR	3		●	●	●		●	●	●	●	
Sosa Family Selection	DR	4		●	●	●			●	●	●	
SP Maduro +	Ni	4							●		●	
Spanish Honduran Red Label	Ho	3		●	●	●			●	●	●	●
Speakeasy +	DR US	3 4				● 		● ●	● ●	 ●	● ●	 ●
Special Jamaican	DR	1		●	●	●		●	●		●	●
Spirit Valley +	Ni	5			●	●			●	●		
Strelsky +	DR	1					●		●		●	
Suave	DR	3			●				●		●	
Suerdieck	Br	3	●	●	●		●					
T.J. +	Ho	2,3			●	●		●	●	●		●
Tabacalera	Ph	3		●	●	●		●	●			●
Tabacon Vintage Selection +	Ho	5			●			●	●	●	●	
Tabacos San Jose	Ni US	2			●	●		●	●	●	●	●
Tabacos Universo	Ho	3			●	●		●	●		●	●
Taino +	DR	5			●	●	●		●		●	
Taino +	PR	5								●		

HANDMADE CIGARS: INDEX

Brand	Made in	Strength	Cigarillo	Panatela	Corona	Lonsdale	Grand Corona	Figurado	Robusto-Toro	Churchill	Double Corona	Giant
Tamayo y Pareto +	DR	2			●			●	●		●	
Tamboril	DR	2,4		●	●			●	●	●		●
Tamboril Cordova Coll. +	DR	3		●	●				●	●		
Tamboril Fore +	DR	4							●			
Tampa Tropics +	US	3						●	●		●	
Tatou +	Mx	1			●							
Te-Amo	Mx	3	●	●	●	●	●	●	●		●	●
Te-Amo Segundo	Mx	3		●	●	●	●		●		●	
Temple Hall	Ja	3		●	●	●		●	●		●	
Tena y Vega	Ho	4			●	●			●		●	
Tenorio +	DR	3		●	●		●	●	●		●	
Terri Welles Signature +	Gu	1									●	
Tesoro +	DR	4			●		●		●		●	●
Tesoros de Copan	Ho	2		●	●		●		●		●	
Third Millenium +	DR	3						●	●	●	●	
Thomas Hinds Cabinet Sel. +	Ni	4			●	●			●		●	
Thomas Hinds Honduran Sel.	Ho	4			●	●		●	●		●	●
Thomas Hinds Nicaraguan Sel.	Ni	2			●	●		●	●		●	

HANDMADE CIGARS: INDEX

Brand	Made in	Strength	Cigarilo	Panatela	Corona	Lonsdale	Grand Corona	Figurado	Robusto-Toro	Churchill	Double Corona	Giant
Thomas Hinds Vintage I +	Ni	4			•	•			•		•	
Tia Martia	DR	2	•	•			•		•		•	
Tiburon	Ho	1	•	•								
Tipo +	DR	3		•					•			
Todo El Mundo	DR	2		•				•	•		•	
Tooth of the Dog	Ni	3						•	•		•	
Topper Centennial	DR	3				•			•		•	
Topper Grande	Ni	4			•	•			•		•	
Torcedor	Ni	1				•			•		•	•
Torcedor +	Mx	5							•		•	
Toro Bravo +	DR	3		•		•			•	•	•	
Torquino +	DR	2		•					•		•	
Tradicionales +	US	2		•	•	•	•	•	•		•	
Tresado	DR	5			•	•	•			•		•
Troya	DR	3,4		•	•	•		•	•	•	•	
12 Stars +	DR	1	•	•	•	•			•	•		•
Ultimate Dominican +	DR	2			•		•		•	•		
Universo +	Ho	3			•	•		•	•		•	•
V Centennial	Ho	3		•	•	•		•	•	•		•
V Centennial 500 +	DR	5		•	•			•	•	•		•

HANDMADE CIGARS: INDEX

Brand	Made in	Strength	Cigarillo	Panatela	Corona	Lonsdale	Grand Corona	Figurado	Robusto-Toro	Churchill	Double Corona	Giant
V.M. Santana/ Connecticut	DR	1			●			●	●		●	
V.M. Santana/ Sumatra +	DR	1			●				●		●	
Valle del Sol +	Mx	3			●				●		●	
Van Winkle +	DR	3								●		
Vanilla Delight +	DR	3			●							
Vanilla Sweets +	US	2		●	●	●	●		●			
Vargas	Cl	1		●	●		●		●	●	●	
Vega del Rey +	DR	3			●				●		●	
Vegas Cubano +	Ni	5							●		●	
Ventura +	Ni	2			●	●			●		●	●
Veracruz	Mx	1		●	●	●		●	●	●		
Victor Sinclair	DR	3			●		●	●	●		●	
Victor Sinclair Grand Res. +	DR	5		●			●	●				
Victor Sinclair Vintage Select +	DR	5			●				●	●	●	
Victory Spirit	Ni	1			●				●	●		
Villa +	DR	3			●				●		●	
Villar y Villar	Ni	4		●	●	●	●	●	●	●	●	●
Villega Reales	DR	3			●	●			●	●		
VIP Club Coll. +	DR	1			●		●		●		●	
Virtuoso Toraño	Ho	2			●	●			●			●

HANDMADE CIGARS: INDEX

Brand	Made in	Strength	Cigarillo	Panatela	Corona	Lonsdale	Grand Corona	Figurado	Robusto-Toro	Churchill	Double Corona	Giant
VSOP Vintage Reserve +	DR	1			●	●		●	●		●	
Vueltabajo	DR	2			●	●		●	●	●		●
Wall Street Portfolio +	Ho	3			●	●		●	●		●	
West Indies Vanilla	In	5	●	●	●	●						
Wild Javanos +	In	3		●	●				●	●		
Xclusivo +	US	4		●		●		●	●		●	●
Xilado +	US	5		●	●	●		●	●	●		●
Xotica +	US	1				●			●			
Xquisito +	Ni	2				●			●	●	●	
Yulerdi +	DR	1				●			●	●		
Yumuri	DR	1			●	●			●	●		
Yumuri 1492	DR	2			●	●			●	●		
Zelo de Cuba +	DR	3			●	●		●			●	
Zino	Ho	1	●	●	●	●	●		●		●	

4.
HANDMADE CIGARS:
LISTINGS BY BRAND

This section provides the details on 961 brands of cigars
marketed nationally in the United States, a net increase of **95%**
(and 468 brands) from the 1997 edition! Each brand listing
includes notes on country of manufacture, the origin of the
tobaccos used, shapes, names, lengths, ring gauges, wrapper
color and a brief description *as supplied by the manufacturers
and/or distributors of these brands.* Ring gauges for some
brands of cigarillos were not available.

Please note that while a cigar may be manufactured in one
country, it may contain tobaccos from many nations. The
designation "handmade" indicates the use of long-filler tobacco
unless otherwise noted.

Although manufacturers have recognized more than 70 shades
of wrapper color, six major color groupings are used here.
Their abbreviations include:

- ‣ DC = Double Claro: green, also known as American
    Market Selection or "AMS."
- ‣ Cl = Claro: a very light tan color.
- ‣ CC = Colorado Claro: a medium brown common to
    many cigars on this list.
- ‣ Co = Colorado: reddish-brown.
- ‣ CM = Colorado Maduro: dark brown.
- ‣ Ma = Maduro: very dark brown or black (also known
    as "double Maduro" or "Oscuro.")

Many manufacturers call their wrapper colors "Natural" or "English Market Selection." These colors cover a wide range of browns and we have generally grouped them in the "CC" range. Darker wrappers such as those from Cameroon show up most often in the "CM" category.

Shape designations are based on our shape chart in section 1.03. Careful readers will note the freedom with which manufacturers attach names of shapes to cigars which do not resemble that shape at all! For easier comparison, all lengths were rounded to the shortest eighth of an inch, although some manufacturers list sizes in 16ths or even 32nds of an inch.

Although hundreds of brands are listed, house brands of cigar lounges or individual tobacco stores do not appear. In general, all of the brands listed are available to retailers through wholesale distribution channels.

Readers who would like to see their favorite brand listed in the 1999 edition can call or write the compilers as noted after the Table of Contents.

A.T. COFINO
Handmade in Saõ Goncalo dos Campos, Brazil.

Wrapper: Ecuador   Binder: Brazil   Filler: Brazil

Shape	Name	Lgth	Ring	Wrapper
Corona	Corona	5½	42	CC
Lonsdale	Lonsdale	6½	42	CC
Churchill	Churchill	7	46	CC
Robusto	Robusto	5	52	CC

| Robusto | Rothschild | 5½ | 50 | CC |
| Double Corona | Double Corona | 7½ | 50 | CC |

Here is a medium-to-full-bodied cigar produced in a small town in the Bahia state of Brazil. It features an Ecuadorian-grown, Connecticut-seed wrapper around native Brazilian tobaccos and is offered in boxes of 20 except for the Corona and Lonsdale sizes, which are offered in 20s.

ABSOLUTO
Handmade in Tamboril, Dominican Republic.

Wrapper: Ecuador   *Binder: Dom. Rep.*   *Filler: Dom. Rep.*

Shape	Name	Lgth	Ring	Wrapper
Double Corona	Xtra Churchill	7½	52	CC
Toro	Xtra Robusto	6	52	CC
Grand Corona	Corona Suprema	6½	46	CC

Introduced in 1997, this brand offers a medium-bodied smoke in three larger sizes, featuring an Ecuadorian-grown wrapper.

ACAPA SWEETS
Handmade in Santiago, Dominican Republic.

Wrapper: Indonesia   *Binder: Dom. Rep.*   *Filler: Dom. Rep.*

Shape	Name		Lgth	Ring	Wrapper
Panatela	Panatela	*(tube available)*	6	38	CC
Corona	Corona	*(tube available)*	5½	44	CC
Cigarillo	Ladyfinger		4	26	CC

This is a new brand in 1997, with your choice of flavors in a medium-bodied style. You can choose from Amaretto Creme and Vanilla Bean to start with Cognac, Irish Creme, mocha and rum on the way! Acapas are available in either individual cellophane sleeves or in tubes, packed in boxes of 25.

HANDMADE CIGARS: BRAND LISTINGS

AGUILA
Handmade in Santiago, Dominican Republic.

Wrapper: USA/Connecticut   Binder: Dom. Rep.   Filler: Dom. Rep.

Shape	Name	Lgth	Ring	Wrapper
Corona	Coronita	5½	40	CC
Lonsdale	Brevas 44	7½	44	CC
Grand Corona	Brevas 46	6½	46	CC
Double Corona	Brevas 50	7½	50	CC
Robusto	Petit Gordo	4¾	50	CC

Created in 1989, this is a mild-to-medium-bodied cigar, which is hand-made in Santiago de los Caballeros, Dominican Republic. The Connecticut wrappers are aged for 5-7 years before production.

AL-CAPONE
Handmade in Esteli, Nicaragua.

Wrapper: Brazil   Binder: Nicaragua   Filler: Nicaragua

Shape	Name	Lgth	Ring	Wrapper
Robusto	Robusto	4½	50	CM
Lonsdale	Corona Grande	6¾	43	CM
Toro	Toro	6	50	CM

This is a 1996 extension of the long-time cigarillo brand produced in Germany. Named for the corpulent Chicago-based gangster of the 1920s, the brand is not surprising in its medium-bodied flavor, but it also exhibits a slightly sweet taste. It is offered in boxes of 25.

ALAMO
Handmade in Danli, Honduras.

Wrapper: Ecuador   Binder: Honduras   Filler: Honduras

Shape	Name	Lgth	Ring	Wrapper
Giant	Travis	8½	52	CC

HANDMADE CIGARS: BRAND LISTINGS

Double Corona	Crockett	7	50	CC
Churchill	Bonham	6¾	46	CC
Toro	Bowie	6	50	CC
Robusto	Esparza	5	50	CC
Lonsdale	Stockton	6½	42	CC

Named in honor of the famed mission in San Antonio, Texas where Texan
freedom fighters fell in a battle against the Mexican army in 1836, this brand
celebrates six members of the garrison, including well-known figures such as
Col. William Barrett Travis, Jim Bowie and Davey Crockett. The cigars
themselves are of medium body and slightly spicy. Scheduled for introduction in
1998, they will be available in boxes of 25.

ALHAMBRA
Handmade in Manila, the Philippines.

Wrapper: Indonesia   *Binder: Philippines*   *Filler: Philippines*

Shape	Name	Lgth	Ring	Wrapper
Corona	Corona	5	42	CM
Giant	Corona Grande	8¼	47	CM
Giant	Double Corona	8½	50	CM
Lonsdale	Duque	6½	42	CM
Toro	Especiale	6½	50	CM

Introduced in 1970, Alhambra cigars are handmade in the well-respected
factories of the Philippine islands and are packed in bundles of 25 cigars each. A
well-made, mild-bodied cigar with a Javan wrapper, it is modestly priced.

ALPHA CANDELA CUBANA
Handmade in Miami, Florida, USA.
Wrapper: Brazil or USA/Connecticut

Binder: Nicaragua   *Filler: Dominican Republic, Nicaragua*

Shape	Name	Lgth	Ring	Wrapper
Small Panatela	Senorita	5	30	CC-Ma

HANDMADE CIGARS: BRAND LISTINGS

Panatela	Panatela	6	36	CC-Ma
Lonsdale	No. 1	6½	42	CC-Ma
Grand Corona	Corona Extra	6	46	CC-Ma
Robusto	Wavell	5	48	CC-Ma
Robusto	Robusto	5	50	CC-Ma
Churchill	Churchill	7	48	CC-Ma
Double Corona	Presidente	7½	52	CC-Ma
Torpedo	Torpedo	6½	52	CC-Ma

Sought after? That's an understatement! Known as "Alpha" for a long time, the actual name is Candela Cubana, but they are combined here for ease of reference. This is a medium-bodied smoke with intense flavors, thanks in part to the Brazilian-grown, Sumatra-seed natural wrappers or Connecticut Broadleaf maduro leaves.

ALVARO
Handmade in Las Palmas, the Canary Islands of Spain.
Wrapper: USA/Connecticut   Binder: Mexico   Filler: Brazil, Dom. Rep.

Shape	Name	Lgth	Ring	Wrapper
Corona	Brevas	5¼	41	CC
Short Panatela	Saudos	4¾	39	CC
Corona	Cedros	5¼	41	CC
Short Panatela	Regalos	5	39	CC

Alvaro cigars are handmade in the historic Canary Islands, where the tradition of cigar making goes back for hundreds of years. This brand is very mild in body and is offered in boxes of 25.

AMOROSO
Handmade in Danli, Honduras.
Wrapper: Ecuador   Binder: Dom. Rep.   Filler: Dom. Rep., Mexico

HANDMADE CIGARS: BRAND LISTINGS

Shape	Name	Lgth	Ring	Wrapper
Double Corona	Churchill	7	50	CM
Lonsdale	Lonsdale	6½	44	CM
Giant	Presidente	8½	52	CM
Robusto	Robusto	4¾	50	CM
Toro	Toro	6	50	CM

Here is a new cigar for 1997, with a mild-bodied flavor in the most popular sizes. Thanks to the unique blend of leaves from three nations, you'll find it easy to enjoy in boxes of 10 or 20.

ANACAONA
Handmade in Santiago, Dominican Republic.

Wrapper: Dom. Rep. or Indonesia   *Binder: Dom. Rep.*   *Filler: Dom. Rep.*

Shape	Name	Lgth	Ring	Wrapper
Robusto	Robusto	5	50	CM-Ma
Toro	Toro	6	50	CM-Ma
Lonsdale	Lonsdale	6½	44	CM-Ma
Churchill	Churchill	7	47	CM-Ma
Torpedo	Torpedo	6½	52	CM-Ma

Introduced in 1997, this brand offers a choice of wrappers: an Indonesian natural wrapper yielding a mild-bodied flavor and a Dominican-grown maduro wrapper that provides a mild-to-medium-bodied flavor. It is offered in either bundles or boxes of 25.

ANCLA Y CAZADOR
Handmade in Esteli, Nicaragua.

Wrapper: Indonesia   *Binder: Indonesia*   *Filler: Nicaragua*

Shape	Name	Lgth	Ring	Wrapper
Corona	Seleccion	5½	42	CM

HANDMADE CIGARS: BRAND LISTINGS

Robusto	Robusto	5	50	CM
Torpedo	Pincourt	6	52	CM
Double Corona	Churchill	7	49	CM

A rich, medium-to-full-bodied flavor is the reward for this brand, introduced in late 1997. Although all of the sizes are available in boxes of 25, you can carry the Seleccion with you easily in their special boxes of five.

ANDROS
Handmade in Santiago, Dominican Republic.

Wrapper: Indonesia *Binder: Dom. Rep.* *Filler: Dom. Rep.*

Shape	*Name*	*Lgth*	*Ring*	*Wrapper*
Long Panatela	Long Panatela	7¾	38	CM
Giant	Giant	8	50	CM
Robusto	Robusto	4½	52	CM
Toro	Toro	6	50	CM
Corona Extra	Corona Extra	5½	46	CM
Churchill	Grand Corona	6¾	46	CM
Corona	Corona	5¼	42	CM
Petit Corona	Petit Corona	4	42	CM

You'll find this brand in special, plexi-topped wood boxes of 25 cigars each. Andros features a Sumatra-grown wrapper, Cuban-seed filler and a medium-bodied flavor.

ANDUJAR
Handmade in Santiago, Dominican Republic.

Wrapper: USA/Connecticut *Binder: Dom. Rep.* *Filler: Dom. Rep.*

Shape	*Name*	*Lgth*	*Ring*	*Wrapper*
Cigarillo	Romana	5	25	CC
Double Corona	Santiago	7½	50	CC

Giant	Azua	9	46	CC
Lonsdale	Macorix	6½	44	CC
Panatela	Samana	6	38	CC
Robusto	Vega	5	50	CC

Introduced in 1994, this line is the special favorite of Oscar Rodriguez, who developed the much-loved Oscar brand. Full-bodied, this line has a clean, gustatory flavor enhanced by each and every draw. The captivating aroma and exciting after-taste make this the perfect cigar for the most special moments. Andujar cigars are offered uncellophaned in all-cedar cabinets for only the truly serious smoker.

ANDULLEROS
Handmade, with short filler, in Santiago, Dominican Republic.

Wrapper: Indonesia   Binder: Dom. Rep.   Filler: Dom. Rep.

Shape	Name	Lgth	Ring	Wrapper
Giant	Churchill	8	50	CM
Double Corona	Presidente	7	50	CM
Grand Corona	Doble Corona	6½	46	CM
Robusto	Robusto	5½	50	CM
Long Corona	Lonsdale	6	44	CM

Here is a short filler, handmade cigar which offers a medium-bodied smoke in an inexpensive package of 25.

ANILLO DE ORO
Handmade in Tamboril, Dominican Republic.

Wrapper: Ecuador   Binder: Dom. Rep.   Filler: Dom. Rep.

Shape	Name	Lgth	Ring	Wrapper
Grand Corona	Churchill	6½	46	CC-Stripe
Giant	President	8	50	CC-Stripe
Long Corona	Corona	7	44	CC-Stripe

HANDMADE CIGARS: BRAND LISTINGS

Lonsdale	Coronita	6½	44	CC-Stripe
Long Panatela	Panatela	7½	38	CC
Robusto	Torito	5	50	CC-Stripe
Slim Panatela	Palmas	7	33	CC
Cigarillo	Especiales	5	26	CC

This cigar was introduced in 1969, and offers a mild-bodied taste. It features a Connecticut-seed wrapper grown in Ecuador and binder and Corojo filler tobaccos from the Dominican Republic.

ANILLO DE PLATA
Handmade in Danli, Honduras.

Wrapper: Ecuador   *Binder: Honduras*
Filler: Dominican Republic, Honduras, Nicaragua

Shape	Name	Lgth	Ring	Wrapper
Torpedo	Torpedo	7	54	CC
Giant	President	8	50	CC
Double Corona	Churchill	6⅞	49	CC
Toro	Toro	6	50	CC
Robusto	Robusto	5	50	CC
Lonsdale	Cetro	6¼	44	CC

This cigar was introduced in December 1996, with a mild-to-medium-bodied blend of leaves from four nations. It is presented in boxes of 25.

ANTELO
Handmade in Miami, Florida, USA.

Wrapper: USA/Connecticut   *Binder: Mexico*   *Filler: Dom. Rep.*

Shape	Name	Lgth	Ring	Wrapper
Double Corona	Presidente	7⅝	50	Cl-Ma
Churchill	Churchill	7	46	Cl-Ma

Lonsdale	No. 1	6¾	42	Cl-Ma
Corona	Cetros	5¾	42	Cl-Ma
Cigarillo	Senoritas	4⅝	28	Cl-Ma
Panatela	Panatela	6⅞	36	Cl-Ma
Corona Extra	Wavell	5⅛	46	Cl-Ma
Giant Corona	Double Corona	7½	42	Cl-Ma
Churchill	Super Cazadore	7½	46	Cl-Ma

These cigars are made by hand in a small factory in Miami, using imported leaf. The taste ranges from mild (Senoritas and Panatelas) to medium (No. 1 and Cetros) to heavy (all other shapes).

ANTILLAS TORO BRAVO
Handmade in Navarette, Dominican Republic.

Wrapper: Indonesia		*Binder: Dom. Rep.*			*Filler: Dom. Rep.*
Shape	*Name*		*Lgth*	*Ring*	*Wrapper*
	Tripa Larga line:				
Double Corona	Churchill		7¾	50	CC
Churchill	No. 1866		6¾	46	CC
Corona Extra	Real Condado		5½	46	CC
Corona	Tabantillas No. 4		5½	42	CC
Petit Corona	Romeros		4½	42	CC
	Tripa Corta line:				
Corona	Brevas		5½	42	CC
Lonsdale	Tabantillas No. 3		6¾	42	CC
Robusto	Corona		5½	50	CC
Corona	Papayo		5¼	42	CC
Churchill	Gavillero		5	30	CC

HANDMADE CIGARS: BRAND LISTINGS

This cigar was introduced in 1997 and offers a medium-to-full-bodied taste in boxes or bundles of 25, featuring a Sumatran-grown wrapper, matched with Dominican leaves.

ANTONIO Y CLEOPATRA PRIVATE RESERVE
Hand-rolled in La Romana, Dominican Republic.

Wrapper: Indonesia   *Binder: USA/Pennsylvania*   *Filler: Dom. Rep., Jamaica*

Shape	Name		Lgth	Ring	Wrapper
Double Corona	Emperadore		7	50	CC
Toro	Double Corona		6¼	48	CC
Long Corona	Lonsdale		6⅛	44	CC
Grand Corona	Palma	*(tubed)*	6½	46	CC

The famous brand of Antonio y Cleopatra, named for the legendary Roman and Egyptian lovers of antiquity (together, more or less, from 44-31 B.C.E.), again graces a hand-rolled cigar! Introduced in late 1997, this four-shape range is machine-bunched with the Javan wrapper rolled by hand. It is mild-to-medium in body.

APERITIF
Handmade in Santiago, Dominican Republic.

Wrapper: USA/Connecticut   *Binder: Dom. Rep.*   *Filler: Dom. Rep.*

Shape	Name	Lgth	Ring	Wrapper
Small Panatela	Aperitif	4	30	CC

This is a 1997-introduced brand of small cigars made with care at the La Aurora factory in the Dominican Republic. It is medium-to-full-bodied and offered in dignified wood boxes of 30.

AQUA D'T
Handmade in Danli, Honduras.

Wrapper: Ecuador   *Binder: Dom. Rep.*   *Filler: Dom. Rep., Honduras, Nicaragua*

Shape	Name	Lgth	Ring	Wrapper
Double Corona	Churchill	7	50	CM

HANDMADE CIGARS: BRAND LISTINGS

Robusto	Robusto	5	50	CM
Lonsdale	Lonsdale	6½	44	CM
Corona	Corona	5½	44	CM

Introduced in 1997, this is a mild-to-medium-bodied brand, offered in boxes of 25. Each cigar is protected in individual cellophane sleeves; you'll know it right away by the four-color, sea-serpent decoration on each box.

ARANGO STATESMAN
Handmade in Danli and San Pedro Sula, Honduras.

Wrapper: Ecuador   *Binder: Dom. Rep.*   *Filler: Dom. Rep., Honduras*

Shape	Name	Lgth	Ring	Wrapper
Churchill	Barrister	7½	46	CC-Ma
Corona	Counselor	5	40	CC-Ma
Petit Corona	Executor	6	43	CC-Ma

Introduced in 1988, these are medium-bodied, handmade cigars, which should not be confused with its sister brand, the Arango Sportsman, which is a flavored machine-made cigar. The Statesman is quite aromatic, with just a hint of vanilla flavor to charm the smoker.

ARMENTER RESERVAS
Handmade in Las Palmas, the Canary Islands of Spain.

Wrapper: Ecuador   *Binder: Dominican Republic*
Filler: Brazil, Canary Islands, Dominican Republic, Nicaragua

Shape	Name	Lgth	Ring	Wrapper
Pyramid	Reserva No. 1	7	52	CC
Long Panatela	Reserva No. 2	7½	39	CC
Robusto	Reserva No. 3	4⅝	50	CC
Corona	Reserva No. 4	5⅝	42	CC
Lonsdale	Reserva No. 5	6⅝	42	CC
Churchill	Reserva No. 6	7	46	CC

HANDMADE CIGARS: BRAND LISTINGS

Double Corona	Reserva No. 7	7½	50	CC

This mild-bodied blend of tobaccos from five nations was introduced in 1996. The wrapper is a Connecticut-seed leaf grown in Ecuador and gives a luxurious finish to these stunning smokes, offered in boxes of 25 except for the Reserva No. 1, offered in 20s.

AROMAS DE SAN ANDRES
Handmade in San Andres Tuxtla, Mexico.

Wrapper: Mexico   *Binder: Mexico*   *Filler: Mexico*

Shape	Name		Lgth	Ring	Wrapper
Lonsdale	Gourmet	(tubed)	6⅛	42	CM
Toro	Afficiando		6	50	CM
Double Corona	Maximillian		7½	52	CM
Robusto	Robusto		5	50	CM
Double Corona	Imperial	(tubed)	7	50	CM
Grand Corona	Crowns		6½	47	CM
Long Corona	Sceptors		6	44	CM

Produced by Tabacos San Andres S.A. de C.V., this line is composed of all-Mexican tobacco of interesting origins. Although all grown in the famous San Andres Valley, the filler and binder are native seed, while the wrapper leaf is Sumatran-type tobacco which is also grown in the S.A. Valley.

AROMELLA
Handmade in San Andres Tuxtla, Mexico.

Wrapper: Mexico   *Binder: Mexico*   *Filler: Mexico*

Shape	Name	Lgth	Ring	Wrapper
Short Panatela	Petite Corona	4¾	38	CC-Ma
Long Corona	Corona Superior	6¼	42	CC-Ma

Introduced in 1994, this brand is flavored, with vanilla, rum or anisette. It is offered in boxes of 25.

HANDMADE CIGARS: BRAND LISTINGS

ARTURO FUENTE
Handmade in Santiago, Dominican Republic.
Wrapper: USA/Connecticut, Cameroon

Binder: Dominican Republic   Filler: Dominican Republic

Shape	Name	Lgth	Ring	Wrapper
Corona	Brevas Royale /medium filler/	5½	42	CC-Ma
Giant	Canones	8½	52	CC-Ma
Robusto	Chateau Fuente	4½	50	CC-Ma
Churchill	Churchill	7¼	48	CC-Ma
Grand Corona	Corona Imperial	6½	46	CC-Ma
Corona Extra	Cuban Corona	5¼	45	CC-Ma
Lonsdale	Curly Head /medium filler/	6½	43	CC-Ma
Lonsdale	Curly Head Deluxe /medium filler/	6½	43	CC-Ma
Toro	Double Chateau Fuente	6¾	50	CC-Ma
Lonsdale	Fumas	7	44	CC-Ma
Long Panatela	Panatela Fina	7	38	CC-Ma
Short Panatela	Petit Corona	5	38	CC-Ma
Lonsdale	Seleccion Privada No. 1	6¾	44	CM-Ma
Robusto	Rothschild	4½	50	CC-Ma
Double Corona	Chateau Fuente Royal Salute	7⅝	54	CC-Ma
Lonsdale	Spanish Lonsdale	6½	42	CM-Ma
Grand Corona	Flor Fina 8-5-8	6	47	CM-Ma
	Hemingway Series:			*(perfecto tips)*
Robusto	Hemingway Short Story	4	48	CM
Robusto	Hemingway Best Seller	5	55	CM

HANDMADE CIGARS: BRAND LISTINGS

Double Corona	Hemingway Untold Story	7½	53	Ma
Churchill	Hemingway Classic	7	48	CM
Grand Corona	Hemingway Signature	6	47	CM
Giant	Hemingway Masterpiece	9	52	CM

Arturo Fuente learned the art of growing and processing tobacco and the making of premium, handmade cigars in Cuba at the end of the 19th century, producing his own line in 1912. Today, his son Carlos and grandson, Carlos, Jr. oversee the more than 500 rollers who manufacture more than 24 million cigars every year. Their line offers a medium-to-full-bodied taste, with the celebrated Hemingway series a little mellower, thanks to an additional 140 days of aging. Until recently, most of the natural-wrapped cigars featured Cameroon leaves, with Connecticut leaf used for maduros; more Connecticut leaf is now in use due to production difficulties in Cameroon.

ARTUS
Handmade in San Andres Tuxtla, Mexico.

Wrapper: Mexico   *Binder: Mexico*   *Filler: Mexico*

Shape	Name	Lgth	Ring	Wrapper
Lonsdale	Lonsdale	6½	42	CM-Ma
Long Corona	Corona	6	42	CM-Ma
Toro	Toro	6	50	CM-Ma
Double Corona	Double Corona	7	50	CM-Ma
Robusto	Robusto	5	50	CM-Ma
Robusto	Rothschild	4½	50	CM-Ma

Mmmm, good! Here is a mild-bodied, all-Mexican cigar which is new for 1997. You can have your pick of wrappers: natural or maduro and you'll find Artus in carefully-built, all-cedar boxes of 25.

ARUBA
Handmade in Santiago, Dominican Republic.

Wrapper: Indonesia   *Binder: Dom. Rep.*   *Filler: Dom. Rep.*

HANDMADE CIGARS: BRAND LISTINGS

Shape	Name	Lgth	Ring	Wrapper
Double Corona	Churchill	7	50	CM
Toro	Toro	6	50	CM
Robusto	Robusto	5	50	CM
Corona	Corona	5½	42	CM
Lonsdale	Lonsdale	6½	44	CM

You don't have to go there to buy it, silly . . . but Aruba will give you the mild-bodied, pleasant experience you'd enjoy if you were in Aruba . . . and you can get 25 of these 1997-introduced Arubas in a single box!

ASHÉ
Handmade in Tamboril, Dominican Republic.

Wrapper: Ecuador   Binder: Dom. Rep.   Filler: Dom. Rep.

Shape	Name	Lgth	Ring	Wrapper
Corona	Corona	5½	42	CM
Robusto	Robusto	5	50	CM
Grand Corona	Classic	6	46	CM
Toro	Churchill	6½	52	CM
Lonsdale	Lonsdale	7	44	CM
Giant	Gigante	8	50	CM

Here is a mild blend, introduced in 1996, that offers a Piloto Cubano filler combined with an Ecuadorian, Connecticut-seed wrapper and Dominican Olor binder, packed in elegant all-cedar boxes of 25.

ASHTON
Handmade in Santiago, Dominican Republic.

Wrapper: USA/Connecticut   Binder: Dom. Rep.   Filler: Dom. Rep.

Shape	Name	Lgth	Ring	Wrapper
Double Corona	Churchill	7½	52	CC

HANDMADE CIGARS: BRAND LISTINGS

Churchill	Prime Minister	6⅞	48	CC
Lonsdale	8-9-8	6½	44	CC
Panatela	Panatela	6	36	CC
Corona	Corona	5¼	44	CC
Slim Panatela	Cordial	5	30	CC
Toro	Double Magnum	6	50	CC
Robusto	Magnum	5	50	CC
Panatela	Elegante	6½	35	CC
	Aged Cabinet Selection:			
Perfecto	No. 1	9	52	CC
Perfecto	No. 2	7	48	CC
Perfecto	No. 3	6	47	CC
Robusto	No. 6	5½	52	CC
Toro	No. 7	6¼	52	CC
Double Corona	No. 8	7	49	CC
Double Corona	No. 10	7½	52	CC
	Maduro:			
Double Corona	No. 60	7½	52	Ma
Churchill	No. 50	7	48	Ma
Toro	No. 40	6	50	Ma
Lonsdale	No. 30	6¾	44	Ma
Corona	No. 20	5½	44	Ma
Robusto	No. 10	5	50	Ma

Robert Levin of Holt's Tobacconist of Philadelphia, Pennsylvania set out to create a great cigar in 1985 . . . and he succeeded. Ashton cigars are manufactured without compromise, blending six tobaccos: Dominican filler and Dominican-grown, Cuban-seed binder leaves with perfect shade-grown wrapper leaves from the Connecticut Valley. The maduro wrappers are longer-aged

Connecticut Broadleaf. The unique range of sizes includes three large perfecto-shaped cigars - tapered at both ends - in the Cabinet Selection series.

ASTRAL
Handmade in Danli, Honduras.

Wrapper: Ecuador   *Binder: Dom. Rep.*   *Filler: Dom. Rep., Nicaragua*

Shape	Name	Lgth	Ring	Wrapper
Lonsdale	Lujos	6½	44	CM
Double Corona	Maestro	7½	52	CM
Robusto	Besos	5	52	CM
Churchill	Favorito	7	48	CM
Churchill	Perfeccion	7	48	CM

More than three years of planning went into the production of this new brand, introduced in 1995 and made in Danli, Honduras. Medium in body, the Connecticut-seed wrappers give this line an elegant appearance, with silky expresso and cream flavors. Special features of this line include the gentle taper of the foot of the Favorito size and the narrowed head of the Perfeccion size. Astral cigars are presented in stunning Mahogany boxes which underscore the total commitment to quality in the manufacturing process.

AVO
Handmade in Santiago, Dominican Republic.

Wrapper: USA/Connecticut   *Binder: Dom. Rep.*   *Filler: Dom. Rep.*

Shape	Name	Lgth	Ring	Wrapper
Lonsdale	Avo No. 1	6¾	42	Co
Toro	Avo No. 2	6	50	Co
Double Corona	Avo No. 3	7½	50	Co
Long Panatela	Avo No. 4	7	38	Co
Grand Corona	Avo No. 5	6⅞	46	Co
Panatela	Avo No. 6	6½	36	Co
Long Corona	Avo No. 7	6	44	Co

HANDMADE CIGARS: BRAND LISTINGS

Corona	Avo No. 8	5½	40	Co
Robusto	Avo No. 9	4¾	48	Co
Pyramid	Pyramid	7	54	Co
Torpedo	Belicoso	6	48	Co
Torpedo	Petit Belicoso	5¼	46	Co
	XO Series:			
Churchill	Maestoso	7	48	CC
Robusto	Intermezzo	5½	50	CC
Long Corona	Preludio	6	40	CC

The perfectly-balanced marriage of five different tobaccos, mostly from the Cibao Valley of the Dominican Republic, gives the Avo line - introduced in 1987 - a rich flavor in a mild-bodied cigar. The newer XO Series offers a richer blend of six tobaccos, using a Dominican-grown, Havana-seed binder with the Connecticut Shade wrapper.

AZ
Handmade in San Andres Tuxtla, Mexico.

Wrapper: Mexico   Binder: Mexico   Filler: Mexico

Shape	Name	Lgth	Ring	Wrapper
Small Panatela	Cordial	4¼	30	CM
Petit Corona	Petit Corona	5	42	CM
Long Corona	Corona	6	44	CM
Robusto	Robusto	5	50	CM
Toro	Toro	6	50	CM
Double Corona	Churchill	7	50	CM
Long Corona	Bolero	6	42	Stripe
Double Corona	Phenom	7½	52	CM

Here's a well-known brand in other countries, but introduced to the U.S. in 1996, featuring all-Mexican tobaccos and a full-bodied taste. All of the shapes use a natural wrapper, except for the Bolero, which offers a double-wrapped "barber pole" style. Maduro-wrapped versions of these shapes are also planned for introduction soon.

AZTECA DOMINICAN MADURO
Handmade in San Andres Tuxtla, Mexico.

Wrapper: Dom. Rep.   Binder: Dom. Rep.   Filler: Honduras

Shape	Name	Lgth	Ring	Wrapper
Perfecto	Perfecto	5¾	48	Ma

Here is a medium-to-full-bodied, rich tasting cigar made with a Dominican-grown, maduro wrapper and long-filler leaves, offered in a box of 24 or bundles of 25.

BACCARAT HAVANA SELECTION
Handmade in Danli, Honduras.

Wrapper: Honduras   Binder: Mexico   Filler: Honduras

Shape	Name	Lgth	Ring	Wrapper
Small Panatela	Bonitas	4½	30	CC
Double Corona	Churchill	7	50	CC-Ma
Long Corona	Luchadore	6	43	CC
Lonsdale	No. 1	7	44	CC
Panatela	Panatela	6	38	CC
Corona	Petit Corona	5½	42	CC
Small Panatela	Platinum	4⅞	32	CC
Pyramid	Polo	7	52	CC
Robusto	Rothschild	5	50	CC-Ma

This fine cigar series was formally introduced in 1978, but actually dates back as far as 1871 when it was supervised by Carl Upmann. The mild body produced by the blending of the Havana-seed fillers, Mexican binder and Connecticut-seed wrapper are sweetened by the use of a special sealing gum in the cigar's cap.

HANDMADE CIGARS: BRAND LISTINGS

BAGATELLE
Handmade in Danli, Honduras.

Wrapper: Indonesia   *Binder: Honduras*   *Filler: Honduras*

Shape	Name	Lgth	Ring	Wrapper
Churchill	Churchill	7	48	CC
Lonsdale	Lonsdale	6½	44	CC
Giant	Presidente	8½	52	CC
Robusto	Robusto	5	50	CC
Toro	Toro	6	50	CC

Here is a medium-bodied blend of leaves, including a Sumatra wrapper and Cuban-seed tobaccos grown in Honduras. Introduced in 1997, you can try them in value-priced boxes of 10 or 20.

BAHIA
Handmade in San Jose, Costa Rica.

Wrapper: Ecuador   *Binder: Nicaragua*   *Filler: Nicaragua*

Shape	Name	Lgth	Ring	Wrapper
Giant	Double Corona	8½	50	CC
Double Corona	Corona Gigante	7	54	CC
Torpedo	No. 2	6½	54	CC
Toro	Esplendido	6	50	CC
Robusto	Robusto	5	50	CC
Corona	No. 4	5½	42	CC

Tony Borhani introduced the Bahia brand in December 1994, and now offers his 1989 crop vintage selection. The entire production of only 490,000 cigars was aged for nine months after rolling and only then released for sale. Packed uncellophaned in slide-top cabinets, Bahia is a limited production cigar of the highest quality and full bodied in taste. When the 1998 Vintage is introduced, it will feature aged tobaccos harvested in 1992.

HANDMADE CIGARS: BRAND LISTINGS

BAHIA GOLD
Handmade in San Jose, Costa Rica.

Wrapper: Ecuador   *Binder: Dom. Rep.*   *Filler: Dom. Rep.*

Shape	Name	Lgth	Ring	Wrapper
Churchill	Churchill	6⅞	48	CC
Torpedo	No. 2	6½	54	CC
Robusto	Robusto	5	50	CC
Corona	No. 4	5½	42	CC

The Tabacalera Tambor in Costa Rica is the creation point for this 1997-introduced series of full-bodied cigars, featuring a Connecticut-seed wrapper.

BAHIA MADURO
Handmade in San Jose, Costa Rica.

Wrapper: USA/Connecticut   *Binder: USA/Conn.*   *Filler: Dom. Rep., Nicaragua*

Shape	Name	Lgth	Ring	Wrapper
Double Corona	Corona Gigantes	7	54	Ma
Torpedo	Torpedo	6½	54	Ma
Robusto	Panchos	5½	52	Ma
Robusto	Robustos	5	50	Ma

At long last! A maduro-wrapped Bahia from Tony Borhani and the Tabacalera Tambor! Note the unusual binder, using Connecticut Broadleaf to underscore the rich maduro taste of this full-bodied cigar introduced in late 1997.

BAHIA TRINIDAD
Handmade in San Jose, Costa Rica.

Wrapper: Ecuador   *Binder: Ecuador*   *Filler: Dom. Rep., Nicaragua*

Shape	Name	Lgth	Ring	Wrapper
Double Corona	Corona Gigantes	7	54	CC
Giant	A	8⅞	48	CC
Torpedo	No. 2	6½	54	CC

HANDMADE CIGARS: BRAND LISTINGS

Robusto	Panchos	5½	52	CC
Robusto	Robustos	5	50	CC
Lonsdale	Elegantes	6½	42	CC

This is a mild-bodied smoke, first made available in 1997. The Ecuadorian-grown wrapper and binder are from Sumatran seed, with Cuban-seed Dominican and Nicaraguan-grown filler leaves. Once rolled, Bahia Trinidads are aged for an additional 120 days to ensure perfect draw and flavor.

BALBOA
Handmade in Colon, Panama.

Wrapper: Honduras   *Binder: Mexico*
Filler: Dominican Republic, Honduras, Panama

Shape	Name	Lgth	Ring	Wrapper
Giant	Viajante	8½	52	CC-Ma
Churchill	Churchill	7	48	CC-Ma
Lonsdale	No. 1	7	43	CC-Ma
Lonsdale	No. 2	6½	43	CC-Ma
Corona	No. 4	5½	43	CC-Ma
Long Panatela	Palma Extra	7	36	CC-Ma

This cigar is offered in bundles of 25 cigars each and is a full-bodied, even heavy, smoke.

BALI HAI
Handmade in Malan, Indonesia.

Wrapper: Indonesia   *Binder: Indonesia*   *Filler: Indonesia*

Shape	Name	Lgth	Ring	Wrapper
Churchill	Sultan	7	48	CC
Toro	Black Bull	6½	50	CC
Pyramid	Krakatau	6	52	CC
Robusto	Buddha	5	50	CC

Long Corona	Java Special	6	42	CC

The Sumatra wrapper and Indonesian filler make this brand mild-to-medium in body. This 1997-introduced cigar is offered in spectacular, 20-count solid wood boxes from Kalimantan; the cigars are swathed in hand-woven Batik cloth.

BALLENA SUPREMA

Handmade in Danli, Honduras and San Andres Tuxtla, Mexico.

DANLI COLLECTION:

Wrapper: USA/Connecticut   *Binder: Mexico*   *Filler: Dom. Rep., Mexico*

SAN ANDRES COLLECTION:

Wrapper: USA/Connecticut   *Binder: Mexico*   *Filler: Mexico*

Shape	Name	Lgth	Ring	Wrapper
	Danli Collection, handmade in Honduras:			
Robusto	Consuelo	5	50	CC
Churchill	Alma	7	47	CC
Lonsdale	Ventaja	6⅞	44	CC
Giant	Encanto	8	50	CC
Pyramid	Capitan	7	54	CC
	San Andres Collection, handmade in Mexico:			
Robusto	Cordura	5	52	CC
Churchill	Concordia	7	48	CC
Lonsdale	Cortes	7	42	CC
Double Corona	Esperanza	7	50	CC
Torpedo	Patron	6½	52	CC

These "Great Whale" cigars are the product of the McClelland Tobacco Company, justly famous for pipe tobaccos for many years. Both lines debuted in 1996 and are meticulously crafted, with the Honduran blend offering a mild-to-medium-bodied taste and the Mexican style a medium-to-full bodied flavor. Both styles are presented in individual cellophane sleeves packed in elegant cedar boxes.

BANCES
Handmade in Cofradia, Honduras.

Wrapper: Ecuador, USA/Connecticut   Binder: Honduras
Filler: Dominican Republic, Honduras and Nicaragua

Shape	Name	Lgth	Ring	Wrapper
Corona	Brevas	5½	43	CM-Ma
Lonsdale	Cazadores	6¼	44	CM-Ma
Churchill	Corona Immensas	6¾	48	CM-Ma
Panatela	El Prados	6¼	36	CM-Ma
Giant	Presidents	8½	52	CM-Ma
Panatela	Uniques	5½	38	CM-Ma

Bances cigars are now, for the most part, handmade in Honduras under the same supervision as the famous Hoyo de Monterrey and Punch lines. This is a true value cigar, with the same great smoking qualities of its more famous sister lines.

BANDERA
Handmade in Santiago, Dominican Republic.

Wrapper: Cameroon   Binder: Ecuador   Filler: Dom. Rep.

Shape	Name		Lgth	Ring	Wrapper
Long Corona	Petit Corona	(tubed)	6	42	CM
Long Corona	Corona	(tubed)	6	44	CM
Grand Corona	Double Corona	(tubed)	6	46	CM
Robusto	Robusto	(tubed)	5½	50	CM
Double Corona	Churchill	(tubed)	7½	50	CM
Pyramid	Pyramide		6½	53	CM

HANDMADE CIGARS: BRAND LISTINGS

Introduced in 1996, this brand offers a medium body with leaves from three nations. Each cigar is uniquely packed in cellophane sleeves and then, for most sizes, in an acrylic tube!

BANDOLEROS
Handmade in Santiago, Dominican Republic.

Wrapper: Dom. Rep.　　　　*Binder: Dom. Rep.*　　　　*Filler: Dom. Rep.*

Shape	Name	Lgth	Ring	Wrapper
Slim Panatela	4-Pack	5	30	CM

These small cigars are easy to smoke and come in handy packs for pocket or purse. The flavor is full-bodied, thanks to the all-Cuban seed construction.

BAUZA
Handmade in Santiago, Dominican Republic.

Wrapper: Ecuador　　　　*Binder: Mexico*　　　*Filler: Dom. Rep., Nicaragua*

Shape	Name	Lgth	Ring	Wrapper
Churchill	Casa Grande	6¾	48	CM
Double Corona	Fabuloso	7½	50	CM
Corona	Grecos	5½	42	CM
Lonsdale	Jaguar	6½	42	CM
Lonsdale	Medalla d'Oro No. 1	6⅞	44	CM
Short Panatela	Petit Corona	5	38	CM
Double Corona	Presidente /combination filler/	7½	50	CM
Robusto	Robusto	5½	50	CM

Introduced in 1980, these medium-to-full-bodied cigars are high in quality and high in value. Enveloped in Ecuadorian wrappers, nine sizes are offered, eight of which are in elegant wooden boxes and one in a bundle of 25 cigars with combination filler.

HANDMADE CIGARS: BRAND LISTINGS

BELINDA
Handmade in Cofradia, Honduras.
Wrapper: Ecuador, Honduras and USA/Connecticut

Binder: Honduras   *Filler: Dominican Republic, Honduras*

Shape	Name	Lgth	Ring	Wrapper
Panatela	Belinda	6½	36	CM
Corona	Breva Conserva	5½	43	CM-Ma
Corona Extra	Cabinet	5⅝	45	CM
Long Corona	Corona Grande	6¼	44	CM-Ma
Short Panatela	Dina	5	36	CM
Cigarillo	Mina	5⅜	28	CM
Churchill	Ramon	7¼	47	CM
Toro	Excellente	6	50	CM-Ma
Double Corona	Prime Minister	7½	50	CM-Ma
Robusto	Medaglia D'Oro	4½	50	CC
Robusto	Robusto	4½	50	CM-Ma
Long Corona	Spanish Twist	6¼	43	CM-Ma
Grand Corona	Vintage Corona	6¼	45	CM-Ma
Long Corona	Humidores	6	43	CM

This old Cuban brand has been successfully re-introduced in 1994 as a medium-to-heavy bodied cigar wrapped in Ecuadorian, Honduran or USA/Connecticut leaves, depending on the shade. It is expertly made and presented in all-cedar boxes that continue the aging process. Of note is the new Humidores model, presented in a glass humidor containing 20 cigars, and the Vintage Corona, presented in an ammunition crate of 105 cigars!

BELLERO
Handmade in Ocotal, Nicaragua.
Wrapper: Ecuador   *Binder: Ecuador*   *Filler: Ecuador, Nicaragua*

HANDMADE CIGARS: BRAND LISTINGS

Shape	Name	Lgth	Ring	Wrapper
Double Corona	Churchill	7½	50	CC
Churchill	Imperial	6¾	46	CC
Petit Corona	Petit Corona	5	42	CC
Long Panatela	Panatela	7	36	CC
Robusto	Robusto	5	50	CC

Here is a mild-to-medium-bodied blend with a Connecticut-seed wrapper introduced in 1996. It is offered in boxes of 25.

BELMONDO
Handmade in San Andres Tuxtla, Mexico.

Wrapper: Mexico   *Binder: Mexico*   *Filler: Mexico*

Shape	Name	Lgth	Ring	Wrapper
Giant	Presidente	8½	52	CC
Robusto	Robusto	5	50	CC
Toro	Toro	6	50	CC
Lonsdale	Lonsdale	6½	44	CC
Double Corona	Churchill	7	50	CC

This is a medium-bodied collection of magnificent, 1997-introduced cigars with Sumatra-seed wrappers and Cuban-seed filler and binder leaves from the fields of the San Andres Valley of Mexico, offered in boxes of 10 or 20.

BEN MIGUEL
Handmade in Santo Domingo, Dominican Republic.

Wrapper: Ecuador or Indonesia   Binder: Dom. Rep.   *Filler: Dom. Rep.*

Shape	Name	Lgth	Ring	Wrapper
Double Corona	Presidente	7½	50	CC-CM
Churchill	Churchill	7	48	CC-CM
Long Panatela	Panatela	7½	38	CC-CM

BERING

CIGARS FOR THE SHREWD INVESTOR.

THESE FINE, HANDMADE CIGARS IMPORTED FROM HONDURAS RECEIVE

"EXCELLENT" RATINGS IN BLIND TASTE TESTS. EACH BERING CIGAR

IS CAREFULLY ROLLED USING ONLY THE FINEST LONG-FILLER TOBACCOS,

A NATURAL-LEAF BINDER, AND SPECIALLY SELECTED AGED WRAPPERS.

THE RESULT IS A CIGAR WITH A SMOOTH DRAW AND A RICH TASTE.

BERINGS NOW COME IN FIFTEEN POPULAR SHAPES.

BERING BY SWISHER INTERNATIONAL, INC.

HANDMADE CIGARS: BRAND LISTINGS

Robusto	Toro	5½	50	CC-CM
Robusto	Robusto	4½	50	CC-CM
Lonsdale	Corona	6½	44	CC-CM

This is a new brand in 1997 and features either a Connecticut-seed wrapper grown in Ecuador or a Sumatra wrapper. Either way, the blend with Cuban-seed filler tobaccos produces a milt-to-medium-bodied taste, offered in boxes of 25.

BERING
Handmade in Cofradia and Danli, Honduras.
Wrapper: Honduras, USA/Connecticut — Binder: Honduras
Filler: Dominican Republic, Honduras, Mexico, Nicaragua

Shape	Name		Lgth	Ring	Wrapper
Giant	Grande		8½	52	CC
Lonsdale	Barons		7¼	42	CC-Ma
Lonsdale	Casinos	(tubed)	7⅛	42	DC-CC
Grand Corona	Cazadores		6¼	45	CC'
Grand Corona	Corona Grande		6¼	46	DC-CC
Long Corona	Corona Royale	(tubed)	6	41	CC
Corona Extra	Coronados		5⅛	45	DC-CC
Small Panatela	No. 8		4¼	32	CC
Slim Panatela	Gold No. 1		6¼	33	CC
Toro	Hispanos		6	50	CC-Ma
Corona	Imperials	(tubed)	5½	42	CC
Lonsdale	Inmensas		7⅛	45	CC-Ma
Long Corona	Plazas		6	43	DC-CC
Pyramid	Torpedo		7	54	CC
Robusto	Robusto		4¾	50	CC

HANDMADE CIGARS: BRAND LISTINGS

Bering is a premium handmade cigar imported from Honduras. This blend of specially selected Cuban-seed, long-leaf tobaccos is the reason for the incredibly smooth draw, spicy aroma and full, rich taste. Berings are available in 15 shapes and a variety of wrappers and in a variety of packaging: 3s, 4s, 5s, 15s, 25s and 50s.

Bering fans alert: Look for the new Bering Dominican Hallmark Selection, a medium-to-full-bodied cigar featuring a Connecticut wrapper, in four sizes in 1998.

BEVERLY HILLS - VIP
Handmade in Danli, Honduras.

Wrapper: Ecuador   Binder: Nicaragua   Filler: Honduras

Shape	Name	Lgth	Ring	Wrapper
Short Panatela	No. 535	5	35	CC
Long Corona	No. 644	6	44	CC
Double Corona	No. 749	7	49	CC
Robusto	No. 550	5	50	CC
Giant	No. 854	8	54	CC

This is a handmade cigar with a Connecticut-seed wrapper and tobaccos of three different nations in the blend. The brand offers a smooth draw and mild body, and is offered in all-cedar boxes of 25.

BIARRITZ
Handmade in Santiago, Dominican Republic.

Wrapper: Dom. Rep.   Binder: Dom. Rep.   Filler: Dom. Rep.

Shape	Name	Lgth	Ring	Wrapper
Double Corona	Churchill	7½	50	CC
Robusto	Rothschild	4½	50	CC
Long Corona	Corona	6	44	CC

HANDMADE CIGARS: BRAND LISTINGS

Introduced in 1997, this is a medium-bodied cigar with a Sumatra-seed wrapper and all Dominican-grown leaves. It is offered in protective cellophane sleeves inside all-cedar boxes of 25.

BIG BUTT
Handmade in Esteli, Nicaragua.

Wrapper: Indonesia *Binder: Nicaragua* *Filler: Nicaragua*

Shape	Name	Lgth	Ring	Wrapper
Double Corona	El Jefe	7½	54	CM
Toro	Don Gordo	6	54	CM
Robusto	Gordito	4¾	54	CM

This brand honors the memory of Don Carlos Santiago, better known as "Don Gordo," a master roller who produced cigars in Cuba until the time of nationalization; he died in 1994. These big-ring cigars offer a medium-to-full body and are packed in elegant cedar cases in individual cellophane sleeves, and accompany a wide line of clothing and fashion accessories.

BIG CHIEF
Handmade in Danli, Honduras.

Wrapper: USA/Connecticut *Binder: Honduras* *Filler: Honduras*

Shape	Name	Lgth	Ring	Wrapper
Torpedo	Torpedo	7	54	CM
Giant	Presidente	8	50	CM
Double Corona	Churchill	7	49	CM
Toro	Toro	6	50	CM
Robusto	Robusto	5	50	CM
Long Corona	Cetro	6	43	CM

Here is a heavy, full-flavored cigar introduced in 1997. The natural wrapper is from Connecticut and the powerful taste comes from the all-Honduran filler.

HANDMADE CIGARS: BRAND LISTINGS

BIJAO
Handmade in Santiago, Dominican Republic.

Wrapper: Indonesia Binder: Dom. Rep. Filler: Dom. Rep.

Shape	Name	Lgth	Ring	Wrapper
Double Corona	Churchill	7½	50	CC
Robusto	Robusto	5	50	CC

Created in 1997, this is a medium-to-full-bodied blend of Sumatra wrappers with Dominican Olor and Piloto Cubano filler leaves. It is offered in boxes of 25.

BIJAO CLASSICO
Handmade in Santiago, Dominican Republic.

Wrapper: Ecuador Binder: Dom. Rep. Filler: Dom. Rep.

Shape	Name	Lgth	Ring	Wrapper
Double Corona	Churchill	7½	50	CC
Robusto	Robusto	5	50	CC

Here is a 1997-introduced, medium-bodied brand that combines a Sumatra wrapper with binder and filler leaves from the Dominican Republic. Look for it in all-cedar, cabinet-style boxes of 25.

BLACK LABEL
Handmade in San Andres Tuxtla, Mexico.

Wrapper: Mexico Binder: Honduras Filler: Mexico

Shape	Name	Lgth	Ring	Wrapper
Long Corona	Acapulco	6	42	CC-Ma
Giant	Cancun	8	52	CC-Ma
Panatela	Guadalajara	6⅝	35	CC-Ma
Double Corona	Jalisco	6⅞	54	CC-Ma
Double Corona	Monterrey	7½	50	CC-Ma
Robusto	Robusto	4¾	50	CC-Ma
Slim Panatela	Tijuana	5	32	CC-Ma

HANDMADE CIGARS: BRAND LISTINGS

Toro	Toro	6	50	CC-Ma
Grand Corona	Veracruz	6⅝	46	CC-Ma

This bundle brand is a medium-bodied cigar, using primarily Mexican tobaccos in both natural and maduro wrapper colors. An excellent value, these long-filler cigars are available in bundles of 10 or 25 cigars.

BLAIR GOLD LABEL
Handmade in Danli, Honduras.

Wrapper: Ecuador   *Binder: Honduras*   *Filler: Honduras*

Shape	Name	Lgth	Ring	Wrapper
Giant	Presidente	8½	52	CC
Churchill	Churchill	7	48	CC
Toro	Robusto	6	50	CC
Robusto	Rothschild	4¾	50	CC
Lonsdale	Lonsdale	6½	44	CC

Introduced in 1996, this brand is offered in five handmade sizes, featuring an Ecuadorian-grown, Connecticut-seed wrapper. The taste is considered to be medium-to-full-bodied and is presented in individual cellophane sleeves and packed in boxes of 25.

BLAIR SILVER LABEL
Handmade in Las Palmas, the Canary Islands of Spain.

Wrapper: USA/Connecticut   *Binder: Canary Islands*   *Filler: Brazil, Dom. Rep.*

Shape	Name	Lgth	Ring	Wrapper
Churchill	Churchill	7	48	CC
Toro	Toro	6	50	CC
Robusto	Rothschild	5	52	CC

New in 1997, this edition of the Blair line is mild-bodied and slightly spicy. It is offered in boxes of 25.

HANDMADE CIGARS: BRAND LISTINGS

BLUE CHIP
Handmade in the USA.

Wrapper: Dom. Rep. *Binder: Dom. Rep.* *Filler: Dom. Rep.*

Shape	Name	Lgth	Ring	Wrapper
Robusto	Robusto	4⅞	50	CC

Check it out! Here's a 1997-introduced, medium-bodied cigar in one size. It offers a complex taste with a hint of coffee-style flavor on the finish, thanks to a blend of three-year aged tobaccos. It is elegantly presented in a 20-cigar cube.

BLUE LABEL
Handmade in Danli, Honduras.

Wrapper: Honduras *Binder: Honduras* *Filler: Honduras*

Shape	Name	Lgth	Ring	Wrapper
Toro	Bulvon	6⅝	54	CC-Ma
Churchill	Churchill	6⅞	48	CC
Slim Panatela	Finos	7	30	CC
Giant	Imperial	8	52	CC-Ma
Lonsdale	No. 1	6⅝	44	CC
Long Corona	No. 2	6	42	CC
Panatela	Palma	6⅞	35	CC
Double Corona	Presidente	7½	50	CC-Ma
Robusto	Rothschild	4¾	50	CC-Ma
Toro	Toro	6¼	50	CC-Ma

These high-quality cigars are made by hand from leaves grown in Honduras. Mild-to-medium-bodied in taste, they are attractively packaged in bundles of 10 or 25 cigars.

BOGAR
Handmade in Danli, Honduras.

Wrapper: Indonesia *Binder: Honduras* *Filler: Dom. Rep., Honduras, Mexico*

HANDMADE CIGARS: BRAND LISTINGS

Shape	Name	Lgth	Ring	Wrapper
Corona	Corona	5½	42	CC
Corona	Toro	5½	44	CC
Robusto	Short Churchill	5	50	CC
Grand Corona	Corona Gorda I	6	46	CC
Toro	Corona Gorda II	6	50	CC
Double Corona	Churchill	7	50	CC

Introduced in 1996, this is a full-bodied cigar with a four-nation blend of leaves, featuring a Sumatra-seed wrapper. Each cigar is presented in individual cellophane sleeves, inside a vanished, all-cedar box of 25.

BOHIO
Handmade in Tamboril, Dominican Republic.
Wrapper: Indonesia, USA/Connecticut

Binder: Dominican Republic   *Filler: Dominican Republic*

Shape	Name	Lgth	Ring	Wrapper
Double Corona	Presidentes	7½	50	CC-Ma
Churchill	Churchills	7	46	CC-Ma
Long Corona	Coronas	6	44	CC-Ma
Robusto	Robustos	5	50	CC-Ma
Corona	Petit-Coronas	5½	42	CC-Ma
Torpedo	Torpedos	7	54	CC-Ma

Introduced in 1997, this brand offers a choice of Sumatra wrapper or a Connecticut maduro wrapper, combined with Dominican-grown binder and fillers for a mild-to-medium smoke. Each cigar is sleeved in cellophane and packed in cedar boxes of 24.

BOHIO
Handmade in Santo Domingo, Dominican Republic.
Wrapper: Ecuador   *Binder: Dom. Rep.*   *Filler: Dom. Rep.*

HANDMADE CIGARS: BRAND LISTINGS

Shape	Name	Lgth	Ring	Wrapper
Double Corona	Don Felipe	7½	50	CC
Lonsdale	Imperial	6¾	44	CC
Long Panatela	Grand Panatella	7½	38	CC
Robusto	Toro	5½	50	CC
Robusto	Robusto	4½	50	CC

A completely different brand of Bohio, this creation of the Los Gringos Cigar Company offers a mild-to-medium-bodied taste, featuring a Connecticut-seed wrapper and Piloto Cubano filler leaves. Introduced in 1997, it is offered in protective cellophane sleeves and packaged in cedar boxes of 25.

BOLIVAR
Handmade in Santiago, Dominican Republic.

Wrapper: Cameroon   Binder: Mexico   Filler: Dom. Rep., Mexico

Shape	Name	Lgth	Ring	Wrapper
Panatela	Panatela	6	38	CC
Grand Corona	Corona Gorda	6¼	47	CC
Lonsdale	Lonsdale	6½	43	CC

Long a famous Cuban brand, but rarely seen in the U.S., this version of Bolivar debuted in 1997. It offers a mild to medium flavor in three popular sizes, available in boxes of 25.

BOOM BOOM EL CAMPEON
Handmade in Miami, Florida, USA.

Wrapper: Mexico   Binder: Dom. Rep.   Filler: Dom. Rep.

Shape	Name	Lgth	Ring	Wrapper
Short Panatela	Bantamweight	5	38	CC
Corona	Lightweight	5½	44	CC

HANDMADE CIGARS: BRAND LISTINGS

Ray "Boom Boom" Mancini, a charismatic lightweight boxing champion of the 1980s, is the inspiration behind this series of mild-bodied cigars. The line is offered in flavored versions, including Amaretto, cafe, chocolate, cognac and vanilla.

BOQUILLA
Handmade in Union City, New Jersey, USA.
Wrapper: Dominican Republic, Mexico, USA/Connecticut
Binder: Mexico   *Filler: Dominican Republic*

Shape	Name	Lgth	Ring	Wrapper
Giant	Churchill	8	50	CC-Ma
Double Corona	Silverano	7	50	CC-Ma
Toro	Torito	6½	50	CC-Ma
Churchill	Imperiale	7½	46	CC-Ma
Lonsdale	Presidente	6½	44	CC-Ma
Long Corona	Senadore	6	44	CC-Ma
Long Panatela	Ninfa	7	36	CC-Ma
Lonsdale	Fuma	7	44	CC-Ma
Torpedo	Torpedo	6	54	CC-Ma
Pyramid	Pyramid	5½	46	CC-Ma
Robusto	Robusto	5	50	CC-Ma

This cigar is made by a small factory of the same name. These are medium-to-full bodied cigars, with an increased number of sizes and wrappers available for 1997.

BOSS
Handmade in Santo Domingo, Dominican Republic.
Wrapper: Indonesia   *Binder: Dom. Rep.*   *Filler: Dom. Rep.*

Shape	Name	Lgth	Ring	Wrapper
Robusto	Robusto	5½	50	CM
Lonsdale	Lonsdale	6½	42	CM

Toro	Toro	6½	50	CM
Churchill	Churchill	6⅞	47	CM

This brand is new for 1997 and features a Sumatra wrapper around a three-leaf filler, offering a medium-bodied flavor. It is presented uncellophaned in cedar cabinets of 25.

BOYERO
Handmade in Santiago, Dominican Republic.

Wrapper: Indonesia   *Binder: Dom. Rep.*   *Filler: Dom. Rep.*

Shape	Name	Lgth	Ring	Wrapper
Double Corona	Churchill	7½	50	CC
Robusto	Rothschild	4½	50	CC
Corona	Petit Corona	5½	42	CC

Introduced in late 1996, this is a mild blend of leaves available in three popular shapes. The Dominican-grown interior tobaccos include Olor binders and Piloto Cubano fillers.

BOYERO PRIMERO
Handmade in Santiago, Dominican Republic.

Wrapper: Indonesia   *Binder: Dom. Rep.*   *Filler: Dom. Rep.*

Shape	Name	Lgth	Ring	Wrapper
Double Corona	Churchill	7½	50	CC
Robusto	Robusto	5	50	CC
Corona	Alquise	6	44	CC

Also introduced in late 1996, this version of Boyero offers a medium-bodied taste with a slightly stronger blend of Olor and Piloto Cubano binder and filler leaves, respectively.

BRAVOS
Handmade in San Andres Tuxtla, Mexico.

Wrapper: Mexico   *Binder: Mexico*   *Filler: Mexico*

HANDMADE CIGARS: BRAND LISTINGS

Shape	Name	Lgth	Ring	Wrapper
Corona	Corona	5½	42	CM

This single-size brand is made from all-long filler tobaccos and is medium-to-full bodied in flavor. Modestly priced, it is offered in bundles or boxes of 25.

BRAVOS
Handmade in Las Palmas, the Canary Islands of Spain.
Wrapper: Indonesia   Binder: Indonesia   Filler: Canary Islands, Dom. Rep.

Shape	Name	Lgth	Ring	Wrapper
Double Corona	Churchill	7¼	50	CC
Toro	Toro	6	50	CC
Robusto	Robusto	5	50	CC
Lonsdale	Lonsdale	6½	43	CC

Here is a medium-bodied brand from the Canary Islands, featuring a Sumatra wrapper, Java binder and filler tobaccos from the Canary Islands and the Dominican Republic. Introduced in 1997, it is offered in boxes of 25.

BRETON LEGEND SERIES
Handmade in the Dominican Republic.
Wrapper: Indonesia   Binder: Dom. Rep.   Filler: Dom. Rep.

Shape	Name	Lgth	Ring	Wrapper
Giant	Churchill	8	50	CM
Double Corona	Presidente	7	50	CM
Grand Corona	Doble Corona	6½	46	CM
Robusto	Robusto	5½	50	CM
Long Corona	Lonsdale	6	44	CM
Long Panatela	Panatela Larga	7	36	CM
Panatela	Panetela	5½	36	CM
Pyramid	Piramide I	5½	50	CM

Torpedo	Classic No. 1	7	50	CM
Torpedo	Classic No. 2	6½	42	CM
Pyramid	Piramide II	7	50	CM

Here is a full-bodied cigar with a Sumatra wrapper, offered in boxes of 25, except for the Classic line (20 per box) and Piramide II (12 per box).

BRIONES
Handmade in Danli, Honduras.
Wrapper: Ecuador

Binder: Nicaragua   *Filler: Dominican Republic, Honduras, Nicaragua*

Shape	Name	Lgth	Ring	Wrapper
Robusto	Robusto	5	50	CC
Toro	No. 1	6	52	CC
Churchill	Churchill	7	48	CC
Double Corona	Presidente	7½	50	CC
Lonsdale	Lonsdale	6½	42	CC
Torpedo	Torpedo	6½	52	CC

From the Tabacalera San Cristobal comes this blend of leaves from four nations that provides a mild-to-medium-bodied flavor for this brand, introduced in 1997. It is offered in boxes of 25.

BUFIDO
Handmade in San Andres Tuxtla, Mexico.
Wrapper: Mexico   *Binder: Mexico*   *Filler: Mexico*

Shape	Name	Lgth	Ring	Wrapper
Double Corona	W. Churchill	7	50	CM-Ma
Toro	Corona Rotunda	6¼	50	CM-Ma
Robusto	Robusto	5	50	CM-Ma
Long Corona	Lonsdale	6¼	42	CM-Ma

HANDMADE CIGARS: BRAND LISTINGS

Petit Corona	Petite Corona	5	42	CM-Ma

This is a new brand for 1997, offering a modestly-priced, mediuim-bodied smoke in bundles of 25 in either natural or maduro wrapper.

BULLDOG
Handmade in Santiago, Dominican Republic.

Wrapper: USA/Connecticut   Binder: Dom. Rep.   Filler: Dom. Rep.

Shape	Name	Lgth	Ring	Wrapper
Corona	Corona	5½	44	CC
Toro	Toro	6	50	CC
Double Corona	Churchill	7	50	CC

Introduced in 1996, this medium-bodied cigar will not bark or bite! It's sure to become man's best friend in bundles of 25.

BURMA
Handmade in Yangon, Myanmar.

Wrapper: Myanmar   Binder: Myanmar   Filler: Myanmar

Shape	Name	Lgth	Ring	Wrapper
Corona	Corona	5½	44	CC

Myanmar? Think Burma and you'll know that the Sittang River Valley is the origination point for the tobaccos in this brand, introduced to the U.S. market in 1997. This is a full-bodied brand and is offered in hand-lacquered boxes of 25 or 50 with a silk liner inside.

BUSTILLO
Handmade in Tampa, Florida, USA.

Wrapper: Honduras   Binder: Honduras   Filler: Honduras

Shape	Name	Lgth	Ring	Wrapper
Robusto	John McKay Super Rothschilds	4½	49	CM

Robusto	Coppola Cafe Robusto	4½	49	Ma

Here is a zesty blend of seven-year-aged Cuban-seed Honduran wrappers, offering a medium body in the John McKay Super Rothschilds and a full-bodied taste in the Coppola Cafe Robusto shape.

BUTERA ROYAL VINTAGE
Handmade in La Romana, Dominican Republic.

Wrapper: USA/Connecticut   Binder: Indonesia   *Filler: Dom. Rep.*

Shape	Name	Lgth	Ring	Wrapper
Robusto	Bravo Corto	4½	50	CC
Lonsdale	Cedro Fino	6½	44	CC
Toro	Dorado 652	6	52	CC
Churchill	Capo Grande	7½	48	CC
Corona	Fumo Dolce	5½	44	CC
Panatela	Mira Bella	6¾	38	CC
Toro	Cornetta No. 1	6	52	CC

Introduced in 1993, Butera Royal Vintage are true-blended, premium cigars handmade in the Dominican Republic by "first-row" cigar makers. Six distinctive whole-leaf tobaccos from three different countries are blended, including four specific types of long-filler leaves from the rarest Dominican crops. Every cigar is well-aged to maturity in cabinets of fine Spanish cedar and packaged in beautiful Mahogany chests. The spicy, flavorful blend is considered medium in body.

C.A.O.
Handmade in Danli, Honduras.
Wrapper: Costa Rica, USA/Connecticut

Binder: Honduras   *Filler: Mexico, Nicaragua*

Shape	Name	Lgth	Ring	Wrapper
Petit Corona	Petit Corona	5	40	CC
Long Corona	Corona	6	42	CC-Ma
Lonsdale	Lonsdale	7	44	CC

Robusto	Robusto	4½	50	CC-Ma
Toro	Corona Gorda	6	50	CC-Ma
Giant	Churchill	8	50	CC-Ma
Pyramid	Triangulare	7½	54	CC-Ma

Introduced in 1995, this medium-bodied cigar line can be enjoyed at any time of the day, with its blend of Cuban-seed tobaccos in the filler and binder and a Connecticut shade wrapper. The maduro-wrapped cigars utilize Connecticut Broadleaf-seed tobaccos grown in Costa Rica.

C.A.O. GOLD
Handmade in Esteli, Nicaragua.

Wrapper: Ecuador   *Binder: Nicaragua*   *Filler: Nicaragua*

Shape	Name	Lgth	Ring	Wrapper
Corona	Corona	5½	42	Co
Robusto	Robusto	5	50	Co
Toro	Corona Gorda	6½	50	Co
Churchill	Churchill	7	48	Co
Double Corona	Double Corona	7½	54	Co

Introduced in 1996, this brand features a Connecticut Shade-seed wrapper and a mild-to-medium taste. Box-pressed, these cigars are offered in elegant boxes of 25.

C.C.I. ROYAL SATIN SELECTION
Handmade in Danli, Honduras.

Wrapper: Ecuador   *Binder: Dom. Rep.*   *Filler: Honduras, Nicaragua*

Shape	Name	Lgth	Ring	Wrapper
Double Corona	No. 1	7½	50	CM
Churchill	No. 2	7	48	CM
Toro	No. 3	6	50	CM
Long Corona	No. 4	6¼	44	CM

Robusto	No. 5	5	50	CM
Torpedo	No. 6	7	54	CM
Double Corona	No. 7	7¾	50	CM

This line of small-batch cigars from Cigar Club International was introduced in 1995 and has a medium body and features Havana-seed filler tobaccos from Honduras and Nicaragua. It offers a vibrant aroma and its even burn generates a solid grey-white ash.

CABALLEROS
Handmade in Santiago, Dominican Republic.

Wrapper: USA/Connecticut   *Binder: Dom. Rep.*   *Filler: Dom. Rep.*

Shape	Name	Lgth	Ring	Wrapper
Double Corona	Churchill	7	50	CC
Robusto	Rothschild	5	50	CC
Churchill	Double Corona	6¾	48	CC
Corona	Corona	5¾	43	CC
Corona	Petit Corona	5½	42	CC

Introduced in 1993, these are mild-to-medium bodied cigars with much flavor, produced with long filler and made completely by hand. Imported from the Dominican Republic, Caballeros cigars are offered in individual cellophane sleeves inside cedarwood boxes of 25.

CABAÑAS
Handmade in La Romana, Dominican Republic.

Wrapper: USA/Connecticut   *Binder: Dom. Rep.*   *Filler: Dom. Rep.*

Shape	Name	Lgth	Ring	Wrapper
Corona	Coronas	5½	42	Ma
Toro	Exquisitos	6½	48	Ma
Lonsdale	Premiers	6⅝	42	Ma
Grand Corona	Royales	5⅝	46	Ma

HANDMADE CIGARS: BRAND LISTINGS

Fans of the darkest wrapper shades will not be disappointed by Cabanas, one of the oldest names in cigars; the flavorful Connecticut wrappers are essentially black. But the blend offers a mild and pleasant taste and is presented in boxes of 25.

CACIQUE
Handmade in Santiago, Dominican Republic.

Wrapper: USA/Connecticut   Binder: Dom. Rep.   Filler: Dom. Rep.

Shape	Name	Lgth	Ring	Wrapper
Panatela	Jaraqua	6¾	36	CC
Long Corona	Tainos	6	42	CC
Lonsdale	Siboneyes	6¾	43	CC
Churchill	Caribes	6⅞	46	CC
Double Corona	Incas	7½	50	CC
Robusto	Azteca	4¾	50	CC-Ma
Toro	Apaches	6	50	CC-Ma
Torpedo	Torpedo	6	52	CC

The Cacique is handmade in the Dominican Republic. It is blended with Dominican Havana-seed "ligero" and "seco" filler. It has a Havana-seed binder and is topped off with authentic Connecticut Shade wrapper. This combination of fine tobacco gives Cacique a full tobacco flavor, yet it is mild in strength.

CALEYES
Handmade in Santiago, Dominican Republic.

Wrapper: Indonesia   Binder: Dom. Rep.   Filler: Dom. Rep.

Shape	Name	Lgth	Ring	Wrapper
Double Corona	Executive	7½	50	CC
Churchill	Churchill	7	48	CC
Long Panatela	Panatelas	7	36	CC
Robusto	Robusto	5	50	CC
Lonsdale	No. 2	6¾	43	CC

| Corona | No. 4 | 5½ | 42 | CC |
| Torpedo | Torpedo | 6 | 54 | CC |

New for 1997, this is a mild blend of Cameroon-seed wrapper grown in Indonesia and Dominican binders and filler, offered in all-cedar boxes.

CALIXTO LOPEZ

Handmade in Manila, the Philippines.

Wrapper: Indonesia   *Binder: Philippines*   *Filler: Philippines*

Shape	Name	Lgth	Ring	Wrapper
Corona	Corona Exquisito	5⅜	43	CM
Giant Corona	Czar	8	45	CM
Giant	Gigante	8½	50	CM
Lonsdale	Lonsdale Suprema	6¾	42	CM
Grand Corona	Corona No. 1	6⅜	45	CM
Toro	Nobles Extra Fino	6½	50	CM
Long Panatela	Palma Royales	7¼	36	CM

Created in 1980 and offering a mild-bodied smoke, the Calixto Lopez line utilizes the best in Southeast Asian tobacco. The main element is home-grown Philippine tobacco from the highly-respected Isabela Valley on the northernmost Philippine island of Luzon, combined with a Java-grown wrapper.

CALLE OCHO

Handmade in Santiago, Dominican Republic.

Wrapper: Ecuador   *Binder: Indonesia*

Filler: Dominican Republic, Mexico, Nicaragua

Shape	Name		Lgth	Ring	Wrapper
Robusto	Gordito	*(tubed)*	5	50	CI
Lonsdale	Perfect Corona	*(tubed)*	6½	42	CI
Double Corona	Churchill	*(tubed)*	7¼	50	CI
Torpedo	Torpedo	*(tubed)*	6½	54	CI

HANDMADE CIGARS: BRAND LISTINGS

Created in 1994, this is a mild-bodied blend of leaves from five nations! Named for the epicenter of the Cuban population in Miami - 8th Street or *Calle Ocho* in Spanish - this brand is offered in glass tubes and packed in boxes of 25.

Please note that the limited-edition "Calle Ocho Perez Family Reunion" brand, which featured unique Candela wrappers in Churchill (7 x 50) and Corona (6½ x 42) shapes was produced in 1997 only and is no longer available.

CAMACHO
Handmade in Danli, Honduras.
Wrapper: Honduras and USA/Connecticut

Binder: Honduras   Filler: Honduras

Shape	Name	Lgth	Ring	Wrapper
Giant	El Cesar	8½	52	Cl-CC-Ma
Double Corona	Executives	7½	50	Cl-CC-Ma
Churchill	Churchill	7	48	Cl-CC-Ma
Lonsdale	No. 1	7	44	Cl-CC-Ma
Robusto	Monarca	5	50	Cl-CC-Ma
Lonsdale	Cetros	6½	44	Cl-CC-Ma
Long Panatela	Pan Especial	7	36	Cl-CC-Ma
Panatela	Elegantes	6½	38	Cl-CC-Ma
Long Corona	Palmas	6	43	Cl-CC-Ma
Corona	Nacionales	5½	44	Cl-CC-Ma
Lonsdale	Cazadores	6½	44	Cl-CC-Ma
Slim Panatela	Conchitas	5½	32	Cl-CC-Ma

This outstanding full-bodied brand was originated in the 1960s and first produced in Nicaragua before moving production to Honduras. It offers connoisseurs a wide range of sizes and features tobaccos primarily from the Jamastran Valley of Honduras. Connecticut wrappers are used for the claro series when available and maduro wrappers are often in short supply for this brand.

HANDMADE CIGARS: BRAND LISTINGS

CAMMANO
Handmade in Santiago, Dominican Republic.

Wrapper: Ecuador   Binder: Dom. Rep.   Filler: Dom. Rep.

Shape	Name	Lgth	Ring	Wrapper
Toro	Double Corona	6	50	CC
Torpedo	Torpedo	7	54	CC
Double Corona	Churchill	7	50	CC
Long Panatela	Lancero	7½	38	CC
Robusto	Robusto	5	50	CC

This is a rarely-seen, but much-desired brand which offers a mild-to-medium body with a Connecticut-seed wrapper.

CAMMARATA
Handmade in Tampa, Florida, USA.
See tobacco blending notes for each group.

Shape	Name	Lgth	Ring	Wrapper
I: Wrapper: Honduras Binder: Dom. Rep.				*Filler: Dom. Rep.*
Robusto	Rothschild	5¾	50	CM
Churchill	Lonsdale	7	46	CM
Double Corona	Churchill	6¾	50	CM
Long Panatela	St. Julien Panatella	7	36	CM
II: Wrapper: Honduras Binder: Honduras				*Filler: Honduras*
Robusto	Rothschild Maduro	4	50	Ma
III: Wrapper: USA/Conn. Binder: Honduras				*Filler: Honduras*
Toro	Varsalona No. 4	6	50	CC
Double Corona	JFK	7½	49	CC
Churchill	Special Series No. 2	6¾	46	CC
Petit Corona	Special Series No. 1	5	44	CC

HANDMADE CIGARS: BRAND LISTINGS

IV: Wrapper: Honduras	Binder: Honduras			Filler: Honduras
Robusto	Havana 5x52	5	52	CM
Double Corona	Havava 7½x52	7½	52	CM
V: Wrapper: USA/Conn.	Binder: Honduras			Filler: Honduras
Pyramid	Havana Pyramid	5	57	CC
VI: Wrapper: Honduras	Binder: Honduras			Filler: Honduras
Toro	Cuban Robusto Maduro	6	54	Ma
VII: Wrapper: USA/Conn.	Binder: Honduras			Filler: Honduras
Double Corona	Cuban Double Corona	7½	54	CC

Carmela Cammarata Varsalona is one of the few cigar rollers left from Ybor City, a West Tampa neighborhood that once hosted 300 cigar factories and 30,000 workers in the 1920s and '30s. She now rolls up to 300 cigars per day, with blends based on Cuban-seed tobaccos from the Dominican Republic, Honduras and the USA. The all-Honduras blends are full-bodied, while the multi-nation blends offer a medium strength.

CAMORRA IMPORTED LIMITED RESERVE
Handmade in Danli, Honduras.

Wrapper: Ecuador	Binder: Honduras			Filler: Honduras
Shape	Name	Lgth	Ring	Wrapper
Slim Panatela	Capri	5½	32	CM
Panatela	Napoli	6⅛	38	CM
Pyramid	Padova	5	48	CM
Robusto	Roma	5	50	CM
Corona	Genova	5½	44	CM
Lonsdale	Venizia	6½	44	CM
Churchill	San Remo	7	48	CM

Camorra Imported Limited Reserve cigars debuted in 1995 as one of the finest super-premium cigars made in Honduras. This unique blend of the finest available Honduran tobacco is blended with a smooth and oily Ecuadorian wrapper for a medium-bodied taste. Note the sweet initial taste, produced by the addition of sugar added to the vegetable gum used to seal the cap.

CAMORRA LIMITED RESERVE DOMINICAN VINTAGE
Handmade in Villa Gonzalez, Dominican Republic.

Wrapper: Dom. Rep.   *Binder: Dom. Rep.*   *Filler: Dom. Rep.*

Shape	Name	Lgth	Ring	Wrapper
Robusto	Robusto	5	50	Ma
Torpedo	Torpedo	6	50	Ma
Giant	Double Corona	8	50	Ma

New for 1997, this is a medium-to-full-bodied cigar available in maduro wrapper only. It is presented in individual cellophane sleeves in an all-cedar boxes of 25.

CAMPEONES
Handmade in Villa Gonzalez, Dominican Republic.

Wrapper: Cameroon or Ecuador   *Binder: Indonesia*   *Filler: Dom. Rep., Honduras*

Shape	Name	Lgth	Ring	Wrapper
Giant	Soberanos	8	52	CC-CM
Torpedo	Piramides	6¼	56	CC-CM
Double Corona	Churchills	7	50	CC-CM
Lonsdale	No. 1	6⅞	44	CC-CM
Toro	Doble Corona	6	50	CC-CM
Robusto	Robusto	5	50	CC-CM

This brand was introduced in 1995 and offers a medium-bodied smoke in a choice of Ecuadorian or Cameroon wrapper. You can find it in either boxes or bundles of 25.

CANARIA D'ORO
Handmade in Santiago, Dominican Republic.

Wrapper: Mexico   *Binder: Mexico*   *Filler: Dom. Rep., Mexico*

HANDMADE CIGARS: BRAND LISTINGS

Shape	Name	Lgth	Ring	Wrapper
Small Panatela	Babies	4⅛	32	CC
Slim Panatela	Finos	6	31	CC
Robusto	Rothschild	4½	50	Ma
Corona	Coronas	5½	43	CC
Lonsdale	Lonsdales	6½	43	CC
Robusto	Inmensos	5½	49	CC
Lonsdale	Supremos	7	45	CC

Made by hand in the Dominican Republic, this line has a creamy, medium-to-full-bodied taste with lots of aroma. Mexican tobaccos dominate the blend (including a Sumatra-seed wrapper), combined with Dominican leaf in the filler blend. It is offered in beautifully-colored boxes of 25.

CANONERO
Handmade in Saõ Goncalo dos Campos, Brazil.
Wrapper: Brazil, Ecuador, USA/Connecticut

Binder: Brazil   Filler: Brazil

Shape	Name	Lgth	Ring	Wrapper
Double Corona	No. 1: Double Corona	7½	50	CC-Ma
Robusto	No. 2: Rothschild	5½	50	CC-Ma
Robusto	No. 3: Robusto	5	52	CC-Ma
Churchill	No. 4: Churchill	7	46	CC-Ma
Lonsdale	No. 10: Lonsdale	6½	42	CC-Ma
Petit Corona	No. 20: Corona	5½	42	CC-Ma
Short Panatela	No. 30: Potra	4¼	38	CC-Ma

This line began in 1995 and under the supervision of master blender Arthur Toraño and now offers a unique variety of three different wrappers combined with all-Brazilian binder and fillers. The result is a mild-bodied taste in the Connecticut-wrapped "Classico" line, a mild-to-medium-bodied flavor in the Ecuadorian-wrapped "Mediano" line and a medium-bodied, but intensely-flavored

"Oscuro" line that features a Brazilian Mata Fina wrapper.

CAOBA
Handmade in Santiago, Dominican Republic.

Wrapper: Ecuador   *Binder: Dom. Rep.*   *Filler: Dom. Rep.*

Shape	Name	Lgth	Ring	Wrapper
Long Panatela	Panetela No. 1	7½	36	CC
Panatela	Panetela No. 2	6¾	36	CC
Robusto	Robusto	5	50	CC
Corona Extra	Pendejo	5½	46	CC
Cigarillo	Petit	4¼	26	CC
Double Corona	5-Star	7	50	CC
Churchill	4-Star	7	46	CC
Grand Corona	3-Star	6¼	46	CC
Corona	2-Star	5½	42	CC
Petit Corona	1-Star	5	42	CC
Torpedo	Torpedo	6	50	CC

This brand was started under a different name in 1992, but still offers the same mild-to-medium body. Caoba cigars are presented in individual cellophane sleeves and packed in all-cedar cabinets.

CAOBA GOLD
Handmade in Santiago, Dominican Republic.

Wrapper: USA/Connecticut   *Binder: Dom. Rep.*   *Filler: Dom. Rep.*

Shape	Name	Lgth	Ring	Wrapper
Churchill	No. 1	7	46	CC
Long Corona	No. 2	6¼	44	CC
Corona	No. 3	5½	42	CC
Long Panatela	Panetela No. 1	7½	36	CC

Panatela	Panetela No. 2	6	36	CC
Churchill	Esplendido	7	47	CC
Robusto	Robusto	5	50	CC
Double Corona	Especial	7	50	CC
Torpedo	Torpedo	6	50	CC

This brand was introduced in 1997. It offers a mild body and a Connecticut wrapper in boxes of 24, except the Especial, which is offered in boxes of 36.

CAOBA PLATINUM
Handmade in Santiago, Dominican Republic.

Wrapper: Ecuador   *Binder: Dom. Rep.*   *Filler: Dom. Rep.*

Shape	Name	Lgth	Ring	Wrapper
Churchill	No. 1	7	46	CC
Long Corona	No. 2	6¼	44	CC
Corona	No. 3	5½	42	CC
Long Panatela	Panetela No. 1	7½	36	CC
Panatela	Panetela No. 2	6	36	CC
Churchill	Esplendido	7	47	CC
Robusto	Robusto	5	50	CC
Double Corona	Especial	7	50	CC
Torpedo	Torpedo	6	50	CC

This new Caoba brand was also introduced in early 1997. It offers a mild-to-medium body and an Ecuadorian-grown wrapper in boxes of 24, except the Especial, which is offered in boxes of 36.

CAONABO
Handmade in Villa Gonzalez, Dominican Republic.
Wrapper: USA/Connecticut or Cameroon

Binder: Dominican Republic   *Filler: Dominican Republic*

HANDMADE CIGARS: BRAND LISTINGS

Shape	Name	Lgth	Ring	Wrapper
	Available with Connecticut wrapper:			
Small Panatela	Helenas	5	30	CC
Long Panatela	Caciques	7½	38	CC
Corona	Naborias	5½	42	CC-Ma
Long Panatela	Nitainos	7	36	CC
Long Corona	Guanines	6	44	CC
Robusto	Petit Premier	4½	50	CC-Ma
Double Corona	Grand Premier	7½	50	CC-Ma
	Available with Cameroon wrapper:			
Torpedo	Grand Jefe	6	54	CM
Torpedo	Jaragua	7	44	CM
Torpedo	Higuey	5	48	CM

This brand debuted in 1996 and is named for the chief of the Taino tribe who resisted Spanish settlement on La Española island in 1493 and 1495. It offers a mild-to-medium body and exquisite construction and is offered in cedar boxes of 25. New for 1997 is the three-figurado series with Cameroon wrappers and three maduro-wrapped shapes.

CAPOTE

Handmade in Tenerife, the Canary Islands of Spain.

Wrapper: USA/Connecticut   Binder: Dom. Rep.   Filler: Dom. Rep.

Shape	Name	Lgth	Ring	Wrapper
Double Corona	No. 1	7	50	CC
Toro	No. 2	6	50	CC
Lonsdale	No. 3	6½	43	CC
Panatela	No. 4	5½	39	CC

This brand was introduced in 1996, offering a mild-to-medium body with a Connecticut Shade wrapper in boxes of 25.

HANDMADE CIGARS: BRAND LISTINGS

CAPRICHO CUBANO
BY PROFESOR SILA
Handmade in Santiago, Dominican Republic.

Wrapper: Cameroon   *Binder: Indonesia*   *Filler: Dom. Rep.*

Shape	Name	Lgth	Ring	Wrapper
Corona	Corona	5½	42	CM
Grand Corona	Gran Corona	6	45	CM
Robusto	Robusto	5	50	CM
Double Corona	Double Corona	7½	50	CM

Introduced in late 1997, this is a medium-to-full-bodied blend of African, Asian and Caribbean tobaccos that features a Cameroon wrapper. Each cigar is wrapped in cedar sheets and packed into all-cedar boxes of 25.

CARA MIA
Handmade in Las Palmas, the Canary Islands of Spain.

Wrapper: Ecuador   *Binder: Canary Islands*   *Filler: Canary Islands*

Shape	Name	Lgth	Ring	Wrapper
Pyramid	Pyramid	7	52	Co
Double Corona	Churchill	7	50	Co
Toro	Toro	6	50	Co
Lonsdale	Lonsdale	6½	42	Co
Corona	Corona	5½	42	Co

Cara Mia was introduced in late 1995 as a new brand from the Canary Islands of Spain, one of the world's celebrated cigar-making regions. This is a medium-bodied cigar with excellent construction, featuring a Connecticut-seed wrapper grown in Ecuador and cured to a rich Colorado shade. Cara Mia cigars are packed uncellophaned in all-cedarwood boxes of 25.

HANDMADE CIGARS: BRAND LISTINGS

CARABANA
Handmade in Danli, Honduras.

Wrapper: USA/Connecticut   Binder: USA/Pennsylvania
Filler: Dominican Republic, Nicaragua, USA/Pennsylvania

Shape	Name	Lgth	Ring	Wrapper
Corona	Corona	5½	42	CC-Ma
Lonsdale	Lonsdale	6½	43	CC-Ma
Toro	Toro	6	49	CC-Ma
Robusto	Robusto	5	50	CC-Ma

This is a new brand for 1997, offering a mild-to-medium-bodied taste in boxes of 25. Two different Connecticut wrappers are available: shade-grown for a lighter color and flavor and Connecticut Broadleaf for a beautiful, flavorful, maduro wrapper. There is also a special "Cristal" version of the Corona shape, using a glass tube and incorporating a Sumatra-seed wrapper and Mexican binder with the brand's normal filler blend.

CARBONELL
Handmade in Santiago, Dominican Republic.

Wrapper: Indonesia   Binder: Dom. Rep.   Filler: Dom. Rep.

Shape	Name	Lgth	Ring	Wrapper
Cigarillo	Palmaritos	4	28	CC
Small Panatela	Demi Tasse	5	30	CC
Slim Panatela	Panatella Thins	7	32	CC
Panatela	Panatella	6	36	CC
Long Panatela	Panatella Grande	7½	38	CC
Corona	Palma Short	5½	42	CC
Lonsdale	Palma	6½	42	CC
Lonsdale	Palma Extra	7	42	CC
Lonsdale	Corona	6½	44	CC
Churchill	Churchill	6⅞	46	CC

HANDMADE CIGARS: BRAND LISTINGS

Double Corona	Presidente	7½	50	CC
Robusto	Toro	5½	50	CC
Giant	Soberano	8½	52	CC
Giant	Gigante	10	56	CC
Torpedo	Piramide Breve	5½	56	CC
Torpedo	Piramide	7½	64	CC
Torpedo	Piramide Gigante	8	68	CC

Here is the largest-selling brand in the Dominican Republic, widely available in the United States in 1996. Created in 1907, it is produced in Santiago and features an Indonesian wrapper. Carbonell cigars are mild with exquisite flavor, devoid of any bitterness.

CARLIN
Handmade in Esteli, Nicaragua.

Wrapper: Nicaragua   *Binder: Nicaragua*   *Filler: Nicaragua*

Shape	Name	Lgth	Ring	Wrapper
Giant	Gigante	8	52	CM
Churchill	Churchill	7	48	CM
Toro	Toro	6	50	CM
Corona	Corona	5½	43	CM
Robusto	Robusto	4¾	52	CM

Introduced as a Dominican-made cigar in 1995, this brand is now made in Nicaragua and incorporates only Nicaraguan leaves. The full, robust flavor comes from the blending of three filler tobaccos, coddled by a beautiful Jalapa wrapper. Carlins are easily enjoyed, thanks to their outstanding construction.

CARLOS OLIVA
Handmade in Ocotal, Nicaragua.

Wrapper: Ecuador   *Binder: Mexico*   *Filler: Dom. Rep., Nicaragua*

HANDMADE CIGARS: BRAND LISTINGS

Shape	Name	Lgth	Ring	Wrapper
Grand Corona	Elegante	6½	46	CC-Ma
Robusto	Toro	5	50	CC
Double Corona	Sabanero	7	50	CC-Ma
Torpedo	Torpedo	6	52	CC-Ma
Giant	Grandioso	8¼	52	CC

Here is a 1997-introduced, medium-to-full-bodied cigar of flawless construction. It features a Sumatra-seed wrapper and is available in protective cellophane sleeves inside all-cedar boxes of 25.

CARLOS TORAÑO DOMINICAN SELECTION
Handmade in Santiago, Dominican Republic.

Wrapper: USA/Connecticut   *Binder: Mexico*   *Filler: Dom. Rep.*

Shape	Name	Lgth	Ring	Wrapper
Toro	Carlos I	6	50	CM
Lonsdale	Carlos II	6¾	43	CM
Double Corona	Carlos III	7½	52	CM
Corona	Carlos IV	5¾	43	CM
Grand Corona	Carlos V	6	46	CM
Churchill	Carlos VI	7	48	CM
Robusto	Carlos VII	4¾	52	CM
Panatela	Carlos VIII	6½	36	CM

More than two years in the making, Carlos Toraño cigars debuted in 1995. They are mild in body and are distributed in France, Germany, Great Britain and the Netherlands in addition to the United States.

CARLOS TORAÑO NICARAGUAN SELECTION
Handmade in Esteli, Nicaragua.

Wrapper: Indonesia   *Binder: Nicaragua*   *Filler: Nicaragua*

Great Cigars Since 43 B.C.*

Virtuoso
Toraño
Honduras

Carlos Toraño
*Dominican
Selection*

Carlos Toraño
*Nicaragua
Selection*

Grand Nica
Toraño
Nicaragua

CARLOS
TORAÑO

Since 1916

Toraño Cigars. Good Taste Runs In the Family.

www.torano.com

*Before Castro

HANDMADE CIGARS: BRAND LISTINGS

Shape	Name	Lgth	Ring	Wrapper
Toro	Double Corona	6¼	50	CM
Long Corona	Cetros	6	44	CM
Churchill	Churchill	7	48	CM
Robusto	Robusto	5	50	CM
Double Corona	Presidente	7½	52	CM
Torpedo	Torpedo	6½	54	CM

New in 1997, this is a medium-bodied cigar with the excellent construction and perfect draw that has become a trademark of the Toraño brands. It is offered in individual cellophane sleeves in all-cedar cabinets of 25.

CARMEN GOLD LABEL
Handmade in Danli, Honduras.
Wrapper: USA/Connecticut *Binder: Honduras or Nicaragua*
Filler: Dominican Republic, Honduras, Nicaragua

Shape	Name	Lgth	Ring	Wrapper
Churchill	Churchill	7	50	CM
Corona	Corona	5¼	42	CM
Double Corona	Presidente	7¾	50	CM
Robusto	Robusto	5	50	CM
Toro	Toro	6	50	CM

Here's a familiar name to opera fans . . . and cigar fans. This is a mild-to-medium-bodied blend made by hand in Honduras and attractively boxed in elegant all-cedar boxes of 25.

CARMEN PLATINUM LABEL
Handmade in Miami, Florida, USA.
Wrapper: USA/Connecticut *Binder: Dom. Rep.* *Filler: Dom. Rep.*

HANDMADE CIGARS: BRAND LISTINGS

Shape	Name	Lgth	Ring	Wrapper
Long Corona	Corona	6	44	CC-Ma
Robusto	Robusto	5	50	CC-Ma
Grand Corona	No. 1	6½	46	CC-Ma
Churchill	Ejecutivo	7	48	CC-Ma
Double Corona	Churchill	7¼	50	CC-Ma
Giant	Presidente	8	52	CC-Ma

Introduced in 1997, this is a Miami-made, mild-bodied cigar that is available in either a natural or maduro wrapper. Each cigar is protected in an individual cellophane sleeve and offered in boxes of 25.

CARMEN WHITE LABEL
Handmade in Santo Domingo, Dominican Republic.

Wrapper: Ecuador   *Binder: Dom. Rep.*   *Filler: Dom. Rep.*

Shape	Name	Lgth	Ring	Wrapper
Short Panatela	Petite Corona	5	38	CC
Corona	Corona	5½	44	CC
Robusto	Robusto	5	50	CC
Churchill	Ejecutivo	6¾	48	CC
Double Corona	Churchill	7	50	CC
Giant	Presidente	8	50	CC

This brand was introduced in 1996 and offers a mild-bodied flavor, packed in boxes of 25.

CARNIVAL HAVANA
Handmade in Esteli, Nicaragua.

Wrapper: Ecuador   *Binder: Nicaragua*   *Filler: Dom. Rep.*

Shape	Name	Lgth	Ring	Wrapper
Lonsdale	No. 1	7	43	CC

Panatela	Panatela	5½	38	CC
Robusto	Robusto	5	50	CC
Toro	Double Corona	6	48	CC
Churchill	Churchill	7	48	CC
Double Corona	President	7½	52	CC
Torpedo	Torpedo	6½	54	CC

Introduced in 1997, this is a premium brand featuring a Connecticut-seed wrapper and a medium-bodied flavor. Enjoy it in all-cedar boxes of 25, or for those replenishing their humidors, in bundles of 25.

CARNIVAL HAVANA SUPREME
Handmade in Esteli, Nicaragua.

Wrapper: Indonesia   *Binder: Nicaragua*   *Filler: Nicaragua*

Shape	Name	Lgth	Ring	Wrapper
Churchill	Churchill	7	48	CM
Toro	Toro	6	50	CM
Robusto	Robusto	4¾	50	CM
Corona	Corona	5½	44	CM
Torpedo	Torpedo	6¾	54	CM
Pyramid	Pyramide	7	50	CM
Giant	Viagante	8½	52	CM
Double Corona	Presidente	7½	52	CM

These cigars feature Cuban-seed Sumatra wrappers, but are mild in body and presented either in cedar boxes or bundles of 25.

CARRINGTON
Handmade in Santo Domingo, Dominican Republic.
Wrapper: USA/Connecticut or Panama

Binder: Dominican Republic   *Filler: Dominican Republic*

HANDMADE CIGARS: BRAND LISTINGS

Shape	Name	Lgth	Ring	Wrapper
Double Corona	No. 1	7½	50	DC-Cl-Ma
Long Corona	No. 2	6	42	Cl-Ma
Long Panatela	No. 3	7	36	Cl-Ma
Corona	No. 4	5½	40	Cl
Churchill	No. 5	6⅞	46	Cl
Robusto	No. 6	4½	50	Cl
Toro	No. 7	6	50	Cl
Pyramid	No. 8	6⅞	60	Cl

Introduced in 1984, Carrington cigars offer a mild to medium taste, with a solid core of spice and a nice, toasty flavor. The wrapper is Connecticut Shade tobacco or Panamanian maduro, with Dominican filler and binders. Check out the No. 8, a pyramid-shape with one of the largest ring gauges (60) of any cigar available.

CASA BLANCA
Handmade in Santiago, Dominican Republic.

Wrapper: USA/Connecticut   Binder: Mexico   Filler: Dom. Rep.

Shape	Name	Lgth	Ring	Wrapper
Short Panatela	Bonita	4	36	CC
Corona	Corona	5½	42	CC
Toro	DeLuxe	6	50	CC-Ma
Robusto	Half Jeroboam	5	66	CC-Ma
Giant	Jeroboam	10	66	CC-Ma
Lonsdale	Lonsdale	6½	42	CC-Ma
Double Corona	Magnum	7	60	CC-Ma
Panatela	Panatela	6	35	CC
Double Corona	President	7½	50	CC-Ma

HANDMADE CIGARS: BRAND LISTINGS

This line, which means "White House" in English, offers an extremely mild taste in a variety of sizes. Particularly noteworthy are the giant 66-ring Half Jeroboam and Jeroboam, the thickest straight-sided cigars offered on the U.S. market.

CASA BLANCA RESERVE
Handmade in Santiago, Dominican Republic.

Wrapper: Ecuador   Binder: Mexico   Filler: Dom. Rep.

Shape	Name	Lgth	Ring	Wrapper
Double Corona	No. 1	7½	50	CC
Toro	No. 2	6	50	CC
Lonsdale	No. 3	6½	42	CC
Corona	No. 4	5½	43	CC

"The best of the best" is the idea behind this upgraded selection of Casa Blanca, the Reserve Collection. Introduced in 1996, this elegant, mild line is offered in all-cedar cabinets of 25 cigars each.

CASA BUENA
Handmade in Las Palmas, the Canary Islands of Spain.

Wrapper: USA/Connecticut   Binder: Dom. Rep.   Filler: Brazil, Dom. Rep.

Shape	Name	Lgth	Ring	Wrapper
Double Corona	Especiales No. 1	7½	50	CC
Toro	Especiales No. 2	6	50	CC
Lonsdale	Especiales No. 3	6½	43	CC
Robusto	Especiales No. 4	4¾	50	CC

This brand was introduced in 1996, but refined for 1997. You'll enjoy a new blend from the Canary Islands that offers a mild-bodied smoke, with some slightly spicy interior tobaccos and Connecticut wrapper, offered in boxes of 25.

CASA DE GONZALEZ
Handmade in Santa Rosa de Copan, Honduras.

Wrapper: USA/Connecticut   Binder: Honduras   Filler: Honduras

HANDMADE CIGARS: BRAND LISTINGS

Shape	Name	Lgth	Ring	Wrapper
Double Corona	Churchill	7	50	CC
Toro	Corona Gorda	6	50	CC
Long Corona	Corona	6	44	CC
Robusto	Robusto	5	50	CC
Petit Corona	Petit Corona	5	42	CC
Panatela	Panatela	6	38	CC
Torpedo	Torpedo	6½	54	CC
Cigarillo	Senora's	4⅛	25	CC

From the famed "La Flor de Copan" factory in Santa Rosa de Copan, Honduras comes this new brand for 1997. You can try it in standard boxes of 25, or in hard-carved humidor boxes of 25, 50 or 75. Production of this mild-to-medium-bodied cigar is limited to 600,000 annually. Look for a Nicaraguan-produced "Casa de Gonzalez" line in 1998.

CASA DE KLAFTER
Handmade in Miami, Florida, USA.

Wrapper: Ecuador   *Binder: Ecuador*
Filler: Dominican Republic, Honduras, Mexico, Nicaragua

Shape	Name	Lgth	Ring	Wrapper
Short Panatela	Corona	5	38	CC-Co-Ma
Robusto	Robusto	5	50	CC-Co-Ma
Toro	Toro	6	50	CC-Co-Ma
Lonsdale	Lonsdale	6½	42	CC-Co-Ma
Long Panatela	Long Panatela	7½	36	CC-Co-Ma
Churchill	Churchill	7½	46	CC-Co-Ma
Double Corona	Double Corona	7½	54	CC-Co-Ma
Double Corona	Special Corona	7¼	50	CC-Co-Ma

HANDMADE CIGARS: BRAND LISTINGS

Created in 1995, this Miami-made blend of tobaccos from five nations offers a full range of flavors from mild to full-bodied thanks to three different styles of wrappers: natural, rosado and maduro.

CASA DE NICARAGUA
Handmade in Nicaragua.

Wrapper: Indonesia   *Binder: Nicaragua*   *Filler: Nicaragua*

Shape	Name	Lgth	Ring	Wrapper
Robusto	Rothschild	5	50	CC
Long Corona	Corona	6	43	CC
Toro	Toro	6	50	CC-Ma
Lonsdale	Double Corona	7	44	CC-Ma
Double Corona	Churchill	7	49	CC
Double Corona	Presidente	7½	52	CC
Giant	Gigante	8	54	CC-Ma
Giant	Viajante	8½	52	CC

These are well-constructed cigars, offered in all-cedar boxes of 25. The body is mild, thanks to an Indonesian wrapper.

CASA MARTIN
Handmade in Las Palmas, the Canary Islands of Spain.

Wrapper: Indonesia   *Binder: Dom. Rep.*   *Filler: Dom. Rep.*

Shape	Name	Lgth	Ring	Wrapper
Corona	Corona	5½	42	CC
Robusto	Robusto	4¾	48	CC
Lonsdale	Numero Uno	6⅝	43	CC
Toro	Governor	6	50	CC
Churchill	Churchill	7	46	CC
Churchill	Double Corona	7½	48	CC

HANDMADE CIGARS: BRAND LISTINGS

Formerly made in the Dominican Republic, this brand was remade in 1996. These cigars are mild to medium in strength, with a Ecuador-grown, Connecticut-seed wrapper and Dominican binder and filler tobaccos. The Casa Martin line is offered in bundles of 25 cigars.

CASCADA
Handmade in San Andres Tuxtla, Mexico.

Wrapper: Mexico *Binder: Mexico* *Filler: Mexico*

Shape	Name	Lgth	Ring	Wrapper
Robusto	Robusto	5	50	CC
Toro	Toro	6	50	CC
Lonsdale	Lonsdale	6½	42	CC
Double Corona	Churchill	7	52	CC

Here is an all-Mexican cigar, offering a medium-to-full-bodied taste. Introduced in 1997, it is packed in individual cellophane sleeves inside cedar boxes of 25.

CASILLAS
Handmade in Sacramento, California, and Reno, Nevada, USA.

Wrapper: Ecuador or USA/Connecticut; Mexico *Binder: Ecuador or Mexico*
Filler: Dominican Republic, Honduras, Mexico, Nicaragua

Shape	Name	Lgth	Ring	Wrapper
Double Corona	Cuban Round	7½	54	CM-Ma
Double Corona	Churchill	7½	50	CM-Ma
Torpedo	Torpedo	7	58	CM-Ma
Toro	Casillas No. 1	6½	56	CM-Ma
Toro	Double Corona	6½	50	CM-Ma
Slim Panatela	Cubanito	6	34	CM-Ma
Long Corona	Corona Long	6	44	CM-Ma
Panatela	Panatela	6½	36	CM-Ma
Toro	Toro	6½	52	CM-Ma

HANDMADE CIGARS: BRAND LISTINGS

Corona Extra	Rothschild	5	46	CM-Ma
Petit Corona	Petit Cetros	5	42	CM-Ma
Panatela	Pencil	5½	36	CM-Ma
Giant	Jacaranda	8½	56	CM-Ma
Churchill	Presidente	7	46	CM-Ma
Toro	Robusto	6¼	52	CM-Ma
Giant	Super Cazadores	8½	52	CM-Ma
Churchill	Cazadores	7½	46	CM-Ma
Robusto	Fuma	4¼	52	CM-Ma
Robusto	Palmitas	4¼	52	CM-Ma
Robusto	Tornquito	4¼	52	CM-Ma

This blend of long-filler tobaccos is assembled under the direction of Macario Casillas, a Cuban native who began rolling cigars at age 13. He supervises three other ex-Cuban nationals who share his passion for quality and the medium-to-full bodied taste and smooth finish that characterizes the Casillas brand. The wrappers vary with Ecuador or U.S.-grown leaves for the natural-shade sizes and a Mexican-grown leaf for the maduro-wrapped shapes.

CASTAÑO
Handmade in Cofradia and Danli, Honduras.

Wrapper: Ecuador   *Binder: USA/Connecticut*   *Filler: Honduras*

Shape	Name	Lgth	Ring	Wrapper
Double Corona	Imperiales	7¼	54	CC
Churchill	Corona Immensa	6⅞	48	CC
Robusto	Magnificos	5½	50	CC
Grand Corona	Corona Royale	6¼	45	CC
Corona	Corona Especial	5½	43	CC

Introduced in 1997, this is a full-bodied cigar with subtle flavors. It offers a Sumatra-seed wrapper and is presented uncellophaned in all-cedar boxes of 25.

HANDMADE CIGARS: BRAND LISTINGS

CAVANA
Handmade in Bronx, New York, USA.

Wrapper: Mexico | Binder: Dom. Rep. | Filler: Honduras, Mexico

Shape	Name	Lgth	Ring	Wrapper
Giant	El Grande	8	50	CM-Ma
Double Corona	Churchill	7	50	CM-Ma
Lonsdale	No. 1 Imperial	7	45	CM-Ma
Slim Panatela	Panatela	6	30	CM-Ma
Toro	No. 2 Double Corona	6	50	CM-Ma
Grand Corona	No. 3	6	45	CM-Ma
Robusto	Robusto	5	50	CM-Ma
Petit Corona	No. 4 Queen	5	41	CM-Ma

Here is an all long-filler, handmade brand that offers two tastes: a mild body with the natural wrapper and a full body with the Mexican maduro wrapper.
Introduced in 1996, it is in limited distribution and offered in cellophane sleeves in air-tight cases of five, or in boxes of 25.

CECIL BROOKS III
Handmade in Miami, Florida, USA.

Wrapper: Indonesia | Binder: Indonesia | Filler: Mexico

Shape	Name	Lgth	Ring	Wrapper
Double Corona	Churchill	6¾	50	Ma
Double Corona	Presidente	7¼	50	Ma
Robusto	Robusto	5	50	Ma

This all-maduro brand was created in 1997, and offers a medium-to-full bodied taste available in boxes of 25.

HANDMADE CIGARS: BRAND LISTINGS

CEDAR JOE
Handmade in Danli, Honduras.

Wrapper: Honduras   *Binder: Honduras*   *Filler: Honduras*

Shape	Name	Lgth	Ring	Wrapper
Robusto	Rothchild	4½	50	CM
Lonsdale	Corona Gorda	6½	44	CM
Double Corona	Aristo	7½	52	CM
Torpedo	Mega Torpedo	7½	64	CM
Pyramid	Club Pyramid	5½	52	CM

A 1994 creation, the Cedar Joe line offers a mild-to-medium-bodied smoke in a fine value line. The three straight-sided shapes and the two shaped styles are each offered in boxes of 10.

CEDAR JOE DULCE
Handmade in Danli, Honduras.

Wrapper: Honduras   *Binder: Honduras*   *Filler: Honduras*

Shape	Name	Lgth	Ring	Wrapper
Robusto	Rothschild	4½	50	CM
Lonsdale	Corona Gorda	6½	44	CM
Double Corona	Aristo	7½	52	CM
Double Corona	Churchill	6⅞	49	CM

Here is a sweetened version of the Cedar Joe blend, mild in body and, available in ten-packs.

CEDROS
Handmade in Santiago, Dominican Republic.

Wrapper: USA/Connecticut   *Binder: Dom. Rep.*   *Filler: Dom. Rep.*

Shape	Name	Lgth	Ring	Wrapper
Toro	Churchill	6½	50	CC
Churchill	Presidente	6⅞	46	CC

| Robusto | Robusto | 5 | 50 | CC |
| Corona | Corona Supreme | 5½ | 42 | CC |

Created by Jim and Kathi Brown-Martin in 1994, this is a mild blend of Dominican leaves with a Connecticut Shade wrapper, offered in individual cellophane sleeves presented in cedar cabinets of 25.

CELESTINO VEGA
Handmade in Jakarta, Indonesia.

Wrapper: Indonesia   *Binder: Indonesia*   *Filler: Dom. Rep., Indonesia*

Shape	Name	Lgth	Ring	Wrapper
Perfecto	Senator	4	48	CC
Robusto	Rothchild	5	50	CC
Toro	Super Rothchild	6	50	CC
Lonsdale	Cuban Corona	6½	42	CC
Perfecto	Cuban Perfecto	6	48	CC
Double Corona	Churchill	7	50	CC

These handmade, long-filler cigars feature Indonesian tobaccos grown on the islands of Java and Sumatra. Javan wrappers are used on all models and these cigars offer a full, flavorful taste and are uniquely packaged not only in boxes of 25, but also in triangular boxes of 21!

CERDAN
Handmade in Santiago, Dominican Republic.

Wrapper: USA/Connecticut   *Binder: Dom. Rep.*   *Filler: Dom. Rep.*

Shape	Name	Lgth	Ring	Wrapper
Long Panatela	Juan Carlos	7	37	CC
Corona	Ejecutivo	5½	42	CC
Lonsdale	Gables	7½	40	CC
Corona	Napoleon	5½	44	CC
Lonsdale	Welles	6¾	44	CC

HANDMADE CIGARS: BRAND LISTINGS

Grand Corona	Chamberlain	6	45	CC
Churchill	Churchill	7	48	CC
Double Corona	Don Juan	7½	50	CC
Robusto	Robusto	5½	50	CC
	Cedar Selection:			
Slim Panatela	Gemma	6	32	CC
Giant Corona	Don Jose	7½	42	CC
Churchill	Don Ramon	7½	48	CC
Toro	Don Jordi	6½	54	CC
Giant Corona	Don Roberto	8	44	CC
Giant	Gran Cerdan	10	54	CC
Lonsdale	Don Alberto	6½	44	CC
Robusto	Robusto	5½	52	CC

Wildly popular in Europe since its introduction in 1981, Cerdan cigars debuted in the United States in 1996. This brand, the creation of Juan Cerdan Soto, offers a mild-to-medium body in plywood boxes of 25, or all-cedar cabinets of 25.

CERVANTES
Handmade in Danli, Honduras.

Wrapper: Honduras   *Binder: Honduras*   *Filler: Honduras*

Shape	*Name*	*Lgth*	*Ring*	*Wrapper*
Lonsdale	Churchill	7¼	45	CC
Grand Corona	Corona	6¼	46	CC
Long Corona	Senadores	6	42	CC

Cervantes are handmade cigars of excellent quality, made in Honduras of all-Honduran tobacco. They are medium in taste, and presented in boxes of 25.

HANDMADE CIGARS: BRAND LISTINGS

CHACARO BLACK STALLION
Handmade in San Pedro Sula, Honduras.

Wrapper: Ecuador   Binder: Honduras   Filler: Honduras

Shape	Name	Lgth	Ring	Wrapper
Robusto	Celebration	5	50	CC
Long Corona	Classic	6¼	44	CC
Toro	Trophy	6	50	CC
Toro	Darkhan's Blue Ribbon	6	54	CC
Corona	Filly	5½	43	CC
Corona	Colt	5½	43	Ma

Here is a medium-to-full-bodied brand introduced in 1996 that celebrates Darkhan, a champion Black Arabian stallion, owned by Roy and Charlotte Ivy of Chacaro So-Black Arabians. You can salute this award-winning horse with a box of 25 of these beauties.

CHAIRMAN'S CHOICE
Handmade in Danli, Honduras.

Wrapper: Ecuador   Binder: Honduras   Filler: Honduras

Shape	Name	Lgth	Ring	Wrapper
Corona	V.P.	5½	42	CC
Robusto	Director	5	50	CC
Toro	Treasurer	6	50	CC
Churchill	President	6⅞	46	CC
Double Corona	CEO	7¾	50	CC
Torpedo	Chairman	7	54	CC

Here is a medium-bodied brand introduced in 1996. The names of the shapes are common enough in big corporations, but is it proper to offer the Chairman a torpedo?

HANDMADE CIGARS: BRAND LISTINGS

CHARLES FAIRMORN
Handmade in Danli, Honduras.

Wrapper: Honduras   Binder: Honduras   Filler: Honduras

Shape	Name	Lgth	Ring	Wrapper
Double Corona	Churchill	6⅞	49	CM
Long Corona	Coronas	6¼	44	CM
Panatela	Elegante	6¾	38	CM
Small Panatela	Super Fino	4½	32	CM

Sought after since their introduction in 1979, the Charles Fairmorn line from Honduras is a medium-to-full-bodied cigar which is available in four sizes. It is made by hand from selected Cuban-seed leaves and offered in boxes of 25.

CHARLES FAIRMORN BELMORE
Handmade in Santiago, Dominican Republic.

Wrapper: USA/Connecticut   Binder: Dom. Rep.   Filler: Dom. Rep.

Shape	Name	Lgth	Ring	Wrapper
Panatela	Petit Corona	5⅝	38	CC
Long Panatela	Panatela	7	36	CC
Robusto	Robusto	4¾	50	CC
Lonsdale	Elegante	7	43	CC
Churchill	Churchill	6⅞	46	CC
Toro	Matador	6	50	CC
Double Corona	Presidente	7½	50	CC
Torpedo	Piramide	7½	64	CC

This series, introduced in 1991, is produced in Santiago de los Caballeros in the Dominican Republic and uses only the smoothest Connecticut wrappers. These cigars are of medium body and are offered in boxes of 25, except for the Piramide shape, offered in 20s.

HANDMADE CIGARS: BRAND LISTINGS

CHARLES FAIRMORN CONNSHADE
Handmade, with short filler, in Dingelstadt, Germany.

Wrapper: USA/Connecticut　　　　　　　　　　　　　*Binder: Indonesia*
Filler: Brazil, Dominican Republic, Honduras, Indonesia

Shape	Name	Lgth	Ring	Wrapper
Short Panatela	Senorita	4½	35	CC
Petit Corona	Corona	4¾	42	CC
Slim Panatela	Panatela	6	32	CC

This is a mild-bodied, handmade brand that features short filler tobaccos from four nations surrounded by a Java binder and a Connecticut-grown wrapper. It is presented in boxes of 20, except for the Panatela, available in boxes of 10.

CHARLES THE GREAT
Handmade in Santa Rosa de Copan, Honduras.

Wrapper: USA/Connecticut　　　　*Binder: Honduras*　　　　　　*Filler: Honduras*

Shape	Name	Lgth	Ring	Wrapper
Double Corona	Madrid	7½	50	CC
Toro	Barcelona	6	50	CC
Grand Corona	Valencia	6¾	46	CC
Robusto	Granada	5	50	CC
Long Corona	Toledo	6	42	CC
Petit Corona	Cordoba	5⅛	42	CC

Charles The Great, better known as Charlemagne, was born in 742 and ruled what is now France and part of western Germany from 768-814 and through conquest and a close relationship with Pope Leo III helped to found the Holy Roman Empire, which he ruled until his death in 814. The cigars are not as old as Charlemagne, but were produced decades ago as a clear Havana, and has recently been resurrected by the Finck Cigar Company of San Antonio, Texas. It utilizes the brand's original box and label art and presents these medium-bodied cigars in all-wooden boxes of 25.

HANDMADE CIGARS: BRAND LISTINGS

CHATEAU AMARETTO
Handmade, with medium filler, in Santiago, Dominican Republic.

Wrapper: Indonesia   Binder: Dom. Rep.   Filler: Dom. Rep.

Shape	Name	Lgth	Ring	Wrapper
Long Corona		6	42	CM
Long Corona		6	44	CM

This is a medium-bodied cigar, available in two sizes, and introduced in 1996. It utilizes all-Dominican filler and is offered in bundles of 25.

CHESSMAN ROYAL RESERVE
Handmade in Miami, Florida, USA.

Wrapper: Ecuador   Binder: Ecuador
Filler: Dominican Republic, Honduras, Nicaragua

Shape	Name	Lgth	Ring	Wrapper
Long Corona	Pawn	6	42	CC-Ma
Toro	Knight	6	52	CC-Ma
Lonsdale	Bishop	6½	44	CC-Ma
Robusto	Rook	5	52	CC-Ma
Churchill	Queen	7	47	CC-Ma
Giant	King	8	52	CC-Ma
Giant	Check Mate	6	60	CC-Ma
Torpedo	The Castle	6½	54	CC-Ma

Named for chess pieces and the game-ending situation, this is a medium-bodied blend of leaves from four nations, created in 1997. The brand is offered in boxes of 25 cigars each.

CHEVERE
Handmade in Kingston, Jamaica.

Wrapper: USA/Connecticut   Binder: Dom. Rep.   Filler: Dom. Rep.

Christiano Leone '
Director's Selection

HOLLYWOOD SERIES Limited Production   **DIRECTOR'S CHOICE SERIES** Extremely Limited Produc

Vanity Fairs   5" x 50

Divas   6" x 42

Producers   8 1/2" x

Vanilla Divas   6" x 42

Agents   7 1/2"

Glamours   6" x 50

Actors   6 1/2"

Elegantes   6 1/2" x 46

Directors   4" x 4

Celebrities   7 1/2" x 50

WRAPPER: SUMATRA   BINDER: DOMINICAN   FILLER: DOMINICAN

Hand made long filler vintage premium cigars

HANDMADE CIGARS: BRAND LISTINGS

Shape	Name	Lgth	Ring	Wrapper
Double Corona	Kingston	7	49	CC
Grand Corona	Montego	6½	45	CC
Giant	Ocho Rios	8	49	CC
Corona	Port Antonio	5½	43	CC
Lonsdale	Spanish Town	6½	42	CC

Chevere cigars are quality, hand-made products of Jamaica, offering good construction and a mild body. Introduced in 1990, the brand's shapes offer a natural wrapper, in bundles of 12 or 25 cigars each.

CHRISTIANO LEONÉ DIRECTOR'S SELECTION
Handmade in Santiago, Dominican Republic.

Wrapper: Indonesia   *Binder: Dom. Rep.*   *Filler: Dom. Rep.*

Shape	Name	Lgth	Ring	Wrapper
	Hollywood Series:			
Long Corona	Divas	6	42	CC
Long Corona	Vanilla Divas	6	42	CC
Robusto	Vanity Fairs	5	50	CC
Toro	Glamours	6	50	CC
Grand Corona	Elegantes	6½	46	CC
Double Corona	Celebrities	7½	50	CC
	Director's Choice Series:			
Long Panatela	Agents	7½	38	CC
Perfecto	Directors	4	44	CC
Giant	Producers	8½	52	CC
Torpedo	Actors	6½	52	CC

Hooray for Hollywood! This brand celebrates the stage, film and television with shape names about performers and those that surround them. The cigars themselves are carefully made, available only in limited quantities and offer Sumatran wrappers to complement Dominican-grown fillers and binder. Medium in body, both lines were introduced in 1996 and are presented in boxes of 25.

CHURCHILL
Handmade in Esteli, Nicaragua.

Wrapper: Ecuador   *Binder: Nicaragua*   *Filler: Nicaragua*

Shape	Name	Lgth	Ring	Wrapper
Giant	Presidente	8	50	CM
Double Corona	Prime Minister	7¼	54	CM
Toro	Senator	6	50	CM
Corona	No. 3	5⅝	44	CM
Robusto	Robusto	4¾	50	CM

Named for the great statesman and British Prime Minister Sir Winston Churchill (1874-1965), this brand celebrates perhaps the world's most famous cigar smoker. Almost always seen with his trademark double corona — or larger — cigar, Churchill achieved much greatness in a long life that included two stints as the leader of his beloved Great Britain (1940-45 and 1951-55). His picture adorns the box of this medium-bodied, all long-filler cigar, which is offered in boxes of 25.

CIBAO
Handmade in Santiago, Dominican Republic.

Wrapper: Indonesia or USA/Connecticut   *Binder: Dom. Rep.*
Filler: Dominican Republic

Shape	Name	Lgth	Ring	Wrapper
Torpedo	Torpedo 6	6	54	CC-CM
Torpedo	Torpedo 7	7	54	CC-CM
Double Corona	Presidente	7½	50	CC-CM
Churchill	Churchill	6⅞	46	CC-CM
Toro	Toro	6	48	CC-CM
Long Corona	Lonsdale	6	44	CC-CM

Robusto	Robusto	5	50	CC-CM
Petit Corona	Petit Coronas	5	42	CC-CM
Short Panatela	Selecto	5	38	CC-CM

Debuting in 1997, there are two versions of this brand: one with a Connecticut wrapper and one with a Sumatra wrapper. Both are mild in strength and are offered in cedar boxes of 25.

CIELO UMO
Handmade in Jakarta, Indonesia.

Wrapper: Indonesia   *Binder: Indonesia*   *Filler: Dom. Rep., Honduras*

Shape	*Name*	*Lgth*	*Ring*	*Wrapper*
Small Panatela	Centennial	4	32	CC
Slim Panatela	Panatella	7	30	CC
Lonsdale	Corona	6½	44	CC
Giant Corona	Lonsdale	8½	44	CC
Lonsdale	Corona Grande	7	42	CC
Robusto	Delicados	4¾	50	CC

Here is a medium-to-full-bodied smoke, featuring a Sumatra wrapper. Each cigar is individually cellophaned and packed in either Indonesian wood boxes or in black acrylic cases.

CIFUENTES
Handmade in Kingston, Jamaica.
Wrapper: Mexico or USA/Connecticut

Binder: "Jember"   *Filler: Dominican Republic*

Shape	*Name*	*Lgth*	*Ring*	*Wrapper*
Double Corona	Churchill	7¼	49	CC
Toro	Toro	6	49	CC
Lonsdale	Fancytail	6¾	42	CC
Torpedo	Belicoso	6¼	50	CC

Robusto	Maduro	4¾	49	Ma
Robusto	Rothschild	4¾	49	CC

The famous name - and face - of Ramon Cifuentes, who took over the Partagas brand in Cuba in 1889 after the death of its founder, adorn this brand, completely remade for 1997. Cigars under this brand name were produced in Havana until nationalization; today's version is mild-to-medium-bodied and beautifully constructed. The Fancytail shape has a twisted head, while the Maduro shape uses a Mexican wrapper leaf rather than the standard shade-grown Connecticut leaf. Cifuentes is available in boxes of 25 for the Churchill, Toro and Fancytail shape and in 20s for all other shapes.

CIGAR COMPADRES
Handmade in Haina, Dominican Republic.
Wrapper: Indonesia and USA/Connecticut

Binder: Dominican Republic   *Filler: Dominican Republic*

Shape	Name	Lgth	Ring	Wrapper
Giant	Presidente	8	50	CC
Double Corona	Churchill	7	50	CC
Robusto	Robusto	5	50	CC
Long Corona	Lonsdale	6	44	CC
Pyramid	Piramide	6	56	CC
Grand Corona	Grand Corona	6½	46	CC

Created in 1996, this line offers a choice of Connecticut or Sumatra wrapper for a mild-to-medium or medium-bodied taste. Enjoy in boxes of 25.

THE CIGAR CONNECTION - NICARAGUA
Handmade in Esteli, Nicaragua.

Wrapper: Ecuador   *Binder: Nicaragua*   *Filler: Nicaragua*

Shape	Name	Lgth	Ring	Wrapper
Churchill	Doble Corona	7½	48	CC
Robusto	Robusto	5½	50	CC

HANDMADE CIGARS: BRAND LISTINGS

Introduced in 1997, this is a mild-to-medium-bodied smoke featuring Habana criollo leaves in the filler. It is offered in boxes of 25.

CIGARROS CIBAO
Handmade in Santiago, Dominican Republic.

Wrapper: Indonesia　　　　　*Binder: Dom. Rep.*　　　　　*Filler: Dom. Rep.*

Shape	Name	Lgth	Ring	Wrapper
Robusto	Gordito	4½	52	CC
Churchill	Quimosabe	6¾	46	CC
Corona	Caballero	5¼	42	CC
Petit Corona	Muchacho	4	42	CC
Slim Panatela	Flecha	5	30	CC
Double Corona	Tubano	7¾	50	CC

This mild-bodied brand debuted in 1996, offering a flavorful blend in boxes of 25. The cigars are well protected: each is paper-wrapped and each row is separated by foil sheets.

CIMMARON
Handmade, with medium filler, in Tamboril, Dominican Republic.

Wrapper: Indonesia　　　　　*Binder: Dom. Rep.*　　　　　*Filler: Dom. Rep.*

Shape	Name	Lgth	Ring	Wrapper
Corona	No. I	5½	42	CM
Robusto	No. II	4¾	52	CM
Long Corona	No. III	6	44	CM
Churchill	No. IV	6⅞	46	CM
Toro	No. V	6½	50	CM
Toro	No. VI	6½	52	CM
Robusto	No. VII	5	50	CM

HANDMADE CIGARS: BRAND LISTINGS

Here is an value-priced, handmade cigar from the Dominican Republic. Introduced in 1997, it features a Sumatra wrapper and a mild-to-medium-bodied taste in bundles of 25.

CIMERO
Handmade in Tamboril, Dominican Republic.

Wrapper: USA/Connecticut   *Binder: Dom. Rep.*   *Filler: Dom. Rep.*

Shape	Name	Lgth	Ring	Wrapper
Double Corona	Churchill	7	50	CC
Toro	Toro	6	50	CC
Robusto	Rothchild	5	50	CC
Churchill	Lonsdale	6⅞	46	CC
Long Corona	Corona Grande	6	44	CC
Corona	Corona	5½	42	CC

The brand name translates into English as "on top of the mountain." So find your favorite heights, sit a spell and light up this mild-to-medium-bodied brand re-introduced in 1995 after its original debut in the 1960s. It features a genuine Connecticut wrapper combined with Cuban-seed filler leaves packed in 5x5 all-cedar cabinets of 25.

CINCO VEGAS
Handmade in Esteli, Nicaragua.

Wrapper: Indonesia   *Binder: Indonesia*   *Filler: Dom.Rep., Nicaragua*

Shape	Name	Lgth	Ring	Wrapper
Double Corona	Churchill	7	52	CC
Torpedo	Torpedo	6	50	CC
Torpedo	Piramide	6½	46	CC
Toro	Doble Corona	6	48	CC
Panatela	Panatela	6	38	CC
Corona	Corona	5½	44	CC
Robusto	Robusto	5	50	CC

Small Panatela	Petite	5	34	CC

This brand, whose name means "five farms" in Spanish, was originally made in 1890 in Cuba. The Sumatra-grown wrapper and binder gives this new brand a rich, but mild-to-medium-bodied flavor. It is offered in boxes of 25 cigars each, except for the Piramide shape, offered in 10s.

CINCO VEGAS VINTAGE SELECTION
Handmade in Esteli, Nicaragua.

Wrapper: Brazil   *Binder: Indonesia*   *Filler: Dom.Rep., Nicaragua*

Shape	Name	Lgth	Ring	Wrapper
Double Corona	Churchill	7	52	CC
Torpedo	Torpedo	6	50	CC
Torpedo	Piramide	6½	46	CC
Toro	Doble Corona	6	48	CC
Panatela	Panatela	6	38	CC
Corona	Corona	5½	44	CC
Robusto	Robusto	5	50	CC

This is a mild-bodied version of the Cinco Vegas brand, with a Brazilian wrapper and a blend of leaves from three other nations inside. It is offered in boxes of 25.

CISSO
Handmade in Santiago, Dominican Republic.

Wrapper: USA/Connecticut   *Binder: Dom. Rep.*   *Filler: Dom. Rep.*

Shape	Name	Lgth	Ring	Wrapper
Double Corona	Churchill	7	50	CC
Toro	Joven	6	50	CC
Robusto	Robusto	5	50	CC
Torpedo	Torpedo	6	50	CC
Grand Corona	Preferido	6	46	CC

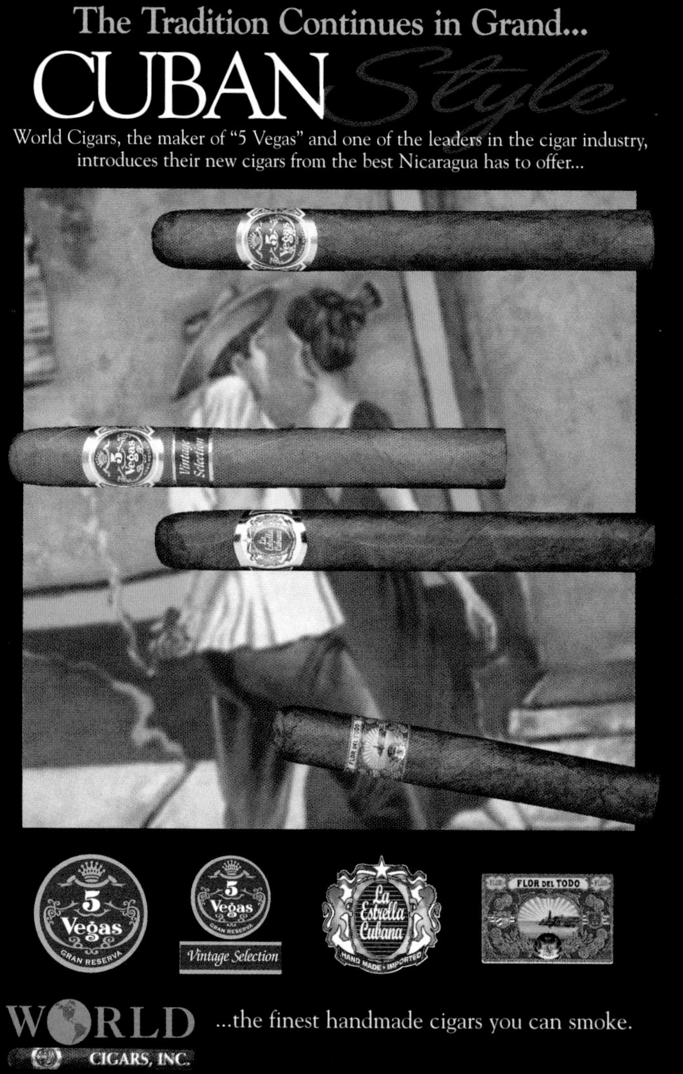

The Tradition Continues in Grand...
CUBAN *Style*

World Cigars, the maker of "5 Vegas" and one of the leaders in the cigar industry, introduces their new cigars from the best Nicaragua has to offer...

Corona	Corona	5½	42	CC
Short Panatela	Petit	4½	36	CC
Panatela	Panetela	6½	36	CC

Introduced in late 1996, this brand offers a mild-to-medium flavor with a genuine Connecticut wrapper. It is offered in all-cedar boxes of 25.

CISSO PREMIUM LOMA
Handmade in Santiago, Dominican Republic.

Wrapper: Indonesia   *Binder: Dom. Rep.*   *Filler: Dom. Rep.*

Shape	Name	Lgth	Ring	Wrapper
Toro	No. 1	6	50	CC
Robusto	No. 2	5	50	CC
Long Corona	No. 3	6	44	CC

This is a medium-bodied cigar introduced in late 1996. It offers a Sumatra-grown wrapper combined with Dominican leaves for a medium-bodied taste.

CLIPPER GOLD RESERVE
Handmade in Santiago, Dominican Republic.
Wrapper: Indonesia, USA/Connecticut

Binder: Dominican Republic   *Filler: Dominican Republic*

Shape	Name	Lgth	Ring	Wrapper
Lonsdale	Hampton	6¾	44	CC-Ma
Robusto	Barrington	5	50	CC-Ma
Double Corona	Port Royale	7½	50	CC-Ma
Churchill	Mystic	6¾	53	CC-Ma

Introduced in 1996, Clipper Gold Reserve offers a medium-to-full-bodied taste in a choice of natural or maduro wrapper, offered in all-cedar boxes of 25.

HANDMADE CIGARS: BRAND LISTINGS

CLASSICO DE CONTINENTAL
Handmade in Villa Gonzalez, Dominican Republic.

Wrapper: Indonesia *Binder: Dom. Rep.* *Filler: Dom. Rep.*

Shape	Name	Lgth	Ring	Wrapper
Grand Corona	Palma a Reserve	6½	46	CC
Long Corona	Long Corona	6	44	CC
Robusto	Robusto	5	50	CC
Churchill	Churchill	7½	48	CC
	Handmade with mixed filler:			
Long Corona	Long Corona	6	44	CC
Robusto	Robusto	5	50	CC
Churchill	Churchill	7½	48	CC
	Handmade with short filler:			
Long Corona	J. Barton Classico	6	42	CC

Introduced in late 1997, this line replaces an earlier Classico de Continental line of medium-bodied cigars from Nicaragua. This new line is medium-to-full bodied in flavor, thanks to its Sumatran wrapper and Dominican binder and filler. These new cigars are offered in individual cellophane sleeves in varnished cedar boxes.

CLASSICO DE CONTINENTAL
Handmade in Danli, Honduras.

Wrapper: Honduras *Binder: Honduras* *Filler: Honduras*

Shape	Name	Lgth	Ring	Wrapper
Toro	Robusto Grande	6	50	CM
Corona Extra	Edgar Corona	5½	46	CM

These cigars offer plenty of smoking pleasure in larger ring sizes, with a medium-bodied flavor. Made of all-Cuban seed tobaccos, this series – introduced in 1997 – is available in bundles or boxes of 25.

HANDMADE CIGARS: BRAND LISTINGS

CLEMENTINE
Handmade in Danli, Honduras.

Wrapper: Honduras   *Binder: Honduras*   *Filler: Honduras, Nicaragua*

Shape	Name	Lgth	Ring	Wrapper
Long Corona	Coronas	6¼	44	CM-Ma
Double Corona	Churchills	7	50	CM-Ma
Giant	Inmensas	8	54	CM
Lonsdale	No. 1	7	44	CM-Ma
Corona	No. 4	5½	44	CM-Ma
Double Corona	Presidente	7¾	50	CM-Ma
Robusto	Rothschild	5	50	CM-Ma
Toro	Toro	6	50	CM-Ma
Giant	Viajante	8½	52	CM

This is a long-filler, bundle cigar which was introduced in 1991 and offers a full-bodied taste. The name of the brand supposedly came from the favorite song of the buyers who were looking for tobacco on the backroads of Central America when the brand was introduced. Please . . .

CLUB SWEETS
Handmade, with short filler, in Mexico City, Mexico.

Wrapper: Mexico   *Binder: Nicaragua*   *Filler: Dom. Rep., Mexico*

Shape	Name	Lgth	Ring	Wrapper
Corona	Mocha	5	44	CM
Corona	Vanilla	5	44	CM

Introduced in 1997, this series offers mild, handmade, short-filler cigars with a strong flavor. The brand is presented with bands and in bundles of 25 cigars.

HANDMADE CIGARS: BRAND LISTINGS

COHIBA
Handmade in Santiago, Dominican Republic.

Wrapper: Cameroon   Binder: "Jember"   Filler: Dom. Rep.

Shape	Name		Lgth	Ring	Wrapper
Robusto	Robusto		5	49	CM
Double Corona	Churchill		7	49	CM
Lonsdale	Corona Especiale		6½	42	CM
Grand Corona	Lonsdale Grande		6¼	47	CM
Corona Extra	Robusto Fino		4¾	47	CM
Corona	Corona		5⅛	42	CM
Petit Corona	Corona Minor		4	42	CM
Corona	Crystal Corona	(tubed)	5½	42	CM
Pyramid	Triangulo		6	54	CM

This is an all-new Cohiba for 1997. General Cigar had produced a three-size, unbanded Cohiba for 20 years, but this new, medium-to-full-bodied blend has more of everything, including sizes and taste. The Corona Especiale is finished with a twisted head and the Crystal Corona is packaged in a glass tube. The product of five years of research, it is offered in a beautiful mahogany box.

COJIMAR
Handmade in Santo Domingo, Dominican Republic.

Wrapper: USA/Connecticut   Binder: Dom. Rep   Filler: Dom. Rep.

Shape	Name	Lgth	Ring	Wrapper
Torpedo	Torpedo	6	54	CC
Giant	Presidente	8	50	CC
Lonsdale	Coronitas	6¾	44	CC
Panatela	Laguitos	6¾	38	CC
Panatela	Cortaditos	6¾	38	Stripe
Robusto	Toro	5½	50	CC

HANDMADE CIGARS: BRAND LISTINGS

Small Panatela	Senoritas	5	30	CC

This cigar debuted in 1996. It now offers a range of popular sizes in a mild-bodied style. Note that the Senoritas shape is also available with vanilla flavoring.

COLORADO
Handmade in Santiago, Dominican Republic.

Wrapper: Indonesia   *Binder: Dom. Rep.*   *Filler: Dom. Rep.*

Shape	Name	Lgth	Ring	Wrapper
Long Corona	Lonsdale	6	42	Co
Long Corona	Corona	6	44	Co
Toro	Robusto	6	50	Co
Double Corona	Churchill	7½	50	Co
Torpedo	Torpedo	7	54	Co
Robusto	Rothchild	4½	50	Co
Giant	Presidente	8	52	Co
Long Panatela	Panatela	7½	38	Co

Colorado is a medium-bodied, premium cigar originally created in 1994. Now made in the Dominican Republic, it offers an all long-filler blend which is presented in individual cellophane sleeves and in all-cedar boxes of 25.

COLUMBUS
Handmade in the Dominican Republic.
Wrapper: Indonesia or USA/Connecticut

Binder: Dominican Republic   *Filler: Dominican Republic*

Shape	Name	Lgth	Ring	Wrapper
Double Corona	Corona Gorda	7	50	CC
Robusto	Robusto	5½	50	CC
Grand Corona	Doble Corona	6½	46	CC

Long Corona	Corona	6	44	CC

This is a medium-bodied cigar, made by hand in the Dominican Republic, and offered in boxes of 25.

COMMANDANTE
Handmade, with short filler, in Licey, Dominican Republic.

Wrapper: Indonesia   *Binder: Dom. Rep.*   *Filler: Dom. Rep.*

Shape	Name	Lgth	Ring	Wrapper
Giant	Churchill	8	48	Ma
Grand Corona	Double Corona	6½	46	Ma
Long Corona	Diplomatico	6	44	Ma
Robusto	Robusto	5	50	Ma

Well made, albeit with short filler, and offering a medium-bodied taste, Commandante featured Piloto Cubano filler tobaccos and is offered in elegant boxes of 25.

CONDAL
Handmade in Las Palmas, the Canary Islands of Spain.

Wrapper: USA/Connecticut   *Binder: Mexico*   *Filler: Brazil, Dom. Rep.*

Shape	Name	Lgth	Ring	Wrapper
Lonsdale	No. 1	6⅝	42	CI
Corona	No. 3	5⅝	42	CI
Corona	No. 4	5¼	42	CI
Corona	No. 5	6	42	CI
Panatela	No. 6	6¼	35	CI
Lonsdale	Inmenso	7¼	42	CI
Churchill	No. 10	7	46	CI
Robusto	Robusto	5½	50	CI
Double Corona	Churchill	7½	50	CI

HANDMADE CIGARS: BRAND LISTINGS

Condal cigars are all handmade and are extremely mild; they are offered in boxes of 25.

CONFEDERACION SUIZA
Handmade in Cofradia, Honduras.

Wrapper: Ecuador   *Binder: Honduras*   *Filler: Dom. Rep., Honduras, Nicaragua*

Shape	Name	Lgth	Ring	Wrapper
Long Corona	Delamain	6¼	44	CM

Here is a flavor-filled, handmade, medium-bodied cigar from one of the world's most outstanding factories. You can try them in cedar chests of 50.

CONNOISSEUR'S CHOICE
Handmade in Canca la Piedra, Dominican Republic.

Wrapper: Indonesia   *Binder: Dom. Rep.*   *Filler: Dom. Rep.*

Shape	Name	Lgth	Ring	Wrapper
Double Corona	Churchill	7	50	CM
Toro	Toro	6	50	CM
Robusto	Rothschild	4½	50	CM
Lonsdale	Twain	6½	44	CM
Corona	Petit Corona	5½	42	CM

This 1997-introduced brand presents a mild-to-medium-bodied taste, offered in individual cellophane sleeves and packed in all-cedar boxes of 25. The surprise? Twenty-five different bands picturing 25 cigar connoisseurs including Winston Churchill, Edward VII, Ulysses S. Grant, Rudyard Kipling, Groucho Marx, George Sand, Daniel Webster and others. Collect them all!

CONQUISTADOR
Handmade in Veracruz, Mexico.

Wrapper: Mexico   *Binder: Honduras*   *Filler: Dom. Rep., Mexico*

Shape	Name	Lgth	Ring	Wrapper
Short Panatela	Chico	4¾	38	CC-Ma

Lonsdale	Lonsdale	6½	40	CC-Ma
Corona	Corona	5½	42	CC-Ma
Lonsdale	Corona Extra	6¾	44	CC-Ma
Grand Corona	Corona Gorda	6	46	CC-Ma
Robusto	Robusto	5	50	CC-Ma
Churchill	Churchill	7¼	48	CC-Ma
Giant	Immensa	8	52	CC-Ma
Torpedo	Belicoso	5½	54	CC-Ma
Long Corona	Aromatic	6¼	42	CC-Ma
	Made with short filler:			
Churchill	Fumas	7	48	CC-Ma

This all-Mexican brand offers a medium-bodied flavor in its Sumatra-seed, natural-wrapped version and a medium-to-full strength in the maduro-wrapped edition. Introduced in 1997, it is offered in individual cellophane sleeves in all-cedar boxes of 25. The Aromatic shape is flavored.

CONUCOS
Handmade in Santiago, Dominican Republic.

Wrapper: USA/Connecticut   Binder: Dom. Rep.   Filler: Dom. Rep., Honduras

Shape	Name	Lgth	Ring	Wrapper
Long Corona	Panatelas	5⅞	40	CC
Corona	Coronas	5¼	42	CC
Robusto	Robustos	5	50	CC
Long Corona	Celebracion	6¼	44	CC

New for 1996, this brand offers a smooth, mild body thanks to the blending of a genuine Connecticut wrapper with a Dominican binder and Dominican and Honduran filler leaves.

HANDMADE CIGARS: BRAND LISTINGS

COPA HAVANA
Handmade in Danli, Honduras.
Wrapper: Cameroon, Ecuador or USA/Connecticut

Binder: Nicaragua   Filler: Nicaragua

Shape	Name	Lgth	Ring	Wrapper
Long Corona	Corona	6	43	CC-CM-Ma
Robusto	Robusto	5	50	CC-CM-Ma
Corona Extra	Torito	5½	47	CC-CM-Ma
Toro	Toro	6	54	CC-CM-Ma
Churchill	Churchill	7	47	CC-CM-Ma
Torpedo	Torpedo	7	54	CC-CM-Ma
Pyramid	Pyramid	6½	52	CC-CM-Ma

Introduced in 1996, the Copa Havana brand offers a choice of wrappers: Cameroon, Ecuadorian Rosado or genuine Connecticut Broadleaf in a maduro shade. The wrappers provide a choice of strengths, from medium to full-bodied.

COSSACK
Handmade in Esteli, Nicaragua.

Wrapper: Indonesia   Binder: Nicaragua   Filler: Nicaragua

Shape	Name	Lgth	Ring	Wrapper
Giant	Tsar	8	54	CM
Churchill	Mongol	7	48	CM
Robusto	Baltic	5½	50	CM
Lonsdale	Kiev	6½	43	CM
Torpedo	Torpedo	6½	50	CM

You don't need a Russian fur hat to enjoy this medium-bodied brand, introduced in 1996! It features a Java wrapper and each cigar is presented in a cellophane sleeve and then packed in a cedar cabinet.

HANDMADE CIGARS: BRAND LISTINGS

COTICAS
Handmade in Villa Gonzalez, Dominican Republic.

Wrapper: Indonesia   Binder: Dom. Rep.   Filler: Dom. Rep.

Shape	Name	Lgth	Ring	Wrapper
Double Corona	Churchill	7½	50	CC
Lonsdale	Corona	6½	44	CC
Churchill	Double Corona	7	48	CC
Corona	Petit Corona	5½	42	CC
Robusto	Rothschild	4½	50	CC
Toro	Toro	6	50	CC

Named for the Coticas bird, this blend offers a medium flavor featuring a Sumatra wrapper and Piloto Cubano filler leaves. Introduced in 1995, it is presented in individual cellophane sleeves and packed in cedar boxes of 25 cigars each.

CREDO
Handmade in Santiago, Dominican Republic.

Wrapper: USA/Connecticut   Binder: Dom. Rep., Mexico   Filler: Dom. Rep.

Shape	Name	Lgth	Ring	Wrapper
Slim Panatela	Jubilante	5	34	CC
Corona	Anthanor	5¾	42	CC
Churchill	Magnificat	6⅞	46	CC
Robusto	Arcane	5	50	CC
Double Corona	Pythagoras	7	50	CC

The Credo cigar line has been designed by the famous Belaubre family with a French flair. Their recipe produces a medium-strength smoke that is very smooth. Only the finest ingredients are used after being meticulously cured. The Magnificat, Arcane and Pythagoras models utilize a Dominican binder, while the Jubilate and Anthanor include a Mexican binder. The finished product, created in 1993, is offered in beautiful boxes imported from France.

HANDMADE CIGARS: BRAND LISTINGS

CREDO LIGAS
Handmade in Danli, Honduras.

Wrapper: Indonesia   *Binder: Honduras*   *Filler: Honduras*

Shape	Name	Lgth	Ring	Wrapper
Slim Panatela	No. 1 Demi-Tasse	5½	32	CC
Robusto	No. 2 Robusto	5	50	CC
Corona	No. 3 Corona	5¾	43	CC
Churchill	No. 4 Churchill	7	48	CC
Giant	No. 5 Double Corona	8	52	CC

This new line of the Credo brand was introduced in mid-1997. It offers a medium-to-full-bodied flavor in five popular shapes, and is offered in cellophane sleeves in a colorfully-adorned box that features the masks of comedy and tragedy.

CREMOSA CUBANOS
Handmade in Santiago, Dominican Republic.

Wrapper: Indonesia   *Binder: Dom. Rep.*   *Filler: Dom. Rep.*

Shape	Name	Lgth	Ring	Wrapper
Robusto	Robusto	5	50	CC
Corona	Corona	5½	43	CC
Lonsdale	Lonsdale	6¾	44	CC
Toro	Toro	6	50	CC
Torpedo	Torpedo	6	52	CC
Double Corona	Churchill	7	50	CC

Introduced in 1997, this is a medium-bodied brand, which mixes Dominican leaves with a Sumatra wrapper for a flavorful taste. You can experience it in boxes of 25.

HANDMADE CIGARS: BRAND LISTINGS

CRESTON
Handmade in San Pedro Sula, Honduras.

Wrapper: Cameroon   Binder: Honduras   Filler: Honduras

Shape	Name	Lgth	Ring	Wrapper
Giant	Presidente	9	52	CM
Double Corona	Churchill	7	49	CM
Robusto	Rothschild	4¾	50	CM
Corona	Corona	5½	42	CM
Long Corona	Senatore	6	43	CM

Introduced in 1997, this is a full-flavored version of the Creston line, including the very light sweet cap, thanks to a finishing dot of cane sugar syrup added at the end of the rolling process. It's not easy to find these cigars, but well worth it if you can!

CRESTON "LOS MONTES"
Handmade in San Pedro Sula, Honduras.

Wrapper: Indonesia   Binder: Dom. Rep.   Filler: Dom. Rep.

Shape	Name	Lgth	Ring	Wrapper
Corona	Montecito	5½	42	CC
Lonsdale	Montecasino	6½	42	CC
Lonsdale	Montelargo	7	42	CC

Here is a full-bodied, rich-tasting cigar made of Cuban-seed tobaccos and an Indonesian-shade wrapper. It is offered in all-cedar boxes of 25.

CRESTON PRESTIGE CUVÈE
Handmade in San Pedro Sula, Honduras.

Wrapper: Ecuador   Binder: Honduras   Filler: Honduras

Shape	Name	Lgth	Ring	Wrapper
	Ultra Premium with Habana Sweet Cap:			
Slim Panatela	Lady Creston	5½	32	CC

HANDMADE CIGARS: BRAND LISTINGS

Panatela	Squire Creston	6⅛	38	CC
Robusto	Sir Creston	5	50	CC
Corona	Baron Creston	5½	44	CC
Lonsdale	Duke of Creston	6½	44	CC
Churchill	Lord Creston	7	48	CC
	Limited Reserve Old Habana style:			*(Honduran puro)*
Robusto	Caballero	5	50	CM
Long Corona	Senor	6	43	CM
Toro	El Rey	6	50	CM
	Special:			
Pyramid	Pyramide Especial	6½	54	CC
Pyramid	Pyramide Nuevo	7	52	CC
Giant	Farouk Gigante	9	60	CC

This is a new cigar which offers a treat for smokers upon lighting: a sweet burst from a special sugar solution introduced into the vegetable gum used to seal the cap. This unique taste is only the beginning of a smooth and elegant smoke. The Prestige Cuvee is medium in body, while the Limited Reserve is medium-to-full in body, using all Honduran tobaccos. The Special cigars are very limited in supply and provide the enthusiast with pleasures of two hours or more at a sitting.

CRISPIN PATIÑO
Handmade in Cumana, Venezuela.

Wrapper: Honduras   *Binder: Venezuela*   *Filler: Venezuela*

Shape	Name	Lgth	Ring	Wrapper
Grand Corona	No. 3	6⅛	46	CM
Corona Extra	No. 2	5½	46	CM
Petit Corona	No. 1	4¾	42	CM
Robusto	Robusto	5	50	CM
Double Corona	Double Corona	7	50	CM

HANDMADE CIGARS: BRAND LISTINGS

Introduced to the U.S. market in 1996, this has been a popular Venezuelan brand since 1928. Mild in body and made of Venezuelan filler and binder with seven-year-old Honduran wrapper, it is produced with pride by the Patiño family, which started making cigars in 1900.

CRISTAL DE LEON
Handmade in Danli, Honduras.
Wrapper: Honduras or USA/Connecticut

Binder: Costa Rica   *Filler: Dominican Republic, Honduras*

Shape	Name		Lgth	Ring	Wrapper
Corona	Cristals	(tubed)	5½	43	CC

Introduced in 1996, this is a handmade, all long-filler cigar from Honduras, featuring either a Sumatra-seed wrapper grown in Honduras for a medium-bodied taste or a Connecticut wrapper, which gives a mild-to-medium bodied flavor. The packaging is absolutely unique: each cigar is presented in an air-tight glass tube, topped by a Honduran penny!

CRISTAL DE VENEZUELA
Handmade in Cumana, Venezuela.

Wrapper: Venezuela   *Binder: Venezuela*   *Filler: Venezuela*

Shape	Name	Lgth	Ring	Wrapper
Giant	Immensa	8	52	CM
Double Corona	Churchill Signature	7½	52	CM
Double Corona	Churchill	7	50	CM
Toro	Presidente	6¼	48	CM
Robusto	Robusto Primero	5¾	52	CM
Robusto	Robusto	5¾	50	CM
Robusto	Corona	5½	48	CM
Corona Extra	Purito	4¾	46	CM
Slim Panatela	Purito Panatella	5	34	CM

HANDMADE CIGARS: BRAND LISTINGS

	Perlas series:			
Corona	Corona Especial No. 3	5¾	44	CM
Corona	Corona Pura No. 2	5¾	40	CM
Petit Corona	Hombres	4¾	44	CM
Panatela	Aceros	5¾	38	CM

This brand has been around, in one form or another, since 1893 and even today is only available in limited quantities and in a limited number of the shapes listed above at any one time. Made of all-Venezuelan tobacco, it offers a medium-bodied taste and is presented in boxes of 25 except for the Purito and Purito Panatella, which are packed in 50s.

CROWN ACHIEVEMENT
Handmade in Danli, Honduras.
Wrapper: Ecuador

Binder: Dominican Republic   *Filler: Costa Rica, Honduras, Nicaragua*

Shape	Name	Lgth	Ring	Wrapper
Giant	Churchill	8	50	CI
Corona	Corona	5½	42	CI
Churchill	Double Corona	7	48	CI
Grand Corona	Grand Corona	6	46	CI
Lonsdale	Lonsdale	6½	42	CI
Torpedo	Rat Tail	5¾	50	CI
Robusto	Robusto	4½	50	CI

Here is a new, medium-bodied brand for 1997. It is blessed with excellent construction and aged leaves from five nations, offered in cedar boxes of 25.

CROWN CLASSICS
Handmade in Danli, Honduras.

Wrapper: Honduras   *Binder: Honduras*   *Filler: Honduras*

HANDMADE CIGARS: BRAND LISTINGS

Shape	Name	Lgth	Ring	Wrapper
Lonsdale		6⅝	44	CM
Robusto		4¾	50	CM-Ma
Toro		6¼	50	CM
Double Corona		7½	50	CM
Giant		8	52	CM

This is an old brand, without shape names, that first appeared around 10. It is medium-bodied and features all-Honduran tobaccos, offered in bundles of 25.

CRUZ REAL
Handmade in Vera Cruz, Mexico.

Wrapper: Mexico   Binder: Mexico   Filler: Mexico

Shape	Name	Lgth	Ring	Wrapper
Lonsdale	No. 1	6⅝	42	CC-Ma
Long Corona	No. 2	6	42	CC-Ma
Panatela	No. 3	6⅝	35	CC-Ma
Double Corona	No. 14	7½	50	CC-Ma
Toro	No. 19	6	50	CC-Ma
Robusto	No. 24	4½	50	CC-Ma
Robusto	No. 25	5½	52	CC-Ma
Giant	No. 28	8½	54	CC-Ma

Cruz Real is a true "puro" using wrapper, binder and filler from Mexico. The fine combination of Mexican-grown Sumatra-seed wrappers (Cuban-seed for maduro) and San Andres binder and fillers are the perfect union for this lightly spicy, mild-to-medium-bodied cigar, which was introduced in 1994. You can enjoy them in boxes of 10 or 25, or in a hand-carved humidor filled with 60 of these great cigars!

HANDMADE CIGARS: BRAND LISTINGS

CRUZ REAL SPECIAL EDITION
Handmade in Vera Cruz, Mexico.

Wrapper: Mexico   Binder: Mexico   Filler: Mexico

Shape	Name	Lgth	Ring	Wrapper
Double Corona	Emperador	7½	50	CC
Toro	Canciller	6	50	CC
Long Corona	Ministro	6	42	CC

This superb, specially-made cigar offers tobaccos from Mexico blended to provide a mild-to-medium-bodied taste, offered in boxes of 25.

CRUZADO RESERVA ESPECIAL
Handmade in Danli, Honduras.

Wrapper: Ecuador   Binder: Dom. Rep.   Filler: Nicaragua

Shape	Name	Lgth	Ring	Wrapper
Double Corona	Churchill	7	49	CM
Lonsdale	Corona	6½	42	CM
Toro	Toro	6	50	CM
Robusto	Robusto	5	52	CM

This is a mild-bodied cigar, introduced in 1997. It features a shiny Indonesian wrapper and is presented in individual cellophane sleeves in boxes of 20.

CRUZADO RESERVA GRANDE
Handmade in Jalapa, Nicaragua.

Wrapper: Indonesia   Binder: Nicaragua   Filler: Nicaragua

Shape	Name	Lgth	Ring	Wrapper
Double Corona	Churchill	7	49	CM
Toro	Toro	6	50	CM
Robusto	Robusto	5	50	CM
Torpedo	Belicoso	6	54	CM

HANDMADE CIGARS: BRAND LISTINGS

The range may be small — just four shapes — but don't try these if you're on a cigar diet! All are impressive in size and construction, with a mild-bodied flavor and a fat ring gauge! These "grande" cigars are packed in cellophane sleeves and presented in all-cedar boxes of 20 cigars each, except for the Belicoso shape, available in bundles of 4, 8, 10 and 12.

CU-AVANA
Handmade in Santiago, Dominican Republic.

Wrapper: Indonesia   Binder: Dom. Rep.   Filler: Dom. Rep.

Shape	Name	Lgth	Ring	Wrapper
Robusto	Robusto	5	50	CC
Long Corona	Cu-Abano Light	6	42	CC
Double Corona	Cu-Abano	7	50	CC
Churchill	Gentleman's Day	7	46	CC
Short Panatela	Lady's Night	5	36	CC

Here is a mild-to-medium-bodied cigar, introduced in 1997. The wrapper is genuine Sumatra-grown and you can enjoy Cu-Avana in cedar boxes of 25.

CUBAN SANDWICH
Handmade, with short filler, in Santiago, Dominican Republic.

Wrapper: USA/Connecticut   Binder: Dom. Rep.   Filler: Dom. Rep.

Shape	Name	Lgth	Ring	Wrapper
Corona	No. 4	5¾	43	Ma
Corona	Breva	5½	44	CC-Ma
Lonsdale	Cetros	6¾	44	CC-Ma
Double Corona	Churchill	7	50	CC-Ma
Toro	Toro	6	50	CC-Ma

Here is a modestly-priced, short-filler cigar from one of the Dominican Republic's finest factories. The short filler is the center of the "sandwich" formed by the binder and results in a pleasant, mild-to-medium-bodied smoke. It if offered in natural and maduro wrapper shades in boxes or bundles of 25.

HANDMADE CIGARS: BRAND LISTINGS

CUBANA ROYALE
Handmade in San Clemente, California, USA.

Wrapper: Brazil, Mexico   Binder: Honduras   Filler: Honduras, Nicaragua

Shape	Name	Lgth	Ring	Wrapper
Grand Corona	Corona	5¾	46	CC-Ma
Lonsdale	El Cubano	6¾	44	CC-Ma
Robusto	Robusto	5	50	CC-Ma
Robusto	Monerico	5½	52	CC-Ma
Toro	Havana	6½	50	CC-Ma
Double Corona	Churchill	7¼	50	CC-Ma
Double Corona	Presidente	7¾	52	CC-Ma
Pyramid	Pyramid	6¾	56	CC-Ma
Panatela	Vanilla Sweet	6¾	38	CC
Panatela	Sweet Panatella	6¾	36	CC
Slim Panatela	Sweet Linda	5¾	32	CC

Made by hand in a small factory in Southern California, these are quality, hard-to-find cigars with a full body and a choice of natural-shade wrappers from Brazil (Sumatra-seed) or maduro wrapper from Mexico. Cubana Royale cigars are available in boxes of 25, wrapped in raw tobacco leaves!

CUBITA
Handmade in Santiago, Dominican Republic.

Wrapper: USA/Connecticut   Binder: Dom. Rep.   Filler: Dom. Rep.

Shape	Name	Lgth	Ring	Wrapper
Double Corona	No. 2000	7	50	CC
Corona	No. 500	5½	43	CC
Lonsdale	No. 8-9-8	6¾	43	CC
Panatela	No. 2	6¼	38	CC
Toro	No. 700	6	50	CC

Small Panatela	Delicias	5⅛	30	CC

Introduced in 1986, this is a medium-to-heavy bodied cigar, with excellent construction. The six-shape brand uses only aged tobaccos and offers these cigars in beautiful cedar cases of 25 cigars each.

CUESTA-REY
Handmade in Santiago, Dominican Republic.
Wrapper: Cameroon and USA/Connecticut
Binder: Dominican Republic   *Filler: Dominican Republic*

Shape	Name		Lgth	Ring	Wrapper
	Cabinet Selection:				
Giant	No. 1		8½	52	CC-Ma
Long Panatela	No. 2		7	36	CC-Ma
Lonsdale	No. 95		6¼	42	CC-Ma
Double Corona	No. 898		7	49	CC-Ma
Lonsdale	No. 1884		6¾	44	CC-Ma
	Centennial Collection:				
Giant	Dominican No. 1		8½	52	CC-Ma
Churchill	Dominican No. 2		7¼	48	CC-Ma
Long Panatela	Dominican No. 3		7	36	CC-Ma
Lonsdale	Dominican No. 4		6½	42	CC-Ma
Corona	Dominican No. 5		5½	43	CC-Ma
Robusto	Dominican No. 7		4½	50	CC-Ma
Toro	Dominican No. 60		6	50	CC-Ma
Churchill	Aristocrat	*(tubed)*	7¼	48	CC
Long Corona	Captiva	*(tubed)*	6⅛	42	CC
Long Panatela	Rivera	*(tubed)*	7	35	CC
Small Panatela	Cameo		4¼	32	CC
Robusto	Robusto No. 7		4½	50	CC-Ma

Giant	Individual	(boxed)	8½	52	CC

Backed by more than a century of experience in the manufacture of handmade cigars since 1884, the Cuesta-Rey selection offers both mild-to-medium (Cabinet) and medium-bodied (Centennial) cigars. Connecticut Shade wrappers are used for all models except Cabinet Selection No. 95, which uses a Cameroon wrapper. Connecticut Broadleaf tobacco is used for all of the maduro wrappers.

CUPIDO
Handmade in Esteli, Nicaragua.

Wrapper: Indonesia   *Binder: Nicaragua*   *Filler: Nicaragua*

Shape	*Name*	*Lgth*	*Ring*	*Wrapper*
Churchill	Churchill	7	48	CM

There's only one size, but what a size it is! Mild-to-medium in body, but without a trace of bitterness, the secret is in the blending of Cuban-seed ligero leaves in the filler, combined with the Sumatran-grown wrapper. Production is limited; where available, Cupido cigars are offered in elegant all-cedar boxes of 25.

CUSANO ESTATE RESERVE
Handmade in Villa Gonzalez, Dominican Republic.

Wrapper: Indonesia   *Binder: Dom. Rep.*   *Filler: Dom. Rep.*

Shape	*Name*	*Lgth*	*Ring*	*Wrapper*
Toro	Toro Grande	6	52	Ma
Giant	Double Robusto	8	52	Ma

A product of careful blending, this special reserve selection offers a medium-to-full bodied taste with two-year aged Cuban-seed leaves in the filler. It is presented in boxes of 25.

CUSANO HERMANOS
Handmade in Santiago, Dominican Republic.
Wrapper: USA/Connecticut, Dominican Republic

Binder: Dominican Republic   *Filler: Dominican Republic*

Puff the Magic!

HANDMADE CIGARS: BRAND LISTINGS

Shape	Name	Lgth	Ring	Wrapper
Robusto	Bullet	4	50	CC-Ma
Robusto	Robusto	5	50	CC-Ma
Long Corona	Corona	6	44	CC-Ma
Churchill	Churchill	6⅞	46	CC-Ma
Pyramid	Pyramid	6	55	CC-Ma

This brand debuted in 1996, with a full-bodied taste and a smooth draw based on a blend of five tobaccos. The Dominican-grown maduro wrapper adds a spicy finish compared to the Connecticut Shade-wrapped models.

CUSANO ROMANI
Handmade in Santiago, Dominican Republic.
Wrapper: USA/Connecticut   Binder: Dom. Rep.   Filler: Dom. Rep.

Shape	Name	Lgth	Ring	Wrapper
Pyramid	Pyramid	6	54	CC

A single roller is specially appointed to create this pyramid shape, introduced in 1996. Five tobaccos - two Dominican-seed and two Cuban-seed - are combined with the elegant Connecticut Shade wrappers to create a smooth smoke with medium-to-full body and a pleasant aroma.

CUSANO SELECTION
Handmade in Santiago, Dominican Republic.
Wrapper: Indonesia   Binder: Dom. Rep.   Filler: Dom. Rep.

Shape	Name	Lgth	Ring	Wrapper
Torpedo	Torpedo	6½	53	Ma
Toro	Toro	6½	50	Ma
Robusto	Robusto	5	50	Ma

This all-maduro line debuted in 1996, with Indonesian wrappers and a medium-to-full-bodied taste. The Cusano Selection is offered in individual cellophane sleeves and packed in boxes of 25.

HANDMADE CIGARS: BRAND LISTINGS

DA VINCI
Handmade in Danli, Honduras.

Wrapper: Ecuador   *Binder: Dominican Republic*
Filler: Dominican Republic, Honduras, Nicaragua

Shape	Name	Lgth	Ring	Wrapper
Pyramid	Renaissance	7	54	CC
Giant	Leonardo	8½	52	CC
Churchill	Ginerva de Benci	7	48	CC
Toro	Monalisa	6	50	CC
Long Corona	Cecilia Gallerani	6	43	CC
Robusto	Madonna	5	50	CC

These masterpieces seek to reach the level of achievement of its namesake, the brilliant Italian artist and scientist who lived from 1452-1519. A full line of personal and smoking accessories is topped by the Connecticut Shade-seed wrapped cigar line, each of which offers a mild-to-medium body. The all-cedar boxes each feature a different Da Vinci painting (except for the Renaissance model), including a notebook self-portrait for the Leonardo model. Besides the boxes of 25, Da Vincis are also available in handy four-packs.

DA VINCI
Handmade in Esteli, Nicaragua.

Wrapper: Ecuador   *Binder: Nicaragua*   *Filler: Dom. Rep., Nicaragua*

Shape	Name	Lgth	Ring	Wrapper
Pyramid	Figurado	7	54	CC
Giant	Maestro	8½	52	CC
Churchill	Mezzanote	7	48	CC
Toro	Dolce Vita	6	50	CC
Long Corona	Bambina	6	43	CC
Robusto	Quadro	5	50	CC

HANDMADE CIGARS: BRAND LISTINGS

New in 1997, this second Da Vinci line offers a medium body and is offered in boxes of 25 or in packages of four for cigar lovers who need their masterpieces with them on the go!

DALALY DIAMANTES
Handmade in Esteli, Nicaragua.

Wrapper: USA/Connecticut   Binder: Nicaragua   Filler: Dom. Rep., Nicaragua

Shape	Name	Lgth	Ring	Wrapper
Giant	Presidente	8½	52	CC
Double Corona	Churchill	7	50	CC
Lonsdale	No. 1	6½	44	CC
Toro	Corona	6	50	CC
Robusto	Robusto	5	50	CC

This brand was introduced in 1997 and offers a smooth, mild-to-medium-bodied flavor with a Connecticut wrapper and Cuban-seed binder and fillers.

DANIEL MARSHALL ARTIST DOMINICAN RESERVE
Handmade in Santiago, Dominican Republic.

Wrapper: USA/Connecticut   Binder: Mexico   Filler: Dom. Rep.

Shape	Name	Lgth	Ring	Wrapper
Robusto	Robusto	5	50	CC
Long Corona	Corona	6	44	CC
Churchill	Churchill	7	48	CC

This brand is a special selection, aged for an additional 12 months, of the standard D. Marshall Signature cigars. Personally picked by Daniel Marshall himself, these are truly the "cream of the crop" and available only by special request.

DANIEL MARSHALL SIGNATURE/DOMINICAN RESERVE
Handmade in Santiago, Dominican Republic.

Wrapper: USA/Connecticut   Binder: Mexico   Filler: Dom. Rep.

HANDMADE CIGARS: BRAND LISTINGS

Shape	Name	Lgth	Ring	Wrapper
Robusto	Robusto	5	50	CC
Long Corona	Corona	6	44	CC
Churchill	Churchill	7	48	CC

A perfect complement to the famous D.Marshall humidors, this 1996-introduced brand was developed to Mr. Marshall's personal standards. It offers a medium-to-full body and consists entirely of three to four-year-old tobaccos.

DANIEL MARSHALL SIGNATURE/HONDURAN RESERVE
Handmade in Danli, Honduras.

Wrapper: USA/Connecticut   Binder: Honduras   Filler: Honduras, Nicaragua

Shape	Name	Lgth	Ring	Wrapper
Robusto	Robusto	5	50	CC
Long Corona	Corona	6½	44	CC
Double Corona	Churchill	7½	50	CC

Created in 1996, this cigar exhibits none of the harshness which sometimes accompanies Honduran-made cigars. It boasts a Connecticut Shade wrapper and has a medium-to-full body; it is presented in all-cedar boxes of 25.

DANIEL MARSHALL SIGNATURE/SUMATRA LIMITED RESERVE
Handmade in Santiago, Dominican Republic.

Wrapper: Indonesia   Binder: Dom. Rep.   Filler: Dom. Rep.

Shape	Name	Lgth	Ring	Wrapper
Robusto	Robusto	5	50	CC
Long Corona	Corona	6	44	CC
Churchill	Churchill	7	48	CC

You cannot stop the expanding cigar empire of the energetic Daniel Marshall, you can only hope to contain him! New for 1997, this line offers a medium-bodied smoke in three popular sizes, offered in all-cedar boxes of 25.

HANDMADE CIGARS: BRAND LISTINGS

DANLYS
Handmade in Danli, Honduras.

Wrapper: Honduras   *Binder: Mexico*   *Filler: Honduras, Mexico*

Shape	Name	Lgth	Ring	Wrapper
Toro	Churchill	6½	52	CM
Short Panatela	Petit	4¼	38	CM
Churchill	Panatella	6¾	48	CM
Toro	Toro	6⅛	50	CM
Grand Corona	No. 1	6½	46	CM
Corona	No. 4	5½	44	CM

This is a fairly old brand, dating from 1972. It is medium-to-full in body and is offered in natural wrapper shades, in economical bundles of 20.

DANTE
Handmade in Santiago, Dominican Republic.

Wrapper: Dom. Rep.   *Binder: Dom. Rep.*   *Filler: Dom. Rep.*

Shape	Name	Lgth	Ring	Wrapper
Robusto	Robusto	5	50	Ma
Long Corona	Corona	6	44	Ma
Slim Panatela	Panatela	6	32	Ma
Double Corona	Churchill	7	50	Ma

These dark-colored cigars are the perfect tribute to the equally dark but brilliant mind of Italian poet Dante Alighieri (1265-1321), who wrote the thunderous "Commedia" (The Divine Comedy) over the last 20 years before his death. The cigars are medium-to-full-bodied, using only eight-year-old tobaccos. Offered in boxes of 25, each chest includes an illustration of a portion of Dante's work as interpreted by Michelangelo.

DAVIDOFF
Handmade in Santiago, Dominican Republic.

Wrapper: USA/Connecticut   *Binder: Dom. Rep.*   *Filler: Dom. Rep.*

IN CIGARS WE MAKE THE BOOKS

DANTE
INTERNATIONAL CIGARS S.A.
• DOMINICAN REPUBLIC •

HANDMADE CIGARS: BRAND LISTINGS

Shape	Name	Lgth	Ring	Wrapper
Long Panatela	No. 1	7½	38	CC
Panatela	No. 2	6	38	CC
Slim Panatela	No. 3	5⅛	30	CC
Panatela	Tubos	6	38	CC
Cigarillo	Ambassadrice	4½	26	CC
	Aniversario Series:			
Giant	Aniversario No. 1	8⅔	48	CC
Churchill	Aniversario No. 2	7	48	CC
	Grand Cru Series:			
Lonsdale	Grand Cru No. 1	6⅛	43	CC
Corona	Grand Cru No. 2	5⅝	43	CC
Petit Corona	Grand Cru No. 3	5	43	CC
Petit Corona	Grand Cru No. 4	4⅝	41	CC
Petit Corona	Grand Cru No. 5	4	41	CC
	Special Series:			
Culebras	Special "C"	6½	33	CC
Double Corona	Double "R"	7½	50	CC
Robusto	Special "R"	4⅞	50	CC
Pyramid	Special "T"	6	52	CC
	Thousand Series:			
Small Panatela	1000	4⅝	34	CC
Petit Corona	2000	5	43	CC
Slim Panatela	3000	7	33	CC
Long Corona	4000	6⅛	42	CC
Grand Corona	5000	5⅝	46	CC

HANDMADE CIGARS: BRAND LISTINGS

A carefully controlled series of events leads to the production of a Davidoff cigar. This celebrated brand, first created in Cuba in 1946, requires tobaccos which have been aged up to four years and only the finest leaves are used in a factory which is solely dedicated to the creation of this brand. Four different blends are used to create the five different series: the large-sized, but mild and light Anniversarios; the mild, delicate and aromatic Nos. 1-2-3, Tubos and Ambassadrice; the fuller-bodied, but still mild "Thousand" series; and the fullest-bodied Grand Cru and Special ranges, which share the same blend.

DE COSSIO
Handmade in Danli, Honduras.

Wrapper: Honduras   Binder: Dom. Rep.   Filler: Honduras

Shape	Name	Lgth	Ring	Wrapper
Double Corona	Churchill	7½	50	CM
Corona	Corona	5½	42	CM
Lonsdale	Lonsdale	6½	42	CM
Robusto	Robusto	4½	52	CM
Toro	Short Churchill	6	50	CM

New for 1997, this is a medium-bodied cigar made in Honduras and offered in boxes of 25.

DE ORTEGA
Handmade in Tamboril, Dominican Republic.
Wrapper: Indonesia or USA/Connecticut

Binder: Dominican Republic   Filler: Dominican Republic

Shape	Name	Lgth	Ring	Wrapper
	El Emperador:			
Toro	Hemingway	6½	48	CI-CC
	Reserva 21:			
Torpedo		7	54	CI-CC
Torpedo		7	52	CI-CC

HANDMADE CIGARS: BRAND LISTINGS

Robusto		5	50	CC
Corona Extra		5	46	CC
Churchill		7	48	CC
	Reserva 21 Lights:			
Panatela		6	36	CI

Here is a new brand group for 1997, offering a variety of flavors. The Emperador line is full-bodied, the Reserva 21 line is medium-bodied and the Lights style is mild in flavor. All are offered in boxes of 25.

DEBERTO & MARTINEZ
Handmade in Danli, Honduras and Tampa, Florida, USA.

Wrapper: Cameroon   *Binder: Honduras*   *Filler: Honduras*

Shape	*Name*	*Lgth*	*Ring*	*Wrapper*
Grand Corona	No. 1	6½	46	CM
Robusto	Robusto	5½	50	CM
Double Corona	Churchill	7½	50	CM

Introduced in 1996, this limited-production cigar offers a medium-bodied smoke in three of the most popular sizes. Each is available in front-latched, all-cedar boxes of 25.

DEFIANT
Handmade in San Pedro Sula, Honduras.

Wrapper: Ecuador   *Binder: Nicaragua*   *Filler: Honduras, Nicaragua*

Shape	*Name*	*Lgth*	*Ring*	*Wrapper*
Robusto	Robusto	4¾	50	CC
Long Corona	Corona	6	44	CC
Toro	Toro	6	50	CC
Double Corona	Presidente	7½	52	CC
Pyramid	Pyramid	6½	52	CC

HANDMADE CIGARS: BRAND LISTINGS

This brand was introduced in 1996 and offers a smooth, medium-bodied taste, presented in boxes of 25 cigars.

DEL SOL

Handmade, with short filler, in Santiago, Dominican Republic.

Wrapper: Dom. Rep.   Binder: Dom. Rep.   Filler: Dom. Rep.

Shape	Name	Lgth	Ring	Wrapper
Double Corona	Churchill	7½	50	CC
Robusto	Robusto	5	50	CC

Here is a value-priced, bundled cigar offering a medium-bodied blend of short filler leaves, offered in cellophane sleeves in bundles of 25.

DEL VALLE
Handmade in Danli, Honduras.

Wrapper: Ecuador   Binder: Nicaragua   Filler: Costa Rica, Honduras

Shape	Name	Lgth	Ring	Wrapper
Petit Corona	Corona	5	44	CC
Robusto	Robusto	5	50	CC
Double Corona	Churchill	7	49	CC
Torpedo	Torpedo	6	52	CC
Giant	Presidente	8	50	CC

Introduced in 1996, this is a medium-to-full-bodied cigar with a blend of four nations in the blend. It is presented in individual cellophane sleeves in boxes of 25.

DIAMANTE
Handmade in Tamboril, Dominican Republic.

Wrapper: USA/Connecticut   Binder: Dom. Rep.   Filler: Dom. Rep.

Shape	Name	Lgth	Ring	Wrapper
Double Corona	Double Corona	7½	50	CC-Ma
Churchill	Churchill	6⅞	46	CC-Ma

Toro	Toro	6	50	CC-Ma
Lonsdale	Lonsdale	6¾	42	CC-Ma
Long Corona	Corona	6	44	CC-Ma
Corona	Petit Corona	5¾	42	CC-Ma

This brand has been around in various configurations in prior years, but is now available in a mild blend of Cuban-seed fillers grown in the Cibao and Yaque valleys, with a genuine Connecticut-grown wrapper.

DIAMOND CROWN
Handmade in Santiago, Dominican Republic.

Wrapper: USA/Connecticut   *Binder: Dom. Rep.*   *Filler: Dom. Rep.*

Shape	Name	Lgth	Ring	Wrapper
Giant	No. 1	8½	54	CC
Double Corona	No. 2	7½	54	CC
Toro	No. 3	6½	54	CC
Robusto	No. 4	5½	54	CC
Robusto	No. 5	4½	54	CC

This mild-bodied, all-54 ring series is an impossible-to-find, 1996-introduced product of the Tabacalera A. Fuente y Cia., made for the J.C. Newman Cigar Co. of Tampa, Florida. You can find these cigars in elegantly-appointed boxes of 15.

DIANA SILVIUS
Handmade in Santiago, Dominican Republic.

Wrapper: USA/Connecticut   *Binder: Dom. Rep.*   *Filler: Dom. Rep.*

Shape	Name	Lgth	Ring	Wrapper
Double Corona	Diana Churchill	7	50	CC
Robusto	Diana Robusto	4⅞	52	CC
Churchill	Diana 2000	6¾	46	CC
Lonsdale	Diana Corona	6½	42	CC

Introduced in 1990, this is a superb smoke which is medium in body and rich in flavor. Diana Silvius cigars strike a subtle balance between taste and aroma. The blend of four filler tobaccos, predominantly Cuban-seed leaves grown in the Dominican Republic, produces a smooth finish that leaves a hint of sweetness on the palate. Every one of these cigars is handmade by the master rollers of Tabacalera A. Fuente y Cia.

DIEGO DE OCAMPO
Handmade in Santiago, Dominican Republic.

Wrapper: Indonesia   *Binder: Dom. Rep.*   *Filler: Dom. Rep.*

Shape	Name	Lgth	Ring	Wrapper
Corona	Corona	5½	43	CC
Robusto	Robusto	5	50	CC
Lonsdale	Lonsdale	6½	43	CC
Toro	Toro	6	50	CC
Double Corona	Churchill	7½	50	CC

Introduced in 1997, Diego de Ocampo offers a medium-bodied taste, well-balanced between the delicate Indonesian wrapper and Dominican-grown wrapper and filler leaves.

DIEGO SILANG
Handmade in Manila, the Philippines.

Wrapper: Philippines   *Binder: Philippines*   *Filler: Philippines*

Shape	Name	Lgth	Ring	Wrapper
Double Corona	El Presidente	7½	52	CC
Churchill	Churchill	7	47	CC
Lonsdale	Diego Primo	7	44	CC
Corona	Corona	5½	44	CC
Robusto	Diego Quinto	5	52	CC
Short Panatela	Gabriela	5	35	CC

HANDMADE CIGARS: BRAND LISTINGS

This brand, one of the latest in the long and storied history of cigar-making in the Philippines, debuted in 1996. All of the leaves are grown in the Ilocos Valley of the Philippines, with Sumatra seeds used for the wrappers and Cuban seeds for the binder and filler. The result is a mild-to-medium bodied smoke, packed in boxes of 25.

DIGNITY
Handmade in Santiago, Dominican Republic.

Wrapper: USA/Connecticut   Binder: Dom. Rep.   Filler: Dom. Rep.

Shape	Name	Lgth	Ring	Wrapper
Corona	Corona	5½	44	CC
Toro	Toro	6	50	CC
Double Corona	Churchill	7	50	CC

Here is a medium-bodied, exceptionally smooth cigar with an elegant Connecticut wrapper, offered in bundles of 25.

DOMINGOLD
Handmade in Santiago, Dominican Republic.

Wrapper: Cameroon   Binder: USA/Connecticut   Filler: Brazil, Dom. Rep.

Shape	Name	Lgth	Ring	Wrapper
Toro	Toro	6	50	CC
Long Corona	Lonsdale	6¼	42	CC
Robusto	Robusto	5	50	CC
Corona	Corona	5½	42	CC
Double Corona	Churchill	7	50	CC

These bundles of 20 cigars are seconds of one of the finest cigar factories in the Dominican Republic. You'll be hard-pressed to tell the difference between these medium-strength cigars and their more-famous siblings.

DOMINICAN DELICIAS
Handmade in Santiago, Dominican Republic.

Wrapper: Honduras   Binder: Dom. Rep.   Filler: Dom. Rep.

HANDMADE CIGARS: BRAND LISTINGS

Shape	Name	Lgth	Ring	Wrapper
Robusto	Selection 701	5	50	CM
Double Corona	Selection 702	7¼	50	CM
Lonsdale	Selection 703	6½	42	CM
Long Corona	Selection 704	6	42	CM
Corona	Selection 705	5½	42	CM
Toro	Selection 706	6	50	CM

Sometimes also identified as "Dominican Escudo," this is a mild-to-medium-bodied cigar offered in bundles of 10 or boxes of 25.

DOMINICAN ELITES
Handmade in Tamboril, Dominican Republic.
Wrapper: Indonesia   *Binder: Dom. Rep.*   *Filler: Dom. Rep.*

Shape	Name	Lgth	Ring	Wrapper
Robusto	Toro	5½	50	CM
Lonsdale	Lonsdale	6½	42	CM-Stripe
Churchill	Churchill	7	47	CM
Double Corona	Presidente	7½	50	CM
Torpedo	Torpedo	6	52	CM

These elegant cigars offer medium strength in flavor from leaves aged for three or more years, including a Sumatran-grown wrapper. The "Barber Pole"-wrapped Lonsdale shape incorporates a genuine Connecticut wrapper with the Sumatra wrapper. Introduced in 1997, this line is presented in all-cedar chest-style boxes, with each cigar protected in an individual cellophane sleeve.

DOMINICAN ESTATES
Handmade in the Dominican Republic.
Wrapper: USA/Connecticut   *Binder: Mexico*   *Filler: Dom. Rep.*

HANDMADE CIGARS: BRAND LISTINGS

Shape	Name	Lgth	Ring	Wrapper
Toro	Corona Gorda	6	50	CC
Double Corona	Double Corona	7	50	CC
Corona	Full Corona	5½	43	CC
Lonsdale	Lonsdale	6½	43	CC
Robusto	Robusto	4½	50	CC

These cigars are mild to the taste, thanks to their Connecticut wrappers, and very well constructed for an easy draw.

DOMINICAN MADURO SPECIAL
Handmade in San Pedro Sula, Honduras.
Wrapper: Indonesia   *Binder: Dom. Rep.*   *Filler: Dom. Rep.*

Shape	Name	Lgth	Ring	Wrapper
Double Corona	Churchill	7	50	Ma
Toro	Double Corona	6	50	Ma
Robusto	Robusto	5	50	Ma

The deep brown Indonesian-shade wrapper adds to the Cuban-seed Dominican binder and filler for a full-bodied taste. This brand is offered in boxes of 25.

DOMINICAN ORIGINAL
Handmade in Santiago, Dominican Republic.
Wrapper: USA/Connecticut   *Binder: Dom. Rep.*   *Filler: Dom. Rep.*

Shape	Name	Lgth	Ring	Wrapper
Long Corona	Cetros	6	44	CC
Churchill	Churchill	6⅞	46	CC-Ma
Giant	Fat Tub	10	66	CC-Ma
Robusto	Gorilla	5	66	CC-Ma
Giant	King Kong	8½	52	CC-Ma
Small Panatela	Miniatures	4¼	32	CC

HANDMADE CIGARS: BRAND LISTINGS

Double Corona	Monster	7	60	CC-Ma
Lonsdale	No. 1	6¾	43	CC-Ma
Corona	No. 2	5¾	43	CC-Ma
Long Panatela	Palma Fina	7	37	CC-Ma
Pyramid	Piramide	6½	56	CC-Ma
Double Corona	Presidente	7½	50	CC-Ma
Robusto	Robusto	4½	50	CC-Ma
Torpedo	Torpedo	7	50	CC-Ma

Talk about sizes! Here is the brand for the lover of unusual, especially large sizes. The Connecticut wrapper and Dominican filler give these cigars a mild taste, and they are offered in bundle packs.

DOMINICAN SELECTION
Handmade in Santiago, Dominican Republic.

Wrapper: USA/Connecticut   Binder: Mexico   Filler: Dom. Rep., Nicaragua

Shape	Name	Lgth	Ring	Wrapper
Giant	Presidente	8	50	CC
Double Corona	El Grande	7	60	CC
Double Corona	Churchill	7	49	CC
Toro	Regulares	6	50	CC
Lonsdale	No. 1	6¾	43	CC
Panatela	No. 3	6¾	38	CC
Corona	No. 4	5½	43	CC
Robusto	Rothschilds	4¾	49	CC
Panatela	Super Fino	6	35	CC

If you're looking for excellent value in a beautifully-made cigar, this is your brand! It features a genuine Connecticut wrapper and a medium-bodied flavor, offered in bundles of 25 cigars each.

HANDMADE CIGARS: BRAND LISTINGS

DOMINICAN SPECIALS
Handmade, with mixed filler, in Santiago, Dominican Republic.

Wrapper: USA/Connecticut   *Binder: Dom. Rep.*   *Filler: Dom. Rep.*

Shape	Name	Lgth	Ring	Wrapper
Double Corona	Churchill	7	50	CC-Ma
Toro	Toro	6	50	CC-Ma
Lonsdale	Fuma	6⅞	43	CC-Ma
Corona	Breva	5½	43	CC-Ma

Here is a modestly-priced, high-quality bundled cigar from the Dominican Republic. Introduced in 1996, it offers a mild taste with a Connecticut Broadleaf wrapper. The filler is a sandwich of long-filler surrounding a short-filler core.

DOMINICANA SUPERBA
Handmade in Santiago, Dominican Republic.

Wrapper: Dom. Rep.   *Binder: Dom. Rep.*   *Filler: Dom. Rep.*

Shape	Name	Lgth	Ring	Wrapper
Giant	No. 1	8½	52	CC-Ma
Double Corona	No. 2	7	49	CC-Ma
Lonsdale	No. 3	6¾	44	CC-Ma
Robusto	No. 4	4½	50	CC-Ma
Corona	No. 5	5½	43	CC-Ma
Double Corona	No. 6	7½	50	CC-Ma

Introduced in 1989, these are mild cigars of very high quality, offered in conveniently-packaged (and priced) bundles of 20 cigars each.

DOMINICO
Handmade in Santiago, Dominican Republic.

Wrapper: Indonesia   *Binder: Dom. Rep.*   *Filler: Dom. Rep.*

HANDMADE CIGARS: BRAND LISTINGS

Shape	Name	Lgth	Ring	Wrapper
Pyramid	No. 700	7½	60	CC
Giant	No. 701	8½	52	CC
Churchill	No. 702	7	48	CC
Toro	No. 703	6	50	CC
Lonsdale	No. 704	7	43	CC
Corona	No. 705	5½	43	CC
Robusto	No. 706	4¾	52	CC

These high-quality bundled cigars debuted in 1994 and now feature an Indonesian-grown wrapper with a Dominican Olor binder and a Cuban-seed, Dominican-grown filler. They offer a mild to medium body and an excellent value.

DOMINIQUE
Handmade in Santiago, Dominican Republic.
Wrapper: USA/Connecticut   Binder: Dom. Rep.   Filler: Dom. Rep.

Shape	Name	Lgth	Ring	Wrapper
Giant	No. 52	8½	52	CI-CC-Ma
Lonsdale	No. 74	7	43	CI-CC-Ma
Grand Corona	Madison	6	46	CI-CC-Ma
Corona	Nacionales	5½	42	CC
Double Corona	Pierce	6⅞	49	CI-CC-Ma
Robusto	Toro	4½	50	CC-Ma

These bundles are made by the famous Tabacalera A. Fuente in the Dominican Republic. They of high quality and moderate pricing, offering a mild flavor in packages of 25 cigars each.

DOMINO PARK
Handmade in Santiago, Dominican Republic.
Wrapper: Indonesia   Binder: Indonesia   Filler: Dom. Rep., Indonesia

HANDMADE CIGARS: BRAND LISTINGS

Shape	Name		Lgth	Ring	Wrapper
Robusto	Robusto	*(tubed)*	5	50	CC
Lonsdale	Corona	*(tubed)*	6½	42	CC
Double Corona	Churchill	*(tubed)*	7	50	CC
Torpedo	Torpedo	*(tubed)*	6½	54	CC

Introduced in 1995 by the Caribbean Cigar Company, this is a medium-to-full-bodied, glass-tubed cigar which salutes Domino Park, a traditional meeting place in Miami's "Little Havana" district, and are offered in boxes of 25.

DON ALBERTO
Handmade in Licey, Dominican Republic.

CLASSICO DOMINICAN SERIES:
Wrapper: Dom. Rep.   *Binder: Dom. Rep.*   *Filler: Dom. Rep.*

ORO DE HABANA SERIES:
Wrapper: USA/Connecticut   *Binder: Dom. Rep.*   *Filler: Dom. Rep.*

ROYAL SERIES:
Wrapper: Dominican Republic and USA/Connecticut
Binder: Dominican Republic   *Filler: Dominican Republic*

SUPERIOR HABANA:
Wrapper: USA/Connecticut   *Binder: Dom. Rep.*   *Filler: Dom. Rep.*

Shape	Name	Lgth	Ring	Wrapper
	Superior Habana series:			
Pyramid	Piramid	6½	53	CC
Robusto	Robusto	5	50	CC
Giant	Churchill	8	48	CC
Grand Corona	Double Corona	6½	46	CC
Lonsdale	Corona	7	44	CC
Long Panatela	Panatela	7½	38	CC

HANDMADE CIGARS: BRAND LISTINGS

Small Panetela	Reina	5	30	CC
	Oro de Habana series:			
Pyramid	Piramid	6½	53	CC
Robusto	Robusto	5	50	CC
Giant	Churchill	8	48	CC
Grand Corona	Double Corona	6½	46	CC
Lonsdale	Corona	7	44	CC
	Classico Dominican series:			
Pyramid	Piramid	6½	53	Ma
Robusto	Robusto	5	50	Ma
Giant	Churchill	8	48	Ma
Grand Corona	Double Corona	6½	46	Ma
Lonsdale	Corona	7	44	Ma
Long Panetela	Panatela	7½	38	Ma
Small Panetela	Reina	5	30	Ma
	Royal series:			
Pyramid	Piramid	6½	53	Stripe
Giant	Presidential	8	48	Stripe
Lonsdale	Corona	7	44	Stripe
Robusto	Robusto	5	50	Stripe

Created in 1996, here is a series offering different blends and tastes, all within the mild-to-medium range. All feature binder and filler tobaccos from the Dominican Republic, with genuine Connecticut wrappers used on the Oro de Havana (mild-to-medium-bodied) and Superior Habana (medium bodied) series. The Royal series offers the "barber pole" double wrapper style, utilizing Connecticut and Dominican leaves for a medium-bodied taste. The Classico Dominican uses a Dominican-grown maduro wrapper and a mild-bodied flavor.

HANDMADE CIGARS: BRAND LISTINGS

DON ANTONIO
Handmade in Dingelstadt, Germany.

Wrapper: Indonesia   Binder: Indonesia   Filler: Brazil, Honduras, Indonesia

Shape	Name	Lgth	Ring	Wrapper
Double Corona	Churchill	6⅞	49	CC
Lonsdale	Lonsdale	6¼	44	CC
Perfecto	Perfecto Grande	6¾	45	CC
Panatela	Panatela Larga	6	38	CC
Robusto	Robusto	5	50	CC
Corona Extra	Torpelito	4⅞	46	CC
Perfecto	Perfecto	5⅛	45	CC

Here is a three-country blend of tobaccos that produces a mild-bodied flavor in this 1997-introduced brand. Handmade with all long-filler leaves, it is presented in individual cellophane sleeves in wood boxes of 20.

DON ANTONIO
Handmade in Dingelstadt, Germany.

Wrapper: Brazil, Indonesia   Binder: Indonesia
Filler: Brazil, Dominican Republic, Honduras, Indonesia

Shape	Name	Lgth	Ring	Wrapper
Slim Panatela	El Gusto (tubes available)	6⅛	33	CC-CM
Short Panatela	El Toro	4⅜	38	CC-CM
Cigarillo	Carmen	4½	20	CC-CM
Cigarillo	El Cerro	3½	25	CC-CM
Cigarillo	El Lupo	3	20	CC-CM
Panatela	La Verdad (tubes available)	5½	35	CC-CM

Here is a rarity: a handmade, 100% tobacco, dry-cure cigar from Germany. Other shapes in the Don Antonio line are machine-produced, but these are made by hand and offered a mild to medium flavor depending on your choice of wrapper: mild Indonesian leaf grown in Sumatra, or the strong Brazilian leaf from the Bahia region.

DON ARMANDO
Handmade in Tamboril, Dominican Republic.

Wrapper: USA/Connecticut   Binder: Dom. Rep.   Filler: Dom. Rep.

Shape	Name	Lgth	Ring	Wrapper
	Premium Series:			
Double Corona	Churchill	7	50	CC
Long Panatela	Mirage	7	38	CC
Lonsdale	Lonsdale	6¾	44	CC
Robusto	Toros	5	50	CC
Corona Extra	Corona Extra	5½	44	CC
Small Panatela	Illusion	5	30	CC
	Classic Series:			
Double Corona	Churchill	7	50	CC
Lonsdale	Lonsdale	6¾	44	CC
Robusto	Robusto	5	50	CC
Corona	Corona Extra	5½	44	CC

This version of Don Armando debuted in 1997, offering a mild-to-medium-bodied flavor. It is presented in individual cellophane sleeves and packed in boxes of 25. Note the Mirage shape has a double wrapper of Connecticut and Sumatra leaves and the Illusion has a vanilla-flavored, sweet tip.

DON ARMANDO
Handmade in Santa Rosa de Copan, Honduras.

Wrapper: Honduras   Binder: Honduras   Filler: Honduras

Shape	Name	Lgth	Ring	Wrapper
Giant	Viajante	8½	50	CM
Double Corona	Embajadores	7¾	50	CM

Long Corona	Corona Gorda	6¼	44	CM
Toro	Toro	6	50	CM
Corona Extra	Corona Extra	5½	46	CM
Corona	Bonitas	5½	42	CM
Robusto	Rothschild	4½	50	CM
Double Corona	Churchill	7	50	CM
Panatela	Lindas	5⅝	38	CM
Panatela	Palma Extra	6¾	35	CM
Corona	No. 4	5½	44	CM
Double Corona	Soberanos	7¾	52	CM
Lonsdale	Cazadores	6½	44	CM
Corona	No. 2	5¾	44	CM
Giant	Grandioso	7½	60	CM

This brand was introduced in 1996 and is produced at the La Flor de Copan factory in Santa Rosa de Copan. It offers a mild body and is presented in boxes of 20 cigars each.

DON AUGUSTO

Handmade in Tamboril, Dominican Republic.

Wrapper: Indonesia or USA/Connecticut   Binder: Dom. Rep.   Filler: Dom. Rep.

Shape	Name	Lgth	Ring	Wrapper
Corona	Petit Corona	5½	42	CC-CM
Robusto	Robusto	5	50	CC-CM
Toro	Toro	6½	50	CC-CM
Grand Corona	Corona Grande	6	46	CC-CM
Giant	Churchill	8	50	CC-CM
Robusto	Colossus Jr.	4¾	60	CC-CM
Toro	Magnum	6	54	CC-CM

Double Corona	Double Corona	7½	52	CC-CM
Lonsdale	Corona	6½	44	CC-CM
Giant	Colossus	9½	60	CC-CM

Introduced in 1997, this brand now offers two wrapper shades for your consideration: a U.S.-grown Connecticut wrapper and a genuine Sumatra wrapper. In either case, this is a mild-to-medium-bodied cigar, offered in boxes of 25.

DON BARCO
Handmade in Santiago, Dominican Republic.

Wrapper: Indonesia   *Binder: Dom. Rep.*   *Filler: Dom. Rep.*

Shape	Name	Lgth	Ring	Wrapper
Double Corona	Galeon	7¾	50	CC
Toro	Admiral	6	50	CC
Robusto	Capitan	5	50	CC
Churchill	Marinero	6¾	46	CC

Introduced in 1996, this is a medium-bodied cigar from the Dominican Republic, offered in boxes of 20 cigars each.

DON BARTOLO
Handmade in Manila, the Philippines.

Wrapper: Indonesia   *Binder: Philippines*   *Filler: Philippines*

Shape	Name	Lgth	Ring	Wrapper
Corona	Corona	5½	44	CC
Robusto	Robusto	5	52	CC
Churchill	Churchill	7	47	CC
Double Corona	Double Corona	7	52	CC

Philippine tobacco is the core of this 1996-introduced cigar, with Sumatran wrappers on all sizes except for the Corona, which features a Javan wrapper. The result is a mild to medium-bodied smoke, offered in boxes of 25.

HANDMADE CIGARS: BRAND LISTINGS

DON BIENVE
Hand-rolled, with short filler, in San Juan, Puerto Rico.

Wrapper: Puerto Rico   *Binder: Homogenized tobacco leaf*   *Filler: Puerto Rico*

Shape	Name	Lgth	Ring	Wrapper
Long Corona	Cazadore	6	42	CM

Here is an inexpensive, mild, machine-bunched and hand-rolled cigar, with short filler, from Puerto Rico. It is offered in bundles of 25.

DON CARLOS
Handmade in Santiago, Dominican Republic.

Wrapper: Cameroon   *Binder: Dom. Rep.*   *Filler: Dom. Rep.*

Shape	Name	Lgth	Ring	Wrapper
Corona	No. 3	5½	44	CM
Robusto	Robusto	5¼	50	CM
Robusto	Double Robusto	5¾	52	CM
Toro	Presidente	6½	50	CM

Here is the result of careful planning and brilliant execution in the making of a new brand from the workshops of Tabacalera A. Fuente. The flawless construction and smooth taste of this medium-bodied cigar make it a rewarding experience from the beginning.

DON CARLOS
Handmade in Danli, Honduras.

Wrapper: Ecuador   *Binder: Nicaragua*   *Filler: Mexico, Nicaragua*

Shape	Name	Lgth	Ring	Wrapper
Double Corona	Churchill	7	49	CC
Robusto	Rothchild	5	50	CC
Corona	Corona	5½	42	CC
Pyramid	Pyramid	5½	52	CC
Pyramid	Super Pyramid	7½	64	CC

HANDMADE CIGARS: BRAND LISTINGS

Here is a new cigar in 1997, with a mild body and a blend that features a Sumatra-seed wrapper grown in Ecuador. It is offered in boxes of 25.

DON CISSO
Handmade, with short filler, in Santiago, Dominican Republic.

Wrapper: Indonesia   *Binder: Dom. Rep.*   *Filler: Dom. Rep.*

Shape	Name	Lgth	Ring	Wrapper
Toro	No. 1	6	50	CC
Robusto	No. 2	5	50	CC
Long Corona	No. 3	6	44	CC

This is a short-fill, bundled cigar that offers a mild-to-medium taste. It is available in economical bundles of 25 cigars each.

DON CORLEONE
Handmade in Danli, Honduras.

Wrapper: Ecuador   *Binder: Honduras*   *Filler: Dom. Rep., Honduras*

Shape	Name	Lgth	Ring	Wrapper
Torpedo	Torpedo	7	54	CC
Giant	Presidente	8	50	CC
Double Corona	Churchill	6⅞	49	CC
Toro	Toro	6	50	CC
Robusto	Robusto	5	50	CC
Long Corona	Cetro	6¼	44	CC

A cigar you can't refuse? Why not! It's a mild cigar with a rich flavor that salutes the famous Mario Puzo character from his novel *The Godfather.* It is offered in boxes of 25.

DON DIEGO
Handmade in La Romana, Dominican Republic.

Wrapper: USA/Connecticut   *Binder: Dom. Rep.*   *Filler: Brazil, Dom. Rep.*

HANDMADE CIGARS: BRAND LISTINGS

Shape	Name		Lgth	Ring	Wrapper
Small Panatela	Babies		5	33	CM
Toro	Coronas Bravas		6½	48	CC
Petit Corona	Coronas Major	*(tubed)*	5	42	CC
Corona	Coronas		5⅝	42	DC-CC
Toro	Grandes		6	50	CC
Panatela	Grecos		6½	38	CC
Lonsdale	Lonsdales		6⅝	42	DC-CC
Churchill	Monarchs	*(tubed)*	7¼	46	CC
Petit Corona	Petit Coronas		5⅛	42	DC-CC
Panatela	Royal Palmas	*(tubed)*	6⅛	36	CC
	Machine-made, with short filler:				
Cigarillo	Preludes		4	28	CC

Well-known for its mild taste, Don Diego cigars have earned a wide following, thanks to their consistency of construction, accessible strength and excellent value for the money. Fans of rarely-seen Candela wrappers on handmade cigars will find three major shapes available. This brand originated in 1964 in the Canary Islands, but production was moved to the Dominican Republic in 1982.

DON DOMINGUEZ
Handmade in Santiago, Dominican Republic

Wrapper: Indonesia   *Binder: Dom. Rep.*   *Filler: Dom. Rep.*

Shape	Name	Lgth	Ring	Wrapper
Double Corona	Churchill	7½	50	CC
Robusto	Robusto	5	50	CC
Corona	Robusto Fino	5½	42	CC
Grand Corona	Lonsdale	6½	46	CC

HANDMADE CIGARS: BRAND LISTINGS

Here is a full-bodied, no-holds-barred cigar from the Dominican Republic. All of the leaves are of Cuban-seed origin and the finished product is presented in modestly-priced bundles of 25.

DON ELEGANTE
Handmade in Miami, Florida, USA.
Wrapper: Indonesia, USA/Connecticut

Binder: Dominican Republic   Filler: Dominican Republic

Shape	Name	Lgth	Ring	Wrapper
Churchill	Churchill	6⅞	46	CC-Ma
Double Corona	Presidente	7⅝	50	CC-Ma
Robusto	Robusto	5	50	CC-Ma
Corona Extra	Wavell	5⅛	46	CC-Ma
Torpedo	Torpedo	6	52	CC-Ma

Take your choice of wrappers with this Miami-made brand: a mild-bodied blend featuring a Connecticut Shade wrapper, a mild-to-medium-bodied blend with a Sumatran wrapper or a maduro-wrapped, medium-bodied blend using Connecticut Broadleaf. Each cigar is sleeved in cellophane and presented in boxes of 25.

DON ERNESTO
Handmade in Las Palmas, the Canary Islands of Spain.
Wrapper: Indonesia   *Binder: Indonesia*
Filler: Brazil, Canary Islands, Dominican Republic

Shape	Name	Lgth	Ring	Wrapper
Toro	Nuncio	6	50	CC
Robusto	Habanero	5½	48	CC
Robusto	Epicurean	4¾	52	CC

Long available in Europe, this brand was introduced to the United States in 1997. It is a medium-bodied cigar blended by Don Ernesto Gonzalez and offered in boxes of 25.

HANDMADE CIGARS: BRAND LISTINGS

DON ESTEBAN
Handmade in Santiago, Dominican Republic.

Wrapper: Ecuador, Dom. Rep.   Binder: Dom. Rep.   Filler: Dom. Rep.

Shape	Name	Lgth	Ring	Wrapper
Giant	President	8	50	CC-Ma
Double Corona	Churchill	7½	49	CC-Ma
Toro	Emperador	6	50	CC-Ma
Robusto	Robusto	5	50	CC-Ma
Lonsdale	Elegante	6½	44	CC-Ma
Corona	Puritano	5½	42	CC-Ma

Re-blended for 1996, this medium-bodied cigar offers a Ecuadorian-grown wrapper in the natural shade and a Dominican-grown wrapper for the maduro shade.

DON FAUSTO
Handmade in Moca, Dominican Republic.

Wrapper: Indonesia   Binder: Dom. Rep.   Filler: Dom. Rep.

Shape	Name	Lgth	Ring	Wrapper
Churchill	Churchills	7	48	CM
Toro	Toro	6	50	CM
Corona	Corona	5¾	42	CM
Panatela	Petit Corona	6	38	CM
Slim Panatela	Panatela	5	34	CM

This is a medium-bodied cigar introduced in 1997. It offers a Sumatra wrapper and Dominican filler and binder in boxes of 25.

DON FIFE
Handmade in Danli, Honduras.
Wrapper: Ecuador or USA/Connecticut

Binder: Honduras   *Filler: Honduras*

HANDMADE CIGARS: BRAND LISTINGS

Shape	Name	Lgth	Ring	Wrapper
Churchill	Churchill	7	48	CM
Lonsdale	Numero 1	7	43	CM
Lonsdale	Double Corona	6½	44	CM
Toro	Corona Gorda	6	50	CM
Robusto	Robusto	5	48	CM
Corona	Petit Cetro	5½	43	CM
Small Panatela	Petit	4½	30	CM

This brand is mild-to-medium in body and was introduced in 1996. Made by hand in Danli, Honduras, Don Fife cigars are offered in seven favorite sizes and presented in elegant cedar boxes of 25.

DON FRANCISCO
Handmade in San Andres Tuxtla, Mexico.
Wrapper: Indonesia or USA/Connecticut   *Binder: Mexico*   *Filler: Mexico*

Shape	Name	Lgth	Ring	Wrapper
Robusto	Robusto	5	50	CC
Double Corona	Churchill	7	50	CC
Lonsdale	Lonsdale	6½	42	CC

San Andres Tuxtla is the closest point on the Mexican peninsula to Cuba. So it's no wonder that Cuban-seed tobaccos power this full-bodied cigar, introduced in 1996 and offered in boxes of 25.

DON FRANCISCO RESERVE
Handmade in El Paraiso, Honduras.
Wrapper: Honduras or USA/Connecticut
Binder: Honduras   *Filler: Ecuador, Honduras*

Shape	Name	Lgth	Ring	Wrapper
Robusto	Robusto	5	50	CM-Ma
Double Corona	Churchill	7	50	CM-Ma

Lonsdale	Lonsdale	6½	42	CM-Ma

Here is a 1996-introduced brand, offering a medium-bodied flavor thanks to its blend of Honduran tobaccos with wrapper leaf from Honduras or Connecticut. Although in limited production, it offers a welcome aroma and mellow taste to those who are able to enjoy it.

DON GUILLERMO
Handmade in Santiago, Dominican Republic.

Wrapper: USA/Connecticut   *Binder: Dom. Rep.*   *Filler: Dom. Rep.*

Shape	Name	Lgth	Ring	Wrapper
Churchill	No. I	6⅞	46	CC
Robusto	Compa	5	50	CC-Ma
Giant	Don Guillermo	8½	50	CC
Long Corona	No. IV	6	44	CC-Ma

A 1997 offering from SJI Wholesale, this is a medium-bodied cigar that is offered with a real Connecticut-grown wrapper in four sizes and two wrapper shades. Depth in the taste of the cigar is provided by the use of Cuban-seed tobaccos in the filler.

DON JIVAN CLASSICO
Handmade in Santiago, Dominican Republic.

Wrapper: USA/Connecticut   *Binder: Dom. Rep.*   *Filler: Dom. Rep.*

Shape	Name	Lgth	Ring	Wrapper
Long Corona	Corona	6	44	CC
Churchill	Grand Corona	6¾	46	CC
Robusto	Robusto	5½	50	CC
Double Corona	Double Corona	7½	52	CC

Inspired by Jivan Tabibian, the gregarious owner of famous Remi restaurant in Santa Monica, California, this is a 1996-introduced, medium-bodied smoke. Noteworthy for its label artwork by artist Milton Glazer, Don Jivan is offered without cellophane in all-cedar boxes of 25.

HANDMADE CIGARS: BRAND LISTINGS

DON JOSE
Handmade in Danli, Honduras.

Wrapper: Honduras   *Binder: Honduras*   *Filler: Honduras*

Shape	Name	Lgth	Ring	Wrapper
Giant	El Grandee	8½	52	CC-Ma
Double Corona	San Marco	7	50	CC-Ma
Toro	Turbo	6	50	CC-Ma
Long Corona	Granada	6	43	CC-Ma
Robusto	Valrico	4½	50	CC-Ma

These Honduran handmades provide a rich taste in both a natural and maduro wrapper. The tobaccos are all grown in Honduras of Cuban-seed origin and are offered in bundles of 20 cigars each.

DON JUAN
Handmade in Ocotal, Nicaragua.

Wrapper: Ecuador   *Binder: Nicaragua*   *Filler: Dom. Rep., Nicaragua*

Shape	Name	Lgth	Ring	Wrapper
Panatela	Lindas	5½	38	CM
Long Corona	Cetros	6	43	CM
Panatela	Palma Fina	6⅞	36	CM
Robusto	Robusto	5	50	CM
Lonsdale	No. 1	6⅝	44	CM
Toro	Matador	6	50	CM
Double Corona	Churchill	7	49	CM
Giant	Presidente	8½	50	CM

Introduced in 1992, Don Juan is a handmade cigar from Nicaragua. The filler is Nicaraguan, with a Dominican Havana-seed binder and a Connecticut Shade wrapper. Cigar connoisseurs consider this a medium-strength cigar.

HANDMADE CIGARS: BRAND LISTINGS

DON JUAN PLATINUM
Handmade in Santiago, Dominican Republic.

Wrapper: USA/Connecticut   *Binder: Dom. Rep.*   *Filler: Dom. Rep., Nicaragua*

Shape	Name	Lgth	Ring	Wrapper
Panatela	Linda	5½	38	CC
Long Corona	Cetro	6	43	CC
Robusto	Robusto	5	50	CC
Lonsdale	No. 1	6⅝	44	CC
Toro	Matador	6	50	CC
Double Corona	Churchill	7	49	CC
Giant	Presidente	8½	50	CC
Torpedo	Torpedo	6	52	CC

Introduced in 1997, here is the work of Pedro Martin, who blended this medium-bodied masterpiece. You can find it in individual cellophane sleeves inside all-cedar boxes of 25.

DON JULIAN
Handmade in Ocotal, Nicaragua.

Wrapper: Ecuador   *Binder: Dom. Rep.*   *Filler: Dom. Rep.*

Shape	Name	Lgth	Ring	Wrapper
Double Corona	Churchill	7½	50	CC
Churchill	Doble Corona	7	48	CC
Toro	Robusto	5	52	CC
Panatela	Panatela	7	36	CC

Made in Nicaragua, this brand offers a mild-to-medium bodied smoke with Connecticut-seed wrappers in boxes of 25.

HANDMADE CIGARS: BRAND LISTINGS

DON JULIO
Handmade in Santiago, Domincan Republic.

Wrapper: USA/Connecticut   Binder: Dom. Rep.   Filler: Dom. Rep.

Shape	Name	Lgth	Ring	Wrapper
Lonsdale	Corona Deluxe	7	44	CC
Toro	Fabulosos	6	50	CC
Corona	Miramar	5¾	43	CC
Robusto	Private Stock No. 1	4½	50	CC
Giant	Supremos	8½	52	CC

Don Julio cigars are handmade, bundled cigars produced in the Dominican Republic. These cigars are mild-bodied, easy to draw, yet exceptionally flavorful. The composition of select Cuban-seed tobaccos took several months to develop, giving Don Julio its delicate taste.

DON LEO
Handmade in Villa Gonzalez, Dominican Republic.

Wrapper: USA/Connecticut   Binder: Dom. Rep.   Filler: Dom. Rep.

Shape	Name	Lgth	Ring	Wrapper
Double Corona	Churchill	7½	50	CM
Lonsdale	Corona	6½	44	CM
Churchill	Double Corona	7	48	CM
Long Panatela	Panatela	7	36	CM
Corona	Petite Corona	5½	42	CM
Torpedo	Piramide	6¾	52	CM
Giant	Presidente	8	52	CM
Toro	Robusto	6	50	CM
Robusto	Rothschild	4½	50	CM
Toro	Toro	6	52	CM

THESE PREMIUM IMPORTED CIGARS FEATURE CAREFULLY SELECTED TOBACCOS AT A PRICE THAT'S AS PLEASING AS THEIR TASTE AND AROMA.

SABROSO FROM NICARAGUA
Fine handmade cigars with carefully selected long-filler tobacco and natural leaf wrapper offer an easy draw and full-bodied taste.

LA PRIMADORA FROM HONDURAS
Enjoy the mild, easy smoke of this cigar – carefully rolled by craftsmen using a premium long-filler blend and natural leaf wrapper.

DON JULIO FROM THE DOMINICAN REPUBLIC
These hand-rolled cigars have a mild, pleasing taste and are made with long filler and a premium wrapper.

SWISHER INTERNATIONAL, INC.

HANDMADE CIGARS: BRAND LISTINGS

Don Leo is a handmade, long-filler cigar from the recently established Puros de Villa Gonzalez factory near Santiago. The blend of leaves from the Dominican and the Connecticut wrapper provide a mild-to-medium body.

DON LIMA
Handmade in Danli, Honduras.

Wrapper: Indonesia   *Binder: Dom. Rep.*   *Filler: Dom. Rep.*

Shape	Name	Lgth	Ring	Wrapper
Corona	Corona	5½	42	CM
Long Panatela	Lancero	7½	38	CM
Robusto	Robusto	5	50	CM
Churchill	Churchill	7	48	CM

These are mild-to-medium-bodied cigars introduced in 1997. The wrapper is Cameroon-seed grown in Indonesia, Cuban-seed filler leaves are used and this brand is available in either all-cedar boxes or economical bundles of 25.

DON LINO
Handmade in Esteli, Nicaragua.

Wrapper: Indonesia   *Binder: Nicaragua*   *Filler: Nicaragua*

Shape	Name	Lgth	Ring	Wrapper
Double Corona	Churchill	7½	50	CC
Lonsdale	No. 1	6½	44	CC
Corona Extra	Toros	5½	46	CC
Robusto	Robusto	5½	50	CC
Small Panatela	Epicure	5	34	CC
Robusto	Rothchild	4½	50	CC

Don Lino are premium, hand-rolled cigars from Nicaragua, first introduced from Honduras in 1990. The brand is now made in Nicaragua and is known for its mild-bodied taste and consistent smooth flavors, thanks to an Indonesian-grown wrapper and Nicaraguan-grown fillers and binders.

A good cigar speaks for itself

we're
here
only to
turn on
the vOlume

Don Lino

MIAMI
Cigar
& Company

Hand made in Nicaragua

HANDMADE CIGARS: BRAND LISTINGS

DON LINO ORO
Handmade in Santiago, Dominican Republic.

Wrapper: Dom. Rep.   Binder: Dom. Rep.   Filler: Dom. Rep.

Shape	Name	Lgth	Ring	Wrapper
Long Corona	Lonsdale	6	42	CM
Churchill	Churchill	6⅞	46	CM
Panatela	Panetelas	6½	36	CM
Robusto	Toros	5½	50	CM

Introduced in 1991, but now produced in the Dominican Republic, this is a full-bodied version of the Don Lino line with 100% Dominican leaf from Corojo seeds that originated in Cuba. You can enjoy these gems in boxes of 25, or in special packages of 3 or 5 for the Lonsdale shape.

DON MANOLO COLLECTION
Handmade in Santiago, Dominican Republic.
Wrapper: Dominican Republic, Indonesia, USA/Connecticut

Binder: Dominican Republic   Filler: Dominican Republic

Shape	Name	Lgth	Ring	Wrapper
	Series 1–Maduro:			
Robusto	Robusto	5½	50	Ma
Grand Corona	Corona Grande	6¾	46	Ma
Double Corona	Churchill	7	50	Ma
	Series 2–Connecticut:			
Long Corona	Lonsdale	6	44	CC
Robusto	Robusto	5	50	CC
Double Corona	Churchill	7½	52	CC
Long Panatela	Panatela	7	38	CC
	Series 3–Sumatra:			
Robusto	Robusto	5	50	CM

Long Corona	Lonsdale	6	44	CM
Double Corona	Churchill	7	50	CM
Pyramid	Pyramid	6	54	CM

This brand made its debut in 1996, with a medium-to-full-bodied maduro group, a mild-to-medium-bodied Connecticut-wrapped line and a medium-bodied, Sumatra-wrapped series. All are available in boxes of 25 except for the Pyramid shape, offered in bundles of 10.

DON MARCOS

Handmade in La Romana, Dominican Republic.

Wrapper: USA/Connecticut   Binder: Dom. Rep.   *Filler: Dom. Rep.*

Shape	Name		Lgth	Ring	Wrapper
Slim Panatela	Baby		5¼	33	CM
Corona	Coronas		5½	42	CC
Toro	Toros		6	50	CC
Torpedo	Torpedos		6	50	CC
Panatela	Naturals	(tubed)	6	38	CC
Lonsdale	Cetros		6½	42	CC
Toro	Double Corona		6½	48	CC
Churchill	Monarchs		7	46	CC

This brand was one of the best-sellers in the western U.S. during the 1960s and 1970s and was re-introduced in a big way in 1995. Well made and easy to smoke, the Don Marcos line has a mild to medium body and an inviting Connecticut Shade wrapper.

DON MARIANO

Handmade in Santiago, Dominican Republic.

Wrapper: USA/Connecticut   Binder: Dom. Rep.   *Filler: Dom. Rep.*

Shape	Name	Lgth	Ring	Wrapper
Corona	Indios	5½	40	CC

Robusto	Gran Corona	5½	48	CC
Corona	Pandukas	5¾	42	CC
Lonsdale	Pelas Corona	6½	44	CC
Lonsdale	Nobles	6¾	42	CC
Panatela	Panatelas	6¾	36	CC
Churchill	X&T Churchills	7	46	CC
Double Corona	Conquistadores	7½	50	CC
Long Panatela	No. 1	7½	38	CC
Churchill	Connoisseur	8¼	48	CC

A product of the cigar artisans of the Dominican Republic, Don Mariano cigars are created only in limited quantities. The blend of aged tobaccos, led by the Connecticut Shade wrappers, offer a smooth smoke with subtle aromas and medium body. This brand, introduced in 1985, is offered in all-mahogany boxes, interleaved with cedar to provide the finest-possible environment for these premium cigars.

DON MATEO
Handmade in Danli, Honduras.

Wrapper: Mexico   *Binder: Mexico*   *Filler: Nicaragua*

Shape	Name	Lgth	Ring	Wrapper
Slim Panatela	No. 1	7	30	CC
Panatela	No. 2	6⅞	35	CC
Long Corona	No. 3	6	42	CC
Corona	No. 4	5½	44	CC
Lonsdale	No. 5	6⅝	44	CC
Churchill	No. 6	6⅞	48	CC
Robusto	No. 7	4¾	50	CC-Ma
Toro	No. 8	6¼	50	CC-Ma
Double Corona	No. 9	7½	50	CC-Ma

Giant	No. 10	8	52	CC-Ma
Toro	No. 11	6⅝	54	CC-Ma

A medium-bodied taste in a banded, bundled cigar is the promise of the well-made and modestly-priced Don Mateo line. The Mexican wrapper is available in both natural and maduro wrappers for most sizes.

DON MELO
Handmade in Santa Rosa de Copan, Honduras.

Wrapper: Honduras   *Binder: Honduras*   *Filler: Honduras*

Shape	Name	Lgth	Ring	Wrapper
Giant	Presidente	8½	50	Ma
Double Corona	Churchill	7	49	Ma
Long Corona	Corona Gorda	6¼	44	Ma
Long Corona	No. 2	6	42	Ma
Corona Extra	Corona Extra	5½	46	Ma
Corona	Petit Corona	5½	42	Ma
Robusto	Nom Plus	4¾	50	Ma
Petit Corona	Cremas	4½	42	Ma

This line honors the father of the Honduran cigar trade, who was the first Honduran national to open a cigar factory in that country in 1896. From humble origins in 1789, the cigar trade has grown considerably in the town of Santa Rosa de Copan and this medium-to-full-bodied smoke, wrapped in all-black leaf, salutes that success.

DON MELO CENTENARIO
Handmade in Santa Rosa de Copan, Honduras.

Wrapper: Honduras   *Binder: Honduras*   *Filler: Honduras*

Shape	Name	Lgth	Ring	Wrapper
Churchill	Liga A	7	48	CM
Toro	Liga B	6	55	CM

| Long Corona | Liga C | 6 | 44 | CM |
| Robusto | Liga D | 5 | 52 | CM |

Here is a limited edition, centennial salute to the man (Don Melo Bueso) who help found the modern Honduran cigar industry. Only 2,000 boxes of each size will be made of this medium-bodied smoke. Even the boxes will be special: hand-crafted in Caoba wood with a removable tray of Spanish cedarwood.

DON NOBERTO
Handmade in Ocotal, Nicaragua.

Wrapper: Indonesia 　　　*Binder: Nicaragua* 　　　*Filler: Honduras*

Shape	*Name*	*Lgth*	*Ring*	*Wrapper*
Double Corona	Churchill	7½	50	CC
Petit Corona	Petit Corona	5	42	CC
Robusto	Corona	5	48	CC
Churchill	Double Corona	7	48	CC
Toro	Robusto	6	50	CC
Long Panatela	Panatela	7	36	CC
Robusto	Torito	5	52	CC

This blend changed in 1997, and now offers a mild-to-medium-bodied flavor, offered in boxes of 25.

DON OTILIO
Handmade in Santiago, Dominican Republic.

Wrapper: Ecuador 　　*Binder: Dom. Rep.* 　*Filler: Dom. Rep., Honduras*

Shape	*Name*	*Lgth*	*Ring*	*Wrapper*
Robusto	Robusto	5	50	CC-Ma
Giant	Presidente	8	50	CC-Ma
Churchill	Churchill	7½	49	CC-Ma
Torpedo	Toro	6½	53	CC-Ma

| Long Corona | Cetro | 6 | 44 | CC-Ma |
| Pyramid | Pyramide | 6⅞ | 52 | CC-Ma |

Introduced in 1996, this brand is named for a long-time tobacco grower in the Dominican Republic. Don Otilio is a mild-to-medium-bodied blend of Dominican and Honduran filler, Cuban-seed binder and an Ecuadorian-grown wrapper.

DON PABLO
Handmade in Las Vegas, Nevada, USA.

Wrapper: USA/Connecticut   *Binder: Dominican Republic*
Filler: Brazil, Dominican Republic, Ecuador, Mexico

Shape	Name	Lgth	Ring	Wrapper
Slim Panatela	Pencil	7	32	CC
Slim Panatela	Panatela	7	34	CC
Lonsdale	Panatela Especial	7	40	CC-Ma
Corona	Corona	5¾	42	CC
Toro	Monterico	5¾	52	CC-Ma
Toro	Cuban Round	6	48	CC-Ma
Churchill	Imperial	6¾	46	CC-Ma
Double Corona	Cuban Round Largo	7½	50	CC-Ma
Giant	El Cubano	8½	52	CC
Torpedo	Torpedo	6¾	58	CC-Ma
Double Corona	Largo Cognac	7½	50	CC
Toro	Monterico Cognac	5¾	52	CC
Double Corona	Corona Grande	7½	50	CC
Churchill	Emperador	7	46	CC

These are mild to medium-bodied cigars of good quality, handmade in a storefront on the Las Vegas strip. Fully in keeping with its location, this small factory offers some gaudy specialties, including the Largo and Monterico sizes made with five-year-aged tobaccos cured with 20-year-old cognac. You can also have cigars cured with rum or brandy or sweetened for a modest charge!

HANDMADE CIGARS: BRAND LISTINGS

DON PATRICIO
Handmade in Managua, Nicaragua.

Wrapper: Nicaragua   *Binder: Nicaragua*   *Filler: Nicaragua*

Shape	Name	Lgth	Ring	Wrapper
Double Corona	Presidente	7	50	Ma
Toro	Toro	6	50	Ma
Lonsdale	Lonsdale	6¼	44	Ma
Robusto	Robusto	5	50	Ma
Corona	Corona	5½	42	Ma

Here is a mild-bodied cigar with excellent construction from 18-month-aged leaves, available in slide-top, all-cedar boxes of 25 cigars each.

DON PEPE
Handmade in Cruz des Almas, Brazil.

Wrapper: Brazil   *Binder: Brazil*   *Filler: Brazil*

Shape	Name	Lgth	Ring	Wrapper
Double Corona	Double Corona	7½	50	CM
Robusto	Robusto	5	50	CM
Short Panatela	Half Corona	4⅜	35	CM
Slim Panatela	Slim Panatela	5⅛	30	CM
Long Corona	Petit Lonsdale	6	40	CM
Churchill	Churchill	7	47	CM

Introduced in 1994, this brand is produced by the famed Suerdieck factory in Brazil. The wrapper is a Sumatran-seed tobacco, with native Brazilian leaves used for the binder and filler to blend into a mild-bodied cigar.

DON PRIAMO
Handmade in Navarette, Dominican Republic.

Wrapper: Indonesia   *Binder: Dom. Rep.*   *Filler: Dom. Rep.*

HANDMADE CIGARS: BRAND LISTINGS

Shape	Name	Lgth	Ring	Wrapper
Giant	Emilio	8½	52	CC
Double Corona	Churchill	7½	50	CC
Robusto	Robusto	5	50	CC
Grand Corona	Extra Corona	6	46	CC
Long Corona	Lonsdale	6	44	CC
Torpedo	Torpedo	6¼	52	CC

Don Priamo cigars were introduced in early 1997 and named in honor of Priamo Reyes, patriarch of the Reyes tobacco family. These cigars offer a mild taste, packaged in all-cedar, slide-top boxes of 25.

DON PUPO
Handmade in Santiago, Dominican Republic.

Wrapper: Dom. Rep. *Binder: Dom. Rep.* *Filler: Dom. Rep.*

Shape	Name	Lgth	Ring	Wrapper
Slim Panatela	Habaneras	5½	30	CC
Slim Panatela	Lindas	7	30	CC
Long Panatela	Panetelas	7	36	CC
Long Panatela	Elegantes	8	38	CC
Long Corona	Cor. Constantin	6	41	CC
Corona	Petit Coronas	5½	42	CC
Long Corona	Cetros	6	44	CC
Perfecto	Perfecto	7	48	CC
Robusto	Robusto	5	50	CC
Toro	Churchill	6½	50	CC
Double Corona	Presidente	6⅞	54	CC

HANDMADE CIGARS: BRAND LISTINGS

Here is an all-Dominican cigar using three-year aged tobaccos and a mild-to-medium flavor. It is offered in boxes of 10 (Presidente), 20 (sizes) or 25 (Habaneras, Lindas and Panetelas only) cigars each.

DON QUIJOTE
Handmade in Cumana, Venezuela.

Wrapper: Honduras   *Binder: Venezula*   *Filler: Venezuela*

Shape	Name	Lgth	Ring	Wrapper
Grand Corona	Churchill	6⅝	46	CC
Corona	No. 5	5½	42	CC
Panatela	Carolinas	6½	38	CC

Introduced in 1996, this unique brand from Venezuela is made under the supervision of master cigar maker Vladimir Perez and offered in boxes of 25.

DON QUIXOTE
Handmade in Santa Rosa de Copan, Honduras.

Wrapper: Ecuador   *Binder: Honduras*   *Filler: Honduras*

Shape	Name	Lgth	Ring	Wrapper
Double Corona	Churchill	7	50	CM
Robusto	Nom Plus	4¾	50	CM
Lonsdale	Corona Gorda	6½	44	CM
Toro	Toro	6	50	CM
Small Panatela	Muneca/Princess	4	30	CM
Panatela	Panatela	6¾	35	CM

Here is a medium-to-full-bodied cigar introduced in 1997. It features a Sumatra-seed wrapper and binder and filler leaves that are aged at least 1½ years. It is offered in boxes of 25.

DON RAFAEL
Handmade in Tamboril, Dominican Republic.

Wrapper: Ecuador, Indonesia   *Binder: Dom. Rep.*   *Filler: Dom. Rep.*

Shape	Name	Lgth	Ring	Wrapper
Long Corona	Petit Corona	6	42	CM-Ma
Long Corona	Lonsdale	6	44	CM-Ma
Grand Corona	Corona	6	46	CM-Ma
Robusto	Short Robusto	4½	50	CM-Ma
Robusto	Long Robusto	5½	50	CM-Ma
Double Corona	Churchill	7½	50	CM-Ma
Toro	Toro	6	54	CM-Ma

This cigar offers a medium-bodied taste, featuring Ecuadorian-grown Connecticut-seed wrappers and maduro wrappers from Sumatra. Introduced in 1997, it is presented in boxes of 25.

DON RENE
Handmade in Miami, Florida, USA.

Wrapper: Ecuador   *Binder: Honduras*   *Filler: Dom. Rep., Nicaragua*

Shape	Name	Lgth	Ring	Wrapper
Torpedo	Torpedo	6½	54	CC-Ma
Corona Extra	Toro	5½	46	CC-Ma
Double Corona	Churchill	7¼	50	CC
Lonsdale	Corona	6½	44	CC
Corona	Coronita	5½	42	CC-Ma
Robusto	Robusto	5½	50	CC-Ma
Long Panatela	Lancero	7	38	CC
Small Panatela	Senoritas	5	30	CC

This brand debuted in 1996. It offers a mild-to-medium-bodied flavor, with each cigar protected in individual cellophane sleeves. Each shape is presented in all-cedar boxes of 25. The Senoritas and Coronaita shapes are also available in a handy five-pack, while the Robusto shape is available in a four-pack.

HANDMADE CIGARS: BRAND LISTINGS

DON RENE VINTAGE
Handmade in Santiago, Dominican Republic.

Wrapper: Indonesia   Binder: Dom. Rep.   Filler: Dom. Rep.

Shape	Name	Lgth	Ring	Wrapper
Double Corona	Churchill	7½	50	CC
Robusto	Rothschild	4½	50	CC
Long Corona	Corona	6	44	CC

This vintage selection is mild-to-medium in flavor and offered in all-cedar boxes of 25.

DON REX
Handmade in El Paraiso, Honduras.

Wrapper: Honduras   Binder: Honduras   Filler: Dom. Rep., Honduras, Nicaragua

Shape	Name	Lgth	Ring	Wrapper
Petit Corona	Blount	5	42	CC
Lonsdale	Cetro	6½	44	CC
Robusto	Corona	5½	50	CC
Long Panatela	Panetela Larga	7	36	CC
Double Corona	Presidente	7½	50	CC

Don Rex is an old brand name now attached to a new cigar in 1997. This model offers a medium-to-full-bodied taste thanks to a Honduran-grown wrapper and filler, plus leaves from the Dominican Republic and Nicaragua.

DON RICARDO HONDURAN SELECTION
Handmade in San Andres Tuxtla, Mexico.

Wrapper: Honduras   Binder: Honduras   Filler: Mexico

Shape	Name	Lgth	Ring	Wrapper
Toro	Toro	6½	52	CM

HANDMADE CIGARS: BRAND LISTINGS

Well known in markets outside the U.S., this medium-to-full-bodied cigar is finally available in 1997. It is offered in bundles of 25 or boxes of 24.

DON SALVADOR
Handmade in Esteli, Nicaragua.

Wrapper: Nicaragua   *Binder: Nicaragua*   *Filler: Nicaragua*

Shape	Name	Lgth	Ring	Wrapper
Panatela	Elegante	6½	38	CM
Corona	Seleccion	5½	42	CM
Long Corona	Cazador	6¼	44	CM
Robusto	Consul	5	52	CM
Giant	Presidente	8	54	CM
Double Corona	Churchill	7	49	CM
Toro	Toro	6	50	CM

Introduced in 1996, this brand features all-Nicaraguan tobacco in a medium-to-full-bodied smoke, offered in boxes of 25.

DON SALVADOR
Handmade in Ocotal, Nicaragua.

Wrapper: Nicaragua   *Binder: Nicaragua*   *Filler: Nicaragua*

Shape	Name	Lgth	Ring	Wrapper
Giant	Presidente	8½	52	CM
Double Corona	Churchill	7	49	CM
Lonsdale	Gran Corona	6½	42	CM
Toro	Toro	6	50	CM
Robusto	Robusto	4½	50	CM
Torpedo	Torpedo	6	50	CM

This is a mild-to-medium-bodied cigar which features all-Nicaraguan tobacco. It was introduced in 1993 and offered in all-cedar boxes of 25.

HANDMADE CIGARS: BRAND LISTINGS

DON SALVATORE
Handmade in Danli, Honduras.

Wrapper: Ecuador *Binder: Mexico* *Filler: Honduras, Nicaragua*

Shape	Name	Lgth	Ring	Wrapper
Giant	Suberano	8	50	CC
Double Corona	Churchill	7	49	CC
Toro	Toro	6	50	CC
Robusto	Rothschild	5	50	CC
Corona	No. 4	5½	42	CC

This is a medium-to-full-bodied smoke featuring Cuban-seed filler tobaccos and offered in boxes of 25.

DON SIXTO
Handmade in Danli, Honduras.

Wrapper: Ecuador *Binder: Honduras* *Filler: Honduras, Nicaragua*

Shape	Name	Lgth	Ring	Wrapper
Double Corona	Presidente	8	50	CC
Double Corona	Churchill	6⅞	49	CC
Toro	Toro	6	50	CC
Robusto	Robusto	4¾	50	CC
Long Corona	Corona	6	43	CC
Panatela	Panatela	6½	38	CC
Small Panatela	Senorita	4½	30	CC
Pyramid	Torpedo	7	54	CC

Introduced in 1997, this is a medium-bodied brand with a Connecticut-seed wrapper and a blend of binder and filler leaves from three nations. A tribute to Sixto Plasencia Juarez, one of the patriarchs of the Cuban cigar industry, Don Sixto cigars are offered in individual cellophane sleeves packed in all-cedar boxes.

HANDMADE CIGARS: BRAND LISTINGS

DON SUERTE
Handmade in Tamboril, Dominican Republic.

Wrapper: Dom. Rep. or Indonesia   Binder: Dom. Rep.   Filler: Dom. Rep.

Shape	Name	Lgth	Ring	Wrapper
Double Corona	Presidente	7½	50	CM
Robusto	Robusto	5	50	CM
Grand Corona	Suave	6½	46	CM
Long Panatela	Panatela	7	38	CM
Long Corona	Corona Extra	6	42	CM
Torpedo	Torpedo	6½	54	CM

Take your choice of Dominican-grown or Indonesian wrappers on this mild-to-medium-bodied brand, offered in boxes of 25.

DON TITO
Handmade in Miami, Florida, USA.

Wrapper: Ecuador   Binder: Nicaragua
Filler: Dominican Republic, Honduras, Nicaragua

Shape	Name	Lgth	Ring	Wrapper
Double Corona	Churchill	7	50	CC-Ma
Double Corona	Double Corona	7¾	49	CC-Ma
Lonsdale	No. 1	6¾	43	CC-Ma
Lonsdale	No. 2	6½	43	CC-Ma
Long Panatela	Panatela	7	38	CC
Pyramid	Piramides	7¼	66	CC-Ma
Robusto	Robusto	5	50	CC-Ma
Grand Corona	Taino	6¼	46	CC-Ma
Torpedo	Torpedo	6½	60	CC-Ma

Don Tito was a new brand in 1996, from the "Little Havana" area of Miami, sporting a balanced blend that provides a rich, full-bodied taste. The brand has some of the largest sizes you can find anywhere and is presented in boxes of 25.

DON TOMAS
Handmade in Danli, Honduras.

Wrapper: Honduras   *Binder: Mexico*   *Filler: Dom. Rep., Mexico, Nicaragua*

Shape	Name		Lgth	Ring	Wrapper
Double Corona	Presidentes		7½	50	CM-Ma
Torpedo	Torpedo		7	48	CM
Long Panatela	Panatela Largas		7	36	CM
Lonsdale	Corona Grandes	(tubed)	6½	44	CM
Lonsdale	Cetros No. 2		6½	44	CM-Ma
Toro	Corona Gordas		6	52	CM
Robusto	Coronas		5½	50	CM-Ma
Corona Extra	Toros		5½	46	CM
Petit Corona	Blunts		5	42	CM
Robusto	Rothschild		4½	50	CM-Ma

Don Tomas cigars are justly famous for their medium-to-full-bodied taste and silky construction. Havana-seed tobaccos are gathered from four nations, eventually ending as the top-quality cigars which are so well known to smokers worldwide. The natural wrappers utilize Honduran-grown Connecticut-seed leaves and a blended filler surrounded by a Mexican binder.

DON TOMAS INTERNATIONAL SELECTION
Handmade in Danli, Honduras.

Wrapper: Indonesia   *Binder: Dom.Rep.*   *Filler: Dom.Rep., Mexico, Nicaragua*

Shape	Name	Lgth	Ring	Wrapper
Lonsdale	No. 1	6½	44	CM
Robusto	No. 2	5½	50	CM
Corona	No. 3	5½	42	CM
Toro	No. 5	6	52	CM

HANDMADE CIGARS: BRAND LISTINGS

The Special Edition is newly blended in 1997 and combines leaves from four nations to produce an effortless draw filled with rich flavors for a full-bodied smoke.

DON TOMAS SPECIAL EDITION
Handmade in Danli, Honduras.

Wrapper: Honduras   Binder: Mexico   Filler: Dom. Rep., Mexico, Nicaragua

Shape	Name	Lgth	Ring	Wrapper
Double Corona	No. 100	7½	50	CC
Lonsdale	No. 200	6½	44	CC
Robusto	No. 300	5	50	CC
Long Panatela	No. 400	7	36	CC
Corona Extra	No. 500	5½	46	CC
Toro	No. 600	6	52	CC

Distinctive, smooth drawing and opulent is the Don Tomas Special Edition. This is a medium-bodied but slightly spicy cigar, offered in boxes of 25.

DON TUTO HABANOS
Handmade in Llano Bonito, Costa Rica.

Wrapper: Indonesia   Binder: Costa Rica   Filler: Costa Rica, Nicaragua

Shape	Name	Lgth	Ring	Wrapper
Lonsdale	Presidente	6½	44	CC-CM
Long Corona	Coronas	6	42	CC-CM
Robusto	Robusto	5	50	CC-CM
Pyramid	Piramides	7	44	CC-CM
Double Corona	El Mambi	7½	50	CC-CM

Introduced in 1996, this namesake brand of the family-owned Factory Don Tuto in Costa Rica offers a medium-to-full-bodied taste. The Indonesian-grown wrapper comes from Cameroon-seed or from Cuban-seed. The brand is presented in boxes of 2, 5, 10 and 25, with each cigar individually packed in a cellophane sleeve.

HANDMADE CIGARS: BRAND LISTINGS

DON XAVIER
Handmade in Las Palmas, the Canary Islands of Spain.
Wrapper: USA/Connecticut   *Binder: Canary Islands*
Filler: Brazil, Canary Islands, Dominican Republic

Shape	Name	Lgth	Ring	Wrapper
Long Panatela	Panatela	7½	39	CC
Panatela	Petit Panatela	5⅝	39	CC
Lonsdale	Lonsdale	6⅝	42	CC
Corona	Petit Lonsdale	5⅝	42	CC
Churchill	Gran Corona	7	46	CC
Corona Extra	Corona	5⅝	46	CC
Double Corona	Churchill	7½	50	CC
Robusto	Robusto	4⅝	50	CC
Pyramid	Pyramid	7	52	CC
Cigarillo	Petit	4	29	CC

The flagship of the Marcos Miguel line, this is a mild blend of tobaccos of four nations in a variety of shapes. Introduced in the current range in 1996, Don Xavier cigars are offered in boxes of 5, 10 and 25 cigars each.

DON YÀNES
Handmade in Cumana, Venezuela.
Wrapper: USA/Connecticut   *Binder: Venezuela*   *Filler: Venezuela*

Shape	Name	Lgth	Ring	Wrapper
Double Corona	Double Corona	7	50	CM
Robusto	Robusto	5	50	CM
Corona	Corona	5½	42	CM
Petit Corona	No. 4	5	42	CM
Panatela	Majico	6¼	38	CM
Long Corona	No. 1	6¼	42	CM

HANDMADE CIGARS: BRAND LISTINGS

Here is an old Venezuelan standard, introduced to the U.S. market in 1996. This is an all long-filler cigar which is made by hand and is considered full-bodied.

DOS REINAS
Handmade in Esteli, Nicaragua.

Wrapper: Indonesia   Binder: Indonesia   Filler: Mexico, Nicaragua

Shape	Name	Lgth	Ring	Wrapper
Corona	Corona	5¾	42	CC
Toro	Corona Extra	6	52	CC
Robusto	Robusto	5	52	CC
Torpedo	Torpedo	5¾	54	CC
Churchill	Churchill	7	48	CC
Pyramid	Piramide	6⅞	54	CC

This brand was introduced in 1997 and features Cuban-seed filler leaves, combined with an Indonesian wrapper for a medium-to-full-bodied smoke. Each cigar is wrapped in cellophane and then packed into all-cedar boxes of 25.

DOS RIOS
Handmade in Esteli, Nicaragua.

Wrapper: Ecuador   Binder: Nicaragua   Filler: Dom. Rep., Nicaragua

Shape	Name	Lgth	Ring	Wrapper
Long Corona	Especial	5⅞	44	CC
Grand Corona	Rios Extra	6½	46	CC
Robusto	Robusto	5	50	CC
Toro	Toro	6	50	CC
Double Corona	Esplendido	7	50	CC
Pyramid	Pyramid	6½	52	CC

New for 1997, this is a full-bodied cigar from Nick's Cigar Company of Miami. It features a Sumatra-seed wrapper grown in Ecuador an is presented in slide-top cedar cabinets of 25.

HANDMADE CIGARS: BRAND LISTINGS

DOUBLE HAPPINESS
Handmade in Manila, the Philippines.

Wrapper: Brazil   *Binder: Philippines*   *Filler: Philippines*

Shape	Name		Lgth	Ring	Wrapper
Pyramid	Nirvana		6	52	CC
Toro	Euphoria		6½	50	CC
Robusto	Bliss		5¼	48	CC
Perfecto	Rapture		5	50	CC
Churchill	Ecstacy		7	47	CC
Corona	Sublime	*(tubed)*	5½	44	CC

This brand is debuted in 1995 and handmade in Manila, the Philippines, with a Brazil-grown, Sumatra-seed wrapper and an Isabela binder and filler, grown in the Philippines. Each shape is presented in a magnificent varnished Narra wood box of 26 (really!, except for the Sublime, offered in 20s), including a hand-sewn crushed velvet liner!

DUARTE 1884
Handmade in Santiago, Dominican Republic.

Wrapper: Indonesia   *Binder: Dom. Rep.*   *Filler: Dom. Rep.*

Shape	Name	Lgth	Ring	Wrapper
Corona	Corona	5¼	42	CM
Robusto	Robusto	5½	50	CM
Churchill	Grand Corona	6¾	46	CM
Double Corona	Presidente	7½	50	CM

Here is a new brand for 1997, offering a Sumatran wrapper with Piloto Cubano filler for a medium-bodied taste. It is offered in value-priced bundles of 25.

DULCE DIAMANTE
Handmade in Danli, Honduras.
Wrapper: Honduras or Indonesia
Binder: Honduras or Nicaragua   *Filler: Honduras or Nicaragua*

HANDMADE CIGARS: BRAND LISTINGS

Shape	Name	Lgth	Ring	Wrapper
	Wrapper: Indonesia Binder: Honduras			*Filler: Honduras*
Small Panatela	Baguette	4½	30	CC
	Wrapper: Honduras Binder: Nicaragua			*Filler: Honduras*
Petit Corona	Heart	5	42	CM
	Wrapper: Honduras Binder: Honduras			*Filler: Honduras*
Double Corona	Marquise	7	49	Ma
	Wrapper: Honduras Binder: Nicaragua			*Filler: Nicaragua*
Robusto	Brilliant	5	50	CM
	Wrapper: Indonesia Binder: Honduras			*Filler: Nicaragua*
Toro	Emerald	6	50	CC

Introduced in 1996, this unusual brand utilizes a different blend for each shape! The overall effect is a medium-bodied smoke for all shapes except the Baguette, which is mild-bodied. It is presented in boxes of 25.

DULCE MARIA
Handmade in Navarette, Dominican Republic.

Wrapper: Indonesia   *Binder: Dom. Rep.*   *Filler: Dom. Rep.*

Shape	Name	Lgth	Ring	Wrapper
Churchill	Churchill	7	48	CC
Robusto	Robusto	5	50	CC
Lonsdale	Corona Grande	6½	44	CC
Long Corona	Corona	6	44	CC

Here is a new-for-1997 cigar that offers a mild-to-medium-bodied flavor and is offered at a modest price for excellent value. "Sweet Mary" is presented in bundles of 25.

HANDMADE CIGARS: BRAND LISTINGS

DUNHILL
Handmade in Las Palmas, the Canary Islands of Spain.

Wrapper: USA/Connecticut   Binder: Dom. Rep.   Filler: Dom. Rep.

Shape	Name	Lgth	Ring	Wrapper
Robusto	Coronas Extra	5½	50	CC
Lonsdale	Corona Grandes	6½	43	CC
Corona	Coronas	5½	43	CC
Lonsdale	Lonsdale Grandes	7½	42	CC
Slim Panatela	Panatelas	6	30	CC

This hand-rolled cigar debuted in 1986 and is mild enough for the casual smoker, yet its distinctive taste will satisfy the connoisseur. The tobacco blend and binder are now grown in the Dominican Republic and finished with a genuine Connecticut wrapper.

DUNHILL
Handmade in La Romana, Dominican Republic.

Wrapper: USA/Connecticut   Binder: Dom. Rep.   Filler: Brazil, Dom. Rep.

Shape	Name		Lgth	Ring	Wrapper
Double Corona	Peravias		7	50	CI
Toro	Condados		6	48	CI
Lonsdale	Diamantes		6⅝	42	CI
Panatela	Samanas		6½	38	CI
Corona	Valverdes		5½	42	CI
Robusto	Altamiras	*(tubed)*	5	48	CI
Churchill	Cabreras	*(tubed)*	7	48	CI
Corona	Tabaras	*(tubed)*	5½	42	CI
Robusto	Romanos		4½	50	CI
Torpedo	Centenas		6	50	CI
Giant	Esplendido		8½	52	CI

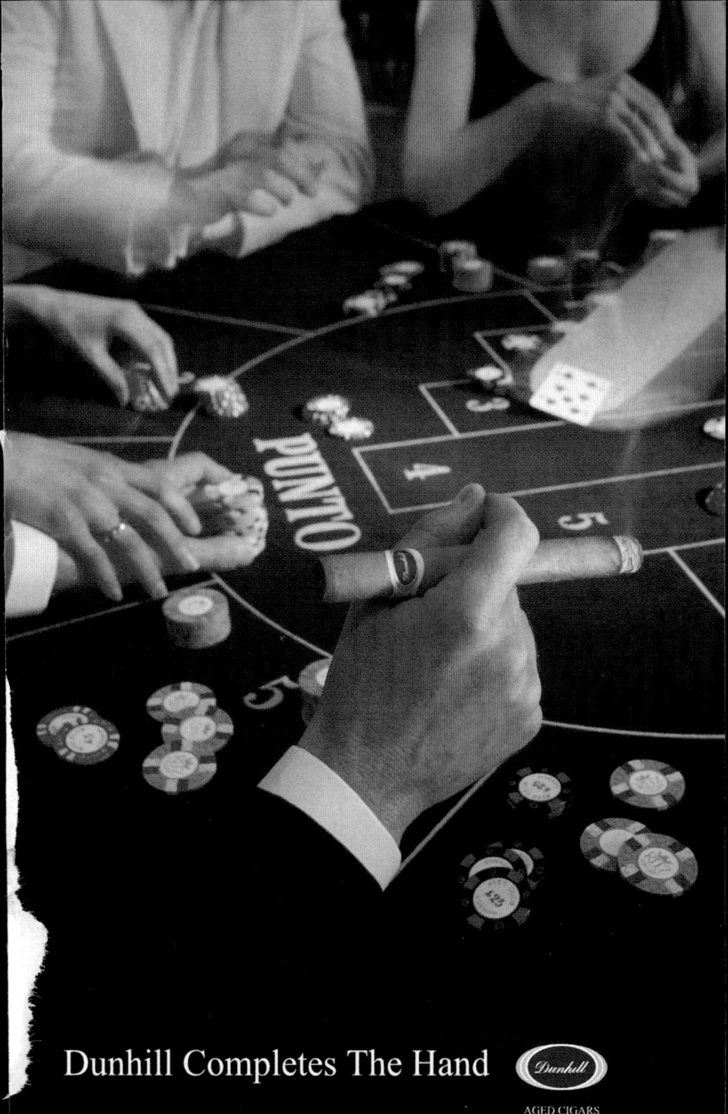
PUNTO
Dunhill Completes The Hand
Dunhill
AGED CIGARS

Petit Corona	Caleta		4	42	Cl

Introduced in 1989, Dunhill's master cigar makers roll a special selection of Piloto Cubano and Olor tobaccos from the Cibao Valley of the Dominican Republic. Wrapping the blend in a Dominican binder, the bunch is then finished with the finest quality Connecticut shade-grown leaf from the Windsor Valley. Prior to final packaging, these cigars are aged in cedar-lined rooms to provide the final mellowing of their mild-to-medium-bodied flavor.

DUO
Handmade in Tamboril, Dominican Republic.
Wrapper: Dominican Republic and USA/Connecticut
Binder: Dominican Republic   *Filler: Dominican Republic*

Shape	Name	Lgth	Ring	Wrapper
Lonsdale	Lonsdale	7	44	Dual
Double Corona	Churchill	7½	50	Dual

Like both natural and maduro wrappers? Here's your chance to enjoy both in the same cigar! The Duo, which debuted in 1997, offers the top half of the cigar wrapped in a Colorado Claro-shade Connecticut wrapper and the bottom in a maduro shade Dominican-grown wrapper. The result? A mild-to-medium-bodied smoke whose flavor is "renewed" halfway through! It is offered in boxes of 25.

888
Handmade, with short filler, in Mexico City, Mexico.
Wrapper: Mexico   *Binder: Mexico*   *Filler: Mexico*

Shape	Name	Lgth	Ring	Wrapper
Corona	No. 1	5¼	40	CM
Toro	No. 2	6¼	50	CM

Here is a five-flavor cigar: Guarapo (a traditional Cuban sugar-cane drink), Gold Label Vanilla, Chocolate, rum and Cappuccino, with a light-to-medium body introduced in 1997. The flavor is added through the curing process and the cigars are available in bundles of 25.

HANDMADE CIGARS: BRAND LISTINGS

898 COLLECTION
Handmade in Kingston, Jamaica.

Wrapper: USA/Connecticut   Binder: Dom. Rep.   Filler: Dom. Rep.

Shape	Name	Lgth	Ring	Wrapper
Double Corona	Churchill	7½	49	CC
Corona	Corona	5½	42	CC
Lonsdale	Lonsdale	6½	42	CC
Lonsdale	Monarch	6¾	45	CC
Robusto	Robusto	5½	49	CC

Introduced in 1991 and made completely by hand in Kingston, Jamaica, the 898 Collection is uncompromising in its commitment to quality of construction and ease in smoking. These are mild-bodied cigars, offered in boxes of 25 cigars each.

1861
Handmade in Canca la Piedra, Dominican Republic.

Wrapper: Indonesia   Binder: Dom. Rep.   Filler: Dom.Rep.

Shape	Name	Lgth	Ring	Wrapper
Giant	President	8	50	CM
Double Corona	Churchill	7	50	CM
Robusto	Grant	5½	50	CM
Lonsdale	Lincoln	6½	46	CM
Corona	Davis	6	44	CM

Civil War fans unite! Here is a mild-to-medium-bodied brand introduced in 1997, with 25 different bands depicting Civil War heroes from North and South . . . Abraham Lincoln, Jefferson Davis, Ulysses S. Grant, Robert E. Lee, William Tecumseh Sherman, James Longstreet, Philip Sheridan and many more! Each cigar is sleeved in cellophane and boxed in varnished boxes of 25 cigars.

HANDMADE CIGARS: BRAND LISTINGS

1876
Handmade in Santiago, Dominican Republic.

Wrapper: USA/Connecticut   *Binder: Dom. Rep.*   *Filler: Dom.Rep.*

Shape	Name	Lgth	Ring	Wrapper
Slim Panatela	Kelly's	5	30	CC
Long Panatela	Panatela	7	36	CC
Corona	Corona	5½	42	CC
Long Corona	Corona Grande	6	44	CC
Robusto	Robusto	5	50	CC
Churchill	Churchill	7	46	CC
Double Corona	Presidente	7½	50	CC
Pyramid	Piramide	7	54	CC

Introduced in 1995, this is a mild-to-medium blend of leaves, available in bundles or tins of 25 cigars.

1881
Handmade in Manila, the Philippines.

Wrapper: Indonesia/Java   *Binder: Philippines*   *Filler: Dom.Rep., Philippines*

Shape	Name	Lgth	Ring	Wrapper
Corona	Corona	5½	44	CM
Robusto	Robusto	5	50	CM
Giant Corona	Centennial	7½	42	CM
Giant	Double Corona	8½	50	CM

The Philippine cigar industry is hundreds of years old and La Flor de la Isabella was formally incorporated in 1881 - hence the name of this brand. It offers excellent craftsmanship and a medium-bodied taste.

EDGAR
Handmade in Santiago, Dominican Republic.

Wrapper: Indonesia, USA/Connecticut   *Binder: Dom. Rep.*   *Filler: Dom. Rep.*

HANDMADE CIGARS: BRAND LISTINGS

Shape	Name	Lgth	Ring	Wrapper
Double Corona	Churchill	7½	50	CC-Ma
Grand Corona	Corona	6	46	CC-Ma
Corona	Lonsdale	6	44	CC-Ma
Robusto	Robusto	5½	50	CC-Ma

Here is a medium-bodied smoke, introduced in 1997 and offered in your choice of a Connecticut-grown natural-shade wrapper or an Indonesian-grown maduro-shade wrapper. You can find it in boxes of 25.

EDGAR PRIVATE RESERVE
Handmade in Indonesia.

Wrapper: Brazil, Indonesia   *Binder: not disclosed*   *Filler: not disclosed*

Shape	Name	Lgth	Ring	Wrapper
Double Corona	No. 1	7⅛	50	CM-Ma
Grand Corona	No. 2	6¼	45	CM-Ma
Long Corona	No. 3	6	42	CM-Ma
Robusto	No. 4	5	50	CM-Ma
Lonsdale	No. 5	7¼	40	CM-Ma

This brand is brand new in 1997 and offers a medium-bodied taste in two wrapper shades (both Indonesian-grown) in boxes of 25.

EL CAMPEON SUAVE
Handmade in the Dominican Republic.

Wrapper: Dom. Rep.   *Binder: Dom. Rep.*   *Filler: Dom. Rep.*

Shape	Name	Lgth	Ring	Wrapper
Corona	Corona	5½	42	CM
Robusto	Robusto	4¾	50	CM
Churchill	Churchill	6¾	46	CM

HANDMADE CIGARS: BRAND LISTINGS

This brand is hard to find, but rewards those who do with a full-bodied taste, offered in boxes of 25.

EL CANELO
Handmade in Miami, Florida, USA.
Origin of wrapper, binder and filler leaves varies, depending on availability.

Shape	Name	Lgth	Ring	Wrapper
Giant	Viajantes	8½	52	CC-Ma
Giant	Embajadores	8	50	CC
Giant	Soberano	8	50	CC
Churchill	Sargentos	7½	46	CC
Churchill	Olympic	7½	46	CC
Churchill	Presidentes	7½	46	CC-Ma
Churchill	Churchills	7	48	CC-Ma
Long Corona	Smokers	7	43	CC-Ma
Toro	Toros	6	50	CC
Robusto	Nom-Plus	4¾	50	CC-Ma
Lonsdale	Infiesta No. 1	7	43	CC-Ma
Long Corona	San Marcos	6	44	CC-Ma
Long Panatela	Elegante	7	36	CC
Corona	Fumas	5½	43	CC-Ma
Slim Panatela	Panatela Rabito	7	30	CC-Ma
Slim Panatela	St. Georges	7	30	CC-Ma
Slim Panatela	St. Augustine	5½	30	CC-Ma
Corona	Corona	5½	42	CC-Ma
Robusto	Robusto	5½	50	CC

These are mild-to-medium cigars with Connecticut wrappers, made in a small factory in the Little Havana section of Miami.

HANDMADE CIGARS: BRAND LISTINGS

EL CID
Handmade in Bahia, Brazil.

Wrapper: Indonesia   *Binder: Dom. Rep.*   *Filler: Brazil, Dom. Rep., Indonesia*

Shape	Name	Lgth	Ring	Wrapper
Double Corona	Presidente	7½	50	CC
Toro	Double Corona	6¼	50	CC
Churchill	Churchill	6⅞	48	CC
Lonsdale	Lonsdale	6½	44	CC

Named for the legendary Spanish warrior Rodrigo Diaz de Bivar (c. 1043-1099), whose exploits were recounted in the epic poem "Poema del Cid," this brand was introduced in late 1997 and offers a medium-to-full-bodied taste.

EL CREDITO
Handmade in Miami, Florida, USA.

Wrapper: Ecuador   *Binder: Nicaragua*   *Filler: Dom. Rep., Nicaragua*

Shape	Name	Lgth	Ring	Wrapper
Giant	Gigantes	9	49	CC-Ma
Giant	Senadores	8	52	CC-Ma
Double Corona	Monarchs	7¼	54	CC-Ma
Double Corona	Imperiales	7¾	49	CC-Ma
Double Corona	Churchill	7	50	CC-Ma
Churchill	Supremos	7½	48	CC-Ma
Toro	Small Churchill	6	52	CC-Ma
Robusto	Rothchild	5	50	CC-Ma
Grand Corona	Corona Extra	6¼	46	CC-Ma
Giant Corona	Corona Grande	7¾	44	CC-Ma
Lonsdale	No. 1	6¾	43	CC-Ma
Long Corona	Cetros	6¼	43	CC-Ma
Corona	Nacionales	5½	43	CC-Ma

Small Panatela	Small Corona	4½	40	CC-Ma
Long Panatela	Panetelas	7	37	CC-Ma
	Made with short filler:			
Churchill	Super Habanero	7½	46	CC-Ma
Lonsdale	Fumas	6¾	44	CC-Ma

This is a medium-bodied smoke, made in the famous El Credito factory in Miami and offered in bundles of 25 cigars each.

EL DIABLO
Handmade in Santiago, Dominican Republic.

Wrapper: Dom. Rep.   *Binder: Dom. Rep.*   *Filler: Dom. Rep.*

Shape	*Name*	*Lgth*	*Ring*	*Wrapper*
Torpedo	Torpedo	6	52	CM
Robusto	Robusto	5	50	CM
Corona Extra	Corona	5½	46	CM

Ready for "The Devil"? This is a medium-to-full-bodied cigar with all-Dominican tobacco and a balanced flavor. Introduced in 1996, it is offered in boxes of 25, except for the Torpedo, available in boxes of 10.

EL DIAMANTE
Handmade in Jalapa, Nicaragua.

EXESO SELECTION:

Wrapper: Ecuador   *Binder: Indonesia*   *Filler: Dom. Rep.*

SELECTO SELECTION:

Wrapper: Indonesia   *Binder: Indonesia*   *Filler: Dom. Rep., Nicaragua*

ESPECIAL SELECTION:

Wrapper: Ecuador   *Binder: Indonesia*   *Filler: Dom. Rep., Honduras, Nicaragua*

HANDMADE CIGARS: BRAND LISTINGS

Shape	Name	Lgth	Ring	Wrapper
	Exeso Selection:			
Torpedo	Torpedo	6½	54	CC
Double Corona	Churchill	7	50	CC
Toro	Toro	6	49	CC
Lonsdale	Palma	6½	44	CC
Robusto	Rothchild	5½	50	CC
Corona	Corona	5½	43	CC
	Selecto Selection:			
Torpedo	Torpedo	6½	54	CC
Double Corona	Churchill	7	50	CC
Toro	Toro	6	49	CC
Lonsdale	Palma	6½	44	CC
Robusto	Rothchild	5½	50	CC
Corona	Corona	5½	43	CC
	Especial Selection:			
Double Corona	Churchill	7	50	CC
Toro	Toro	6	50	CC
Lonsdale	Palma	6½	44	CC
Long Corona	Corona	6	43	CC

Take your choice of sizes and tastes! The Exeso Selection offers a Connecticut-seed wrapper with a mild flavor; the Selecto group is medium-bodied with a Sumatra wrapper and the Especial Selection has a Connecticut-seed wrapper and is full-bodied. The Exeso and Selecto selections are available in either bundles or boxes of 25; the Especial line is available in boxes of 25 only.

HANDMADE CIGARS: BRAND LISTINGS

EL DORADO GOLD RESERVE
Handmade in Danli, Honduras.

Wrapper: Indonesia *Binder: Costa Rica* *Filler: Brazil, Dom. Rep., Mexico*

Shape	Name	Lgth	Ring	Wrapper
Robusto	Robusto	4¾	50	CM
Lonsdale	Lonsdale	6⅝	44	CM
Churchill	Churchill	7	48	CM
Giant	Presidente	8	52	CM

Not your sister's cigar! Here is a 1997-introduced, *full-bodied* cigar that celebrates the legend of El Dorado (literally, "the gilded"), a king of a fabulously wealthy city located by early explorers of the Amazon regions in South America. While the cigar is not covered in gold, it does offer strong flavor in boxes of 25.

EL EMPERADOR
Handmade in Navarette, Dominican Republic.

Wrapper: Indonesia *Binder: Dom. Rep.* *Filler: Dom. Rep.*

Shape	Name	Lgth	Ring	Wrapper
Double Corona	Esplendidos	7	50	Ma
Double Corona	Churchill	7	50	Ma
Toro	Torpedo	6	50	Ma
Robusto	Robusto	5½	50	Ma
Churchill	Double Corona	6¾	48	Ma

This is a medium-bodied, all-maduro line, introduced in 1996. It features a Sumatra wrapper and a Dominican-grown Olor binder. It is available in handcrafted, Spanish Cedar boxes of 25.

EL FIDEL
Handmade in Villa Gonzalez, Dominican Republic.

Wrapper: Indonesia *Binder: Dom. Rep.* *Filler: Dom. Rep.*

Shape	Name	Lgth	Ring	Wrapper
Robusto	Peasant	5	50	CC
Long Corona	Revolutionary	6	44	CC
Double Corona	Dictator	7	50	CC

Here is a not too subtle salute to Fidel Castro, leader of the Cuban Revolution in 1959 and the head of the Cuban state since that time. In seeming contrast to the fiery Castro, this blend is rather mild and is offered in slide-top cedar boxes of 25.

ELEGANTE
Handmade in Danli, Honduras.

Wrapper: Ecuador   Binder: Honduras   Filler: Dom. Rep., Honduras

Shape	Name	Lgth	Ring	Wrapper
Churchill	Grande	8	48	CC
Churchill	Especial	7	48	CC
Lonsdale	Centimo	7	44	CC
Long Panatela	Panatela Larga	7	36	CC
Long Corona	Petit Cetro	6	42	CC
Robusto	Queen	5	50	CC

Originally made in Tampa beginning in 1985 and now made in Honduras, this is a medium-bodied combination of Cuban seed, Dominican long filler, wrapped in a light Ecuadorian-grown leaf, and offered in boxes of 25.

EL ESENCIAL
Handmade in Tamboril, Dominican Republic.

Wrapper: Indonesia   Binder: Dom. Rep.   Filler: Dom. Rep.

Shape	Name	Lgth	Ring	Wrapper
Corona	Corona	5½	42	CM
Churchill	Lonsdale	6¾	46	CM
Toro	Robusto	6	50	CM

| Double Corona | Churchill | 7½ | 50 | CM |

Here is a full-bodied brand introduced in 1996. The wrapper is from Sumatra and the filler in all Piloto Cubano tobacco. You can find it in cellophane sleeves in either bundles or boxes of 25.

EL ESENCIAL WHITE LABEL
Handmade, with mixed filler, in Tamboril, Dominican Republic.

Wrapper: Indonesia   Binder: Dom. Rep.   Filler: Dom. Rep.

Shape	Name	Lgth	Ring	Wrapper
Corona	Corona	5½	42	CM
Churchill	Lonsdale	6¾	46	CM
Toro	Robusto	6	50	CM
Double Corona	Churchill	7½	50	CM

This blend is medium-to-full-bodied, introduced in 1996. The filler is a mixed "sandwich" of long-filler and cut leaves and is offered in bundles of 25.

EL FARO
Handmade in Navarette, Dominican Republic.

Wrapper: Indonesia   Binder: Dom. Rep.   Filler: Dom. Rep.

Shape	Name	Lgth	Ring	Wrapper
Giant	Emilio	8½	52	CC
Double Corona	Churchill	7½	50	CC
Robusto	Robusto	5	50	CC
Grand Corona	Extra Corona	6	46	CC
Long Corona	Lonsdale	6	44	CC
Torpedo	Torpedo	6¼	52	CC

Named for the El Faro Lighthouse near Santo Domingo, this cigar presents a full-bodied taste. Introduced in 1997, it is offered in all-cedar boxes of 25.

HANDMADE CIGARS: BRAND LISTINGS

EL GATO
Handmade in Cumana, Venezuela.
Wrapper: Ecuador or Venezuela

Binder: Honduras or Venezuela   *Filler: Honduras, Venezuela*

Shape	Name	Lgth	Ring	Wrapper
Corona	Corona	5½	42	CC-CM
Robusto	Robusto	5	50	CC-CM
Grand Corona	Corona Gorda	6⅛	46	CC-CM
Double Corona	Double Corona	7½	50	CC-CM

Introduced in 1989, you can take your choice of wrapper shades: light, featuring an Ecuadorian wrapper and Honduran binder, or dark, with a Venezuelan wrapper and binder. Both offer a medium-bodied smoke, available in boxes of 25.

EL GAUCHO
Handmade in Danli, Honduras.

Wrapper: Honduras   *Binder: Honduras*   *Filler: Honduras*

Shape	Name	Lgth	Ring	Wrapper
Giant	Ganza	8	54	CM
Churchill	Pampas	7¼	46	CM
Double Corona	Bolas	6¾	50	CM
Long Corona	Corral	6	44	CM
Robusto	Ponchos	4½	52	CM

This new brand for 1997 offers a heavy-bodied cigar in an all-Honduran blend. Each shape is presented in all-cedar cabinets.

EL INCOMPARABLE
Handmade in Danli, Honduras.

Wrapper: Ecuador   *Binder: Nicaragua*   *Filler: Dom. Rep., Mexico, Nicaragua*

HANDMADE CIGARS: BRAND LISTINGS

Shape	Name	Lgth	Ring	Wrapper
Long Corona	Corona	6	44	CC
Robusto	Robusto	4½	50	CC
Double Corona	Churchill	7	49	CC
Torpedo	Torpedo	7	56	CC

This is a fairly new brand, introduced in 1996, which is unique for its process that imbues the tobacco with 21-year-old Glenfarclas single malt scotch whisky. These full-bodied and spicy cigars are offered in equally stunning packaging, in a five-pack of aluminum tubes to ensure absolute, perfect freshness.

EL MURAZO
Handmade in Santiago, Dominican Republic.
Wrapper: USA/Connecticut   Binder: Dom. Rep.   Filler: Dom. Rep.

Shape	Name	Lgth	Ring	Wrapper
Double Corona	Churchill	7½	50	CM
Churchill	Double Corona	7	48	CM
Toro	Robusto	6	50	CM
Robusto	Rothchild	4½	50	CM

Here is a new cigar for 1997, named for the mountain which overlooks the Santiago area in the Dominican Republic. It features a Dominican Olor binder, Dominican-grown, Piloto Cubano filler and a Connecticut wrapper. It offers a mild and creamy taste which is offered in cedar cabinets of 25.

EL NOBLE
Handmade in Santiago, Dominican Republic.
Wrapper: Indonesia   Binder: Dom. Rep.   Filler: Dom. Rep.

Shape	Name	Lgth	Ring	Wrapper
Grand Corona	Corona	6	46	CM
Robusto	Robusto	5	50	CM
Churchill	Churchill	7	50	CM

HANDMADE CIGARS: BRAND LISTINGS

Here is a new brand for 1997 with a mild body and outstanding construction and draw. It is offered in individual cellophane sleeves packed inside all-cedar boxes of 25.

EL PARAISO
Handmade in Danli, Honduras.

Wrapper: Ecuador   *Binder: Mexico*   *Filler: Costa Rica, Honduras, Nicaragua*

Shape	Name	Lgth	Ring	Wrapper
Giant	Grande	8½	52	CC-Ma
Double Corona	Presidente	7½	50	CC
Torpedo	Torpedo	7	54	CC-Ma
Churchill	Double Corona	7	46	CC
Panatela	Panatelas	6½	36	CC
Toro	Toro	6	50	CC-Ma
Corona	Corona	5¾	43	CC
Robusto	Robustos	4¾	52	CC-Ma
Slim Panatela	Pequenos	5	30	CC

Tobaccos from five nations go into the creation of El Paraiso, which results in a medium-bodied blend and excellent construction. Packed in cedar boxes of 18, 25 or 50 - depending on size - this brand is also modestly priced.

EL REY DEL MUNDO
Handmade in Cofradia, Honduras.
Wrapper: Ecuador, USA/Connecticut

Binder: Honduras   *Filler: Dominican Republic, Honduras*

Shape	Name	Lgth	Ring	Wrapper
Robusto	Robusto	5	54	Ma
Toro	Robusto Larga	6	54	Ma
Double Corona	Robusto Suprema	7¼	54	Ma
Robusto	Robusto Zavalla	5	54	CM
Robusto	Rothschilde	5	50	CM

Grand Corona	Rectangulares	5⅝	45	CM
Panatela	Tino	5½	38	CM
Lonsdale	Cedars	7	43	CM
Toro	Choix Supreme	6⅛	49	CM
Grand Corona	Corona	5⅝	45	CM
Giant	Coronation	8½	52	CM
Double Corona	Double Corona	7	49	CM
Torpedo	Flor de Llaneza	6½	54	CM
Pyramid	Flor de LaVonda	6½	52	CM
Double Corona	Flor del Mundo	7¼	54	CM
Petit Corona	Petit Lonsdale	4⅝	43	CM
Churchill	Corona Inmensa	7¼	47	CM-Ma
Slim Panatela	Plantations	6½	30	CC
Cigarillo	Elegantes	5⅜	29	CC
Short Panatela	Reynitas	5	38	CC
Small Panatela	Cafe au Lait	4½	35	CC

This name means "The King of the World" in Spanish and it lives up to its name with its excellent construction and strong flavor from the Honduran filler and binder and Sumatran-seed Ecuadorian wrapper. Launched in its current form in 1994, a total of 47 sizes are planned, of which 21 are currently in production. The "Lights" group is mild in strength, with a Connecticut wrapper, Honduran binder and filler tobacco from the Dominican Republic.

EL REY DE FLOREZ

Handmade in Tamboril, Dominican Republic.

Wrapper: Dom. Rep. *Binder: Dom. Rep.* *Filler: Dom. Rep.*

Shape	*Name*	*Lgth*	*Ring*	*Wrapper*
Double Corona	Presidente	7½	50	CM
Grand Corona	Suave	6½	46	CM

Lonsdale	Panatella	7	40	CM
Robusto	Robusto	5	50	CM
Long Corona	Corona Extra	6	42	CM
Perfecto	Petite Perfecto	4½	46	CM

"The King of Florez" was crowned in 1997 and offers a smooth, full-bodied flavor. These outstanding cigars are presented without cellophane in elegant, all-cedar boxes.

EL RICO HABANO
Handmade in Miami, Florida, USA and Villa Gonzalez, Dominican Republic.

Wrapper: Ecuador   *Binder: Nicaragua*   *Filler: Honduras, Nicaragua*

Shape	Name	Lgth	Ring	Wrapper
Double Corona	Gran Habanero Deluxe	7¾	50	CM
Churchill	Double Coronas	7	47	CM
Corona Extra	Gran Coronas	5¾	46	CM
Long Corona	Lonsdale Extra	6¼	44	CM
Corona	Coronas	5¾	42	CM
Petit Corona	Petit Habanos	5	40	CM
Robusto	Habano Club	5	48	CM
Long Panatela	No. 1	7½	38	CM

This is a heavy-bodied cigar produced with imported Havana-seed tobaccos and made by hand in Ernesto Carrillo's famous El Credito cigar factory in Miami and the new El Credito facility in Villa Gonzalez, Dominican Republic. They are the most robust of the family of brands which includes La Hoja Selecta (mild) and La Gloria Cubana (medium-bodied).

EL SABINAR
Handmade in Villa Gonzalez, Dominican Republic.

Wrapper: Indonesia   *Binder: Dom. Rep.*   *Filler: Dom. Rep.*

HANDMADE CIGARS: BRAND LISTINGS

Shape	Name	Lgth	Ring	Wrapper
Churchill	1492	6¾	46	CC
Robusto	No. 3	4½	52	CC
Corona	No. 4	5¼	42	CC
Corona Extra	No. 5	5½	46	CC

This is a new brand for 1996, offering a medium-bodied blend. The wrapper is a Sumatra-seed leaf grown in Ecuador. El Sabinar cigars are offered in cellophane sleeves inside cedar cabinets of 25, with the No. 3 also offered in boxes of 10.

EL SIG ROPES
Handmade in San Jose, Costa Rica.

Wrapper: Ecuador   Binder: Nicaragua   Filler: Nicaragua

Shape	Name	Lgth	Ring	Wrapper
Churchill	Corona Grande	7	48	CC
Lonsdale	Corona Corona	6½	42	CC
Toro	Corona Gordo	6	50	CC

First released in 1997, this limited-edition cigar is a joint venture project of Aaron Sigmond, founding editor-in-chief of *Smoke* magazine and respected cigar maker Tony Borhani. Offering a medium-to-full flavor, El Sig Ropes are available in all-cedar boxes of 25 or cabinets of 50. Each case is personally signed and dated by the roller.

EL SOL
Handmade in Santiago, Dominican Republic
and Tampa, Florida, USA

Wrapper: USA/Connecticut   Binder: Dom. Rep.   Filler: Dom. Rep.

Shape	Name	Lgth	Ring	Wrapper
Corona	Brevas	5½	42	CC-Co-Ma
Lonsdale	Corona Imperial	6¼	43	DC-CC-Co-Ma
Grand Corona	Palma Imperial	6½	46	CC-Co-Ma

HANDMADE CIGARS: BRAND LISTINGS

Double Corona	Churchill	7	50	CC-Co-Ma
Double Corona	Emperador	7¾	50	CC-Co-Ma
Robusto	Rothschild	4½	50	CC-Co-Ma
Lonsdale	Londres Deluxe *(short filler)*	6½	43	CC-Co-Ma

This brand dates back all the way to 1928! In its current form, it offers a mild smoke and is made both in Tampa and in the Dominican Republic.

EL SUBLIMADO
Handmade in Danli, Honduras.

Wrapper: Ecuador   *Binder: Dom. Rep.*   *Filler: Dom. Rep.*

Shape	Name	Lgth	Ring	Wrapper
Long Corona	Corona	6	44	CC
Robusto	Robusto	4½	50	CC
Torpedo	Torpedo	7	56	CC
Double Corona	Churchill	7	49	CC

With its mild-to-medium body and totally unique flavor, El Sublimado cigars have earned a place in the hearts of discriminating smokers. Three-year-old leaves from the Cibao Valley of the Dominican Republic are mellowed with 50-year-old Noces d'Or cognac following a secret (and patented) method which enhances the flavor and combined with Connecticut-seed wrappers grown in Ecuador. The unusual packaging of this 1993-inaugurated brand offers these cigars in boxes of five aluminum tubes to ensure absolute freshness and peak of flavor.

EL TIGRE
Handmade in Danli, Honduras.

Wrapper: Indonesia   *Binder: Nicaragua*   *Filler: Honduras, Mexico*

Shape	Name	Lgth	Ring	Wrapper
Long Corona	Lonsdale	6	42	CM
Robusto	Robusto	5	50	CM
Double Corona	Churchill	7	49	CM

HANDMADE CIGARS: BRAND LISTINGS

Giant	Double Corona	8½	52	CM
Torpedo	Pyramid	6	52	CM

"The Tiger" roars with a medium-to-full-bodied flavor and features a Sumatra wrapper. Introduced in 1996, El Tigre is offered in elegant, all-cedar boxes of 25 cigars each.

EL TIGRE
Handmade in Ocotal, Nicaragua.

Wrapper: Ecuador	Binder: Nicaragua			Filler: Nicaragua
Shape	*Name*	*Lgth*	*Ring*	*Wrapper*
Robusto	Robusto	4¾	50	CM
Giant	Churchill	8½	42	CM
Corona	Corona	5½	42	CM
Toro	Toro	6	50	CM

More roar! This shade of The Tiger has only a mild bite, thanks to its Sumatra-seed wrapper grown in Ecuador and Nicargauan binder and filler. It is presented in all-cedar boxes of 25.

EL TROFEO HABANO
Handmade in Tamboril, Dominican Republic.

Wrapper: Indonesia	Binder: Dom. Rep.			Filler: Dom. Rep.
Shape	*Name*	*Lgth*	*Ring*	*Wrapper*
Short Panatela	Panatela Fina	5	36	CC
Petit Corona	Corona	5	44	CC
Lonsdale	Corona Grande	6½	44	CC
Robusto	Robusto	5	50	CC
Double Corona	Double Corona	7	50	CC

Here is a mild cigar with rich flavor, introduced in 1996. It is offered in bundles of 25 or 50 cigars or in boxes of 24 cigars each.

HANDMADE CIGARS: BRAND LISTINGS

EL TROFEO HABANO VINTAGE
Handmade in Tamboril, Dominican Republic.

Wrapper: Ecuador, Indonesia   Binder: Dom. Rep.   Filler: Dom. Rep.

Shape	Name	Lgth	Ring	Wrapper
Petit Corona	Corona	5	44	CC-Ma
Lonsdale	Corona Grande	6½	44	CC-Ma
Robusto	Robusto	5	50	CC-Ma
Double Corona	Double Corona	7	50	CC-Ma

Here is a mild cigar with big flavor, offered without cellophane in boxes of 25. You have your choice of wrappers: Ecuadorian-grown, Connecticut-seed natural shade wrapper or a maduro wrapper grown in Sumatra for this 1997-introduced cigar.

EL TURQUITO
Handmade in Danli, Honduras.

Wrapper: Ecuador   Binder: Honduras   Filler: Nicaragua

Shape	Name	Lgth	Ring	Wrapper
Long Corona	Corona	6	42	CC
Long Corona	Lonsdale	6¼	42	CC
Giant	Presidente	8	52	CC
Robusto	Robusto	5	50	CC
Double Corona	Churchill	7½	50	CC

New in 1997, this is a medium-bodied blend that features a Connecticut-seed wrapper. It is offered in boxes of 25.

EL UNICORNIO
Handmade in Antigua, Guatemala.

Shape	Name	Lgth	Ring	Wrapper
Robusto	Rothchild	4½	50	CM
Toro	Toro	6	50	CM

Giant	Viajante	8½	52	CM
Lonsdale	Corona	6½	44	CM
Giant	Presidente	8½	52	CM

Here is "the Unicorn," an all-long filler, handmade cigar from Guatemala, offering a full-bodied taste in boxes of 25.

EL VALLE DORADO
Handmade in Esteli, Nicaragua.

Wrapper: Indonesia   *Binder: Nicaragua*   *Filler: Honduras, Nicaragua*

Shape	Name	Lgth	Ring	Wrapper
Long Corona	Cetro	6¼	44	CC
Churchill	Churchill	7	48	CC
Double Corona	Presidente	7½	50	CC
Robusto	Robusto	5	50	CC
Toro	Toro	6	50	CC

Here is a new brand for 1997, with a mild-to-medium body, offered in boxes of 25.

ENCANTO
Handmade in Santa Rosa de Copan, Honduras.

Wrapper: Honduras   *Binder: Honduras*   *Filler: Honduras*

Shape	Name	Lgth	Ring	Wrapper
Giant	Grandioso	8	60	CM
Giant	Viajante	8½	52	CM
Double Corona	Churchill Claro	6⅞	49	CM-Ma
Lonsdale	Elegante	7	44	CM
Toro	Toro	6	50	CM-Ma
Lonsdale	Corona Larga	6¼	44	CM

HANDMADE CIGARS: BRAND LISTINGS

Long Corona	Cetro Claro	6	42	CM-Ma
Robusto	Rothschild	4½	50	CM-Ma
Corona	Petit Corona	5½	42	CM
Long Corona	Luchadore	6¼	44	CM
Panatela	Palma Fina	6¾	36	CM
Small Panatela	Princessa	4½	30	CM

This is a very well made cigar, introduced in 1977, offering a medium-to-heavy bodied taste in a variety of sizes and wrappers. It is offered in boxes of 25, except for the Princessa, offered in 50s.

ENTRE RIOS
Handmade in Santiago, Dominican Republic.

Wrapper: Indonesia   Binder: Dom. Rep.   Filler: Dom. Rep.

Shape	Name	Lgth	Ring	Wrapper
Toro	Toro	6½	50	CC
Corona	Corona	5½	42	CC

Here is a new brand, introduced in 1997 and made in Santiago, the Dominican Republic. It features a Sumatra wrapper, Olor binder and filler and a mild-to-medium-bodied taste.

ENTREPRENEUR
Handmade in Santiago, Dominican Republic.

Wrapper: Indonesia   Binder: Dom. Rep.   Filler: Dom. Rep.

Shape	Name	Lgth	Ring	Wrapper
Double Corona	Churchill	7½	50	CC
Churchill	Grand Corona	6¾	46	CC
Toro	Toro	6	50	CC
Lonsdale	Lonsdale	6½	44	CC
Robusto	Robusto	5	50	CC

HANDMADE CIGARS: BRAND LISTINGS

Corona	Corona	5½	42	CC

This is a mild-to-medium-bodied smoke, featuring a Sumatra wrapper. Introduced in 1997, it is offered in individual cellophane sleeves and packed in boxes of 25.

ESCUDO CUBANO
Handmade in Villa Gonzalez, Dominican Republic.

Wrapper: Indonesia   *Binder: Dom. Rep.*   *Filler: Dom. Rep.*

Shape	Name	Lgth	Ring	Wrapper
Double Corona	Churchill	7	50	CC
Torpedo	Torpedo	5½	52	CC
Lonsdale	No. 1	6½	44	CC
Corona Extra	Gran Corona	5¾	46	CC
Long Panatela	Lancero	7¾	38	CC
Robusto	Robusto	5	50	CC

This line of Escudo Cubano was introduced in early 1997, and offers a mild-to-medium-bodied taste in boxes of 25.

ESCUDO CUBANO
Handmade in Esteli, Nicaragua.

Wrapper: Ecuador   *Binder: Nicaragua*   *Filler: Nicaragua*

Shape	Name	Lgth	Ring	Wrapper
Giant	Presidente	8½	52	CC
Double Corona	Churchill	7	50	CC
Lonsdale	No. 1	6½	44	CC
Torpedo	Torpedo	7½	54	CC
Pyramid	Piramide	7	50	CC
Long Panatela	Lancero	7	38	CC
Robusto	Robusto	5	50	CC

HANDMADE CIGARS: BRAND LISTINGS

Introduced in 1996, this is a mild blend of tobaccos, including a Connecticut-seed wrapper grown in Ecuador and binder grown in the Jalapa Valley. These cigars are presented in unique cedar boxes of 25, featuring a plexiglass top!

ESPADA DE ORO
Handmade in Danli, Honduras.

Wrapper: Honduras   *Binder: Honduras*   *Filler: Honduras*

Shape	Name	Lgth	Ring	Wrapper
Giant	Viajante	8½	52	Ma
Giant	Presidente	8½	50	Ma
Double Corona	Executive	7¾	50	Ma
Torpedo	Torpedo	7	54	Ma
Double Corona	Monarch	7	52	Ma
Long Corona	Corona Gorda	6¼	44	Ma
Panatela	Palma Fina	6⅞	36	Ma
Long Corona	Vintage	6	43	Ma
Robusto	Rothschild	5	50	Ma

Created in 1992, this is a Honduran "puro" that offers a medium-bodied taste, thanks to a specially-selected blend of Cuban-seed tobaccos grown in Honduras. It is offered in specially-constructed boxes of 10, 20 and 25 cigars each.

ESPANOLA GOLD LABEL
Handmade in Santiago, Dominican Republic.

Wrapper: USA/Connecticut   *Binder: Dom. Rep.*   *Filler: Dom. Rep.*

Shape	Name	Lgth	Ring	Wrapper
Panatela	Torito	6	36	CC
Corona	Corona	5½	42	CC
Churchill	Excellente	6⅞	46	CC
Robusto	Robusto	5	50	CC

HANDMADE CIGARS: BRAND LISTINGS

Lonsdale	Lonsdale	7	44	CC
Toro	Sassoun	6	50	CC
Torpedo	Belicoso	5½	52	CC
Double Corona	Churchill	6¾	50	CC
Double Corona	Presidente	7	50	CC

Silky smooth Connecticut shade-grown wrappers encase this mild blend from the Dominican Republic. Debuting in 1996, the eight shapes of this original Espanola series are presented without cellophane in cedar cabinets of 25 cigars.

ESPANOLA GREEN LABEL
Handmade in Santiago, Dominican Republic.

Wrapper: USA/Connecticut   Binder: Dom. Rep.   Filler: Dom. Rep.

Shape	Name	Lgth	Ring	Wrapper
Panatela	Torito	6	36	CC
Corona	Corona	5½	42	CC
Lonsdale	Lonsdale	6½	42	CC
Churchill	Excellente	6⅞	46	CC
Long Corona	Corona Grande	6	44	CC
Churchill	Churchill	6¾	50	CC
Robusto	Robusto	5	50	CC
Toro	Sassoun	6	50	CC
Double Corona	Double Corona	7½	50	CC
Torpedo	Belicoso	5½	52	CC
Giant	Fabuloso	8	52	CC

Formerly known as the Reserve Series, this line was introduced in 1996 and offers a more robust taste, generally judged to be medium in strength. It is presented in 5x5 packaging in all-cedar cabinet boxes of 25.

ESPAÑOLA

Only One
Brand
Can Fill
These
Bands...

Red
Gold
Reserve

JM
Tobacco Co.

HANDMADE CIGARS: BRAND LISTINGS

ESPANOLA RED LABEL
Handmade in Santiago, Dominican Republic.

Wrapper: Indonesia   *Binder: Dom. Rep.*   *Filler: Dom. Rep.*

Shape	Name	Lgth	Ring	Wrapper
Panatela	Torito	6	36	CM
Corona	Corona	5½	42	CM
Churchill	Excellente	6⅞	46	CM
Robusto	Robusto	5	50	CM
Lonsdale	Lonsdale	7	44	CM
Torpedo	Belicoso	5½	52	CM
Toro	Sassoun	6	50	CM
Double Corona	Churchill	6¾	50	CM
Double Corona	Presidente	7	50	CM
Giant	Fabuloso	8	52	CM

With a Sumatra wrapper and the fullest body of the entire Espanola line, this cigar — introduced in 1997 — offers every conceivable size for the convenience of all smokers. Like its siblings, it is presented nude in five-row packaging inside all-cedar cabinet boxes.

ESPINOSA CLASSICO
Handmade in Tegucigalpa, Honduras.

Wrapper: Ecuador   *Binder: Nicaragua*   *Filler: Dom. Rep.*

Shape	Name	Lgth	Ring	Wrapper
Corona	Corona	5½	44	CC
Long Corona	Lonsdale	6	44	CC
Robusto	Robusto	5	50	CC
Double Corona	Churchill	7½	50	CC

Introduced in 1997, this is a medium-bodied brand that features a Connecticut-seed wrapper and Dominican-grown Olor and Piloto Cubano filler leaves. It is attractively presented in all-cedar cabinets of 25 cigars each.

ESPINOSA GOLD
Handmade in Santiago, Dominican Republic.

Wrapper: Indonesia　　　　*Binder: Dom. Rep.*　　　　*Filler: Dom. Rep.*

Shape	Name	Lgth	Ring	Wrapper
Corona	Corona	5½	44	CC
Long Corona	Lonsdale	6	44	CC
Robusto	Robusto	5	50	CC
Double Corona	Churchill	7½	50	CC

Here is a new brand for 1997, with a medium-to-full bodied flavor and wrapper from Sumatra. It is offered in an all-cedar box of 25.

ESTEVAN REY CABINET SELECTION
Handmade in Tamboril, Dominican Republic.

Wrapper: Ecuador　　　　*Binder: Dom. Rep.*　　　　*Filler: Dom. Rep.*

Shape	Name	Lgth	Ring	Wrapper
Long Corona	Corona	6	42	CC
Robusto	Robusto	5	50	CC
Double Corona	Churchill	7½	50	CC

Introduced in 1997, this is a medium-bodied cigar with Piloto Cubano filler leaves and an Ecuadorian wrapper. Each cigar is protected in an individual cellophane sleeve and packed in boxes of 25.

ESTEVAN REY PREMIUM SELECTION
Handmade in Tamboril, Dominican Republic.

Wrapper: Dom. Rep.　　　　*Binder: Dom. Rep.*　　　　*Filler: Dom. Rep.*

Shape	Name	Lgth	Ring	Wrapper
Long Corona	Corona	6	42	CC
Robusto	Robusto	5	50	CC

Double Corona	Churchill	7½	50	CC

Here is a mild-to-medium bodied, all-Dominican leaf cigar, also introduced in 1997. Slightly milder than the Cabinet Selection of this brand, it is also offered in cellophane sleeves and packed in boxes of 25.

ESTRADA Y ARGUETA
Handmade in Esteli, Nicaragua.

Wrapper: Nicaragua *Binder: Nicaragua* *Filler: Nicaragua*

Shape	Name	Lgth	Ring	Wrapper
Short Panatela	No. 438	4¼	38	CM
Robusto	No. 452	4½	52	CM
Corona	No. 544	5½	44	CM
Churchill	No. 648	6¾	48	CM
Toro	No. 650	6¼	50	CM
Toro	No. 652	6½	52	CM
Double Corona	No. 754	7¼	54	CM
Giant	No. 852	8½	52	CM
Torpedo	Figurado	6¾	54	CM
Corona	Mini Fuma	5½	44	CM

Here is a full-bodied, all-Nicaraguan cigar that is modestly priced and available in every popular size. It is offered in bundles of 25.

ESTRELLA
Handmade in San Andres Tuxtla, Mexico.

Wrapper: Indonesia or Mexico *Binder: Mexico* *Filler: Mexico*

Shape	Name	Lgth	Ring	Wrapper
Double Corona	Churchill	7	50	CC-Ma
Toro	Toro	6	50	CC-Ma
Robusto	Robusto	5	50	CC-Ma

HANDMADE CIGARS: BRAND LISTINGS

Long Corona	Corona Especial	6	44	CC-Ma

Here is a mild cigar, with a choice of Sumatra (natural) or Mexican (maduro) wrapper, introduced in 1997. It is offered in individual cellophane sleeves in boxes of 25.

ESTRELLA BLANCA
Handmade, with short filler, in San Andres Tuxtla, Mexico.

Wrapper: Mexico   Binder: Mexico   Filler: Mexico

Shape	Name	Lgth	Ring	Wrapper
Robusto	Robusto	5	50	CC
Long Corona	Lonsdale	6¼	42	CC
Corona	Corona	5½	41	CC

New for 1997, this is a mild-bodied brand offered in value-priced boxes of 25.

EVELIO
Handmade in Danli, Honduras.

Wrapper: Ecuador   Binder: Nicaragua

Filler: Honduras, Mexico, Nicaragua

Shape	Name	Lgth	Ring	Wrapper
Corona	Corona	5¾	42	CC
Churchill	Double Corona	7⅝	47	CC
Lonsdale	No. 1	7	44	CC
Robusto	Robusto	4¾	54	CC
Toro	Robusto Larga	6	54	CC
Pyramid	Torpedo	7	54	CC

The lifetime of expertise which resides in master roller Evelio Oviedo is the secret behind this brand, introduced in 1996. This is a full-bodied but smooth smoke in six of the most popular sizes, prepared in the same all-by-hand method that Oviedo knew from his days in Cuba at the H. Upmann factory in Havana. Evelio cigars are presented in all-cedar boxes of 25.

HANDMADE CIGARS: BRAND LISTINGS

EVITA
Handmade in Santiago, Dominican Republic.

Wrapper: Indonesia   *Binder: Dom. Rep.*   *Filler: Dom. Rep.*

Shape	Name	Lgth	Ring	Wrapper
Long Corona	Corona	6	44	CC
Grand Corona	Extra Corona	6	46	CC
Giant	Double Corona	8½	52	CC
Robusto	Robusto	5	50	CC
Churchill	Churchill	7½	48	CC
Torpedo	Torpedo	6½	52	CC
Double Corona	Presidente	7½	50	CC
Churchill	Lancero	7	46	CC
Long Panatela	Panatella	7	36	CC

Don't cry for this brand, Argentina! A 1997 tribute to the former first lady of Argentina, Evita Peron (1919-52), this is a mild-to-medium-bodied brand offered in boxes of 25s.

EXCALIBUR
BY HOYO DE MONTERREY
Handmade in Cofradia, Honduras.

Wrapper: USA/Connecticut   *Binder: Honduras*
Filler: Dominican Republic, Honduras and Nicaragua

Shape	Name	Lgth	Ring	Wrapper
Double Corona	No. I	7¼	54	CC-Ma
Churchill	No. II	6¾	47	CC-Ma
Toro	No. III	6⅛	48	CC-Ma
Grand Corona	No. IV	5⅝	46	CC-Ma
Grand Corona	No. V	6¼	45	CC-Ma
Panatela	No. VI	5½	38	CC-Ma
Petit Corona	No. VII	5	43	CC-Ma

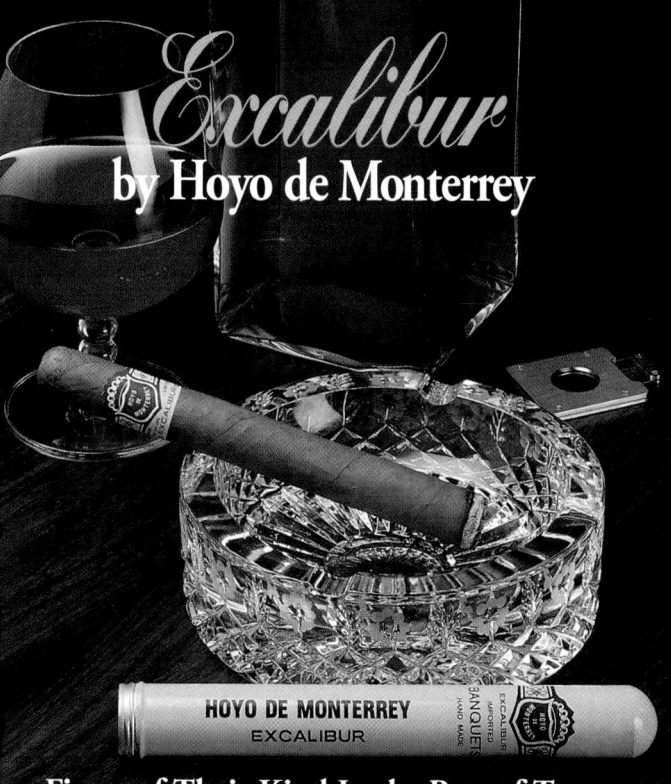

Excalibur
by Hoyo de Monterrey

Finest of Their Kind In the Best of Taste

...ce 1845 our master cigar-makers developed a ...hnique to marry the full-bodied flavor of the ...glish market wrapper with the supreme mild-... ...s of the Claro into a world-class, hand-made ...ar like Excalibur.

...r craftsmen make sure that every precious ...g-filler leaf, binder and wrapper that goes into ...h Excalibur is hand-bunched in the

traditional, time-honored way, then packed in a Spanish cedar Boite Nature Box to enhance the seasoning and taste to guarantee a classic smoke that is truly the finest of its kind.

Available at Fine Tobacconists Everywhere. There are eight sizes and shapes available in English Claro and Rich Maduro to satisfy the most discriminating smoker.

Imported by Danby-Palacio Division
VILLAZON & CO., INC.

Churchill	Banquets	*(tubed)*	6¾	48	CC
Cigarillo	Miniatures		3	22	CC

Excalibur cigars are handmade in Honduras and are the choicest cigars picked from the famous Hoyo de Monterrey line of fine cigars. A new shape, the Miniature, joins the initial eight shapes, and all are wrapped in beautiful Connecticut Shade wrappers, which gives each and every Excalibur cigar a robust, but exquisitely smooth taste.

EXCELSIOR
Handmade in San Andres Tuxtla, Mexico.

Wrapper: USA/Connecticut   *Binder: Mexico*   *Filler: Dom. Rep., Mexico*

Shape	Name	Lgth	Ring	Wrapper
Long Corona	No. 1	6¼	42	CC
Lonsdale	No. 2	6¾	44	CC
Robusto	No. 3	5½	52	CC
Churchill	No. 4	7	48	CC
Giant	No. 5	8	50	CC
Giant	Individuale	8½	52	CC

This brand was introduced in 1996, offering a blend of tobaccos and a medium-bodied flavor in boxes of 25 cigars each, except for the Individuale, which is offered in boxes of 10.

EXPRESS IMPORTS
Handmade in Danli, Honduras.

Wrapper: Mexico   *Binder: Mexico*   *Filler: Nicaragua*

Shape	Name	Lgth	Ring	Wrapper
Slim Panatela	No. 1	7	30	CC-Ma
Slim Panatela	No. 2	6⅞	30	CC-Ma
Long Corona	No. 3	6	42	CC-Ma
Corona	No. 4	5½	42	CC-Ma

Lonsdale	No. 5	6⅝	44	CC-Ma
Churchill	No. 6	6⅞	48	CC-Ma
Robusto	No. 7	4¾	50	CC-Ma
Toro	No. 8	6¼	50	CC-Ma
Double Corona	No. 9	7½	50	CC-Ma
Giant	No. 10	8	52	CC-Ma
Torpedo	No. 11	6⅝	54	CC-Ma

This is a medium-bodied cigar, available in both natural and maduro wrappers, since 1992. It is offered in bundles of 25.

F.D. GRAVE
Handmade in Danli, Honduras.

Wrapper: USA/Connecticut   Binder: USA/Connecticut   Filler: Honduras, Indonesia

Shape	Name	Lgth	Ring	Wrapper
Double Corona	Churchill	7¾	50	CM
Double Corona	Corona Grande	7	52	CM
Long Corona	Lonsdale	6¼	44	CM
Robusto	Robusto	5	50	CM

One of the most respected names in U.S. cigar history is back with an all-handmade line of exceptional quality, made in Honduras. Introduced in late 1995, the four-shape line is full-bodied in taste and offers a Connecticut Broadleaf wrapper and filler, to complement the Honduran and Indonesian fillers. The F.D. Grave series are presented in individual cellophane sleeves inside an all-wood cabinet box.

FAMOUS PRIVATE SELECTION
Handmade in Santiago, Dominican Republic.

Wrapper: USA/Connecticut   Binder: Dom. Rep.   Filler: Dom. Rep.

Shape	Name	Lgth	Ring	Wrapper
Double Corona	Presidente	7½	50	CC

HANDMADE CIGARS: BRAND LISTINGS

Torpedo	Torpedo	6½	50	CC
Grand Corona	Corona Gorda	6½	46	CC
Long Corona	Lonsdale	6	42	CC
Toro	Toro	6	50	CC
Robusto	Robusto	5	50	CC

First available in 1997, this mild-bodied brand offers a rich flavor and excellent construction at a very agreeable price. You'll find it presented in cedar cabinets of 25 cigars each.

THE FAMOUS RUM RUNNER
Handmade, with medium filler, in Jakarta, Indonesia.

Wrapper: Indonesia   *Binder: Indonesia*
Filler: Columbia, Dominican Republic, Indonesia

Shape	Name	Lgth	Ring	Wrapper
Cigarillo	Treasures	3⅝	20	CM
Short Panatela	Wench	4½	36	CM
Petit Corona	Bucaneer	4¾	42	CM
Lonsdale	Pirate	7	42	CM

This is a flavored cigar produced by the Caribbean Cigar Company and introduced in 1994. Made by hand, it uses medium filler and offers a mild and sweet flavor. Not surprisingly, the black and gold band features the skull-and-crossbones emblem of pirate ships of yore!

FANTASTIC FLAVOR CIGARS
Handmade, with short filler, in Tampa, Florida, USA.

Wrapper: Ecuador   *Binder: Dom. Rep.*   *Filler: Ecuador*

Shape	Name	Lgth	Ring	Wrapper
Corona	Viva Vanilla	5½	42	CC
Corona	Ariva Amaretto	5½	42	CC
Corona	Cha-Cha Cherry	5½	42	CC

HANDMADE CIGARS: BRAND LISTINGS

Corona	Rhumba Rum	5½	42	CC

New for 1997, this four-flavor brand offers a rich taste and a modest price. Made by hand with short filler tobaccos, it is offered in individual cellophane sleeves in boxes of 25.

FAT CAT
Handmade in Tamboril, Dominican Republic.

Wrapper: Indonesia   *Binder: Dom. Rep.*   *Filler: Dom. Rep.*

Shape	*Name*	*Lgth*	*Ring*	*Wrapper*
Robusto	Robusto	5	52	CC
Long Corona	Corona	6	44	CC
Double Corona	Churchill	7	50	CC
Toro	Toro	6	50	Ma
Giant	Grand Reserve	8	50	Ma
Torpedo	Torpedo	6¾	54	CC

These are "fat" cigars indeed, as all but one has a ring gauge of 50 or more. Offered in "Fat Pacs" of five cigars, or in boxes or 10 or 25 depending on size, this is a full-bodied brand with silky Sumatra wrappers.

FELIPE GREGORIO
Handmade in Danli, Honduras.

Wrapper: Honduras   *Binder: Honduras*   *Filler: Honduras*

Shape	*Name*	*Lgth*	*Ring*	*Wrapper*
Double Corona	Glorioso	7¾	50	CM
Churchill	Suntouso	7	48	CM
Torpedo	Belicoso	6	54	CM
Corona	Sereno	5¾	42	CM
Robusto	Robusto	5	52	CM
Petit Corona	Nino	4¼	44	CM

HANDMADE CIGARS: BRAND LISTINGS

Introduced in 1992, this brand shows off the efforts of a single plantation in Honduras - Jamastram - in the famous valley of the same name. Their Havana-seed tobaccos offer full-bodied, but mellow flavor with an elegant, sweet aroma.

FELIPE II
Handmade in Danli, Honduras.

Wrapper: Indonesia	Binder: Honduras			Filler: Honduras
Shape	Name	Lgth	Ring	Wrapper
Double Corona	Reserva A	7¾	50	CM
Torpedo	Reserva B	6	52	CM
Churchill	Reserva X	7	48	CM
Toro	Reserva D	6	50	CM
Robusto	Reserva R	5	50	CM
Corona	Reserva C	5½	42	CM
Petit Corona	Reserva N	4	44	CM

New for 1997, this is a medium-to-full-bodied cigar with peppery highlights and offered in a fabulous cabinet-style box. The Sumatra-grown wrapper complements the Cuban-seed binder and filler and the perfect construction for an enjoyable experience every time you light one up.

FIGHTING COCK
Handmade in Manila, the Philippines.

Wrapper: Indonesia	Binder: Philippines			Filler: Philippines
Shape	Name	Lgth	Ring	Wrapper
Pyramid	Sidewinder	6	52	CM
Toro	Texas Red	6½	50	CM
Robusto	Smokin' Lulu	5¼	48	CM
Perfecto	Rooster Arturo	5	50	CM
Churchill	C.O.D.	7	47	CM
Corona	Fly Boy (tubed)	5½	44	CM

Felipe Gregorio

Enjoy a Dream

HANDMADE CIGARS: BRAND LISTINGS

Introduced in 1995, these hand-made, Manila-manufactured cigars offer a medium-bodied taste, combining a Javan sun-grown wrapper with Philippine Isabela binder and filler. The brand is presented in stunning varnished wooden boxes of 25, each equipped with a hand-sewn, crushed velvet liner (except for the Fly Boy shape, offered in 20s). The shapes are named after actual champion roosters!

FIRST PRIMING
Handmade in Danli, Honduras.

Wrapper: Honduras   *Binder: Honduras*   *Filler: Honduras*

Shape	Name	Lgth	Ring	Wrapper
Giant	Grandees	8½	52	CC-Ma
Double Corona	Largos	7½	50	CC-Ma

This is a medium-bodied cigar, made of all Honduran tobacco. An excellent value, it is offered in modestly-priced bundles of 25.

FITTIPALDI
Handmade in Santiago, Dominican Republic.

Wrapper: Dom. Rep.   *Binder: Dom. Rep.*   *Filler: Dom. Rep.*

Shape	Name	Lgth	Ring	Wrapper
Giant	Presidente	8	50	CM
Torpedo	Torpedo	6¾	54	CM
Toro	Toro	6	50	CM
Robusto	Robusto	4½	50	CM
Churchill	Churchill	7	48	CM
Lonsdale	Lonsdale	6½	42	CM
Long Corona	Corona	6	44	CM
Cigarillo	Para Ella	5	28	CM

Yes, this brand is owned by famous Brazilian racer Emerson Fittipaldi, winner of Formula 1 world championships in 1972 and 1974 and the Indianapolis 500 in 1989 and 1993. The band features the checkered flag, symbol of victory in racing and the cigars themselves are produced in conjunction with the much-respected Sosa & Vilar Corporation. The blend is mild-to-medium in strength, featuring a Sumatra-seed wrapper. Fittipaldi cigars are presented in cellophane sleeves and packed in all-cedar cabinets of 25.

FLAMENCO PURO
Handmade in Los Angeles, California, USA.

Wrapper: Honduras   *Binder: Mexico*   *Filler: Dom. Rep., Mexico*

Shape	Name	Lgth	Ring	Wrapper
Torpedo	Torpedo	6½	52	CM
Toro	Churchill	6½	52	CM
Corona	Corona	6	44	CM
Robusto	Robusto	5	52	CM

Decision-time: do you prefer the mild-bodied flavor of this 1996-introduced brand, or prefer it in a flavored version of either Bacardi Rum or vanilla. In either case, it comes in a box of 25.

FLOR CUBANA
Handmade in Danli, Honduras.

Wrapper: Cameroon   *Binder: Indonesia*   *Filler: Dom. Rep., Nicaragua*

Shape	Name	Lgth	Ring	Wrapper
Double Corona	Presidente	7½	50	CC
Churchill	Churchill	7	48	CC
Lonsdale	Lonsdale	7	44	CC
Corona	Corona	5½	44	CC
Robusto	Robusto	5	50	CC
Long Panatela	Panatela	7½	38	CC

This is a mild to medium-bodied smoke featuring a natural wrapper and leaves from four nations, presented in individual cellophane sleeves in boxes of 25.

HANDMADE CIGARS: BRAND LISTINGS

FLOR DE AMOR
Handmade in Esteli, Nicaragua.

Wrapper: Indonesia   Binder: Indonesia   Filler: Mexico, Nicaragua

Shape	Name	Lgth	Ring	Wrapper
Toro	Corona	5¾	52	CC
Toro	Corona Extra	6	52	CC
Robusto	Robusto	5	52	CC
Torpedo	Torpedo	5¾	54	CC
Churchill	Churchill	7	48	CC

Introduced in 1997, this is a mild-bodied cigar featuring Cuban-seed filler tobaccos, offered in protective cellophane sleeves and packed in all-cedar boxes of 25.

FLOR DE CONSUEGRA
Handmade in Cofradia, Honduras.

Wrapper: Honduras   Binder: Honduras   Filler: Honduras

Shape	Name	Lgth	Ring	Wrapper
Corona	Corona	5½	42	CM
Churchill	Corona Inmensa	7¼	47	CM
Grand Corona	Cuban Corona	5⅝	45	CM
Lonsdale	Lonsdale	6½	42	CM
Short Panatela	Panatela	5⅝	38	CM
Giant	President	8½	49	CM
Robusto	Robusto	4½	50	CM
Grand Corona	Corona Grande	6¼	45	CM
Long Corona	Corona Extra	6	42	CM

This looks like a heavy-bodied cigar, and it is. It is marked by a rich, deep-brown colored, Havana-seed wrapper. Not for the timid!

HANDMADE CIGARS: BRAND LISTINGS

FLOR DE DIOS
Handmade in Esteli, Nicaragua.

Wrapper: Nicaragua *Binder: Nicaragua* *Filler: Nicaragua*

Shape	Name	Lgth	Ring	Wrapper
Double Corona	Churchill	7	50	CM
Toro	Toro	6	50	CM
Robusto	Robusto	5	50	CM

Here is an all-Nicaraguan brand offering a medium-bodied smoke in three of the most popular sizes. Introduced in 1997, it is offered in boxes of 25.

FLOR DE FARACH
Handmade in Esteli, Nicaragua.

Wrapper: Ecuador *Binder: Honduran*
Filler: Dominican Republic, Honduras, Nicaragua

Shape	Name	Lgth	Ring	Wrapper
Double Corona	Francisco	7¼	54	CC
Churchill	Churchill	7	48	CC
Torpedo	Momotombo	6¾	54	CC
Pyramid	Momotomito	7	52	CC
Pyramid	Lonsdale	6½	43	CC
Corona	Corona	5½	44	CC
Robusto	Robusto	4½	54	CC
Toro	Regios	6½	54	CC
Short Panatela	Petit Lancero	4¼	39	CC

Here is the revival of an ancient Cuban brand which dates from 1903, much appreciated until it disappeared in 1960. In 1996, a Nicaraguan version of the Flor de Farach was introduced. It's a medium-to-full-bodied cigar, with a beautiful Sumatra-seed wrapper grown in Ecuador and a rich flavor.

HANDMADE CIGARS: BRAND LISTINGS

FLOR DE FILIPINAS
Handmade in Manila, the Philippines.

Wrapper: Philippines   *Binder: Philippines*   *Filler: Philippines*

Shape	Name	Lgth	Ring	Wrapper
Pyramid	Cortado	5⅝	50	CC
Churchill	Churchill	6¾	47	CC
Lonsdale	Coronas Largas	6¾	44	CC
Corona	Coronas	5½	44	CC
Panatela	Cetros	5⅞	39	CC
Short Panatela	Half Corona	4	39	CC
Short Panatela	Panatellas	4⅞	35	CC

Introduced in 1996, this is an inexpensive, medium-bodied but handmade brand from the Philippines. Made from Philippine Isabela tobacco in the binder and filler, it is covered in a Philippine Cagayan Valley wrapper and offered in boxes of 25.

FLOR DE FLOREZ
Handmade in Danli, Honduras.

Wrapper: Honduras   *Binder: Honduras*   *Filler: Honduras*

Shape	Name	Lgth	Ring	Wrapper
Double Corona	Presidente	7	49	CM
Lonsdale	Cetros No. 2	6½	44	CM
Toro	Corona	6	49	CM
Robusto	Rothchild	4⅞	47	CM
Petit Corona	Blunt	5	42	CM

Essentially a family secret, American smokers discovered Flor de Florez in 1995. Now produced in Honduras, these cigars are mild to medium in body, using an all-Honduran blend, including a Connecticut Shade-seed wrapper.

HANDMADE CIGARS: BRAND LISTINGS

FLOR DE FLOREZ CABINET SELECTION
Handmade in Managua, Nicaragua.

Wrapper: Nicaragua   *Binder: Nicaragua*   *Filler: Nicaragua*

Shape	Name	Lgth	Ring	Wrapper
Double Corona	Gigantes	7½	49	CM
Churchill	Sir Winston	7	47	CM
Torpedo	Belicoso	6½	52	CM
Corona Extra	Florez-Florez	5½	46	CM
Robusto	Robusto	5	50	CM
Petit Corona	Coronita	5	42	CM

This is a new line from Flor de Florez, introduced in 1996. This is an all-Nicaraguan cigar, offering a medium-to-full-bodied flavor with rich spices in the taste, offered in boxes of 25.

FLOR DE FLOREZ MIAMI BLEND
Handmade in Miami, Florida, USA.

Wrapper: Ecuador   *Binder: Mexico*   *Filler: Brazil, Honduras, Nicaragua*

Shape	Name	Lgth	Ring	Wrapper
Double Corona	Double Corona	7½	49	CC
Churchill	Churchill	7	47	CC
Torpedo	Torpedo	6	52	CC
Toro	Toro	6	50	CC
Long Panatela	Panatela	7	38	CC
Grand Corona	Corona	6½	46	CC
Robusto	Robusto	5	50	CC

Viva Miami! This new blend, offered for the first time in 1997, offers a medium-to-full-bodied taste, perfect for evenings on the *Calle Ocho*. It is presented without cellophane in all-cedar, slide-top cabinets of 25.

HANDMADE CIGARS: BRAND LISTINGS

FLOR DE GONZALEZ
Handmade in Miami, Florida, USA.
Wrapper: Ecuador

Binder: Dom. Rep. or Honduras   Filler: Dom. Rep., Honduras, Nicaragua

Shape	Name	Lgth	Ring	Wrapper
Double Corona	Churchill	7	50	CC-Ma
Toro	Extra Corona	6	50	CC-Ma
Double Corona	Magnum	7	60	CC-Ma
Lonsdale	No. 1	6¾	44	CC-Ma
Corona	No. 4	5½	44	CC-Ma
Pyramid	Piramide No. 2	7	62	CC-Ma
Double Corona	Presidente	7½	50	CC-Ma
Torpedo	Torpedo	6¼	52	CC-Ma
Robusto	Wavell	5	50	CC-Ma
Giant	Monster	9	60	CC-Ma
Giant	Gigante	9	50	CC-Ma
Panatela	Panatela	6¾	38	CC-Ma

This brand was introduced in 1996, made in the Miami area and offering a wide range, including some really, really big ring gauges. Available in both natural and maduro wrappers, the body is mild and all shapes are offered in boxes of 25.

FLOR DE HONDURAS
Handmade in Danli, Honduras.

Wrapper: Honduras   Binder: Honduras   Filler: Honduras

Shape	Name	Lgth	Ring	Wrapper
Giant	Viajantes	8½	52	CM-Ma
Torpedo	Torpedo	7	54	CM-Ma
Double Corona	Churchill	7	49	CM-Ma
Toro	Toro	6	50	CM-Ma

| Lonsdale | Corona | 6¾ | 43 | CM |
| Robusto | Robustos | 5 | 50 | CM-Ma |

This brand was introduced in 1996. It offers a mild-bodied taste and is conveniently packaged in triangular bundles of 25.

FLOR DE JALAPA
Handmade in Esteli, Nicaragua.

Wrapper: Ecuador   *Binder: Nicaragua*   *Filler: Nicaragua*

Shape	Name	Lgth	Ring	Wrapper
Giant	Presidente	8½	52	CM
Toro	Toro	6	50	CM
Long Corona	Grand Corona	6	44	CM
Churchill	Churchill	7	48	CM
Robusto	Robusto	4¾	50	CM

This brand was introduced in January 1996. It is light to medium in strength and uses a Havana-seed wrapper, grown in Ecuador. These cigars are offered in boxes of 25.

FLOR DE LOS REYES
Handmade in Navarette, Dominican Republic.

Wrapper: Indonesia   *Binder: Dom. Rep.*   *Filler: Dom. Rep.*

Shape	Name	Lgth	Ring	Wrapper
Giant	Emilio	8½	52	CM
Double Corona	Churchill	7½	50	CM
Robusto	Robusto	5	50	CM
Long Corona	Extra Corona	6	44	CM
Grand Corona	Lonsdale	6	46	CM
Torpedo	Torpedo	6¼	48	CM

HANDMADE CIGARS: BRAND LISTINGS

Introduced in 1997 by the Blue Springs, Missouri-based Grand Cigar Company, this is a medium-bodied cigar with a hint of spice on the finish. The Sumatra wrapper is combined with Cuban-seed tobaccos in the binder and filler. Flor de Los Reyes cigars are offered in individual cellophane sleeves inside all-cedar boxes of 25. A Connecticut-wrapped version, mild-to-medium in strength, is also planned.

FLOR DE MANILA
Handmade in Manila, the Philippines.

Wrapper: Philippines   Binder: Philippines   Filler: Philippines

Shape	Name	Lgth	Ring	Wrapper
Churchill	Churchill	7	47	CC
Lonsdale	Coronas Largas	7	44	CC
Corona	Coronas	5½	44	CC
Long Panatela	Cetros Largos	7½	39	CC
Panatela	Cetros	6	39	CC
Corona	Londres	5¾	44	CC
Panatela	Panatela	5¾	35	CC
Torpedo	Cortado	5	50	CC

This is a mild to medium-bodied cigar in very limited distribution, which blends Cuban-seed tobaccos grown in the Philippines for a pleasant, unique taste.

FLOR DE MEXICO
Handmade in San Andres Tuxtla, Mexico.

Wrapper: Mexico   Binder: Mexico   Filler: Mexico

Shape	Name	Lgth	Ring	Wrapper
Toro	Churchill	6½	52	CM
Toro	Toro	6⅛	50	CM
Grand Corona	No. 1	6½	46	CM
Churchill	No. 2	6¾	48	CM
Short Panatela	No. 3	4⅛	38	CM

HANDMADE CIGARS: BRAND LISTINGS

Corona	No. 4	5½	44	CM

Created in 1979, this is a full-bodied cigar made in Mexico and offered in
bundles of 20 cigars each.

FLOR DE NICARAGUA
Handmade in Esteli, Nicaragua.

Wrapper: Nicaragua *Binder: Nicaragua* *Filler: Nicaragua*

Shape	Name	Lgth	Ring	Wrapper
Giant	Presidente	8	54	CC-Ma
Giant	Viajante	8½	52	CC-Ma
Double Corona	Presidente Corto	7¼	54	CC-Ma
Double Corona	Viajante Corto	7	52	CC-Ma
Double Corona	Emperador	7¾	50	CC-Ma
Double Corona	Emperador Corto	7½	50	CC-Ma
Churchill	Churchill	6⅞	48	CC-Ma
Churchill	No. 11	7½	46	CC-Ma
Toro	Duke	6	50	CC-Ma
Long Panatela	No. 9	8	38	CC-Ma
Long Panatela	No. 9 Corto	7	38	CC-Ma
Corona Extra	Corona Extra	5½	46	CC-Ma
Robusto	Consul	4½	52	CC-Ma
Lonsdale	No. 1	6⅝	44	CC-Ma
Lonsdale	No. 10	6½	43	CC-Ma
Long Corona	No. 3	6	44	CC-Ma
Corona	Nacional	5½	44	CC-Ma
Panatela	No. 5	6⅞	35	CC-Ma
Long Corona	No. 6	6	41	CC-Ma
Corona	Seleccion B	5½	42	CC-Ma

HANDMADE CIGARS: BRAND LISTINGS

Slim Panatela	No. 7	7	30	CC-Ma
Panatela	Elegante	6½	38	CC-Ma
Petit Corona	No. 2	4½	42	CC-Ma
Short Panatela	Petits	5½	38	CC-Ma
Slim Panatela	Senoritas	5½	34	CC-Ma
Small Panatela	Piccolino	4⅛	30	CC-Ma
Toro	Corona	5⅝	48	CC-Ma

Introduced in 1995, the 27-shape Flor de Nicaragua range is a Nicaraguan puro. These mild-bodied cigars use filler and binder leaf from the Jalapa Valley of Nicaragua, combined with Nicaraguan wrappers.

FLOR DE ORO
Handmade in Esteli, Nicaragua.

Wrapper: Indonesia   *Binder: Indonesia*   *Filler: Nicaragua*

Shape	Name	Lgth	Ring	Wrapper
Lonsdale	No. 1	6½	44	CC
Giant	Presidente	8½	52	CC
Robusto	Robusto	5	50	CC
Torpedo	Torpedo	6½	54	CC
Double Corona	Churchill	7	50	CC

This is a new cigar in 1997, with a mild-to-medium-bodied taste and offered in cellophane sleeves in all-cedar boxes of 25.

FLOR DE PALICIO
Handmade in Cofradia, Honduras.

Wrapper: Ecuador, Indonesia   *Binder: Honduras*
Filler: Dominican Republic, Honduras and Nicaragua

Shape	Name	Lgth	Ring	Wrapper
Lonsdale	No. 1	7	40	CM

| Long Corona | No. 2 | 6 | 42 | CM-Ma |
| Churchill | Corona | 6¾ | 48 | CM-Ma |

This is a handmade, medium-bodied cigar, created under the supervision of the master cigar makers who manufacture Hoyo de Monterrey and Punch. This elegant brand is offered in equally elegant boxes of 25 each.

FLOR DE SELVA
Handmade in Danli, Honduras.

Wrapper: Ecuador   *Binder: Honduras*   *Filler: Honduras*

Shape	Name	Lgth	Ring	Wrapper
Small Panatela	Panatela	4½	30	CC
Robusto	Robusto	4¾	50	CC
Long Corona	Fino	6	44	CC
Robusto	Corona	5½	48	CC
Churchill	Churchill	7	49	CC
Double Corona	Double Corona	7½	52	CC

This brand debuted in Europe in 1994 and in the U.S. in 1997. It offers a medium body, featuring a Connecticut-seed wrapper grown in Ecuador. It is presented in cellophane and packed in all-cedar boxes of three, ten and 25.

FLOR DEL CARIBE
Handmade in Danli, Honduras.

Wrapper: Ecuador and Indonesia   *Binder: Honduras*
Filler: Dominican Republic, Honduras and Nicaragua

Shape	Name	Lgth	Ring	Wrapper
Corona	Duques	5½	42	CM-Ma
Churchill	Super Cetro	7	46	CM-Ma
Double Corona	Sovereign	7	52	CM-Ma

HANDMADE CIGARS: BRAND LISTINGS

This brand is offered in elegant boxes of 25 cigars each. The medium-to-full-bodied range was reduced from six to three sizes in 1996, with a maduro wrapper now available for all sizes.

FLOR DEL TODO
Handmade in Esteli, Nicaragua.

Wrapper: Indonesia or Nicaragua   Binder: Indonesia   Filler: Dom. Rep., Nicaragua

Shape	Name	Lgth	Ring	Wrapper
Double Corona	Churchill	7½	50	CC-Ma
Double Corona	Presidente	7	50	CC-Ma
Toro	Toro	6	50	CC-Ma
Corona	Corona	5½	44	CC-Ma
Robusto	Robusto	5	50	CC-Ma
Panatela	Palma	6	38	CC-Ma
Slim Panatela	Petite	5	34	CC-Ma

Here is a new brand for 1997, offered in either bundles or boxes of 25. It has a full-bodied flavor and a modest price. Check it out!

FONSECA
Handmade in Santiago, Dominican Republic.

Wrapper: USA/Connecticut   Binder: Mexico   Filler: Dom. Rep.

Shape	Name	Lgth	Ring	Wrapper
Long Corona	8-9-8	6	43	Co
Grand Corona	7-9-9	6½	46	Co-Ma
Double Corona	10-10	7	50	Co-Ma
Robusto	5-50	5	50	Co-Ma
Petit Corona	2-2	4¼	40	Co-Ma
Pyramid	Triangular	5½	56	Co

One of the world's most famous names in Port is also a respected name in cigars. Medium in body, this refined, cabinet-selection brand debuted in 1962 and was re-introduced in its current blend in 1991. It is blended from the choicest tobaccos grown in the Cibao Valley of the Dominican Republic. The wrapper is outstanding Connecticut Shade (natural) or Connecticut Broadleaf (maduro) leaf. The Triangular shape is one of the hardest to make and offers a rich flavor, concentrated by its conical shape.

FONTICIELLA
Handmade in Santiago, Dominican Republic.

Wrapper: Ecuador   Binder: Brazil   Filler: Dom. Rep., Honduras

Shape	Name	Lgth	Ring	Wrapper
Lonsdale	Corona Classicos	6½	44	CC-Ma
Long Panatela	Palma Fina	7	38	CC-Ma
Small Panatela	Damas	5	32	CC-Ma
Torpedo	Imperial	6½	52	CC-Ma
Churchill	No. 1	7	46	CC-Ma
Double Corona	Embajadores	7	50	CC-Ma
Torpedo	Ejecutivos	6	52	CC-Ma
Robusto	Acendados	5	50	CC-Ma

Here is an old brand name in a new blend, introduced in 1997. This is a medium-bodied smoke, offered in individual cellophane sleeves and packed in boxes of 25.

FRANCISCO HERNANDEZ
Handmade, with medium filler, in Navarette, Dominican Republic.

Wrapper: Indonesia   Binder: Dom. Rep.   Filler: Dom. Rep.

Shape	Name	Lgth	Ring	Wrapper
Corona	Corona	5	43	CC
Toro	Toro	6½	50	CC
Churchill	Churchill	7¼	48	CC
Long Corona	Petro	6	44	CC

HANDMADE CIGARS: BRAND LISTINGS

Here is a fine example of a "Cuban Sandwich"-style cigar in which medium and short filler is surrounded by long filler leaves, then bound and wrapped into a medium-bodied smoke. The cigars are then protected in individual cellophane sleeves before being packed in plywood boxes.

FREE CUBA
Handmade in Santiago, Dominican Republic.

Wrapper: Indonesia   Binder: Indonesia   Filler: Dom. Rep., Indonesia, Nicaragua

Shape	Name		Lgth	Ring	Wrapper
Robusto	Robusto	(tubed)	5	50	CM
Lonsdale	Corona	(tubed)	6½	42	CM
Double Corona	Churchill	(tubed)	7¼	50	CM
Torpedo	Torpedo	(tubed)	6½	54	CM

This brand was introduced in 1996 by the Caribbean Cigar Company, headquartered in Florida. Thanks to its Sumatra wrapper and blended filler, Free Cuba belies its fiery name with a medium-to-full-bodied flavor, offered in individual glass tubes inside carefully-crafted boxes of 25.

FUEGO CUBANO
Handmade in Los Angeles, California, USA.

Wrapper: Indonesia   Binder: Ecuador   Filler: Dom. Rep.

Shape	Name	Lgth	Ring	Wrapper
Slim Panatela	Palmita	6	34	CC
Petit Corona	Panetella	5	40	CC
Robusto	Cuba Libre	5	48	CC
Corona	Corona	5½	42	CC
Robusto	Robusto	5	50	CC
Grand Corona	Toro	6	46	CC
Lonsdale	Lonsdale	6½	44	CC
Toro	Double Corona	6½	48	CC
Double Corona	Churchill	7	50	CC

Toro	Corona Grande	6	52	CC
Torpedo	Torpedo	6	52	CC
Giant	Presidente	8	50	CC
Corona Extra	Companion	3½	46	CC
	Made with short filler:			
Grand Corona	Fuma	6½	46	CC

"Cuban Fire" is the name of this brand, with offers a medium-bodied smoke thanks to Cuba-seed filler leaves and a Cameroon-seed Indonesian wrapper. Introduced in 1997, it is presented in an all-cedar box.

FUEGO CUBANO GOLD EDITION
Handmade in Los Angeles, California, USA.

Wrapper: Ecuador   *Binder: Ecuador*   *Filler: Dom. Rep.*

Shape	Name	Lgth	Ring	Wrapper
Slim Panatela	Palmita	6	34	CC
Petit Corona	Panetella	5	40	CC
Robusto	Cuba Libre	5	48	CC
Corona	Corona	5½	42	CC
Robusto	Robusto	5	50	CC
Grand Corona	Toro	6	46	CC
Lonsdale	Lonsdale	6½	44	CC
Toro	Double Corona	6½	48	CC
Double Corona	Churchill	7	50	CC
Toro	Corona Grande	6	52	CC
Torpedo	Torpedo	6	52	CC
Giant	Presidente	8	50	CC

HANDMADE CIGARS: BRAND LISTINGS

First available in 1997, this is a medium-bodied cigar with Cuban-seed filler tobaccos grown in the Dominican Republic and a golden Ecuador-grown wrapper. It is offered in all-cedar boxes of 25.

FUEGO CUBANO PLATINUM EDITION
Handmade in Los Angeles, California, USA.

Wrapper: USA/Connecticut   Binder: Ecuador   *Filler: Dom. Rep.*

Shape	Name	Lgth	Ring	Wrapper
Slim Panatela	Palmita	6	34	CC
Petit Corona	Panetella	5	40	CC
Robusto	Cuba Libre	5	48	CC
Corona	Corona	5½	42	CC
Robusto	Robusto	5	50	CC
Grand Corona	Toro	6	46	CC
Lonsdale	Lonsdale	6½	44	CC
Toro	Double Corona	6½	48	CC
Double Corona	Churchill	7	50	CC
Toro	Corona Grande	6	52	CC
Torpedo	Torpedo	6	52	CC
Giant	Presidente	8	50	CC

This is a medium-to-full-bodied smoke that debuted in 1997. It is also presented in boxes of 25.

FUNDADORES JAMAICA
Handmade in Kingston, Jamaica.

Wrapper: Ecuador or USA/Connecticut   *Binder: Mexico*
Filler: Dominican Republic, Jamaica

Shape	Name	Lgth	Ring	Wrapper
Double Corona	Churchill	7½	49	CC-Ma
Toro	Robusto Gorda	6	50	CC-Ma

Fundadores
Pride of Jamaica

Santa Cruz
Jamaican Heritage

Barrington House
Premium Cigars, Ltd.

Kingston 5, Jamaica W.I.

Home of Award Winning Cigars

1980 - Prague
1980 - Buenos Aires   1981 - London
1982 - Lisbon   1982 - Brussels
1983 - Rome   1984 - Madrid

The quality of aged and matured tobacco used,
the skill and experience in choosing the blend, and
the craft that has been expressed in their production by
hand for four decades are your assurance that these
exquisite cigars are unsurpassed in richness, aroma
and smoking satisfaction.

We are also the creators & manufacturers of private
label super premium cigars for world renowned resorts,
cigar bars, exclusive golf clubs and championship
sporting events.

George Campbell
Factory Manager

Barrington G. Adams
C.E.O.

Lonsdale	Lonsdale	6½	42	CC-Ma
Corona	Corona	5½	42	CC-Ma
Robusto	Petit Robusto	4	50	CC-Ma

This brand is produced by the Combined Tobacco Co. of Kingston, Jamaica and offers mild, rich flavors. Offered in wood boxes of 25, Connecticut Shade or Connecticut-seed (grown in Ecuador) wrappers are offered in both a natural and maduro style.

GALANTE CLASE
Handmade in Danli, Honduras.

Wrapper: Ecuador   Binder: Dom. Rep.   Filler: Honduras

Shape	Name	Lgth	Ring	Wrapper
Double Corona	Churchill	7	49	CC
Robusto	Rothchild	5	50	CC
Toro	Toro	6	50	CC
Giant	Soberano	8	50	CC
Corona	No. 4	5½	42	CC
Slim Panatela	Muneca/Petit	5⅜	34	CC
Small Panatela	Muneca/Tico	4½	30	CC

Here is a mild-to-medium-bodied brand with Sumatra-seed wrappers grown in Ecuador. Introduced in 1997, it is offered in boxes of 25.

GALIANO
Handmade in Santiago, Dominican Republic.

Wrapper: USA/Connecticut   Binder: Dom. Rep.   Filler: Dom. Rep.

Shape	Name	Lgth	Ring	Wrapper
Double Corona	Presidente	7½	50	CC
Corona	Corona	5¾	43	CC
Churchill	Churchill	7	48	CC

HANDMADE CIGARS: BRAND LISTINGS

Toro	Toro	6	50	CC
Lonsdale	No. 1	7	43	CC
Robusto	Robusto	4¾	52	CC
Short Panatela	Petit Corona	5	36	CC
Long Panatela	Panatela	7	36	CC

Originally introduced in 1994, this is a mild-to-medium-bodied brand which is in national distribution in the U.S. for the first time in 1996. Very well constructed, it features a genuine Connecticut Shade wrapper and is packed in all-cedar cabinets of 25.

GALLARDO
Handmade in Danli, Honduras.

Wrapper: Indonesia   Binder: Honduras   Filler: Honduras, Nicaragua

Shape	Name	Lgth	Ring	Wrapper
Toro	Missles	6	54	CM
Giant	Soberano	8	50	CM
Double Corona	Churchill	7	49	CM
Toro	Toro	6	50	CM
Robusto	Rothschild	5	50	CM
Corona	No. 4	5½	42	CM
Long Panatela	Palma Fina	7	38	CM

Introduced in 1997, this is a medium-bodied cigar that is offered in all-cedar cabinets of 25 cigars. A portion of the sales price of each box is used to support an experimental organic tree farm on the north coast of Honduras.

GARGOYLE
Handmade in Manila, Philippines.

Wrapper: Philippines   Binder: Philippines   Filler: Philippines

HANDMADE CIGARS: BRAND LISTINGS

Shape	Name	Lgth	Ring	Wrapper
Double Corona	Bacchus	7¼	50	CM
Robusto	Florentine	5	50	CM
Corona	Parisian	5¾	42	CM

This all-Philippine brand debuted in 1995 and offers a mild flavor in three popular sizes. Each is available in boxes of 25, with each cigar protected in cellophane sleeves.

GARMEISTER
Handmade in Eureka Springs, Arkansas.

Wrapper: Ecuador   *Binder: Indonesia*   *Filler: Dom. Rep., Indonesia*

Shape	Name	Lgth	Ring	Wrapper
Robusto	Robusto	5	50	CC
Toro	Corona Grande	6	48	CC
Torpedo	Torpedo	6½	52	CC
Double Corona	Garmeister	7	58	CC

Here is the story of some folks who learned how to roll cigars on the kitchen table and are now developing a growing following in the mid-South area. Introduced in 1995, Garmeister cigars utilize a flavorful Connecticut-seed wrapper and blend it with leaves from the Dominican Republic and Indonesia for a mild taste, offered in bundles of 25.

GARO
Handmade in Santiago, Dominican Republic.

Wrapper: USA/Connecticut   *Binder: Dom. Rep.*   *Filler: Dom. Rep.*

Shape	Name	Lgth	Ring	Wrapper
Double Corona	Presidente	7½	50	CC
Churchill	Churchill	7	48	CC
Toro	Opus	6	50	CC
Lonsdale	Numero Uno	7	43	CC

Robusto	Robusto	4¾	52	CC
Torpedo	Torpedo	6¼	52	CC
Corona	Corona	5¾	43	CC
Long Panatela	Panatela	7	36	CC

First available in 1996, the Garo line is made by hand in the Dominican Republic, offering a mild-to-medium body. It uses only Cuban-seed long filler, combined with a Dominican Olor binder and genuine Connecticut Shade-grown wrapper leaves. Even the band is elegant, employing the famous "Fleur de Lis" design.

GARO MADURO
Handmade in Santiago, Dominican Republic.

Wrapper: Brazil   *Binder: Dom. Rep.*   *Filler: Dom. Rep.*

Shape	Name	Lgth	Ring	Wrapper
Torpedo	Baritone	4½	52	Ma
Robusto	Alto	5	50	Ma
Torpedo	Tenor	5½	52	Ma
Torpedo	Soprano	6½	52	Ma

Here is a 1997-introduced, all-maduro line which offers a full-bodied smoke, thanks to its Brazilian wrapper, which is aged for more than three years. It is offered in boxes of 25.

GARO VERDE
Handmade in Santiago, Dominican Republic.

Wrapper: Indonesia   *Binder: Dom. Rep.*   *Filler: Dom. Rep.*

Shape	Name	Lgth	Ring	Wrapper
Double Corona	Verde 1	7½	50	CC
Toro	Verde 2	6½	50	CC
Robusto	Verde 3	5	50	CC
Corona	Verde 4	5½	42	CC

HANDMADE CIGARS: BRAND LISTINGS

The Garo "green" line offers a medium-to-full-bodied taste featuring a Sumatra wrapper and Cuban-seed filler leaves grown in the Dominican Republic. Introduced in 1997, it offers four popular sizes and is available in boxes of 25.

GARCIA Y VEGA
Handmade in Kingston, Jamaica.

Wrapper: USA/Connecticut   *Binder: Mexico*   *Filler: Dom. Rep., Mexico*

Shape	Name	Lgth	Ring	Wrapper
Churchill	Churchill	7	45	CC
Lonsdale	Lonsdale	6½	42	CC
Panatela	Corona	5½	38	CC

Garcia y Vega has been a famous name in cigars since it was introduced in 1882. In 1996, a new handmade series was introduced to complement the existing machine-made line with a Connecticut Shade wrapper and offering a medium body.

GATO
Handmade in Santiago, Dominican Republic.

Wrapper: Indonesia   *Binder: Dom. Rep.*   *Filler: Dom. Rep.*

Shape	Name	Lgth	Ring	Wrapper
Corona	Corona	5½	42	CC
Long Corona	Corona Grande	6	44	CC
Robusto	Robusto	5	50	CC
Double Corona	Presidente	7½	50	CC

This is a medium-bodied blend, available in a choice of packaging: bundles, boxes or amatista jars.

GEOFFREY RED
Handmade in Santiago, Dominican Republic.

Wrapper: Indonesia   *Binder: Ecuador*   *Filler: Dom. Rep.*

HANDMADE CIGARS: BRAND LISTINGS

Shape	Name	Lgth	Ring	Wrapper
Long Corona	Corona	6	44	CC
Toro	Double Corona	6	48	CC
Robusto	Robusto	5	50	CC
Double Corona	Churchill	7	50	CC

Geoffrey Red made its debut in 1997 as a mild-bodied and slight sweet-tasting smoke, featuring a Sumatra wrapper. It is offered in individual cellophane sleeves in either boxes or bundles of 25.

GILBERTO OLIVA
Handmade in Ocotal, Nicaragua.
Wrapper: Costa Rica, USA/Connecticut
Binder: Dominican Republic   *Filler: Dominican Republic, Nicaragua*

Shape	Name	Lgth	Ring	Wrapper
Lonsdale	No. 1	6½	44	CC
Robusto	Robusto	5½	50	CC-Ma
Double Corona	Churchill	7	50	CC-Ma
Toro	Viajante	6	52	CC
Torpedo	Torpedo	6	52	CC-Ma

Although this brand was new in 1996, it has already established a reputation for quality. Here is a medium-bodied, richly flavored cigar in both a natural (Connecticut) and maduro-shade (Costa Rican) wrapper in the most popular sizes. The line is complemented by the elegant, all-cedar boxes in which 25 cigars are held.

GILFRANCO DOMINICAN
Handmade, with medium filler, in Santiago, Dominican Republic.
Wrapper: Indonesia   *Binder: Dom. Rep.*   *Filler: Dom. Rep.*

Shape	Name	Lgth	Ring	Wrapper
Robusto	Robustos	5½	50	CC

HANDMADE CIGARS: BRAND LISTINGS

Grand Corona	Grandes	6	46	CC	
Double Corona	Churchills	7½	50	CC	

Here is a medium-filler, medium-bodied cigar with an Olor binder and Piloto Cubano filler. It is offered in individual cellophane sleeves in bundles of 25.

GILFRANCO VANILLA BOMBERS
Handmade, with short filler, in San Juan, Puerto Rico.

Wrapper: Puerto Rico   Binder: Homogenized tobacco leaf   Filler: Puerto Rico

Shape	Name	Lgth	Ring	Wrapper
Perfecto	Perfecto	4¾	44	CM

Here is a medium-bodied flavored cigar that is imbued with vanilla and walnut oil and offer a brightly-flavored taste in boxes of 100.

GIOCONDA
Handmade in Danli, Honduras.

Wrapper: USA/Connecticut   Binder: Honduras
Filler: Dominican Republic, Honduras, Nicaragua

Shape	Name	Lgth	Ring	Wrapper
Double Corona	President	7¼	54	CC
Long Corona	Lonsdale	6¼	44	CC
Churchill	Churchill	6¾	48	CC
Robusto	Robusto	4½	50	CC

New life was given to this brand by Vincent & Tampa Cigar Co.'s Mario Garrido. It is now made in Honduras and offers a medium-bodied blend, presented in boxes of 25.

GISPERT
Handmade in Danli, Honduras.

Wrapper: Ecuador   Binder: Dominican Republic
Filler: Dominican Republic, Honduras, Nicaragua

HANDMADE CIGARS: BRAND LISTINGS

Shape	Name	Lgth	Ring	Wrapper
Double Corona	Churchill	7½	50	CM
Toro	Toro	6	50	CM
Robusto	Robusto	5	52	CM
Lonsdale	Lonsdale	6½	44	CM

Introduced in 1996, this is a Honduran version of an old Cuban brand with excellent construction and a mild-to-medium-bodied taste. The wrapper is Connecticut-seed grown in Ecuador and each box of 25 is packed in cedar. The brand is only available in limited distribution to members of the Tobacconists' Association of America (TAA).

GITANO
Handmade in Santiago, Dominican Republic.

Wrapper: Brazil   Binder: Philippines   Filler: Brazil, Dom. Rep.

Shape	Name	Lgth	Ring	Wrapper
Long Panatela	Panatela	7¾	38	Ma
Giant	Presidente	8	50	Ma
Robusto	Robusto	4½	52	Ma
Toro	Toro	6	50	Ma
Corona Extra	Double Corona	5½	46	Ma
Churchill	Corona Extra	6¾	46	Ma
Corona	Corona	5¼	42	Ma
Petit Corona	Petit Corona	4	42	Ma

New in 1997, this is an all-maduro line that features a Brazilian wrapper and a Philippines binder. It is medium-bodied and presented in boxes of 25 cigars each.

GLORIA PALMERA
Handmade in Las Palmas, Canary Islands of Spain.

Wrapper: USA/Connecticut   Binder: Indonesia
Filler: Brazil, Canary Islands, Dominican Republic

HANDMADE CIGARS: BRAND LISTINGS

Shape	Name	Lgth	Ring	Wrapper
Double Corona	Doble Corona	7½	50	CC
Toro	Toro	6	50	CC
Robusto	Robusto	5	50	CC
Lonsdale	Lonsdale	6½	43	CC

Introduced in 1996, this is a mild-bodied cigar which offers a genuine
Connecticut wrapper, presented in boxes of 25.

GRAN HABANO
Handmade in Canca la Piedra, Dominican Republic.

Wrapper: Indonesia   *Binder: Dom. Rep.*   *Filler: Dom. Rep.*

Shape	Name	Lgth	Ring	Wrapper
Double Corona	Churchill	7	50	CC
Toro	Toro	6	50	CC
Robusto	Robusto	5	50	CC
Long Corona	Corona	6	44	CC
Corona	Petit Corona	5½	42	CC

New in 1997, this is a medium-to-full-bodied cigar which features a Sumatra
wrapper, Olor binder and Piloto Cubano filler leaves. It is presented in
cellophane sleeves and packed in all-cedar cabinets.

GRAN RESERVE SUAREZ
Handmade in the Dominican Republic.
Wrapper: Indonesia, USA/Connecticut

Binder: Dominican Republic   *Filler: Dominican Republic*

Shape	Name	Lgth	Ring	Wrapper
Robusto	Robusto	5	50	CC-CM
Double Corona	Presidente	7½	52	CC-CM
Grand Corona	Royal Corona	6½	46	CC-CM

HANDMADE CIGARS: BRAND LISTINGS

Long Panatela	Lonsdale	7	36	CC-CM
Pyramid	Torpedo Royale	7	50	CC-CM
Torpedo	Especial No. 1	7	50	CC-CM

Take your choice of Connecticut or Sumatra wrappers in this medium
(Connecticut) to full (Sumatra)-bodied line, available in boxes of 25 except for
the Torpedo Royale (12 to the box) and Especial No. 1 (20 per box).

GRAND CRUZ
Handmade in Licey, Dominican Republic.

Wrapper: Indonesia   *Binder: Dom. Rep.*   *Filler: Dom. Rep.*

Shape	Name	Lgth	Ring	Wrapper
Giant	Presidente	8	50	Ma
Lonsdale	Corona	7	44	Ma
Grand Corona	Double Corona	6½	46	Ma
Pyramid	Piramid	6½	53	Ma
Robusto	Robusto	5	50	Ma
Long Corona	Diplomatico	6	44	Ma

Here is an all-maduro line with a medium-to-full body. The Indonesian maduro
wrapper is complemented by Cuban-seed, Dominican-grown binder and fillers.
The line is presented is boxes of 25.

GRAND NICA
Handmade in Esteli, Nicaragua.

Wrapper: Nicaragua   *Binder: Nicaragua*   *Filler: Nicaragua*

Shape	Name	Lgth	Ring	Wrapper
Toro	Toro	6	50	CM
Lonsdale	Lonsdale	6½	44	CM
Double Corona	Churchill	7	52	CM
Robusto	Robusto	5	52	CM

| Giant | Gigante | 8 | 54 | CM |
| Torpedo | Torpedo | 6½ | 54 | CM |

Introduced in 1996, this all-Nicaraguan line features all-Cuban seed tobaccos and offers a medium-to-full-bodied taste. It is offered in all-cedar cabinets of 25 cigars, each protected by cellophane sleeves.

THE GRIFFIN'S
Handmade in Santiago, Dominican Republic.

Wrapper: USA/Connecticut   Binder: Dom. Rep.   Filler: Dom. Rep.

Shape	Name	Lgth	Ring	Wrapper
Long Panatela	No. 100	7	38	CC
Lonsdale	No. 200	7	44	CC
Long Corona	No. 300	6¼	44	CC
Panatela	No. 400	6	38	CC
Corona	No. 500	5	43	CC
Slim Panatela	Privilege	5	31	CC
Giant	Prestige	7½	50	CC
Robusto	Robusto	5	50	CC

While the mythical character of the Griffin gives this brand its name, the effort which gives the cigars their high quality is very real. The filler includes three different Cibao Valley tobaccos combined with a Dominican binder and Connecticut wrapper to give it a mildly spicy, flavorful taste.

GUARANTEED JAMAICA
Handmade, with medium and long filler, in Kingston, Jamaica.

Wrapper: USA/Connecticut   Binder: Mexico
Filler: Dominican Republic, Jamaica, Mexico

Shape	Name	Lgth	Ring	Wrapper
Grand Corona	Petit Churchill	6	45	CC
Petit Corona	Corona	5	40	CC

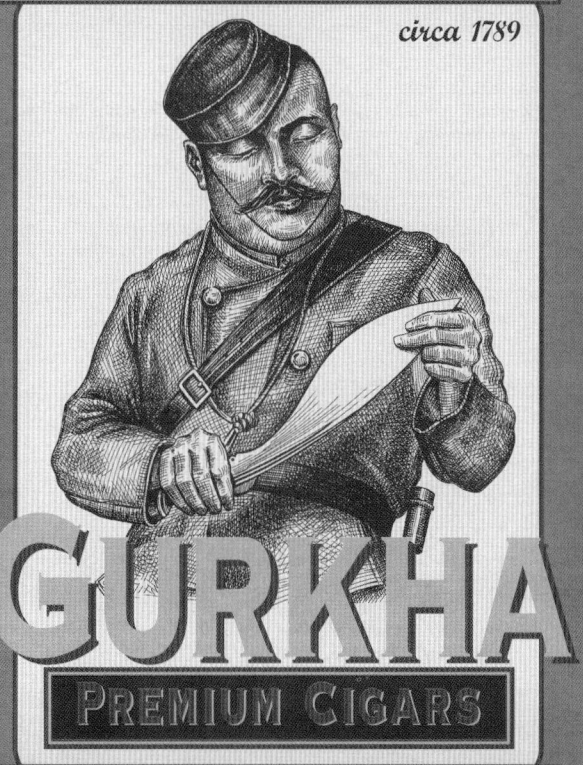

· HAND ROLLED ·

circa 1789

GURKHA

PREMIUM CIGARS

DOMINICAN REPUBLIC

STEEPED IN LEGEND AND HISTORY, THE GURKHA CIGAR, CREATED MORE THAN A CENTURY AGO, HAS NOW BEEN REBORN. METICULOUSLY HAND-CRAFTED OUT OF DOMINICAN TOBACCO FROM CUBAN PILOT SEED, A DOMINICAN BINDER AND A FIVE YEAR-OLD CONNECTICUT WRAPPER, SMOKED WITH LOUIS XIII COGNAC. THE RESULT IS A CIGAR THAT BOASTS A RICH, CREAMY FLAVOR WITH A HINT OF SPICE AND A PLEASANTLY LIGHT FINISH. ONLY LIMITED QUANTITIES AVAILABLE.

Distributed by Miami Cigars Inc.

Robusto	Robusto	5	50	CC

These are well-made, high-quality cigars from the Combined Tobacco Co. factory in Kingston, Jamaica. The Connecticut wrapper surrounds a Mexican binder and a combination of medium and long-filler leaves to give this brand a mild-to-medium, rich taste in boxes of 25.

GURKHA
Handmade in Tamboril, Dominican Republic.

Wrapper: USA/Connecticut   *Binder: Dom. Rep.*   *Filler: Dom. Rep.*

Shape	Name	Lgth	Ring	Wrapper
Double Corona	Double Corona	7	50	CC
Robusto	Robusto	5	50	CC
Grand Corona	Churchill	6½	46	CC
Long Corona	Corona	6	44	CC
Torpedo	Torpedo	6¼	53	CC
Lonsdale	Lonsdale	7	42	CC
Petit Corona	Petit Corona	5	42	CC
Pyramid	Pyramid	6½	53	CC
Toro	Collector's Tin	6	50	CC

The Gurkha brand has been around, in one form or another, since 1887. That's as long as the Gurkhas, a Nepalese tribe who fought for the British in World Wars I and II, have been around. This edition shows a mild-to-medium body, with a Connecticut wrapper and a light finish. It is presented in boxes of 25, except for the Pyramids (bundles of 25) and the Collector's Tin (tin of 25). Limited to about 600,000 cigars per year, Gurkhas are hard to find, yet plentiful compared to the 25,000-unit Gurkha Vintage line, which is slated for U.S. distribution in the near future.

H M
Handmade in Manila, the Philippines.

Wrapper: Indonesia   *Binder: Philippines*   *Filler: Philippines*

HANDMADE CIGARS: BRAND LISTINGS

Shape	Name	Lgth	Ring	Wrapper
Corona	Petit Corona	5½	42	CC
Toro	Torito	5¾	52	CC
Churchill	Doble Corona	7	47	CC
Lonsdale	Corona	7	42	CC
Double Corona	Churchill	7½	52	CC
Corona	Special Havana Corona	5½	44	CC

H M stands for Humberto Mendoza and this tribute to the late Cuban farmer is a
mild blend of tobaccos featuring an Indonesian wrapper grown in Java and
offered in beautiful Narra wood boxes of 25. A Connecticut-wrapped edition is
also planned.

H. UPMANN
Handmade in the La Romana, Dominican Republic.

Wrapper: Indonesia   Binder: Dom. Rep.   Filler: Dom. Rep.

Shape	Name		Lgth	Ring	Wrapper
Grand Corona	Churchills		5⅝	46	CM
Churchill	Corona Imperiales		7	46	CM
Petit Corona	Corona Major	(tubed)	5	42	CM
Corona	Coronas		5½	42	CM
Corona	Corona Cristals (glass tube)		5½	42	CM
Toro	Coronas Bravas		6½	48	CM
Long Panatela	El Prado		7	36	CM
Lonsdale	Lonsdales		6⅝	42	CM
Churchill	Monarch	(tubed)	7	46	CM
Panatela	Naturales	(tubed)	6⅙	36	CM
Lonsdale	No. 2000		7	42	CM

Panatela	Panatela Cristal *(glass tube)*	6¾	38	CM
Robusto	Pequenos No. 100	4½	50	CM
Corona Extra	Pequenos No. 200	4½	46	CM
Petit Corona	Pequenos No. 300	4½	42	CM
Petit Corona	Petit Coronas	5	42	CM
Panatela	Extra Finos Gold *(tubed)*	6¾	38	CM
Panatela	Finos Gold *(tubed)*	6⅛	36	CM
Petit Corona	Tubos Gold *(tubed)*	5	42	CM
Machine-made with short-filler:				
Cigarillo	Aperitif	4	28	CM
Small Panatela	Demi Tasse	4½	33	CM

Legendary is the only way to describe the H. Upmann brand, originated in Cuba in 1844. Today's Dominican-produced Upmann appeared in the U.S. for the first time in 1975 and combines a medium-bodied taste with first-class construction and a consistency – even through a change in wrapper tobacco from Cameroon to Indonesia – which makes this brand a dependable favorite of smokers everywhere.

H. UPMANN CABINET SELECTION
Handmade in La Romana, Dominican Republic.

Wrapper: Indonesia   *Binder: Dom. Rep.*   *Filler: Dom. Rep.*

Shape	Name	Lgth	Ring	Wrapper
Giant	Columbo	8	50	CM
Robusto	Corsario	5½	50	CM
Robusto	Robusto	4¾	50	CM

The larger girth of these marvelous cigars affords the smoker a full volume of smoke and a richness of taste and aroma that smaller-ring cigars cannot provide. The enthusiast will appreciate the "boite nature" packaging of 50 cigars per box.

HANDMADE CIGARS: BRAND LISTINGS

H. UPMANN CHAIRMAN'S RESERVE
Handmade in La Romana, Dominican Republic.

Wrapper: USA/Connecticut   Binder: Dom. Rep.   Filler: Brazil, Dom. Rep.

Shape	Name	Lgth	Ring	Wrapper
Long Panatela	Chairman's Reserve	7½	38	CC
Churchill	Churchill	6¾	48	CC
Double Corona	Double Corona	7	50	CC
Robusto	Robusto	5	50	CC
Torpedo	Torpedo	6	50	CC

This new brand, introduced in 1996, offers smokers a chance to sample the blend made for Consolidated Cigar Corporation's owner, Ron Perelman. It is medium-bodied and elegantly made; the Chairman's Reserve is individually boxed in a mahogany slide-top case! The other shapes are available in 20s.

HABANA GOLD
Handmade in Danli, Honduras.

Wrappers: Black Label—Indonesia; White Label—Nicaragua

Binder: Nicaragua   Filler: Nicaragua

Shape	Name	Lgth	Ring	Wrapper
Petit Corona	Petite Corona	5	42	CC-CM
Long Corona	Corona	6	44	CC-CM
Robusto	Robusto	5	50	CC-CM
Pyramid	Torpedo	6	52	CC-CM
Double Corona	Churchill	7	52	CC-CM
Churchill	Double Corona	7½	46	CC-CM
Giant	Presidente	8½	52	CC-CM
Torpedo	No. 2	6⅛	52	CC-CM

Cuban-seed tobaccos are married with wrappers from Nicaragua (White Label) or Sumatra-grown leaves (Black Label) to create a distinctive new brand: Habana Gold. Medium in body, these cigars continue to age as they are offered in cellophane sleeves inside beautiful cedar boxes.

HABANA GOLD STERLING VINTAGE
Handmade in San Pedro Sula, Honduras.

Wrapper: Ecuador *Binder: Ecuador* *Filler: Nicaragua*

Shape	Name	Lgth	Ring	Wrapper
Petit Corona	Petite Corona	5	42	CM
Long Corona	Corona	6	44	CM
Robusto	Robusto	5	50	CM
Pyramid	Torpedo	6	52	CM
Double Corona	Churchill	7	52	CM
Churchill	Double Corona	7½	46	CM
Giant	Presidente	8½	52	CM
Torpedo	No. 2	6⅛	52	CM

This new blend includes an Ecuador-grown wrapper and binder, offering dark, full flavor, thanks to the specially aged wrapper leaf. The taste is nothing less than "sterling."

HABANICA
Handmade in Condega, Nicaragua.

Wrapper: Nicaragua *Binder: Nicaragua* *Filler: Nicaragua*

Shape	Name	Lgth	Ring	Wrapper
Churchill	Serie 747	7	47	CM
Grand Corona	Serie 646	6	46	CM
Panatela	Serie 638	6	38	CM
Corona Extra	Serie 546	5¼	46	CM
Robusto	Serie 550	5	50	CM
Torpedo	Serie T	6	52	CM

HANDMADE CIGARS: BRAND LISTINGS

Created in 1995, this is a medium-bodied smoke that is smooth and non-acidic. Made in Condega, Nicaragua, it combines choice Havana-seed tobaccos grown in nearby Jalapa to create a pleasant, rich taste.

HAMILTONS
Handmade in La Romana, Dominican Republic.

Wrapper: Indonesia   Binder: Dom. Rep.   Filler: Dom. Rep.

Shape	Name	Lgth	Ring	Wrapper
Churchill	George I	7½	48	CC
Robusto	George II	5	50	CC
Torpedo	George III	6	50	CC
Lonsdale	George IV	6½	44	CC
Corona	George V	5½	42	CC
Long Panatela	George VI	7½	38	CC
Cigarillo	George VII	4½	28	CC
Panatela	George VIII	6¾	38	CC

This brand debuted in 1996, established by the noted actor and celebrity George Hamilton, a man who is never without his trademark tan. These eight sizes are made in the Consolidated Cigar Company factory in the Dominican Republic, and differ from the separate series produced by Tabacos Dominicanos. This is a medium-to-full-bodied blend and is available only at selected retailers.

HAMILTONS HOUSE
Handmade in Tamboril, Dominican Republic.

Wrapper: Indonesia   Binder: Dom. Rep.   Filler: Dom. Rep.

Shape	Name	Lgth	Ring	Wrapper
Robusto	Robusto	5	52	CC
Long Corona	Corona	6	44	CC
Toro	Toro	6	50	CC
Double Corona	Double Corona	7	50	CC
Torpedo	Torpedo	6	54	CC

HANDMADE CIGARS: BRAND LISTINGS

Beautifully made, but not quite as deeply tanned as George Hamilton himself, this is a medium-bodied range introduced in late 1997. You can enjoy them in elegant boxes of 25.

HAMILTONS RESERVE
Handmade in Santiago, Dominican Republic.

Wrapper: USA/Connecticut   *Binder: Dom. Rep.*   *Filler: Dom. Rep.*

Shape	Name	Lgth	Ring	Wrapper
Cigarillo	Lady H	5	26	CC
Panatela	Ashley	5½	38	CC
Long Panatela	Zorro	7½	38	CC
Corona	Corona	5½	42	CC
Churchill	Don Jorge	7	48	CC
Robusto	Robusto	5	50	CC
Double Corona	King George	7½	50	CC
Giant	Lord H	9¼	50	CC
Torpedo	Torpedo	6⅛	52	CC

A 1996 companion brand to the Hamiltons brand above, this nine-shape line is produced at the Tabadom factory in Santiago. This is a full-bodied blend with a smooth Connecticut wrapper.

HABANOS HATUEY
Handmade in Santiago, Dominican Republic.

Wrapper: USA/Connecticut   *Binder: Dom. Rep.*   *Filler: Dom. Rep.*

Shape	Name	Lgth	Ring	Wrapper
Lonsdale	Lonsdale	6½	44	CC
Corona	Corona	5½	42	CC
Churchill	Churchill	6⅞	48	CC
Robusto	Robusto	5	48	CC

HANDMADE CIGARS: BRAND LISTINGS

This medium-bodied brand was introduced in 1995 and offers excellent construction and lots of flavor. It is offered in boxes of 25.

HANNIBAL
Handmade in Mission Escuba, Indonesia.

Wrapper: Indonesia   *Binder: Indonesia*   *Filler: Indonesia*

Shape	Name	Lgth	Ring	Wrapper
Churchill	El Supremo	7	47	CC
Lonsdale	Excelsior	7	44	Ma
Petit Corona	Excelencia	5	44	CC
Pyramid	El Jumbo	5½	44	CC
Corona	Imperiales Corona	5½	44	CC
Double Corona	Premo del Premo	7½	52	CC
Robusto	Obelisco	5½	52	CC
Robusto	Poco de Paz	5	52	CC
Perfecto	Barracuda	5	52	CC
Panatela	La Fortuna	6	35	CC
Short Panatela	Excelencia Infanta	4	39	CC
Panatela	Contessa	6	39	CC
Long Panatela	Prima Donna	7½	39	CC
Robusto	Poco Dulce	5	52	CC
Double Corona	Premo del Mundo	7	52	CC
	Handmade with short filler:			
Giant	Emperador	15	125	CC
Lonsdale	Sensacionales	6¾	44	CC
Cigarillo	Duquesa	4½	20	CC
Short Panatela	Valentino Casanova	5	35	CC
Corona	Christobal Colon	5¼	44	CC

HANDMADE CIGARS: BRAND LISTINGS

Available in the U.S. in 1997, the foundations of this brand go back to 1586 when Havana seeds and cuttings were planted at the Mission Escuba in Indonesia. These are medium and medium-to-full bodied cigars, handmade in some unusual shapes including the trumpet-style El Jumbo and the perfecto-tipped Barracuda, which also has a pigtail head. For a test of patience, try the gigantic Emperador with a ring gauge of 125, the largest available anywhere. The Poco Dulce and Premo del Mundo sizes are blended for a fuller-bodied flavor. All of the tobaccos are aged for at least two years.

HASA REY
Handmade in Danli, Honduras.

Wrapper: Honduras   *Binder: Honduras*   *Filler: Honduras*

Shape	Name	Lgth	Ring	Wrapper
Toro	Churchill	6½	52	CM
Short Panatela	Petit	4¼	38	CM
Toro	Toro	6⅛	50	CM
Grand Corona	No. 1	6½	46	CM
Corona	No. 4	5½	44	CM

The name is a phonetic version of the Yiddish word "chazarai," (pronounced HAAS-a-RYE) originally referring to junk or trash, but now in use as a general reference to goods or "stuff." This cigar stuff dates from 1969 and is a full-bodied bundle of 25 cigars. Stuff one in your mouth and light up!

HAVANA
Handmade in Union City, New Jersey, USA.
Wrapper: Dominican Republic, Mexico, USA/Connecticut
Binder: Mexico, USA/Connecticut   *Filler: Dominican Republic, Honduras*

Shape	Name	Lgth	Ring	Wrapper
Giant	Churchill	8	50	CC-Ma
Double Corona	Silverano	7	50	CC-Ma
Toro	Torito	6½	50	CC-Ma
Churchill	Imperiale	7½	46	CC-Ma

Lonsdale	Presidente	6½	44	CC-Ma
Long Corona	Senadore	6	44	CC-Ma
Long Panatela	Ninfa	7	36	CC-Ma
Lonsdale	Fuma	7	44	CC-Ma
Torpedo	Torpedo	6	54	CC-Ma
Pyramid	Pyramid	5½	46	CC-Ma
Robusto	Robusto	5	50	CC-Ma

This cigar is made by the Boquilla cigar factory in Union City. These are medium-to-full bodied cigars – now banded – with a wider range of shapes and wrappers available.

HAVANA 7
Handmade in Miami, Florida, USA.

Wrapper: Ecuador   Binder: Dom. Rep.   Filler: Honduras, Nicaragua

Shape	Name	Lgth	Ring	Wrapper
Double Corona	President	7½	50	CC
Double Corona	Churchill	7	50	CC
Churchill	Double Corona	6¾	46	CC
Grand Corona	7 Classic	6½	46	CC
Lonsdale	Corona	6½	44	CC
Corona	Petite Corona No. 4	5½	43	CC
Robusto	Robusto	5	50	CC
Torpedo	Torpedo	6½	52	CC

Here is a 1996-introduced series offering a medium-to-full body. Not always easy to find, this carefully-made line is offered in cedar boxes of 25.

HAVANA BLENDS
Handmade in Santiago, Dominican Republic.
Wrapper: Dominican Republic or Indonesia
Binder: Dominican Republic   Filler: Dominican Republic

HANDMADE CIGARS: BRAND LISTINGS

Shape	Name	Lgth	Ring	Wrapper
Giant	Churchill	8	50	CM
Robusto	Robusto	5½	50	CM
Grand Corona	Double Corona	6½	46	CM
Long Corona	Corona	6	44	CM
Long Panatela	Lancero	7	36	CM
Panatela	Monarch	6	36	CM
Slim Panatela	Panetela	5	30	CM

Here is a mild-to-medium-bodied brand introduced in 1997, already featured on national television, offered in boxes of 25.

HAVANA CLASE
Handmade in San Pedro Sula, Honduras.

Wrapper: Ecuador   *Binder: Nicaragua*   *Filler: Nicaragua*

Shape	Name	Lgth	Ring	Wrapper
Double Corona	Churchill	7	50	CC
Robusto	Rothchild	5½	50	CC
Lonsdale	Corona Gorda	6½	44	CC
Corona	Corona	5½	42	CC

Introduced in 1997, this is a medium-bodied cigar that features Cuban-seed filler leaves and Sumatra-seed wrappers. It is offered in boxes of 25.

HAVANA CLASSICO
Handmade in Santiago, Dominican Republic.

Wrapper: USA/Connecticut, Pennsylvania   *Binder: Ecuador*
Filler: Colombia, Dominican Republic, Indonesia

Shape	Name		Lgth	Ring	Wrapper
Robusto	Robusto	*(tubed)*	5	50	CC-Ma
Lonsdale	Corona Classic	*(tubed)*	6½	42	CC-Ma

| Double Corona | Churchill | (tubed) | 7¼ | 50 | CC-Ma |
| Torpedo | Torpedo | (tubed) | 6½ | 54 | CC-Ma |

This brand was created in 1994 and is a featured maduro-wrapped brand of the Caribbean Cigar Company. This is a full-bodied brand which utilizes a Pennsylvania-grown wrapper. The newer Connecticut-wrapped version offers a medium-bodied taste. You can take your choice in elegant boxes of 25, with each cigar encased in individual glass tubes!

HAVANA COOL
Handmade, with short filler, in Esteli, Nicaragua.

Wrapper: Nicaragua   Binder: Nicaragua   Filler: Nicaragua

Shape	Name	Lgth	Ring	Wrapper
Long Corona	Alhambra	6	44	CM
Robusto	Granada	5	50	CM
Churchill	Riviera	7	48	CM
Short Panatela	Salamanca	4	38	CM

This is a medium-to-full bodied smoke introduced in 1996 and made with all-Nicaraguan tobacco and offered in boxes of 25.

HAVANA KING
Handmade in Santiago, Dominican Republic.

Wrapper: Dom. Rep.   Binder: Dom. Rep.   Filler: Dom. Rep.

Shape	Name	Lgth	Ring	Wrapper
Double Corona	Presidente	7½	50	CC
Churchill	Churchill	6⅞	46	CC
Long Corona	Corona	6	44	CC
Torpedo	Torpedo	6	52	CC
Robusto	Robusto	5	50	CC

Here is a mild-bodied brand featuring all-Dominican tobaccos and offered in protective cellophane sleeves inside boxes of bundles of 25.

HANDMADE CIGARS: BRAND LISTINGS

HAVANA KING
Handmade in Santiago, Dominican Republic.

Wrapper: Dom. Rep.   Binder: Dom. Rep.   Filler: Dom. Rep.

Shape	Name	Lgth	Ring	Wrapper
Double Corona	Presidente	7½	50	CC
Churchill	Churchill	6⅞	46	CC
Long Corona	Corona	6	44	CC
Torpedo	Torpedo	6	52	CC
Robusto	Robusto	5	50	CC
Small Panatela	Rosas	5	30	CC

This brand is a little richer than its sibling above, with a medium-to-full-bodied blend of all-Dominican tobaccos offered in protective cellophane sleeves inside boxes of bundles of 25.

HAVANA RESERVE
BY DON LINO
Handmade in Santiago, Dominican Republic.

Wrapper: USA/Connecticut   Binder: Dom. Rep.   Filler: Dom. Rep.

Shape	Name	Lgth	Ring	Wrapper
Lonsdale	No. 1	6½	44	CC
Corona Extra	Toros	5½	46	CC
Long Panatela	Panatela	6	36	CC
Double Corona	Churchill	7½	50	CC
Petit Corona	Petit Corona	4¾	40	CC
Robusto	Robustos	4¾	50	CC

Introduced in 1993, Havana Reserve was made in Honduras through 1996. In 1997, production was moved to the Dominican Republic. It is a handmade cigar with Dominican long filler and binder that assures consistent, medium-bodied taste and burning qualities. The wrapper is selected from only the finest Connecticut leaf for the unique taste that is only found in Havana Reserve.

HANDMADE CIGARS: BRAND LISTINGS

HAVANA ROYALE
Handmade in Santiago, Dominican Republic.

Wrapper: Indonesia   Binder: Dom. Rep.   Filler: Dom. Rep.

Shape	Name	Lgth	Ring	Wrapper
Torpedo	Torpedo	6	54	CC
Giant	Presidente	8	50	CC
Churchill	Churchill	7	48	CC
Toro	Royale	6	50	CC
Long Corona	Gran Corona	6	44	CC
Robusto	Robusto	4½	50	CC

Sumatra wrapper? Cuban-seed binder and filler? Mild-to-medium-bodied taste! Olé! New in 1997, Havana Royales are presented in elegant, cedar-chest-style boxes of 25 cigars each, individually protected by cellophane sleeves.

HAVANA SELECT
Handmade in Esteli, Nicaragua.

Wrapper: Indonesia   Binder: Nicaragua   Filler: Dom. Rep.

Shape	Name	Lgth	Ring	Wrapper
Robusto	Robusto	5	50	CM
Robusto	Corona Gorda	5½	50	CM
Torpedo	Torpedo	6	54	CM
Long Corona	Corona	6	44	CM
Toro	Capone	6	60	CM
Toro	Toro	6½	50	CM
Double Corona	Churchill	7½	50	CM
Giant	Presidente	8	52	CM

Here is a full-bodied brand introduced in 1997 and offering a Sumatra wrapper and Piloto Cubano filler in a variety of shapes. Check out the fat Capone shape, or any of the others in boxes of 25.

HANDMADE CIGARS: BRAND LISTINGS

HAVANA SUNRISE
Handmade in Miami, Florida, USA.
Wrapper: Ecuador or USA/Connecticut

Binder: Dom. Rep.   Filler: Dom. Rep., Honduras, Indonesia, Nicaragua

Shape	Name	Lgth	Ring	Wrapper
Cigarillo	Panatela - Cache	5	28	Co
Robusto	Robusto	5	50	Co
Torpedo	Torpedo	6	54	Co
Long Corona	Corona	6	44	Co
Toro	Double Corona	6	48	Co
Toro	Emperador	6¼	54	Co
Churchill	Havana	6¾	46	Co
Torpedo	Pyramid	7	60	Co
Long Panatela	Lancero	7½	38	Co
Double Corona	Churchill	7½	50	Co
Giant	Presidente	8	52	Co

Created in the heart of "Little Havana" in Miami, Havana Sunrise cigars were introduced in 1996. Offering a medium-to-full-bodied flavor, they are presented in handsome cedar boxes of 25, where the cigars continue to age and obtain an even more elegant finish. The Churchill, Lancero and Panatela-Cache sizes are offered in boxes of 15.

HAVANA VERDE
Handmade in Danli, Honduras.

Wrapper: Indonesia   Binder: Honduras   Filler: Dom. Rep., Honduras

Shape	Name	Lgth	Ring	Wrapper
Robusto	Robusto	5	50	CC
Double Corona	Churchill	7	50	CC
Double Corona	Double Corona	7½	52	CC
Grand Corona	Corona Gorda	6	46	CC

HANDMADE CIGARS: BRAND LISTINGS

This brand debuted in late 1996, offering a medium-to-full body that features a Sumatra-seed wrapper. It is presented in varnished, all-cedar boxes of 25.

HEAVEN
Handmade in Santiago, Dominican Republic.

Wrapper: Ecuador   Binder: Dom. Rep.   Filler: Dom. Rep.

Shape	Name	Lgth	Ring	Wrapper
Double Corona	Scarface	7	50	CC-Ma
Torpedo	Machiavelli	6	54	CC-Ma
Long Corona	Bugsy	6	44	CC-Ma
Robusto	Sun Tzu	5	50	CC-Ma

Introduced in 1996, this is two lines within one brand: the Cloud Nine series offers a natural-shade wrapper with a medium-bodied flavor, while the Private Reserve has a Ecuadorian-grown maduro wrapper, which is medium-to-full in body. Either way, you can enjoy these cigars in boxes of 25.

HEAVENLY VANILLA
Handmade in Santiago, Dominican Republic.

Wrapper: USA/Connecticut   Binder: Dom. Rep.   Filler: Dom. Rep.

Shape	Name	Lgth	Ring	Wrapper
Small Panatela	Heavenly Vanilla	5	30	CC

This is a 1997-introduced, all-vanilla flavored cigar with a sweet tip, offered in boxes of 25.

HECHO A MANO DOMINICANA
Handmade in Santiago, Dominican Republic.

Wrapper: Indonesia   Binder: Dom. Rep.   Filler: Dom. Rep.

Shape	Name	Lgth	Ring	Wrapper
Robusto	No. 550	5½	50	CC
Grand Corona	No. 646	6½	46	CC
Long Corona	No. 644	6	44	CC

Double Corona	No. 750	7	50	CC

Introduced in 1997, this "made by hand"-named cigar offers a mild-to-medium body in boxes of 25.

HENRY CLAY
Handmade in La Romana, Dominican Republic.

Wrapper: USA/Connecticut   *Binder: Dom. Rep.*   *Filler: Dom. Rep.*

Shape	Name	Lgth	Ring	Wrapper
Corona	Brevas	5½	42	Ma
Corona Extra	Brevas a la Conserva	5⅝	46	Ma
Churchill	Brevas Finas	6½	48	Ma

There aren't a lot of sizes in this brand, but don't tell that to its devoted followers, who are lovers of its medium-bodied taste and Connecticut Broadleaf maduro wrappers. Undoubtedly named for the famous American politician of the same name (U.S. senator from Kentucky 1806-07, 1810-11, 1831-42, 1849-52; U.S. representative and Speaker of the House 1811-14, 1815-21, 1823-25; U.S. secretary of state 1825-29), this brand originated in Cuba and the Henry Clay factory in Havana is still pictured on the brand's box.

HENRY GEORGE
Handmade in Santiago, Dominican Republic.

Wrapper: USA/Connecticut   *Binder: Dom. Rep.*   *Filler: Dom. Rep.*

Shape	Name	Lgth	Ring	Wrapper
Double Corona	Double Corona	7½	49	CC
Lonsdale	Lonsdale	7	44	CC
Toro	Toro	6½	50	CC

Created in 1997, this is a medium-to-full-bodied brand, named after the famous American economist and New York mayoral candidate Henry George (1839-1897). If you prefer his cigar to his economic theories, you'll find it in bundles of 25.

HANDMADE CIGARS: BRAND LISTINGS

HERMOSA FLOR
Handmade in the Jalapa Valley, Nicaragua.

Wrapper: Indonesia   *Binder: Nicaragua*   *Filler: Nicaragua*

Shape	Name	Lgth	Ring	Wrapper
Double Corona	Viajante	7	54	CC-Ma
Double Corona	Presidente	7½	50	CC-Ma
Toro	Toro	6	50	CC-Ma
Lonsdale	No. 3	6½	44	CC-Ma
Robusto	Corona	5½	48	CC-Ma
Robusto	Robusto	4½	52	CC-Ma

Created in 1995, this medium-bodied cigar is offered with a Sumatra-grown wrapper in either shade and binder and filler leaves from Nicaragua. You can find it in all-cedar cabinets of 25 cigars each.

HIDALGO
Handmade, with mixed filler, in Colon, Panama.

Wrapper: Ecuador   *Binder: Mexico*

Filler: Dominican Republic, Honduras, Panama

Shape	Name	Lgth	Ring	Wrapper
Lonsdale	Cazadore	7	44	CC
Lonsdale	Fuma	7	44	Ma
Corona	Corona	5½	42	CC-Ma
Churchill	Double Corona	7	48	CC-Ma
Giant	Monarch	8½	52	CC-Ma

These medium-bodied cigars use mixed filler (long and short) and are offered in bundles of 20 cigars each.

HIDALGOS
Handmade in Veracruz, Mexico.

Wrapper: Mexico   *Binder: Mexico*   *Filler: Mexico*

HANDMADE CIGARS: BRAND LISTINGS

Shape	Name	Lgth	Ring	Wrapper
Robusto	Robusto	5	50	CC-Ma
Double Corona	Churchill	6¾	50	CC-Ma
Double Corona	Double Corona	7¼	50	CC-Ma

This product of the Escudo Habanero tobacco conglomerate is an all-Mexican cigar with a mild-to-medium taste. Introduced in 1997, it is offered in individual cellophane sleeves in boxes of 25.

HOBO
Handmade in Santiago, Dominican Republic.

Wrapper: Ecuador or Indonesia   Binder: Dom. Rep.   Filler: Dom. Rep.

Shape	Name	Lgth	Ring	Wrapper
Short Panatela	Compadre	5	38	CC
Petit Corona	El Rey	5	42	CC
Grand Corona	Amigo	6	46	CC
Robusto	Matador	5	50	CC
Double Corona	Patron	7	50	CC

This is a flavored brand, available in almond brandy, chocolate, cognac, rum, vanilla and sweet styles. It's a mild-bodied smoke, available in boxes of 25.

HOJA CUBANA
Handmade in Esteli, Nicaragua.

Wrapper: Ecuador   Binder: Honduras   Filler: Dom. Rep. Honduras, Nicaragua

Shape	Name	Lgth	Ring	Wrapper
Petit Corona	Punch	4	44	CM
Long Corona	Corona	6	44	CM
Robusto	Robusto	5	50	CM
Toro	Epicure	6	50	CM
Double Corona	Churchill	7	50	CM

Torpedo	Torpedo	6½	54	CM

This is a new cigar in 1997, with medium body. It offers a smooth draw and features an Ecuadorian-grown Rosado wrapper. It is presented in all-cedar, slide-top cabinet-style boxes of 25.

HOJA DE HONDURAS
Handmade in Danli, Honduras.

Wrapper: Ecuador *Binder: Honduras* *Filler: Honduras*

Shape	Name	Lgth	Ring	Wrapper
Double Corona	Churchill	7	50	CC
Giant	General	8½	52	CC
Giant	Inmensas	8	54	CC
Lonsdale	Number 1	7	43	CC
Long Panatela	Palma Extra	7	36	CC
Corona	Reyes	5½	42	CC
Toro	Toro	6	50	CC

These are medium-to-full bodied cigars, well constructed and offered in boxes of 25.

HOJA DE MEXICALI
Handmade in San Andres Tuxtla, Mexico.

Wrapper: Mexico *Binder: Mexico* *Filler: Mexico*

Shape	Name	Lgth	Ring	Wrapper
Lonsdale	Lonsdale	6⅝	42	CM
Long Corona	Royal Corona	6	42	CM
Double Corona	Soberano	7½	50	CM
Toro	Toro	6	50	CM-Ma
Giant	Viajante	8½	52	CM-Ma

HANDMADE CIGARS: BRAND LISTINGS

This Mexican "puro" is a heavy-bodied cigar created in 1985 with all-San Andres Valley tobaccos, offered in convenient bundles of 25 cigars each.

HOJA DE NICARAGUA
Handmade in Esteli, Nicaragua.

Wrapper: Nicaragua   *Binder: Nicaragua*   *Filler: Nicaragua*

Shape	Name	Lgth	Ring	Wrapper
Double Corona	Churchill	7	48	CM-Ma
Robusto	Consul	4½	52	CM-Ma
Toro	Corona	6	48	CM-Ma
Long Corona	Numero 3	6	44	CM-Ma
Long Corona	Numero 6	6	41	CM-Ma
Double Corona	Presidente	8	54	CM-Ma
Giant	Viajante	8½	52	CM-Ma
Double Corona	Diplomatico	7	52	CC-Ma
Panatela	Petits	5½	38	CC-Ma

Here is an all-Nicaraguan cigar offered in elegant boxes of 25, offering a spicy, medium-bodied taste thanks to a blend of Cuban-seed tobaccos.

HOJA DE ORO
Handmade in San Andres Tuxtla, Mexico.

Wrapper: Mexico   *Binder: Mexico*   *Filler: Mexico*

Shape	Name	Lgth	Ring	Wrapper
Double Corona	No. 100	7	50	CC-Ma
Double Corona	No. 101	7½	50	CC-Ma
Toro	No. 103	6	50	CC-Ma
Lonsdale	No. 104	6¾	45	CC-Ma
Robusto	No. 105	4½	50	CC-Ma
Grand Corona	No. 106	6	45	CC-Ma

Corona Extra	No. 107		5	45	CC-Ma

Another product of the famous San Andres Valley in Mexico, the Hoja de Oro line utilizes all-Mexican tobacco, including filler tobacco from San Andres mixed with Cuban-seed leaf grown in the northern part of the Mexican state of Veracruz. The binder is San Andres-grown while the wrapper is Sumatran-seed, also grown in the San Andres Valley.

HOJA REAL
Handmade in San Andres Tuxtla, Mexico.

Wrapper: Indonesia   *Binder: Mexico*   *Filler: Mexico*

Shape	Name	Lgth	Ring	Wrapper
Double Corona	Churchill	7½	50	CC
Robusto	Robusto	5½	50	CC
Long Corona	No. 1	6¼	44	CC

This brand has been around since about 1992, but available in the U.S. beginning in 1997. It combines a Sumatra wrapper with Mexican binder and filler tobaccos for a medium-bodied flavor. Each all-cedar box is numbered and personally signed by the master blender as proof of its quality.

HOMBRE DE ORO
Handmade in Villa Gonzalez, Dominican Republic.

Wrapper: Ecuador   *Binder: Mexico*   *Filler: Dom. Rep.*

Shape	Name	Lgth	Ring	Wrapper
Double Corona	Churchills	7½	50	CC
Lonsdale	Corona	6½	44	CC
Churchill	Double Corona	7	48	CC
Corona	Petit Corona	5½	42	CC
Robusto	Rothschild	4½	50	CC
Toro	Toro	6	50	CC

HANDMADE CIGARS: BRAND LISTINGS

This is a new cigar in 1997 offering a mild-bodied flavor that features Cuban-seed filler leaves grown in the Dominican Republic. It is presented in individual cellophane sleeves in cedar boxes of 25.

HONDURAS CUBAN TOBACCOS
Handmade in Danli, Honduras.

Wrappers: Costa Rica, Ecuador, Mexico, USA/Connecticut
Binders: Costa Rica, Dom. Rep., Honduras, Indonesia
Mexico, Nicaragua, USA/Pennsylvania
Fillers: Brazil, Costa Rica, Dom. Rep., Ecuador, Honduras,
Indonesia, Mexico, Nicaragua, Puerto Rico, USA/Connecticut

Shape	Name	Lgth	Ring	Wrapper
Torpedo	Torpedo: 1	7½	64	Varies
Torpedo	Torpedo: 2	7	64	Varies
Pyramid	Piramides: 1	6½	54	Varies
Pyramid	Piramides: 2	6	52	Varies
Pyramid	Piramides: 3	5½	52	Varies
Giant	Gigantes: 1	8	54	Varies
Giant	Gigantes: 2	11	50	Varies
Giant	Double Corona: 1	8½	52	Varies
Double Corona	Double Corona: 2	7½	52	Varies
Double Corona	Double Corona: 3	7	52	Varies
Double Corona	Churchill: 1	7¾	50	Varies
Double Corona	Churchill: 2	7	50	Varies
Double Corona	Churchill: 3	7	49	Varies
Double Corona	Churchill: 4	6⅞	49	Varies
Churchill	Churchill: 5	7	47	Varies
Toro	Toro: 1	6	54	Varies
Toro	Toro: 2	6	52	Varies

HANDMADE CIGARS: BRAND LISTINGS

Robusto	Robusto: 1	5¼	52	Varies
Robusto	Robusto: 2	5	50	Varies
Robusto	Robusto: 3	4½	50	Varies
Lonsdale	Lonsdale: 1	6½	44	Varies
Lonsdale	Lonsdale: 2	6½	43	Varies
Corona	Corona: 1	6	43	Varies
Corona	Corona: 2	6	42	Varies
Corona	Corona: 3	5½	42	Varies
Long Panatela	Palmas: 1	7	38	Varies
Panatela	Palmas: 2	6⅞	36	Varies
Slim Panatela	Petit	5½	34	Varies

The Honduras Cuban Tobaccos company in Danli, Honduras produces private label cigars from 15 different blends using leaves from around the world. HCT also offers its clients a choice of brand names, if desired, including CONQUISTADOR, DON CHRISTOBAL, DON RAMON and SEÑORIAL. Whether in bundles or boxes of 5, 10 or 25 cigars, these brands are high in quality and are even occasionally offered for public sale under one or more of the afore-mentioned brand names.

HONDURAS SPECIAL
Handmade in Danli, Honduras.

Wrapper: Honduras   *Binder: Honduras*   *Filler: Honduras*

Shape	Name	Lgth	Ring	Wrapper
Giant	No. 201	8½	52	CM
Short Panatela	No. 202	4½	36	CM
Double Corona	No. 203	7½	50	CM
Toro	No. 204	6	50	CM
Robusto	No. 205	4½	50	CM
Lonsdale	No. 206	6⅝	44	CM
Corona	No. 207	5½	42	CM

HANDMADE CIGARS: BRAND LISTINGS

Panatela	No. 208	6⅞	35	CM
Panatela	No. 209	6	36	CM
Corona Extra	No. 210	5½	46	CM

This hard-to-find brand is medium-bodied and sells quickly, thanks to its packaging in bundles of just 10 cigars, which keeps the modest price within reach of every smoker.

HOYO DE CORTEZ CORTO
Handmade, with medium filler, in Santiago, Dominican Republic.
Wrapper: Indonesia   Binder: Dom. Rep.   Filler: Dom. Rep.

Shape	Name	Lgth	Ring	Wrapper
Double Corona	Churchill	7½	52	CC
Churchill	Corona Gorda	7	48	CC
Robusto	Robusto	5	50	CC
Lonsdale	Panatela	6½	44	CC

Introduced in 1997, this is a value-priced cigar with a medium-bodied flavor and a Sumatra wrapper.

HOYO DE CORTEZ ESCOGIDO
Handmade in Santiago, Dominican Republic.
Wrapper: Indonesia   Binder: Dom. Rep.   Filler: Dom. Rep.

Shape	Name	Lgth	Ring	Wrapper
Double Corona	Churchill	7½	52	CC
Churchill	Gran Corona	7	48	CC
Robusto	Robusto	5	50	CC
Lonsdale	Panatela	6½	44	CC
Torpedo	Torpedo	7	54	CC

HANDMADE CIGARS: BRAND LISTINGS

This brand debuted in 1997 and offers a medium body, featuring a Sumatra-grown wrapper. It is presented in individual cellophane sleeves in all-cedar boxes of 25.

HOYO DE CORTEZ PREMERA CALIDAD
Handmade in Santiago, Dominican Republic.

Wrapper: Ecuador   *Binder: Dom. Rep.*   *Filler: Dom. Rep.*

Shape	Name	Lgth	Ring	Wrapper
Double Corona	Churchill	7½	52	CC
Churchill	Gran Corona	7	48	CC
Robusto	Robusto	5	50	CC
Torpedo	Torpedo	7	54	CC

Here is a 1997-introduced brand with a medium body and a Connecticut-seed wrapper grown in Ecuador. It is offered in protective cellophane sleeves and packed in all-cedar boxes of 25.

HOYO DE HONDURAS
Handmade in Danli, Honduras.

Wrapper: Honduras   *Binder: Honduras*   *Filler: Honduras*

Shape	Name	Lgth	Ring	Wrapper
Grand Corona	No. 1	6½	46	CM
Corona	No. 4	5½	44	CM
Toro	Churchill	6½	52	CM
Short Panatela	Petit	4¼	38	CM
Churchill	Presidente	6¾	48	CM
Toro	Toro	6⅛	50	CM

Created in 1985, this is an all-Honduran, full-bodied cigar, offered in economical bundles of 20.

HANDMADE CIGARS: BRAND LISTINGS

HOYO DE MONTERREY
Handmade in Cofradia, Honduras.

Wrapper: Ecuador or USA/Connecticut *Binder: Honduras*
Filler: Dominican Republic, Honduras and Nicaragua

Shape	Name	Lgth	Ring	Wrapper
Giant	Presidents	8½	52	CC-Ma
Double Corona	Sultans	7¼	54	CC-Ma
Churchill	Double Coronas	6¾	48	CC-Ma
Toro	Governors	6⅛	50	CC-Ma
Corona	Cafe Royales (tubed)	5⅝	43	CC-Ma
Small Panatela	Petit	4¾	31	CC-Ma
Grand Corona	Churchills	6¼	45	CC-Ma
Lonsdale	No. 1	6½	43	CC-Ma
Corona Extra	Coronas	5⅝	46	CC-Ma
Robusto	Rothschilds	4½	50	CC-Ma
Churchill	Cuban Largos	7¼	47	CC-Ma
Grand Corona	Dreams	5¾	46	CC-Ma
Corona	Super Hoyos	5½	44	CC-Ma
Long Corona	Ambassadors	6¼	44	CC-Ma
Slim Panatela	Largo Elegantes	7¼	34	CC-Ma
Cigarillo	Margaritas	5¼	29	CC-Ma
Corona	No. 55	5¼	43	CC-Ma
Panatela	Delights	6¼	37	CC-Ma
Short Panatela	Demitasse	4	39	CC-Ma
Petit Corona	Sabrosos	5	40	CC-Ma

This ancient brand began in Cuba but first appeared in a Honduran-manufactured blend in 1969. Hoyo de Monterrey cigars are medium-to-heavy in flavor. Handmade in Honduras, these are truly quality cigars with a large variety of sizes to give exceptional satisfaction to the smoker. The tobaccos are blended from four nations, including the Cuban-seed Honduran binder and Sumatra-seed wrappers from Ecuador. The maduro wrappers use only the finest Connecticut broadleaf available.

HUGO CASSAR
Handmade in Danli, Honduras.

Wrapper: Indonesia		Binder: Honduras			Filler: Honduras, Mexico
Shape	*Name*		*Lgth*	*Ring*	*Wrapper*
Robusto	No. 1		4¾	50	CC
Corona Extra	No. 2		5½	46	CC
Lonsdale	No. 3		6¾	44	CC
Churchill	No. 4		7	48	CC
Double Corona	No. 5		6¾	54	CC
Double Corona	No. 6		7½	50	CC
Giant	No. 7		8	52	CC

A careful blend and smooth draw is the mark of these cigars, which are expertly crafted, medium in body and packaged in bundles of 25 cigars. An excellent value.

HUGO CASSAR
Handmade in San Andres Tuxtla, Mexico.

Wrapper: Mexico		Binder: Mexico			Filler: Mexico
Shape	*Name*		*Lgth*	*Ring*	*Wrapper*
Robusto	Rothschild		4½	50	CC
Robusto	Robusto		5½	52	CC
Long Corona	Corona		6	42	CC
Toro	Toro		6½	50	CC
Double Corona	Churchill		7½	50	CC

Here is an all-Mexican brand with a Sumatra-seed, natural-shade, full-bodied wrapper grown in Mexico, offering a medium-to-full-bodied taste. You can find these modestly-priced line in all-cedar boxes of 25.

HUGO CASSAR
Handmade in San Andres Tuxtla, Mexico.

Wrapper: Mexico   *Binder: Mexico*   *Filler: Mexico*

Shape	Name	Lgth	Ring	Wrapper
Robusto	Tulum	4¾	50	CC-Ma
Long Corona	Monterey	6	42	CC-Ma
Panatela	Durango	6¾	36	CC-Ma
Double Corona	Veracruz	7	54	CC-Ma
Double Corona	Yucatan	7½	50	CC-Ma
Giant	Sierra Madre	8	52	CC-Ma

These cigars are Mexican puros, offered in both a natural and maduro wrapper. They offer a spicy, sweet flavor, with medium body, and are packaged in bundles of 25 cigars each.

HUGO CASSAR DIAMOND DOMINICAN
Handmade in Villa Gonzalez, Dominican Republic.

Wrapper: USA/Connecticut   *Binder: Dom. Rep.*   *Filler: Dom. Rep.*

Shape	Name	Lgth	Ring	Wrapper
Robusto	Robusto	4¾	50	CC
Corona	Corona	5½	42	CC
Grand Corona	Grand Corona	6	46	CC
Toro	Toro	6½	52	CC
Lonsdale	Lonsdale	7	44	CC
Giant	El Presidente	8	50	CC

This careful blend of aged tobaccos, introduced in 1996, produces a cigar which is filled with a rich spiciness, with cocoa flavors and a mild-to-medium body, and offered in specially-constructed cedar boxes of 20 (except for El Presidente, available in 10s).

HANDMADE CIGARS: BRAND LISTINGS

HUGO CASSAR DIAMOND DOMINICAN MYSTIQUE
Handmade in Villa Gonzalez, Dominican Republic.
Wrapper: Dominican Republic and USA/Connecticut
Binder: Dominican Republic   Filler: Dominican Republic

Shape	Name	Lgth	Ring	Wrapper
Torpedo	Torpedo	6	53	Stripe
Toro	Toro	6¼	50	Stripe
Lonsdale	Lonsdale	7	44	Stripe
Giant	Churchill	8	50	Stripe

Talk about unique! Here is a "barber pole" of a cigar with a double wrapper: Connecticut Shade and a Dominican brewleaf, surrounding Dominican binder and filler tobaccos, for a medium body. Introduced in 1996, there's no doubting the popularity of this new concept in cigar making, which is presented in bundles or all-cedar boxes of 20 (except for the Torpedo, available in boxes of 24).

HUGO CASSAR DIAMOND HONDURAN
Handmade in Danli, Honduras.
Wrapper: Ecuador   Binder: Dom. Rep.   Filler: Nicaragua

Shape	Name	Lgth	Ring	Wrapper
Robusto	Robusto	5	50	CC
Corona	Corona	5½	44	CC
Torpedo	Torpedo	6	53	CC
Toro	Double Corona	6½	52	CC
Grand Corona	Lonsdale	6⅝	46	CC
Double Corona	Presidente	7	49	CC
Double Corona	Chairman	7¾	50	CC

A luxury cigar that has all of the characteristics of the finest cigars made today. The filler is a special blend of aged tobaccos, bonded with a special Dominican binder. The reddish-brown, Ecuadorian shade-grown wrappers create a cigar that offers a sweet, medium-to-full-bodied taste and is slightly aromatic.

Cigar Legends: Hugo Cassar

Hugo Cassar is a very brave fellow.

Brave because he has put his family's name on 16 lines of cigars, leaving no doubt about who is responsible for the blending, production and ultimately, the smoking experience of those who try them.

Brave because he introduced the radical "barber pole" style cigar, the Hugo Cassar Mystique. The combination of the intertwined Connecticut and Dominican wrappers presents an unmistakable contrast – in appearance and taste – to the 1,000 or so other brands on the market. Developed in 1995, the Mystique offers a continuously reinvigorated flavor, as well as a visual experience unlike any other cigar. Today, there are imitators to be sure, but there is also a clear recognition of the leader in this unusual style. You can try the inventor's work in Dominican or Honduran-made editions.

Brave because all of this effort came as an outgrowth of his highly-successful clove and natural-tobacco cigarette business founded in the early 1980s. At a time when the mass-market cigarettes had all but eliminated those with all-natural construction, Cassar offered an alternative which has found an expanding market among smokers who recognize and appreciate quality.

All of this from a man born on the island of Malta, who endured World War II bombing of the island during his youth. Next to that, is it any wonder that Hugo rarely even blinks when introducing a new cigar? Viva Hugo!

HANDMADE CIGARS: BRAND LISTINGS

Hugo Cassar Diamond Honduran Mystique Classic
Handmade in Danli, Honduras.
Wrapper: Costa Rica and Ecuador

Binder: Dominican Republic   *Filler: Nicaragua*

Shape	Name	Lgth	Ring	Wrapper
Long Corona	Corona	6	44	CM
Toro	Toro	6½	52	CM
Torpedo	Torpedo	6	53	CM
Churchill	Churchill	7¾	47	CM

Introduced in 1996, this is a deeply-colored, beautifully-prepared "barber pole" cigar. It is a medium-to-full-bodied smoke with a double wrapper from Costa Rica (maduro shade) and Ecuador (natural shade). These cigars are elegantly presented in perfectly-fitted, all-cedar boxes of 20 cigars each.

Hugo Cassar Private Collection
Handmade in Tamboril, Dominican Republic.

Wrapper: Dom. Rep.   *Binder: Dom. Rep.*   *Filler: Dom. Rep.*

Shape	Name	Lgth	Ring	Wrapper
Robusto	Robusto	5	50	CC
Long Corona	Corona	6	42	CC
Torpedo	Torpedo	6	48	CC
Toro	Toro	6½	52	CC
Double Corona	Presidente	7½	49	CC

Here is a mild cigar introduced in 1996. It features all Dominican tobacco, is elegantly prepared and presented in stunning all-cedar boxes of 25 cigars.

Hugo Cassar Private Collection
Handmade in Danli, Honduras.

Wrapper: Ecuador   *Binder: Dom. Rep.*   *Filler: Mexico, Nicaragua*

HANDMADE CIGARS: BRAND LISTINGS

Shape	Name	Lgth	Ring	Wrapper
Robusto	Robusto	4¾	52	CC
Long Corona	Matador	6	42	CC
Toro	Elegantes	6	50	CC
Lonsdale	Imperial	7	44	CC
Double Corona	Emperador	7¾	47	CC

Beautifully finished, this is a full-bodied smoke with tobaccos from four nations. The cigars are presented in precisely-finished cedar boxes of 25 cigars each.

HUGO CASSAR PRIVATE COLLECTION
Handmade in Kudus, Indonesia.

Wrapper: Indonesia   *Binder: Indonesia*   *Filler: Brazil, Dom. Rep., Jamaica*

Shape	Name	Lgth	Ring	Wrapper
Toro	Toros	6	50	CC
Churchill	Churchill	7½	46	CC
Small Panatela	Petite Corona	4½	34	CC
Cigarillo	Mini	3¾	26	CC

Introduced in 1997, this is a medium-bodied cigar. The Toro and Churchill shapes have a Javan wrapper and filler from the Dominican Republic and Jamaica only, while the Petite Corona and Mini shapes add a Brazilian leaf in the filler and feature a Sumatran wrapper.

HUGO CASSAR PRIVATE COLLECTION
Handmade in San Andres Tuxtla, Mexico.

Wrapper: Mexico   *Binder: Mexico*   *Filler: Mexico*

Shape	Name	Lgth	Ring	Wrapper
Robusto	Rothschild	4½	50	Ma
Long Corona	Corona	6	42	Ma
Toro	Toro	6½	50	Ma

| Robusto | Robusto | 5½ | 52 | Ma |
| Double Corona | Churchill | 7½ | 50 | Ma |

From the fertile San Andres Valley comes the Hugo Cassar Private Collection. These are full-bodied cigars with all-Mexican tobacco, packed in cedar boxes to maintain them at the peak of flavor. The maduro wrappers are Mexican-grown, Cuban-seed leaves.

HUGO GOLD
Handmade in Esteli, Nicaragua.

Wrapper: Nicaragua   *Binder: Nicaragua*   *Filler: Nicaragua*

Shape	Name	Lgth	Ring	Wrapper
Long Corona	Corona	6	44	CM
Robusto	Robusto	5	52	CM
Toro	Toro	6	50	CM
Churchill	Churchill	6⅞	48	CM
Giant	Gigante	8	54	CM

This is the gold standard in Nicaraguan cigars, with a medium body and all-Nicaraguan tobaccos. The wrapper is Cuban-seed and you can find this elegant cigar in all-cedar boxes of 24.

HUGO SIGNATURE SERIES
Handmade in Villa Gonzalez, Dominican Republic.

Wrapper: Indonesia or Mexico   Binder: Dom. Rep.   Filler: Dom. Rep.

Shape	Name	Lgth	Ring	Wrapper
	Natural wrapper:			
Toro	Toro	6¼	50	CC
Lonsdale	Lonsdale	7	44	CC
Giant	Churchill	8	50	CC

	Maduro wrapper:			
Robusto	Robusto	5	52	Ma
Toro	Toro	6	50	Ma
Churchill	Lonsdale	7	48	Ma
Giant	Churchill	8	54	Ma

This is a medium-bodied cigar introduced in 1997. You can have your choice of a natural wrapper grown in Indonesia, or a yummy maduro wrapper from Mexico. In either case, these well-made cigars are offered in boxes of 24.

HUGO SIGNATURE SERIES
Handmade in Esteli, Nicaragua.

Wrapper: Indonesia   Binder: Nicaragua   Filler: Nicaragua

Shape	Name	Lgth	Ring	Wrapper
Lonsdale	Lonsdale	6¾	44	CC
Corona	Corona	5½	42	CC
Toro	Toro	6	50	CC
Robusto	Robusto	4¾	52	CC
Churchill	Churchill	7	48	CC
Giant	Gigante	8	54	CC

More Hugo! Just when you thought he's come up with every conceivable style of smoke from the Dominican Republic, Honduras and Mexico, here's a signature series from Nicaragua! It's a medium-bodied smoke introduced in 1996, presented upright in honeycombed boxes of 25.

HURRICANOS
Handmade in Danli, Honduras.

Wrapper: Ecuador   Binder: Honduras   Filler: Honduras, Nicaragua

Shape	Name	Lgth	Ring	Wrapper
Double Corona	Churchill	7	49	CM
Toro	Short Churchill	6	50	CM

Lonsdale	Lonsdale	7	43	CM
Robusto	Robusto	5	50	CM
Corona	Corona	5½	42	CM

It's a hurricane! This brand, new in 1997, stormed its way to popular acclaim when first introduced and is now delighting smokers with a medium-bodied taste. It is presented in cellophane sleeves, packed in cedar boxes of 25.

IDEAL
Handmade in San Juan, Puerto Rico.
Wrapper: USA/Pennsylvania

Binder: USA/Pennsylvania   *Filler: Dom. Rep., Puerto Rico*

Shape	Name	Lgth	Ring	Wrapper
Churchill	Cazadores No. 5	7	46	CM
Long Corona	Cazadores No. 6	6	42	CM

Here is a value-priced, handmade and medium-bodied brand with Pennsylvania wrapper and binder and a blended filler. It is offered in economical bundles of 25.

IL FIORE D'ORO
Handmade in Danli, Honduras.
Wrapper: Honduras   *Binder: Honduras*
Filler: Dominican Republic, Honduras, Mexico, Nicaragua

Shape	Name	Lgth	Ring	Wrapper
Giant	Presidente	8½	52	CM
Toro	Toro	6	50	CM
Churchill	Churchill	7	48	CM
Robusto	Robusto	4¾	50	CM
Long Corona	Corona Gordo	6	44	CM

New for 1997, this is a full-bodied line with a Connecticut-seed wrapper and filler tobaccos featuring Cuban-seed leaves. It is offered in boxes of 25.

HANDMADE CIGARS: BRAND LISTINGS

IMPERIO CUBANO
Handmade in Miami, Florida, USA.

Wrapper: Ecuador   Binder: Mexico   Filler: Dom. Rep.

Shape	Name	Lgth	Ring	Wrapper
Torpedo	Torpedo	6¼	54	CC
Churchill	Churchill	6¾	48	CC
Toro	Toro	6	50	CC
Robusto	Robusto	5	50	CC
Lonsdale	Lonsdale	6¾	43	CC
Corona	Corona	5½	43	CC

From Little Havana in Miami comes this brand, introduced in 1996, available only in limited distribution and with limited production. Master cigar maker Juan Sosa offers a medium-bodied flavor in this brand, thanks in part to a Connecticut-seed wrapper grown in Ecuador.

INDIAN ANNIVERSARY LIMITED RESERVE SERIES A
Handmade in Danli, Honduras.

Wrapper: Ecuador   Binder: Mexico   Filler: Honduras, Nicaragua

Shape	Name	Lgth	Ring	Wrapper
Robusto	The Bear	5	50	CM
Pyramid	The Bison	6½	54	CM
Churchill	The Buffalo	7	47	CM

Introduced in 1997, here is a specially-aged brand with exquisite construction and a full-bodied flavor. It features a Sumatra-seed wrapper and is offered in boxes of 25.

INDIAN CLASSIC
Handmade in Danli, Honduras.
Wrapper: Ecuador, USA/Connecticut

Binder: Mexico   Filler: Honduras, Nicaragua

HANDMADE CIGARS: BRAND LISTINGS

Shape	Name	Lgth	Ring	Wrapper
Double Corona	Chief	7½	52	CM
Long Corona	Warrior	6	42	CM
Robusto	Boxer	4½	50	CM-Ma
Pyramid	Teepee	5½	52	CM-Ma
Toro	Tomahawk	6	52	CM-Ma
Slim Panatela	Arrow	5½	34	CM

Here is a much-celebrated 1995 addition to the cigar scene, offering a medium-bodied taste in an exquisitely-crafted cigar. The brand features an Ecuadorian-grown, Sumatra-seed wrapper and Mexican Morron binder and is offered in all-cedar boxes of 25. The glorious maduro series debuted in 1997 and features a Connecticut Broadleaf wrapper and a medium-to-full-bodied taste.

INDIAN HEAD
Handmade in Danli, Honduras.

Wrapper: Ecuador   *Binder: Honduras*   *Filler: Dom. Rep., Honduras*

Shape	Name	Lgth	Ring	Wrapper
Small Panatela	Princesse	4½	30	CC
Slim Panatela	Petit Coronas	5½	34	CC
Panatela	Lindas	5½	38	CC
Corona	No. 4	5½	42	CC-Ma
Slim Panatela	Pinceles	7	30	CC
Long Corona	No. 2	6	43	CC-Ma
Panatela	Panatelas	6⅞	35	CC
Long Corona	Corona Gorda	6¼	44	CC-Ma
Robusto	Rothschild	5	50	CC-Ma
Lonsdale	No. 1	7	43	CC-Ma
Long Panatela	Palma de Mayorca	8	38	CC
Toro	Toros	6	50	CC-Ma

HANDMADE CIGARS: BRAND LISTINGS

Churchill	Corona Grande	7½	46	CC
Double Corona	Churchills	6⅞	49	CC-Ma
Double Corona	Monarch	7	52	CC-Ma
Double Corona	Soberanos	7¾	50	CC-Ma
Giant	Viajantes	8½	52	CC-Ma
Giant	Gigantes	8	54	CC-Ma
Torpedo	Torpedos	7	54	CC
	Mixed filler:			
Lonsdale	Fumas	7	44	CC
Long Corona	Cazadores	6¼	44	CC

Indian Head cigars are mild-to-medium in strength using Honduran filler and binder tobaccos combined with a Ecuador-grown, Connecticut-seed wrapper (natural and maduro). They are presented in bundles of 25 cigars each. The mixed-filler Fumas is noteworthy for its twisted head.

INDIAN PRINCESS
Handmade in Danli, Honduras.

Wrapper: Ecuador   *Binder: Honduras*   *Filler: Honduras*

Shape	Name	Lgth	Ring	Wrapper
Giant	Chief	8	52	CC
Churchill	Churchill	6⅞	48	CC
Corona	Corona	5½	43	CC
Corona Extra	Corona Extra	5½	46	CC
Long Corona	Long Corona	6	42	CC
Double Corona	Presidente	7½	50	CC
Robusto	Rothschild	4¾	50	CC
Toro	Toro	6¼	50	CC

HANDMADE CIGARS: BRAND LISTINGS

This is a medium-bodied brand introduced in 1996. It is offered in value-priced bunldes of 25.

INDIGO
Handmade in Santiago, Dominican Republic.

Wrapper: Indonesia   *Binder: Dom. Rep.*   *Filler: Dom. Rep.*

Shape	Name	Lgth	Ring	Wrapper
	Natural shape:			
Corona	Corona	5½	42	CM
Long Corona	Corona Grande	6	42	CM
Grand Corona	Gran Corona	6	46	CM
Robusto	Robusto	5	48	CM
Robusto	Robusto Gordo	5	50	CM
Churchill	Churchill	7	47	CM
Toro	Toro	6	50	CM
Toro	Gran Indigo	6	60	CM
	Box pressed:			
Corona	Corona	5½	42	CM
Lonsdale	Lonsdale	6½	42	CM
Robusto	Robusto	5	48	CM
Grand Corona	Gran Corona	6	46	CM
Churchill	Churchill	7	47	CM
Torpedo	Torpedo	6	52	CM

Introduced in 1997, Indigo offers eight outstanding shapes including the police baton-sized Gran Indigo. This is a medium-bodied brand offered in two groups: round-shaped and box-pressed.

INFIESTA
Handmade in St. Augustine, Florida, USA.
Origin of wrapper, binder and filler leaves varies, depending on availability.

HANDMADE CIGARS: BRAND LISTINGS

Shape	Name	Lgth	Ring	Wrapper
Giant	Soberanos	8	50	DC-CC-Ma
Small Panatela	Miniatures	4½	30	DC-CC-Ma
Churchill	Churchill	7	48	DC-CC-Ma
Toro	Governos	6	50	DC-CC-Ma
Lonsdale	Cetros No. 1	7	43	DC-CC-Ma
Lonsdale	Cetros No. 2	6½	42	DC-CC-Ma
Long Panatela	Panatelas No. 3	7	36	DC-CC-Ma
Slim Panatela	Panatelas Rabito	7	30	DC-CC-Ma
Long Corona	San Marcos	6	44	DC-CC-Ma
Lonsdale	Fumas	7	44	DC-CC-Ma
Churchill	Cazadores	7	46	DC-CC-Ma
Corona	No. 4	5½	42	DC-CC-Ma

This all-long filler brand is made by hand under the supervision of the El Canelo factory of Miami, Florida.

INSURGENTES
Handmade, with short fuller, in San Andres Tuxtla, Mexico.
Wrapper: Mexico   Binder: Mexico   Filler: Mexico

Shape	Name	Lgth	Ring	Wrapper
Corona	Petite Corona	5½	41	CM

Here is a single size, short-filler brand which offers a medium-bodied, somewhat earthy flavor at a modest price.

INTERNATIONAL
Handmade in Miami, Florida, USA.
Wrapper: Ecuador   Binder: Dom. Rep.   Filler: Dom. Rep., Indonesia

Shape	Name	Lgth	Ring	Wrapper
Robusto	Robusto	4¾	50	CC

Long Corona	Corona	6	44	CC
Toro	Toro	6	50	CC
Double Corona	Presidente	7½	52	CC
Torpedo	Torpedo	6¼	52	CC

Introduced in 1996 and formerly known as Alta Gracia, this Miami-based brand offers a medium-bodied taste in a slightly sweet blend, presented in boxes of 25.

IRACEMA
Handmade in Cruz des Almas, Brazil.

Wrapper: Brazil   *Binder: Brazil*   *Filler: Brazil*

Shape	Name	Lgth	Ring	Wrapper
Corona	Santana	5⅜	43	CM
Corona	Autentico-Fumas	5¼	44	CM
Lonsdale	Macumba	6½	42	CM
Corona	Mata Fina Especial	5¼	44	CM
Cigarillo	Santo Amaro	3½	25	CM
	Machine-made:			
Cigarillo	Cigarrilhas	3⅛	28	CM

Introduced about 1960, this cigar is a product of the famous Suerdieck Charutos e Cigarrilhas Ltda. factory in Brazil. The range offers a medium-bodied flavor in four shapes. The tobaccos are all Brazilian grown, including Mata Fina leaf for the wrappers of the Macumba and Mata Fina shapes offering up a seductive, tropical aroma.

ISABELLA
Handmade in Santiago, Dominican Republic.

Wrapper: Indonesia   *Binder: Dom. Rep.*   *Filler: Dom. Rep.*

Shape	Name	Lgth	Ring	Wrapper
Double Corona	Churchill	7	50	CM
Toro	Toro	6	50	CM

Robusto	Robusto	5	50	CM
Corona	Corona	5½	42	CM
Lonsdale	Lonsdale	6½	44	CM

New for 1997, this is a mild-bodied cigar . . . but with character, thanks to its Sumatra wrapper. You can guess which character it is after enjoying a box of 25!

ISLAND AMARETTO
Handmade, with medium filler, in Jakarta, Indonesia.

Wrapper: Indonesia   *Binder: Indonesia*
Filler: Colombia, Dominican Republic, Indonesia

Shape	Name	Lgth	Ring	Wrapper
Cigarillo	Treasures	3⅝	20	CM
Short Panatela	Bellissima	4½	36	CM
Petit Corona	Bella	4¾	42	CM
Lonsdale	Grand Bella	7	42	CM

This is a flavored cigar produced by the Caribbean Cigar Company and introduced in 1995. It is handmade using 100% tobacco, but with medium filler instead of long filler leaves. It has a full-bodied taste and is offered in boxes of 25 cigars each.

ISLANDS
Handmade in Malan, Indonesia.

Wrapper: Indonesia   *Binder: Indonesia*   *Filler: Indonesia*

Shape	Name	Lgth	Ring	Wrapper
Churchill	Lombok	7	48	CC
Toro	Sumbawa	6½	50	CC
Pyramid	Komodo	6	52	CC
Robusto	Borneo	5	50	CC
Long Corona	Sumatra	6	42	CC

HANDMADE CIGARS: BRAND LISTINGS

If the green-skinned, red-lipped, moustache-bearing mascot isn't enough to draw your attention, check out the Rattan-patterned bamboo boxes and hand-woven Batik cloth in which the cigars are packed. Oh, yes, this 1997-introduced brand is mild in flavor thanks to its all-Indonesian leaves.

J. CORTES
Handmade in Santo Domingo, Dominican Republic.
Wrapper: USA/Connecticut
Binder: Dominican Republic   Filler: Brazil, Dominican Republic, Indonesia

Shape	Name	Lgth	Ring	Wrapper
Slim Panatela	No. 2	5	32	CC
Corona	No. 3	5½	40	CC
Toro	No. 6	6½	45	CC

J. Cortes is an old Belgian brand, which started in 1926. The handmade, all-long-filler shapes were introduced in 1994 and offer a mild taste. They are presented uncellophaned in all-cedar boxes of 25.

J. L. FERRER 1891
Handmade in the Dominican Republic.
Wrapper: USA/Connecticut   Binder: Dom. Rep.   Filler: Dom. Rep.

Shape	Name	Lgth	Ring	Wrapper
Torpedo	Torpedo	6½	54	CC
Robusto	Entracto	5	50	CC
Lonsdale	Churchill	7	44	CC
Toro	Robusto	6	50	CC
Corona	Corona	5½	42	CC

Here is a medium-bodied cigar with Dominican Olor and Piloto Cubano filler leaves, offered in boxes of 25 or in special plexi-topped display cases of 20.

HANDMADE CIGARS: BRAND LISTINGS

JAMAICA BAY
Hand-rolled in Kingston, Jamaica.

Wrapper: USA/Connecticut   Binder: Mexico   Filler: Dom. Rep., Mexico

Shape	Name	Lgth	Ring	Wrapper
Double Corona	No. 100	7½	49	CC
Toro	No. 200	6	50	CC
Lonsdale	No. 300	6¾	45	CC
Lonsdale	No. 400	6½	42	CC
Panatela	No. 500	6¾	38	CC
Corona	No. 600	5½	42	CC

These are mild cigars, machine-bunched and then hand-wrapped with
Connecticut Shade leaves. They are offered only in limited distribution, in
bundles of 20 cigars each.

JAMAICA GEM
Handmade in Kingston, Jamaica.

Wrapper: Mexico   Binder: Mexico   Filler: Jamaica, Mexico

Shape	Name	Lgth	Ring	Wrapper
Petit Corona	Petit Corona	5	40	CC
Slim Panatela	Palma	6¾	34	CC
Corona	Corona	5½	40	CC
Long Corona	Royal Corona	6	40	CC
Lonsdale	Corona Grande	6½	42	CC
Giant	Churchill	8	51	CC
Lonsdale	Double Corona	7	45	CC
Grand Corona	Magnum	6	47	CC
Double Corona	Giant Corona	7½	49	CC
Slim Panatela	Palmitas	6	30	CC

HANDMADE CIGARS: BRAND LISTINGS

This cigar was created in 1983 and is made in Jamaica, but with a Mexican-grown, Connecticut-seed wrapper. It is medium-to-full in body and offered in bundles of 25 cigars each.

JAMAICA GOLD
Handmade in Santa Rosa de Copan, Honduras.

Wrapper: Honduras   *Binder: Honduras*   *Filler: Honduras*

Shape	Name	Lgth	Ring	Wrapper
Double Corona	Prince	7¾	50	CM
Panatela	Earl	6¾	38	CM
Lonsdale	Baron	6½	44	CM
Long Corona	Queen	6¼	43	CM
Panatela	Count	5½	38	CM
Corona	Duke	5½	43	CM
Small Panatela	Dutchess	4½	30	CM
Toro	King	6	50	CM
Torpedo	Torpedo	7	52	CM

Created in 1982, this is a mild-to-medium-bodied cigar, with a Connecticut-seed wrapper. The brand is offered in all-wooden boxes of 25 cigars, plus a ten-pack for the Prince size and a 120-count box for the Dutchess shape.

JAMAICA HERITAGE
Handmade in Kingston, Jamaica.

Wrapper: Ecuador   *Binder: Mexico*
Filler: Dominican Republic, Jamaica, Mexico

Shape	Name	Lgth	Ring	Wrapper
Double Corona	No. 100	7½	49	CC-Ma
Giant	No. 102	8	50	CC-Ma
Toro	No. 200	6	50	CC-Ma
Grand Corona	No. 500	6	45	CC-Ma

Lonsdale	No. 400	6½	42	CC-Ma
Corona	No. 700	5½	42	CC-Ma

From one of the finest factories in Kingston, Jamaica comes Jamaica Heritage, a celebration of the famous Jamaican cigar industry. These cigars offer a mild, rich taste and are available in bundles of 25.

JIMENEZ
Handmade in Bronx, New York.
Wrapper: Cameroon or USA/Connecticut
Binder: Indonesia   Filler: Colombia, Dom. Rep.

Shape	Name	Lgth	Ring	Wrapper
Long Corona	Corona	6	44	CC
Toro	Toro	6	54	CC
Cigarillo	Masterpiece	7	28	Ma
Robusto	Robusto	5	50	CC
Torpedo	Torpedo	6½	52	CC
Petit Corona	Petite Corona	5	42	CC
Lonsdale	No. 1	6½	42	CC
Churchill	Churchill	7	47	CC-CM
Double Corona	Fabuloso	7	54	CM

Introduced in 1997, this is a medium-bodied brand with a choice of wrappers in the larger sizes, offered in packs of 25. Pick one up on your way to see the Bronx Bombers at Yankee Stadium!

JOHN AYLESBURY
Handmade in Danli, Honduras.
Wrapper: Honduras, Mexico   Binder: Honduras   Filler: Honduras

Shape	Name	Lgth	Ring	Wrapper
Toro	Churchill	6⅝	49	CC-Ma

HANDMADE CIGARS: BRAND LISTINGS

Lonsdale	Pinceles	7	43	CC
Long Corona	Puritos	6	43	CC
Panatela	Morning	5½	39	CC
Panatela	Panatela XTR	6¾	36	CC
Small Panatela	Picos	4½	32	CC
Toro	Rothschild	6	50	CC-Ma

Introduced in 1978, the John Aylesbury Honduran series has a medium body and a subtle aroma. All seven sizes are offered with a Honduran-grown wrapper, while the maduro-wrapped shapes feature a Mexican leaf.

JOHN AYLESBURY PREMIUM
Handmade in La Romana, Dominican Republic.

Wrapper: USA/Connecticut   Binder: Dom. Rep.   Filler: Dom. Rep.

Shape	Name	Lgth	Ring	Wrapper
Slim Panatela	Panatela	6	32	CC
Lonsdale	Lonsdale	6⅝	42	CC
Corona	Corona	5½	42	CC
Panatela	Elegante	6¾	38	CC
Churchill	Churchill	7	46	CC
Robusto	Rothschild	4½	50	CC

The John Aylesbury Premium line offers a mild-bodied smoke in a beautifully-constructed cigar that debuted in 1991. These cigars are matured and then offered in graceful, solid mahogany boxes.

JOHN HAY
Handmade in Santiago, Dominican Republic.

Wrapper: Indonesia   Binder: Honduras or Nicaragua   Filler: Honduras, Nicaragua

Shape	Name	Lgth	Ring	Wrapper
Double Corona	Churchill	7	50	CM

Lonsdale	Corona	6½	42	CM
Giant	President	8	52	CM
Toro	Robusto Largo	6	50	CM
Robusto	Robusto	5	50	CM

Here is a tribute to U.S. Secretary of State John Hay (1838-1905), who served from 1898-1905 and was noted for beginning the first U.S. contacts with China. The brand, introduced in 1997, features a picture of Hay on the all-cedar box, which encloses 25 medium-bodied smokes.

JOHN T'S
Handmade in the Dominican Republic.

Wrapper: Dom. Rep.   *Binder: Dom. Rep.*   *Filler: Pipe tobaccos*

Shape	Name		Lgth	Ring	Wrapper
Panatela	Brown Gold	(tubed)	5½	38	CC
Panatela	Cherry Cream	(tubed)	5½	38	CC
Panatela	Capuccino	(tubed)	5½	38	CC
Panatela	Cafe Ole	(tubed)	5½	38	CC
Panatela	Amaretto	(tubed)	5½	38	CC

Nicknamed "The Crowdpleaser," this brand has been created to offer a more pleasant, sweeter aroma than most cigars. The result is a mild smoke with considerable flavor (take your pick!) in a panatela shape packed in bundles of 20 tubes. Unusual to say the least!

JOSE BENITO
Handmade in Santiago, Dominican Republic.

Wrapper: Indonesia   *Binder: Dom. Rep.*   *Filler: Dom. Rep.*

Shape	Name	Lgth	Ring	Wrapper
Double Corona	Presidente	7¾	50	CM
Double Corona	Churchill	7	50	CM
Lonsdale	Corona	6¾	43	CM

Panatela	Panatela	6¾	38	CM
Long Corona	Palma	6	43	CM
Panatela	Petite	5½	38	CM
Robusto	Rothschild	4¾	50	CM
Small Panatela	Chico	4¼	32	CM
Cigarillo	Havanitos	5	25	CM
Giant	Magnum	8¾	60	CM

Since its introduction in the 1970s, every Jose Benito cigar is the result of individually-chosen long-filler tobacco blended from the finest Dominican farms and specially selected Indonesian wrapper leaves. They result in a medium-bodied smoke, upholding the family's tradition of excellence in tobacco which began in the mid-1800s.

JOSÉ GIRBÉS
Handmade in Santiago, Dominican Republic.

Wrapper: USA/Connecticut   Binder: Dom. Rep.   Filler: Dom. Rep.

Shape	Name	Lgth	Ring	Wrapper
Corona	Corona	5½	43	CC
Robusto	Robusto	5	50	CC
Lonsdale	Lonsdale	6½	43	CC
Toro	Toro	6	50	CC
Double Corona	Churchill	7½	50	CC
Pyramid	Piramide	6	52	CC
Cigarillo	Purito	4	24	CC
Cigarillo	Petite Panetela	5	28	CC

This richly-flavored, medium-bodied cigar is handmade in the Doninican Republic and features a Dominican binder and filler and a genuine Connecticut-grown wrapper.

HANDMADE CIGARS: BRAND LISTINGS

JOSE L. PIEDRA
Handmade in Esteli, Nicaragua.

Wrapper: Nicaragua *Binder: Nicaragua* *Filler: Nicaragua*

Shape	Name	Lgth	Ring	Wrapper
Double Corona	Emperador	7½	50	CC
Robusto	Excelentes	5	50	CC
Churchill	Gran Presidente	6⅞	46	CC
Robusto	Robusto	5½	52	CC

An old Cuban brand still in production today, this is a Nicaraguan-made, long-filler, handmade cigar that offers full-bodied flavor. Introduced in 1996, it is presented in cedar boxes of 25.

JOSE LLOPIS
Handmade in Colon, Panama.

Wrapper: Ecuador *Binder: Mexico*
Filler: Dominican Republic, Honduras, Panama

Shape	Name	Lgth	Ring	Wrapper
Giant	Viajante	8½	52	CC-Ma
Churchill	Churchill	7	48	CC-Ma
Lonsdale	No. 1	7	43	CC-Ma
Lonsdale	No. 2	6½	43	CC-Ma
Corona	No. 4	5½	43	CC-Ma
Long Panatela	Palma Extra	7	36	CC-Ma
Robusto	Rothschild	4¾	50	CC-Ma
Double Corona	Soberano	7¼	52	CC-Ma

Introduced in 1984, this cigar is offered in bundles of 20 and is medium in strength; it should not be confused with its milder sibling brand, Jose Llopis Gold.

HANDMADE CIGARS: BRAND LISTINGS

JOSE LLOPIS GOLD
Handmade in Colon, Panama.

Wrapper: USA/Connecticut　　　　　　　　　　　　*Binder: Mexico*
　　　　　　　Filler: Dominican Republic, Honduras, Panama

Shape	Name	Lgth	Ring	Wrapper
Giant	Viajante	8½	52	CC-Ma
Churchill	Churchill	7	48	CC-Ma
Lonsdale	No. 1	7	43	CC-Ma
Lonsdale	No. 2	6½	43	CC-Ma
Long Panatela	Palma Extra	7	36	CC-Ma
Corona	No. 4	5½	43	CC-Ma
Robusto	Rothschild	4½	50	CC-Ma

Created in 1989, this well-respected brand is all handmade and wrapped in
Connecticut shade-grown leaves (natural) or Connecticut Broadleaf (maduro). All
of its sizes are offered in cedar boxes. This mild-bodied cigar is distinctive for its
gold band.

JOSE MARTI
Handmade in Santiago, Dominican Republic.

Wrapper: USA/Connecticut　　　　*Binder: Dom. Rep.*　　　　*Filler: Dom. Rep.*

Shape	Name	Lgth	Ring	Wrapper
Slim Panatela	Creme	6	34	CC
Corona	Corona	5½	42	CC
Lonsdale	Palma	7	42	CC
Lonsdale	Maceo	6⅞	44	CC
Robusto	Robusto	5½	50	CC
Double Corona	Jose Marti	7½	50	CC

Introduced in 1994, Jose Marti is a very mild, sweet cigar with a golden brown
Connecticut wrapper. It offers excellent draw, a silky, smooth taste and a
wonderful aroma. Offered in boxes of 20.

HANDMADE CIGARS: BRAND LISTINGS

JOSE MARTI
Handmade in Esteli, Nicaragua.

Wrapper: Ecuador   *Binder: Honduras*
Filler: Dominican Republic, Honduras, Nicaragua

Shape	Name	Lgth	Ring	Wrapper
Double Corona	Don Juan	7¼	54	CC
Lonsdale	Lonsdale	6½	44	CC
Churchill	Valentino	7	48	CC
Torpedo	Masaya Figurado	6¾	54	CC
Pyramid	Trinidad Piramide	7	48	CC
Short Panatela	Petite Lancero	4½	38	CC
Corona	Remedios	5½	44	CC
Robusto	Robusto	4½	52	CC
Giant	Rey del Rey	8½	52	CC
Toro	Robusto Extra	6½	52	CC

This is a new, 1996 blend for the Jose Marti brand, offering a spicy, full-bodied taste and showing off an Ecuadorian-grown, Sumatra-seed wrapper. The brand has an excellent array of shapes and sizes, including two shaped cigars.

JOSE R. OLIVA
Handmade in Ocotal, Nicaragua.

Wrapper: Indonesia   *Binder: Nicaragua*   *Filler: Nicaragua*

Shape	Name	Lgth	Ring	Wrapper
Giant	Presidente	8	52	CC
Double Corona	Churchill	7	50	CC-Ma
Robusto	Rothschild	5	50	CC-Ma
Torpedo	Belicoso	6	52	CC-Ma
Toro	Double Corona	6½	48	CC
Corona	Lonsdale	5¾	43	CC

HANDMADE CIGARS: BRAND LISTINGS

From the famous house of Oliva comes this "JRO" cigar, a mild-to-medium-bodied beauty which features a Sumatra wrapper. You can find them in cellophane sleeves inside all-cedar boxes of 25.

JOYA DE HONDURAS
Handmade in Danli, Honduras.

Wrapper: Ecuador   *Binder: Nicaragua*   *Filler: Honduras*

Shape	Name	Lgth	Ring	Wrapper
Corona	Cuatro	5½	42	CM
Long Corona	Cetros	6	44	CM
Double Corona	Churchill	7	50	CM
Giant	Soberano	8½	54	CM
Long Panatela	Palma	7	38	CM
Toro	Toro	6	50	CM
Pyramid	Pyramid	5½	52	CM
Robusto	Robusto	5	50	CM
Torpedo	Torpedo	6	52	CM

This is an old brand which has now been revived in a mild-to-medium-bodied range and offering a size of interest to almost every smoker. Made by hand in Honduras, these cigars are offered in all-wood boxes of 25.

JOYA DEL REY
Handmade in Danli, Honduras.

Wrapper: Indonesia   *Binder: Honduras*   *Filler: Dom. Rep., Nicaragua*

Shape	Name		Lgth	Ring	Wrapper
Robusto	Robusto Grande	(tubed)	4¾	50	CC
Corona	Corona Grande	(tubed)	5½	42	CC
Toro	Toro Grande	(tubed)	6	50	CC
Double Corona	Churchill Grande	(tubed)	7	49	CC
Long Panatela	No. 35		7	35	CC

HANDMADE CIGARS: BRAND LISTINGS

HANDMADE CIGARS: BRAND LISTINGS

Corona	No. 42	5½	42	CC
Lonsdale	No. 43	7	43	CC
Double Corona	No. 49	7	49	CC
Toro	No. 50	6	50	CC
Giant	No. 52	8½	52	CC

The translation of this brand name means "Gems of the King." This is a medium-bodied brand using Cuban-seed tobaccos for the binder and filler. Joya del Rey cigars are offered in all-cedar boxes of 25.

JOYA DE NICARAGUA
Handmade in Esteli, Nicaragua.

Wrapper: Ecuador, Costa Rica   Binder: Nicaragua   Filler: Nicaragua

Shape	Name	Lgth	Ring	Wrapper
Giant	Viajante	8½	52	CC
Churchill	Churchill	6⅞	49	CC
Toro	Toro	6	50	CC
Slim Panatela	Senorita	5½	34	CC
Small Panatela	Piccolino	4½	30	CC
Panatela	Petit	5½	38	CC
Robusto	Consul	4½	52	CC
Lonsdale	No. 1	6⅝	44	CC
Panatela	No. 5	6⅞	35	CC
Long Corona	No. 6	6	42	CC
	Maduro Deluxe:			
Double Corona	Presidente	7½	50	Ma
Toro	Toro	6	50	Ma
Robusto	Robusto	4¾	52	Ma

HANDMADE CIGARS: BRAND LISTINGS

Always popular since its introduction in the 1970s, this cigar was newly blended in 1996. The standard series now sports a mild taste thanks to an Ecuadorian-grown, Connecticut-seed wrapper, while the Costa Rica-grown maduro line is a full-bodied smoke. These cigars are meticulously cured and skillfully rolled which makes them truly the "Jewel of Nicaragua."

JOYA DEL CIBAO
Handmade in Tamboril, Dominican Republic.

Wrapper: Indonesia *Binder: Dom. Rep.* *Filler: Dom. Rep.*

Shape	Name	Lgth	Ring	Wrapper
Double Corona	Santiagos	7½	50	CM
Robusto	Navarettes	5	50	CM
Lonsdale	Cancas	6¾	42	CM
Corona	Quinguas	5¾	42	CM

Here is a full-bodied brand which was introduced in 1996. It offers a Sumatra-grown wrapper and is presented in boxes of 25.

J-R ULTIMATE
Handmade in Cofradia, Honduras.

Wrapper: Honduras *Binder: Honduras* *Filler: Honduras*

Shape	Name		Lgth	Ring	Wrapper
Lonsdale	Cetro		7	42	DC-CC-CM-Ma
Grand Corona	Corona		5⅝	45	DC-CC-CM-Ma
Grand Corona	Corona Tubos	*(tubed)*	5⅝	45	CC
Churchill	Double Corona		6¾	48	DC-CC-CM-Ma
Giant	Estelo Individuel		8½	52	CM
Cigarillo	Habanellas		5	28	CC
Double Corona	No. 1		7¼	54	CC-CM-Ma
Long Corona	No. 5		6⅛	44	DC-CC-CM-Ma
Giant Corona	No. 10		8¼	47	CC-CM

HANDMADE CIGARS: BRAND LISTINGS

Toro	Padron	6	54	CC-Ma
Panatela	Palma Extra	6⅞	38	CC-CM-Ma
Panatela	Petit Cetro	5½	38	CC-CM-Ma
Petit Corona	Petit Corona	4⅝	43	CC-CM-Ma
Giant	President	8½	52	CC-CM-Ma
Robusto	Rothschild	4½	50	CC-CM-Ma
Panatela	Slims	6⅞	36	CC-CM-Ma
Giant Corona	Super Cetro	8¼	43	CC
Toro	Toro	6	50	DC-CC-CM-Ma

This is a full-bodied cigar with Havana-seed wrappers in multiple shades. Made in Cofradia, Honduras, these cigars are carefully aged for at least one year and packed uncellophaned in thick cedar cases.

JUAN CLEMENTE
Handmade in Santiago, Dominican Republic.

Wrapper: USA/Connecticut   Binder: Dom.Rep.   Filler: Dom.Rep.

Shape	Name	Lgth	Ring	Wrapper
	Classic:			
Petit Corona	Corona	5	42	Co
Long Corona	Grand Corona	6	42	Co
Panatela	Panatela	6½	34	Co
Long Panatela	Especiale	7½	38	Co
Churchill	Churchill	6⅞	46	Co
Cigarillo	Demi Tasse	3⅝	34	Co
Small Panatela	"530"	5	30	Co
Petit Corona	Demi-Corona	4	40	Co
Robusto	Rothschild	4⅞	50	Co
Giant	Gigante	9	50	Co

Giant	Gargantua	13	50	Co
Cigarillo	Mini	4⅛	22	Co
Panatela	Especiale No. 2	6	38	Co
	Club Selection:			
Toro	No. 1	6	50	Co
Corona Extra	No. 2	4½	46	Co
Lonsdale	No. 3	7	44	Co
Corona	No. 4	5¾	42	Co
Torpedo	Obelisco	6	54	Co

Sought after since 1982, this is the product of a small cigar factory that has only one, ultra-demanding client. The Juan Clemente Classic line offers a full, round, medium-bodied smoke with complex flavors and spices. The vintage "Club Selection" line is a more robust blend, with four years of aging that creates a rich, smooth character for an exquisite cigar for the connoisseur.

JUAN DOLIO
Handmade in the Dominican Republic.

Wrapper: Indonesia   *Binder: Dom. Rep.*   *Filler: Dom. Rep.*

Shape	Name	Lgth	Ring	Wrapper
Double Corona	Senator	7	50	CM
Lonsdale	Elegante	6½	44	CM
Robusto	Principe	5	50	CM
Petit Corona	Corona	5	44	CM

Juan Dolio has been sold in the Dominican Republic as a domestic cigar as far back as 1876. Now exported to the United States, it features a Sumatra wrapper, Dominican-grown Olor binder and Dominican-grown Olor and Piloto Cubano leaves in the filler. It is considered medium-bodied.

HANDMADE CIGARS: BRAND LISTINGS

JUAN GUILLERMO DE ROBLES
Handmade in Dingelstadt, Germany.

Wrapper: Dom. Rep.   Binder: Dom. Rep.   Filler: Dom. Rep.

Shape	Name	Lgth	Ring	Wrapper
Double Corona	Churchill	7	49	CC
Toro	Lonsdale	6½	49	CC
Panatela	Panatella Larga	6	38	CC
Robusto	Robusto	5	50	CC

This is a handmade cigar from Germany, with a mild taste and all-Dominican leaves. It is offered in slide-top cedar boxes of 10 or 25.

JUAN LOPEZ
Handmade in Danli, Honduras.

Wrapper: Ecuador   Binder: Honduras   Filler: Honduras

Shape	Name	Lgth	Ring	Wrapper
Giant	No. 300	8½	52	CM
Double Corona	No. 301	7½	50	CM
Toro	No. 302	6	50	CM
Lonsdale	No. 303	6½	42	CM
Corona	No. 304	5½	42	CM

Recognize the brand name? It's a famous old Havana brand, produced for the U.S. market since the mid-1980s as a bundle cigar of good quality. The all-handmade blend of Honduras tobaccos plus an Ecuadorian-grown, Connecticut-seed wrapper is offered in 25-cigar packs and has a medium-to-full body.

JUAN Y RAMON
Handmade in Villa Gonzalez, Dominican Republic.
Wrapper: Dominican Republic or USA/Connecticut

Binder: Dominican Republic   Filler: Dominican Republic

HANDMADE CIGARS: BRAND LISTINGS

Shape	Name	Lgth	Ring	Wrapper
Toro	Short Churchill	6½	50	CC-Ma
Pyramid	Figurado	6¼	53	CC-Ma
Double Corona	Churchill	7½	50	CC-Ma
Corona	Corona	5½	42	CC
Long Corona	Grand Corona	6	44	CC-Ma
Panatela	Panatela	6	38	CC
Robusto	Rothschild	5	50	CC-Ma
Small Panatela	Fino	5	30	CC-Ma

Introduced in 1996, this is a medium-bodied blend of Piloto Cubano and Olor leaves in the filler surrounded by a Connecticut Shade-grown wrapper (maduros are Dominican-grown). Elegantly packaged, Juan y Ramon cigars are available in all-cedar boxes of 20, except for the Figurado, offered in 24s.

JUSTINO
Handmade in Santiago, Dominican Republic.

Wrapper: USA/Connecticut   Binder: Dom. Rep.   Filler: Dom. Rep.

Shape	Name	Lgth	Ring	Wrapper
Robusto	Ponton	5	50	CC
Corona	Candelones	5¾	43	CC
Torpedo	Navarette	6¼	52	CC
Churchill	Mejia	7	48	CC

Here is a mild-bodied cigar in four popular shapes. The Connecticut wrapper is combined with Olor binders and Piloto Cubano filler leaves for a smooth draw and presented in boxes of ten or 20.

HANDMADE CIGARS: BRAND LISTINGS

KENNEDY
Handmade in Santiago, Dominican Republic.

Wrapper: Indonesia *Binder: Dom. Rep.* *Wrapper: Dom. Rep.*

Shape	Name	Lgth	Ring	Wrapper
Double Corona	President	7½	50	Ma
Robusto	Robusto	5	50	Ma
Churchill	Churchill	6¾	48	Ma
Long Corona	Corona	6	44	Ma

These are medium-bodied, well-made cigars that feature Indonesian wrappers and are presented in boxes of 25.

KEY WEST HAVANA GOLD LABEL
Handmade in Santiago, Dominican Republic.

Wrapper: USA/Connecticut *Binder: Dom. Rep.* *Wrapper: Dom. Rep.*

Shape	Name	Lgth	Ring	Wrapper
Slim Panatela	Amelia	5	30	CC
Long Panatela	Marti	7	38	CC
Long Corona	Estella	6	44	CC
Robusto	Cortez	5	50	CC
Double Corona	Sanchez	7½	50	CC
Pyramid	Piramide	7	54	CC

Introduced in 1994, this brand has become a Key West tradition! It offers a mild-to-medium-bodied flavor, packed in bundles or tins of 25 cigars each.

KING COBRA
Handmade in Santiago, Dominican Republic.

Wrapper: Indonesia or USA/Connecticut *Binder: Dom. Rep.* *Filler: Dom. Rep.*

Shape	Name	Lgth	Ring	Wrapper
Grand Corona	Primo	6	46	CC-Ma

Robusto	Robusto	5	50	CC-Ma
Toro	Presidente	6½	50	CC-Ma
Double Corona	Supremo	7	50	CC-Ma
Double Corona	Churchill	7½	50	CC-Ma

Here is a full-bodied brand, available in your choice of Connecticut (natural) or Indonesian (maduro) wrappers. Introduced in 1997, you can find this cigar in hand-carved boxes of 25.

KING DOMINICAN
Handmade in Santiago, Dominican Republic.

Wrapper: USA/Connecticut   Binder: Honduras
Wrapper: Brazil, Dominican Republic

Shape	Name	Lgth	Ring	Wrapper
Lonsdale	No. 1	6½	42	CC-Ma
Corona	No. 2	5½	42	CC-Ma
Panatela	No. 3	6¾	38	CC
Panatela	No. 5	5½	38	CC
Robusto	No. 6	4¾	50	CC-Ma
Giant	No. 7	8½	52	CC-Ma
Double Corona	No. 8	7	60	CC-Ma
Giant	No. 9	10	66	CC-Ma
Double Corona	No. 10	7½	49	CC-Ma
Robusto	No. 13	5	66	CC-Ma

A full, yet deliciously mild bundled cigar, introduced in 1989. The natural-wrapped version has a smooth herbal character, while the maduro wrapper offers a rich earthiness to the palate. These delicate flavors and the line's smooth draw are truly unique, as are its range in some of the largest available ring gauges.

HANDMADE CIGARS: BRAND LISTINGS

KING RICHARD
Handmade in Miami, Florida, USA.

Wrapper: USA/Connecticut   Binder: USA/Connecticut   Filler: Dom. Rep.

Shape	Name	Lgth	Ring	Wrapper
Double Corona	Royal Tycoon	7	50	CM-Ma
Churchill	Royal Churchill	6⅞	46	CM-Ma
Lonsdale	Royal Duke	6¾	42	CM-Ma
Torpedo	Royal Stud	6	52	CM-Ma
Robusto	Royal Knight	5	50	CM-Ma
Panatela	Royal Madame	6⅞	36	CM

Take your choice of natural or maduro wrappers in this brand, created in 1996 in Little Havana. The taste varies between mild-to-medium (Stud, Madame), medium (Duke, Knight) and full-bodied (Tycoon, Churchill).

KINGS CLUB
Handmade in Danli, Honduras.

Wrapper: USA/Connecticut   Binder: Dom. Rep.   Filler: Dom. Rep.

Shape	Name	Lgth	Ring	Wrapper
Pyramid	Alfonso XII	7	50	CC-Ma
Giant	King Ferdinand	8½	52	CC-Ma
Robusto	Henry VII	4½	50	CC-Ma
Lonsdale	King Philip	6¼	44	CC-Ma
Toro	Louis XIV	6	50	CC-Ma
Churchill	King Arthur	7	48	CC-Ma

Here is a new brand for 1997, named after great royals of the past. Cigar history buffs will not be surprised that the largest cigar is named after Ferdinand of Spain, one of the most important monarchs in the promotion of tobacco after its discovery by Columbus. The cigars themselves are medium-bodied and feature a blend of Dominican-grown Piloto Cubano filler leaves. The Kings Club is offered in all-cedar boxes of 25.

Churchills and Double Coronas

These larger shapes are much loved for the full flavor they can deliver. The dimensions of these shapes include:

- Churchill   6¾-7⅞ inches long; 46-48 ring.
- Double Corona   6¾-7¾ inches long; 49-54 ring.

Pictured opposite, from left to right, are:

                                                (shape)

- **NAPA DOMINICAN RESERVE** *Churchill*
  (Dominican Republic) 7½ x 50   Double Corona

- **DON PEPE** *Double Corona*
  (Brazil)   7½ x 50   Double Corona

- **HAMILTONS** *George I*
  (Dominican Republic) 7½ x 48   Churchill

- **MATCH PLAY** *Olympic*
  (Dominican Republic) 7½ x 50   Double Corona

- **CREDO LIGAS** *No. 4–Churchill*
  (Honduras)   7 x 48   Churchill

- **ULTIMATE DOMINICAN CLASSIC** *Churchill*
  (Dominican Republic) 7 x 48   Churchill

- **GRAND NICA** *Churchill*
  (Nicaragua)   7 x 52   Double Corona

HANDMADE CIGARS: BRAND LISTINGS

KINGSTON
Handmade in San Andres Tuxtla, Mexico.

Wrapper: Mexico   Binder: Mexico   Filler: Mexico

Shape	Name	Lgth	Ring	Wrapper
Lonsdale	Corona Grande	6⅝	42	CC-Ma
Double Corona	Giant Corona	7½	50	CC-Ma
Panatela	Panatela	6½	35	CC-Ma
Long Corona	Royal Corona	6	42	CC-Ma
Toro	Toro	6	50	CC-Ma
Robusto	Rothschild	4½	50	CC-Ma
Giant	Viajante	8½	50	Ma

All of the tobacco in this brand is grown in Mexico, with the wrapper grown from Sumatran seeds. It is full-bodied and offered in bundles of 25.

KISKEYA
Handmade, with mixed filler, in Santiago, Dominican Republic.

Wrapper: Ecuador   Binder: Dom. Rep.   Filler: Dom. Rep., Nicaragua

Shape	Name	Lgth	Ring	Wrapper
Corona	Corona	5½	42	CC
Long Corona	No. 2	6	42	CC
Robusto	Robusto	5	50	CC
Long Corona	Cetros	6¼	44	CC
Lonsdale	No. 1	6¾	44	CC
Toro	Toros	6	50	CC
Churchill	Churchills	7	48	CC
Double Corona	Presidentes	7½	50	CC

These cigars are handmade with sandwich filler, with natural wrappers of Ecuador-grown, Connecticut-seed tobacco. Medium in body, they are packed in boxes of 25 cigars.

HANDMADE CIGARS: BRAND LISTINGS

L'ATTITUDE 18

Handmade, with mixed filler, in Santiago, Dominican Republic.

Wrapper: Indonesia   Binder: Dom. Rep.   Filler: Dom. Rep.

Shape	Name	Lgth	Ring	Wrapper
Robusto	Robusto	5½	50	CM
Corona	Corona	5¼	42	CM
Long Corona	Lonsdale	6¾	42	CM

Here is a mixed-filler cigar with a high-quality Sumatra wrapper and a medium-bodied taste. Introduced in 1996, L'Attitude cigars are offered in cellophane sleeves in bundles of 25.

LA AURORA

Handmade in Santiago, Dominican Republic.

Wrapper: Cameroon   Binder: Dom. Rep.   Filler: Dom. Rep.

Shape	Name	Lgth	Ring	Wrapper
Short Panatela	Petit Coronas	4½	37	CM
Corona	Aurora No. 4	5¼	43	CM
Short Panatela	Coronas	5	38	CM
Long Corona	Cetros	6⅜	41	CM
Toro	Bristol Especiales	6⅜	48	CM
Panatela	Palmas Extra	6¾	35	CM
Short Panatela	Sublimes *(tubed)*	5	38	CM
Robusto	Robusto	5	50	CM
Double Corona	Doble Corona	7½	50	CM
Small Panatela	Finos	4	30	CM
Toro	Gran Corona	6½	50	CM
Torpedo	Belicoso	6¼	52	CM
Torpedo	Petit Belicoso	5	52	CM

HANDMADE CIGARS: BRAND LISTINGS

Respected since its introduction in 1903, La Aurora is a medium-bodied cigar offering a unique blend of Dominican fillers and binder, completed with a rare Cameroon wrapper for a soft, accessible taste. Take your choice of sizes in boxes of 25, or in five-packs in the Cetro, Corona or Doble Corona shapes.

LA AVIDA
Handmade in Miami, Florida, USA.

Wrapper: Indonesia   Binder: Dom. Rep.   Filler: Dom. Rep.

Shape	Name	Lgth	Ring	Wrapper
Long Corona	No. 2	6	44	CC
Robusto	Rothchild	5	50	CC
Toro	Toro	6	50	CC
Churchill	Churchill	7	46	CC
Double Corona	Soberano	7½	50	CC

Created in 1997, this medium-bodied cigar features a Sumatra wrapper. Each is presented in an individual cellophane sleeve, packed in cedar boxes of 20.

LA BAMBA
Handmade in Santiago, Dominican Republic.

Wrapper: USA/Connecticut   Binder: Dom. Rep.   Filler: Dom. Rep.

Shape	Name	Lgth	Ring	Wrapper
Giant	Presidente	8	50	CC
Double Corona	Churchill	7½	50	CC
Lonsdale	Lonsdale	6½	44	CC
Robusto	Robusto	4½	50	CC
Toro	Toro	6	50	CC

Sing along with Ritchie Valens now! Oh, you're *smoking* a La Bamba. With your voice, it's just as well . . . by now, you're enjoying the mild taste of this 1997-introduced brand with a genuine U.S.-grown, Connecticut wrapper.. When you're finished, you can tell us whether you opted for the single-row box of 10 or the double-row box of 20!

HANDMADE CIGARS: BRAND LISTINGS

LA COBRA CUBANA
Handmade in San Andres Tuxtla, Mexico.

Wrapper: Indonesia   Binder: Honduras   Filler: Dom. Rep., Ecuador, Honduras

Shape	Name	Lgth	Ring	Wrapper
Robusto	Robusto	5	50	CC-Ma
Long Corona	Corona	6	44	CC-Ma
Toro	La Cobra No. 1	6	52	CC-Ma
Slim Panatela	Veracruz	6	32	CC-Ma
Panatela	Panatela	6½	38	CC-Ma
Churchill	Cubana	6¾	46	CC-Ma
Double Corona	Churchill	7	50	CC-Ma
Giant	Presidente	8	52	CC-Ma
Torpedo	Torpedo	6	50	CC-Ma
Torpedo	Torpedo Grande	7½	60	CC-Ma

Introduced in 1995, this is a mild-to-medium-bodied cigar, enveloped in a Connecticut-seed wrapper grown in Ecuador. The brand is available in your choice of a natural or maduro wrapper and it is offered in boxes or bundles of 25. The Veracruz shape is available in a flavored version, in your choice of sweet, amaretto or rum tastes.

LA CONCHA
Handmade in Santiago, Dominican Republic.

Wrapper: Indonesia   Binder: Dom. Rep.   Filler: Dom. Rep.

Shape	Name	Lgth	Ring	Wrapper
Long Corona	Lonsdale	6	44	CC
Double Corona	Double Corona	7½	50	CC
Churchill	Churchill	7	46	CC
Torpedo	Torpedo	7	54	CC
Robusto	Robusto	5½	50	CC

HANDMADE CIGARS: BRAND LISTINGS

Introduced in 1997, this is a mild-to-medium-bodied brand which combines a Sumatra wrapper with Dominican-grown Olor and Piloto Cubano leaves. It is offered in boxes of 25.

LA COSECHA
Handmade in Esteli, Nicaragua.

Wrapper: Indonesia　　　　　*Binder: Nicaragua*　　　　　*Filler: Nicaragua*

Shape	Name	Lgth	Ring	Wrapper
Robusto	Robusto	4¾	50	CC
Corona	Corona	5½	42	CC
Toro	Toro	6	50	CC
Double Corona	Churchill	7	50	CC

Here is a 1997-introduced, mild-bodied cigar that features a Cameroon-seed wrapper, available in boxes of 25.

LA DAMITA
Handmade in Bayamon, Puerto Rico.

Wrapper: USA/Pennsylvania　　　*Binder: Puerto Rico*　　　　*Filler: Puerto Rico*

Shape	Name	Lgth	Ring	Wrapper
Slim Panatela	Panatella	6¾	34	CC

This is a mild-bodied cigar, offered in modestly-priced bundles of 25.

LA DILIGENCIA
Handmade in Danli, Honduras.

Wrapper: USA/Connecticut　　　　　　　*Binder: Dominican Republic*
Filler: Dominican Republic, Honduras, Nicaragua

Shape	Name	Lgth	Ring	Wrapper
Giant	Presidente	8½	52	CC
Toro	Toro	6	50	CC
Long Corona	Grand Corona	6	44	CC

| Churchill | Churchill | 7 | 48 | CC |
| Robusto | Robusto | 4¾ | 50 | CC |

This brand was introduced in 1996 and offers a light to medium body, thanks to a blend of tobaccos from four nations. La Diligencia offers lots of flavor and is packaged in boxes of 25 cigars each.

LA DIVA
Handmade in Villa Gonzalez, Dominican Republic.

Wrapper: USA/Connecticut   *Binder: Dom. Rep.*   *Filler: Dom. Rep.*

Shape	Name	Lgth	Ring	Wrapper
Long Corona	Corona	6	44	CC
Robusto	Robusto	4½	50	CC
Giant	Churchill	8	50	CC
Torpedo	Torpedo	7	54	CC

This cigar was introduced in 1996 and is unique for the process which imbues the leaves with the essence of the marvelous Cognac Pierre Ferrand. Combined with Connecticut Shade wrappers and Dominican leaves in the interior of the cigar, the blend has a medium body and is offered in either glass tubes, elegant wooden boxes or individually cellophaned in bundles of 25.

LA EMINENCIA
Handmade in Danli, Honduras.

Wrapper: Ecuador   *Binder: Honduras*
Filler: Brazil, Dominican Republic, Honduras, Nicaragua

Shape	Name	Lgth	Ring	Wrapper
Giant	Supreme	8½	52	CC-Ma
Toro	After Dinner	6⅛	50	CC-Ma
Robusto	Rothschild	4½	50	CC-Ma
Churchill	Corona Inmensa	7¼	46	CC-Ma
Grand Corona	Fumas No. 1	6½	46	CC-Ma
Corona Extra	Robusto	5⅝	46	CC-Ma

Corona	Fancy Cubanitas	5½	44	CC-Ma
Long Panatela	Palmas	7	38	CC-Ma
Torpedo	Torpedo	6¾	54	CC-Ma
Pyramid	Pyramid	7	50	CC-Ma

Back in distribution in 1996 after a short absence, La Eminencia is made by hand in Honduras and by machine in Tampa, Florida. The handmade blend is mild to medium-bodied, with both natural and maduro wrappers available in all sizes.

LA ESTRELLA CUBANA
Handmade in Esteli, Nicaragua.

Wrapper: Nicaragua   *Binder: Nicaragua*   *Filler: Nicaragua*

Shape	Name	Lgth	Ring	Wrapper
Double Corona	Churchill	7	52	CM-Ma
Toro	Torpedo	6	50	CM-Ma
Toro	Gran Corona	6	48	CM-Ma
Panatela	Panetela	6	38	CM-Ma
Corona	Corona	5½	44	CM-Ma
Robusto	Robusto	5	50	CM-Ma

Fans of full-bodied cigars will enjoy this all-Nicaraguan brand, which is offered in natural and maduro (actually, oscuro!) shade wrappers in boxes of 25.

LA FABULOSO
Handmade in Danli, Honduras.

Wrapper: Honduras   *Binder: Honduras*   *Filler: Honduras*

Shape	Name	Lgth	Ring	Wrapper
Grand Corona	No. 1	6½	46	CM
Corona	No. 4	5½	44	CM
Toro	Churchill	6½	52	CM

Short Panatela	Petit	4¼	38	CM
Churchill	Presidente	6¾	48	CM
Toro	Toro	6⅛	50	CM

Created in the early 1970s, this is a mild-to-medium-bodied cigar, offered in economical bundles of 20.

LA FAMA
Handmade in Las Palmas, the Canary Islands of Spain.

Wrapper: USA/Connecticut   Binder: Mexico   Filler: Brazil, Dom. Rep.

Shape	Name	Lgth	Ring	Wrapper
Corona	Gran Fama	6½	41	CC
Corona	Corona Fama Platas	6½	41	CC
Petit Corona	Fama Coronas	5⅛	40	CC
Panatela	Solera	5½	39	CC
Long Corona	Royal	6¼	43	CC
Grand Corona	Cedros	6½	47	CC
Double Corona	Churchill	7	50	CC

This brand is very mild in body and is made by hand in the Canary Islands. It is offered in elegant boxes of 25 cigars each.

LA FAVORITA
Handmade in Tenerife, the Canary Islands of Spain.

Wrapper: USA/Connecticut   Binder: Mexico   Filler: Brazil, Dom. Rep.

Shape	Name	Lgth	Ring	Wrapper
Double Corona	Doble Corona	7½	50	CC
Toro	Toro	6	50	CC
Robusto	Robusto	4¾	50	CC
Lonsdale	Lonsdale	6½	43	CC

HANDMADE CIGARS: BRAND LISTINGS

Here is a new brand for 1997, with a mild body and offered in beautifully-appointed cedar boxes of 25.

LA FAVORITA
Handmade in Danli, Honduras.

Wrapper: Ecuador   *Binder: Honduras*   *Filler: Nicaragua*

Shape	Name	Lgth	Ring	Wrapper
Long Corona	La Francesca	6	43	CC
Panatela	La Patricia	6	38	CC
Slim Panatela	La Blanca	5½	32	CC

This brand dates from 1991, and offers a uniquely mild taste, with just a hint of vanilla scent. The flavored scent comes from the box in which the cigars are packed.

LA FINCA
Handmade in Esteli, Nicaragua.

Wrapper: Nicaragua   *Binder: Nicaragua*   *Filler: Nicaragua*

Shape	Name	Lgth	Ring	Wrapper
Double Corona	Bolivares	7½	50	CM
Grand Corona	Cazadore	6½	45	CM
Corona	Corona	5½	42	CM
Corona	Crystales	5⅝	44	CM
Grand Corona	Fuma	6½	46	CM
Corona Extra	Fuma Corta	5½	46	CM
Pyramid	Figurado	6¾	54	CM
Giant	Gran Finca	8½	52	CM
Toro	Joya	6	50	CM
Pyramid	Pyramides	7	48	CM
Robusto	Robusto	4½	50	CM
Lonsdale	Romeo	6½	42	CM

HANDMADE CIGARS: BRAND LISTINGS

Churchill	Valentino	6¾	48	CM

This is a Nicaraguan "puro" featuring all Nicaraguan tobaccos from the Jamastran Valley. A heavy-bodied cigar, La Finca shapes are offered in boxes of 25 cigars each.

LA FLOR DE ARMANDO MENDEZ
Handmade in Tampa, Florida, USA.

Wrapper: USA/Connecticut   Binder: Honduras   Filler: Honduras

Shape	Name	Lgth	Ring	Wrapper
Toro	La Flor de A. Mendez	6	50	CM

This is a medium-bodied blend, offered in six-packs from the respected Cammarata Cigar Factory in the Ybor City section of Tampa, Florida.

LA FLOR DE CUBA
Handmade in Bayamon, Puerto Rico.

Wrapper: Cameroon   Binder: Dom. Rep.
Filler: Dominican Republic, Puerto Rico

Shape	Name	Lgth	Ring	Wrapper
Churchill	Selectos	7	46	CM
Grand Corona	Embajadores	6¼	46	CM
Double Corona	Esplendido	7	50	CM

This is a medium-to-heavy-bodied cigar, featuring a Cameroon wrapper and offered in boxes of 25.

LA FLOR DE NAVARETTE
Handmade in Santiago, Dominican Republic.

Wrapper: Indonesia   Binder: Dom. Rep.   Filler: Dom. Rep.

Shape	Name	Lgth	Ring	Wrapper
Double Corona	Churchill	7½	50	CC
Long Corona	Lonsdale	6	44	CC

Robusto	Robusto	5	50	CC

Offered in cellophane sleeves in bundles of 25, this is a medium-bodied cigar with a Sumatra wrapper, introduced in 1997.

LA FLOR DOMINICANA
Handmade in Santiago, Dominican Republic.

Wrapper: USA/Connecticut, Mexico   Binder: Dom. Rep.   Filler: Dom. Rep.

Shape	Name	Lgth	Ring	Wrapper
	Premium:			
Churchill	Mambises	6⅞	48	CC
Robusto	Maceo	5	48	CC
Lonsdale	Alcalde	6½	44	CC
Corona	Insurrectos	5½	42	CC
Petit Corona	Macheteros	4	40	CC
Slim Panatela	Diplomaticos	5	30	CC
Torpedo	Figurados	6½	52	Ma
Lonsdale	Lonsdale	6½	44	Ma
Robusto	Robusto	5	48	Ma
	Reserva Especial:			
Double Corona	Churchill	6⅞	49	CC
Robusto	Robusto	5	48	CC
Robusto	Belicoso	5½	52	CC
Torpedo	Figurado	6½	52	CC

Introduced in 1994, Cuban-seed tobaccos from the Cibao Valley of the Dominican Republic are the stuff of which La Flor Dominicana cigars are founded. These leaves are wrapped with Connecticut Shade leaves to produce a mild-to-medium bodied cigar of ultimate quality from Santiago, in the Dominican Republic. The Mexican maduro-wrapped line is new for 1997. The Reserva Especial line has a medium-to-full-bodied taste, with a creamy flavor and a touch of pepper.

HANDMADE CIGARS: BRAND LISTINGS

LA FONTANA VINTAGE
Handmade in Danli, Honduras.

Wrapper: USA/Connecticut   Binder: Mexico   Filler: Honduras

Shape	Name	Lgth	Ring	Wrapper
Corona	Verdi	5½	44	CC
Robusto	Galileo	5	50	CC
Lonsdale	Puccini	6½	44	CC
Churchill	Da Vinci	6⅞	48	CC
Double Corona	Michelangelo	7½	52	CC
Slim Panatela	Rossini	5½	33	CC
Pyramid	Mona Lisa	4¾	46	CC
Torpedo	Belicoso	6	54	CC
Panatela	Dante	5½	38	CC

This is a mild blend which debuted in 1993. It is constructed of Honduran-grown tobaccos in the binder and a light Connecticut wrapper. This creation of master blender Tino Argudin includes two new, shaped sizes for 1997 and is offered in elegant 25-cigar boxes.

LA GIANNA HAVANA
Handmade in Esteli, Nicaragua.

Wrapper: Nicaragua   Binder: Nicaragua   Filler: Nicaragua

Shape	Name	Lgth	Ring	Wrapper
	Classic Series:			
Long Corona	No. 2	6¼	44	CM
Double Corona	Churchill	7	49	CM
Robusto	Rothchild	5	50	CM
Torpedo	Torpedo	6	54	CM
Torpedo	Bellabusto	5	52	CM
	Graciella Collection:			

HANDMADE CIGARS: BRAND LISTINGS

Long Corona	No. 2	6¼	44	CM
Double Corona	Churchill	7	49	CM
Robusto	Rothchild	5	50	CM
Torpedo	Torpedo	6	54	CM
Torpedo	Bellabusto	5	52	CM
	Ebony Selection:			
Long Corona	No. 2	6¼	44	Ma
Double Corona	Churchill	7	49	Ma
Robusto	Rothchild	5	50	Ma
Torpedo	Torpedo	6	54	Ma
Torpedo	Bellabusto	5	52	Ma

The Classic line was introduced in 1996, with the Graciella and Ebony series debuting in 1997. The brand offers a mild-bodied taste in the Classic line, thanks to a Connecticut-seed wrapper, and medium-bodied flavor in the other lines (Sumatra-seed wrapper in the Graciella series) in five popular shapes. The aging process continues in the elegant cedar boxes in which La Gianna cigars are presented.

LA GLORIA CUBANA
Handmade in Miami, Florida, USA and Villa Gonzalez, Dominican Republic.

Wrapper: Ecuador   Binder: Nicaragua   Filler: Dom.Rep., Nicaragua

Shape	Name	Lgth	Ring	Wrapper
Giant	Crown Imperial	9	49	DC-CC-Ma
Giant	Soberano	8	52	DC-CC-Ma
Double Corona	Charlemagne	7¼	54	DC-CC-Ma
Double Corona	Double Corona	7¾	49	DC-CC-Ma
Double Corona	Churchill	7	50	DC-CC-Ma
Churchill	Glorias Inmensas	7½	48	DC-CC-Ma

HANDMADE CIGARS: BRAND LISTINGS

Toro	Corona Gorda	6	52	DC-CC-Ma
Robusto	Wavell	5	50	DC-CC-Ma
Grand Corona	Glorias Extra	6¼	46	DC-CC-Ma
Giant Corona	Coronas Extra Larga	7¾	44	DC-CC-Ma
Lonsdale	Medaille D'Or No. 1	6¾	43	DC-CC-Ma
Long Corona	Medaille D'Or No. 2	6¼	43	DC-CC-Ma
Corona	Glorias	5½	43	DC-CC-Ma
Small Panatela	Minutos	4½	40	DC-CC-Ma
Long Panatela	Panatela De'Luxe	7	37	DC-CC-Ma
Cigarillo	Medaille D'Or No. 3	7	28	DC-CC-Ma
Panatela	Medaille D'Or No. 4	6	32	DC-CC-Ma
Torpedo	Torpedo No. 1	6½	Tpr	DC-CC-Ma
Pyramid	Piramides	7¼	Tpr	DC-CC-Ma

This is a medium-bodied smoke of absolutely exquisite quality made in the El Credito factory in Miami, Florida (primarily for local sale only) and in a new facility in Villa Gonzalez, Dominican Republic. All sizes are offered in boxes of 25, except for the Crown Imperial and the Piramides, which are offered in boxes of 10.

LA HABANERA
Handmade in Santiago, Dominican Republic.

Wrapper: USA/Connecticut   *Binder: Dom. Rep.*   *Filler: Dom. Rep.*

Shape	Name	Lgth	Ring	Wrapper
Churchill	Churchill	6⅞	46	Cl
Long Corona	Diplomaticos	6	44	Cl
Lonsdale	Elegante	6¾	42	Cl
Robusto	Emperadores	5½	50	Cl
Small Panatela	Especiale	5	30	Cl
Double Corona	Presidente	7½	50	Cl

Corona	Puritanos	5¾	42	Cl
Long Panatela	Selectos	7	36	Cl

This is an old brand name from 1902 that now combines a genuine Connecticut wrapper with Dominican-grown binder and fillers for a mild-to-medium-bodied taste. La Habanera is presented in colorful boxes of 25.

LA HOJA DEL SABOR
Handmade in Tamboril, Dominican Republic.
Wrapper: Indonesia or USA Connecticut

Binder: Dominican Republic   *Filler: Dominican Republic*

Shape	Name	Lgth	Ring	Wrapper
Torpedo	Torpedo	6½	52	CC-Ma
Double Corona	Churchill	7	50	CC-Ma
Toro	Corona Gorda	6	52	CC-Ma
	Sweetness added:			
Corona	Corona	5½	44	CC-Ma
Slim Panatela	Petite	5	34	CC-Ma

New for 1997, this brand offers a choice of Sumatra wrapper in natural and maduro shades or Connecticut leaf, making for a medium-bodied taste in the lighter shades and medium-to-full bodied in the maduro-wrapped version. It is presented in individual cellophane sleeves in a colorful, paper-wrapped box.

LA HOJA RICA
Handmade in Santiago, Dominican Republic.
Wrapper: Indonesia   *Binder: Indonesia*   *Filler: Dominican Republic*

Shape	Name	Lgth	Ring	Wrapper
Churchill	Churchill	6¾	48	CM
Toro	Toro	6	50	CM
Corona Extra	Corona	5½	46	CM
Robusto	Robusto	4½	52	CM

HANDMADE CIGARS: BRAND LISTINGS

New in 1997, this hand-made line offers a medium-to-full-bodied smoke with Dominican-grown Olor and Piloto Cubano leaves powering the filler. Each cigar is wrapped in cellophane and each size is offered in all-cedar boxes of 20.

LA HOJA RICA
Handmade in Esteli, Nicaragua.

Wrapper: Nicaragua *Binder: Nicaragua* *Filler: Nicaragua*

Shape	Name	Lgth	Ring	Wrapper
Giant	Churchill	8⅞	48	CM
Long Corona	Gran Corona	6	44	CM
Corona Extra	Corona	6	41	CM
Robusto	Robusto	4½	52	CM

Also new in 1997, this line is medium in body and features Nicaraguan tobacco. Wonderfully constructed, each cigar is sleeved in cellophane and each size is presented in all-cedar boxes of 25.

LA HOJA SELECTA
Handmade in Miami, Florida, USA.

Wrapper: USA/Connecticut *Binder: Ecuador* *Filler: Dom.Rep., Nicaragua*

Shape	Name	Lgth	Ring	Wrapper
Double Corona	Chateau Sovereign	7½	52	CI
Churchill	Cosiac	7	48	CI
Toro	Choix Supreme	6	50	CI
Robusto	Palais Royals	4¾	50	CI
Lonsdale	Selectos No. 1	6½	42	CI
Corona	Cetros de Oro	5¾	43	CI
Panatela	Bel Aires	6¾	38	CI
Slim Panatela	Geneves	6½	32	CI

HANDMADE CIGARS: BRAND LISTINGS

These are the mildest cigars produced by the El Credito factory in Miami, Florida, thanks to their Connecticut Shade wrappers and filler tobaccos from the Dominican Republic.

LA ISLA
Handmade in Bayamon, Puerto Rico.

Wrapper: USA/Pennsylvania   *Binder: Puerto Rico*   *Filler: Puerto Rico*

Shape	Name	Lgth	Ring	Wrapper
Grand Corona	Fat Corona	5¾	46	CC

This is a heavy, full-bodied cigar that offers a Pennsylvania-grown wrapper and is available in boxes of 25.

LA ISLA
Handmade in Union City, New Jersey, USA.

Wrapper: USA/Connecticut   *Binder: Dominican Republic*
Filler: Costa Rica, Dominican Republic, Honduras, Mexico

Shape	Name	Lgth	Ring	Wrapper
Churchill	Churchill	7⅛	46	CC-Ma
Robusto	Soberanos Cortos	5½	50	CC-Ma
Giant	Soberanos	8	50	CC-Ma
Giant	Presidente	8	50	CC-Ma
Churchill	Especiale	7	46	CC-Ma
Churchill	Corona	7	46	CC-Ma
Panatela	Panatela	6¼	35	CC-Ma
Long Panatela	Palmas	7	35	CC-Ma
Lonsdale	Fumas	6¾	44	CC-Ma
Lonsdale	No. 1	7⅛	42	CC-Ma
Long Corona	No. 2	6¼	40	CC-Ma
Corona	No. 4	5½	40	CC-Ma

HANDMADE CIGARS: BRAND LISTINGS

These medium-to-full-bodied cigars are handmade in a small store in Union City, New Jersey. The wide variety of sizes – 12 in all – are enveloped in Connecticut-grown leaves, including Connecticut Broadleaf tobaccos for the maduro wrappers.

LA LUNA DE LA HABANA
Handmade in Miami, Florida, USA.

LA LUNA CONNECTICUT:

Wrapper: Ecuador   *Binder: Ecuador*   *Filler: Dom. Rep., Ecuador, Honduras*

LA LUNA CASJUCA:

Wrapper: Ecuador   *Binder: Ecuador*   *Filler: Dom. Rep., Ecuador, Honduras*

LA LUNA INDONESIA:
Wrapper: Indonesia

Binder: Ecuador   *Filler: Dom. Rep., Ecuador, Honduras, Indonesia*

LA LUNA MADURO:

Wrapper: Ecuador   *Binder: Ecuador*   *Filler: Dom. Rep., Honduras, Ecuador*

LA LUNA SUMATRA:

Wrapper: Indonesia   *Binder: Indonesia*   *Filler: Dom. Rep., Honduras, Indonesia*

Shape	Name	Lgth	Ring	Wrapper
	La Luna Connecticut:			
Double Corona	Churchill	7	50	CC
Lonsdale	Especiale No. 1	6½	42	CC
	La Luna Casjuca:			
Robusto	Robusto	5	50	CC
Double Corona	Churchill	7	50	CC
Lonsdale	Corona	6¾	44	CC
Lonsdale	Especiale No. 1	6½	42	CC
	La Luna Indonesia:			
Robusto	Robusto	5	50	CC

HANDMADE CIGARS: BRAND LISTINGS

Double Corona	Churchill	7	50	CC
Lonsdale	Corona	6¾	44	CC
Lonsdale	Especiale No. 1	6½	42	CC
	La Luna Maduro:			
Robusto	Robusto	5	50	Ma
Double Corona	Churchill	7	50	Ma
Lonsdale	Corona	6¾	44	Ma
Lonsdale	Especiale No. 1	6½	42	Ma
	La Luna Sumatra:			
Robusto	Robusto	5	50	CC
Double Corona	Churchill	7	50	CC
Lonsdale	Corona	6¾	44	CC

This is a complicated brand because it is offered in five separate versions. The Connecticut line is the lightest, offering a mild-to-medium-bodied taste, with the La Luna Casjuca next at medium-to-full-bodied. The Indonesia, Maduro and Sumatra lines are all full-bodied. These are beautifully-made cigars which are offered in boxes of 25.

LA LUNDA
Handmade in San Andres Tuxtla, Mexico.

Wrapper: Mexico   Binder: Mexico   Filler: Mexico

Shape	Name	Lgth	Ring	Wrapper
Double Corona	Immensa	7½	52	CC-Ma
Torpedo	Belisco	5½	44	CC-Ma
Double Corona	Churchill	7¼	50	CC-Ma
Robusto	Robusto	5	50	CC-Ma
Grand Corona	Corona Gorda	6	46	CC-Ma
Lonsdale	Corona Especial	7	44	CC-Ma
Corona	Corona	5½	42	CC-Ma

HANDMADE CIGARS: BRAND LISTINGS

Lonsdale	Lonsdale	6½	40	CC-Ma
Short Panatela	Petite Corona	5	36	CC-Ma
	Made with short filler:			
Churchill	Presidente	7	48	CC-Ma

Introduced in 1994, this all-Mexican brand offers a medium-bodied smoke presented in boxes of 25, except for the Presidente size, which is offered in bundles.

LA LUNDA DE SANTA MARIA
Handmade in Santa Maria, Panama.

Wrapper: Panama   *Binder: Panama*   *Filler: Panama*

Shape	Name	Lgth	Ring	Wrapper
Toro	Presidente	6¼	48	Ma

This brand, which was first produced back in 1922, is offered today in only one shape. The flavor is medium-bodied and the cigars are presented in boxes of 25.

LA MAXIMILIANA
Handmade in Danli, Honduras.

Wrapper: Indonesia   *Binder: Honduras*   *Filler: Nicaragua*

Shape	Name	Lgth	Ring	Wrapper
Double Corona	Perfectus	7	50	CC
Lonsdale	Fumas	7	44	CC
Toro	Optimus	6	48	CC
Long Corona	Luxus	6	43	CC
Corona	Dulcis	5½	42	CC

Introduced in 1996, this brand offers a medium body and a spicy taste, thanks to its Sumatra-grown wrapper, combined with Honduran and Nicaraguan leaves inside. La Maximiliana cigars are presented in a traditional box-pressed format in individual cellophane sleeves.

HANDMADE CIGARS: BRAND LISTINGS

LA NATIVE
Handmade in Danli, Honduras.

Wrapper: Nicaragua   *Binder: Honduras*   *Filler: Honduras, Nicaragua*

Shape	Name	Lgth	Ring	Wrapper
Giant	Gigantes	8	52	CM
Churchill	Corona Grande	7½	46	CM
Churchill	Churchill	6⅞	49	CM
Robusto	Rothchild	5	50	CM
Toro	Toro	6	50	CM
Long Corona	Cetros	6	43	CM
Small Panatela	Super Fino	4½	30	CM

These Honduran-made cigars were introduced in 1994 and offer a very smooth draw with a medium-bodied taste and excellent construction. La Native is offered in boxes of 10 and 20.

LA NUBIA
Handmade in Las Palmas, the Canary Islands of Spain.

Wrapper: USA/Connecticut   *Binder: Indonesia*
Filler: Brazil, Dominican Republic

Shape	Name	Lgth	Ring	Wrapper
Short Panatela	Viuditas	4	35	CC
Small Panatela	Panatelas	4¾	32	CC
Small Panatela	Senoritas	4	32	CC
Petit Corona	Petit	4½	40	CC
Corona	No. 13	5⅛	42	CC
Lonsdale	No. 15	5⅞	43	CC
Lonsdale	No. 17	6½	44	CC
Robusto	Robusto	4¾	50	CC
Double Corona	Churchill	7½	50	CC

HANDMADE CIGARS: BRAND LISTINGS

First manufactured way back in 1925, this is a mild-bodied blend of tobaccos from four nations. La Nubia cigars are offered in boxes of 25 except for the Viuditas and Panatelas shapes (20) and Senoritas (30).

LA PALMA DE ORO

Handmade in Las Palmas, the Canary Islands of Spain.

Wrapper: Indonesia or USA/Connecticut   *Binder: Brazil*
Filler: Dominican Republic, Spain

Shape	Name	Lgth	Ring	Wrapper
Short Panatela	Palma	5¼	38	CC
Long Panatela	Lancero	7	38	CC
Corona	Cafe	5½	44	CC
Robusto	Robusto	5	50	CC
Churchill	Don Ricardo	6¾	46	CC
Double Corona	Double Corona	6¾	50	CC
Toro	Don Jorge	6¼	54	CC
Double Corona	Superior	7½	54	CC

These cigars, available in the U.S. beginning in 1997, offer a mild body with a hint of spice on the finish. Depending on availability, you have your choice of either Connecticut-grown or Java-grown wrappers in boxes of 10.

LA PALOMA

Handmade in Santiago, Dominican Republic.

Wrapper: Ecuador   *Binder: Dom. Rep.*   *Filler: Dom. Rep.*

Shape	Name	Lgth	Ring	Wrapper
Double Corona	Churchill	7	50	CM
Toro	Toro	6	50	CM
Robusto	Wavell	5	50	CM
Lonsdale	No. 2	6½	42	CM
Giant	Presidente	8½	52	CM

Petit Corona	Petite		4½	40	CM

Here is a new brand for 1997, made at the MATASA factory in Santiago, home to dozens of outstanding brands. This one is only in limited production and the remarkable result of the blend of Connecticut-seed wrapper with Dominican-grown filler and binder leaves is a pleasing, medium-bodied smoke. If you can find it, it will be in boxes of 10 or 20.

LA PANTERA PREDATOR DIAMOND COLLECTION
Handmade in Danli, Honduras.

Wrapper: Indonesia   *Binder: Honduras*   *Filler: Costa Rica, Honduras*

Shape	Name	Lgth	Ring	Wrapper
Double Corona	Churchill	7	50	CM
Corona	No. 4	5½	42	CM
Long Panatela	Palma Fina	7	38	CM
Pyramid	Pyramid	5½	52	CM
Robusto	Rothchild	5	50	CM
Toro	Toro	6	50	CM
Torpedo	Torpedo	7	54	CM
Giant	Gigante	8½	54	CM

Known simply as "La Pantera" since introduction in 1996, the Predator Diamond Collection is a mellow, mild-to-medium bodied cigar, thanks to its Sumatra-seed wrapper, offered in wooden boxes of 25.

LA PANTERA PREDATOR EMERALD COLLECTION
Handmade in Esteli, Nicaragua.

Wrapper: Indonesia   *Binder: Nicaragua*   *Filler: Dom. Rep., Nicaragua*

Shape	Name	Lgth	Ring	Wrapper
Double Corona	Churchill	7	50	CM
Robusto	Rothschild	5	50	CM
Torpedo	Torpedo	6½	54	CM

Grand Corona	Lancero No. 1	6½	46	CM

Here is the strongest of the Predator blends, the green-banded, full-bodied Emerald Collection. The Sumatra wrapper is well-matched with the Nicaraguan and Dominican tobaccos for a powerful flavor, available in boxes of 25.

LA PANTERA PREDATOR SAPPHIRE COLLECTION
Handmade in Danli, Honduras.

Wrapper: Indonesia *Binder: Dom. Rep.* *Filler: Honduras, Nicaragua*

Shape	Name	Lgth	Ring	Wrapper
Double Corona	Churchill	7	50	CM
Corona	No. 4	5½	42	CM
Long Panatela	Palma Fina	7	38	CM
Robusto	Rothchild	5	50	CM
Torpedo	Misile	6	54	CM
Giant	Soberano	8	52	CM

This is a stronger blend than its sister brand, the Predator Diamond Collection. Spicier and more robust, this is a medium-bodied cigar which features aged tobaccos and is offered in cedar cabinets of 25.

LA PERLA
Handmade in Esteli, Nicaragua.

Wrapper: Nicaragua *Binder: Nicaragua* *Filler: Nicaragua*

Shape	Name	Lgth	Ring	Wrapper
Churchill	Churchill	7	48	CM
Toro	Deluxe	6	50	CM
Lonsdale	Perlas	6½	40	CM

"The Pearl" is new for 1997 and offers a mild-to-medium-bodied flavor in an all-Nicaraguan-grown, Cuban-seed blend. It is presented in all-cedar boxes of 25 cigars each.

Robustos and Toros

These are very popular sizes as enthusiasts look for the flavor of a larger ring gauge of a Churchill or Double Corona combined with shorter lengths for a shorter smoke. The dimensions of these shapes include:

- Robusto   4½-5½ inches long; 48-54 ring.
- Toro   5⅝-6⅝ inches long; 48-54 ring.

Pictured opposite, from left to right:

		(shape)
MAYORGA *Toro*		
(Nicaragua)	6 x 50	Toro
ROLANDO *No. 3*		
(Dominican Republic)	6 x 50	Toro
CRUZADO RESERVA ESPECIAL *Toro*		
(Honduras)	6 x 50	Toro
LA PERLA HABANA *Toro*		
(Dominican Republic)	6 x 50	Toro
PHEASANT *Robusto*		
(Honduras)	5¼ x 54	Robusto
FUEGO CUBANO *Robusto*		
(United States)	5 x 50	Robusto
EL REY DE FLOREZ *Robusto*		
(Dominican Republic)	5 x 50	Robusto

HANDMADE CIGARS: BRAND LISTINGS

LA PERLA HABANA
Handmade in Santiago, Dominican Republic.

Wrapper: Indonesia   Binder: Indonesia   Filler: Dom. Rep.

Shape	Name	Lgth	Ring	Wrapper
Corona	Coronas	5¾	43	CC
Lonsdale	Lonsdales	6¾	43	CC
Robusto	Robustos	4¾	52	CC
Toro	Toros	6	50	CC
Double Corona	Double Coronas	7½	52	CC
Torpedo	Figurados	6½	52	CC

Here is a new brand in 1997, with a medium body and a famous old Cuban name. This reincarnation of the "Pearl of Havana" is presented in cellophane sleeves and packed in cedar boxes of 25.

LA PLATA
Handmade in Los Angeles, California, USA; Cofradia, Honduras and Villa Gonzalez, Dominican Republic.

LA PLATA SELECTION:
Wrapper: Indonesia, Mexico

Binder: Indonesia   Filler: Dominican Republic, Indonesia

PREMIUM SELECTION:
Wrapper: USA/Connecticut   Binder: Honduras   Filler: Dom.Rep., Honduras

DOMINICAN SELECTION:
Wrapper: Dom. Rep.   Binder: Dom. Rep.   Filler: Dom. Rep.

Shape	Name	Lgth	Ring	Wrapper
	La Plata Selection:			
Giant	Rockets	8	50	CC-Ma
Double Corona	Enterprise	7	52	CC-Ma
Lonsdale	Internationals	7	42	CC

HANDMADE CIGARS: BRAND LISTINGS

Churchill	Victor No. 1	7	46	CC-Ma
Toro	Jr. Enterprise	6	52	CC
Lonsdale	Numero Dos	6½	42	CC
Long Corona	Magnificos	6	42	Ma
Long Panatela	Reinas	7	34	CC
Slim Panatela	Tito Specials	6	34	CC
Short Panatela	Dessert Specials	5	36	CC-Ma
Torpedo	Torpedo	6	54	CC-Ma
Robusto	Victor No. 2	5	50	CC-Ma
Long Panatela	Victor No. 3	7	38	CC
Corona Extra	Jr. Smoker /short filler/	5½	46	CC
Short Panatela	Ninos	4	38	CC
Petit Corona	Jr. Magnificos /short filler/	5	42	Ma
	Premium Selection:			
Giant	Prime Minister	8	50	Ma
Double Corona	Royal Wilshire	7	52	Ma
Robusto	Robusto Uno	4½	52	Ma
Long Corona	Magnificos	6	44	Ma
Robusto	Hercules	5½	54	CI
Panatela	Ashford Classic	6	34	CI
Short Panatela	Dessert Specials	5	36	CI
Long Corona	Grand Classic	6	44	CI
Double Corona	Enterprise Classic	7	52	CI
Toro	Jr. Enterprise Classic	6	52	CI
	Dominican Selection:			
Petit Corona	Petit Corona	4¾	40	CC
Robusto	Robusto	4¾	52	CC

Toro	Toro	6	50	CC
Double Corona	Double Corona	7	52	CC

Founded in 1947, the popular La Plata line now requires both a Los Angeles factory and help from Villazon's master cigar makers in Honduras to help meet the demand! The original series offers a wide range of sizes and flavors, with strength from mild through full-bodied with Indonesian wrappers in natural shades and Mexican leaf for maduro-wrapped shapes. The newer Premium Selection offers either Connecticut wrappers in either claro (mild to medium body) or maduro (full body) shades. The Dominican Selection was introduced in 1997 and offers a medium-to-full-bodied smoke with a glorious Dominican-grown Rosado wrapper and a glamorous red band.

LA PRIMADORA
Handmade in Danli, Honduras.
Wrapper: Ecuador or Mexico   Binder: Indonesia   Filler: Honduras, Nicaragua

Shape	Name	Lgth	Ring	Wrapper
Giant	Emperor	8½	50	CC-Ma
Toro	Solitaire	6	50	CC-Ma
Robusto	Starbrite	4½	50	CC-Ma
Panatela	Falcon	6½	34	CC-Ma
Lonsdale	Excellentes	6½	42	CC-Ma
Corona	Petite Cetros	5½	42	CC-Ma

La Primadora is a mild-bodied cigar with a unique and slightly spicy blend of long-filler tobaccos. These imported cigars are well constructed, with a consistent finish and offered in bundles of 25 cigars each.

LA PRIMERA
Handmade in Santiago, Dominican Republic.
Wrapper: Ecuador   Binder: Nicaragua   Filler: Dom.Rep., Nicaragua

Shape	Name	Lgth	Ring	Wrapper
Giant	Presidente	8½	52	CC
Double Corona	Churchill	7	50	CC

HANDMADE CIGARS: BRAND LISTINGS

Toro	Toro	6	50	CC
Lonsdale	Cetro Grande	6¾	44	CC
Robusto	Rothschild	5	50	CC
Corona	Petite Corona	5¾	43	CC

This brand was introduced in 1996 from one of the most respected factories in the Dominican Republic. It offers a medium-flavored blend with considerable smoothness and is offered in wooden boxes of 25.

LA PRUEBA FLAVORED CIGARS
Handmade in San Andres Tuxtla, Mexico.

Wrapper: Mexico *Binder: Mexico* *Filler: Mexico*

Shape	*Name*	*Lgth*	*Ring*	*Wrapper*
Corona	Corona	5½	42	CC

Take your choice of cherry, chocolate, coffee, rum, tequila or vanilla, imbued into the tobacco prior to rolling and an additional injection of flavor after rolling, but before packaging. All of the tobacco used for these cigars is at least two years old to allow the curing process to take place. These mild-to-medium-bodied cigars feature Sumatra-seed wrappers and are offered in bundles of 25.

LA REAL
Handmade in Condega, Nicaragua.

Wrapper: Nicaragua *Binder: Nicaragua* *Filler: Nicaragua*

Shape	*Name*	*Lgth*	*Ring*	*Wrapper*
Double Corona	Imperiales	7	50	CM
Robusto	Baron	5	50	CM

This is an all-Nicaraguan, full-bodied smoke which debuted in 1995. It's for the serious smoker, though: packed without cellophane and in boxes of 50. Light 'em up!

HANDMADE CIGARS: BRAND LISTINGS

LA REGENTA
Handmade in Las Palmas, the Canary Islands of Spain.
Wrapper: USA/Connecticut

Binder: Dominican Republic   *Filler: Brazil, Canary Islands, Dominican Republic*

Shape	Name	Lgth	Ring	Wrapper
Giant	Individual	8	50	CI
Double Corona	Premiers	7½	50	CI
Churchill	Gran Corona	7¼	46	CI
Pyramid	Piramide	7	52	CI
Lonsdale	No. 1	6¾	42	CI
Robusto	Especial No. 2	4¾	50	CI
Corona	No. 3	5¾	42	CI
Petit Corona	No. 4	5⅛	42	CI
Petit Corona	No. 5	4½	42	CI

One of the famous brands from the Canary Islands, the La Regenta line is famous for its perfect construction, easy draw and mild taste in every shape. A very old brand that had been out of sight for several years, it was returned to the U.S. market by the Marcos Miguel Tobacco Corp. in late 1996. You can find it today in elegant boxes of 25.

LA REGIONAL
Handmade in Las Palmas, the Canary Islands of Spain.

Wrapper: Ecuador   *Binder: Mexico*   *Filler: Nicaragua*

Shape	Name	Lgth	Ring	Wrapper
Double Corona	Monarch	7¼	50	CC
Churchill	Churchill	6⅞	46	CC
Lonsdale	Lonsdale	6⅝	42	CC
Corona	Corona	5⅝	42	CC
Panatela	Delicioso	6⅝	36	CC
Slim Panatela	Palmas	5½	33	CC

HANDMADE CIGARS: BRAND LISTINGS

Toro	Matador	6⅛	50	CC

Here is a full-bodied brand introduced in 1995 and produced in one of the world's historic cigar regions: the Canary Islands of Spain. The blend is Nicaraguan and Mexican tobaccos with a Connecticut Shade-seed wrapper grown in Ecuador.

LA RESTINA
Handmade in Bayamon, Puerto Rico.
Wrapper: USA/Pennsylvania   Binder: Puerto Rico   Filler: Puerto Rico

Shape	Name	Lgth	Ring	Wrapper
Long Corona	Cazadores	6	44	CM
Double Corona	No. 1	7	50	CM

La Restina is a medium-to-heavy bodied cigar, offered in boxes of 25.

LA TRADICION CABINET SELECTION
Handmade in Miami, Florida, USA and Esteli, Nicaragua.
Wrapper: Ecuador or USA/Connecticut   Binder: Ecuador
Filler: Dominican Republic, Honduras, Nicaragua

Shape	Name	Lgth	Ring	Wrapper
Long Panatela	Lanceros	7¼	38	CC-CM-Ma
Long Corona	Coronas	6	44	CC-CM-Ma
Robusto	Robustos	5	50	CC-CM-Ma
Double Corona	Churchills	7	49	CC-CM-Ma
Double Corona	Double Coronas	7⅝	50	CC-CM-Ma
Torpedo	Torpedoes	6½	54	CC-CM-Ma
Torpedo	Gran Torpedo	7½	60	CC-CM-Ma
Toro	Elite	6	60	CC-CM-Ma

Introduced in 1995, this is a medium-to-full-bodied series from Nick's Cigar Company of Miami, Florida. You can take your choice of wrappers from Connecticut or Ecuador in natural, rosado or maduro wrappers and enjoy them from slide-top, all-cedar boxes of 25.

HANDMADE CIGARS: BRAND LISTINGS

LA TRADICION CUBANA
Handmade in Miami and Tampa, Florida, USA.
Wrapper: Ecuador, Mexico

Binder: Honduras   *Filler: Dominican Republic, Honduras*

Shape	Name	Lgth	Ring	Wrapper
Double Corona	Churchill	7	49	CC-CM-Ma
Long Corona	Corona	6	44	CC-CM-Ma
Double Corona	Double Corona	7⅝	50	CC-CM-Ma
Long Panatela	Lanceros	7¼	38	CC-CM-Ma
Robusto	Robusto	5	50	CC-CM-Ma
Torpedo	Torpedo	6½	54	CC-CM-Ma
Torpedo	Gran Torpedo	7½	60	CC-CM-Ma
Small Panatela	Lunchour	5	32	CC

Introduced in 1996, this brand is made by a small factory which prizes quality above all else. Offered in boxes of 25, the blend has a medium-to-full body in an Ecuadorian natural-shade wrapper or Mexican maduro wrapper. The Lunchour shape is available in either a rum or vanilla flavor, if desired.

LA UNICA
Handmade in Santiago, Dominican Republic.
Wrapper: USA/Connecticut   *Binder: Dom. Rep.*   *Filler: Dom. Rep.*

Shape	Name	Lgth	Ring	Wrapper
Giant	No. 100	8½	52	CI-Ma
Double Corona	No. 200	7	49	CI-Ma
Lonsdale	No. 300	6¾	44	CI-Ma
Robusto	No. 400	4½	50	CI-Ma
Corona	No. 500	5½	42	CI-Ma

Introduced in 1986, this brand has a mild flavor and aroma in a well-constructed cigar, with a natural or maduro wrapper. An excellent value, these long-filler cigars are packaged in bundles of 20 cigars each.

HANDMADE CIGARS: BRAND LISTINGS

LA VELEZA
Handmade in Tamboril, Dominican Republic.

Wrapper: Indonesia   Binder: Dom. Rep.   Filler: Dom. Rep.

Shape	Name	Lgth	Ring	Wrapper
Robusto		5	50	CC
Long Corona		6	44	CC
Toro		6	50	CC
Churchill		7	46	CC
Double Corona		7½	50	CC
Torpedo		7	54	CC

First marketed in 1997, this brand has no shape names, but features a tasty Sumatran wrapper for a mild-to-medium-bodied flavor. It is offered in value-priced bundles of 10 or 25 cigars, except for the Torpedo shape, offered in bundles of 10 or 20 only.

LA VENGA
Handmade in Honduras.

Wrapper: Ecuador, Indonesia   Binder: Honduras
Filler: Dominican Republic, Honduras and Nicaragua

Shape	Name	Lgth	Ring	Wrapper
Corona	No. 10	5½	43	CC
Robusto	No. 37	4½	50	CC-Ma
Double Corona	No. 59	7¼	54	CC-Ma
Long Corona	No. 60	6¼	44	CC-Ma
Toro	No. 61	6¼	50	CC-Ma
Corona Extra	No. 62	5½	47	CC-Ma
Churchill	No. 63	7¼	46	CC-Ma
Churchill	No. 70	6¾	48	CC-Ma
Giant	No. 80	8½	52	CC-Ma

HANDMADE CIGARS: BRAND LISTINGS

	Short-filler tobacco:			
Corona	Fuma	5½	44	CC-Ma

The complex blend of this cigar provides a medium-to-full bodied taste and is offered in economically-priced bundles of 25.

LA VIEJA HABANA
Handmade in Santiago, Dominican Republic.
Wrapper: Ecuador   *Binder: Ecuador*   *Filler: Dom. Rep., Honduras, Nicaragua*

Shape	Name	Lgth	Ring	Wrapper
Torpedo	Bullet	4½	54	CC
Torpedo	Gran Torpedo	6½	54	CC
Torpedo	Torpedo	5	54	CC
Double Corona	Churchill	7	50	CC
Toro	Toro	6	50	CC
Robusto	Gran Rothchild	5	54	CC
Lonsdale	Lonsdale	6¾	42	CC
Long Corona	Corona Grande	6	44	CC

Named for the old city of Havana — "La Vieja Habana" — this brand offers a powerful, full-bodied taste with plenty of large shapes in the line. Introduced in 1994, the blend includes a choice of Connecticut or Ecuadorian wrappers.

LADY JANE
Handmade in Danli, Honduras.
Wrapper: Indonesia   *Binder: Honduras*   *Filler: Honduras, Mexico*

Shape	Name	Lgth	Ring	Wrapper
Long Corona	Princesa	6¼	44	CC
Corona	Petit Corona	5½	42	CC

HANDMADE CIGARS: BRAND LISTINGS

There are just two shapes in this brand, but they offer a pleasant, mild-bodied flavor with a Sumatra wrapper. Lady Jane cigars are presented in cellophane sleeves in boxes of 25.

LAMBS CLUB
Handmade in Santiago, Dominican Republic.

Wrapper: Ecuador *Binder: Honduras* *Filler: Brazil, Dom. Rep.*

Shape	Name	Lgth	Ring	Wrapper
Double Corona	Churchill	7	50	CC
Long Corona	Corona Extra	6½	43	CC
Toro	Toro	6	50	CC
Robusto	Rothschild	4¾	50	CC
Petit Corona	Chico	4½	40	CC

Lambs Club is a super-premium Dominican cigar, handmade by one of the most respected manufacturers in that country. Its rich, flavorful character is derived from the finest Dominican Olor and Piloto tobaccos, which together with a smooth Ecuadorian wrapper, develops a spicy, medium-bodied taste.

LANCELOT
Handmade in San Andres Tuxtla, Mexico.

Wrapper: Mexico *Binder: Mexico* *Filler: Mexico*

Shape	Name	Lgth	Ring	Wrapper
Lonsdale	Lancer	6½	42	CM-Ma
Long Corona	Principe	6	44	CM-Ma
Toro	Centenario	6	50	CM-Ma
Double Corona	Grand Marquis	7	50	CM-Ma
Robusto	Caballero	5	50	CM-Ma
Giant	Monarca	8	52	CM-Ma

A salute to the Age of Chivalry, this is a mild-bodied, all-Mexican cigar which is new for 1997. You can have your pick of wrappers: natural or maduro and you'll find Lancelots in carefully-built, all-cedar boxes of 25.

HANDMADE CIGARS: BRAND LISTINGS

LARGO Y ZORRO
Handmade in the Dominican Republic and Nicaragua.

BOHICA SERIES:

Wrapper: Nicaragua　　　　*Binder: Nicaragua*　　　　*Filler: Nicaragua*

LAS MUJERES SERIES:
Wrapper: Ecuador or USA/Connecticut

Binder: Dominican Republic　　　　*Filler: Dominican Republic, Honduras*

RIO FUERTE SERIES:

Wrapper: Dom. Rep.　　　　*Binder: Dom. Rep.*　　　　*Filler: Dom. Rep.*

Shape	Name	Lgth	Ring	Wrapper
	Bohica series, made in Nicaragua:			
Robusto	Robusto	5	50	CM
Toro	Toro	6⅛	52	CM
Churchill	Churchill	7⅜	47	CM
	Las Mujeres series, made in the Dominican Republic:			
Robusto	Robusto	5	50	CC
Toro	Churchill	6½	52	CC
Torpedo	Torpedo	6½	54	CC
	Rio Fuerte series, made in the Dominican Republic:			
Robusto	Corditos	5	50	CM
Torpedo	Conos	6	53	CM
Churchill	Churchill	7	48	CM
Giant	La Reina	8	50	CM

This direct-order brand first appeared in 1996. The Bohica line is considered mild, while the Las Mujeres group is medium-bodied and the Rio Fuerte is full-bodied. Connecticut wrappers are used for the Las Mujeres group except for the Robusto shape, for which Ecuadorian-grown leaf is employed. All of the shapes are offered in three-packs or in boxes of 25.

HANDMADE CIGARS: BRAND LISTINGS

LARS TETENS PHAT CIGARS
Handmade in New York, New York.
Wrapper: Cameroon and USA/Connecticut
Binder: Dominican Republic   Filler: Dominican Republic

Shape	Name	Lgth	Ring	Wrapper
	Evolving series:			
Toro		5¾	48	CM
Toro		5¾	50	CM
Robusto		5	50	CM
Double Corona		6¾	54	CM
Grand Corona		6	46	CM
Torpedo		6	60	CM
Giant		8	46	CM
Giant		8	50	CM
Churchill		7¾	46	CM
	Phat Cigars:			
Double Corona	Body Shop	7½	50	CI
Long Panatela	Saint Ash	7½	38	CI
Double Corona	VII	7	50	CI
Double Corona	ChurchHill	7½	50	CI
Torpedo	Asadachi	6	60	CI
Toro	Brief XTC	6	50	CI
Lonsdale	Sun Fook KA	6½	44	CI
Long Corona	Royal	6	44	CI
Robusto	Shorty	5½	50	CI
Panatela	Slim	6¼	36	CI

HANDMADE CIGARS: BRAND LISTINGS

	Musashi:			
Double Corona	Two Skies	7½	52	CI
Double Corona	Katana	7½	52	CI
Robusto	5 Rings	5¼	50	CI
Robusto	Wakizashi	5	50	CI
	Tesshu Torac:			
Double Corona	Fusako	7	66	CC
Toro	Seizan	6	50	CC
Robusto	Yamaoka	5	50	CC
	Grass:			
Torpedo	Da Joint	5	36	CM
Torpedo	Grass			CM
	Rare & Expensive:			
Lonsdale		7	44-7	CM
Long Panatela		8	34-9	CM
Long Panatela		7	38	CM
Double Corona		7½	50-6	CM

This mysterious, 1995-introduced brand is hard to find, expensive and utterly impossible to explain. The cigars are rolled in New York with constantly changing shapes, names, sizes and blend; this listing is a snapshot of the brand at the time of publication. The relative strengths of the series include Tesshu: mild to medium; Phat: medium; Evolving and Musashi: medium to full, and Grass and Rare: full-bodied. Some of the lines are treated with special oils; the Rare line is reportedly made with pre-embargo Cuban tobacco. Some lines have shape names and some do not. Some people like these cigars, some do not. They are, however, unique. And no other brand can claim any bands that rival this one for size, color or the quality of artwork, perhaps a collector's item in the making.

HANDMADE CIGARS: BRAND LISTINGS

LAS CABRILLAS
Handmade in Danli, Honduras.

Wrapper: USA/Connecticut   Binder: Mexico   Filler: Nicaragua

Shape	Name	Lgth	Ring	Wrapper
Small Panatela	Pizarro	5½	32	CC
Double Corona	Maximilian	7	56	CC-Ma
Giant	Columbus	8¼	52	CC-Ma
Double Corona	Balboa	7½	54	CC-Ma
Double Corona	De Soto	6⅞	50	CC-Ma
Robusto	Cortez	4¾	50	CC-Ma
Lonsdale	Ponce de Leon	6¾	44	CC-Ma
Churchill	Vasco de Gama	7	48	CC-Ma
Long Corona	Magellan	6	42	CC
Panatela	Coronado	6⅞	35	CC

The explorers of the "New World" are saluted in this brand, which debuted in 1993 and which offers a medium-bodied taste. New in 1997 is the Maximilian, a double corona, which will be offered in boxes of 20, and the Vasco de Gama, which like the rest of the brand – except Columbus (10s) and Pizarro (60s) – is available in boxes of 25.

LAS VEGAS CIGAR CO.
Handmade in Las Vegas, Nevada, USA.

Wrapper: Ecuador, Mexico   Binder: Dom. Rep.   Filler: Dom. Rep., Mexico

Shape	Name	Lgth	Ring	Wrapper
Long Panatela	Palma	7	38	CI
Robusto	Rothchild	4½	50	CI-Ma
Small Panatela	Nix	5	30	CI
Corona	Corona	5¾	42	CI-Ma
Corona	Montefino	5¾	52	CI-Ma
Slim Panatela	Pencil	6¾	30	CI

HANDMADE CIGARS: BRAND LISTINGS

Toro	Punch		6½	52	Cl-Ma
Lonsdale	Corona Largo		6¾	44	Cl-Ma
Lonsdale	Fuma	*(short filler)*	6¾	46	Cl
Panatela	Panatela		6¾	36	Cl
Double Corona	Churchill		7½	50	Cl-Ma
Churchill	Imperial		7	46	Cl-Ma
Giant	Excalibur		8¾	52	Cl-Ma
Giant	El Rey		9	60	Cl-Ma
Toro	El Rey Corto		5	62	Cl-Ma
Torpedo	Torpedo		7	60	Cl-Ma
Lonsdale	Rum		6¾	44	Cl-Ma

You'll find this small factory in a storefront on the famous Las Vegas Strip. The body varies from mild (Corona, Corona Largo) to heavy (Excalibur, El Rey), with the majority of the sizes rated as medium. Note the large number of shapes with big ring gauges.

LAZARUS
Handmade in San Andres Tuxtla, Mexico.

Wrapper: Mexico   Binder: Mexico   Filler: Mexico

Shape	Name	Lgth	Ring	Wrapper
Churchill	Excalibur	6¾	46	CM-Ma
Long Corona	Siglo	6	44	CM-Ma
Toro	Delicioso	6	52	CM-Ma
Double Corona	Glorioso	7	50	CM-Ma
Robusto	Bravo	5	52	CM-Ma
Churchill	Esplendido	7½	46	CM-Ma
Giant	Royal	8	52	CM-Ma
Long Panatela	Lancero	6¾	38	CM

HANDMADE CIGARS: BRAND LISTINGS

This is a mild-bodied, all-Mexican cigar which is new for 1997. You can have your pick of wrappers: natural or maduro and you'll find Lazarus in carefully-built, all-cedar boxes of 25.

LEGACY
Handmade in Danli, Honduras.

Wrapper: Ecuador   *Binder: Honduras*   *Filler: Honduras*

Shape	Name	Lgth	Ring	Wrapper
Giant	No. 6 Napoleon	8½	52	CC-Ma
Double Corona	No. 5 Monarch	7	52	CC-Ma
Churchill	No. 4 Corona Grande	7½	46	CC
Lonsdale	No. 3 Elegante	7	43	CC
Robusto	No. 2 Rothchild	5	50	CC-Ma
Long Corona	No. 1 Super Cetro	6	43	CC

This is a premium, imported cigar offered in unique 18-pack bundles. Made entirely by hand with high-quality, long-filler tobaccos, the price is just as captivating as the medium-bodied taste.

LEGEND•ARIO
Handmade in Danli, Honduras.

Wrapper: Ecuador   *Binder: Honduras*   *Filler: Honduras*

Shape	Name	Lgth	Ring	Wrapper
Churchill	Churchill	7	48	CC
Lonsdale	No. 1	6½	44	CC
Corona	No. 4	5½	44	CC
Toro	Super Rothschild	6	50	CC
Robusto	Rothschild	5	50	CC

Introduced in 1996, this brand offers five classic shapes in a medium-bodied blend matching an Ecuadorian-grown wrapper with Honduran binder and filler leaves.

HANDMADE CIGARS: BRAND LISTINGS

LEGION
Handmade in Esteli, Nicaragua.

Wrapper: Ecuador   Binder: Nicaragua   Filler: Nicaragua

Shape	Name	Lgth	Ring	Wrapper
Giant	No. 852	8	52	CI
Churchill	No. 748	7	48	CI
Toro	No. 650	6	50	CI
Robusto	No. 450	4¾	50	CI
Lonsdale	No. 644	6½	44	CI
Corona	No. 544	5½	44	CI
Toro	No. 654	6	54	CI
Double Corona	No. 752	7	52	CI

New in 1997, this is a medium-bodied brand with an elegant aroma, offered in boxes of 25.

LEMPIRA
Handmade in Danli, Honduras.

Wrapper: Ecuador   Binder: Dom. Rep.   Filler: Honduras, Nicaragua

Shape	Name	Lgth	Ring	Wrapper
Corona	Coronas	5½	42	Co
Robusto	Robusto	5	50	Co
Lonsdale	Lonsdale	6½	44	Co
Long Panatela	Lanceros	7½	38	Co
Toro	Toro	6	50	Co
Churchill	Churchills	7	48	Co
Double Corona	Presidents	7¾	50	Co

The Lempira is manufactured in Honduras using a blended filler from Honduras and Nicaragua, adding a binder from the Dominican Republic for extra flavor.

HANDMADE CIGARS: BRAND LISTINGS

The wrapper is Ecuadorian-grown, Connecticut Shade. This is a medium-strength cigar with lots of flavor.

LEON
Handmade in Los Angeles, California, USA.

Wrapper: Ecuador   Binder & Filler: Central American blend

Shape	Name	Lgth	Ring	Wrapper
Lonsdale	Cazadores	7	44	Ma
Lonsdale	Cetro	6½	44	CC
Churchill	Cubarro	7	46	CC
Lonsdale	Fuma	7	44	Ma
Long Panatela	Panetelas	7	36	CC
Double Corona	Presidentes	7½	50	CC-Ma
Lonsdale	Numero 4	6½	44	Ma
Toro	Tronquito	5¾	50	CC-Ma
Giant	Gigante	8	52	Ma

In a nondescript shop on 6th Street in midtown Los Angeles is Roberto Leon, putting together handmade, medium-bodied cigars that are favored by enthusiasts who appreciate quality and value. One common sight: motorcycle-mounted police lighting up a Presidentes for the road!

LEON
Handmade, with short filler, in Santiago, Dominican Republic.

Wrapper: Indonesia   Binder: Dom. Rep.   Filler: Dom. Rep.

Shape	Name	Lgth	Ring	Wrapper
Double Corona	Churchill	7	50	CC
Lonsdale	No. 1	6½	44	CC
Churchill	Gran Corona	6¾	46	CC
Robusto	Robusto	5	50	CC

HANDMADE CIGARS: BRAND LISTINGS

This brand was introduced in 1996, offering a medium body. It is presented with unique packaging, as the cedar box of 20 is topped with plexiglass, giving a full view of the precious gems inside!

LEON JIMENES
Handmade in the Santiago, Dominican Republic.

Wrapper: USA/Connecticut   *Binder: Dom. Rep.*   *Filler: Dom. Rep.*

Shape	Name	Lgth	Ring	Wrapper
Double Corona	No. 1	7½	50	CM
Churchill	No. 2	7	47	CM
Lonsdale	No. 3	6½	42	CM
Corona	No. 4	5⅝	42	CM
Short Panatela	No. 5	5	38	CM
Robusto	Robusto	5½	50	CM
Pyramid	Torpedo	6	58	CM
Torpedo	Gran Corona	6½	50	CM
Torpedo	Belicoso	6¼	52	CM
Robusto	Petit Belicoso	5	52	CM
Churchill	Churchill De Luxe	7	47	CM
Lonsdale	Cristal (tubed)	6½	42	CM
Small Panatela	Petites	4	30	CM

Introduced in the 1970s, Leon Jimenes is a hand-made, full-bodied cigar with Dominican fillers and binder, encased in a Connecticut wrapper that provides excellent balance and an exquisite aroma. The brand is presented in individual cellophane sleeves, packed in elegant all-cedar boxes of 5, 10 or 25 in most shapes.

LEW'S SMOKERS
Handmade in Cofradia, Honduras.

Wrapper: Honduras   *Binder: Mexico*   *Filler: Honduras*

HANDMADE CIGARS: BRAND LISTINGS

Shape	Name	Lgth	Ring	Wrapper
Churchill	Sunday Special	7	48	CM
Long Corona	Pop's Choice	6	44	CM

This brand debuted in 1996, created by the endlessly creative Lew Rothman, who puts his name on a medium-bodied blend of Havana seed fillers, Mexican binder and Connecticut-seed wrappers grown in Honduras. The gimmick? A special sweetening of the gum used to seal the cap, to give a sweet taste upon lighting!

LEYENDA
Handmade in Tamboril, Dominican Republic.

Wrapper: Indonesia   Binder: Indonesia   Filler: Dominican Republic

Shape	Name	Lgth	Ring	Wrapper
Double Corona	Churchill	7	50	CM
Torpedo	Piramide	6	53	CM
Long Corona	Corona	6	44	CM
Robusto	Robusto	5	50	CM

This brand was introduced in 1997 and has a mild-bodied flavor. Made with long-filler tobaccos only, each cigar is protected in a cellophane sleeve and each size is offered in boxes of 25.

LICENCIADOS
Handmade in Santiago, Dominican Republic.

Wrapper: USA/Connecticut   Binder: Dom. Rep.   Filler: Dom. Rep.

Shape	Name	Lgth	Ring	Wrapper
Double Corona	Churchill	7	50	CM
Long Corona	Excellentes	6¾	43	CM
Small Panatela	Expreso	4½	35	CM
Torpedo	Figurado	6	56	CM
Corona	No. 4	5¾	43	CM

HANDMADE CIGARS: BRAND LISTINGS

Long Panatela	Panatela Linda	7	38	CM
Giant	Presidentes	8	50	CM
Giant	Soberanos	8½	52	CM
Toro	Toro	6	50	CM
Robusto	Wavell	5	50	CC-Ma
Corona	No. 200	5¾	43	Ma
Lonsdale	No. 300	6¾	43	Ma
Toro	No. 400	6	50	Ma
Giant	No. 500	8	50	Ma

Introduced in 1988, this veteran handmade brand has earned a reputation for excellence in taste, construction and value. The wide range of shapes and medium-bodied flavor makes it accessible to many smokers. It is offered in colorful boxes of 25.

LICEY
Handmade in Licey, Dominican Republic.

Wrapper: Indonesia   *Binder: Dom. Rep.*   *Filler: Dom. Rep.*

Shape	Name	Lgth	Ring	Wrapper
Giant	Churchill	8	48	Ma
Long Corona	Diplomatico	6	44	Ma
Pyramid	Piramid	6½	53	Ma
Robusto	Robusto	5	50	Ma
Grand Corona	Double Corona	6½	46	Ma

Named for the city of its birth, this cigar offers a mild-bodied flavor in an all-maduro line. Look for it in elegant cedar cabinets of 25.

LITTLE HAVANA CIGAR FACTORY
Handmade in Chicago, Illinois, USA.

Wrapper: Dom. Rep.   *Binder: Dom. Rep.*   *Filler: Dom. Rep.*

HANDMADE CIGARS: BRAND LISTINGS

Shape	Name	Lgth	Ring	Wrapper
Slim Panatela	Petit	5	32	CM
Corona	Fino	5½	42	CM
Panatela	Panatella	6	36	CM
Panatela	Chocolate Sensation	6	36	CM
Robusto	Santiago	5	50	CM
Robusto	Señor Julio	5½	52	CM
Grand Corona	Fuma	6	46	CM
Grand Corona	Monte Rico	6	46	CM
Toro	Cueste de Oro	6	50	CM
Double Corona	Favorito	7	50	CM
Double Corona	Maestro	7¾	52	CM
Torpedo	Torpedo	6	54	CM
Torpedo	Gran Torpedo	7	54	CM

From the Windy City comes this brand, whose history dates back to the tobacco fields of Cuba in 1938. Today's version uses all Dominican tobacco and offers a medium-bodied blend of leaves.

LONE WOLF
Handmade in Santiago, Dominican Republic.

LOBO ROJO:

Wrapper: Indonesia   *Binder: Dom. Rep.*   *Filler: Dom. Rep.*

SIGNATURE SELECT:

Wrapper: USA/Connecticut   *Binder: Dom. Rep.*   *Filler: Dom. Rep.*

VINTAGE SERIES:

Wrapper: Indonesia   *Binder: Dom. Rep.*   *Filler: Dom. Rep.*

HANDMADE CIGARS: BRAND LISTINGS

Shape	Name	Lgth	Ring	Wrapper
	Lobo Rojo:			
Robusto	Robusto	5	50	Co
Short Panatela	Petit Corona	5	38	Co
Lonsdale	Lonsdale	6⅜	44	Co
Torpedo	Belicoso	6¼	52	Co
Churchill	Churchill	6⅝	48	Co
Double Corona	Double Corona	7½	50	Co
	Signature Select:			
Robusto	Robusto	5	50	CC
Corona	Corona	5½	44	CC
Toro	Toro	6	50	CC
Torpedo	Triangular	6	52	CC
Double Corona	Churchill	7	50	CC
	Vintage Series:			
Robusto	Robusto	4½	50	CC
Corona	Corona	5½	42	CC
Toro	Toro	6	50	CC
Torpedo	Torpedo	6	52	CC
Churchill	Churchill	6¾	48	CC
Double Corona	Double Corona	7½	50	CC

Lone Wolf is a 1996-created brand developed by well-known film and television stars Jim Belushi and Chuck Norris. Three different Dominican manufacturers are involved in the making of these cigars, which offer a taste for every palate. Belushi's Lobo Rojo ("Red Wolf") series features a Cameroon-seed wrapper and is considered mild-to-medium in strength. The Signature Select blend was chosen by Norris for its medium-bodied taste and complex blend of flavors. It is offered in traditional 8-9-8 varnished boxes. The Vintage Series has a mild-to-medium strength of flavor using two-year aged Dominican filler and an Indonesian wrapper.

LOS NICAS
Handmade in Esteli, Nicaragua.

Wrapper: Nicaragua　　　　*Binder: Nicaragua*　　　　*Filler: Nicaragua*

Shape	Name	Lgth	Ring	Wrapper
Robusto	Robusto	5	50	CC
Corona	Corona	5½	42	CC
Toro	Grande Robusto	6	50	CC
Double Corona	Presidente	7	50	CC

Here is a new cigar in 1997, with a medium body. It is available in today's most popular shapes (look at those 50-ring sizes!) and offered in bundles of 25 or in boxes of 5 or 25.

LUNA AZUL
Handmade in Navarette, Dominican Republic.

Wrapper: Indonesia　　　　*Binder: Dom. Rep.*　　　　*Filler: Dom. Rep.*

Shape	Name	Lgth	Ring	Wrapper
Double Corona	Churchill	7½	50	CM
Robusto	Robusto	5½	50	CM
Grand Corona	Corona Grande	6¾	46	CM
Lonsdale	Corona	6¼	44	CM
Corona	Petite Corona	5½	42	CM
Churchill	Lonsdale	6¾	48	CM

The idea behind the name? "Cigars this good come only once in a blue moon!" This is a medium-bodied blend, offered in cedar boxes of 25, in bundles of 25 or in special cedar carry cases of three cigars in the Corona Grande and Churchill sizes.

HANDMADE CIGARS: BRAND LISTINGS

MACABI
Handmade in Santiago, Dominican Republic.

Wrapper: USA/Connecticut   Binder: Mexico   Filler: Dom. Rep., Nicaragua

Shape	Name	Lgth	Ring	Wrapper
Double Corona	Super Corona	7¾	52	Co
Double Corona	Double Corona	6⅞	49	Co
Lonsdale	No. 1	6¾	44	Co
Torpedo	Belicoso Fino	6¼	52	Co
Toro	Corona Extra	6	50	Co
Corona	Media Corona	5½	43	Co
Robusto	Royal Corona	5	50	Co

Introduced in 1995, this brand – launched as the "pride of Miami" – has been made in Santiago, Dominican Republic beginning in 1997. Handmade in the centuries-old tradition and under the watchful eye of master cigar maker Juan Sosa, Macabi brings a medium-bodied flavor to connoisseurs of fine cigars. Very smooth and slightly spicy, these gems are offered uncellophaned in slide-top cedar boxes.

MACANUDO
Handmade in Santiago, Dominican Republic
and in Kingston, Jamaica.

Wrapper: USA/Connecticut   Binder: Mexico   Filler: Dom. Rep., Jamaica, Mexico

Shape	Name		Lgth	Ring	Wrapper
	Handmade in Jamaica:				
Small Panatela	Ascot		4⅛	32	Cl
Short Panatela	Caviar		4	36	Cl
Slim Panatela	Claybourne		6	31	DC-Cl
Short Panatela	Petit Corona		5	38	Cl
Corona	Duke of Devon		5½	42	DC-Cl-Ma
Long Panatela	Portofino	(tubed)	7	34	Cl

HANDMADE CIGARS: BRAND LISTINGS

Corona	Hampton Court (tubed)	5¾	43	CI
Robusto	Hyde Park	5½	49	CI-Ma
Lonsdale	Baron de Rothschild	6½	42	DC-CI-Ma
Robusto	Crystal (tubed)	5½	50	CI
Torpedo	Duke of Windsor	6	50	CI
Giant	Prince of Wales	8	52	CI
Cigarillo	Miniature	3¾	24	CI
	Handmade in the Dominican Republic:			
Double Corona	Prince Philip	7½	49	DC-CI-Ma
	Vintage Cabinet Selection, handmade in Jamaica:			
Double Corona	I	7½	49	CM
Lonsdale	II	6½	43	CM
Corona	III	5½	43	CM
Corona Extra	IV	4½	47	CM
Robusto	V	5½	49	CM
Torpedo	VI	6	52	CM
Long Panatela	VII	7½	38	CM
Robusto	VIII (tubed)	5½	50	CM
Churchill	XX	7	47	CM

An exceptionally consistent cigar, made with Connecticut Shade wrappers that have been aged for at least three years. The cigar has a silky feel to the hand and has a taste which is only found in a Macanudo. The Vintage Cabinet Selection cigars are each more than four years in the making and include filler leaves from the Dominican Republic and Mexico. Vintage Cabinet cigars have been offered only in the following years: 1979, 1984, 1988 and 1993.

MACARENA

Handmade in Las Palmas, the Canary Islands of Spain.

Wrapper: USA/Connecticut   Binder: Indonesia   Filler: Brazil, Dom. Rep., Indonesia

MACARENA Cigars

A cigar hand made with delicacy
and care which only Spanish
women are capable of putting
into such a task.

Due to this, Macarena cigars are
quite unique, and can be set
aside for connoisseurs.

When you think of a great cigar
think of Macarena.

What CAN YOU EXPECT
from the hands
of a Spanish WOMAN?

Always a MASTERPIECE

THE GREEN BOX

HANDMADE CIGARS: BRAND LISTINGS

Shape	Name	Lgth	Ring	Wrapper
Double Corona	Doble Corona	7½	50	CC
Toro	Toro	6	50	CC
Robusto	Robusto	5	50	CC
Lonsdale	Lonsdale	6½	43	CC

Yes, it's a cigar inspired by the dance craze of the mid-90s, the "macarena."
Although smoking this brand might not make you a better dancer, it will certainly
mark you as a keen observer of pop culture! The blend is mild and this 1997-
introduced brand is offered in boxes of 25 cigars each.

MADAME MARSHALL
BY DANIEL MARSHALL
Handmade in Santiago, Dominican Republic.

Wrapper: Cameroon   *Filler: Dominican Republic*

Shape	Name	Lgth	Ring	Wrapper
Small Panatela	Madame Marshall	4	30	CC

New for 1997, this is a small but very well made cigar from the Dominican
Republic. It has a medium-bodied taste thanks to the Cameroon wrapper and is
offered in elegant, all-cedar boxes.

MADRIGAL HABANA
Handmade in San Andres Tuxtla, Mexico.

Wrapper: Mexico   *Binder: Mexico*   *Filler: Mexico*

Shape	Name	Lgth	Ring	Wrapper
Giant	Monarch	8	54	CC-Ma
Double Corona	Imperial	7½	52	CC-Ma
Robusto	Robusto	5	52	CC-Ma
Toro	Governor	6	50	CC-Ma
Lonsdale	Classic Corona	7	44	CC-Ma
Corona	Petit Corona	5½	42	CC-Ma

HANDMADE CIGARS: BRAND LISTINGS

Re-introduced in 1996, this is an old Havana brand which had been kicked around by several cigar manufacturers since the 1970s and was produced primarily in Honduras. In 1985, Brick-Hanauer acquired the brand and found the right formula for a new, mild smoke featuring all-Mexican tobacco. The blend includes Connecticut Shade-seed tobacco for the natural wrappers and Jaltepec leaves for the maduro wrappers. Even the box speaks elegance: it is an exact copy of a 1927 box of Madrigal, then made in Havana.

MAESTRO
Handmade in San Diego, California, USA

Wrapper: Ecuador   Binder: Ecuador   Filler: Honduras, Mexico

Shape	Name	Lgth	Ring	Wrapper
Torpedo	No. 1	6	54	Ma
Toro	No. 2	6½	50	Ma
Robusto	No. 3	4¾	52	Ma
Grand Corona	No. 4	5¾	46	Ma

California, here I come! Experienced Cuban hands direct the making of these cigars in the lively Cuban Cigar Factory in the Gaslamp District of San Diego. You can see them rolling, then try the finished result — a full-bodied, all-maduro series with a rich flavor, offered in boxes of 25.

MAESTRO CUBANO
Handmade in Danli, Honduras.

Wrapper: Indonesia   Binder: Honduras   Filler: Honduras, Mexico

Shape	Name	Lgth	Ring	Wrapper
Robusto	Robusto	5	50	CC
Double Corona	Churchill Original Label	7½	52	CC
Torpedo	Torpido Figurado	6	52	CC
Long Corona	Lonsdale	6¼	44	CC

This brand debuted in late 1996 and offers a medium-bodied taste. It features a Sumatra-seed wrapper and a two-nation interior blend that is presented in varnished, all-cedar boxes of 25.

COMME IL FAUT

AS IT SHOULD BE; PERFECT.

HANDMADE CIGARS: BRAND LISTINGS

MAESTRO DE LA PALMA
Handmade in Las Palmas, the Canary Islands of Spain.
Wrapper: Indonesia or USA/Connecticut
Binder: Canary Islands   Filler: Canary Islands

Shape	Name	Lgth	Ring	Wrapper
Robusto	Santa Cruz	4¾	50	CM-Ma
Corona Extra	Urbano	5½	46	CM-Ma
Grand Corona	Punta Gorda	6½	46	CM
Double Corona	El Paso	7¼	50	CM

Here is a 1997-introduced, mild-bodied cigar available in English Market Selection (Connecticut) or maduro leaf (Indonesia). You can find it in boxes of 25.

MAKER'S MARK
Handmade in Navarette, Dominican Republic.
Wrapper: Indonesia   Binder: Dom. Rep.   Filler: Dom. Rep.

Shape	Name	Lgth	Ring	Wrapper
Toro	Robusto	6	50	CM

The famous bourbon, frozen into a cigar?!? Not quite . . . this is a medium-to-full-bodied, long-filler, quality cigar which is imbued with the luscious taste of famous Maker's Mark bourbon over a 5-7 day process. It features a Sumatra wrapper and is offered in individual glass tubes, in "Amatista"-style glass jars or in re-supply boxes of 25.

MANIFIESTO
Handmade in Villa Gonzalez, Dominican Republic.
Wrapper: Indonesia   Binder: Dom. Rep.   Filler: Dom. Rep.

Shape	Name	Lgth	Ring	Wrapper
Giant	Presidente	8	52	CC
Torpedo	Torpedo	6	52	CC
Toro	Toro	6	54	CC

Double Corona	Churchill	7½	50	CC
Toro	Robusto	6	50	CC
Robusto	Rothschild	4½	50	CC
Churchill	Double Corona	7	48	CC
Torpedo	Torpedo No. 2	7	44	CC
Lonsdale	Corona	6½	44	CC
Corona	Petit Corona	5½	42	CC
Long Panatela	Panetela	7	36	CC

Here is a new brand for 1997, with a medium-bodied flavor and a Sumatra wrapper. It is offered in all-cedar boxes of 10 in five shapes and in 25s in all shapes.

MANUEL CASALS
Handmade in Vera Cruz, Mexico.

Wrapper: Mexico   Binder: Mexico   Filler: Mexico

Shape	Name	Lgth	Ring	Wrapper
Double Corona	Churchill	7¼	52	CM
Grand Corona	No. 1	6¼	46	CM
Toro	No. 3	6	52	CM
Petit Corona	No. 4	5	42	CM

Here is a medium-bodied cigar introduced in 1997. It features all-Mexican tobaccos and is presented in boxes of 25.

MARIA MANCINI
Handmade in Cofradia, Honduras.

Wrapper: Honduras   Binder: Honduras   Filler: Honduras

Shape	Name	Lgth	Ring	Wrapper
Double Corona	Clemenceau	7	49	CC-CM
Corona	Corona Classico	5½	43	CC-CM

Long Corona	Corona Larga	6¼	43	CC-CM
Robusto	De Gaulle	5	50	CM
Lonsdale	Grandee	6¾	43	CC-CM
Panatela	Palma Delgado	7	39	CC-CM

This is a heavy-bodied, all-Honduran blend, featuring Cuban-seed tobaccos that produce a full-flavored taste with an easy draw.

MARIO PALOMINO
Handmade in Kingston, Jamaica.

Wrapper: USA/Connecticut   *Binder: Mexico*   *Filler: Jamaica*

Shape	Name	Lgth	Ring	Wrapper
Slim Panatela	Buccaneers	5½	32	CC
Petit Corona	Petit Corona	5	41	CC
Slim Panatela	Rapier	6	32	CC
Long Corona	Festivale	6	41	CC
Lonsdale	Cetro	6½	42	CC
Grand Corona	Corona Immensa	6	47	CC
Lonsdale	Caballero	7½	45	CC
Double Corona	Presidente	7½	49	CC
Giant	Churchill	8	52	CC

These cigars are manufactured by The Palomino Brothers Tobacco Co. in Jamaica. The blend features Jamaican filler and in combination with the Mexican binder and Connecticut Shade wrapper produce a heavy, full-bodied flavor.

MARQUEZ MENDOZA
Handmade in Villa Gonzalez, Dominican Republic.

Wrapper: Ecuador   *Binder: Dom. Rep.*   *Filler: Dom. Rep.*

Shape	Name	Lgth	Ring	Wrapper
Double Corona	Marquez I	7½	50	CC

HANDMADE CIGARS: BRAND LISTINGS

Toro	Marquez II	6	50	CC
Robusto	Marquez III	5	52	CC
Long Panatela	Marquez IV	7	36	CC

Introduced in 1997, this brand offers a mild-bodied smoke with a Connecticut-seed wrapper, offered in boxes of 25.

MARSH 1840
Handmade in Danli, Honduras.

Wrapper: USA/Connecticut   *Binder: USA/Pennsylvania*
Filler: Dominican Republic, Nicaragua, USA/Pennsylvania

Shape	Name	Lgth	Ring	Wrapper
Lonsdale	Lonsdale	6½	43	CC-Ma

A grand old name in U.S. cigar making – M. Marsh & Son – again adorns a handmade cigar for the first time in more than 70 years! This new handmade cigar is offered in one classic size only and presents a mild-to-medium taste with its blend of U.S.-grown, Dominican and Nicaraguan tobaccos. The available wrappers include shade-grown Connecticut and Connecticut Broadleaf for the maduro version. You can find it boxes of 25.

MASTER BRADLEY'S PREMIUM DOMINICAN
Handmade in Santiago, Dominican Republic.

Wrapper: Indonesia   *Binder: Dom. Rep.*   *Filler: Dom. Rep.*

Shape	Name	Lgth	Ring	Wrapper
Long Corona	Breva	6	44	CC
Robusto	Toro	5	50	CC
Churchill	Churchill	7	48	CC

Introduced in 1997, here is a mild-to-medium-bodied, value-priced bundle of 20 cigars, each protected in an individual cellophane sleeve. The wrapper is genuine Sumatra, with a blend of Dominican-grown leaves inside.

HANDMADE CIGARS: BRAND LISTINGS

MATACAN
Handmade in San Andres Tuxtla, Mexico.

Wrapper: Mexico   *Binder: Mexico*   *Filler: Mexico, Nicaragua*

Shape	Name	Lgth	Ring	Wrapper
Double Corona	No. 1	7½	50	CC-Ma
Toro	No. 2	6	50	CC-Ma
Grand Corona	No. 3	6⅝	46	CC-Ma
Lonsdale	No. 4	6⅝	42	CC-Ma
Long Corona	No. 5	6	42	CC-Ma
Panatela	No. 6	6⅝	35	CC-Ma
Robusto	No. 7	4¾	50	CC-Ma
Giant	No. 8	8	52	CC-Ma
Small Panatela	No. 9	5	32	CC-Ma
Double Corona	No. 10	6⅞	54	CC-Ma

Good value, good quality and a medium-bodied taste led by San Andres Valley tobaccos is the promise of Matacan. These cigars are offered in bundles of 20.

MATADOR
Handmade in Danli, Honduras.

Wrapper: Ecuador   *Binder: Honduras*   *Filler: Dom. Rep., Nicaragua*

Shape	Name	Lgth	Ring	Wrapper
Robusto	Robusto	4¾	54	CC
Corona	Corona	5¾	42	CC
Toro	Doble Corona	6	54	CC
Lonsdale	No. 1	7	44	CC
Churchill	Churchill	7⅞	48	CC
Torpedo	Torpedo	6	52	CC

HANDMADE CIGARS: BRAND LISTINGS

Here is a rarely-seen, but highly respected brand with medium body and excellent construction. The brand is offered in boxes of 25.

M.A.T.A.S.A. SECONDS
Handmade in Santiago, Dominican Republic.

Wrapper: USA/Connecticut *Binder: Mexico* *Filler: Dom. Rep.*

Shape	Name	Lgth	Ring	Wrapper
Small Panatela	Chico	4	32	CC
Double Corona	Churchill	7	50	CC
Long Corona	Corona	6	43	CC
Giant	King Kong	8½	52	CC
Lonsdale	No. 2	6½	43	CC-Ma
Corona	No. 4	5½	43	CC-Ma
Short Panatela	No. 5	5	35	CC
Panatela	No. 21	5½	38	CC
Toro	No. 502	6	54	CC
Grand Corona	No. 505	6½	45	CC
Long Panatela	Palma Fina	7	36	CC
Toro	Regulare	6	50	CC
Short Panatela	Palmita	5	38	CC
Grand Corona	Seniors	6	46	CC
Panatela	Super Fino	6	36	CC-Ma
Robusto	Wavell	4½	50	CC

``MATASA'' is a highly-respected name in the cigar trade as it is the name of one of the Dominican Republic's finest cigar manufacturing groups. These seconds are overruns of some of the factory's "big name" cigars, and are very mild with a beautiful Connecticut wrapper.

HANDMADE CIGARS: BRAND LISTINGS

MATCH PLAY
Handmade in the Santiago, Dominican Republic.

Wrapper: Ecuador   Binder: Dom. Rep.   Filler: Dom. Rep.

Shape	Name	Lgth	Ring	Wrapper
Robusto	Cypress	4¾	50	CC
Long Corona	St. Andrews	6¼	44	CC
Toro	Turnberry	6	50	CC
Churchill	Prestwick	6⅞	46	CC
Double Corona	Olympic	7½	50	CC
Pyramid	Troon	7	54	CC

This brand was introduced in 1995; it is a handmade, medium-bodied cigar that is the product of a balanced blend from four distinctly different tobaccos. It is enhanced by a Connecticut Seed wrapper that has a unique growing cycle and final processing procedure. Its golf-themed band is further reflected in the shape names taken from some of the world's great golf courses.

MATCH PLAY SERIE MEDALLISTA
Handmade in Santiago, Dominican Republic.

Wrapper: USA/Connecticut   Binder: Dom. Rep.   Filler: Dom. Rep.

Shape	Name	Lgth	Ring	Wrapper
Torpedo	No. 18	5¾	44	CC
Torpedo	No. 36	6	46	CC
Torpedo	No. 36	5½	48	CC
Torpedo	No. 72	6	52	CC

No, the heads of the cigars aren't shaped like golf clubs, but they might as well be! Here's a totally unique, all-torpedo line which celebrates the number of holes completed after one (18), two (36), three (54) or four (72) rounds of a golf tournament. The line offers a medium-to-full flavor and is offered in slide-top boxes of 25.

HANDMADE CIGARS: BRAND LISTINGS

MAXIM'S
BY PIERRE CARDIN
Handmade in Santiago, Dominican Republic.

Wrapper: USA/Connecticut   Binder: Dom. Rep.   Filler: Dom. Rep.

Shape	Name	Lgth	Ring	Wrapper
Double Corona	Omnibus	7	52	CC
Lonsdale	Royale	7	43	CC
Toro	Bistrot	6½	49	CC
Churchill	Imperial	7½	48	CC
Corona	Belle Epoque	5½	40	CC
Slim Panatela	Sehm	5	34	CC

Elegant is the word for this brand, introduced in 1997. It is medium-bodied and features a genuine Connecticut wrapper. Maxim's is presented in protective cellophane sleeves and packaged in all-cedar boxes of 25.

MAXIUS
Handmade in Santiago, Dominican Republic.
Wrapper: Indonesia or USA/Connecticut

Binder: Dominican Republic   Filler: Dominican Republic

Shape	Name	Lgth	Ring	Wrapper
	Sumatra line:			
Robusto	Robusto	5	50	CC
Lonsdale	Lonsdale	6½	44	CC
Churchill	Churchill	7	47	CC
Double Corona	Double Corona	7½	50	CC
	Connecticut line:			
Long Corona	Corona	6	44	CC
Robusto	Robusto	5	50	CC
Slim Panatela	Panatella	7	32	CC

Churchill	Churchill	6⅞	46	CC

This brand was new in 1996 and offers two different styles: the Sumatra line, which is medium-to-full in body and has a spicy finish, and the Connecticut line, which is mild-to-medium in body and slightly sweet. Both are products of the finest manufacturing facilities in the Dominican Republic.

MAYA
Handmade in Danli, Honduras.

Wrapper: Ecuador   *Binder: Honduras*   *Filler: Dom. Rep., Honduras*

Shape	Name	Lgth	Ring	Wrapper
Slim Panatela	Petit	5½	34	CI
Robusto	Robusto	5	50	CI-Ma
Torpedo	Torpedo	7	54	CI
Double Corona	Executives	7¾	50	CI-Ma
Churchill	Churchills	6⅞	49	CI-Ma
Lonsdale	Elegantes	7	43	CI
Long Corona	Corona	6¼	44	CI-Ma
Long Corona	Cetros	6	43	CI
Panatela	Palma Fina	6⅞	36	CI
Corona	Petit Coronas	5½	42	CI
Toro	Matador	6	50	CI-Ma
Giant	Viajantes	8½	52	CI

Introduced in the mid-1980s, the Maya brand is a Honduran, handmade, long-filler cigar with predominantly Honduran filler blended with Dominican Havana seed tobaccos. Maya's Havana-seed binder and Ecuadorian-grown, Connecticut-seed wrapper complete this mild-to-medium strength cigar.

MAYORGA
Handmade in Esteli, Nicaragua.

Wrapper: Indonesia   *Binder: Nicaragua*   *Filler: Nicaragua*

HANDMADE CIGARS: BRAND LISTINGS

Shape	Name	Lgth	Ring	Wrapper
Robusto	Robusto	4¾	50	CC
Corona	Corona	5½	44	CC
Toro	Toro	6	50	CC
Churchill	Churchill	7	48	CC
Torpedo	Torpedo	6¾	54	CC

Get ready for unbounded pleasure in this brand, introduced in 1997. It offers a Sumatra wrapper and Nicaraguan-grown, Cuban-seed binder and filler leaves. It has a medium body and rich, sometimes spicy flavors. You can find it carefully packaged in all-cedar boxes of 25.

MEDAL OF HONOR
Handmade in Danli, Honduras.

Wrapper: USA/Connecticut   Binder: Honduras   Filler: Honduras

Shape	Name	Lgth	Ring	Wrapper
Lonsdale	No. 300	6½	42	CC-Ma
Double Corona	No. 500	7½	50	CC-Ma
Giant	No. 700	8½	52	CC-Ma

A new standard for value, this premium bundle was introduced in 1995 and is 100% handmade in Honduras, using excellent-quality, long-filler tobaccos and distinctive packaging. These cigars are available in a choice of a Connecticut Shade or maduro wrapper.

MEMPHIS BLUE
Handmade in Veracruz, Mexico.

Wrapper: Indonesia   Binder: Mexico   Filler: Dom. Rep., Honduras, Mexico

Shape	Name	Lgth	Ring	Wrapper
Double Corona	Churchill	7	50	CM
Double Corona	Double Corona	7¼	50	CM
Robusto	Robusto	5	50	CM

Long Corona	Corona	6	42	CM

Introduced in 1997, this Mexican-made, medium-bodied brand features a Sumatra wrapper and a three-nation interior blend. You can find it in boxes of 25.

MENDEZ Y LOPEZ
Handmade in Santiago, Dominican Republic.

Wrapper: Indonesia   *Binder: Dom. Rep.*   *Filler: Dom. Rep.*

Shape	Name	Lgth	Ring	Wrapper
Cigarillo	Palmaritos	4	28	CM
Small Panetela	Finos	5	30	CM
Corona	Favorito	5½	42	CM
Robusto	Robusto	5½	50	CM
Panatela	Panetela	6	36	CM
Lonsdale	Latinos	6½	42	CM
Lonsdale	Exclusivos	6½	44	CM
Churchill	Churchill	6⅞	46	CM
Lonsdale	Palma de Mayorca	7	42	CM
Long Panatela	Panetelas Extra	7½	38	CM
Double Corona	Presidentes	7½	50	CM
Giant	Soberanos	8½	52	CM
Giant	Viajante	10	58	CM
Pyramid	Piramide Breve	5½	56	CM
Pyramid	Piramide	7½	64	CM
Torpedo	Piramide Gigante	8	68	CM

This is a very old Cuban brand, now re-constituted as a mild-bodied brand with 16 different shapes, including the stunning Piramide Gigante with its 68-ring diameter at the foot! It debuted in its present form in 1997 and is presented in boxes of 10 or 20 cigars each.

HANDMADE CIGARS: BRAND LISTINGS

MERCEDES
Handmade in Santo Domingo, Dominican Republic.
Wrapper: Indonesia, USA/Connecticut

Binder: Dominican Republic   Filler: Dominican Republic

Shape	Name	Lgth	Ring	Wrapper
Torpedo	No. 1 Torpedo	7	60	CC-Ma
Double Corona	No. 2 Double Corona	7½	52	CC-Ma
Long Panatela	No. 3 Lonsdale	7	38	CC-Ma
Corona	No. 4 Corona	5½	44	CC-Ma
Robusto	No. 5 Robusto	5	50	CC-Ma
Toro	No. 6 Toro	6	50	CC-Ma
Pyramid	No. 7 Pyramid	6	52	CC-Ma
Small Panatela	No. 9 Cordial	5	30	CC

Here is an easy-to-draw, medium-bodied (in Connecticut-grown natural) or medium-to-full-bodied (in Indonesian-grown maduro) cigar introduced into the U.S. in 1996. Available previously in France and the Caribbean, it is presented uncellophaned in all-cedar boxes of 25.

MEXICAN EMPERADOR
Handmade in San Andres Tuxtla, Mexico.

Wrapper: Mexico   Binder: Mexico   Filler: Mexico

Shape	Name	Lgth	Ring	Wrapper
Giant	Emperador	13¾	49	CC

The size says it all! This is a unique product of the famous San Andres Valley region of Mexico, the birthplace of many great brands. Despite its immense length, the 49-ring width makes it an accessible smoke, albeit a time-consuming one. The Emperador is individually packaged in an elegant, slide-top cedar box.

MI FLOR
Handmade in Danli, Honduras.

Wrapper: Ecuador   Binder: Dom. Rep.   Filler: Dom. Rep., Honduras

HANDMADE CIGARS: BRAND LISTINGS

Shape	Name	Lgth	Ring	Wrapper
Double Corona	Presidente	7½	50	CM
Churchill	Churchill	7	48	CM
Toro	Toro	6	50	CM
Long Corona	Cetro	6¼	44	CM
Robusto	Robusto	5	50	CM
Corona	Corona	5½	42	CM

New in 1997, this is a mild-to-medium-bodied cigar with a blend of three nations giving it a distinctive flavor. You will find "my flower" in cellophane sleeves inside all-cedar boxes of 25.

MiCubano
Handmade in Esteli, Nicaragua.

Wrapper: Nicaragua   Binder: Nicaragua   Filler: Nicaragua

Shape	Name		Lgth	Ring	Wrapper
Robusto	No. 450		4¾	50	CM
Corona	No. 542		5½	42	CM
Toro	No. 650		6	50	CM
Lonsdale	No. 644		6½	44	CM
Churchill	No. 748		7	48	CM
Giant	No. 852		8½	52	CM
Toro	Tubo No. 1	(tubed)	6	50	CM

Here, at long last, is a cigar made up of 100 percent Cuban-seed tobacco, which debuted in 1995. Grown in Nicaragua, the filler, binder and wrapper combine for a rich, uninhibited, full-bodied taste that is offered uncellophaned in beautiful all-cedar boxes of 25 cigars each.

HANDMADE CIGARS: BRAND LISTINGS

MIGUELON
Handmade in Manila, the Philippines.

Wrapper: Indonesia   Binder: Philippines   Filler: Philippines

Shape	Name	Lgth	Ring	Wrapper
Corona	Corona	5½	44	CC
Robusto	Robusto	5	52	CC

This is a well-made, medium-bodied cigar, introduced in 1997. It features a Java wrapper and is offered in boxes of 25.

MILLENIUM
Handmade in Santiago, Dominican Republic.

Wrapper: Indonesia   Binder: Dom. Rep.   Filler: Dom. Rep.

Shape	Name	Lgth	Ring	Wrapper
Robusto		5	50	CM
Grand Corona		6½	46	CM
Toro		6	50	CM

Here is a 1997-introduced brand with no shape names, but with a medium-to-full flavor, offered in box of 25.

MOCAMBO
Handmade in San Andres Tuxtla, Mexico.

Wrapper: Mexico   Binder: Mexico   Filler: Mexico

Shape	Name	Lgth	Ring	Wrapper
Double Corona	Churchill	7	50	CC-Ma
Toro	Double Corona	6	51	CC-Ma
Panatela	Empire	6½	39	CC
Giant	Inmensa	8½	50	CC-Ma
Lonsdale	Premier	6⅝	43	CC-Ma
Robusto	Robusto	4½	50	CC-Ma

HANDMADE CIGARS: BRAND LISTINGS

Long Corona	Royal Corona	6	42	CC-Ma
Churchill	S/L	6¾	48	CC-Ma

This is a heavy-bodied cigar, offered with a choice of a natural-colored wrapper or a sweeter, maduro-shade wrapper.

MONTAGUE
Handmade in Pandaan, Indonesia.

Wrapper: Brazil, Indonesia *Binder: Indonesia*
Filler: Brazil, Indonesia

Shape	Name	Lgth	Ring	Wrapper
Double Corona	No. 1	7¼	50	Cl-Ma
Grand Corona	No. 2	6⅔	45	Cl-Ma
Long Corona	No. 3	6	40	Cl-Ma
Robusto	Robustos	5	50	Cl-Ma
Lonsdale	Lanceros	7½	40	Cl-Ma

This Indonesian brand is made by hand with a medium-bodied taste. Two shades of wrapper are available: a light Claro of Indonesian Vorstenlanden tobacco and a deep maduro, of Brazilian Mata Fina, both of which produce a sophisticated and unique flavor.

MONTE CANARIO
Handmade in Las Palmas, the Canary Islands of Spain.

Wrapper: USA/Connecticut *Binder: Dominican Republic*
Filler: Brazil, Canary Islands, Dominican Republic

Shape	Name	Lgth	Ring	Wrapper
Lonsdale	Nuncios	6¾	44	Cl
Lonsdale	Imperiales	6½	42	Cl
Corona	No. 3	5¾	42	Cl
Panatela	Panatela	6	38	Cl
Robusto	Robustos	4¾	50	Cl

THE CONSISTENTLY PERFECT CIGAR.

Every leaf.

Every roll.

Every draw.

Every Montague.®

Only Montague.

| Double Corona | Churchill | 7 | 50 | CI |
| Torpedo | Figurados | 6 | 50 | CI |

Part of the long history of cigar-making in the Canary Islands, the Monte Canario brand has been around in one form or another since the 1920s. It's a mild smoke, featuring a Connecticut wrapper and a blend of leaves from three nations on the interior. It is presented uncellophaned in boxes of 25.

MONTE REAL
Handmade in Santiago, Dominican Republic.

Wrapper: USA/Connecticut   *Binder: Dom. Rep.*   *Filler: Dom. Rep.*

Shape	Name	Lgth	Ring	Wrapper
Double Corona	Churchill	7½	50	CC
Churchill	Grand Corona	6¾	46	CC
Lonsdale	Lonsdale	6½	44	CC
Toro	Toro	6	50	CC
Corona	Corona	5½	42	CC
Robusto	Robusto	5	50	CC

Here is a 1997-introduced brand, with a shiny Connecticut wrapper and a mild-body. It is offered in cellophane sleeves inside boxes or bundles of 25.

MONTE RIO
Handmade in Santiago, Dominican Republic.

Wrapper: Ecuador   *Binder: Dom. Rep.*   *Filler: Dom. Rep.*

Shape	Name	Lgth	Ring	Wrapper
Long Corona	Corona	6	44	CC
Grand Corona	Extra Corona	6	46	CC
Giant	Double Corona	8½	52	CC
Robusto	Robusto	5	50	CC
Churchill	Churchill	7½	48	CC

Torpedo	Torpedo	6½	52	CC

Introduced in 1997, here is a medium-bodied brand offered in six popular sizes in boxes of 25. A series of three bundled sizes (6 inches by 42 ring, 5 inches by 50 ring and 5 inches by 36 ring) with Amaretto, cinnamon, coconut, chocolate, mint, rum or vanilla flavoring is due in 1998.

MONTEBELLO
Handmade in San Andres Tuxtla, Mexico.

Wrapper: USA/Connecticut *Binder: Mexico* *Filler: Mexico*

Shape	Name	Lgth	Ring	Wrapper
Giant	Inmenso	8	52	CC
Double Corona	Embajador	7	50	CC
Robusto	Regio	5¼	50	CC
Grand Corona	Banquero	6½	46	CC
Corona	Corona	5¼	42	CC
Panatela	Panatela	5½	35	CC
Small Panatela	Petit	5	30	CC

Hard to find, this handmade brand is full-bodied with a unique flavor and a spicy finish. If you like them a lot, you can get them in all-cedar boxes of 25. If you'll be smoking only a few, pick up your Montebellos in a cedar box of 10 or a handy carton pack of five!

MONTECASSINO
Handmade in Danli, Honduras.

Wrapper: Honduras *Binder: Honduras* *Filler: Honduras*

Shape	Name	Lgth	Ring	Wrapper
Giant	Imperial	8½	52	CM
Lonsdale	Cazadores	6½	44	CM
Giant	Diamantes	8	50	CM
Lonsdale	No. 225	6½	44	CM

Long Panatela	Picadores	7	35	CM

These cigars are all made by hand and have a mild-to-medium body, despite their all-Honduran tobaccos. Montecassinos are offered in modestly-priced bundles of 25 cigars each.

MONTECRISTO
Handmade in La Romana, Dominican Republic.

Wrapper: USA/Connecticut   *Binder: Dom. Rep.*   *Filler: Dom. Rep.*

Shape	Name		Lgth	Ring	Wrapper
Churchill	Churchill		7	48	CC
Lonsdale	No. 1		6½	44	CC
Torpedo	No. 2		6	50	CC
Corona	No. 3		5½	44	CC
Robusto	Robustos		4¾	50	CC
Lonsdale	Tubos	(tubed)	6⅝	42	CC
Toro	Double Corona		6½	50	CC
Corona Extra	Corona Grande		5¾	46	CC

This famous name in cigars is relatively young, as the brand was originated in 1935 in Cuba. Today's Dominican version, introduced in 1995, offers outstanding craftsmanship and a slow-burning, medium-to-heavy-bodied smoke whose obvious quality is the lasting impression.

MONTECRUZ
Handmade in La Romana, Dominican Republic.
Wrapper: Indonesia, USA/Connecticut

Binder: Dominican Republic   *Filler: Brazil, Dominican Republic*

Shape	Name	Lgth	Ring	Wrapper
Churchill	No. 200	7¼	46	CI-CM
Lonsdale	No. 210	6½	42	DC-CI-CM
Corona	No. 220	5½	42	DC-CI-CM

HANDMADE CIGARS: BRAND LISTINGS

Petit Corona	No. 230		5	42	CM
Long Panatela	No. 255		7	36	Cl-CM
Short Panatela	No. 270		4¾	36	CM
Slim Panatela	No. 276		6	32	CM
Cigarillo	No. 281		6	28	CM
Petit Corona	Cedar Aged		5	42	Cl-CM
Robusto	Robusto		4½	49	CM
Giant	Individuales		8	46	CM
Toro	Colossus		6½	50	CM
Long Corona	Tubos	*(tubed)*	6	42	CM
Panatela	Tubulares	*(tubed)*	6⅛	36	Cl-CM
	Machine-made small cigars:				
Cigarillo	Chicos		4	28	Cl-CM
Slim Panatela	Juniors		5¼	33	Cl-CM
Panatela	Senores		5¾	35	Cl-CM

Originated in 1959 in the Canary Islands of Spain, Montecruz Sun Grown cigars have been hand crafted in La Romana in the Dominican Republic since 1977. The filler is a blend of Dominican-grown Piloto Cubano, Olor and Brazilian tobaccos, while the binder is a Santo Domingo leaf. The cigar is then finished with a Java wrapper known for its silky feel and rich taste. The Natural Claro line, which debuted in 1988, delivers the rich flavor that Montecruz is famous for, but with a milder taste due to the use of a Connecticut Shade wrapper, from the famous Windsor Valley. The number of sizes in production for 1998 has been reduced to increase availability of the more popular shapes.

MONTENEGRO
Handmade in San Andres Tuxtla, Mexico.

Wrapper: Mexico   *Binder: Mexico*   *Filler: Mexico*

Shape	Name		Lgth	Ring	Wrapper
Lonsdale	No. 2	*(tube available)*	6½	42	CM-Ma

Double Corona	Churchill	7	52	CM

Introduced in 1997, this is a mild-bodied cigar featuring a Sumatra-seed wrapper grown in Mexico. It is presented in individual cellophane sleeves, or a glass tube for the No. 2 shape, packed in all-cedar boxes of 25.

MONTERO
Handmade in Santiago, Dominican Republic.

Wrapper: Ecuador *Binder: Dom. Rep.* *Filler: Dom. Rep.*

Shape	Name	Lgth	Ring	Wrapper
Torpedo	Torpedo	7	54	CI
Double Corona	Presidente	7½	50	CI
Churchill	Churchill	6⅞	46	CI
Toro	Toro	6	50	CI
Long Corona	Cetro	6	44	CI
Robusto	Robusto	5	50	CI

The Montero is a premium cigar from the Dominican Republic, introduced in 1995. It is hand made with the long filler and binder from the Dominican Republic and a Connecticut-seed wrapper from Ecuador. Available only in a natural wrapper, the Montero is a medium-bodied cigar.

MONTES DE OCA
Handmade in San Ramon, Costa Rica.

Wrapper: Nicaragua *Binder: Costa Rica* *Filler: Costa Rica*

Shape	Name	Lgth	Ring	Wrapper
Corona	No. 3	5½	42	CC
Long Corona	No. 2	6	44	CC-Ma
Toro	Espindido	6	50	Ma
Churchill	Churchill	7¾	48	CC-Ma

HANDMADE CIGARS: BRAND LISTINGS

This cigar was introduced in 1989, but is only in limited distribution. If you can find it, you'll enjoy a rich, medium-to-full-bodied taste, presented uncellophaned in all-cedar boxes of 25.

MONTES DE ORO
Handmade in San Ramon, Costa Rica.

Wrapper: Nicaragua *Binder: Costa Rica* *Filler: Costa Rica*

Shape	Name	Lgth	Ring	Wrapper
Long Corona	No. 2	6	44	Ma
Churchill	Churchill	7¾	48	Ma

This is a medium-bodied blend of tobaccos introduced in 1996. It is offered in maduro-only bundles of 25 cigars with a natural-wrapped edition coming soon.

MONTESINO
Handmade in Santiago, Dominican Republic.

Wrapper: USA/Connecticut *Binder: Dom. Rep.* *Filler: Dom. Rep.*

Shape	Name	Lgth	Ring	Wrapper
Churchill	Gran Corona	6¾	48	CM-Ma
Lonsdale	No. 1	6⅞	43	CM-Ma
Long Corona	No. 2	6¼	44	CM-Ma
Corona	Diplomatico	5½	42	CM-Ma
Churchill	Napoleon Grande	7	46	CM-Ma
Lonsdale	Fumas	6¾	44	CM

This well-known brand debuted in its current format in 1981 and is handmade in Santiago, Dominican Republic. Its quality of construction and taste, combined with its modest cost, makes it an excellent value.

MONTOYA
Handmade in Danli, Honduras.

Wrapper: Honduras *Binder: Dom. Rep.* *Filler: Dom. Rep.*

HANDMADE CIGARS: BRAND LISTINGS

Shape	Name	Lgth	Ring	Wrapper
Giant	Presidente	8½	52	CC
Double Corona	Churchill	7½	50	CC
Lonsdale	No. 1	6⅞	43	CC
Corona	Petit Corona	5½	43	CC
Robusto	Rothschild	5	50	CC

This is a high-quality cigar, offered in bundles of 25 cigars each. Montoya debuted in 1992 and is considered mild in body.

MOORE & BODE
Handmade in Miami, Florida, USA.

Wrapper: USA/Connecticut   Binder and Filler: Central & South American

Shape	Name	Lgth	Ring	Wrapper
	Miami blend:			
Corona	Bishop	5	41	CI
Grand Corona	Corona	6	46	CI
Lonsdale	Corona Largo	7	44	CI
Slim Panatela	34's	6¾	34	CI
Robusto	Salvadore	5	50	CI
Toro	North Greenway	6¾	50	CI
Double Corona	Number Ten	7½	50	CI
Pyramid	Brass	5½	58	CI
Pyramid	Full Brass	7¼	64	CI
	Flamboyan blend:			
Corona	Bishop	5	41	CI
Grand Corona	Corona	6	46	CI
Lonsdale	Corona Largo	7	44	CI
Slim Panatela	34's	6¾	34	CI

Robusto	Salvadore	5	50	Cl
Toro	North Greenway	6¾	50	Cl
Double Corona	Number Ten	7½	50	Cl
Pyramid	Brass	5½	58	Cl
Pyramid	Full Brass	7¼	64	Cl

There are cigars, and there is the art of the cigar. Moore & Bode cigars are among the foremost expositions of the roller's art, expressed in the highest possible quality of construction. Two series of identical shapes are made; the Miami Blend (introduced 1991) is a mild-to-medium bodied cigar, while the Flamboyan Blend (1995) is medium to heavy.

MORAN
Handmade in Santiago, Dominican Republic.
Wrapper: Indonesia, USA/Connecticut   Binder: Dom. Rep.   Filler: Dom. Rep.

Shape	Name	Lgth	Ring	Wrapper
Petit Corona	Baroness	5	42	CC-Ma
Churchill	Czarina	6¾	48	CC-Ma
Panatela	Debutante	6	38	CC-Ma
Robusto	Duchess	5½	50	CC-Ma
Torpedo	Empress	6½	53	CC-Ma
Double Corona	Grand Dame	7½	50	CC-Ma
Lonsdale	Princess	6¼	44	CC-Ma

We didn't know that a Duchess could be so "robusto" until we saw this brand! Introduced in 1995, each shape in this brand is named for a female member of a royal or feudal court. The cigars are pretty good, too, with a mild-to-medium bodied flavor and a choice of Connecticut-grown natural or Indonesian-grown maduro wrapper.

MOREL
Handmade in Santiago, Dominican Republic.
Wrapper: Indonesia   Binder: Dom. Rep.   Filler: Dom. Rep.

HANDMADE CIGARS: BRAND LISTINGS

Shape	Name	Lgth	Ring	Wrapper
Toro	Toro	6½	50	CC
Corona	Corona	5½	44	CC

This is a new brand for 1997, with a Sumatra wrapper and Dominican-grown Olor binder and filler for a mild-to-medium taste. It is offered in economical bundles of six cigars each.

MORENO MADURO
Handmade in La Romana, Dominican Republic.

Wrapper: Mexico   Binder: Dom. Rep.   Filler: Brazil, Dom. Rep.

Shape	Name	Lgth	Ring	Wrapper
Corona	No. 445	5½	44	Ma
Slim Panatela	No. 326	6	32	Ma
Lonsdale	No. 426	6½	42	Ma
Churchill	No. 467	7¼	46	Ma
Toro	No. 486	6	48	Ma
Double Corona	No. 507	7	50	Ma
Giant	No. 528	8½	52	Ma

These are mild to medium-bodied cigars, wrapped in dark maduro wrappers and featuring a pleasant blend of tobacco from three nations.

MOTTA
Handmade in San Andres Tuxtla, Mexico.

Wrapper: Mexico   Binder: Mexico   Filler: Mexico, Nicaragua

Shape	Name	Lgth	Ring	Wrapper
Toro	Toro	6	50	CC
Robusto	Robusto	5	50	CC
Long Corona	Corona Especial	6	44	CC
Double Corona	Churchill	7	50	CC

HANDMADE CIGARS: BRAND LISTINGS

Introduced in 1996, this is a mild-to-medium-bodied cigar with a Sumatra-seed wrapper and Mexican and Cuban-seed/Nicaraguan-grown leaves in the filler. You can find it in cedar boxes of 25.

MULATO

Handmade, with short filler, in Tamboril, Dominican Republic.

Wrapper: Dom. Rep.   *Binder: Dom. Rep.*   *Filler: Dom. Rep.*

Shape	Name	Lgth	Ring	Wrapper
Corona	Corona	5½	42	Ma

This is a 1996-introduced, medium-to-full-bodied, maduro-wrapped, short-filler cigar from the Dominican Republic. Its special flavor and aroma come from a special treatment of the tobacco with red wine!

MURSULI'S

Handmade in Los Angeles, California, USA.

Wrapper: Ecuador or USA/Connecticut   *Binder: Honduras*
Filler: Dominican Republic, Honduras

Shape	Name	Lgth	Ring	Wrapper
Torpedo	Torpedo Grande	7¼	56	CC-Ma
Torpedo	Torpedo	6	56	CC-Ma
Toro	Churchill	6½	52	CC-Ma
Robusto	Robusto	5	52	CC-Ma
Churchill	Double Corona	7	46	CC
Panatela	Sweet Panatela	6	36	CC
Long Corona	Corona	6	44	CC-Ma
Corona	Sweet Corona	6	44	CC
Grand Corona	Fuma	6½	46	CC-Ma
Toro	Oscar No. 1	6	50	CC
Giant	Cubano	8	50	CC
Double Corona	Presidente	7	50	CC-Ma

Slim Panatela	Linda	5	32	CC
Slim Panatela	Reyna	7	32	CC
Corona	Junior Fuma	5½	44	CC
Short Panatela	Petite Corona	5	38	CC

Blended by veteran cigar maker Oscar Mursuli, these handmade smokes offer a choice of natural wrappers from Connecticut (natural) or maduro-wrapped shapes featuring leaves from Ecuador. In either shade, this is a medium-to-full-bodied cigar, offered in boxes or bundles of 25 cigars each. The Sweet Panatela is dipped in sugar syrup at the end only, while the Corona and Linda are also available in a sweetened style.

NAPA

Handmade in Villa Gonzalez, Dominican Republic, and Esteli, Nicaragua.

DOMINICAN SELECTION:

Wrapper: Dom. Rep.   *Binder: Dom. Rep.*   *Filler: Dom. Rep.*

NICARAGUAN SELECTION:

Wrapper: Indonesia   *Binder: Nicaragua*   *Filler: Nicaragua*

Shape	Name	Lgth	Ring	Wrapper
	Dominican Selection:			
Long Corona	Grand Corona	6	44	CC
Robusto	Rothschild	4½	50	CC
Churchill	Churchill	7	48	CC
Toro	Toro	6	50	CC
Pyramid	Pyramid	6	52	CC
Panatela	Petite Panatela	5½	38	CC
	Nicaraguan Selection:			
Robusto	Double Robusto	5	52	CM
Petit Corona	Petit Corona	5	42	CM

Corona	Corona	5½	44	CM
Robusto	Rothschild	4¾	50	CM
Toro	Toro	6	50	CM
Perfecto	Perfecto	5¾	50	CM
Churchill	Churchill	7½	48	CM

Here is a two-series brand introduced in the final months of 1996 which bears the name of the famous California valley in which some of the world's finest wines are produced. The cigars are equally well crafted, with the Dominican shapes offering a medium-bodied blend marked by a purple band. The Nicaraguan series has a green band and is mild in strength. All of the shapes are presented in all-cedar boxes.

NAPA RESERVE
Handmade in Las Palmas, the Canary Islands of Spain and Santiago, Dominican Republic

CANARY ISLANDS RESERVE:
Wrapper: USA/Connecticut   *Binder: Canary Isl.*   *Filler: Canary Isl., Dom. Rep.*

DOMINICAN RESERVE:
Wrapper: Ecuador   *Binder: Dom. Rep.*   *Filler: Dom. Rep.*

Shape	Name	Lgth	Ring	Wrapper
	Canary Islands Reserve:			
Corona	Corona	5¾	42	CC
Lonsdale	Gran Corona	6¾	44	CC
Robusto	Robusto	4¾	50	CC
Pyramid	Figurado	6	50	CC
Double Corona	Churchill	7	50	CC
	Dominican Reserve:			
Corona	Corona	5½	44	CC
Robusto	Robusto	5	50	CC

Pyramid	Pyramid	6	52	CC
Lonsdale	Lonsdale	7	44	CC
Double Corona	Churchill	7½	50	CC

Debuting in early 1997, this line is designed to be one of the finest, most delicately balanced cigars produced anywhere. The Canary Islands series wrapper is grown in Connecticut and the medium-to-full-bodied cigars are presented in all-cedar boxes to help continue the mellowing of the tobaccos from the factory to the smoker's own living room. The newer Dominican line utilizes an Ecuadorian wrapper and offers a medium-to-full-bodied flavor.

NAPOLEON'S DREAM
Handmade in Danli, Honduras.

Wrapper: Honduras   *Binder: Honduras*   *Filler: Honduras*

Shape	Name	Lgth	Ring	Wrapper
Lonsdale	Cognac	6½	44	CM
Lonsdale	Rum	6½	44	CM
Lonsdale	Southern Comfort	6½	44	CM
Lonsdale	Vanilla	6½	44	CM

You want flavored? Forget it . . . you really want *cured* tobacco which is thoroughly imbued with flavors such as cognac, rum, vanilla and Southern Comfort. That's the secret of this 1997-introduced, all-flavored brand with a mild-to-medium body. The 18-24 month process of introducing these flavors into the tobaccos make this a flavored experience unlike any other available. Napoleon's Dream are also presented properly: in the famous "Cigar Jar" that keeps these flavored smokes from affecting the taste of other, non-flavored cigars. Look for it in tubes of one cigar, gift packs of 12 or full packs of 25 or 75.

NAT SHERMAN
Handmade in the Dominican Republic and Honduras.

EXCHANGE SELECTION:
Wrapper: USA/Connecticut • Binder: Mexico • Filler: Dom. Rep.

HANDMADE CIGARS: BRAND LISTINGS

LANDMARK SELECTION:
Wrapper: Cameroon • Binder: Mexico • Filler: Dom. Rep.

MANHATTAN SELECTION:
Wrapper: Mexico • Binder: Mexico • Filler: Dom. Rep.

GOTHAM SELECTION:
Wrapper: USA/Connecticut • Binder: Dom. Rep. • Filler: Dom. Rep.

VIP SELECTION:
Wrapper: USA/Connecticut • Binder: Dom. Rep. • Filler: Brazil, Dom. Rep.

CITY DESK SELECTION:
Wrapper: Mexico • Binder: Dom. Rep. • Filler: Dom. Rep., Mexico

HOST SELECTION:
Wrapper: Ecuador • Binder: Honduras • Filler: Honduras

METROPOLITAN SELECTION:
Wrapper: USA/Connecticut • Binder: Dom. Rep. • Filler: Dom. Rep.

LSN SELECTION:
Wrapper: USA/Connecticut • Binder: Mexico • Filler: Dom. Rep.

Shape	Name	Lgth	Ring	Wrapper
	Exchange Selection, made in the Dominican Republic:			
Small Panatela	Academy No. 2	5	31	CC
Panatela	Murray Hill No. 7	6	38	CC
Lonsdale	Butterfield No. 8	6½	42	CC
Grand Corona	Trafalgar No. 4	6	47	CC
Double Corona	Oxford No. 5	7	49	CC
Lonsdale	Carpe Diem	6¾	43	CC
	Landmark Selection, made in the Dominican Republic:			
Panatela	Metropole	6	34	CM
Corona	Hampshire	5½	42	CM
Lonsdale	Algonquin	6¾	43	CM

HANDMADE CIGARS: BRAND LISTINGS

Robusto	Vanderbilt	5	47	CM
Double Corona	Dakota	7½	49	CM
	Manhattan Selection, made in the Dominican Republic:			
Cigarillo	Beekman	5¼	28	CM
Slim Panatela	Tribeca	6	31	CM
Panatela	Chelsea	6½	38	CM
Lonsdale	Gramercy	6¾	43	CM
Robusto	Sutton	5½	49	CM
	Gotham Selection, made in the Dominican Republic:			
Slim Panatela	No. 65	6	32	CC
Long Corona	No. 1400	6¼	44	CC
Toro	No. 711	6	50	CC
Double Corona	No. 500	7	50	CC
	VIP Selection, made in the Dominican Republic:			
Panatela	Zigfield "Fancytale"	6¾	38	CC
Corona	Barnum (tubed)	5½	42	CC
Lonsdale	Morgan	7	42	CC
Robusto	Astor	4½	50	CC
Toro	Carnegie	6	48	CC
	City Desk Selection, made in the Dominican Republic:			
Long Corona	Gazette	6	42	Ma
Grand Corona	Dispatch	6½	46	Ma
Toro	Telegraph	6	50	Ma
Double Corona	Tribune	7½	50	Ma
	Host Selection, made in Honduras:			
Small Panatela	Hudson	4⅝	32	CM
Corona	Hamilton	5½	42	CM

HANDMADE CIGARS: BRAND LISTINGS

Lonsdale	Hunter	6	43	CM
Grand Corona	Harrington	6	46	CM
Robusto	Hobart	5	50	CM
Double Corona	Hampton	7	50	CM
Giant Corona	Halstead	8	40	CM
Pyramid	Hanover	5½	56	CM
Pyramid	Huron	4½	44	CM
	Metropolitan Selection, made in the Dominican Republic:			
Corona	Anglers	5½	43	CC
Pyramid	Nautical	7	48	CC
Toro	University	6	50	CC
Pyramid	Explorers	5½	56	CC
Pyramid	Metropolitan	7	60	CC
	LSN Selection, made in the Dominican Republic:			
Slim Panatela	A2	5	31	CC
Lonsdale	A4	6¾	43	CC
Robusto	A6	5½	49	CC
Double Corona	A8	7½	49	CC

Nat Sherman, "tobacconist to the world" for more than six decades, offers enough variety in its series to keep the serious smoker trying new sizes and blends for several months. The Exchange Selection provides a mild, smooth and polished flavor thanks to its Connecticut wrapper; the Landmark Selection is more intensely flavorful and full-bodied due to its Cameroon wrapper; the Manhattan Selection is a lean and racy blend of medium body and a nut-like flavor, finished with a soft, light-tasting Mexican wrapper; the Gotham Selection is the most delicate and mild of the group, finished in a mellow Connecticut wrapper; the VIP Selection offers a rich, crisp aroma along with buttery smoothness in the draw and mild taste; the City Desk Selection uses a dark maduro wrapper to give a full, hearty flavor, but without harshness; and the Host Selection matches a sweet Connecticut wrapper with Cuban-seed filler and binders to provide a solid flavor of medium strength and a rustic aroma.

HANDMADE CIGARS: BRAND LISTINGS

Newer selections include the Metropolitan (introduced in 1995), which offers a medium-to-full-bodied smoke and three shaped sizes, and the LSN Selection (1996), which is also medium-to-full in body, but more spicy.

NATIONAL BRAND
Handmade in Danli, Honduras.

Wrapper: Honduras   *Binder: Mexico*   *Filler: Honduras*

Shape	Name	Lgth	Ring	Wrapper
Giant	Imperial	8½	52	CC-Ma
Double Corona	Churchill	7½	50	CC-Ma
Lonsdale	Lonsdale	6½	42	CC-Ma
Corona	Corona	5½	42	CC
Toro	Super Rothschild	6	50	CC-Ma
Churchill	Soberanos	6⅞	46	CC
Panatela	Royal Palm	6⅞	36	CC

First offered in 1978, this is a Honduran-produced cigar with all Honduran-grown tobacco, including a Connecticut-seed wrapper, offered in bundles of 25 cigars each. It is considered mild-to-medium in strength.

NATIVO
Handmade in Mayaguez, Puerto Rico.

Wrapper: Indonesia   *Binder: Dom. Rep.*   *Filler: Dom. Rep., Puerto Rico*

Shape	Name	Lgth	Ring	Wrapper
Robusto	Robusto	5	50	CC
Grand Corona	Corona Grande	6	46	CC
Torpedo	Figurado	6	52	CC
Lonsdale	Lonsdale	7	44	CC
Churchill	Churchill	7	48	CC

This is a mild-to-medium-bodied blend of Caribbean binder and filler leaves, enveloped by an Indonesian-grown wrapper. Introduced in 1997, it is offered in an all-cedar box of 25.

NAVARRO
Handmade in Esteli, Nicaragua.

Wrapper: Ecuador   *Binder: Nicaragua*   *Filler: Nicaragua*

Shape	Name	Lgth	Ring	Wrapper
Double Corona	Churchill	7	50	CC
Lonsdale	Lonsdale	6½	44	CC
Giant	Presidente	8½	52	CC
Robusto	Robusto	4¾	50	CC
Toro	Toro	6	50	CC

Here is a very well made brand, introduced in 1997, which features a Connecticut-seed wrapper grown in Ecuador, combined with Piloto Cubano leaves grown in Nicaragua. The result is a medium-bodied blend which is offered in conveniently-sized boxes of 10 or 20.

NESTOR 747
Handmade in Danli, Honduras.

Wrapper: Honduras   *Binder: Nicaragua*   *Filler: Honduras, Nicaragua*

Shape	Name	Lgth	Ring	Wrapper
Churchill	747	7⅝	47	CM

This is a full-bodied cigar, developed in 1994, which salutes Nestor Plasencia, one of the world's most prolific cigar makers. His factories in Honduras produce dozens of outstanding brands, including this one, to which he put his name. The 747 is box-pressed, produced in limited quantities, and the plain cedar box understates the quality of the product it presents.

NESTOR 747 SERIES II
Handmade in Danli, Honduras.

Wrapper: Ecuador   *Binder: Honduras*   *Filler: Honduras, Nicaragua*

HANDMADE CIGARS: BRAND LISTINGS

Shape	Name	Lgth	Ring	Wrapper
Robusto	454	4¾	54	CM-Ma
Toro	654	6	54	CM
Churchill	747	7⅝	47	CM

The second generation of the Nester 747 is the three-shape Series II line, also a full-bodied cigar. However, this group uses 1989-vintage leaves and is presented in its original rounded shape in cedar cabinets of 50 cigars each (the 747 is also available in a box of 25). Each completed bunch of 50, tied with a silk ribbon, is aged for nine months after rolling to ensure that the aromas and flavors of the bunch have penetrated each of the cigars.

NEW YORK, NEW YORK
BY TE-AMO
Handmade in San Andres Tuxtla, Mexico.

Wrapper: Mexico　　　　　*Binder: Mexico*　　　　　*Filler: Mexico*

Shape	Name	Lgth	Ring	Wrapper
Lonsdale	Park Avenue	6⅝	42	CC
Corona	Fifth Avenue	5½	44	CC
Grand Corona	7th Avenue	6½	46	CC
Churchill	Broadway	7¼	48	CC
Toro	Wall Street	6	52	CC
Robusto	La Guardia	5	54	CC

A cigar salute to the Big Apple! Given the widespread popularity of Te-Amo in New York – just look at the number of "Te-Amo" signs above newsstands and tobacco shops – it's little wonder that this specially-blended and banded brand was introduced. Medium in body, these cigars are offered in boxes of 25.

NEXTGENERATION
Handmade in Canca la Piedra, Dominican Republic.
Wrapper: Indonesia, USA/Connecticut

Binder: Dominican Republic　　　　　*Filler: Dominican Republic*

HANDMADE CIGARS: BRAND LISTINGS

Shape	Name	Lgth	Ring	Wrapper
Robusto	Robusto	5	50	CC
Churchill	Churchill	7	48	CC
Long Corona	Corona	6	44	CC
Pyramid	Pyramid	7	54	CC

New for 1997, this brand offers a choice of wrappers: Sumatra-grown, with a medium and spicy flavor, or Connecticut, with a mild body. Either way, these are very well made cigars and are offered in four popular sizes in boxes of 25.

NICARAGUA ESPECIAL
Handmade in Ocotal, Nicaragua.

Wrapper: Ecuador   *Binder: Nicaragua*   *Filler: Nicaragua*

Shape	Name	Lgth	Ring	Wrapper
Panatela	No. 1 Linda	5½	38	CC
Long Corona	No. 2 Super Cetro	6	44	CC
Toro	No. 3 Matador	6	50	CC
Double Corona	No. 4 Presidente	7¾	50	CC
Giant	No. 5 Viajante	8½	52	CC

An excellent buy in a handmade, medium-bodied cigar, the Nicaragua Especial debuted in 1992 and offers high-quality construction in a bundle of 25 cigars, in which each cigar is individually wrapped for maximum protection and freshness.

NICARAGUA SUPREMO
Handmade in Esteli, Nicaragua.

Wrapper: Ecuador   *Binder: Nicaragua*   *Filler: Nicaragua*

Shape	Name	Lgth	Ring	Wrapper
Giant	Presidentes	8½	52	CC
Double Corona	Churchill	7	49	CC
Toro	Toro	6	50	CC

| Corona | Gran Corona | 6½ | 42 | CC |
| Robusto | Robusto | 4½ | 50 | CC |

Introduced in 1997, this is a mild-to-medium-bodied cigar presented in beautiful cabinet-style boxes of 25.

NICARO
Handmade in Managua, Nicaragua.

Wrapper: Ecuador *Binder: Nicaragua* *Filler: Dom. Rep.*

Shape	Name	Lgth	Ring	Wrapper
Giant	Presidente	8	50	CM
Double Corona	Churchill	6⅞	49	CM
Toro	Toro	6	50	CM
Robusto	Robusto	5	50	CM
Long Corona	Cetro	6¼	44	CM

Here is a 1997-introduced brand with a medium-to-full-bodied flavor and a blend of leaves from three nations. You can enjoy them in boxes of 25 cigars each.

NICOLE MILLER
Handmade in Tamboril, Dominican Republic.

Wrapper: Indonesia *Binder: Dom. Rep.* *Filler: Dom. Rep.*

Shape	Name	Lgth	Ring	Wrapper
Double Corona	Extravaganza	7½	50	CC
Grand Corona	Aristocrat	6½	46	CC
Robusto	Masterpiece	5	50	CC
Long Corona	Black Tie	6	42	CC
Toro	Gran Amour	6½	54	CC
Long Corona	Vanilla D'Oro	6	42	CC

HANDMADE CIGARS: BRAND LISTINGS

Talk about style! Here's a cigar from the famous designer Nicole Miller, whose cigar ties have been prized by cigar lovers for many years. Well made with a Sumatra-grown wrapper and beautifully packaged, this range varies by size from mild-to-medium in the smaller shapes to medium-to-full in the larger sizes. There is also a vanilla-flavored shape available. The brand was introduced in mid-1997 and is offered in individual cellophane sleeves in all-cedar boxes of 25.

NIÑO VASQUEZ
Handmade in Santiago, Dominican Republic.

Wrapper: Ecuador   Binder: Dom. Rep.   Filler: Dom. Rep.

Shape	Name	Lgth	Ring	Wrapper
Giant	Presidente	8	52	CM
Double Corona	Churchill	7	50	CM
Toro	Governor	6	48	CM
Corona	Corona	5½	42	CM
Robusto	Robusto	5	48	CM
Torpedo	Torpedo	6¼	54	CM

The secret's out! Here is a medium-bodied cigar with tobaccos grown and rolled by the manufacturers of some of the most elegant and famous brands on the market. Don't tell . . . just try 'em, in boxes of bundles of 25, or in a sampler pack of six.

NIVELACUSO PRIVATE RESERVE
Handmade in Santiago, Dominican Republic.

Wrapper: Indonesia   Binder: Dom. Rep.   Filler: Dom. Rep.

Shape	Name	Lgth	Ring	Wrapper
Robusto	Robusto	5	50	CC
Lonsdale	No. 1	7	44	CC
Grand Corona	Grand Corona	6½	46	CC
Giant	Double Corona	8	50	CC

HANDMADE CIGARS: BRAND LISTINGS

Named for the Cuban factory dating acronym (N=1 through O=0), this brand offers a medium-bodied smoke. Introduced in 1996, it is presented in slide-top cedar boxes of 25.

NORDING
Handmade in Danli, Honduras.

Wrapper: USA/Connecticut   *Binder: Nicaragua*   *Filler: Dom. Rep., Nicaragua*

Shape	Name	Lgth	Ring	Wrapper
Toro	Corona Grande	6	50	CC
Double Corona	Presidente	7½	52	CC
Lonsdale	Lonsdale	6¾	43	CC
Corona	Corona	5½	43	CC
Robusto	Robusto	4¾	52	CC

One of Denmark's most distinguished craftsmen, Erik Nording has created cigars of expert manufacture, using Cuban-seed Dominican and Nicaraguan filler, Nicaraguan binder and a Connecticut wrapper. The result is a medium-bodied smoke that was introduced in 1995, packed with a unique humidification system designed by Nording himself.

NOSTALGIA
Handmade in Danli, Honduras.

Wrapper: Honduras   *Binder: Honduras*   *Filler: Honduras*

Shape	Name	Lgth	Ring	Wrapper
Double Corona	Presidente	7½	50	CM
Corona	Corona	5¾	43	CM
Churchill	Churchill	7	48	CM
Robusto	Robusto	5	50	CM
Torpedo	Torpedo	6	54	CM

Introduced in 1997, here is a tribute by Carlos Toraño to his Cuban homeland and memories of growing up among the tobacco fields of the Pinar del Rio. Naturally, this is a full-bodied blend of tobaccos in five of the most popular sizes of all time. You can enjoy them, and the memories, by lighting up one of the beauties, packed in all-cedar cabinets of 25.

O & B DOMINICAN RESERVE
Handmade in Santiago, Dominican Republic.

Wrapper: Indonesia   *Binder: Dom. Rep.*   *Filler: Dom. Rep.*

Shape	Name	Lgth	Ring	Wrapper
Torpedo	Torpedo	6½	53	CC
Pyramid	Piramide	5	52	CC
Giant	Presidente	8	52	CC
Double Corona	Churchill	7½	49	CC
Robusto	Robusto	5	50	CC
Long Corona	Corona	6	44	CC

Introduced in 1997, this is a mild cigar that uses aged tobaccos to ensure the smoothest possible taste. It is offered in all-cedar boxes of 25.

OCHO RIOS
Handmade in Kingston, Jamaica.

Wrapper: Ecuador   *Binder: Dom. Rep.*   *Filler: Dom. Rep., Jamaica*

Shape	Name	Lgth	Ring	Wrapper
Double Corona	President	7	50	CC
Toro	Toro	6	50	CC
Giant	Viajante	8¼	52	CC
Petit Corona	No. 4	5	42	CC
Lonsdale	No. 1	7	43	CC

Originated in 1955, this is a handmade Jamaican cigar of mild body and all long-filler tobaccos, offered in bundles of 25.

HANDMADE CIGARS: BRAND LISTINGS

OCTAVIO TAVARES
Handmade in Santiago, Dominican Republic.
Wrapper: Cameroon, Indonesia, USA/Connecticut
Binder: Dominican Republic   *Filler: Dominican Republic*

Shape	Name	Lgth	Ring	Wrapper
Double Corona	Churchill	7	50	CC-CM-Ma
Toro	Torpedos	6	52	CC-CM-Ma
Robusto	Robusto	5½	50	CC-CM-Ma
Churchill	Double Corona	6¾	48	CC-CM-Ma

Introduced in 1997, this brand honors the memory of master roller Octavio
Tavares, who left Cuba in 1962 and settled in the Dominican Republic. Tobaccos
for the first run of these cigars were harvested in 1995 and aged for two years.
The final blend offers a mild smoke with Connecticut wrappers, a medium-to-full-
bodied flavor with Cameroon wrappers and a full-bodied experience with the
Sumatran-grown maduro wrappers.

OH QUE BUENO
Handmade in Las Palmas, the Canary Islands of Spain.
Wrapper: USA/Connecticut   *Binder: Indonesia*   *Filler: Brazil, Dom.Rep.*

Shape	Name	Lgth	Ring	Wrapper
Lonsdale	No. 1	7	41	CC
Corona	Corona	5¼	41	CC

Very well constructed, this brand blends tobaccos of four nations to produce a
medium-bodied smoke, offered in boxes of 25 cigars each.

OLD FASHIONED
Handmade in Santiago, Dominican Republic
and Kingston, Jamaica.
Wrapper: Cameroon, USA/Connecticut
Binder: Mexico   *Filler: Dominican Republic, Mexico*

HANDMADE CIGARS: BRAND LISTINGS

Shape	Name	Lgth	Ring	Wrapper
Small Panatela	Ascots	4¼	32	CC
Short Panatela	Caviar	4	36	CC
Slim Panatela	Delights	5	34	CM
Lonsdale	No. 31	6¾	43	CM
Corona	No. 32	5¾	43	CM
Slim Panatela	No. 36	6	34	CM
Toro	No. 38	6	49	CM
Double Corona	No. 40	7½	49	CM
Robusto	No. 41	5½	49	CM
Robusto	No. 42	4½	49	CM
Slim Panatela	No. 250	6	31	CC
Slim Panatela	No. 350	7	34	CC
Corona	No. 500	5½	42	CC
Lonsdale	No. 700	6½	42	CC
Churchill	No. 745	7	45	CC
Double Corona	No. 749	7½	49	CC-Ma
Cigarillo	Quill	5	28	CC

Here are seconds of some of the world's finest cigars, varying from mild to medium-to-full in strength. A great value, they are offered in bundles of 20 or 25.

OLD TRINIDAD XVIII CENTURY
Handmade in Las Palmas, the Canary Islands of Spain.

Wrapper: USA/Connecticut   Binder: Brazil   Filler: Dom. Rep., Honduras

Shape	Name	Lgth	Ring	Wrapper
Corona	Corona	5½	42	CC
Robusto	Robusto	5	50	CC

Toro	Toro	6	50	CC
Churchill	Churchill	7	46	CC
Double Corona	Soberano	7½	50	CC

Introduced in 1996, this brand celebrates the Cuban city of Trinidad and offers a mild-to-medium taste, thanks to its Connecticut wrapper, Mata Fina binder and Piloto Cubano filler. It is presented in boxes of 25.

OLIVEROS

Handmade in Santiago, Dominican Republic.
Wrapper: Dominican Republic, Indonesia, USA/Connecticut
Binder: Dominican Republic   *Filler: Dominican Republic*

Shape	Name	Lgth	Ring	Wrapper
Giant	Presidente	8	50	Ma
Perfecto	Diablo	6¼	50	CC-CM
Torpedo	Maestro	6¼	50	CC-CM-Ma
Double Corona	Coronel	7	50	CC-CM-Ma
Toro	Toro	5¾	50	CC-CM-Ma
Perfecto	Tango	4	50	CC-CM
Lonsdale	Dos Perez	6¾	42	CC-CM
Lonsdale	Mulatos	6¾	42	Stripe
Corona	Reyes	5½	42	CC-CM
Short Panatela	Long Lady	5	36	CC-CM
Slim Panatela	Caballeros	8	34	CC-CM

Oliveros cigars have been produced in one form or another since 1927. The current edition offers either a natural wrapper using Connecticut or Javan leaves or a maduro wrapper using Javan tobacco. The natural-wrapped cigars are mild-to-medium in body, while the maduro wrapper offers a medium-to-full-bodied taste. The Mulato cigars, with a "barber pole" look, offer a mild taste thanks to the double-wrapper of Connecticut and Javan maduro leaves.

HANDMADE CIGARS: BRAND LISTINGS

OLOR

Handmade in Santiago, Dominican Republic.

Wrapper: USA/Connecticut   Binder: Dom. Rep.   Filler: Dom. Rep.

Shape	Name	Lgth	Ring	Wrapper
Double Corona	Cacique	7⅝	54	CC-Ma
Robusto	Rothschild	4½	50	CC-Ma
Corona	Momento	5½	43	CC-Ma
Toro	Paco	6	50	Cl-CC-Ma
Lonsdale	Lonsdale	6½	42	CC-Ma
Churchill	Coloso	7¼	48	CC-Ma
Short Panatela	Pronto	4	38	CC

This brand is now in national distribution and has won new friends among many cigar enthusiasts. Individually cellophaned and packed in slide-top cedar cabinets, these cigars are produced by the Tabacalera A. Fuente and are an excellent value and a smooth, medium-bodied smoke.

OLOR VINTAGE

Handmade in Santiago, Dominican Republic.

Wrapper: USA/Connecticut   Binder: Dom. Rep.   Filler: Dom. Rep.

Shape	Name	Lgth	Ring	Wrapper
Double Corona	Presidente	7½	50	CC
Torpedo	Pirimide	6½	50	CC
Grand Corona	Corona Gorda	6½	46	CC
Toro	Toro	6	50	CC
Long Corona	Lonsdale	6	42	CC
Robusto	Robusto	5	50	CC

More Olor! This well-kept secret now has a sibling, introduced in 1997. It is even more refined than the standard series and offers a medium-bodied smoke in all-cedar cabinets of 25.

HANDMADE CIGARS: BRAND LISTINGS

ONE PLUS
Handmade in Navarette, Dominican Republic.

Wrapper: Indonesia   Binder: Dom. Rep.   Filler: Dom. Rep.

Shape	Name	Lgth	Ring	Wrapper
Churchill	Churchill	7½	48	CC
Robusto	Robusto	5½	48	CC
Long Corona	Corona	6	44	CC

Here is a mild-to-medium-bodied brand introduced in 1997, using a specially-aged (four years!) filler and Sumatra wrapper. It is presented in cedar boxes or in bundles of 25.

100 FUEGOS
Handmade in Mexico City, Mexico.

Wrapper: Indonesia   Binder: Nicaragua   Filler: Mexico

Shape	Name	Lgth	Ring	Wrapper
Long Corona	Corona	6	42	CM
Robusto	Robusto	5	50	CM
Double Corona	Churchill	7½	50	CM
Torpedo	Torpedo	6	52	CM

Introduced in 1996, this is a uniquely presented brand. It comes in a special, slant-front box and is available in a standard series with red bands and a specially-aged "special edition" series with blue bands. In either form, this is a medium-to-full-bodied blend protected in individual cellophane sleeves and packed in the afore-mentioned slant-front cedar boxes of 25.

ONYX
Handmade in La Romana, Dominican Republic.

Wrapper: Mexico   Binder: Indonesia   Filler: Dom. Rep., Mexico

Shape	Name	Lgth	Ring	Wrapper
Long Corona	No. 642	6	42	Ma
Grand Corona	No. 646	6⅝	46	Ma

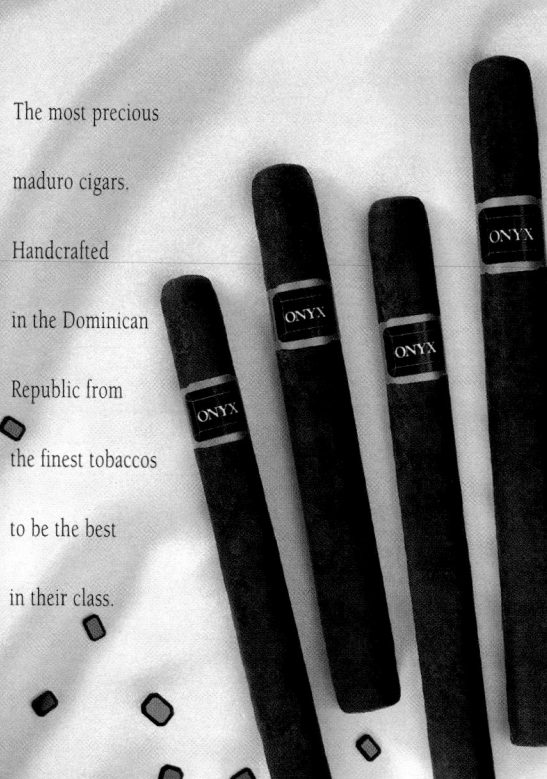

ONYX
The Gem of Maduro

The most precious

maduro cigars.

Handcrafted

in the Dominican

Republic from

the finest tobaccos

to be the best

in their class.

Toro	No. 650	6	50	Ma
Double Corona	No. 750	7½	50	Ma
Giant	No. 852	8	52	Ma

This all-maduro series debuted in 1992 and is hand crafted from the finest tobaccos to be the best in their class. The filler is a Dominican blend of Piloto Cubano and Olor, with some Mexican leaf. A Java leaf is used for the binder, then the cigar is finished with a dark Mexican maduro leaf. The taste is mild with a pleasant spicy note.

OPUS X
Handmade in Santiago, Dominican Republic.

Wrapper: Dom. Rep.   *Binder: Dom. Rep.*   *Filler: Dom. Rep.*

Shape	Name	Lgth	Ring	Wrapper
Toro	Perfecxion No. 2	6⅜	52	CM
Double Corona	Double Corona	7⅝	49	CM
Grand Corona	Fuente Fuente	5⅝	46	CM
Churchill	Reserva d'Chateau	7	48	CM
Petit Corona	Perfecxion No. 8	4⅞	40	CM
Toro	Perfecxion X	6¼	48	CM
Panatela	Petite Lancero	6¼	39	CM
Robusto	Robusto	5¼	50	CM
Lonsdale	No. 1	6½	42	CM
Giant	A	9¼	47	CM

This full-bodied brand was introduced in 1996 and is scarcely available anywhere. A project of the Tabacalera A. Fuente y Cia., this brand features all-Dominican tobacco, including the new wrapper leaf grown on the Fuente's own farm.

ORAMA
Handmade in Tampa, Florida, USA.

Wrapper: Nicaragua   *Binder: Dom. Rep.*   *Filler: Dom. Rep., Honduras*

HANDMADE CIGARS: BRAND LISTINGS

Shape	Name	Lgth	Ring	Wrapper
Lonsdale	Fuma No. 2	6½	44	CM
Lonsdale	Nacional No. 3	6½	44	CM
Giant	Presidente	8½	50	CM
Grand Corona	Churchill	6½	46	CM
Churchill	Panetelas	6¾	46	CM
Robusto	Rothchild	5	50	CM
Grand Corona	Toro	6	47	CM
Churchill	Orama	7	47	CM
Grand Corona	Triada	6½	46	CM
	Made with short filler:			
Long Corona	Fuma No. 1	6	44	CM

Re-introduced in 1997, this brand dates back to the 1920s when Tampa was the center of the cigar industry. It has a mild flavor and is available in sample packs of five cigars and boxes of 25.

ORIENT EXPRESS
Handmade in Danli, Honduras.

Wrapper: Ecuador   Binder: Dom. Rep.   Filler: Mexico, Nicaragua

Shape	Name	Lgth	Ring	Wrapper
Long Panatela	Le Twist 2	8	38	CM
Panatela	No. 2407	6⅞	36	CM
Lonsdale	No. 2418	6⅝	44	CM
Toro	Expresso	6	48	CM
Robusto	No. 2406	5	50	CM
Petit Corona	No. 2414	4	40	CM
Corona	No. 2415	5½	44	CM
Long Corona	Le Twist	6	40	CM

Double Corona	No. 2410	6⅞	49	CM
Double Corona	Le Club	7¾	50	CM

This brand debuted in 1994 and offers the exquisite pleasure of aged filler tobaccos in a mild, slightly aromatic cigar. Please note the unfinished, pigtail heads on the two Le Twist sizes. The quality of the construction extends to the boxes which are made of cedar and offer 10 or 25 cigars each.

ORNELAS
Handmade in San Andres Tuxtla, Mexico.

Wrapper: Mexico   *Binder: Mexico*   *Filler: Mexico*

Shape	Name	Lgth	Ring	Wrapper
Long Corona	LTD al Cognac	6¼	42	Ma
Lonsdale	Ornelas No. 1	6¾	44	CC
Long Corona	Ornelas No. 2	6	44	CC
Long Panatela	Ornelas No. 3	7	38	CC
Petit Corona	Ornelas No. 4	5	44	CC
Panatela	Ornelas No. 5	6	38	CC
Short Panatela	Ornelas No. 6	5	38	CC
Double Corona	Churchill	7	49	CC-Ma
Robusto	Robusto	4¾	49	CC-Ma
Grand Corona	Cafetero Grande	6½	46	Ma
Corona Extra	Cafetero Chico	5½	46	Ma
Slim Panatela	Matinee	6	30	CC
Small Panatela	Matinee Lights	4¾	30	CC
Slim Panatela	ABC Extra	7	30	CC
Giant	250 mm	9½	64	CC
Lonsdale	Ornelas No. 1 Vanilla	6¾	44	CC
Long Corona	Ornelas No. 2 Vanilla	6	44	CC
Long Panatela	Ornelas No. 3 Vanilla	7	38	CC

HANDMADE CIGARS: BRAND LISTINGS

Petit Corona	Ornelas No. 4 Vanilla	5	44	CC
Panatela	Ornelas No. 5 Vanilla	6	38	CC
Short Panatela	Ornelas No. 6 Vanilla	5	38	CC
Slim Panatela	Matinee Vanilla	6	30	CC
Small Panatela	Matinee Lights Vanilla	4¾	30	CC

Re-introduced in 1995, the Ornelas line continues a 60-year tradition. Each of these handmade cigars is a mild Mexico "puro" with special shapes such as the LTD al Cognac line, featuring cognac-treated wrappers, and the eight shapes of vanilla-treated cigars. The huge "250" is one of the largest cigars available anywhere.

ORO DOMINICANO
Handmade in Tamboril, Dominican Republic.

Wrapper: USA/Connecticut   *Binder: Dom. Rep.*   *Filler: Dom. Rep.*

Shape	Name	Lgth	Ring	Wrapper
Toro	No. 1	6½	50	CC-Ma
Robusto	No. 3	5	50	CC-Ma
Long Corona	No. 5	6	42	CC

Here is a new brand for 1998, featuring Piloto Cubano and Olor leaves in the filler, Olor binder and Connecticut or maduro wrappers. Available in three sizes, these are mild to medium-bodied cigars offered in boxes of 25.

ORO 750
Handmade in Santiago, Dominican Republic.

Wrapper: Indonesia   *Binder: Dom. Rep.*   *Filler: Dom. Rep.*

Shape	Name	Lgth	Ring	Wrapper
Churchill	No. 1	7	47	CM
Lonsdale	No. 2	6½	44	CM
Robusto	No. 3	5	50	CM
Toro	No. 4	6⅜	48	CM

HANDMADE CIGARS: BRAND LISTINGS

Corona	No. 5	5½	42	CM

Here is a new brand from Savinelli, already one of the most respected names anywhere in pipes, humidors and cigars! This 1997-introduced brand is medium in body and features a dark Sumatra-grown wrapper in boxes of 25.

OROSI
Handmade in Condega, Nicaragua.

Wrapper: Nicaragua   *Binder: Nicaragua*   *Filler: Nicaragua*

Shape	Name	Lgth	Ring	Wrapper
Double Corona	Oro 700	7	49	CC
Long Corona	Oro 600	6¼	44	CC
Toro	Oro 650	6	50	CC
Corona	Oro 500	5½	42	CC
Robusto	Oro 550	5	50	CC

This brand debuted in 1996, offering a medium-bodied taste. The blend features a Connecticut-seed, Nicaraguan-grown wrapper and is offered in individual cellophane sleeves inside all-cedar boxes of 25.

OSCAR
Handmade in Santiago, Dominican Republic.

Wrapper: USA/Connecticut   *Binder: Dom. Rep.*   *Filler: Dom. Rep.*

Shape	Name	Lgth	Ring	Wrapper
Cigarillo	Oscarito	4	20	CC
Short Panatela	Prince	5	30	CC
Long Panatela	No. 100	7	38	CC
Lonsdale	No. 200	7	44	CC
Long Corona	No. 300	6¼	44	CC
Panatela	No. 400	6	38	CC
Robusto	No. 500	5½	50	CC
Robusto	No. 600	4½	50	CC

Pyramid	No. 700	7	54	CC
Petit Corona	No. 800	4	42	CC
Giant	Supreme	8	48	CC
Giant	Don Oscar	9	46	CC

Introduced in October 1988, the Oscar is medium to full-bodied, offering a rich bouquet. The experience is mouth-filling with its smooth draw and the luxurious indulgence of the taste of the Dominican blend with a flawless Connecticut wrapper. Produced by only the most experienced artisans, Oscars are packed uncellophaned in cedar cabinets. A maduro-wrapped version is coming soon!

PADRON
Handmade in Danli, Honduras and Esteli, Nicaragua.

Wrapper: Nicaragua　　　　*Binder: Nicaragua*　　　　*Filler: Nicaragua*

Shape	Name	Lgth	Ring	Wrapper
Giant	Magnum	9	50	Cl-CM-Ma
Giant Corona	Grand Reserve	8	41	Cl-CM-Ma
Double Corona	Executive	7½	50	Cl-CM-Ma
Churchill	Churchill	6⅞	46	Cl-CM-Ma
Lonsdale	Ambassador	6⅞	42	Cl-CM-Ma
Panatela	Panatela	6⅞	36	Cl-CM-Ma
Long Corona	Palmas	6¼	42	Cl-CM-Ma
Corona	Londres	5½	42	Cl-CM-Ma
Panatela	Chicos	5½	36	Cl-CM-Ma
Corona Extra	Delicias	4⅞	46	Cl-CM-Ma
Robusto	2000	5	50	Cl-CM-Ma
Robusto	3000	5½	52	Cl-CM-Ma
	30th Anniversary Series:			
Double Corona	Diplomatico	7	50	CM
Pyramid	Pyramide	6⅞	52	CM

HANDMADE CIGARS: BRAND LISTINGS

Robusto	Exclusivo	5½	50	CM
Grand Corona	Monarca	6½	46	CM
Lonsdale	Superior	6½	42	CM
Long Corona	Corona	6	42	CM

The Padron family began manufacturing cigars by hand in Miami in 1964 using the experience of their Cuban forefathers who began making cigars in 1853. Only Cuban-seed tobaccos are used in the manufacture of this medium-to-full-bodied range from all Nicaraguan tobaccos in factories in Honduras and Nicaragua. The 30th Anniversary Series was introduced to considerable acclaim in 1994.

PAISANOS
Handmade in La Romana, Dominican Republic.

Wrapper: Dom. Rep.   Binder: Dom. Rep.   Filler: Dom. Rep.

Shape	Name	Lgth	Ring	Wrapper
Corona	No. 1	5½	44	CC
Churchill	No. 2	6⅞	48	CC
Double Corona	No. 3	7½	50	CC
Robusto	No. 4	5	52	CC
Giant	No. 5	8½	52	CC

Here is a 1996-introduced, medium-bodied offering with all Dominican leaves, offered in all-wooden boxes of 25.

PALMAREJO
Handmade in Villa Gonzalez, Dominican Republic.

Wrapper: Indonesia   Binder: Dom. Rep.   Filler: Dom. Rep.

Shape	Name	Lgth	Ring	Wrapper
Double Corona	Churchill	7½	50	CC
Long Corona	Corona	6	44	CC
Corona	Petit Corona	5½	42	CC

| Toro | Robusto | 6 | 50 | CC |
| Robusto | Rothschild | 4½ | 50 | CC |

Here is a premium, medium-bodied brand introduced in 1997. It features a Sumatra wrapper and is offered in all-cedar boxes of 25.

PANABANO
Handmade in Chiriqui, Panama.

Wrapper: Panama   *Binder: Panama*   *Filler: Panama*

Shape	Name	Lgth	Ring	Wrapper
Double Corona	Churchill	7½	50	CC
Robusto	Robusto	5½	50	CC
Grand Corona	Doble Corona	6	46	CC

This cigar was introduced to the U.S. market in 1997 and offers all-Panamanian, Cuban-seed tobacco for a mild-bodied smoke. The presentation is unique as the brand is offered in cellophane-wrapped octagons of 25 cigars each, in addition to boxes of 10 or 25.

PANAMA JONES
Manufacture and components vary by size; see below.

Shape	Name	Lgth	Ring	Wrapper
	Handmade in Chiriqui, Panama: *(Wrapper: Indonesia; Binder: Panama; Filler: Panama)*			
Churchill	Double Corona	6¾	46	CC
	Handmade in San Andres Tuxtla, Mexico: *(Wrapper: Mexico; Binder: Mexico; Filler: Mexico)*			
Corona	Corona	5½	42	CM-Ma
	Handmade in Santiago, Dominican Republic: *(Wrapper: Dom.Rep.; Binder: Dom.Rep.; Filler: Dom.Rep.)*			
Robusto	Robusto	4¾	50	CC
Lonsdale	Lonsdale	6¾	44	CC

HANDMADE CIGARS: BRAND LISTINGS

Talk about complicated! Here's a brand with three different blends from factories in three different countries in just four sizes! The Panama-made Double Corona is considered mild-to-medium bodied; the Mexican-made Coronas are medium-bodied and the Dominican-made sizes are also medium-bodied. Introduced in 1997, Panama Jones cigars are modestly priced, so try them all!

PANOREA
Handmade in Santiago, Dominican Republic.

Wrapper: USA/Connecticut   Binder: Dom. Rep.   Filler: Dom. Rep.

Shape	Name	Lgth	Ring	Wrapper
Double Corona	Churchill	7	50	CM
Robusto	Robusto	5	50	CM
Torpedo	Belicoso	6¼	52	CM
Lonsdale	Lonsdale	6½	42	CM
Corona	Corona	5½	42	CM

Here is a 1997-introduced, medium-to-full-bodied cigar that features Piloto Cubano filler leaves and an Olor binder. It is presented without cellophane in all-cedar boxes of 25.

PANTERA
Handmade, with short filler, in Santiago, Dominican Republic.

Wrapper: Dom. Rep.   Binder: Dom. Rep.   Filler: Dom. Rep.

Shape	Name	Lgth	Ring	Wrapper
Robusto	No. 10	5½	50	CC
Corona Extra	No. 20	5½	46	CC
Corona	No. 30	5½	42	CC
Panatela	No. 40	5½	38	CC

This handmade brand is mild in taste and offered in economical bundles of 25 cigars each.

HANDMADE CIGARS: BRAND LISTINGS

PANTERA DE ORO
Handmade in Esteli, Nicaragua.

Wrapper: Nicaragua   Binder: Nicaragua   Filler: Nicaragua

Shape	Name	Lgth	Ring	Wrapper
Double Corona	Presidente	7	54	Cl-CC-Ma
Double Corona	Churchill	7	50	Cl-CC-Ma
Toro	Toro	6	50	Cl-CC-Ma
Long Corona	Grand Corona	6	44	Cl-CC-Ma
Robusto	Corona Extra	5½	48	Cl-CC-Ma
Robusto	Robusto	5	52	Cl-CC-Ma
Robusto	Rothschild	4½	50	Cl-CC-Ma

Here is a mild-bodied blend of tobaccos, available in a choice of wrappers.
Available in either cellophane sleeves or nude in cedar boxes, an Indonesian-
wrapped version is also available in limited distribution.

PARTAGAS
Handmade in Santiago, Dominican Republic.

Wrapper: Cameroon   Binder: Mexico   Filler: Dom. Rep., Mexico

Shape	Name	Lgth	Ring	Wrapper
Torpedo	Aristocrat	6	50	CM
Cigarillo	Miniatura	3¾	24	CM
Small Panatela	Puritos	4⅛	32	CM
Panatela	No. 6	6	34	CM
Short Panatela	No. 4	5	38	CM
Robusto	Robusto	4½	49	CM
Corona	No. 2	5¾	43	CM
Robusto	Naturales	5½	50	CM
Grand Corona	Maduro	6¼	48	Ma
Lonsdale	No. 1	6¾	43	CM

HANDMADE CIGARS: BRAND LISTINGS

Long Corona	Sabroso	(tubed)	5⅞	44	CM
Lonsdale	Humitube	(tubed)	6¾	43	CM
Grand Corona	Almirantes		6¼	47	CM
Lonsdale	8-9-8		6⅞	44	CM
Double Corona	No. 10		7½	49	CM
Double Corona	Fabuloso		7	52	CM
	Limited Reserve series:				
Lonsdale	Royale		6¾	43	CM
Grand Corona	Regale		6¼	47	CM
Robusto	Robusto		5½	49	CM
Short Panatela	Epicure		5	38	CM
	150 Signature Series:				
Double Corona	AA		7½	49	CM
Lonsdale	A		6¾	43	CM
Grand Corona	B		6½	47	CM
Robusto	C		5½	49	CM
Short Panatela	D		5	38	CM
Toro	Figurado		6	50	CM
Robusto	Robusto		4½	49	CM
Double Corona	Don Ramon		7	52	CM

This famous brand, originated in 1845, continues to use only the highest quality Cameroon wrappers which, combined with tobaccos from the Dominican Republic and Mexico, gives it a spicy, full flavor. In a salute to the brand's 150th anniversary, the limited edition 150th Signature Series debuted in late 1995. Wrapped in specially-cured, 18-year-old Cameroon tobaccos, these cigars are aged an additional four months and presented in unique, varnished cedar boxes of 25, 50 or 100 cigars.

HANDMADE CIGARS: BRAND LISTINGS

PARTICULARES
Handmade in Santiago, Dominican Republic.

Wrapper: Ecuador   Binder: Dom. Rep.   Filler: Dom. Rep., Nicaragua

Shape	Name	Lgth	Ring	Wrapper
Slim Panatela	Petit	5⅝	34	CC
Corona	No. 4	5½	42	CC
Panatela	Panatelas	6⅞	35	CC
Long Corona	Royal Coronas	6¼	43	CC
Robusto	Rothschild	5	50	CC-Ma
Lonsdale	Supremos	7	43	CC
Toro	Matador	6	50	CC-Ma
Churchill	Churchills	6⅞	49	CC
Double Corona	Presidentes	7¾	50	CC
Giant	Viajantes	8½	52	CC-Ma

Introduced in the 1980s, the Particulares was originally made in Honduras and, beginning in 1997, is now manufactured in the Dominican Republic. The wrapper is Connecticut-seed from Ecuador and helps to make this a medium-bodied cigar, offered in boxes of 25.

PASEANA
Handmade in Danli, Honduras.

Wrapper: Honduras   Binder: Honduras   Filler: Honduras, Nicaragua

Shape	Name	Lgth	Ring	Wrapper
Giant	Presidente	8½	50	CM
Torpedo	Torpedo	7	54	CM
Robusto	Robusto	5	50	CM
Churchill	Churchill	7	48	CM
Toro	Toro	6	50	CM
Long Corona	Cetro	6	44	CM

HANDMADE CIGARS: BRAND LISTINGS

A limited-production cigar introduced in 1997, this is a medium-bodied brand. It is offered in individual cellophane sleeves and then packed into all-cedar boxes of 25.

PAUL GARMIRIAN
Handmade in Santiago, Dominican Republic.

Wrapper: USA/Connecticut   *Binder: Dom. Rep.*   *Filler: Dom. Rep.*

Shape	Name	Lgth	Ring	Wrapper
Giant	P.G. Celebration	9	50	CC
Double Corona	P.G. Double Corona	7⅝	50	CC
Torpedo	P.G. Belicoso	6¼	52	CC
Churchill	P.G. Churchill	7	48	CC
Long Panatela	P.G. No. 1	7½	38	CC
Grand Corona	P.G. Corona Grande	6½	46	CC
Torpedo	P.G. Belicoso Fino	5½	52	CC
Lonsdale	P.G. Lonsdale	6½	42	CC
Toro	P.G. Connoisseur	6	50	CC
Robusto	P.G. Epicure	5½	50	CC
Robusto	P.G. Robusto	5	50	CC
Robusto	P.G. No. 2	4¾	48	CC
Corona	P.G. Corona	5½	42	CC
Petit Corona	P.G. Petit Corona	5	43	CC
Short Panatela	P.G. Petit Bouquet	4½	38	CC
Petit Corona	P.G. No. 5	4	40	CC
Petit Corona	P.G. Bombones	3½	43	CC
Panatela	P.G. Especial	5¾	38	CC

"Smooth, subtle, spicy and delicious." That's the response of many smokers who were delighted to enjoy a Dominican-produced cigar which has so many attributes of a high-quality Havana. The characteristics of the P.G. line include a scarce and richly-flavored medium-to-dark reddish-brown Colorado-colored

HANDMADE CIGARS: BRAND LISTINGS

Connecticut Shade wrappers which are the favorite of many connoisseurs. The new Especial shape is specially configured to be of interest to women smokers.

PECADO
Handmade in Tamboril, Dominican Republic.

Wrapper: Indonesia   Binder: Dom. Rep.   Filler: Dom. Rep.

Shape	Name	Lgth	Ring	Wrapper
Torpedo	Torpedo	7	50	CC
Churchill	Churchill	7	48	CC
Toro	Toro	5¾	50	CC
Robusto	Robusto	5	50	CC
Corona	Corona	5½	42	CC

Here is a medium-bodied cigar that includes a Sumatra-grown wrapper, combined with Dominican-grown Olor binders and Piloto Cubano filler. The brand is presented in cellophane sleeves within all-cedar boxes.

PENGUIN
Handmade in Villa Gonzalez, Dominican Republic.

Wrapper: Dominican Republic, USA/Connecticut

Binder: Dominican Republic   Filler: Dominican Republic

Shape	Name	Lgth	Ring	Wrapper
Giant	Emperor	8½	52	CC-CM-Stripe
Double Corona	Empress	7½	50	CC-CM-Stripe
Toro	King	6½	52	CC-CM-Stripe
Lonsdale	Adelie	6½	43	CC-CM-Stripe
Toro	Gentoo	6	48	CC-CM-Stripe
Robusto	Gallapagos	5	50	CC-CM-Stripe

Introduced in 1996, this brand is medium in body and offered in a variety of wrapper shades – natural-shade leaves from Connecticut and darker wrapper from the Dominican Republic – and in a double wrapped version. It is offered in boxes of 25.

HANDMADE CIGARS: BRAND LISTINGS

PERA
Handmade in Esteli, Nicaragua.

Wrapper: Nicaragua   Binder: Nicaragua   Filler: Nicaragua

Shape	Name	Lgth	Ring	Wrapper
Churchill	Churchill	6¾	48	CM
Corona	Corona	5½	44	CM
Double Corona	Double Corona	7	54	CM
Pyramid	Figurado	7½	52	CM
Robusto	Rothschild	4½	52	CM
Toro	Toro	6¼	50	CM

Created in 1996, this all-Nicaraguan line is medium-bodied, with a touch of spice on the finish. Offered in bundles of 25.

PETER STOKKEBYE
Handmade in Santiago, Dominican Republic.

Wrapper: USA/Connecticut   Binder: Proprietary   Filler: Dom. Rep.

Shape	Name	Lgth	Ring	Wrapper
Double Corona	Santa Maria No. 1	7	50	CC
Panatela	Santa Maria No. 2	6¾	38	CC
Corona	Santa Maria No. 3	5½	43	CC

The famous Stokkebye family is now in its eighth generation in the tobacco trade. They were once one of the appointed cigar rollers to Winston Churchill! Their cigars, introduced in 1987, are blended with a delicate balance to simultaneously provide a mild and flavorful smoke.

PETERSON HALLMARK
Handmade in Santiago, Dominican Republic.

Wrapper: USA/Connecticut

Binder: Dominican Republic or Ecuador   Filler: Dominican Republic

Shape	Name	Lgth	Ring	Wrapper
Double Corona	Presidente	7½	50	Cl-Ma

Churchill	Churchill	(tubed)	7	48	Cl-Ma
Toro	Toro	(tubed)	6	50	Cl-Ma
Corona	Corona	(tubed)	5¾	43	Cl-Ma
Petit Corona	Petite Corona	(tubed)	5	43	Cl
Robusto	Robusto	(tubed)	4¾	50	Cl-Ma
Short Panatela	Tres Petite Corona		4½	38	Cl

Famous for pipes for more than 100 years, the Peterson Hallmark Collection brings a medium-bodied taste to this range. The initial Peterson of Dublin line, introduced in 1995, includes seven shapes, made from specially-selected leaf in the Dominican Republic and a wrapper from Connecticut. The maduro line, new for 1997, utilizes a Dominican binder and offers a medium-to-full-bodied taste.

PETRUS
Handmade in Santa Rosa de Copan, Honduras.

Wrapper: Ecuador   *Binder: Honduras*   *Filler: Honduras*

Shape	Name	Lgth	Ring	Wrapper
Double Corona	Double Corona	7¾	50	CC
Long Panatela	Lord Byron	8	38	CC
Double Corona	Churchill	7	50	CC
Long Corona	No. II	6¼	44	DC-CC
Toro	No. III	6	50	CC
Panatela	Palma Fina	6	38	CC
Panatela	No. IV	5⅝	38	CC
Corona Extra	Corona Sublime	5½	46	CC
Torpedo	Antonius	5	52	CC
Petit Corona	Gregorius	5	42	CC
Robusto	Rothschild	4¾	50	CC
Short Panatela	Chantaco	4¾	35	CC
Small Panatela	Duchess	4½	30	CC

HANDMADE CIGARS: BRAND LISTINGS

This outstanding line, which debuted in 1989, adds a new panatela shape for 1997 and a double claro wrapper for the No. II size. These natural-wrapped cigars showcase Ecuadorian-grown leaf. Petrus is a mild-to-medium-bodied cigar with dense, spicy aromas and rich flavors.

PETRUS ETIQUETTE ROUGE
Handmade in Danli, Honduras.

Wrapper: Ecuador   *Binder: Honduras*   *Filler: Dom.Rep., Nicaragua*

Shape	Name	Lgth	Ring	Wrapper
Churchill	RCH 1	7	48	CC
Torpedo	RB 1	7	55	CC
Corona	RCR 1	5¾	44	CC
Robusto	RR 1	5	52	CC

Here is a superior cigar, made in a limited production of 2,000 boxes per shape. Packed in exquisite Caoba wood boxes of 20 cigars, this is a medium-bodied, rich blend created to satisfy the most demanding cigar enthusiast.

PETRUS ORO NEGRO
Handmade in Santa Rosa de Copan, Honduras.

Wrapper: Honduras   *Binder: Honduras*   *Filler: Honduras*

Shape	Name	Lgth	Ring	Wrapper
Double Corona	Double Corona	7¾	50	Ma
Double Corona	Churchill	7	50	Ma
Long Corona	No. II	6¼	44	Ma
Toro	No. III	6	50	Ma
Corona Extra	Corona Sublime	5½	46	Ma
Torpedo	Antonius	5	54	Ma
Robusto	Rothschild	4¾	50	Ma

Introduced in 1996, this cigar is wrapped in a superb Honduran maduro wrapper around a blend of all-Honduran-grown tobaccos. This is a medium-bodied smoke available in all-cedar boxes of 25.

Petrus...
The hunt for the perfect cigar is finally over
Petrus
Petrus
Quality Cigars from Honduras

HANDMADE CIGARS: BRAND LISTINGS

PHEASANT
Handmade in Danli, Honduras.

Wrapper: Ecuador *Binder: Mexico* *Filler: Honduras, Nicaragua*

Shape	Name	Lgth	Ring	Wrapper
Double Corona	Churchill	7½	50	CC
Toro	Toro	6	50	CC
Robusto	Robusto	5¼	54	CC
Lonsdale	Corona	6½	42	CC

Here is a mild-bodied brand with a Connecticut-seed wrapper which was introduced in 1995 and complements the outstanding Pheasant line of Spanish leather cigar and smoking accessories. Each of these styles is offered in elegant boxes of 25.

PHILIPPINE CIGAR COMPANY
Handmade in Manila, the Philippines.

Wrapper: Philippines *Binder: Philippines* *Filler: Philippines*

Shape	Name	Lgth	Ring	Wrapper
Double Corona	Double Corona	7½	52	CM
Churchill	Churchill	6¾	47	CM
Lonsdale	Corona Largas	6¾	44	CM
Corona Extra	Rothschild	5½	46	CM
Corona	Corona	5½	42	CM
Robusto	Robusto	5	52	CM
Torpedo	Cortado	5	52	CM
Short Panatela	Half Corona	4	39	CM

This is a medium-bodied cigar with two-year-old tobaccos grown in the Philippines, available in Narra wood boxes of 25.

HANDMADE CIGARS: BRAND LISTINGS

PHILLIPS & KING GUARDSMEN
Handmade in La Romana, Dominican Republic.

Wrapper: Indonesia   *Binder: Dominican Republic*
Filler: Brazil, Dominican Republic, Mexico

Shape	Name	Lgth	Ring	Wrapper
Giant	No. 1	8	52	CM
Double Corona	No. 2	7½	50	CM
Toro	No. 3	6	50	CM
Robusto	No. 4	4¾	50	CM
Churchill	No. 5	7	48	CM
Corona	No. 6	5½	44	CM
Long Corona	No. 7	6	42	CM
Panatela	No. 8	6	36	CM

The Guardsmen series is the flagship of the famous cigar distribution firm of Phillips & King of Industry, California. It is mild in body, individually wrapped and offered in boxes of 25 cigars each.

PINNACLE
Handmade in Santiago, Dominican Republic.

Wrapper: Indonesia   *Binder: Dom. Rep.*   *Filler: Dom. Rep.*

Shape	Name	Lgth	Ring	Wrapper
Churchill	Imperial Corona	6¾	46	CC
Robusto	Robusto	5	50	CC
Toro	Corona Gorda	6	50	CC

This brand from the Dominican Republic was introduced in 1996. The medium-bodied taste is complemented by the unusual packaging: each cigar is banded, then presented in an individual foil sleeve, which also bears the brand's band. The finished product is sold in elegant, all-cedar boxes of 25.

PIRATA
Handmade in Santiago, Dominican Republic.

HANDMADE CIGARS: BRAND LISTINGS

NATURAL SELECTION:

Wrapper: Indonesia   *Binder: Dom. Rep.*   *Filler: Dom. Rep.*

MADURO SELECTION:

Wrapper: Brazil   *Binder: Brazil*   *Filler: Brazil*

Shape	Name	Lgth	Ring	Wrapper
Churchill	Gran Corona	6¾	46	CC-Ma
Giant	President	8	50	CC-Ma
Robusto	Robusto	4½	52	CC-Ma
Toro	Toro	6	50	CC-Ma
Torpedo	Torpedo	6½	52	CC-Ma

This brand achieved wider recognition in 1997 and offers two medium-bodied blends: one that features an Indonesian wrapper with Dominican interior leaves, the other with all-Brazilian tobaccos. In either case, you can enjoy Pirata in boxes of 25.

PLASENCIA
Handmade in Esteli, Nicaragua.

Wrapper: Ecuador   *Binder: Nicaragua*   *Filler: Nicaragua*

Shape	Name	Lgth	Ring	Wrapper
Double Corona	Presidente	7½	50	CC
Torpedo	Torpedo	7	54	CC
Toro	Toro	6	50	CC
Long Corona	Corona Especial	6	44	CC
Robusto	Robusto	4¾	52	CC

Here is a brand that celebrates the famous name of Plasencia — a name revered throughout the cigar world for the manufacture of outstanding cigars. These cigars are outstanding in their own right, with a medium-bodied taste. They are offered in boxes of 25.

PLAYBOY
BY DON DIEGO
Handmade in La Romana, Dominican Republic.

Wrapper: USA/Connecticut   Binder: Dom. Rep.   Filler: Brazil, Dom. Rep.

Shape	Name	Lgth	Ring	Wrapper
Double Corona	Churchill	7¾	50	CC
Toro	Double Corona	6	52	CC
Churchill	Gran Corona	6¾	48	CC
Robusto	Robusto	5	50	CC
Lonsdale	Lonsdale	6½	42	CC
Grand Corona	Leroy Nieman Selection	6½	46	CC

Here is the 1996-introduced brand named for the famous magazine and entertainment company, produced in cooperation with Consolidated Cigar Company in its La Romana factory. The blend is medium in body and features a dark shade of Connecticut wrapper. The cigars are presented in elegant wooden box, while the Leroy Nieman Selection offers a special Nieman artwork on the inside of just 5,000 boxes; a select number have been signed by the artist.

PLEIADES
Handmade in Santiago, Dominican Republic.

Wrapper: Mexico or USA/Connecticut   Binder: Dom. Rep.   Filler: Dom. Rep.

Shape	Name	Lgth	Ring	Wrapper
Giant	Aldebaran	8½	50	CC
Giant	Saturne	8	46	CC
Giant Corona	Neptune	7½	42	CC
Churchill	Sirius	6⅞	46	CC-Ma
Corona	Centaurus	5¾	42	DC
Corona	Orion	5¾	42	CC
Panatela	Uranus	6⅞	34	CC
Corona	Antares	5½	40	CC

Robusto	Pluton	5	50	CC-Ma
Small Panatela	Perseus	5	34	CC
Cigarillo	Mars	5	28	CC
	Machine-made:			
Cigarillo	Mini	3½	24	CC

Pleiades are exquisite cigars imported from the Dominican Republic. They are created by hand using only the finest long-leaf filler and smooth Connecticut Shade wrappers or Mexican maduro wrappers. Depending on the selection from the 12 available shapes, the richness, quality of taste and aroma will vary from mild and light to a bold, full-bodied flavor. The unusual packaging includes not only an all-cedar box, but each is equipped with a mini-humidifier to keep the cigars in perfect condition!

PLEIADES RESERVE PRIVEE
Handmade in Santiago, Dominican Republic.

Wrapper: USA/Connecticut   Binder: Dom. Rep.   Filler: Dom. Rep.

Shape	Name	Lgth	Ring	Wrapper
Churchill	Sirius	6⅞	46	CC
Robusto	Pluton	5	50	CC

New for 1997, here are glorious examples of the roller's art, using vintage tobaccos from 1991 and 1992 to form beautiful, usually mild-bodied cigars without a hint of harshness. Available only in limited quantities, you can experience them in all-cedar boxes of 16 (Pluton) or 24 (Sirius).

POR LARRAÑAGA
Handmade in La Romana, Dominican Republic.

Wrapper: USA/Connecticut   Binder: Dom. Rep.   Filler: Dom. Rep.

Shape	Name	Lgth	Ring	Wrapper
Lonsdale	Cetros	6⅞	42	CC
Panatela	Delicados	6½	36	CC
Double Corona	Fabulosos	7	50	CC

Corona	Nacionales	5½	42	CC
Short Panatela	Petit Cetro	5	38	CC
Pyramid	Pyramides	6	50	CC
Robusto	Robusto	5	50	CC

This is an ancient brand which first saw production in Cuba in 1834! Today's Dominican version is very mild and limited in production. It is generally available only to tobacconists who are members of the Tobacconists' Association of America (TAA).

POR MATT AMORE
Handmade in Santiago, Dominican Republic.

Wrapper: USA/Connecticut   Binder: Dom. Rep.   Filler: Dom. Rep.

Shape	Name	Lgth	Ring	Wrapper
Double Corona	DJB	7	47	CC
Robusto	Amistad	4½	50	CC
Long Corona	Esperanza	6	43	CC
Toro	MQ	6	50	CC

Known as Por Matamor when introduced in 1996, this is a limited production cigar for the benefit of a discriminating few who appreciate a medium-bodied smoke with excellent construction. These cigars are individually cellophaned and packed in all-cedar boxes of 25.

PORFIRIO
Handmade in Santiago, Dominican Republic.

Wrapper: USA/Connecticut   Binder: Dom. Rep.   Filler: Dom. Rep.

Shape	Name	Lgth	Ring	Wrapper
Corona	Coronas	5½	42	CC
Lonsdale	Lonsdale	6½	42	CC
Robusto	Robusto	5	50	CC
Double Corona	Churchill	7½	50	CC

Giant	Rubi	8½	52	CC

This brand was introduced in 1996, with a mild body and an elegant Connecticut Shade wrapper surrounding Dominican tobaccos. Each cigar is presented in an individual cellophane sleeve and Porfirios are available in cedar cabinets of 25 cigars.

PORTO BELLO
Handmade in Santiago, Dominican Republic.

Wrapper: USA/Connecticut   Binder: Mexico   Filler: Dom. Rep., Honduras

Shape	Name	Lgth	Ring	Wrapper
Giant	No. 1	8½	52	CC
Double Corona	No. 2	7½	50	CC
Churchill	No. 3	6⅞	46	CC
Toro	No. 4	6	50	CC
Lonsdale	No. 5	6¾	42	CC
Long Panatela	No. 6	7½	38	CC
Long Panatela	No. 7	7	36	CC
Corona	No. 8	5¾	42	CC
Robusto	No. 9	5	50	CC
Pyramid	Piramide	7	54	CC

Created in 1988, this is an economical, bundled brand which offers a mild taste in a handmade, all long-filler cigar – including a genuine Connecticut Shade wrapper!

PRESIDENTE
Handmade in Hialeah, Florida, USA.

Wrapper: Ecuador   Binder: Dom. Rep.   Filler: Dom. Rep.

Shape	Name	Lgth	Ring	Wrapper
Panatela	Panetela Azuquita	6	38	CC
Corona	Varadero Havana	5½	44	CC

HANDMADE CIGARS: BRAND LISTINGS

Toro	Corona Excelente	6	48	CC
Robusto	Robusto Clasico	4¾	50	CC
Toro	Robusto Tradicion	5¾	50	CC
Double Corona	Churchill Gold	6¾	50	CC
Double Corona	Toro Matador	7	52	CC
Double Corona	Presidente Platino	7½	54	CC
Torpedo	Torpedo Superior	6½	54	CC
Giant	Embajador Imperial	8	60	CC

Here is a medium-bodied brand introduced in 1996. It offers an enticing aroma in boxes of 25.

PRESIDENTE CACERES
Handmade in Santiago, Dominican Republic.

Wrapper: USA/Connecticut   *Binder: Dom. Rep.*   *Filler: Dom. Rep.*

Shape	*Name*	*Lgth*	*Ring*	*Wrapper*
Churchill	Double Corona	7	48	CM
Toro	Robusto Grande	6	50	CM

You'll enjoy this mild-to-medium-bodied brand, offered to the U.S. market initially in 1996. The brand is managed by the grandchildren of the man for whom this brand is named in Santiago in the heart of the tobacco zone of the Dominican Republic.

PRESTIGIO CUBANO
Handmade in Danli, Honduras.

Wrapper: Ecuador   *Binder: Dom. Rep.*   *Filler: Honduras, Nicaragua*

Shape	*Name*	*Lgth*	*Ring*	*Wrapper*
Torpedo	Torpedo	7	54	CC
Giant	President	8	50	CC
Churchill	Churchill	6⅞	49	CC
Toro	Toro	6	50	CC

HANDMADE CIGARS: BRAND LISTINGS

Robusto	Robusto	5	50	CC
Lonsdale	Cetro	6¼	44	CC

Marvelous! This is a super-premium cigar from Honduras, made at the famous Plasencia factories with a medium-to-heavy taste, introduced in late 1996.

PRIDE OF COPAN
Handmade in Santa Rosa de Copan, Honduras.
Wrapper: USA/Connecticut   Binder: Honduras   Filler: Honduras

Shape	Name	Lgth	Ring	Wrapper
Double Corona	Pride of Copan No. 1	6¾	50	CC
Long Corona	Pride of Copan No. 2	6	44	CC
Short Panatela	Pride of Copan No. 3	5⅜	38	CC
Panatela	Pride of Copan No. 4	5⅞	35	CC
Slim Panatela	Pride of Copan No. 5	6¼	30	CC
Small Panatela	Pride of Copan No. 6	4¾	30	CC
Cigarillo	Pride of Copan No. 7	4⅛	25	CC

A quality, medium-to-full-bodied cigar with quality construction. That's the story of Pride of Copan, created for those who want quality, consistency and value.

PRIDE OF JAMAICA
Handmade in Kingston, Jamaica.
Wrapper: USA/Connecticut   Binder: Mexico
Filler: Dominican Republic, Jamaica, Mexico

Shape	Name	Lgth	Ring	Wrapper
Double Corona	Churchill	7½	49	Ma
Robusto	Robusto	4	50	Ma
Grand Corona	Petit Churchill	6	50	Ma
Lonsdale	Rothschild	6½	42	Ma
Corona	Royal Corona	5½	42	CC-Ma

Robusto	Petit Corona	5	50	CC-Ma

This famous brand continues to be created daily in Kingston, Jamaica and offered in boxes of 25 well-made, much-respected cigars. Connecticut Shade wrapper is used to help give the mild, rich flavor for which Pride of Jamaica is so well known.

PRIMERA DE NICARAGUA
Handmade in Ocotal, Nicaragua.

Wrapper: Nicaragua *Binder: Honduras* *Filler: Honduras, Nicaragua*

Shape	Name	Lgth	Ring	Wrapper
Lonsdale	No. 1	7	44	CM-Ma
Double Corona	Churchill	7	50	CM-Ma
Robusto	Rothschild	5	50	CM-Ma
Toro	Toro	6	50	CM-Ma
Giant	Viajante	8½	52	CM-Ma

Here is a mild-to-medium bodied cigar, produced from all long-filler tobaccos, introduced in 1990. This is one of the first brands to emerge after the civil unrest in Nicaragua and is presented in all-wood boxes of 25.

PRIMO DEL CRISTO
Handmade in Danli, Honduras.

Wrapper: Honduras *Binder: Honduras* *Filler: Honduras*

Shape	Name	Lgth	Ring	Wrapper
Lonsdale	No. 1	7	44	CI-CC-Ma
Toro	Churchills	7	50	CI-CC-Ma
Corona	Coronas	6	42	CI-CC-Ma
Giant	Generals	8½	52	CI-CC-Ma
Giant	Inmensos	8	54	CC-Ma
Long Panatela	Palmas Extra	7	36	CC
Long Panatela	Palmas Reales	8	36	CI-CC

Double Corona	Presidentes	7½	50	CC
Petit Corona	Reyes	5¼	44	Cl-CC-Ma
Robusto	Rothschilds	5	50	Cl-CC-Ma
Toro	Toros	6	50	Cl-CC-Ma

These are well-made cigars that are offered in modestly-priced bundles of 25, with a medium-to-heavy body.

PRIMO DEL REY
Handmade in La Romana, Dominican Republic.

Wrapper: Indonesia   *Binder: Dom. Rep.*   *Filler: Dom. Rep.*

Shape	Name	Lgth	Ring	Wrapper
Long Corona	Cazadores	6	44	Ma
Lonsdale	Chavon	6½	41	CM
Slim Panatela	Panetela Extras	5⅞	34	CM
Panatela	Reales	6⅛	36	CM
Lonsdale	Seleccion No. 1	6¾	42	CM
Long Corona	Seleccion No. 2	6¼	42	Cl-CM
Panatela	Seleccion No. 3	6¾	36	CM
Corona	Seleccion No. 4	5½	42	Cl-CM-Ma
	Machine-made, with short filler:			
Cigarillo	Cortos	4	28	CM

Primo del Rey are first-quality cigars first produced in 1961, offering a mild taste from a unique blend of leaves, notably including a Indonesian wrapper. An excellent value, the entire Primo del Rey series is very well constructed. Please note that some sizes are machine-bunched.

PRIVATE STOCK
Handmade in Santiago, Dominican Republic.

Wrapper: USA/Connecticut   *Binder: Dom. Rep.*   *Filler: Dom. Rep.*

HANDMADE CIGARS: BRAND LISTINGS

Shape	Name	Lgth	Ring	Wrapper
Double Corona	Private Stock No. 1	7¾	48	CC
Toro	Private Stock No. 2	6	48	CC
Slim Panatela	Private Stock No. 3	6½	33	CC
Panatela	Private Stock No. 4	5¾	38	CC
Corona	Private Stock No. 5	5¾	43	CC
Corona Extra	Private Stock No. 6	5¼	46	CC
Petit Corona	Private Stock No. 7	4¾	43	CC
Short Panatela	Private Stock No. 8	4⅝	35	CC
Cigarillo	Private Stock No. 9	4⅝	26	CC
Petit Corona	Private Stock No. 10	4	40	CC
Robusto	Private Stock No. 11	4⅝	50	CC

These cigars are manufactured in one of the most exclusive factories in the world. High standards of quality make the Private Stock label an excellent value for cigars with a mild to medium body.

PRIZE POINTER
Handmade in Santiago, Dominican Republic.

Wrapper: USA/Connecticut   Binder: Dom. Rep.   Filler: Dom. Rep.

Shape	Name	Lgth	Ring	Wrapper
Double Corona	Double Corona	7½	49	CC
Corona	Corona	5½	42	CC
Lonsdale	Lonsdale	7	44	CC
Toro	Toro	6½	50	CC

Stop barking! This is no dog, but a full-bodied cigar created in 1997, offered in bundles of 25.

HANDMADE CIGARS: BRAND LISTINGS

PROFESOR SILA 1934
Handmade in Santiago, Dominican Republic.
Wrapper: USA/Connecticut, Indonesia

Binder: Canary Islands   Filler: Canary Islands

Shape	Name		Lgth	Ring	Wrapper
Robusto	Robusto		4⅝	50	CI
Corona Extra	Presidente		5⅝	45	CI
Long Panatela	Principe		7¼	38	CI
Grand Corona	Excellencia		6½	45	CI
Double Corona	Majestad		7¼	50	CI
Torpedo	Torpedo Reserva		6½	53	CI
Corona Extra	Conde		4	45	CI-Ma
Giant	Double Corona		8	50	CI-Ma
Toro	Churchill	(tubed)	6½	50	CI-Ma

This factory has been producing cigars since 1934 and, as practice makes perfect, were proud to debut this project in 1996. It offers either a light Connecticut wrapper or an Indonesian maduro wrapper and provides a mild-to-medium-bodied smoke in handy 5-packs or in boxes of 25. You'll recognize it right away with its double band!

PROFESOR SILA BABA
Handmade, with short filler, in Santiago, Dominican Republic.

Wrapper: Indonesia   Binder: Dom. Rep.   Filler: Dom. Rep.

Shape	Name	Lgth	Ring	Wrapper
Lonsdale	Baba	6½	42	CI

This is a mild-bodied, short filler, flavored cigar available in Amaretto, bourbon, coffee, Cognac, rum and vanilla styles. Introduced in 1997, Babas are offered in individual cellophane sleeves in flip-top boxes of 25.

P L É I A D E S

HAND-ROLLED TO MEET THE HIGHEST EXPECTATIONS
OF CONNOISSEURS. MADE FROM THE CHOICEST LEAF
AND LONG FILLER IN THE DOMINICAN REPUBLIC.
THEY ARE HAND SELECTED FOR WRAPPER COLOR
AND PACKED IN FLAVOR-ENHANCING CEDAR BOXES.

Imported by Swisher International, Inc.

HANDMADE CIGARS: BRAND LISTINGS

PROFESOR SILA NAVEGADOR
Handmade in Santiago, Dominican Republic.

Wrapper: Ecuador   *Binder: Dom. Rep.*   *Filler: Dom. Rep.*

Shape	Name	Lgth	Ring	Wrapper
Double Corona	Viajante	7⅝	50	CM
Robusto	Robusto	4¾	50	CM
Grand Corona	No. 1	6¼	47	CM
Corona Extra	No. 3	5½	47	CM
Corona Extra	No. 4	5	47	CM
Panatela	Margarita	5¾	38	CM

Here is a new Profesor Sila line for 1997, made by hand in the Dominican Republic. It features a double band and a medium-bodied flavor thanks to its blend of two-year-aged Olor binder and Cuban-seed filler tobaccos.

PROFESOR SILA SANTA MARIA
Handmade in Santiago, Dominican Republic.

Wrapper: Indonesia   *Binder: Dom. Rep., Indonesia*   *Filler: Brazil, Dom. Rep.*

Shape	Name	Lgth	Ring	Wrapper
Corona	Ancla	5½	43	CM
Long Corona	Galeon	5⅞	43	CM
Lonsdale	Timon	6¾	43	CM
Grand Corona	Capitan	6¾	45	CM
Grand Corona	Proa	5¾	45	CM
Double Corona	Admiral	7	50	CM
Robusto	Robusto	4⅞	50	CM
Slim Panatela	Panatella	7	30	CM

New for 1997, the Santa Maria line presents a full-bodied smoke, with a double band, double binder and a Sumatra wrapper, offered in boxes of 25.

HANDMADE CIGARS: BRAND LISTINGS

PROVIDENCIA
Handmade in Licey, Dominican Republic.

Wrapper: Indonesia   *Binder: Dom. Rep.*   *Filler: Dom. Rep.*

Shape	Name	Lgth	Ring	Wrapper
Giant	Presidente	8	50	Ma
Grand Corona	Double Corona	6½	46	Ma
Long Corona	Corona	6	44	Ma
Robusto	Robusto	5	50	Ma

This cigar was introduced in 1997 and the all-maduro range features an Indonesian wrapper combined with Cuban-seed tobaccos grown in the Dominican Republic. The result is a medium-bodied smoke offered in all-cedar boxes of 25.

PUEBLO DOMINICANO
Handmade in Santiago, Dominican Republic.

Wrapper: Indonesia   *Binder: Dom. Rep.*   *Filler: Dom. Rep.*

Shape	Name	Lgth	Ring	Wrapper
Long Panatela	Cabarete	7¾	38	CM
Giant	Barahona	8	50	CM
Robusto	San Pedro de Marcoris	4½	52	CM
Toro	Santo Domingo	6	50	CM
Corona Extra	La Romana	5½	46	CM
Churchill	Siglo V	6¾	46	CM
Corona	Santiago de los Caballeros	5¼	42	CM
Petit Corona	Samana	4	42	CM

Introduced in 1996, this is a medium-to-full-bodied cigar. It features Cuban-seed filler leaves and is offered in cellophane sleeves in boxes of 25. Boxes of ten are available in the Barahona, Samana and San Pedro de Marcoris shapes.

HANDMADE CIGARS: BRAND LISTINGS

PUERTO RICO
Handmade in San Juan, Puerto Rico.
Wrapper: USA/Pennsylvania

Binder: USA/Pennsylvania   Filler: Dominican Republic, Puerto Rico

Shape	Name	Lgth	Ring	Wrapper
Churchill	JFC No. 3	7	46	CM
Long Corona	JFC No. 4	6	42	CM

Value, medium-bodied flavor and a unique blend of Pennsylvania and Caribbean leaves are yours with Puerto Rico brand cigars, offered in bundles of 25.

PUNCH
Handmade in Cofradia, Honduras.
Wrapper: Ecuador, USA/Connecticut   Binder: Honduras
Filler: Dominican Republic, Honduras, Nicaragua

Shape	Name	Lgth	Ring	Wrapper
Giant	Presidents	8½	52	CM-Ma
Churchill	Double Coronas	6¾	48	CM-Ma
Toro	Pitas	6⅛	50	CM-Ma
Long Corona	Punch	6¼	44	CM-Ma
Lonsdale	Lonsdales	6½	43	CM-Ma
Robusto	Rothschilds	4½	50	CM-Ma
Churchill	Casa Grande	7¼	46	CM-Ma
Corona	No. 75	5½	44	CM-Ma
Long Corona	Amatistas	6¼	44	CM-Ma
Slim Panatela	Largo Elegantes	7	32	CM-Ma
Corona	Elites	5¼	44	CM-Ma
Petit Corona	London Club	5	40	CM-Ma
Lonsdale	After Dinner	7¼	45	CM-Ma
Robusto	Super Rothschilds	5¼	50	CM-Ma
Cigarillo	Slim Panatellas	4	28	CM-Ma

HANDMADE CIGARS: BRAND LISTINGS

Corona	Cafe Royal	(tubed)	5⅝	44	CM-Ma
Long Corona	Crystals	(glass jar)	6	43	CM-Ma
	Deluxe Series:				
Double Corona	Chateau "L"		7¼	54	DC-CM-Ma
Corona Extra	Chateau "M"		5¾	46	DC-CM-Ma
Grand Corona	Coronas		6¼	45	DC-CM-Ma
Corona	Royal Coronations	(tubed)	5¼	44	DC-CM-Ma
	Grand Cru Series:				
Toro	Britania		6¼	50	CM
Double Corona	Diademas		7¼	54	CC
Churchill	Monarcas	(tubed)	6¾	48	CM
Giant	Prince Consorts		8½	52	CM
Robusto	Robustos		5¼	50	CM-Ma
Robusto	Superiors		5½	48	CM
Torpedo	No. II		6	50	CM

The world-famous Punch brand is handmade in Honduras since 1969 from Cuban-seed tobaccos grown in Honduras, Nicaragua and the Dominican Republic. This range offers a magnificent, easy smoke with unsurpassed taste and bouquet using Sumatra-seed, Ecuadorian-grown natural wrappers and Connecticut broadleaf for the maduro-wrapped shapes. The Grand Cru series is made from vintage tobaccos aged from 3-5 years under the supervision of Villazon & Co.'s master blenders. Grand Cru cigars are robust in taste, yet sweet with a marvelous bouquet.

PURO NICARAGUA
Handmade in Ocotal, Nicaragua.

Wrapper: Ecuador   Binder: Nicaragua   Filler: Dom. Rep., Nicaragua

Shape	Name	Lgth	Ring	Wrapper
Panatela	Lindas	5½	38	CC
Corona	No. 4	5½	42	CC

Robusto	Rothschild	5	50	CC
Panatela	Panatela Especial	6⅞	35	CC
Long Corona	Corona Gorda	6	44	CC
Lonsdale	No. 1	6⅝	44	CC
Toro	Toro	6	50	CC
Double Corona	Churchill	7	49	CC
Double Corona	Soberano	7¾	50	CC
Giant	Viajantes	8½	52	CC
Giant	Gigantes	8	54	CC

These heavy-bodied cigars are made by hand and use Nicaraguan-grown binder and filler tobaccos. Packaged in bundles of 25 cigars, they are an excellent value.

PURO PLACER
Handmade in Esteli, Nicaragua.

Wrapper: Indonesia   *Binder: Nicaragua*   *Filler: Nicaragua*

Shape	Name	Lgth	Ring	Wrapper
Double Corona	Presidente	7	50	CM
Toro	Grand Corona	6½	48	CM
Toro	Toro	6	50	CM
Long Corona	Lonsdale	6	44	CM
Robusto	Rothchild	5	50	CM

This is a medium-bodied cigar which was introduced in 1997. It features a dark Sumatra-grown wrapper and is offered cellophaned in all-cedar boxes of 25.

PUROFINO BLUE LABEL
Handmade in Danli, Honduras.

Wrapper: Ecuador   *Binder: Mexico*   *Filler: Costa Rica, Mexico, Nicaragua*

HANDMADE CIGARS: BRAND LISTINGS

Shape	Name	Lgth	Ring	Wrapper
Lonsdale	Corona Real	6½	43	CM
Robusto	Robusto Gordo	5¼	52	CM
Double Corona	Churchill	7	50	CM
Pyramid	Piramide	6½	54	CM

Here is a medium-to-full-bodied brand introduced in 1995. The wrapper is Sumatra-seed, grown in Ecuador and you can enjoy it in boxes of 20.

PUROFINO GOLD LABEL
Handmade in Danli, Honduras.
Wrapper: Ecuador   *Binder: Nicaragua*   *Filler: Mexico, Nicaragua*

Shape	Name	Lgth	Ring	Wrapper
Lonsdale	Corona Real	6½	43	CC
Robusto	Robusto Gordo	5¼	52	CC
Double Corona	Churchill	7	50	CC
Pyramid	Piramide	6½	54	CC

Here is the full-bodied big brother to the Blue Label series, also introduced in 1995. The wrapper is Sumatra-seed, grown in Ecuador and is also offered in boxes of 20.

PUROS DON ABREU
Handmade in Santiago, Dominican Republic.
Wrapper: Indonesia or USA/Connecticut
Binder: Dominican Republic   *Filler: Dominican Republic*

Shape	Name	Lgth	Ring	Wrapper
Toro	Big Toros	6½	50	CC-Ma
Grand Corona	Churchill	6½	46	CC-Ma
Churchill	Churchill Plus	8	48	CC-Ma
Lonsdale	Cobra Double Wrap I	7	44	CC-Ma
Toro	Cobra Double Wrap II	6½	50	CC-Ma

HANDMADE CIGARS: BRAND LISTINGS

Lonsdale	Corona	7	44	CC-Ma
Lonsdale	Coronitas	6½	44	CC-Ma
Double Corona	Double Corona	7½	49	CC-Ma
Double Corona	Ejecutivos	7½	50	CC-Ma
Corona	General	5½	42	CC-Ma
Long Panatela	Panatela	7	37	CC-Ma
Corona Extra	Petite	5	46	CC-Ma
Giant	President	8	50	CC-Ma
Robusto	Toros	5	50	CC-Ma
Torpedo	Torpedo	6½	53	CC-Ma

Introduced in 1996, the Puros Don Abreu line presents a medium-bodied flavor in a choice of a Connecticut-grown natural or Indonesian-grown maduro wrapper.

PUROS INDIOS
Handmade in Danli, Honduras.

Wrapper: Ecuador   *Binder: Ecuador*
Filler: Brazil, Dominican Republic, Jamaica, Nicaragua

Shape	Name	Lgth	Ring	Wrapper
Double Corona	Churchill Especial	7¼	53	CM-Ma
Churchill	Presidente	7¼	47	CM-Ma
Churchill	No. 1 Especial	7	48	CM-Ma
Grand Corona	No. 2 Especial	6½	46	CM-Ma
Lonsdale	Nacionales	6½	43	CM-Ma
Toro	Toro Especial	6	53	CM-Ma
Robusto	Rothschild	5	50	CM-Ma
Corona	No. 4 Especial	5½	44	CM-Ma
Long Panatela	Palmas Real	7	39	CM-Ma
Pyramid	Piramide No. 1	7½	60	CM-Ma

Pyramid	Piramide No. 2	6½	46	CM-Ma
Short Panatela	Petit Perla	5	38	CM-Ma
Short Panatela	No. 5 Especial	5	36	CM-Ma
Perfecto	Victoria	7¼	60	CM-Ma
Perfecto	Gran Victoria	10	60	CM
Giant	Chief	18	60	CM

Introduced in 1995, the blending talents of Rolando Reyes are again at work in Puros Indios cigars. Leaves from five nations are blended by hand in Honduras to create a medium-bodied smoke in a wide variety of sizes, including the 18-inch Chief, one of the longest regular-production cigars marketed anywhere.

PUROS NIRVANA
Handmade in Managua, Nicaragua.

Wrapper: Indonesia   Binder: Costa Rica   Filler: Costa Rica, Nicaragua

Shape	Name	Lgth	Ring	Wrapper
Double Corona	Churchill	7½	50	CC
Long Corona	Lonsdale	6¼	44	CC
Toro	Corona Gorda	6	50	CC
Robusto	Robusto	5	50	CC

Introduced in 1997, this is a medium-bodied brand with a Sumatra wrapper. It is offered in slide-top, cedar boxes of bundles of 25.

PUROS POLANCO
Handmade in San Andres Tuxtla, Mexico.

Wrapper: Mexico   Binder: Mexico   Filler: Mexico

Shape	Name	Lgth	Ring	Wrapper
Lonsdale	Lonsdale	6½	43	CM

Here is a medium-bodied cigar made of all-Mexican tobaccos, offering your choice of Amaretto, rum or vanilla flavors, presented in individual glass tubes. Look for an all-long-filler, Dominican-made series in 1998.

HANDMADE CIGARS: BRAND LISTINGS

PUROS TEJERA
Handmade in Villa Gonzalez, Dominican Republic.

Wrapper: USA/Connecticut   *Binder: Dom. Rep.*   *Filler: Dom. Rep.*

Shape	*Name*	*Lgth*	*Ring*	*Wrapper*
Toro	Toro	6	52	CC
Double Corona	Churchill	7½	50	CC
Lonsdale	Corona	6½	44	CC
Corona	Petit Corona	5½	42	CC

Introduced in 1996, this is a mild-to-medium-bodied blend of tobaccos from Connecticut and Cuban-seed leaves grown in the Dominican Republic. You can find it in boxes of 25.

PYRAMID
Handmade in Santiago, Dominican Republic.

Wrapper: Indonesia   *Binder: Dom. Rep.*   *Filler: Dom. Rep.*

Shape	*Name*	*Lgth*	*Ring*	*Wrapper*
Corona	Giza	5½	44	CC
Lonsdale	Chephren	7	44	CC
Robusto	Khufu	5	50	CC
Toro	Mycerinus	6	50	CC
Double Corona	Cheops	7½	50	CC
Torpedo	Great Pyramid	7	50	CC

Introduced in 1997, this brand has shape names that celebrate the Egyptian pyramids of ancient times, the last remaining "wonder" of the ancient world. The blend features a Sumatra wrapper combined with a Dominican Olor binder and Piloto Cubano filler. The strength is medium and the brand is presented in boxes of 25.

QUETZAL
Handmade in La Romana, Dominican Republic.

Wrapper: Dom. Rep.   *Binder: Dom. Rep.*   *Filler: Dom. Rep.*

HANDMADE CIGARS: BRAND LISTINGS

Shape	Name	Lgth	Ring	Wrapper
Giant	No. 1	8	52	CC
Toro	No. 2	6	50	CC
Churchill	No. 3	7	48	CC
Lonsdale	No. 4	6¾	44	CC
Long Corona	No. 5	6	42	CC
Long Panatela	No. 6	7	38	CC

Here is a new brand for 1997, made up of all-Dominican leaves and offering a mild taste in bundles of 25 cigars each.

QUETZAL
Handmade in Danli, Honduras.

Wrapper: Honduras   Binder: Honduras   Filler: Honduras

Shape	Name	Lgth	Ring	Wrapper
Giant	No. 1	8	50	CM
Double Corona	No. 2	7	52	CM
Churchill	No. 3	6⅞	48	CM
Lonsdale	No. 4	6⅝	44	CM
Long Corona	No. 5	6	42	CM
Robusto	No. 6	4¾	50	CM

This is a new, mild brand for 1997 featuring all-Honduran tobaccos and offered in bundles of 25 cigars each.

QUINTERO BLUE RIBBON
Handmade in Ocotal, Nicaragua.

Wrapper: Ecuador   Binder: Nicaragua   Filler: Nicaragua

Shape	Name	Lgth	Ring	Wrapper
Double Corona	No. 500	7½	52	CC
Toro	No. 501	6	50	CC

Robusto	No. 502	4¾	50	CC
Lonsdale	No. 503	6½	44	CC
Corona	No. 504	5½	42	CC

This cigar, which bears the name of an old Cuban brand still in production, debuted in 1994. Its medium body comes from the Cuban-seed binder and filler and a Connecticut-seed wrapper grown in Ecuador. These cigars are offered in bundles of 25 cigars each at modest price, accessible to all smokers.

QUINTIN "Q-ORO"
Handmade in the Dominican Republic, Honduras, Mexico, Nicaragua and Miami, Florida, USA.

MIAMI RESERVE:

Wrapper: Ecuador, USA/Connecticut　　　　　　*Binder: Ecuador*
Filler: Dominican Republic, Honduras, Nicaragua

DOMINICAN REPUBLIC:

Wrapper: Dom. Rep.　　　*Binder: Dom. Rep.*　　　*Filler: Dom. Rep.*

HONDURAS:

Wrapper: Ecuador　　　*Binder: Mexico*　　*Filler: Dom. Rep., Nicaragua*

MEXICO:

Wrapper: Mexico　　　*Binder: Mexico*　　　*Filler: Mexico*

NICARAGUA:

Wrapper: Nicaragua　　　*Binder: Nicaragua*　　　*Filler: Nicaragua*

Shape	Name	Lgth	Ring	Wrapper
	Miami Reserve, made in Miami:			
Long Corona	Corona	6	44	CC-CM-Ma
Robusto	Robusto	5	50	CC-CM-Ma
Toro	Epicure	6	50	CC-CM-Ma
Double Corona	Churchill	7	50	CC-CM-Ma

HANDMADE CIGARS: BRAND LISTINGS

Torpedo	Torpedo	6½	54	CC-CM-Ma
Dominican Republic, made in Santiago:				
Corona	Corona	5½	42	CM
Robusto	Robusto	5	50	CM
Toro	Toro	6½	52	CM
Double Corona	Churchill	7½	50	CM
Torpedo	Torpedo	6	53	CM
Honduras, made in Danli:				
Robusto	Robusto	5	50	CM
Toro	Toro Grande	6	50	CM
Lonsdale	Lonsdale	7	44	CM
Double Corona	Imperial	7	50	CM
Mexico, made in San Andres Tuxtla:				
Robusto	Robusto	4½	50	CM
Toro	Toro	5¾	50	CM
Double Corona	Churchill	6¾	50	CM
Nicaragua, made in Esteli:				
Robusto	Rothschild	4½	52	CM
Lonsdale	Lonsdale	6½	42	CM
Toro	Double Corona	5⅝	48	CM
Double Corona	Churchill	7½	50	CM

Here is an entire family of cigars, all introduced in 1997 and produced in popular sizes in the cigar-making capitals of the world! The Miami Reserve is full-bodied and offers a choice of Ecuador-grown or Connecticut-grown wrappers in natural, English Market Selection, rosado or maduro shades! The Dominican, Mexican and Nicaraguan blends are considered medium-bodied and the Honduran line is mild. All are offered in wood boxes of 25 cigars each.

HANDMADE CIGARS: BRAND LISTINGS

QUIRANTES
Handmade in Tamboril, Dominican Republic.

Wrapper: Indonesia, USA/Connecticut   Binder: Dom. Rep.   Filler: Dom. Rep.

Shape	Name	Lgth	Ring	Wrapper
Robusto	Robusto	4½	50	CC-Ma
Robusto	Robusto	4¾	50	CC-Ma
Petit Corona	Ricky Ray	5	42	CC-Ma
Cigarillo	Little Ray	5½	28	CC-Ma
Robusto	Corona	5½	50	CC-Ma
Lonsdale	No. 1	6¼	44	CC-Ma
Giant	Magnum	8	54	CC-Ma
Churchill	Lonsdale	6¾	46	CC-Ma
Churchill	Gloria Habana	6¾	48	CC-Ma
Pyramid	Pyramid	6	52	CC-Ma
Torpedo	Torpedo	6½	54	CC-Ma
Long Panatela	Lancero	7½	38	CC-Ma
Double Corona	Churchill	7½	50	CC-Ma

This is a full-bodied cigar from Tamboril, Dominican Republic. It is offered in boxes of 25 (or 20 for the Churchill or Ricky Ray) or bundles of 25, with a choice of Connecticut-grown natural wrappers or Sumatran-grown maduro wrappers.

RAMAR
Handmade in Miami, Florida, USA.

Wrapper: Ecuador, Mexico, USA/Connecticut

Binder: Ecuador or Indonesia   Filler: Dom. Rep., Honduras, Nicaragua

Shape	Name	Lgth	Ring	Wrapper
Robusto	Robusto	5¼	50	CC-CM-Ma
Double Corona	Soberano	7½	50	CC-CM-Ma
Toro	Double Corona	6¼	50	CC-CM-Ma

Churchill	Churchill	7	48	CC-CM-Ma
Lonsdale	Seleccion No. 1	6¾	42	CC-CM-Ma
Long Corona	Seleccion No. 2	6¼	42	CC-CM-Ma
Panatela	Seleccion No. 3	6¾	36	CC-CM-Ma
Corona	Petit Corona	5¾	42	CC-CM-Ma
Giant Corona	Palmas	8	40	CC-CM-Ma
Panatela	Lauren	5¾	36	CC-CM-Ma
Pyramid	Piramides	7	60	CC-CM-Ma
Corona Extra	Adan	5½	46	CC-CM-Ma
Giant	Presidente	8¼	50	CC-CM-Ma

Available since 1977, this cigar is getting wider notice in the 1990s, thanks to its high quality in construction and a mild-to-medium-bodied taste. Three wrapper shades are available: Connecticut tobacco for the lightest, Colorado-Claro wrappers; Ecuadorian leaves for the darker "Cafe" selection and Mexican-grown leaves for the maduro shade.

RAMBLING RIVER
Handmade in San Andres Tuxtla, Mexico.

Wrapper: Mexico   Binder: Mexico   Filler: Mexico

Shape	Name	Lgth	Ring	Wrapper
Robusto		4¾	50	Ma
Small Panatela		5	32	Ma
Long Corona		6	42	Ma
Toro		6	50	Ma
Panatela		6⅝	35	Ma
Lonsdale		6⅝	42	Ma
Grand Corona		6⅝	46	Ma
Double Corona		6⅞	54	Ma
Double Corona		7½	50	Ma

HANDMADE CIGARS: BRAND LISTINGS

Giant		8	52	Ma

This brand dates back to the late 1970s and is offered in an all-maduro series. It features all-Mexican tobacco and is medium in body. Although it has no shape names, you can try in boxes of 25!

RAMON ALLONES
Handmade in Santiago, Dominican Republic.

Wrapper: Cameroon   *Binder: Mexico*   *Filler: Dom. Rep., Mexico*

Shape	Name		Lgth	Ring	Wrapper
Petit Corona	D		5	42	CM
Lonsdale	B		6½	42	CM
Lonsdale	A		7	45	CM
Double Corona	Redondos		7	49	CM
Lonsdale	Crystals	(tubed)	6¾	42	CM
Lonsdale	Trumps		6¾	43	CM
Robusto	Naturales		5½	50	CM
Small Panatela	Ramonitos		4¼	32	CM

This brand originated in Cuba way back in 1837. The Dominican version is a medium-to-heavy flavored cigar and is manufactured in the same Santiago, Dominican Republic factory which produces famous Partagas cigars. It is exceptionally well made.

REAL VERACRUZ
Handmade in Veracruz, Mexico.

Wrapper: Mexico   *Binder: Mexico*   *Filler: Mexico*

Shape	Name	Lgth	Ring	Wrapper
Double Corona	Churchill	7¼	52	CC
Petit Corona	No. 4	5	42	CC
Toro	No. 3	6	52	CC
Grand Corona	No. 1	6¼	46	CC

HANDMADE CIGARS: BRAND LISTINGS

Introduced in 1997, this all-Mexican cigar has a medium-to-full-bodied flavor and is offered in cellophane sleeves inside all-cedar boxes of 25.

RED LION

Handmade in Santiago, Dominican Republic.

Wrapper: Dom. Rep.   *Binder: Dom. Rep.*   *Filler: Dom. Rep.*

Shape	Name	Lgth	Ring	Wrapper
Toro	Mature Toro	6	60	CM
Robusto	Puppy Robusto	4½	50	CM
Robusto	Robusto	5½	50	CM
Giant Corona	Lonsdale	7¾	44	CM
Double Corona	Churchill	7	50	CM

Want a fat cigar? How about a long cigar? You can take your choice of styles of these medium-to-full-bodied, all-Dominican blends, introduced in 1996. They are available in boxes of 25, except for the Mature Toro, offered in 15s. Gift boxes of three of five cigars are also available.

REGALOS

Handmade in Danli, Honduras.

Wrapper: Ecuador or Costa Rica

Binder: Dominican Republic   *Filler: Honduras, Nicaragua*

Shape	Name	Lgth	Ring	Wrapper
Long Corona	Lonsdale	6	43	CC-Ma
Churchill	Churchill	7	47	CC-Ma
Robusto	Robusto	5	50	CC-Ma
Giant	Presidente	8½	52	CC-Ma
Toro	Toro	6	54	CC-Ma
Torpedo	Torpedo	6½	54	CC-Ma
Torpedo	Especial	7½	64	CC-Ma

HANDMADE CIGARS: BRAND LISTINGS

This is a beautiful cigar, well constructed and featuring an Ecuadorian-grown, Sumatra-seed wrapper, or a maduro wrapper from Costa Rica. Introduced in 1996, it is medium-to-full-bodied and offered in individual cellophane sleeves and all-wood boxes of 25.

REINA DOMINICANA
Handmade in Tamboril, Dominican Republic.
Wrapper: Ecuador and/or USA/Connecticut

Binder: Dominican Republic · · · · · · · · · · · · · · · · · · Filler: Dominican Republic

Shape	Name	Lgth	Ring	Wrapper
Giant	President	8	50	CC-Stripe
Grand Corona	Churchill	6	46	CC-Stripe
Lonsdale	Corona	7	44	CC-Stripe
Long Panatela	Panatela	7½	38	CC-Stripe
Robusto	Torito	5	50	CC-Stripe

Introduced in 1997, this line offers a choice of an Ecuador-grown wrapper or a double-wrapped Ecuador and Connecticut-wrapped model for a mild-bodied smoke. It is offered in boxes of 25 and it is well worthy of its name as the "Queen of the Dominican."

REMEDIOS
Handmade in Esteli, Nicaragua.
Wrapper: USA/Connecticut · · · · · Binder: Mexico · · · · · Filler: Dom. Rep., Nicaragua

Shape	Name	Lgth	Ring	Wrapper
Toro	Corona Gorda	6⅛	50	CC
Double Corona	Clemenceau	7¼	54	CC
Grand Corona	Corona	5⅝	45	CC
Toro	Don Victor	6	54	CC
Robusto	Robusto	4½	50	CC

Here is a new, super-premium cigar from J-R Tobacco for 1998, designed to compete with the finest cigars on the market. The combination of Connecticut wrapper and Mexican binder complement the blended filler to offer a medium-to-full-bodied smoke. You will find it only in specially-made, all-cedar chests of 50, created to assist in the aging of these cigars when you aren't smoking them! Some of the shapes will also be available in maduro-shade wrappers.

REPEATER

Handmade, with mixed filler, in Danli, Honduras.

Wrapper: Honduras   Binder: Honduras   Filler: Honduras

Shape	Name	Lgth	Ring	Wrapper
Corona	Repeater 100	5½	43	CM
Long Corona	Repeater 200	6	43	CM
Lonsdale	Repeater 300	6½	43	CM
Lonsdale	Havana Twist	7	44	CM
Double Corona	Churchill	7	49	CM

This brand debuted in the late 1960s and utilizes medium-filler tobacco of all-Honduran origin to produce an enjoyable smoke of medium-to-full body.

RESERVA DEL PATRON

Handmade in San Andres Tuxtla, Mexico.

Wrapper: Mexico   Binder: Mexico   Filler: Mexico

Shape	Name	Lgth	Ring	Wrapper
Churchill	Churchill	7¼	47	CM
Corona Extra	Toro	5¼	47	CM
Corona	No. 4	5¼	42	CM

This all-Mexican cigar was introduced in 1997 and provides a medium-bodied, smooth flavor with Sumatra-seed wrappers and criollo filler leaves, offered in all-cedar boxes of 25.

REY DE ZABA

Handmade in the Dominican Republic.

Wrapper: Indonesia   Binder: Dom. Rep.   Filler: Dom. Rep.

HANDMADE CIGARS: BRAND LISTINGS

Shape	Name	Lgth	Ring	Wrapper
Toro	Casadores	6	50	CM
Lonsdale	Lonsdale	6½	42	CM
Robusto	Robusto	5½	50	CM
Long Corona	Churchill	6	44	CM

This medium-to-full-bodied brand, made with considerable skill in the Dominican Republic, is offered in boxes of 25.

REY DEL MAR
Handmade in Navarette, Dominican Republic.

Wrapper: Indonesia   Binder: Dom. Rep.   Filler: Dom. Rep.

Shape	Name	Lgth	Ring	Wrapper
Churchill	Churchill	7	48	CC
Toro	Toro	6	50	CC
Robusto	Robusto	4¾	52	CC
Corona	Corona	5¾	42	CC

Introduced in 1995, this is a medium-to-full-bodied blend of leaves offered in boxes of 25.

RG SANTIAGO DOMINICAN
Handmade in Santiago, Dominican Republic.
Wrapper: Indonesia or USA/Connecticut

Binder: Dominican Republic   Filler: Dominican Republic

Shape	Name	Lgth	Ring	Wrapper
Corona	Corona	5½	43	CC
Robusto	Robusto	5	50	CC
Lonsdale	Lonsdale	6½	43	CC
Toro	Toro	6	50	CC
Double Corona	Churchill	7½	50	CC

DISTRIBUTED BY
SJI WHOLESALE

SJI Wholesale / SJI Tobacco

STEWART - BECKWITH

The Humidor Maker

The Executive Entertainer Series

(408) 298-9910
Fax (408) 293-6506
E-Mail address: stewbeck@ix.netcom.com

Pyramid	Pyramide	7	50	CC
Cigarillo	Petit Panatela	5	28	CC
Cigarillo	Purito	4	24	CC

New in 1997, this is a medium-bodied cigar that features a choice of delicately-flavored Indonesian or genuine Connecticut wrappers to complement the Dominican-grown binder and fillers.

RICO HAVANA
Handmade in Danli, Honduras.

Wrapper: Ecuador   *Binder: Honduras*   *Filler: Dom.Rep., Honduras*

Shape	Name	Lgth	Ring	Wrapper
Giant	Rough Rider	9	50	CC-Ma
Churchill	Churchill	7½	48	CC-Ma
Lonsdale	Plaza	7	44	CC-Ma
Long Corona	Corona	6	42	CC-Ma
Robusto	Duke	4½	50	CC-Ma
Petit Corona	Habanero	4½	42	CC-Ma

A favorite since 1939, this medium-bodied blend of Cuban seed, Dominican-grown long-filler tobaccos combines with an Ecuadorian wrapper for great smoking flavor. Rico Havana is available in natural and maduro wrappers.

RICOS DOMINICANOS
Handmade in Santiago, Dominican Republic.

Wrapper: USA/Connecticut   *Binder: Dominican Republic*
Filler: Brazil, Dominican Republic, Indonesia

Shape	Name	Lgth	Ring	Wrapper
Double Corona	Churchill	7	50	CC-Ma
Toro	Toro	6	50	CC-Ma
Corona	Breva	5½	44	CC-Ma

HANDMADE CIGARS: BRAND LISTINGS

Lonsdale	Centro Largo	6¾	44	CC-Ma

This brand debuted in 1996 and offers a mild-to-medium bodied taste in either a natural or maduro wrapper. It has a rich aroma and, best of all, is an excellent value.

RIGOLETTO
Handmade in Santiago, Dominican Republic.
Wrapper: USA/Connecticut   Binder: Dom. Rep.   Filler: Dom. Rep.

Shape	Name	Lgth	Ring	Wrapper
Churchill	Black Magic	7½	46	CC-Ma
Lonsdale	Black Arrow	6¼	44	CC-Ma
Toro	Dominican Lights	6¼	48	CC-Ma

This brand, which debuted in 1905, is made by hand in the Dominican Republic using Connecticut Shade leaves for natural wrappers and Connecticut Broadleaf tobaccos for the maduro style. Medium in body, it's an underrated smoke.

ROBALI
Handmade in San Jose, Costa Rica.
Wrapper: Ecuador or Indonesia   Binder: Costa Rica   Filler: Costa Rica, Nicaragua

Shape	Name	Lgth	Ring	Wrapper
Giant	Viajante	8	52	CC
Churchill	Double Corona	7	46	CC
Lonsdale	Delgado	6½	44	CC
Robusto	Robusto	5	50	CC
Toro	Corona	6	50	CC
Corona	Esteban	5½	43	CC

New in 1996, Robali carries on the tradition of Costa Rican cigar making. A mild-to-medium-bodied blend with a Connecticut-seed wrapper, these cigars are offered in boxes or bundles of 25 from the Robali de Centro America, S.A. factory.

HANDMADE CIGARS: BRAND LISTINGS

ROBUSTO DE CASA
Handmade in San Andres Tuxtla, Mexico.

Wrapper: Mexico   Binder: Mexico   Filler: Honduras

Shape	Name	Lgth	Ring	Wrapper
Robusto	Robusto	5½	50	CM

Known to European smokers for most of the 1990s, this brand debuted in the U.S. in 1997. It features a Sumatra-seed wrapper grown in Mexico and is medium in body. You can find it in boxes of 24 or bundles of 25.

RODRIGUEZ & MENENDEZ
Handmade in Tampa, Florida, USA.
Wrapper: Dom. Rep., Ecuador, Honduras, USA/Connecticut
Binder: Dom. Rep., Honduras, Nicaragua   Filler: Dom. Rep., Ecuador, Honduras

Shape	Name	Lgth	Ring	Wrapper
Churchill	Fuma	7¼	47	CC-Ma
Lonsdale	Palma	6½	43	CC
Robusto	Rothschild	4⅞	50	Ma
Churchill	Reyna	7¼	47	CC-Ma
Double Corona	No. 5	7	49	CC-Ma
Giant Corona	Imperiales	8	45	CC-Ma
Grand Corona	Gran Corona	6	47	CC-Ma
Slim Panatela	Panatela	5½	34	CC
Double Corona	Super Presidente	8¼	48	CC

Well respected since their introduction in 1981, these are medium-bodied cigars in the natural wrappers and full-bodied in maduro. They are produced in a small factory in the famous Tampa suburb of Ybor City.

ROLANDO
Handmade in Santiago, Dominican Republic.
Wrapper: USA/Connecticut   Binder: Dom. Rep.   Filler: Dom. Rep.

HANDMADE CIGARS: BRAND LISTINGS

Shape	Name	Lgth	Ring	Wrapper
Churchill	No. 2	7½	48	CC
Toro	No. 3	6	50	CC
Long Corona	No. 4	6	43	CC
Robusto	Robusto	4¾	52	CC

Introduced in 1995, meticulously-selected tobaccos and extended aging contribute to the exquisite, mild-to-medium flavor of one of the world's finest cigars. Rolandos are wrapped in the famous Connecticut Shade-grown wrapper, with Dominican filler leaf.

ROLLER'S CHOICE
Handmade in Santiago, Dominican Republic.
Wrapper: USA/Connecticut   Binder: Dom. Rep.   Filler: Dom. Rep.

Shape	Name	Lgth	Ring	Wrapper
Double Corona	RC Double Corona	7	50	CC
Long Corona	RC Corona	6	43	CC
Grand Corona	RC Lonsdale	6½	46	CC
Robusto	RC Robusto	5	50	CC
Petit Corona	RC Pequeno	4¼	40	CC
Corona	RC Fino	5½	41	CC
Torpedo	RC Torpedo	5½	56	CC
Toro	RC Toro	6	50	CC
Corona	RC Cetro	5½	43	CC

While not as well known as some other brands, Roller's Choice was introduced in 1992 and is a well-constructed, mild-bodied cigar produced in one of the Dominican Republic's most dependable factories.

ROLY
Handmade in the Dominican Republic and Honduras.
Wrapper: Mexico   Binder: Dom. Rep.   Filler: Dom. Rep.

HANDMADE CIGARS: BRAND LISTINGS

Shape	Name	Lgth	Ring	Wrapper
Double Corona	Churchill	7¼	53	CM
Churchill	Presidente	7¼	47	CM
Double Corona	Valentino	7	49	CM
Grand Corona	Corona de Lux	6½	46	CM
Corona Extra	No. 4 Extra	5½	45	CM
Lonsdale	Lonsdale	6½	43	CM
Corona	Remedios	5½	43	CM
Toro	Toro Extra	6	53	CM
Robusto	Rothchild	5	50	CM
Short Panatela	Petit Cetro	5	36	CM
Long Panatela	Long Palma	7	39	CM

Here is a brilliantly constructed cigar, available in a variety of shapes. Medium in body, Roly features a Sumatra-seed wrapper and Dominican binder and filler. Look for it in boxes or bundles of 25.

ROMANO'S CONNOISSEUR SERIES
Handmade in Tamboril, Dominican Republic.
Wrapper: Indonesia or USA/Connecticut

Binder: Dominican Republic　　　　　　　　　　Filler: Dominican Republic

Shape	Name	Lgth	Ring	Wrapper
Double Corona	Corona Grande	7½	50	CC
Churchill	Churchill	7	46	CC
Panatela	Panatela	6	38	CC
Robusto	Robusto	5	50	CC

This is a medium-bodied cigar, with Sumatra wrappers on three sizes and a Connecticut wrapper on the Panatela shape. Introduced in 1997, they are offered in boxes of 25.

HANDMADE CIGARS: BRAND LISTINGS

ROMANTICOS
Handmade in Villa Gonzalez, Dominican Republic

Wrapper: USA/Connecticut   *Binder: Dom. Rep.*   *Filler: Dom. Rep.*

Shape	Name	Lgth	Ring	Wrapper
Giant	Marc Anthony	8	50	Co
Double Corona	Valentino	7	48	Co
Corona	Cleopatra	6	44	Co
Robusto	Eros	5	52	Co
Torpedo	Casanova	6½	56	Co

Introduced in 1996, this is a rich-flavored, mild-to-medium bodied blend of long-filler tobaccos, offered in individual cellophane sleeves in elegant cedar cabinets of 25. Check out the shape names: some of the great lovers and love-gods in history!

ROMEO Y JULIETA
Handmade in Santiago, Dominican Republic.

Wrapper: Indonesia   *Binder: USA/Connecticut*   *Filler: Brazil, Dom. Rep.*

Shape	Name	Lgth	Ring	Wrapper
Giant	Monarcas	8	52	CM
Double Corona	Churchills	7	50	CM
Lonsdale	Presidentes	7	43	CM
Robusto	Rothschilds	5	50	CM-Ma
Lonsdale	Cetros	6½	44	CM-Ma
Long Corona	Palmas	6	43	CM
Corona	Coronas	5½	44	CM
Slim Panatela	Delgados	7	32	CM
Panatela	Brevas	5⅝	38	CM
Short Panatela	Panatelas	5¼	35	CM
Small Panatela	Chiquitas	4¼	32	CM
Pyramid	Romeos	6	46	CM

O Romeo, Romeo! wherefore Art Thou Romeo?

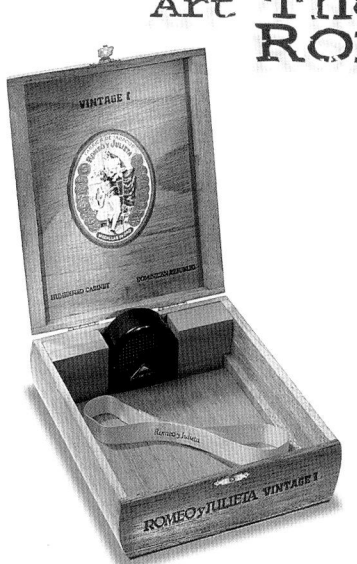

...you have been looking for our Romeo y Julieta® Vintage cigars ...d have been finding a lot of empty boxes like this... well, you're ...alone. It seems that many discriminating cigar smokers are ...able to find these cigars in stock at their local tobacconist.

...why don't we make more? Believe me, we'd love to.

You see, the select Romeo y Julieta Vintage tobacco leaf takes a full three years to age and mature. This is what makes the cigars taste so... well, you know. That's probably why you were looking for them in the first place. And as much as we would like to make more, we simply cannot speed up the process that has produced such a rewarding flavor.

Just as Romeo found Julieta, you will find your true love, and the wait will be worth it.

HANDMADE CIGARS: BRAND LISTINGS

This famous brand originated in Cuba, and this version lives up to its heritage. Made by hand in the Dominican Republic, this line is medium in strength, using tobaccos from many nations to create a complex taste. The shortage of Cameroon wrappers often make these cigars hard to find.

ROMEO Y JULIETA VINTAGE
Handmade in Santiago, Dominican Republic.

Wrapper: USA/Connecticut   Binder: Mexico   Filler: Dom. Rep.

Shape	Name	Lgth	Ring	Wrapper
Long Corona	I	6	43	CC
Grand Corona	II	6	46	CC
Robusto	III	4½	50	CC
Churchill	IV	7	48	CC
Double Corona	V	7½	50	CC
Pyramid	VI	7	60	CC

This is the ultimate cigar! Made with perfectly fermented tobacco, the wrapper is selected for a natural, oily sheen and silky appearance. The binder is aged Mexican leaf and the filler is superbly blended Cuban seed and long-leaf Dominican tobaccos. Introduced in 1993, this is a finesse cigar, mild with very round flavor and made in extremely limited supply.

RONALDO SOMMA
Handmade in Santiago, Dominican Republic.

Wrapper: Indonesia   Binder: Nicaragua   Filler: Dom. Rep.

Shape	Name	Lgth	Ring	Wrapper
Robusto	Robusto	5	50	CC
Toro	Double Corona	6½	48	CC
Torpedo	Torpedo	6½	52	CC
Double Corona	Churchill	7	50	CC
Lonsdale	Corona	6½	44	CC
Toro	Ronaldo	6	50	CC

Giant	Gigante	8	56	CC

Introduced in 1997, this brand offers a mild-to-medium bodied experience, with a Sumatra wrapper and Cuban-seed filler leaves grown in the Dominican Republic. The brand is offered in all-cedar cabinets of 25 cigars each.

ROSA BLANCA RESERVA
Handmade in Esteli, Nicaragua.

Wrapper: Indonesia   Binder: Nicaragua   Filler: Nicaragua

Shape	Name	Lgth	Ring	Wrapper
Corona	Corona	5½	44	CC
Toro	Toro	6	54	CC
Torpedo	Gigante	7	54	CC
Torpedo	Torpedo	5½	56	CC
Churchill	Churchill	7	49	CC

This brand was introduced in 1997 and has a mild-to-medium-bodied flavor. It is offered uncellophaned in cedar boxes of 25.

ROSA CUBA
Handmade, with mixed filler, in Esteli, Nicaragua.

Wrapper: Ecuador   Binder: Dominican Republic
Filler: Dominican Republic, Honduras, Nicaragua

Shape	Name	Lgth	Ring	Wrapper
Short Panatela	Angels	4½	38	CC
Corona	Flor de Rosa	5½	44	CC
Toro	Governor	6⅛	50	CC
Robusto	Herencia	4½	52	CC
Churchill	Mille Fleurs	6¾	48	CC
Grand Corona	Media Noche	6½	46	CC
Toro	Ortiz y Laboy	6½	52	CC

HANDMADE CIGARS: BRAND LISTINGS

Giant	President	8½	52	CC
Double Corona	Sultana	7½	54	CC
Lonsdale	Vargas	6½	44	CC

New for 1996, this line offers a medium-to-full-bodied flavor with a magnificent Ecuador-grown, Sumatra-seed wrapper, in economical bundles of 20.

ROSALONES
Handmade in Esteli, Nicaragua.

Wrapper: Nicaragua   *Binder: Nicaragua*   *Filler: Nicaragua*

Shape	Name	Lgth	Ring	Wrapper
Giant	Presidente	8	54	CC-Ma
Giant	Viajante	8½	52	CC-Ma
Double Corona	Presidente Corto	7¼	54	CC-Ma
Double Corona	Viajante Corto	7	52	CC-Ma
Double Corona	Emperador	7¾	50	CC-Ma
Double Corona	Emperador Corto	7½	50	CC-Ma
Churchill	Churchill	6⅞	48	CC-Ma
Churchill	No. 11	7½	46	CC-Ma
Toro	Duke	6	50	CC-Ma
Long Panatela	No. 9	8	38	CC-Ma
Long Panatela	No. 9 Corto	7	38	CC-Ma
Corona Extra	Corona Extra	5½	46	CC-Ma
Robusto	Consul	4½	52	CC-Ma
Lonsdale	No. 1	6⅝	44	CC-Ma
Lonsdale	No. 10	6½	43	CC-Ma
Long Corona	No. 3	6	44	CC-Ma
Corona	Nacional	5½	44	CC-Ma
Panatela	No. 5	6⅞	35	CC-Ma

Long Corona	No. 6	6	41	CC-Ma
Corona	Seleccion B	5½	42	CC-Ma
Slim Panatela	No. 7	7	30	CC-Ma
Panatela	Elegante	6½	38	CC-Ma
Petit Corona	No. 2	4½	42	CC-Ma
Short Panatela	Petits	5½	38	CC-Ma
Slim Panatela	Senoritas	5½	34	CC-Ma
Small Panatela	Piccolino	4⅛	30	CC-Ma
Toro	Corona	5⅝	48	CC-Ma

This line, introduced in 1983, is primarily produced for the Nicaraguan home market, with some distribution reaching the United States. A 27-shape brand, it is a sister to the U.S.-marketed Flor de Nicaragua range. These are mild-bodied cigars, using filler and binder leaf from the Jalapa Valley of Nicaragua, with Nicaraguan wrappers.

ROSARIO
Handmade in Veracruz, Mexico.

Wrapper: Mexico *Binder: Mexico* *Filler: Mexico*

Shape	Name	Lgth	Ring	Wrapper
Double Corona	Churchill	7	50	CM
Toro	Toro	6	50	CM
Long Corona	Corona	6	42	CM
Lonsdale	Lonsdale	6½	42	CM

Introduced in 1997, this is a Mexican "puro" offering a medium body. You'll find it in protective cellophane sleeves inside all-cedar boxes of 25.

ROSATO
Handmade in Managua, Nicaragua.

Wrapper: Nicaragua *Binder: Nicaragua* *Filler: Nicaragua*

HANDMADE CIGARS: BRAND LISTINGS

Shape	Name	Lgth	Ring	Wrapper
Giant	Presidente	8½	52	CM-Ma
Slim Panatela	Little R	5½	34	CM
Long Corona	Corona	6	48	CM-Ma
Robusto	Robusto	5	52	CM-Ma
Toro	Toro	6	50	CM-Ma
Churchill	Churchill	7½	50	CM-Ma
	Cognac Aged:			
Long Corona	Corona	6	44	CM
Robusto	Robusto	5	52	CM

A full-flavored taste is the promise of Rosato, introduced to the U.S. market in 1997. Offered in cellophane sleeves inside boxes or bundles of 25, it is available in both natural and maduro wrappers.

THE ROUGH RIDER
Handmade in Santo Domingo, Dominican Republic.
Wrapper: Indonesia   *Binder: Dom. Rep.*   *Filler: Dom. Rep.*

Shape	Name	Lgth	Ring	Wrapper
Robusto	Rough Rider	5	48	CC

Who needs sizes? Here's a short, stout cigar introduced in 1997 that delivers a medium-bodied flavor. This brand burns evenly and draws easily; it's perfect for golf or other outdoor activities, such as charging up San Juan Hill!

ROVANOFF
Handmade in Esteli, Nicaragua.
Wrapper: Nicaragua   *Binder: Nicaragua*
Filler: Dominican Republic, Ecuador, Nicaragua

Shape	Name	Lgth	Ring	Wrapper
Giant	Hemingway	8	52	CC

Double Corona	Churchill	7	50	CC
Robusto	Consul	5	50	CC
Churchill	Presidente	7	46	CC
Long Corona	Corona	6	44	CC
Corona	Habana	5½	43	CC
Long Panatela	Lanceros	7½	38	CC

Here is a 1997-introduced brand with a medium-bodied flavor, featuring a Cuban-seed, Jalapa Valley-grown wrapper and a blended filler from three nations. It is offered in boxes of 20.

ROYAL BARBADOS
Handmade in Bridgetown, Barbados.

Wrapper: Ecuador   Binder & Filler: Caribbean blend

Shape	Name	Lgth	Ring	Wrapper
Grand Corona	No. 2	6½	46	CC
Long Corona	No. 3	6⅛	42	CC
Corona	No. 4	5⅛	42	CC
Panatela	No. 6	6⅛	38	CC

This is a limited distribution, light-bodied cigar from Barbados introduced in 1996 and offered in boxes of 25.

ROYAL COURT
Handmade in Danli, Honduras.

Wrapper: Ecuador   Binder: Honduras   Filler: Honduras

Shape	Name	Lgth	Ring	Wrapper
Panatela	No. 1 Petit Corona	5½	38	CC
Panatela	No. 2 Panatela	6⅞	36	CC
Long Corona	No. 3 Cetro	6	43	CC
Double Corona	No. 4 Presidente	7¾	50	CC
Giant	No. 5 Viajante	8½	52	CC

HANDMADE CIGARS: BRAND LISTINGS

Premium quality at modest prices. That's the story of this smooth, mild and flavorful cigar with a natural wrapper which debuted in 1992. Each of the 25 cigars in this bundle is individually wrapped.

ROYAL DOMINICANA
Handmade in the Dominican Republic.

Wrapper: USA/Connecticut   Binder: Mexico   Filler: Dom. Rep.

Shape	Name	Lgth	Ring	Wrapper
Double Corona	Churchill	7¼	50	CC
Grand Corona	Corona	6	46	CC
Corona	Nacional	5½	43	CC
Lonsdale	No. 1	6¾	43	CC
Panatela	Super Fino	6	35	CC
Short Panatela	Mini	4	36	CC

This is a mild-to-medium bodied cigar with a Connecticut wrapper, well-known for its quality construction and reasonable price.

ROYALE GOLD
Handmade in Santo Domingo, Dominican Republic.

Wrapper: Dom. Rep.   Binder: Dom. Rep.   Filler: Dom. Rep.

Shape	Name	Lgth	Ring	Wrapper
Long Panatela	Panetela	7½	38	CM
Long Corona	Lonsdale	6	44	CM
Double Corona	Double Corona	7½	50	CM
Robusto	Robusto	4½	50	CM
Torpedo	Torpedo	6	54	CM

Here is a cigar for the 90s! All Dominican-grown leaf is rolled into a medium-to-heavy-bodied smoke, but without any harshness.

HANDMADE CIGARS: BRAND LISTINGS

ROYALE SALUDO
Handmade in Santiago, Dominican Republic.
Wrapper: USA/Connecticut or Cameroon   Binder: Dom. Rep.   Filler: Dom. Rep.

Shape	Name	Lgth	Ring	Wrapper
Giant	Churchill	8	50	CC-Ma
Robusto	Robusto	5	50	CC-Ma
Long Corona	Lonsdale	6	44	CC-Ma
Grand Corona	Corona	6½	46	CC-Ma
Pyramid	Pyramid	7	50	CC-Ma

Introduced in 1995, this mild-bodied brand features Piloto Cubano filler leaves and Olor binders grown in the Dominican Republic. Choose your favorite wrapper from Connecticut (natural) or Cameroon (maduro) leaves.

ROYALES
Handmade in Santiago, Dominican Republic.
Wrapper: Indonesia   Binder: Brazil   Filler: Brazil, Dom. Rep.

Shape	Name	Lgth	Ring	Wrapper
Giant	No. 1	8	52	CC
Double Corona	No. 2	7½	50	CC
Toro	No. 3	6	50	CC
Robusto	No. 4	5	50	CC
Lonsdale	No. 5	6⅝	44	CC
Long Corona	No. 6	6	42	CC
Panatela	No. 7	6⅞	38	CC

Introduced in 1992, Royales is a careful hand-blend of leaves that produces a mild cigar with a rich bouquet.

ROYAL HONDURAS
Handmade in Danli, Honduras.
Wrapper: Indonesia   Binder: Dom. Rep.   Filler: Honduras

HANDMADE CIGARS: BRAND LISTINGS

Shape	Name	Lgth	Ring	Wrapper
Giant	Czar	8	50	CC
Churchill	Sovereign	7	48	CC
Torpedo	Kings	6⅛	54	CC
Lonsdale	Prince	7	44	CC
Robusto	Majesty	5	50	CC
Corona	Joker	5½	42	CC
Pyramid	Princess	5	38	CC
Toro	Knight	6	50	CC

Royal Honduras was introduced in 1996, with a mild-to-medium flavor in sizes named after characters in a royal court. All are presented in cedar boxes. The two shaped cigars flare from 42 to 54 ring (Kings) and from 32 to 38 (Princess).

ROYAL JAMAICA
Handmade in La Romana, Dominican Republic
and in Maypen, Jamaica

Wrapper: Indonesia   *Binder: Cameroon*   *Filler: Jamaica*

Shape	Name	Lgth	Ring	Wrapper
Slim Panatela	Buccaneer	5½	30	CM-Ma
Lonsdale	Corona Grande	6½	42	CM-Ma
Giant	Churchill	8	51	CM-Ma
Corona	Corona	5½	40	CM-Ma
Grand Corona	Director No. 1	6	46	CM
Lonsdale	Double Corona	7	45	CM
Slim Panatela	Doubloon	7	30	CM
Slim Panatela	Gaucho	5¼	33	CM
Giant	Goliath	9	64	CM
Giant	Individuales	8½	52	CM

Long Corona	New York Plaza	6	40	CM
Grand Corona	Park Lane	6	47	CM
Robusto	Robusto	4½	49	CM
Toro	Toro	6	50	CM
Grand Corona	No. 1 Tube _(tubed)_	6	45	CM
Slim Panatela	No. 2 Tube _(tubed)_	6½	34	CM
Giant	No. 10 Downing Street	10	51	CM

Consistently ranked as one of the tastiest handmade cigars in the world with an abundant variety of shapes and styles, Royal Jamaica is again being made in Jamaica. Transferred to the Dominican Republic in 1988 after Hurricane Gilbert destroyed the factory in Kingston, Consolidated Cigar has opened a new facility in Maypen, Jamaica and production began in late 1996. The filler is predominantly Jamaica-grown tobaccos, with a secret family additive applied during the fermentation process. The Cameroon binder combined with the Java wrapper results in a unique, spicy flavor. A dark Mexican maduro wrapper gives that series a rich taste with a hint of sweetness. The Mexican leaf is heated with steam and aged two weeks to result in a deep brown hue.

ROYAL MANNA
Handmade in Santa Rosa de Copan, Honduras.

Wrapper: Ecuador — _Binder: Honduras_ — _Filler: Honduras_

Shape	Name	Lgth	Ring	Wrapper
Lonsdale	No. 1	7⅛	43	CM
Corona	No. 4	5⅛	42	CM
Panatela	Manchego	6¾	35	CM
Double Corona	Churchill	7½	50	CM
Long Panatela	Largo Extra Fino	8	38	CM
Robusto	Rothschild	4¾	50	CM
Toro	Toro	6	50	CM

This popular brand was introduced in 1972, originally made in the Canary Islands. It is well known for its Connecticut Shade-seed wrapper, excellent construction and a medium-bodied taste.

HANDMADE CIGARS: BRAND LISTINGS

ROYAL NICARAGUAN
Handmade in Esteli, Nicaragua.

Wrapper: Indonesia   *Binder: Nicaragua*   *Filler: Nicaragua*

Shape	Name	Lgth	Ring	Wrapper
Giant	No. 2	8½	52	CC-Ma
Giant	No. 4	8	54	CC
Double Corona	No. 8	7	49	CC-Ma
Lonsdale	No. 10	7	44	CC
Toro	No. 14	6	50	CC
Robusto	No. 20	5	50	CC-Ma

This is a medium-bodied cigar with all long-filler tobacco offered in modestly-priced bundles of 25.

ROYCE
Handmade in Danli, Honduras.

Wrapper: Indonesia   *Binder: Ecuador*   *Filler: Dom. Rep., Honduras*

Shape	Name	Lgth	Ring	Wrapper
Robusto	Robustos	5	50	CC-Ma
Lonsdale	Fumas	7	44	CC-Ma
Toro	Coronas	6	50	CC-Ma
Double Corona	Churchills	7	50	CC-Ma

New in 1997, this Honduran-produced brand is medium-to-full in body and only in limited production. Each cigar is protected in an individual cellophane sleeve and packed in all-cedar boxes of 25.

RUBIROSA
Handmade in Santiago, Dominican Republic.
Wrapper: USA/Connecticut (Claro) or Indonesia (Supremo)
Binder: Dominican Republic   *Filler: Dominican Republic*

HANDMADE CIGARS: BRAND LISTINGS

Shape	Name	Lgth	Ring	Wrapper
	Claro series:			
Double Corona	Maximos	7½	50	CC
Churchill	Extasis	6⅞	46	CC
Robusto	Polo	5	50	CC
Long Corona	Caribe	6	44	CC
Torpedo	Torpedo	6½	53	CC
	Supremo series:			
Double Corona	Maximos	7½	50	CC
Churchill	Extasis	6⅞	46	CC
Torpedo	Torpedo	6½	53	CC
Long Corona	Caribe	6	44	CC
Robusto	Polo	5	50	CC

Named for the famous Dominican playboy Porfirio Rubirosa (1909-65), who charmed, married and befriended many of the most famous and richest women in the world, the Claro line, introduced in 1996, offers a mild taste. The Supremo line, introduced in 1997, offers a medium-bodied flavor. These cigars are presented in boxes made only of Spanish cedar to enhance the aging process.

RUM RAIDER
Handmade in Santiago, Dominican Republic.
Wrapper: Indonesia   *Binder: Dom. Rep.*   *Filler: Dom. Rep.*

Shape	Name	Lgth	Ring	Wrapper
Torpedo	Torpedo	5	56	CM

Here is a thoroughly-soaked, medium-bodied, rum-imbued cigar with a Sumatra wrapper, offered in a large size and available in boxes of 16 (really!).

RUM ROYALE
Handmade, with medium filler, in Santiago, Dominican Republic.
Wrapper: Indonesia   *Binder: Dom. Rep.*   *Filler: Dom. Rep.*

HANDMADE CIGARS: BRAND LISTINGS

Shape	Name	Lgth	Ring	Wrapper
Long Corona		6	42	CM
Long Corona		6	44	CM

This is a medium-bodied, flavored cigar available in two sizes and introduced in 1996. It utilizes all-Dominican filler and is offered in bundles of 25.

SABOR
Handmade in Tamboril, Dominican Republic.
Wrapper: USA/Connecticut   *Binder: Dom. Rep.*   *Filler: Dom. Rep.*

Shape	Name	Lgth	Ring	Wrapper
Small Panatela	Junior	5	34	CC
Panatela	Panatela	6	36	CC
Corona	Petit Corona	5½	42	CC

This is a flavored cigar, introduced in 1997. It offers long-filler tobaccos and a mild body with the taste of vanilla! You can enjoy it in boxes of 25.

SABOR HABANO
Handmade in Esteli, Nicaragua.
Wrapper: Ecuador   *Binder: Nicaragua*   *Filler: Dom. Rep., Nicaragua*

Shape	Name	Lgth	Ring	Wrapper
Long Corona	Cetro	6	44	CC
Robusto	Rothchild	5	50	CC
Toro	Matador	6	50	CC
Double Corona	Churchill	7	49	CC
Giant	Presidente	8½	52	CC

Here is a medium-bodied cigar which matches a Connecticut-seed wrapper grown in Ecuador with a Havana-seed binder from Nicaragua and filler leaves from the Dominican Republic and Nicaragua. New in 1996, Sabor Habano is offered in boxes of 25 cigars each.

HANDMADE CIGARS: BRAND LISTINGS

SABOR HABANO DOMINICAN RESERVE
Handmade in Tamboril, Dominican Republic.

Wrapper: Nicaragua   Binder: Dom. Rep.   Filler: Dom. Rep.

Shape	Name	Lgth	Ring	Wrapper
Long Corona	Cetro	6	44	CC
Robusto	Rothchild	5	50	CC
Toro	Matador	6	50	CC
Double Corona	Churchill	7	50	CC

Introduced in 1997, this is a medium-bodied cigar that features a Sumatra-seed wrapper and an Olor binder. It is presented in cellophane sleeves and packed in boxes of 25.

SABROSO
Handmade in Esteli, Nicaragua.

Wrapper: Ecuador   Binder: Nicaragua   Filler: Nicaragua

Shape	Name	Lgth	Ring	Wrapper
Robusto	Numero Uno	4¾	50	CC
Long Corona	Numero Dos	6	44	CC
Toro	Numero Tres	6	50	CC
Churchill	Numero Cuatro	7	48	CC
Giant	Numero Cinco	8½	52	CC

Introduced in 1996, this value-packed brand from Nicaragua offers a full-bodied taste and an excellent value. Sabroso cigars are packaged in bundles of 25.

ST. CHRISTOBAL
Handmade, with mixed filler, in Santo Domingo, Dom. Rep.

Wrapper: Indonesia   Binder: Dom. Rep.   Filler: Dom. Rep.

Shape	Name	Lgth	Ring	Wrapper
Corona	Corona	5½	42	CM
Robusto	Robusto	5	50	CM

Toro	Toro	6	50	CM
Double Corona	Churchill	6¾	50	CM
Double Corona	Presidente	7	50	CM

Here is a value-priced, medium-to-full-bodied cigar offered in bundles of 25. It features a Sumatra-grown wrapper around a sandwich filler of long leaves surrounding shorter filler tobaccos.

ST. GEORGE
Handmade in Tamboril, Dominican Republic.

Wrapper: Indonesia   Binder: Dom. Rep.   Filler: Dom. Rep.

Shape	Name	Lgth	Ring	Wrapper
Giant	Dragonslayer	8	50	CC
Churchill	Churchill	7	48	CC
Toro	Ascalon	6½	50	CC
Torpedo	Falchion	6	52	CC
Corona Extra	Chevalier	5½	46	CC
Corona	Coronet	5½	42	CC
Robusto	Chivalry	5	50	CC

Here is a mild-to-medium-bodied smoke offered in cabinets of 25 cigars each. Introduced in 1997, this brand is presented uncellophaned by the Tabacalera La Real.

SAINT LUIS REY
Handmade in Danli, Honduras.

Wrapper: Honduras   Binder: Honduras   Filler: Honduras

Shape	Name	Lgth	Ring	Wrapper
Torpedo	Torpedo	6	54	CM
Double Corona	Churchill	7	50	CM
Toro	Serie A	6	50	CM
Lonsdale	Lonsdale	6½	44	CM

HANDMADE CIGARS: BRAND LISTINGS

Introduced at *LE CIGAR NOIR - BEVERLY HILLS* on May 1, 1996, this Honduran version of an old Cuban brand was an immediate hit with everyone who tried it. Full-bodied but smooth on the draw, these cigars blend plenty of flavor with a slow-burning cadre of Honduran-grown, Cuban-seed tobaccos for a relaxing smoke. Saint Luis Rey cigars are individually cellophaned and packed in windowed boxes of 25.

ST. TROPEZ
Handmade in Danli, Honduras.

Wrapper: Ecuador   Binder: Honduras   Filler: Honduras

Shape	Name	Lgth	Ring	Wrapper
Lonsdale	Numero Uno	7	44	CC
Long Corona	Numero Dos	6	43	CC
Corona	Numero Tres	5½	42	CC

This brand was introduced in 1996, offering a mild body and a modest price point. The quality of construction and leaf are all the more appreciated in cigars which are also affordable for an everyday smoke.

SAN ANGELO
Handmade in Villa Gonzalez, Dominican Republic.

Wrapper: USA/Connecticut   Binder: Dom. Rep.   Filler: Dom. Rep.

Shape	Name	Lgth	Ring	Wrapper
Giant Corona	La Reina de San Angelo	8	40	CC
Robusto	Gorditos	5	50	CC

Here is a very old brand, presented in its current form since 1995. It offers a mild blend of leaves available in boxes of 25.

SAN FERNANDO
Handmade in Santa Rosa de Copan, Honduras.

Wrapper: Honduras   Binder: Honduras   Filler: Honduras

Shape	Name	Lgth	Ring	Wrapper
Churchill	Churchill	7	48	CM
Long Corona	Corona	6	44	CM

HANDMADE CIGARS: BRAND LISTINGS

Robusto	Robusto	5	52	CM

This brand was introduced in 1975 and includes all-Honduran tobaccos. Named for one of Honduras's premier tobacco farms, San Fernando is a full-bodied blend.

SAN MARCOS
Handmade in Danli, Honduras.

Wrapper: Honduras   Binder: Honduras   Filler: Honduras

Shape	Name	Lgth	Ring	Wrapper
Giant	Embajadores	8½	52	CC
Churchill	Churchill	7	48	CC
Long Corona	Sabrosos	6	43	CC
Corona	Casa Blanca	5½	42	CC
Robusto	Rothschild	5	50	CC

Here is a full-bodied blend, introduced in 1996, which features a Jamastram Valley-grown wrapper. The five classic shapes are offered, box-pressed, in boxes of 25 cigars each.

SAN VICENTE 50 ANNIVERSARIO SELECCION
Handmade in Esteli, Nicaragua.

Wrapper: Ecuador   Binder: Honduras   Filler: Dom. Rep., Nicaragua

Shape	Name	Lgth	Ring	Wrapper
Giant	Ruilovas	8½	52	CM
Double Corona	Prime Minster	7¼	54	CM
Toro	Barons	6⅛	52	CM
Robusto	Rothschilds	4½	52	CM
Churchill	Gran Corona	6¾	48	CM
Lonsdale	Exquisitos	6½	44	CM
Corona	Royal Coronas	5½	44	CM
Short Panatela	Señoritas	4¼	38	CM

HANDMADE CIGARS: BRAND LISTINGS

This is the 50th anniversary of this respected brand, now made by hand in Nicaragua. The taste of this special blend for the anniversary year is full-bodied, with mild spice flavors; San Vicente is offered in cedar boxes of 25.

SANTA CLARA "1830"
Handmade in San Andres Tuxtla, Mexico.

Wrapper: Mexico　　　　　Binder: Mexico　　　　　Filler: Mexico

Shape	Name		Lgth	Ring	Wrapper
Double Corona	I		7½	52	CC-Ma
Toro	II		6½	48	CC-Ma
Lonsdale	III		6⅝	43	CC-Ma
Corona	IV		5	44	CC-Ma
Long Corona	V		6	44	CC-Ma
Toro	VI		6	51	CC-Ma
Cigarillo	VII		5½	25	CC
Slim Panatela	VIII		6	32	CC
Panatela	Premier Tubes	(tubed)	6¾	38	CC-Ma
Small Panatela	Quino		4¼	30	CC
Robusto	Robusto		4½	50	CC-Ma
Long Corona	Fiesta		6½	42	Stripe
Giant	Magnum		19	60	CC

This is a medium-bodied cigar of all-Mexican tobacco. The wrapper is a unique Sumatran-seed type, which gives this line a unique flavor in both the natural and maduro shades. The Fiesta features the "barber pole" double wrapper style and the new Magnum can be used as a baseball bat if you're not smoking it. At 19 inches long, it's the biggest standard-production cigar available today.

SANTA DAMIANA
Handmade in La Romana, Dominican Republic.

Wrapper: USA/Connecticut　　　Binder: Dom. Rep.　　　Filler: Dom. Rep.

HANDMADE CIGARS: BRAND LISTINGS

Shape	Name	Lgth	Ring	Wrapper
Churchill	Seleccion No. 100	6¾	48	Cl
Corona Extra	Seleccion No. 300	5½	46	Cl
Robusto	Seleccion No. 500	5	50	Cl
Lonsdale	Seleccion No. 700	6½	42	Cl
Double Corona	Seleccion No. 800	7	50	Cl

A beautifully-finished cigar that defines what a "claro" wrapper looks like, Santa Damiana is an elegant, medium-bodied smoke. This brand originated in Cuba and today's Dominican-manufactured cigar was introduced in 1992. It is offered in attractive, slide-top cedar boxes of 25.

SANTA ROSA
Handmade in Santa Rosa de Copan, Honduras.

Wrapper: Ecuador   Binder: Honduras   Filler: Honduras

Shape	Name	Lgth	Ring	Wrapper
Corona	No. 4	5½	42	CC-Ma
Long Corona	Cetros	6	42	CC-Ma
Giant	President	8½	50	CC
Double Corona	Churchill	7	49	CC-Ma
Lonsdale	Corona	6½	44	CC-Ma
Lonsdale	Elegante	7	43	CC-Ma
Slim Panatela	Finas	6½	30	CC
Panatela	Largos	6¾	35	CC
Corona Extra	Regulares	5½	46	CC
Robusto	Sancho Panza	4¾	50	CC-Ma
Torpedo	Torpedo	6½	54	CC-Ma
Toro	Toro	6	50	CC-Ma

Introduced in 1985, the Santa Rosa brand is marked by a beautiful new band, along with an expanded set of shapes. Made in the La Flor de Copan factory in

A Cigar By Any Other Name...
Just Wouldn't Taste The Same.

HANDMADE CIGARS: BRAND LISTINGS

Santa Rosa, Honduras, this is a mild brand with a smooth, easy taste that everyone can enjoy. The wrapper is particularly smooth Ecuadorian-grown leaf from Connecticut Shade seeds.

SANTIAGO
Handmade in Santiago, Dominican Republic.

Wrapper: USA/Connecticut   *Binder: Dom. Rep.*   *Filler: Dom. Rep.*

Shape	Name	Lgth	Ring	Wrapper
Churchill	No. 1	6¾	48	CC
Long Panatela	No. 2	7	36	CC
Grand Corona	No. 3	6¾	46	CC
Corona Extra	No. 4	5½	46	CC
Petit Corona	No. 5	5	40	CC

A beautifully-boxed cigar, the Santiago brand blends mild tobaccos for a very mild body.

SANTIAGO SILK
Handmade in Villa Gonzalez, Dominican Republic.

Wrapper: Ecuador   *Binder: Dom. Rep.*   *Filler: Dom. Rep.*

Shape	Name	Lgth	Ring	Wrapper
Robusto	Robusto	4½	50	CC
Lonsdale	Lonsdale	6½	44	CC
Toro	Toro	6	50	CC
Churchill	Churchill	7	48	CC
Giant	Presidente	8	50	CC
Torpedo	Torpedo	6½	52	CC

Here is a new cigar for 1997, with a medium-bodied flavor thanks to its Connecticut-seed wrapper. It is offered in individual cellophane sleeves inside all-cedar boxes of 25.

HANDMADE CIGARS: BRAND LISTINGS

SANTO DIEGO
Handmade in San Andres Tuxtla, Mexico.

Wrapper: Mexico   *Binder: Mexico*   *Filler: Mexico*

Shape	Name	Lgth	Ring	Wrapper
Petit Corona	Petite Corona	5	42	CM
Lonsdale	Lonsdale	6¼	42	CM
Robusto	Robusto	5	50	CM
Toro	Corona Gorda	6¼	50	CM
Double Corona	Churchill	7	50	CM

This product of San Andres Valley in Mexico is mild-bodied and offered in economical bundles of 25.

SAVINELLI EXTREMELY LIMITED RESERVE
Handmade in Santiago, Dominican Republic.

Wrapper: USA/Connecticut   *Binder: Dom. Rep.*   *Filler: Dom. Rep.*

Shape	Name	Lgth	Ring	Wrapper
Churchill	No. 1 Churchill	7¼	48	CC
Grand Corona	No. 2 Corona Extra	6⅝	46	CC
Long Corona	No. 3 Lonsdale	6¼	43	CC
Toro	No. 4 Double Corona	6	50	CC
Corona	No. 5 Extraordinaire	5½	44	CC
Robusto	No. 6 Robusto	5	49	CC

"Extremely limited" is the key phrase in the name of this brand. Long famous for their high-quality pipes, the Savinelli tradition of craftsmanship is continued in this limited-distribution line of medium-bodied cigars introduced in 1995.

SEBASTIAN RESERVAS
Handmade in Esteli, Nicaragua.

Wrapper: Nicaragua   *Binder: Nicaragua*   *Filler: Nicaragua*

HANDMADE CIGARS: BRAND LISTINGS

Shape	Name	Lgth	Ring	Wrapper
Robusto	Reserva No. 1	5	52	CM
Toro	Reserva No. 2	6	50	CM
Churchill	Reserva No. 3	6⅞	48	CM
Double Corona	Reserva No. 4	7	52	CM
Double Corona	Reserva No. 5	7	54	CM
Double Corona	Reserva No. 6	7½	50	CM
Giant	Reserva No. 7	8	54	CM

Here is a medium-bodied cigar with excellent construction and an easy draw. It was introduced in 1997 and is offered in boxes of 20 cigars each.

SEGOVIA
Handmade in Segovia, Nicaragua.

Wrapper: Nicaragua   Binder: Nicaragua   Filler: Nicaragua

Shape	Name	Lgth	Ring	Wrapper
Double Corona	Crown Royal	7	52	CM
Long Corona	Primo Gorda	6	42	CM
Robusto	Robusto	5	52	CM
Toro	Toro	6	50	CM
Grand Corona	X-O	6¼	46	CM

Cuban seeds from the 1959 crop are the basis of this brand, which seeks to recreate the rich flavors of the Cuban heydey and escape the mediocrity of today's ultra-mild brands. Not surprisingly, this is a full, heavy-bodied cigar, with plenty of strong, ligero leaves inside.

SELECTO PURO DOMINICANO
Handmade in Villa Gonzalez, Dominican Republic.

Wrapper: Indonesia   Binder: Dom. Rep.   Filler: Dom. Rep.

HANDMADE CIGARS: BRAND LISTINGS

Shape	Name	Lgth	Ring	Wrapper
Giant	Selecto Double Corona	8	50	CM
Long Panatela	Selecto Gran Panatela	7¾	38	CM
Churchill	Selecto Gran Corona	6¾	46	CM
Toro	Selecto Toro	6	50	CM
Corona Extra	Selecto Corona	5½	46	CM
Robusto	Selecto Robusto	5½	52	CM
Churchill	Selecto Churchill	7	48	CM
Torpedo	Selecto Torpedo Gran Reserva	6½	52	CM

New from the Dominican Republic in 1997, this limited-distribution brand features two-year-aged tobaccos grown in the Valle de Yaque of the Dominican Republic, combined with a Sumatran-grown wrapper. It has a medium-bodied flavor and is offered in boxes of 25 except for the Selecto Double Corona, offered in boxes of ten.

SEVILLA
Handmade in Honduras.

Wrapper: Ecuador *Binder: Dom. Rep.* *Filler: Dom. Rep., Nicaragua*

Shape	Name	Lgth	Ring	Wrapper
Long Corona	Corona	6	44	CC
Robusto	Robusto	4	50	CC
Toro	Toro	6	50	CC
Churchill	Churchill	7	48	CC
Torpedo	Torpedo	7½	54	CC

Here is a mild brand, introduced in 1997 with a Connecticut-seed wrapper. It is offered in boxes of 25.

SIGLO 21
Handmade in Santiago, Dominican Republic.

Wrapper: Ecuador *Binder: Dom. Rep.* *Filler: Dom. Rep.*

HANDMADE CIGARS: BRAND LISTINGS

Shape	Name	Lgth	Ring	Wrapper
Robusto	No. 1	4½	50	CC-Ma
Lonsdale	No. 2	6½	44	CC-Ma
Toro	No. 3	6	50	CC-Ma
Churchill	No. 4	7	48	CC-Ma
Giant	No. 5	8	50	CC-Ma
Torpedo	No. 6	6¾	52	CC-Ma

Introduced in 1996 as a salute to the 21st century ("siglo" in Spanish). The cigars are medium-bodied, with excellent draw and a marvelous aroma. It is offered in elegant boxes of 25 cigars each.

SIGNATURE COLLECTION
Handmade in Santiago, Dominican Republic.
Wrapper: Ecuador   *Binder: Indonesia*
Filler: Dominican Republic, Honduras, Nicaragua

Shape	Name		Lgth	Ring	Wrapper
Robusto	Robusto	*(tubed)*	5	50	Co
Lonsdale	Corona	*(tubed)*	6½	42	Co
Double Corona	Churchill	*(tubed)*	7¼	50	Co
Torpedo	Torpedo	*(tubed)*	6½	54	Co

Introduced in 1994, the Signature Collection by Santiago Cabana cigars are now made in the Dominican Republic. These glass-encased cigars are made up of Cuban-seed tobaccos from the Dominican Republic, Ecuador, Honduras and Nicaragua plus an Indonesian-grown binder. The result is a medium-bodied cigar with a slow and even burn and a complex bouquet of taste and aroma.

SIGNET
Handmade in La Romana, Dominican Republic.
Wrapper: USA/Connecticut   *Binder: Dom. Rep.*   *Filler: Dom. Rep.*

HANDMADE CIGARS: BRAND LISTINGS

Shape	Name	Lgth	Ring	Wrapper
Robusto	Bedford	4¾	50	CC
Long Corona	Berkeley	6	42	CC
Churchill	Buckingham	7	48	CC

This brand was introduced in 1996 and is offered only in limited distribution. The brand has a mild, rich taste and is presented in cedar boxes of 25.

660 RED
Handmade in Miami, Florida, USA.
Wrapper: Ecuador   Binder: Dom. Rep.   Filler: Honduras, Nicaragua

Shape	Name	Lgth	Ring	Wrapper
Toro	660 Red	6	60	CM

Wow! It's like holding a short police baton, more than a cigar. But light one up and you'll experience a powerful flavor. 660 Reds are offered - if you can find them - in bundles of 15.

SMOK-A-CUBA
Handmade in Santiago, Dominican Republic
and Tampa, Florida, USA.
Wrapper: Indonesia   Binder: Dom. Rep.   Filler: Dom. Rep., Honduras, Mexico

Shape	Name	Lgth	Ring	Wrapper
Robusto	Twins	4½	52	CC
Giant	Solo Memento	9½	50	CC
Giant	Don Gaetano	8	50	CC
Toro	Robusto Grande	6	50	CC
Churchill	Larabie Court	6¾	46	CC
Corona	Recuerdos de Cuba	5¼	42	CC
Petit Corona	Familia	4	42	CC
Long Panatela	Viola Maria	7¾	38	CC

Small Panatela	Los Ninos	4⅛	30	CC
	Made with short filler:			
Robusto	1725 East 7th	5½	50	CC
Lonsdale	La Septima	6¾	42	CC

This new brand for 1997 features a medium-bodied taste, whether made in the Dominican Republic or the USA!

SOCORRO
Handmade in Santiago, Dominican Republic.

Wrapper: Indonesia *Binder: Dom. Rep.* *Filler: Dom. Rep.*

Shape	*Name*	*Lgth*	*Ring*	*Wrapper*
Double Corona	Presidente	7¾	50	CM
Double Corona	Churchill	6¾	50	CM
Toro	Toro	6	50	CM
Robusto	Robusto	5	50	CM

New for 1997, this brand combines a Sumatra wrapper with Cuban-seed binder and filler leaves for a medium-bodied taste. It's available in boxes of 10 or 20.

SOL Y MAR
Handmade in Danli, Honduras.

Wrapper: Ecuador, Indonesia *Binder: Mexico* *Filler: Dom. Rep., Nicaragua*

Shape	*Name*	*Lgth*	*Ring*	*Wrapper*
Double Corona	Churchill	7	50	CC
Pyramid	Torpedo	7	54	CC
Toro	Toro	6	50	CC
Corona	Corona	6	44	CC
Robusto	Robusto	5	50	CC
Perfecto	Figurado	6	46	CC

Perfecto	Figuradito	4½	46	CC

Here is a 1996-introduced brand, with leaves from four nations combining to offer a medium-bodied smoke. Sol y Mar cigars are presented in boxes of 25. A maduro-wrapped version of this brand is scheduled for the near future.

SOLEARES
Handmade in San Jose, Costa Rica.

Wrapper: Indonesia   *Binder: Indonesia*

Filler: Mexico, Nicaragua, Panama

Shape	Name	Lgth	Ring	Wrapper
Giant	Imperial	8	52	CM
Lonsdale	Lonsdale	7	44	CM
Corona	Corona	5¾	44	CM
Robusto	Robusto	5	52	CM
Corona Extra	Petite Corona	4½	46	CM
Churchill	Churchill	7	48	CM

Introduced at *LE CIGAR NOIR-CHICAGO* in December 1996, this is a well-balanced cigar with a strong finish. It offers a medium-bodied flavor in Cuban-style boxes of 24 cigars, except for the Robusto (20) and Imperial (10) shapes.

SOLEARES LIMITED RESERVE
Handmade in San Jose, Costa Rica.

Wrapper: Indonesia   *Binder: Nicaragua*   *Filler: Mexico, Nicaragua*

Shape	Name	Lgth	Ring	Wrapper
Giant	Imperial	8	52	CM
Robusto	Robusto	5	52	CM
Toro	Corona Extra	6	52	CM
Churchill	Churchill	7	48	CM

HANDMADE CIGARS: BRAND LISTINGS

This special reserve line (introduced in 1997) offers a complex, medium-bodied taste, available in boxes of 20 (except for the Imperial shape). It's available in boxes of 10.

SOLEARES SPECIAL RESERVE
Handmade in San Jose, Costa Rica.

Wrapper: Indonesia   *Binder: Nicaragua*   *Filler: Mexico, Nicaragua*

Shape	Name	Lgth	Ring	Wrapper
Giant	Imperial	8	52	CM
Churchill	Double Corona	7¼	46	CM
Robusto	Robusto	5	52	CM
Lonsdale	Gran Corona	6½	44	CM
Churchill	Churchill	7	48	CM

The Special Reserve debuted in 1997 and offers a medium-bodied flavor with a smooth finish thanks to its three-nation blend. It is offered in an all-cedar box of 20 cigars each, except for the Imperial shape which is offered in boxes of 10.

SOSA
Handmade in Santiago, Dominican Republic.
Wrapper: Ecuador, USA/Connecticut

Binder: Honduras   *Filler: Brazil, Dominican Republic*

Shape	Name	Lgth	Ring	Wrapper
Churchill	Churchill	7	49	CC-Ma
Robusto	Wavell	4¾	50	CC-Ma
Lonsdale	Lonsdale	6½	43	CC-Ma
Corona	Brevas	5½	43	CC-Ma
Pyramid	Piramides	7	60	CC-Ma
Panatela	Santa Fe	6	35	CC-Ma
Double Corona	Magnums	7½	52	CC-Ma
Toro	Governor	6	50	CC-Ma

HANDMADE CIGARS: BRAND LISTINGS

Juan Sosa is well known in the cigar trade for excellent products which are modestly priced. Originally made in Miami in 1964 and then in the Dominican Republic since 1974, this line bears his name and does it proud with a medium bodied-smoke and a choice of an Ecuadorian-grown Sumatra-seed wrapper or, for those who prefer maduro, a well-aged Connecticut Broadleaf. Sosa cigars are cellophaned and presented in slide-top cedar boxes.

SOSA FAMILY SELECTION
Handmade in Santiago, Dominican Republic.

Wrapper: USA/Connecticut   Binder: Dom. Rep.   Filler: Dom. Rep.

Shape	Name	Lgth	Ring	Wrapper
Lonsdale	No. 1	6¾	43	Co
Toro	No. 2	6¼	54	Co
Corona	No. 3	5¾	44	Co
Petit Corona	No. 4	5	40	Co
Robusto	No. 5	5	50	Co
Panatela	No. 6	6¼	38	Co
Toro	No. 7	6	50	Co
Churchill	No. 8	6¾	48	Co
Double Corona	No. 9	7¾	52	Co
Slim Panatela	Intermezzo	5	32	Co

The Sosa family tradition of fine cigars is carried on in this line, first introduced in 1995. Medium to full-bodied in flavor, all of these cigars are round – not pressed – and are presented in elegant cabinet-selection boxes.

SP MADURO
Handmade in Esteli, Nicaragua.

Wrapper: Nicaragua   Binder: Nicaragua   Filler: Nicaragua

Shape	Name	Lgth	Ring	Wrapper
Double Corona	Presidente	7	54	Ma
Toro	Toro	6	50	Ma

Robusto	Robusto	5	52	Ma

This all-maduro wrapped line is new for 1997. Unusual in that only maduro wrappers are offered – in the style of of the Henry Clay or Onyx lines from the Dominican – these are medium-to-full-flavored cigars with a rich taste, made of all Nicaraguan-grown leaves.

SPANISH HONDURAN RED LABEL
Handmade in Cofradia, Honduras.

Wrapper: Honduras   *Binder: Honduras*   *Filler: Honduras*

Shape	Name	Lgth	Ring	Wrapper
Giant Corona	Casino	8½	42	CM-Ma
Long Corona	Cetro	6	42	CM-Ma
Toro	Churchill Round	6	49	CM-Ma
Long Panatela	Elegante	7	38	Cl-CM-Ma
Giant	Emperadore	8½	52	CM-Ma
Lonsdale	Londre	7	40	Cl-CM-Ma
Churchill	Lonsdale	6¾	48	Cl-CM-Ma
Double Corona	Magnifico	7¼	54	Cl-CM-Ma
Giant Corona	Presidente	7½	45	Cl-CM-Ma
Robusto	Rothchild	4½	50	CM-Ma
Long Corona	Super Cetro	6¼	44	CM-Ma
Churchill	Wilshire *(glass jar)*	7¼	46	CM-Ma

These bundle-packed cigars are medium in body and easy to recognize thanks to the bright red label. The Wilshire shape is packed in an elegant glass jar, complete with an enclosed cigar cutter.

SPEAKEASY
Handmade in Santiago, Dominican Republic and Miami, Florida, USA.

HANDMADE CIGARS: BRAND LISTINGS

SPEAKEASY CLASSICS:

Wrapper: USA/Connecticut   Binder: Dom. Rep.   Filler: Dom. Rep.

SPEAKEASY GODFATHERS:

Wrapper: Indonesia   Binder: Nicaragua   Filler: Dom. Rep., Ecuador

SPEAKEASY UNTOUCHABLES:

Wrapper: Indonesia   Binder: Dom. Rep.   Filler: Dom. Rep.

SPEAKEASY GANGSTERS:

Wrapper: Ecuador   Binder: Nicaragua   Filler: Dom. Rep.

SPEAKEASY BOOTLEGGERS:

Wrapper: Indonesia   Binder: Dom. Rep.   Filler: Dom. Rep.

Shape	Name	Lgth	Ring	Wrapper
	Speakeasy Classics:			
Robusto	Foxes	4¾	50	CC
Corona	Legs	5½	42	CC
Lonsdale	Bugsys	6¾	44	CC
Double Corona	Machine Guns	7½	50	CC
	Speakeasy Godfathers:			
Churchill	Da Bosses	7	47	CM
Torpedo	Scarfaces	7¼	54	CM
Double Corona	Snorkys	7½	50	CM
Giant	Big Als	8	52	CM
	Speakeasy Untouchables:			
Robusto	Bugs	5	50	CM
Corona	Legs	5½	42	CM
Long Corona	Luckys	6	44	CM
Torpedo	Untouchables	6½	54	CM
Double Corona	Machine Guns	7½	50	CM

HANDMADE CIGARS: BRAND LISTINGS

	Speakeasy Gangsters:			
Robusto	Bugs	5	50	CC
Toro	Luckys	6	50	CC
Torpedo	Untouchables	6½	54	CC
Double Corona	Enforcers	7	50	CC
	Speakeasy Bootleggers:			
Robusto	Bugs	5	50	CM-Ma
Double Corona	Machine Guns	7½	50	CM-Ma
Torpedo	Untouchables	6½	54	CM-Ma

These cigars remember the bad old days of the gangster in Chicago and New York with a series of shapes named for some of the most notorious hoodlums in American history. The Godfathers and Gangsters series are made in Miami and offer a medium-to-full-bodied taste, while the Untouchables, Bootleggers and Classics lines are made in the Dominican Republic and provide a medium-bodied flavor. New for 1997, this line of well-made cigars is presented in individual cellophane sleeves and packed in boxes of 25.

SPECIAL JAMAICAN
Handmade in Santiago, Dominican Republic.

Wrapper: USA/Connecticut   Binder: Mexico   Filler: Dom. Rep.

Shape	Name	Lgth	Ring	Wrapper
Toro	Bonita Obsequio	6	50	CC
Double Corona	Churchill	7	52	CC-Ma
Lonsdale	Fancytale	6½	43	CC
Double Corona	Mayfair	7	60	CC-Ma
Double Corona	Nobles	7	50	CC
Small Panatela	Pica	5	32	CC
Pyramid	Pyramid	7	52	CC
Giant	Rey del Rey	9	60	CC-Ma

HANDMADE CIGARS: BRAND LISTINGS

Lonsdale	A	6½	44	DC-CC-Ma
Long Corona	B	6	44	CC
Corona	C	5½	44	DC-CC
Toro	D	6	50	CC-Ma

This is a mild blend of tobaccos from three nations combined to create a high-quality series of cigars, especially in the larger sizes. The huge "Rey del Rey" shape translates to "King of Kings."

SPIRIT VALLEY
Handmade in the Jalapa Valley, Nicaragua.

Wrapper: Nicaragua *Binder: Nicaragua* *Filler: Nicaragua*

Shape	Name	Lgth	Ring	Wrapper
Long Corona	Corona Grande	6	44	CM-Ma
Toro	Toro	6	50	CM-Ma
Giant Corona	Lonsdale	7½	43	CM-Ma
Robusto	Robusto	5	52	CM-Ma
Churchill	Churchill	6⅞	48	CM-Ma

Here is a full-bodied cigar introduced in 1997. All of the leaves are grown in Nicaragua and you can find this brand with a choice of wrapper shades in boxes of 25.

STRELSKY
Handmade in Tamboril, Dominican Republic.

Wrapper: Ecuador, Indonesia *Binder: Dom. Rep.* *Filler: Dom. Rep.*

Shape	Name	Lgth	Ring	Wrapper
Robusto	Robusto	5	50	CC
Toro	Sophia	6½	50	CC
Double Corona	Ivan	7	50	CC
Double Corona	Czar	7½	50	CC

Grand Corona	Gran Corona	6½	46	CC
Grand Corona	Corona	6	46	CC

Introduced in 1997, this is a mild-bodied brand with a choice of an Ecuadorian or Sumatran wrapper. You can find it mostly on the East Coast in boxes of 25.

SUAVE
Handmade in Villa Gonzalez, Dominican Republic.

Wrapper: USA/Connecticut   Binder: Dom. Rep.   Filler: Dom. Rep.

Shape	Name	Lgth	Ring	Wrapper
Long Corona	Corona	6	44	CC
Robusto	Robusto	4½	50	CC
Double Corona	Churchill	7½	50	CC

Introduced in 1996, this brand offers excellent construction and medium body from a blend of a Connecticut wrapper with two-year-old tobaccos from the Cibao Valley, the heart of the Dominican tobacco-growing zone. Suave cigars are presented either in all-cedar boxes of 25, or in bundles of 25 in individual cellophane sleeves.

SUERDIECK
Made in Cruz des Almas, Brazil.

Wrapper: Brazil   Binder: Brazil   Filler: Brazil

Shape	Name	Lgth	Ring	Wrapper
	Handmade cigars, made in Brazil:			
Slim Panatela	Brasilia	5½	30	CM
Slim Panatela	Caballeros	6	30	CM
Grand Corona	Finos	5¾	46	CM
Petit Corona	Mandarim Pai	5	42	CM
Cigarillo	Nina	6	22	CM
Slim Panatela	Nips	6	32	CM
Slim Panatela	Valencia	6	30	CC

HANDMADE CIGARS: BRAND LISTINGS

Petit Corona	Viajantes	5	40	CM
	Premium series, handmade in Brazil:			
Corona Extra	Corona Brasil Luxo	5½	45	CM
Corona Extra	Corona Imperial Luxo	5½	45	CC
Corona	Mata Fina Especial	5¼	42	CM
Short Panatela	Panatella Fina	5⅜	36	CM
	Cigarillos, handmade in Brazil of 100% tobacco:			
Cigarillo	Beira Mar Finos	5¼	28	CM
Cigarillo	Copacabana	5	29	CC
	Cigarillos, machine-made in Brazil:			
Cigarillo	Palomitas	3½	32	CM
Cigarillo	Palomitas Classics	3½	32	CM
Cigarillo	Palomitas Cherry	3½	32	CM
Cigarillo	Palomitas Clove	3½	32	CM
Cigarillo	Reynitas	3⅛	22	CC-CM

This well-known brand offers a medium-bodied taste of Brazilian tobacco in both handmade and machine-made shapes, famous since 1892. All use home-grown leaf, although the Corona Imperial, Palomitas, Panatela, Copacabana, Reynitas and Valencia shapes use Sumatran-seed tobaccos grown in Brazil.

T.J.
Handmade in San Pedro Sula, Honduras.

Wrapper: Ecuador   *Binder: Honduras*   *Filler: Honduras, Nicaragua*

Shape	Name	Lgth	Ring	Wrapper
Long Corona	Lonsdale	6¼	44	CC
Robusto	Robusto	5	50	CC
Toro	Splendido	6	50	CC
Churchill	Churchill	6¾	48	CC

HANDMADE CIGARS: BRAND LISTINGS

Giant	Grande	8½	52	CC-Ma
Corona	Petite Corona	5½	42	CC-Ma
Lonsdale	Londido	7	44	CC
	SP line:			
Torpedo	Torpedo SP	6¾	54	Ma
Lonsdale	Londido SP	7	44	Ma
Toro	Splendido SP	6	50	Ma
Pyramid	Pyramid SP	6	54	Ma

Introduced in 1996, the T.J. line offers a mild-to-medium-bodied series with an Ecuadorian-grown wrapper and Honduran filler and binder. The SP line is slightly stronger, with a medium-body and a three-year-aged maduro wrapper, plus some Nicaraguan tobacco in the filler.

TABACALERA
Handmade in Manila, the Philippines.

Wrapper: Indonesia   Binder: Philippines   Filler: Dom. Rep., Philippines

Shape	Name	Lgth	Ring	Wrapper
Corona	Corona	5½	42	CM
Lonsdale	Corona Largas	6½	43	CM
Giant	Corona Largas Especiales	8	46	CM
Giant	Double Coronas	8½	50	CM
Short Panatela	Half Corona	4	37	CM
Short Panatela	Panatelas	5	35	CM
Robusto	Robusto	5	50	CM
Pyramid	Pyramid	6	52	CM

The famous history of cigar production in the Philippines is continued with the medium-bodied Tabacalera line, which dates to 1881. Using Southeast Asian tobaccos from the Indonesian island of Java for the wrapper, most of the filler and the binder is home-grown from the province of Isabela, on the island of Luzon, also home to the Philippine capital of Manila.

TABACON VINTAGE SELECTION
Handmade in Santa Rosa de Copan, Honduras.

Wrapper: Indonesia   *Binder: Honduras*   *Filler: Honduras*

Shape	Name	Lgth	Ring	Wrapper
Long Corona	Corona	6¼	44	CC
Robusto	Robusto	5½	50	CC
Torpedo	Belicoso	6	52	CC
Churchill	Churchill	7	48	CC
Double Corona	Double Corona	7¾	50	CC

This is a 1997-introduced cigar with a Sumatra wrapper and a full-bodied flavor. It is offered in boxes of 25.

TABACOS SAN JOSE
Handmade in Miami, Florida, USA and Esteli, Nicaragua.

Wrapper: Ecuador or USA/Connecticut   *Binder: Dominican Republic*
Filler: Brazil, Dominican Republic, Honduras, Nicaragua

Shape	Name	Lgth	Ring	Wrapper
Corona	Corona	5½	44	Co-CC-Ma
Lonsdale	Lonsdale	6½	42	Co-CC-Ma
Robusto	Robusto	4⅞	50	Co-CC-Ma
Toro	Epicure	6	50	Co-CC-Ma
Churchill	Churchill	7	47	Co-CC-Ma
Double Corona	Double Corona	7⅝	50	Co-CC-Ma
Giant	Presidente	8	52	Co-CC-Ma
Torpedo	Torpedo	6½	54	Co-CC-Ma
Torpedo	Gran Torpedo	7½	60	Co-CC-Ma

HANDMADE CIGARS: BRAND LISTINGS

This brand debuted in 1996, offered in three shades of wrapper: Natural and Rosado, both using an Ecuadorian-grown wrapper, and a maduro shade, utilizing Connecticut leaf. The result is a mild-to-medium bodied taste, offered in all-cedar boxes of 25 (except for the Gran Torpedo, offered in 10s).

TABACOS UNIVERSO
Handmade in Danli, Honduras.

Wrapper: Honduras   Binder: Honduras   Filler: Honduras

Shape	Name	Lgth	Ring	Wrapper
Corona	Numero 4	5½	42	CM
Lonsdale	Lonsdale	6½	43	CM
Robusto	Rothchild	5	50	CM
Double Corona	Churchill	7	49	CM
Giant	Soberano	8	50	CM
Torpedo	Misiles	6	52	CM

This is a 1996 introduction, handmade with long-filler tobaccos from Honduras. The body is medium and each shape is offered in boxes of 25, except for the Misiles shape (offered in 10s).

TAINO
BY PROFESOR SILA
Handmade in Santiago, Dominican Republic.

Wrapper: Indonesia   Binder: Dom. Rep.   Filler: Dom. Rep.

Shape	Name	Lgth	Ring	Wrapper
Corona	Corona	5¼	42	CC
Long Corona	Long Corona	6	42	CC
Lonsdale	Lonsdale	6½	42	CC
Corona Extra	Corona Extra	5¾	45	CC
Grand Corona	Gran Corona	6¾	45	CC
Robusto	Robusto	4¾	50	CC

Double Corona	Double Corona	7	50	CC

Introduced in 1997, this is a value-priced, all handmade, full-bodied cigar that is a welcome smoke anytime and on any day. You'll find it presented in attractive flip-top wooden boxes of 25.

TAINO
Handmade in Bayamon, Puerto Rico.
Wrapper: USA/Pennsylvania   Binder: Puerto Rico   Filler: Puerto Rico

Shape	Name	Lgth	Ring	Wrapper
Churchill	Long Fumo	7¼	48	CM

This is a heavy-bodied cigar with a Pennsylvania wrapper, offered in boxes of 25.

TAMAYO Y PARETO
Handmade in Santiago, Dominican Republic.
Wrapper: Ecuador   Binder: Dom. Rep.   Filler: Dom. Rep.

Shape	Name	Lgth	Ring	Wrapper
Double Corona	Churchill	7½	50	CC
Long Corona	Corona	6	44	CC
Pyramid	Piramide	7	54	CC
Toro	Robusto	6	50	CC
Robusto	Rothschild	4½	50	CC
Toro	Toro	6	52	CC

Introduced in 1997, this is a highly-respected new brand with a mild-to-medium taste in boxes of 25, except for the Piramide, offered in 24s.

TAMBORIL
Handmade in Tamboril, Dominican Republic.
Wrapper: USA/Connecticut, Indonesia   Binder: Dom. Rep.   Filler: Dom. Rep.

HANDMADE CIGARS: BRAND LISTINGS

Shape	Name		Lgth	Ring	Wrapper
	Connecticut Collection:				
Giant	Double Corona		8	50	CC
Churchill	Churchill		7	47	CC
Churchill	Diablo	*(perfecto tip)*	7	47	CC
Torpedo	Torpedo		6½	54	CC
Corona	Corona		6	44	CC
Robusto	Robusto		5	52	CC
Short Panatela	Cortadito		5	38	CC
	Sumatra Collection:				
Petit Corona	Coronita		4	44	CC
Long Corona	Corona		6	44	CC
Robusto	Robusto		5	52	CC
Churchill	Churchill		7	47	CC
Churchill	Diablo	*(perfecto tip)*	7	47	CC
Torpedo	Torpedo		6½	54	CC

Here is an exhaustingly produced cigar, introduced in 1996, which offers a choice of wrappers. With a Connecticut wrapper, it presents a mild-to-medium-bodied taste; with a Sumatra wrapper, the taste is medium-to-full-bodied. These are serious cigars made by serious smokers and presented in boxes of 25.

TAMBORIL CORDOVA COLLECTION
Handmade in Tamboril, Dominican Republic.

Wrapper: Indonesia   Binder: Dom. Rep.   Filler: Dom. Rep.

Shape	Name		Lgth	Ring	Wrapper
Corona	Corona		5½	44	CC
Panatela	Panatela		6	38	CC
Petit Corona	Short Diablo	*(perfecto tip)*	4	44	CC

HANDMADE CIGARS: BRAND LISTINGS

Robusto	Robusto		5	50	CC
Toro	Toro		6	50	CC
Churchill	Churchill		7	47	CC
Long Corona	Pyramid		6	44	CC
Robusto	Robustubo	(tubed)	5½	52	CC

Here is a uniquely-finished cigar . . . with just a hint of cocoa! This is a medium-bodied smoke, introduced in 1997 and packed in all-cedar boxes of 25.

TAMBORIL FORE
Handmade, with short filler, in Tamboril, Dominican Republic.
Wrapper: Indonesia   *Binder: Dom. Rep.*   *Filler: Dom. Rep.*

Shape	Name		Lgth	Ring	Wrapper
Robusto	Robusto Grande	(tubed)	5½	52	CC

Introduced in 1997, you'll find this Java-wrapped brand in a glass tube inside a box of 30 cigars, each containing a medium-to-full-bodied, short-filler cigar.

TAMPA TROPICS
Handmade in Tampa, Florida, USA.
Wrapper: Cameroon   *Binder: Dom. Rep.*   *Filler: Dom. Rep., Nicaragua*

Shape	Name	Lgth	Ring	Wrapper
Robusto	Rothschild	5	50	CM
Double Corona	Churchill	7	50	CM
Torpedo	Belicoso	6¼	52	CM

This newest innovation from the Cammarata Cigar Co. of Tampa offers a medium-bodied taste, in boxes of 25.

TATOU
Handmade, with short filler, in Mexico City, Mexico.
Wrapper: Mexico   *Binder: Nicaragua*   *Filler: Dom. Rep., Mexico*

HANDMADE CIGARS: BRAND LISTINGS

Shape	Name	Lgth	Ring	Wrapper
Corona	Amaretto	5	44	CM
Corona	Coconut	5	44	CM
Corona	Rum	5	44	CM
Corona	Vanilla	5	44	CM

New for 1997, this is an all-flavored, all-handmade line of corona-sized cigars. Each has a mild taste, with the flavor elements being added after the rolling process has been completed. Tatou cigars are easy on the pocketbook and are presented in boxes of 25.

TE-AMO
Handmade in San Andres Tuxtla, Mexico.

Wrapper: Mexico   *Binder: Mexico*   *Filler: Mexico*

Shape	Name	Lgth	Ring	Wrapper
Lonsdale	No. 1 Relaxation	6⅝	44	CC-CM-Ma
Long Corona	No. 2 Meditation	6	42	CC-CM-Ma
Panatela	No. 3 Torero	6½	35	CC-CM-Ma
Petit Corona	No. 4	5	42	CC-CM-Ma
Cigarillo	No. 5 Picador	7	27	CC-CM-Ma
Giant	No. 6 CEO	8½	52	CM-Ma
Cigarillo	No. 10 Epicure	5	27	CM
Cigarillo	No. 11 Elegante	5¾	27	CC-CM-Ma
Double Corona	No. 14 Churchill	7½	50	CC-CM-Ma
Double Corona	No. 17 Presidente	7	50	CM-Ma
Robusto	No. 18 Torito	4¾	50	CM-Ma
Toro	No. 19 Toro	6	50	CC-CM-Ma
Long Panatela	No. 24 Caballero	7	35	CM
Double Corona	No. 28 Maximo	7	54	CM-Ma

HANDMADE CIGARS: BRAND LISTINGS

Grand Corona	No. 29 Satisfaction	6	46	CM-Ma
Lonsdale	Celebration *(tubed)*	6⅝	44	CM
Robusto	Robusto	5½	54	CM-Ma
Torpedo	Figurado	6⅝	50	CM-Ma
Pyramid	Piramides	6¼	50	CM-Ma
Pyramid	Gran Piramides	7¼	54	CM-Ma
Perfecto	Double Perfecto	7	48	CM-Ma
	Made with short filler:			
Cigarillo	No. 26 Intermezzo	4	28	CC
Small Panatela	No. 27 Impulse	5	32	CC
Short Panatela	Pauser	5⅜	35	CC
Small Panatela	Purito	4⅞	30	CC

This very popular brand originated in the 1960s and is a product of the San Andres Valley, where all of the tobaccos for this brand are grown. Considered to be medium in strength, the enthusiast has a choice of natural or maduro wrappers, or can choose many of the shapes in the lighter-wrappered and lighter-bodied Te-Amo Lights.

TE-AMO SEGUNDO
Handmade in San Andres Tuxtla, Mexico.

Wrapper: Mexico   *Binder: Mexico*   *Filler: Mexico*

Shape	Name	Lgth	Ring	Wrapper
Panatela	No. 55 Torero	6½	35	CM-Ma
Long Corona	No. 60 Meditation	6	42	CM-Ma
Lonsdale	No. 75 Relaxation	6⅝	44	CM-Ma
Double Corona	No. 90 Presidente	7	50	CM-Ma
Double Corona	No. 110 Churchill	7½	50	CM-Ma
Grand Corona	No. 120 Satisfaction	6	46	CM-Ma
Toro	No. 135 Toro	6	50	CM-Ma

HANDMADE CIGARS: BRAND LISTINGS

These are just what the name suggests: seconds of the regular Te-Amo line produced with the same San Andres Valley tobaccos. Offered in bundles of 20 cigars each, they are good cigars and an even better value.

TEMPLE HALL
Handmade in Kingston, Jamaica.

Wrapper: USA/Connecticut   Binder: Mexico   *Filler: Dom. Rep., Mexico*

Shape	Name	Lgth	Ring	Wrapper
Double Corona	No. 700	7	49	CC
Lonsdale	No. 675	6¾	45	CC
Robusto	No. 550	5½	49	CC
Long Corona	No. 625	6¼	42	CC
Small Panatela	No. 500	5	31	CC
Small Panatela	No. 450	4½	49	Ma
Torpedo	Belicoso	6	50	CC
Lonsdale	Trumps No. 1	6½	42	CC-Ma
Robusto	Trumps No. 2	5½	50	CC
Corona	Trumps No. 3	5½	42	CC-Ma
Double Corona	Trumps No. 4	7½	49	CC

A medium-strength cigar made in Jamaica since 1876, Temple Hall cigars are made and left in a natural, round shape – not pressed. It is an easy-drawing cigar which offers the connoisseur a choice of shapes, and in a few cases, the choice of a natural-shade or maduro-shade wrapper.

TENA Y VEGA
Handmade in Danli, Honduras.

Wrapper: Cameroon   Binder: Honduras   *Filler: Honduras*

Shape	Name	Lgth	Ring	Wrapper
Long Corona	Cetros	6⅛	42	CM
Double Corona	Churchill	7	50	CM
Toro	Double Corona	6	50	CM

Lonsdale	No. 1	6¾	42	CM

These are rather medium-to-heavy bodied, all long-filler cigars. Its distinctive taste is produced by the blending of Honduran origin tobaccos and the hard-to-find, medium-brown Cameroon wrapper.

TENORIO
Handmade in Santiago, Dominican Republic.
Wrapper: Indonesia or USA/Connecticut   Binder: Dom. Rep.   Filler: Dom. Rep.

Shape	Name	Lgth	Ring	Wrapper
Long Corona	Corona	6	44	CI-CC-CM
Robusto	Robusto	5	50	CI-CC-CM
Double Corona	Churchill	7½	50	CI-CC-CM
Toro	Toro	6	50	CI-CC-CM
Torpedo	Torpedo	6½	52	CI-CC-CM
Grand Corona	Extra Corona	6	46	CI-CC-CM
Panatela	Panatela	6	38	CI-CC
Small Panatela	Privilege	5	30	CI-CC

This line offers a choice of wrapper, both providing a medium bodied taste. The interior of these cigars is all Dominican, with both Cuban-seed and Olor leaves in the bunch. Introduced in 1997, Tenorio is available in 5x5-packed cabinets of 25.

TERRI WELLES SIGNATURE SERIES
Handmade in Antigua, Guatemala.
Wrapper: Ecuador   Binder: Dom. Rep.   Filler: Costa Rica, Honduras, Nicaragua

Shape	Name	Lgth	Ring	Wrapper
Double Corona	Churchill	7½	50	CC

This cigar is marketed in tribute to 1981 Playboy magazine "Playmate of the Year" Terri Welles and features her likeness on the band and box. The cigar itself is mild-bodied and offers a creamy flavor.

HANDMADE CIGARS: BRAND LISTINGS

TESORO
Handmade in Santiago, Dominican Republic.

Wrapper: Indonesia · *Binder: Dom. Rep.* · *Filler: Dom. Rep.*

Shape	Name	Lgth	Ring	Wrapper
Giant	Conquistador	8½	52	CM
Double Corona	Don	7½	50	CM
Grand Corona	Gorda	6½	46	CM
Long Corona	Mimosa	6	42	CM
Robusto	Plumpo	5	50	CM
Toro	Polo	6	50	CM

New in 1997, this is a medium-to-full-bodied cigar, offered in economical bundles of 25 cigars each.

TESOROS DE COPAN
Handmade in Santa Rosa de Copan, Honduras.

Wrapper: Honduras · *Binder: Honduras* · *Filler: Honduras*

Shape	Name	Lgth	Ring	Wrapper
Double Corona	Churchill	7	50	CC
Long Corona	Cetros	6¼	44	CC
Toro	Toros	6	50	CC
Corona Extra	Corona	5¼	46	CC
Robusto	Yumbo	4¾	50	CC
Panatela	Lindas	5⅝	38	CC

Created in 1993, Tesoros de Copan cigars are much more than simply a mild-to-medium-bodied cigar with Honduran-grown Connecticut-seed wrappers. Part of the proceeds from the sale of these cigars supports the efforts of the La Ruta Maya Foundation, which is dedicated to the conservation of the Central American rain forests and historic preservation of the remains of the Mayans, who originated the use of tobacco many centuries ago.

HANDMADE CIGARS: BRAND LISTINGS

THIRD MILLENIUM
Handmade in Santiago, Dominican Republic.

Wrapper: Indonesia   *Binder: Ecuador*   *Filler: Dom. Rep.*

Shape	Name	Lgth	Ring	Wrapper
Double Corona	Double Corona	7½	50	CM
Churchill	Preludio I	7	46	CM
Robusto	Preludio II	5½	50	CM
Torpedo	Pyramide	7	56	CM

Hard to find, this is a 1997-introduced cigar which offers medium-bodied flavor presented in varnished all-cedar boxes of 25.

THOMAS HINDS CABINET SELECTION
Handmade in Esteli, Nicaragua.

Wrapper: Nicaragua   *Binder: Nicaragua*   *Filler: Nicaragua*

Shape	Name	Lgth	Ring	Wrapper
Double Corona	Churchill	7	49	CM
Toro	Short Churchill	6	50	CM
Long Corona	Corona Grande	6	44	CM
Robusto	Robusto	5	50	CM
Lonsdale	Lonsdale	7	43	CM
Corona	Corona	5½	42	CM

Here is a creamy, medium-to-full-bodied brand first introduced in 1997. It offers all Nicaraguan-grown leaves protected in individual cellophane sleeves and packed in cedar boxes of 25.

THOMAS HINDS HONDURAN SELECTION
Handmade in Danli, Honduras.

Wrapper: Ecuador   *Binder: Honduras*   *Filler: Honduras*

HANDMADE CIGARS: BRAND LISTINGS

Shape	Name	Lgth	Ring	Wrapper
Giant	Presidente	8½	52	CM
Double Corona	Churchill	7	49	CM
Torpedo	Torpedo	6	52	CM
Toro	Short Churchill	6	50	CM
Lonsdale	Supremos	7	43	CM
Robusto	Robusto	5	50	CM
Long Corona	Royal Corona	6	43	CM
Corona	Corona	5½	42	CM

Introduced in the U.S. in 1994, Thomas Hinds Honduran Selection are premium, hand-rolled cigars. The long-leaf filler and double binder are of Honduran origin, while the wrapper is a spicy Ecuadorian leaf. Look for it in cedar boxes of 25.

THOMAS HINDS NICARAGUAN SELECTION
Handmade in Esteli, Nicaragua.

Wrapper: Ecuador   *Binder: Nicaragua*   *Filler: Nicaragua*

Shape	Name	Lgth	Ring	Wrapper
Torpedo	Torpedo	6	52	CC-Ma
Double Corona	Churchill	7	49	CC-Ma
Lonsdale	Lonsdale Extra	7	43	CC-Ma
Toro	Short Churchill	6	50	CC-Ma
Corona	Corona	5½	42	CC-Ma
Robusto	Robusto	5	50	CC-Ma

First offered in 1995, the Thomas Hinds Nicaraguan Selection showcases filler and binder tobaccos from the Jalapa region of Nicaragua. Easy to smoke thanks to top-quality construction, these cigars are elegantly packaged in handsome all-cedar boxes.

HANDMADE CIGARS: BRAND LISTINGS

THOMAS HINDS VINTAGE I
Handmade in Esteli, Nicaragua.

Wrapper: Nicaragua   *Binder: Nicaragua*   *Filler: Nicaragua*

Shape	Name	Lgth	Ring	Wrapper
Double Corona	Churchill	7	49	CM
Robusto	Robusto	5	50	CM
Lonsdale	Lonsdale	7	43	CM
Corona	Corona	5½	42	CM

New for 1997, this brand offers a medium-to-full-bodied smoke, but without any
harshness. It is presented in individual cellophane sleeves in limited numbers.
Once gone, they will not be replenished, but instead a Vintage II will be
introduced.

TIA MARTIA
Handmade in Santiago, Dominican Republic.

Wrapper: Honduras   *Binder: Mexico*   *Filler: Dom. Rep., Honduras*

Shape	Name	Lgth	Ring	Wrapper
Grand Corona	No. 1	6½	46	CM
Corona	No. 4	5½	44	CM
Toro	Churchill	6½	52	CM
Short Panatela	Petit	4¼	38	CM
Churchill	Presidente	6¾	48	CM
Toro	Toro	6⅛	50	CM

Created in 1978, this is a mild-to-medium blend of leaves from three nations,
offered in modestly-priced bundles of 20.

TIBURON
Handmade in Danli, Honduras.

Wrapper: Ecuador   *Binder: Indonesia*

Filler: Dominican Republic, Honduras, Nicaragua

HANDMADE CIGARS: BRAND LISTINGS

Shape	Name	Lgth	Ring	Wrapper
Slim Panatela	Tiger Shark	6¼	33	CC
Long Corona	Great White	6	42	CC
Corona	Mako	5¼	42	CC

Despite the fierce names of the shapes, these are mild-bodied cigars. They are offered in bundles of 25 cigars each.

TIPO
Handmade in Tamboril, Dominican Republic.
Wrapper: Dom. Rep.   *Binder: Dom. Rep.*   *Filler: Dom. Rep.*

Shape	Name	Lgth	Ring	Wrapper
Toro	Churchill	6	50	CM
Long Corona	Lonsdale	6	44	CM

Here is a reasonably-priced bundled cigar, introduced in 1997. It offers a medium-bodied smoke, thanks to its two-year aged tobaccos, all grown in the Dominican Republic.

TODO EL MUNDO
Handmade in Villa Gonzalez, Dominican Republic.
Wrapper: USA/Connecticut   *Binder: Dom. Rep.*   *Filler: Dom. Rep.*

Shape	Name	Lgth	Ring	Wrapper
Double Corona	Churchill	7½	50	CC
Toro	Toro	6	52	CC
Long Corona	Corona	6	44	CC
Petit Corona	Petit Corona	5½	42	CC
Robusto	Rothschild	4½	50	CC
Torpedo	Torpedo	6	52	CC

Here is a 1996 introduction of a cigar whose names means "all over the world" in Spanish. Thanks to its mild-to-medium body and silky Connecticut wrapper, it probably will achieve popularity "todo el mundo."

HANDMADE CIGARS: BRAND LISTINGS

TOOTH OF THE DOG
Handmade in Esteli, Nicaragua.

Wrapper: Nicaragua   *Binder: Nicaragua*   *Filler: Nicaragua*

Shape	Name	Lgth	Ring	Wrapper
Robusto	Robusto	5	50	CM
Toro	Short Churchill	6	50	CM
Double Corona	Churchill	7	49	CM
Torpedo	Torpedo	6	52	CM

Here is a medium-bodied cigar of all-Nicaraguan origin, offered with an interesting name and an even more interesting box: each holds 25 Tooth of the Dog cigars . . . or is that Teeth of the Dog?

TOPPER CENTENNIAL
Handmade in Santiago, Dominican Republic.

Wrapper: Ecuador   *Binder: Dom. Rep.*   *Filler: Dom. Rep.*

Shape	Name	Lgth	Ring	Wrapper
Double Corona	Churchill	7½	52	CC
Toro	Toro	6	50	CC
Lonsdale	Lonsdale	6¾	43	CC

The Topper Cigar Company was founded in 1896, offering handmade cigars with imported long filler and Connecticut broadleaf wrappers. That tradition is now continued with the Topper Centennial, introduced in 1995. It's a handmade cigar manufactured in the Dominican Republic, providing a medium-bodied smoke, offered in three popular sizes.

TOPPER GRANDE
Handmade in Esteli, Nicaragua.

Wrapper: Indonesia   *Binder: Nicaragua*   *Filler: Nicaragua*

Shape	Name	Lgth	Ring	Wrapper
Double Corona	Churchill	7½	50	CM
Toro	Toro	6	50	CM

Robusto	Robusto	4½	50	CM
Lonsdale	Cetro	6½	43	CM
Corona	Corona	5½	43	CM

Here is an outstanding handmade from an American institution among cigar makers which celebrated its 100th anniversary in 1996. This is a medium-to-full bodied smoke, featuring Indonesian wrappers around aged Nicaraguan leaves.

TORCEDOR
Handmade in Esteli, Nicaragua.

Wrapper: Nicaragua   *Binder: Nicaragua*   *Filler: Honduras*

Shape	Name	Lgth	Ring	Wrapper
Lonsdale	No. 1	7	44	CC
Double Corona	Churchill	7	50	CC
Robusto	Robusto	5	50	CC
Toro	Toro	6	50	CC
Giant	General	8	52	CC

"Torcedor" means cigar roller in Spanish and this 1996-introduced brand salutes them with a mild blend of long-filler tobaccos from Honduras and Nicaragua.

TORCEDOR
Handmade in San Andres Tuxtla, Mexico.

Wrapper: Mexico   *Binder: Mexico*   *Filler: Mexico*

Shape	Name	Lgth	Ring	Wrapper
Robusto	Robusto Extra	5	60	CM-Ma
Toro	Super Toro	6½	60	CM-Ma
Double Corona	Churchill Extra	7½	60	CM-Ma

Here is a new member of the Torcedor family for 1997. It features all Mexican tobacco and a full-bodied taste. You'll find it in boxes of 25 in your choice of natural or maduro wrapper!

Figurados:
Perfectos, Pyramids and Torpedos

These shapes are the most distinctive of all, with flared ends and/or conical heads. Although the dimensions vary, the definitions remain constant:

- Perfectos: A cigar with a conical-shaped head *and* foot.
- Pyramids: A cigar whose ring gauge increases continuously from head to foot. Also known as "triangulars" or "trumpets."
- Torpedos: A cigar with a tapered head that flares out to straight sides. Also known as "belicosos."

Pictured opposite, from left to right:

- **VICTOR SINCLAIR GRAND RESERVE** *Figurado*
  (Dominican Republic) 5 x 46 Corona Extra with a *"perfecto"* foot

- **BIG BUTT** *Don Gordo*
  (Nicaragua) 6 x 54 Perfecto

- **1876** *Piramide*
  (Dominican Republic) 7 x 54 Pyramid

- **CARRINGTON** *No. 8*
  (Dominican Republic) 6⅞ x 60 Pyramid

- **SELECTO PURO DOMINICANO** *Selecto Torpedo Gran Reserva* 6½ x 52 Torpedo

- **HOJA CUBANA** *Torpedo*
  (Nicaragua) 6½ x 54 Torpedo

- **BALI HAI** *Krakatau*
  (Indonesia) 6 x 52 Pyramid

HANDMADE CIGARS: BRAND LISTINGS

TORO BRAVO
Handmade in Tamboril, Dominican Republic.

Wrapper: Indonesia   *Binder: Dom. Rep.*   *Filler: Dom. Rep.*

Shape	Name	Lgth	Ring	Wrapper
Double Corona	Churchill	7	50	CM
Robusto	Robusto	5	50	CM
Churchill	Grande Corona	6¾	46	CM
Long Panatela	Lancero	7¾	38	CM
Lonsdale	No. 1	6½	44	CM

This is a medium-bodied brand introduced in 1997. It features a Sumatra wrapper and is offered in boxes of 25.

TORQUINO
Handmade in Canca la Piedra, Dominican Republic.

Wrapper: Indonesia   *Binder: Dom. Rep.*   *Filler: Dom. Rep.*

Shape	Name	Lgth	Ring	Wrapper
Double Corona	Delicioso	7	50	CC
Toro	Toro	6	50	CC
Robusto	Robusto	5	50	CC
Long Corona	Privada No. 1	6	42	CC

This is a new brand for 1997, offering a mild to medium taste and offered in individual cellophane sleeves in cedar boxes of 25.

TRADICIONALES
Handmade in San Diego, California, USA.

Wrapper: Indonesia   *Binder: Indonesia*   *Filler: Ecuador, Honduras, Mexico*

Shape	Name	Lgth	Ring	Wrapper
Slim Panatela	Fino	5¾	32	CM-Ma
Corona	Corona	5¾	42	CM-Ma

Lonsdale	El Cubano	6¾	44	CM-Ma
Panatela	Panatela	6¾	36	CM-Ma
Robusto	Robusto	5	50	CM-Ma
Grand Corona	Havana	6	46	CM-Ma
Toro	Monterico	5½	52	CM-Ma
Double Corona	Cuban Round Largo	7¼	50	CM-Ma
Double Corona	Presidente	7¾	52	CM-Ma
Torpedo	Torpedo	7	56	CM-Ma

Here is a mild-to-medium-bodied cigar that you can see being made by hand by the Cuban Cigar Factory in San Diego's Gaslamp District! It features a Sumatra wrapper and Java wrapper and is offered in boxes of 25.

TRESADO
Handmade in La Romana, Dominican Republic.

Wrapper: Indonesia   Binder: Dom. Rep.   Filler: Dom. Rep.

Shape	Name	Lgth	Ring	Wrapper
Giant	Seleccion No. 100	8	52	CC
Churchill	Seleccion No. 200	7	48	CC
Grand Corona	Seleccion No. 300	6	46	CC
Lonsdale	Seleccion No. 400	6⅝	44	CC
Corona	Seleccion No. 500	5½	42	CC

Tresado provides handmade quality at a value price. Introduced in 1988, the cigar starts with a Dominican blend and binder, then adds a Javan wrapper for a full-bodied yet mild smoke.

TROYA
Handmade in Santiago, Dominican Republic.

Wrapper: USA/Connecticut   Binder: Dom. Rep.   Filler: Dom. Rep.

HANDMADE CIGARS: BRAND LISTINGS

Shape	Name	Lgth	Ring	Wrapper
Torpedo	No. 81 Torpedo	7	54	CC-Ma
Double Corona	No. 72 Executive	7¾	50	CC-Ma
Churchill	No. 63 Churchill	6⅞	46	CC-Ma
Lonsdale	No. 54 Elegante	7	43	CC-Ma
Long Corona	No. 45 Cetro	6¼	44	CC-Ma
Long Panatela	No. 36 Palma Fina	7	36	CC
Corona	No. 27 Corona	5½	42	CC
Robusto	No. 18 Rothchild	4½	50	CC-Ma
	Troya Clasico:			
Double Corona	No. 72 Executive	7¾	50	CC
Corona	No. 27 Corona	5½	42	CC

Troya is a hand-crafted cigar of the highest quality, introduced in 1985. It has a medium body and a consistency in construction and draw that will reward the connoisseur every time. Troyas are offered in boxes of 25 cigars, in natural and maduro wrappers. The Clasico line of two shapes was created in 1991 and is produced only when truly superior leaves are available to create a fuller taste that is now encased in boxes of 20 cigars each. Look for the newer Clasico band, and note that each box produced is sequentially numbered to ensure quality control and exclusivity.

12 STARS
Handmade in Santiago, Dominican Republic.

Wrapper: USA/Connecticut   Binder: Dom. Rep.   Filler: Dom. Rep.

Shape	Name	Lgth	Ring	Wrapper
Giant	Star 1	8½	50	CC
Churchill	Star 2	8	46	CC
Lonsdale	Star 3	7½	42	CC
Churchill	Star 4	6⅞	46	CC
Corona	Star 5	5¾	42	CC

Corona	Star 6	5¾	42	DC
Churchill	Star 7	6⅞	46	CC
Corona	Star 8	5½	40	CC
Robusto	Star 9	5	50	CC
Small Panatela	Star 10	5	34	CC
Cigarillo	Star 11	5	28	CC
Cigarillo	Star 12	5½	28	CC

This is a very high value brand, offering a generally mild-tasting cigar for a price well below its pedigree. Available in bundles of 25, these are among the finest cigars you can buy, penny for penny, thanks to their just slightly imperfect Connecticut wrappers and carefully selected Dominican binder and filler.

ULTIMATE DOMINICAN
Handmade in Santiago, Dominican Republic.

ULTIMATE CLASSIC:
Wrapper: USA/Connecticut Binder: Dom. Rep. Filler: Dom. Rep.

ULTIMATE GOLD:
Wrapper: Dom. Rep. Binder: Dom. Rep. Filler: Dom. Rep.

Shape	Name	Lgth	Ring	Wrapper
	Ultimate Classic:			
Churchill	Churchill	7	48	CC
Grand Corona	Corona Gorda	6	46	CC
Long Corona	Lonsdale	6	42	CC
Robusto	Robusto	5	50	CC
Petit Corona	Petit Corona	5	40	CC
	Ultimate Gold:			
Churchill	Churchill	7	48	CC

HANDMADE CIGARS: BRAND LISTINGS

Grand Corona	Corona Gorda	6	46	CC
Long Corona	Lonsdale	6	42	CC
Robusto	Robusto	5	50	CC
Petit Corona	Petit Corona	5	40	CC

You'll find this brand, introduced in 1997, in individual cellophane sleeves inside all-cedar, cabinet-style boxes. These are mild-to-medium bodied cigars, with Olor binders and Piloto Cubano filler leaves, all grown in the Dominican Republic.

UNIVERSO
Handmade in Danli, Honduras.

Wrapper: Ecuador   *Binder: Honduras*   *Filler: Dom. Rep., Honduras*

Shape	Name	Lgth	Ring	Wrapper
Corona	No. 4	5½	42	CC
Robusto	Rothschild	5	50	CC
Lonsdale	Lonsdale	6½	43	CC
Double Corona	Churchill	7	49	CC
Giant	Soberanos	8	50	CC
Torpedo	Misiles	6	52	CC

This is a medium-bodied cigar introduced in 1997. It is offered in six popular sizes in boxes of 25.

V CENTENNIAL
Handmade in Danli, Honduras.

Wrapper: USA/Connecticut   *Binder: Mexico*
Filler: Dominican Republic, Honduras, Nicaragua

Shape	Name	Lgth	Ring	Wrapper
Torpedo	Torpedo	7	54	CC
Giant	Presidente	8	50	CC

Churchill	Churchill	7	48	CC-Ma
Long Panatela	No. 1	7½	38	CC
Toro	No. 2	6	50	CC-Ma
Lonsdale	Cetros	6¼	44	CC-Ma
Robusto	Robustos	5	50	CC-Ma
Corona	Coronas	5½	42	CC

V Centennial is handmade in Honduras using the finest tobacco from the Dominican Republic, Nicaragua, Honduras, Mexico and the United States. Selection and processing of this cigar began in 1992. It was introduced in November 1993 and has become one of the top-rated cigars available today. It is considered a medium-bodied cigar.

V CENTENNIAL 500
Handmade in Santiago, Dominican Republic.
Wrapper: USA/Connecticut   Binder: Dominican Republic
Filler: Dominican Republic, Honduras, Mexico, Nicaragua

Shape	Name	Lgth	Ring	Wrapper
Corona	Corona	5½	42	CM
Robusto	Robusto	5	50	CM
Long Corona	Cetro	6¼	44	CM
Toro	No. 2	6	50	CM
Long Panatela	No. 1	7½	38	CM
Churchill	Churchill	7	48	CM
Giant	Presidente	8	50	CM
Torpedo	Torpedo	7	54	CM

A salute to the five centuries since Columbus's voyage to the Caribbean, this is a full-bodied blend of leaves from five nations, available in all-cedar boxes of 20.

HANDMADE CIGARS: BRAND LISTINGS

V.M. Santana Connecticut Collection
Handmade in Santiago, Dominican Republic.

Wrapper: USA/Connecticut   *Binder: Dom. Rep.*   *Filler: Dom. Rep.*

Shape	Name	Lgth	Ring	Wrapper
Robusto	Robusto	5	50	CC
Long Corona	Corona Grande	6	44	CC
Double Corona	Churchill	7	50	CC
Pyramid	Pyramid	6	54	CC

This was a new brand for 1996, with a mild body and a smooth, genuine Connecticut wrapper offered in limited distribution in boxes of 25 cigars each.

V.M. Santana Sumatra Collection
Handmade in Santiago, Dominican Republic.

Wrapper: Indonesia   *Binder: Dom. Rep.*   *Filler: Dom. Rep.*

Shape	Name	Lgth	Ring	Wrapper
Long Corona	Lonsdale	6	44	CM
Robusto	Robusto	5	50	CM
Double Corona	Churchill	7	50	CM

Mild but full of flavor, this blend of a Sumatra wrapper with Dominican Olor and Piloto Cubano leaves must be tasted to be appreciated. You'll find these red-labeled beauties in boxes of 25.

Valle del Sol
Handmade in San Andres Tuxtla, Mexico.

Wrapper: Mexico   *Binder: Mexico*   *Filler: Mexico*

Shape	Name	Lgth	Ring	Wrapper
Double Corona	Churchill	7½	50	CC
Long Corona	Lonsdale	6¼	42	CC
Robusto	Robusto	5	50	CC

Long Corona	Super Gordo	6¼	50	CC

New in 1997, this is a medium-bodied, long-filler brand that is offered in boxes of 25.

VAN WINKLE
Handmade in Navarette, Dominican Republic.

Wrapper: Indonesia   *Binder: Dom. Rep.*   *Filler: Dom. Rep.*

Shape	*Name*	*Lgth*	*Ring*	*Wrapper*
Churchill	Double Corona	6¾	48	CM

The Grand Cigar Company introduced this brand about ten minutes before we went to press. It is a medium-bodied cigar that features a Sumatra wrapper and Dominican-grown Olor binder. The brand is presented in protective cellophane sleeves and packed in elegant, easy-to-carry, all-cedar three-packs.

VANILLA DELIGHT
Handmade, with medium filler, in Santiago, Dominican Republic.

Wrapper: Indonesia   *Binder: Dom. Rep.*   *Filler: Dom. Rep.*

Shape	*Name*	*Lgth*	*Ring*	*Wrapper*
Long Corona		6	42	CM
Long Corona		6	44	CM

This is a medium-bodied cigar, available in two sizes, that was introduced in 1996. It utilizes all-Dominican filler and is offered in bundles of 25.

VANILLA SWEETS
Handmade in San Diego, California, USA.

Wrapper: Ecuador   *Binder: Ecuador*   *Filler: Honduras, Mexico*

Shape	*Name*	*Lgth*	*Ring*	*Wrapper*
Slim Panatela	Coronita	5¾	32	CM
Lonsdale	Especial	6½	40	CM
Petit Corona	Petit Corona	5	42	CM

HANDMADE CIGARS: BRAND LISTINGS

| Corona Extra | Emperador | 5½ | 46 | CM |
| Toro | Corona Grande | 6 | 50 | CM |

Here is a carefully-made, all-long-filler, flavored cigar that starts with Cuban-seed filler leaves and cures them with pure vanilla and a taste of honey. The quality of the result is obvious and you can try them in boxes of 25.

VARGAS
Handmade in Las Palmas, the Canary Islands of Spain.

Wrapper: Indonesia *Binder: Indonesia* *Filler: Canary Islands*

Shape	Name	Lgth	Ring	Wrapper
Churchill	Presidentes	6¾	46	CM
Corona Extra	Senadores	5½	46	CM
Panatela	Diplomaticos	5½	36	CM
Double Corona	Churchill	7½	50	CM
Corona	Capitolios	5⅛	44	CM
Robusto	Robustos	4¾	50	CM
Short Panatela	Cremas	4⅜	39	CM

This is an old brand which was re-introduced in 1996. It is mild in body and has excellent construction of primarily Indonesian leaves, offered in boxes of 25.

VEGA DEL REY
Handmade in Santiago, Dominican Republic.

Wrapper: Dom. Rep. *Binder: Dom. Rep.* *Filler: Dom. Rep.*

Shape	Name	Lgth	Ring	Wrapper
Double Corona	Toro	7	50	CC-Ma
Robusto	Robusto	4¾	52	CC-Ma
Long Corona	Corona	6	42	CC-Ma

This is a new brand in 1997 with all-Dominican-grown tobacco offering a medium-bodied smoke packed in cedar cabinets of 25 cigars each.

HANDMADE CIGARS: BRAND LISTINGS

VEGAS CUBANO
Handmade in Esteli, Nicaragua.

Wrapper: Indonesia   *Binder: Nicaragua*   *Filler: Dom. Rep., Nicaragua*

Shape	Name	Lgth	Ring	Wrapper
Robusto	Robusto	5	50	CC
Toro	Churchill	6	48	CC
Double Corona	President	7	50	CC
	Hand-molded:			
Double Corona	Churchill	6¾	50	Ma

Here is a full-flavored brand, exquisitely presented in shallow cedar boxes of five cigars, each equipped with a plexiglass window lid. The hand-molded shapes are completely hand pressed and no mold is used, a true challenge to the torcedor!

VENTURA
Handmade in Ocotal, Nicaragua.

Wrapper: Ecuador   *Binder: Indonesia*   *Filler: Nicaragua*

Shape	Name	Lgth	Ring	Wrapper
Giant	Presidente	8	50	CC
Double Corona	Churchill	7	49	CC
Toro	Toro	6	50	CC
Robusto	Robusto	5	50	CC
Lonsdale	Lonsdale	6½	44	CC
Corona	Corona	5½	42	CC

Introduced in 1996, this is a mild-to-medium-bodied cigar which features a Connecticut-seed wrapper grown in Ecuador, Sumatra binder plus Cuban-seed, Nicaraguan-grown filler leaves.

VERACRUZ
Handmade in San Andres Tuxtla, Mexico.

Wrapper: Mexico   *Binder: Mexico*   *Filler: Mexico*

HANDMADE CIGARS: BRAND LISTINGS

Shape	Name	Lgth	Ring	Wrapper
Small Panatela	Flor de Veracruz Carinas	4⅝	34	CC
Long Corona	Mina de Veracruz *(tubed)*	6¼	44	CC
Robusto	Corto de Veracruz *(tubed)*	5	50	CC
Robusto	Corta'o de Veracruz *(tubed)*	5	50	Ma
Torpedo	Corridos de Veracruz	4	47	CC
Torpedo	Marques de Veracruz *(tubed)*	5⅛	46	CC
Lonsdale	Poemas de Veracruz *(tubed)*	6¼	44	Ma
Churchill	Veracruz Magnum *(tubed)*	7⅞	48	CC

Introduced in 1994, Veracruz ultra-premium cigars are hand-rolled from a selection of choice Mexican tobaccos. Remarkably mild, yet flavorful with hints of honey, spices and coffee, Veracruz are guaranteed fresh. In fact, each of the larger-sized cigars are individually encased in glass tubes for air-tight safety.

VICTOR SINCLAIR
Handmade in Santiago, Dominican Republic.
Wrapper: Indonesia, USA/Connecticut
Binder: Dominican Republic   *Filler: Dominican Republic*

Shape	Name	Lgth	Ring	Wrapper
Double Corona	Churchill	7½	50	CC-Ma
Robusto	Robusto No. 1	5½	50	CC-Ma
Robusto	Robusto No. 2	4½	50	CC-Ma
Long Corona	Lonsdale	6	44	CC-Ma
Grand Corona	Corona	6	46	CC-Ma
Pyramid	Pyramid	7	54	CC-Ma

Introduced in 1995, this handmade cigar offers two different shades of wrapper: a natural wrapper grown in Connecticut and a maduro wrapper from Indonesia. The blend is medium in body and offered in boxes of 25.

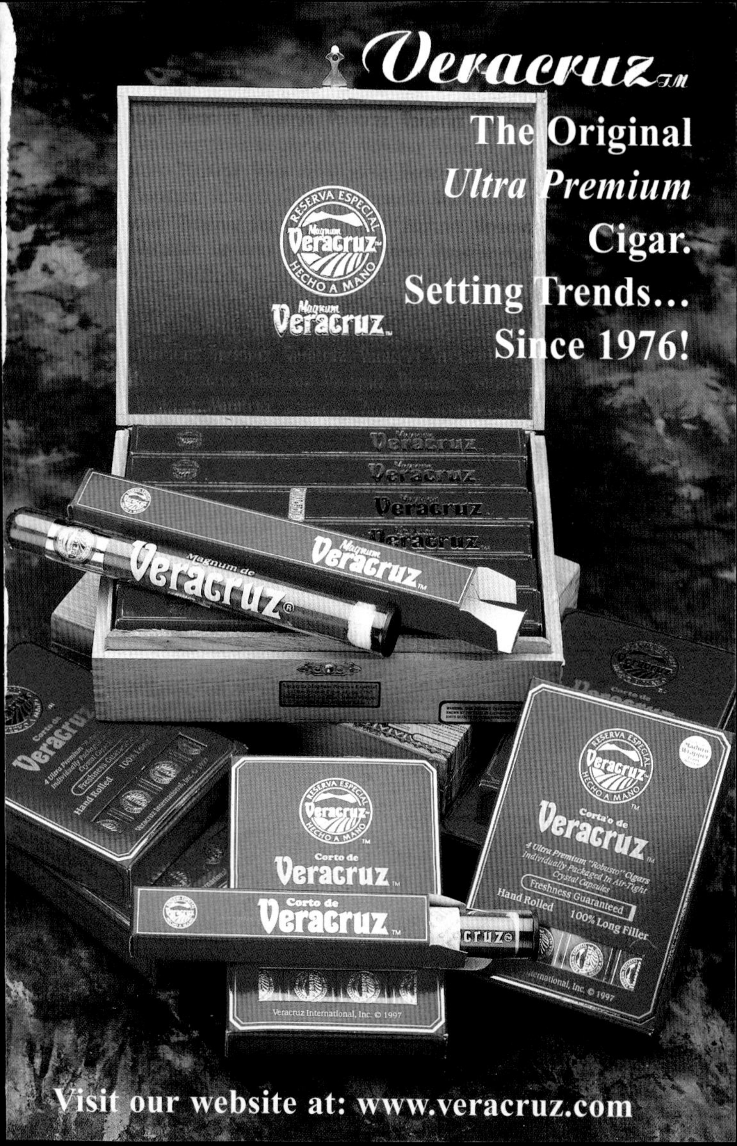
Veracruz TM
The Original
Ultra Premium
Cigar.
Setting Trends...
Since 1976!
RESERVA ESPECIAL
Magnum
Veracruz TM
HECHO A MANO
Magnum
Veracruz TM
Magnum de
Veracruz®
Magnum
Veracruz TM
Corto de
Veracruz TM
Corto de
Veracruz TM
Corta'o de
Veracruz TM
4 Ultra Premium "Robusto" Cigars
Individually Packaged In Air-Tight
Crystal Capsules
Freshness Guaranteed
Hand Rolled
100% Long Filler
Veracruz International, Inc. © 1997
Visit our website at: www.veracruz.com

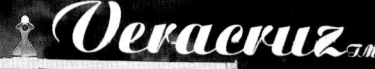

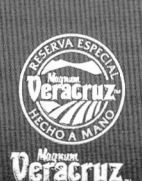

HANDMADE CIGARS: BRAND LISTINGS

VICTOR SINCLAIR GRAND RESERVE
Handmade in Santiago, Dominican Republic.

Wrapper: Indonesia   Binder: Dom. Rep.   Filler: Dom. Rep.

Shape	Name	Lgth	Ring	Wrapper
Long Panatela	Panatela	7	38	Ma
Corona Extra	Figurado	5	46	Ma
Torpedo	Belicoso	5¾	52	Ma
Pyramid	Pyramid	6	54	Ma

This is a full-bodied, Sumatra-clad cigar introduced in 1997. Available in maduro wrappers only, it is offered in boxes of ten (panatela), 15 (figurado and belicoso) or three (pyramid).

VICTOR SINCLAIR VINTAGE SELECT
Handmade in Santiago, Dominican Republic.

Wrapper: Dom. Rep.   Binder: Dom. Rep.   Filler: Dom. Rep.

Shape	Name	Lgth	Ring	Wrapper
Robusto	Robusto No. 1	4½	50	Ma
Robusto	Robusto No. 2	5½	50	Ma
Long Corona	Corona	6	44	Ma
Churchill	Double Corona	7	48	Ma
Double Corona	Churchill	7½	50	Ma

Here is a full-bodied cigar, introduced in 1996. It is offered in maduro wrapper only with all-Cuban seed binder and filler and presented in cedar boxes of 25

VICTORY SPIRIT
Handmade in Esteli, Nicaragua.

Wrapper: Indonesia   Binder: Nicaragua
Filler: Nicaragua and a proprietary Central American leaf

Shape	Name	Lgth	Ring	Wrapper
Corona	Champion	5¾	44	CC

Robusto	Victor	4¾	52	CC
Toro	Laureate	6	50	CC
Churchill	Conqueror	7	48	CC

Here is a special cigar introduced in 1996 under license from the Olympic Council of Ireland. Featuring the five Olympic rings on its Collector's Edition boxes, this is a mild and flavorful blend which features shade-grown, Havana-seed wrappers grown in Indonesia. Victory Spirit cigars are available in commemorative cedar cabinets of 12 (limited quantities) and in special cabinets of 24.

VILLA
Handmade in Villa Gonzalez, Dominican Republic.

Wrapper: Indonesia   *Binder: Dom. Rep.*   *Filler: Dom. Rep.*

Shape	*Name*	*Lgth*	*Ring*	*Wrapper*
Double Corona	Churchill	7½	50	CC
Robusto	Rothschild	4½	50	CC
Long Corona	Corona	6	44	CC

New for 1997, this is a very well constructed, medium-bodied cigar presented in all-cedar boxes of 25

VILLAR Y VILLAR
Handmade in Esteli, Nicaragua.

Wrapper: Ecuador   *Binder: Honduras*
Filler: Dominican Republic, Honduras, Nicaragua

Shape	*Name*	*Lgth*	*Ring*	*Wrapper*
Giant	Bermejos	8½	52	CC
Grand Corona	Cazadores	6½	46	CC
Lonsdale	Figaros	6½	44	CC
Short Panatela	Half Coronas	4½	38	CC
Robusto	Laguitos	4½	52	CC

HANDMADE CIGARS: BRAND LISTINGS

Pyramid	Pyramides	7	50	CC
Petit Corona	Remedios	4½	44	CC
Robusto	Robustos	4½	52	CC
Toro	Toros	6⅛	48	CC
Pyramid	Trumpet	7	48	CC
Corona	Tubos (tubed)	5⅝	44	CC
Churchill	Valentinos	6¾	48	CC
Double Corona	754s	7	54	CC

The romance of the great days of the Cuban cigar industry are re-kindled immediately by the mere mention of this the name of this storied brand. In 1996, it re-appeared as a modestly-priced, medium-to-heavy-bodied cigar with a Sumatra-seed wrapper grown in Ecuador. Originally offered in bundles, it will be presented in cedar boxes of 20 beginning in late 1997.

VILLEGA REALES
Handmade in Moca, Dominican Republic.

Wrapper: Sumatra   *Binder: Dom. Rep.*   *Filler: Dom. Rep.*

Shape	Name	Lgth	Ring	Wrapper
Corona	Corona	5½	43	CM
Churchill	Churchill	7	48	CM
Lonsdale	Lonsdale	7	43	CM
Robusto	Robusto	4¾	52	CM
Toro	Toro	6	50	CM

These handmade cigars were introduced in late 1996 and feature Dominican-grown Piloto Cubano filler leaves and Olor binders coupled with three-year-old Sumatra-grown wrappers. This is a medium-bodied brand produced under the supervision of Raul Diaz de Villega in the Montezuma factory in Moca, near Santiago, in the Dominican Republic.

A BREAK FOR SMOKERS OF HANDMADE/IMPORTED CIGARS.

INTRODUCING SIGLO 21, FLOR DE JALAPA AND LA DILIGENCIA CIGARS.

These exquisite handmade, long-filler cigars are all imported. Each cigar features carefully selected tobaccos for a satisfying taste and aroma.

They come from three of the finest tobacco growing regions of the world - Siglo 21s from the Dominican Republic, Flor de Jalapas from the Jalapa Valley of Nicaragua and La Diligencias from Honduras.

*Imported by
Swisher International, Inc.*

HANDMADE CIGARS: BRAND LISTINGS

VIP CLUB COLLECTION
Handmade in Santiago, Dominican Republic.

Wrapper: Indonesia   Binder: Dom. Rep.   Filler: Dom. Rep.

Shape	Name	Lgth	Ring	Wrapper
Double Corona	Presidente	7½	49	CC
Grand Corona	Suave	6½	47	CC
Robusto	Robusto	5	49	CC
	Flavored shape:			
Long Corona	Corona	6	43	CC

Here is a mild-bodied brand, introduced in 1997. It offers both a standard series and a flavored shape, available in Anisette and vanilla.

VIRTUOSO TORAÑO
Handmade in Danli, Honduras.

Wrapper: Costa Rica, Ecuador   Binder: Honduras
Filler: Costa Rica, Honduras, Nicaragua

Shape	Name	Lgth	Ring	Wrapper
Giant	Presidente	8	52	CC-Ma
Toro	Double Corona	6	50	CC-Ma
Robusto	Robusto	4¾	52	CC-Ma
Lonsdale	Lonsdale	7	44	CC
Long Corona	Cetros	6	43	CC

Introduced in 1995, Virtuoso is a long-filler, all hand-made cigar with a Colorado-Claro wrapper of Connecticut-seed origin grown in Ecuador. This and the blend of leaves from three nations in the filler and binder give this line a mild-to-medium body, but with plenty of taste. The maduro-wrapped shapes utilize leaf grown in Costa Rica.

V.S.O.P. VINTAGE RESERVE
Handmade in Santiago, Dominican Republic.

Wrapper: Indonesia   Binder: Dom. Rep.   Filler: Dom. Rep.

Shape	Name	Lgth	Ring	Wrapper
Double Corona	Churchill	7	50	CC
Robusto	Robusto	5	50	CC
Lonsdale	Lonsdale	6½	42	CC
Torpedo	Torpedo	6	54	CC
Corona	Corona	5½	42	CC

Here is a brand with Dominican Olor binder and filler, wrapped with a Sumatra-grown leaf. The result? A 1997-introduced, mild-bodied cigar with a slight taste of cognac used in the curing process that is offered in individual cellophane sleeves and packed in all-cedar cabinets.

VUELTABAJO
Handmade in Santiago, Dominican Republic.

Wrapper: USA/Connecticut   Binder: Dom. Rep.   Filler: Dom. Rep.

Shape	Name	Lgth	Ring	Wrapper
Giant	Gigante	8½	52	CC
Churchill	Churchill	7	48	CC
Robusto	Robusto	4¾	52	CC
Lonsdale	Lonsdale	7	43	CC
Toro	Toros	6	50	CC
Corona	Corona	5¾	42	CC
Pyramid	Pyramid	6¼	54	CC

Introduced in 1994, the Vueltabajo line is fine enough to bear the name of the most legendary tobacco-growing region in the world. Artfully crafted with a smooth Connecticut Shade wrapper, hand-selected Dominican Olor binder and the richest Dominican Piloto Cubano filler, this cigar is mild-to-medium in strength.

HANDMADE CIGARS: BRAND LISTINGS

WALL STREET PORTFOLIO COLLECTION
Handmade in Danli, Honduras.

Wrapper: Indonesia   *Binder: Honduras*   *Filler: Dom. Rep., Honduras*

Shape	Name	Lgth	Ring	Wrapper
Double Corona	Churchill	7	50	CC
Robusto	Robusto	5	50	CC
Lonsdale	Lonsdale	6½	42	CC
Torpedo	Torpedo	6	54	CC
Corona	Corona	5½	42	CC

Here is a medium-bodied cigar with a Sumatra wrapper and Dominican Olor and Honduran Piloto Cubano filler, introduced in 1997. It is presented in individual cellophane sleeves in elegant all-cedar cabinets of 25 cigars each.

WEST INDIES VANILLA
Handmade, with medium filler, in Jakarta, Indonesia.

Wrapper: Indonesia   *Binder: Indonesia*
Filler: Colombia, Dominican Republic, Indonesia

Shape	Name	Lgth	Ring	Wrapper
Cigarillo	Treasures	3⅜	20	CM
Short Panatela	Carmelita	4½	36	CM
Petit Corona	Carmela	4½	42	CM
Lonsdale	Grand Carmela	7	42	CM

This is a vanilla-flavored cigar produced by the Caribbean Cigar Company and introduced in 1995. It is handmade, but with medium filler instead of long filler leaves. It has a full-bodied taste and is offered in boxes of 25 cigars each.

WILD JAVANOS
Handmade in Java, Indonesia.

Wrapper: Indonesia   *Binder: Indonesia*   *Filler: Indonesia*

HANDMADE CIGARS: BRAND LISTINGS

Shape	Name	Lgth	Ring	Wrapper
Churchill	Argopuro	7	48	CC
Toro	Indopuro	6½	50	CC
Robusto	Stupa	5	50	CC
Long Corona	Puri	6	42	CC
Toro	Besuki	6	50	CC
Slim Panatela	Gadis	6	30	CC

Introduced in 1997 and medium in body, this all-Indonesian cigar is available in bundles of 25 cigars each.

XCLUSIVO
Handmade in Miami, Florida, USA.
Wrapper: Indonesia, Mexico

Binder: Indonesia or Nicaragua   *Filler: Brazil, Indonesia*

Shape	Name	Lgth	Ring	Wrapper
Giant	Gigante	8½	52	CM-Ma
Double Corona	Presidente	7¾	52	CM-Ma
Double Corona	Churchill	7	50	CM-Ma
Toro	Toro	6	50	CM-Ma
Robusto	Rothschild	5	50	CM-Ma
Lonsdale	No. 1	7	44	CM-Ma
Long Panatela	Panatela	7	36	CM-Ma
Pyramid	Piramide	6	52	CM-Ma

This line was introduced in 1996 and is available in natural (Java) and maduro (Mexican) wrappers. It offers a medium-to-full body and is packed in boxes of 25.

HANDMADE CIGARS: BRAND LISTINGS

XILADO
Handmade in Miami, Florida, USA.

Wrapper: Indonesia, Mexico   *Binder: Indonesia*
Filler: Brazil, Dominican Republic, Indonesia

Shape	Name	Lgth	Ring	Wrapper
Toro	Robusto	6	52	CM-Ma
Giant	Elegante	8	50	CM-Ma
Long Corona	Corona Especial	6	42	CM-Ma
Churchill	Imperial	6¾	46	CM-Ma
Torpedo	Torpedo Clasico	7	54	CM-Ma
Torpedo	Campanita	5	54	CM-Ma
Torpedo	Torpedo	6	54	CM-Ma
Lonsdale	Lancero	7½	40	CM-Ma
Long Panatela	Panatela	7	36	CM-Ma

This line debuted in 1996 and is a full-bodied smoke with excellent construction, offered in individual cellophane sleeves and packed in either wood boxes of 25, upright acrylic cases of 25 or the Torpedo in a plastic four-pack! Take your pick of Sumatra-grown natural wrappers or Mexican-grown maduro wrapped smokes.

XOTICA
Handmade, with mixed filler, in Miami, Florida, USA.

Wrapper: Nicaragua   *Binder: Indonesia*   *Filler: Dom. Rep., Indonesia, Nicaragua*

Shape	Name	Lgth	Ring	Wrapper
Long Corona	Corona	6	42	CC
Toro	Toro	6	50	CC

Want flavors? Here is a wild brand, new for 1997, mild in body and made with mixed filler accompanied by a Nicaraguan wrapper. The tobacco is cured prior to rolling and available flavors include (!) amaretto, black cherry, caffe con leche, chocolate, coconut, mango, menthol, piña colada, rum, tequila and vanilla. More are on the way!

HANDMADE CIGARS: BRAND LISTINGS

XQUISITO
Handmade in Esteli, Nicaragua.

Wrapper: Indonesia   *Binder: Nicaragua*   *Filler: Nicaragua*

Shape	Name	Lgth	Ring	Wrapper
Double Corona	Presidente	7½	52	CM
Churchill	Churchill	7	48	CM
Lonsdale	Lonsdale	6¾	43	CM
Robusto	Gran Rothschild	5½	50	CM

Here is a 1996-introduced cigar, with a Sumatran wrapper and a mild-to-medium body. Available in natural wrapper only, Xquisitos are packed in Spanish Cedar, cabinet-style boxes.

YULERDI
Handmade, with short filler, in Santiago, Dominican Republic.

Wrapper: Dom. Rep.   *Binder: Dom. Rep.*   *Filler: Dom. Rep.*

Shape	Name	Lgth	Ring	Wrapper
Robusto	Robusto	5	50	CM
Toro	Toro	6	50	CM
Lonsdale	Lonsdale	6½	44	CM
Churchill	Churchill	7	47	CM

Created in 1997, this is a short-filler brand with a mild body and all Dominican tobacco. Yulerdi is available in individual cellophane sleeves in bundles of 25.

YUMURI
Handmade in Navarrete, Dominican Republic.

Wrapper: USA/Connecticut   *Binder: Dom.Rep.*   *Filler: Dom.Rep.*

Shape	Name	Lgth	Ring	Wrapper
Toro	Toro	6	50	CC
Churchill	Churchill	7	48	CC

Robusto	Robusto	4¾	52	CC
Corona	Corona	5½	43	CC
Lonsdale	Lonsdale	7	43	CC

This brand was introduced late in 1995 and continues to expand its distribution. Mild in body, it features Piloto Cubano filler leaves surrounded by an Olor binder and a Connecticut Shade wrapper. Individually sleeved in cellophane, Yumuri cigars are presented in a hand-varnished boxes of 25.

YUMURI 1492
Handmade in Navarrete, Dominican Republic.

Wrapper: Indonesia   Binder: Dom. Rep.   Filler: Dom. Rep.

Shape	Name	Lgth	Ring	Wrapper
Toro	Toro	6	50	CC
Churchill	Churchill	7	48	CC
Robusto	Robusto	4¾	52	CC
Corona	Corona	5½	43	CC
Lonsdale	Lonsdale	7	43	CC

This second Yumuri style also features a Sumatran wrapper, which helps to produce a mild to medium-bodied taste to the brand.

ZELO DE CUBA
Handmade in Santiago, Dominican Republic.

Wrapper: Indonesia   Binder: Dom. Rep.   Filler: Dom. Rep.

Shape	Name	Lgth	Ring	Wrapper
Double Corona	Churchill	7	50	CM
Toro	Toro	6	50	CM
Robusto	Robusto	5	50	CM
Corona	Corona	5½	42	CM
Lonsdale	Lonsdale	6½	44	CM

Pyramid	Piramid	6	52	CM

Carefully blended to offer a medium-bodied taste, this brand was introduced in 1997. You can enjoy it in boxes of 25!

ZINO

Handmade in Santa Rosa de Copan, Honduras.

Wrapper: Ecuador   *Binder: Honduras*   *Filler: Honduras*

Shape	Name	Lgth	Ring	Wrapper
Cigarillo	Princesse	4¼	25	CC
Panatela	Diamonds	5⅝	38	CC
Lonsdale	Tradition	6¼	44	CC
Double Corona	Veritas	7	49	CC
Panatela	Tubos No. 1 *(tubed)*	6¾	35	CC
	Connoisseur Series:			
Double Corona	Connoisseur 100	7½	52	CC
Toro	Connoisseur 200	6½	48	CC
Grand Corona	Connoisseur 300	5¾	46	CC
	Mouton-Cadet Series:			
Lonsdale	Mouton-Cadet No. 1	6¼	44	CC
Panatela	Mouton-Cadet No. 2	6	35	CC
Panatela	Mouton-Cadet No. 3	5¾	38	CC
Slim Panatela	Mouton-Cadet No. 4	5⅛	30	CC
Petit Corona	Mouton-Cadet No. 5	5	42	CC
Robusto	Mouton-Cadet No. 6	5	50	CC

The subtlety of Davidoff combined with the finest Honduran tobaccos and a Connecticut-seed wrapper is expressed in the Zino line. The Mouton-Cadet series was specially selected for Baronne Philippine de Rothschild, offering a rich aroma and a mild taste.

5.
MASS-MARKET CIGARS: INDEX

Here are 124 machine-made brands of cigars listed in a compact index to country of origin and shapes.

For each brand, a two-letter code designates the country of manufacture:

Be	Belgium	In	Indonesia
Br	Brazil	Mx	Mexico
CI	Canary Islands	Ne	Netherlands
CR	Costa Rica	Ni	Nicaragua
DR	Dominican Republic	PR	Puerto Rico
Ge	Germany	Sz	Switzerland
Ho	Honduras	US	United States

In addition, each line lists (1) whether the brand includes at least one all-tobacco shape and (2) the shape "groups" in which each brand is produced. The 19 standard shapes listed in section 1.03 are broken into ten groups, including:

1. Cigarillo

2. Panatela group
- Small Panatela
- Slim Panatela
- Short Panatela
- Panatela
- Long Panatela

3. Corona group
- Petit Corona
- Corona
- Long Corona

4. Lonsdale group
- Lonsdale
- Giant Corona

5. Grand Corona group
- Corona Extra
- Grand Corona

6. Figurado group
- Culebras
- Perfecto
- Pyramid
- Torpedo

MASS-MARKET CIGARS: INDEX

7. Robusto-Toro group
- Robusto
- Toro

8. Churchill
9. Double Corona
10. Giant

New listings (or brands with name changes) are indicated by the "+" symbol. Additional, detailed information about each of these brands is available in the following section, offering brand listings.

Brand	Made in	All-tobacco	Cigarillo	Panatela	Corona	Lonsdale	Grand Corona	Figurado	Robusto-Toro	Churchill	Double Corona	Giant
Antonio y Cleopatra	PR		●	●	●				●			
Arango Sportsman	US		●	●		●			●	●		
As You Like It	US		●	●								
Balmoral	Ne	●	●	●	●							
Bances	US	●		●	●		●		●			
Ben Bey	US				●							
Ben Franklin	PR				●							
Black & Mild	US			●								
Black Hawk	US						●					
Budd Sweet	US			●	●							
Candlelight	Ge	●	●	●								
Caribbean Rounds	US			●		●						
Casino Club +	US				●		●		●			
Cazadores +	US			●	●							

MASS-MARKET CIGARS: INDEX

Brand	Made in	All-tobacco	Cigarillo	Panatela	Corona	Lonsdale	Grand Corona	Figurado	Robusto-Toro	Churchill	Double Corona	Giant
Charles Denby	US				●							
Cherry Blend	US			●								
Cima	PR				●							
Corps Diplomatique	Be	●		●	●			●				
Cuesta-Rey	US			●	●							
Cyrilla	US			●	●						●	
De Olifant	Ne	●	●	●								
Decision Maduro	US			●	●		●		●			
Dexter Londres	US				●							
Directors	US		●	●	●							
Don Antonio	Ge	●	●	●								
Don Cesar	US				●							
Dry Slitz	US			●								
Dutch Masters	PR US		● ●	●	●		●		●			
1886	PR				●							
El Cauto	US	●			●	●	●					
El Gozo +	CI	●	●	●	●				●			
El Macco	US	●					●					
El Producto	PR			●	●		●		●			
El Trelles	US				●		●	●				
El Verso	US	●	●	●			●					

MASS-MARKET CIGARS: INDEX

Brand	Made in	All-tobacco	Cigarillo	Panatela	Corona	Lonsdale	Grand Corona	Figurado	Robusto-Toro	Churchill	Double Corona	Giant
Emanuelo +	US	●			●		●					
Emerson	US				●							
Evermore	US	●			●		●					
Farnam Drive	US	●					●					
Figaro	US	●				●						
Flor de Borinquen	PR				●							
Florida Queen	US				●							
Garcia Grande	US				●			●	●	●		
Garcia y Vega	DR US		●	●	●							
Gargoyle	US			●								
George Burns Vintage +	DR	●			●		●				●	
Gold & Mild	US			●								
Governor +	US				●							
Harvester	PR				●							
Hauptmann's	US			●	●		●					
Hav-A-Tampa	US		●	●	●							
Havana Blend	US	●	●	●	●	●				●	●	
De Heeren van Ruysdael	Ne	●		●								
Henry the Fourth	US				●		●			●		
Ibold	US	●	●	●	●				●			

MASS-MARKET CIGARS: INDEX

Brand	Made in	All-tobacco	Cigarillo	Panatela	Corona	Lonsdale	Grand Corona	Figurado	Robusto-Toro	Churchill	Double Corona	Giant
J. Cortes	Be	●	●	●								
J-R Famous	US			●	●	●			●			
John Hay +	US	●					●		●			
Jose Melendi	US	●		●	●	●	●		●			
Keep Moving	US				●							
King Edward	US		●	●	●							
La Eminencia	US	●		●	●	●						
La Fendrich	US			●			●					
La Paz	Ne	●	●	●	●							
Lancer	US	●		●								
Le Petit Chateau +	PR	●		●								
Lord Beaconsfield	US			●	●						●	
Lord Clinton	US			●	●							
Lucky Lady +	US	●				●						
Marsh	US			●								
Miflin's Choice	US			●								
Mocha Lights +	US						●					
Moya Gusto	US			●	●	●						
Mr. B +	US						●					
Muniemaker	US	●		●			●	●	●			
Muriel	PR US		● ●	●	●		●					
Nat Cicco's	US			●	●	●					●	

MASS-MARKET CIGARS: INDEX

Brand	Made in	All-tobacco	Cigarillo	Panatela	Corona	Lonsdale	Grand Corona	Figurado	Robusto-Toro	Churchill	Double Corona	Giant
National Cigar	US				●							
Odin	US				●							
Old Hermitage	US	●					●					
Optimo	US			●	●							
Palma	US					●						
Pedro Iglesias	US	●			●	●	●					
Phillies	US		●	●	●							
Phillips & King Cigarren +	Ge	●		●	●		●					
Pollack	US			●								
R.G. Dun	US		●	●	●							
Red Dot	US			●	●							
Rigoletto	US			●	●		●					
Rivalo	PR	●	●		●							
Robert Burns	DR US		●		●							
Roi-Tan	PR			●	●							
Rosedale	US	●					●	●				
Royal Hawaiian +	US	●				●						
Ruy Lopez	US	●		●	●		●					
San Felice	US				●							
Schimmelpennink	Ne	●		●	●							
Sierra Sweet	US			●								

MASS-MARKET CIGARS: INDEX

Brand	Made in	All-tobacco	Cigarillo	Panatela	Corona	Lonsdale	Grand Corona	Figurado	Robusto-Toro	Churchill	Double Corona	Giant
'63 Air-Flo	US				●							
Sweet-Nut +	US			●								
Swisher Sweets	US	●	●	●	●							
Tampa Cub	US				●							
Tampa Nugget	US		●	●	●							
Tampa Resagos	US				●							
Tampa Sweet	US		●	●	●							
Tayo	PR	●			●							
The Cigar Baron	US	●					●	●				
Topper	US	●			●		●	●				
Topstone	US	●		●	●		●			●		
Travis Club Premium	US	●			●		●	●	●		●	
Vasco da Gama	Ge	●			●							
Villa de Cuba	US				●	●						
Villazon Deluxe	US				●							
Villazon Deluxe Aromatics	US			●	●							
White Owl	US		●	●	●							
Willem II	Ne	●			●							
Wm. Ascot	US			●		●						
William Penn	US		●	●	●							
Windsor & Mark IV	US			●	●	●						

MASS-MARKET CIGARS: INDEX

Brand		Made in	All-tobacco	Cigarillo	Panatela	Corona	Lonsdale	Grand Corona	Figurado	Robusto-Toro	Churchill	Double Corona	Giant
Wolf Bros.		US		●	●				●				
Wuhrmann	+	Sz	●		●	●	●	●		●			
X-Rated	+	US			●								
Y.B.		US				●							
Zino		Ne	●	●									
		Sz	●		●	●		●					

6.
MACHINE-MADE CIGARS

This section provides the details on 124 brands of mass-market cigars, generally made by machine for distribution to the widest possible audience in drug stores, supermarkets and, of course, tobacco stores.

Each brand listing includes notes on country of manufacture, shapes, names, lengths, ring gauges and wrapper color *as supplied by the manufacturers and/or distributors of these brands.* Ring gauges for some brands of cigarillos were not available.

Please note that while a cigar may be manufactured in one country, it may contain tobaccos from many nations. All brands utilize short-filler tobaccos unless otherwise noted.

For ease of reference, those brands with at least *one* all-tobacco shape in their line have been grouped together at the front of this section and the remaining brands – those using homogenized (sheet) leaf – follow in alphabetical order in the next grouping.

Although manufacturers have recognized more than 70 shades of wrapper color, six major color classifications are used here. Their abbreviations include:

- ‣ DC = Double Claro: green, also known as "AMS."
- ‣ Cl = Claro: a very light tan color.
- ‣ CC = Colorado Claro: a medium brown common to many cigars on this list.

MACHINE-MADE CIGARS: BRAND LISTINGS

▸ Co = Colorado: reddish-brown.
▸ CM = Colorado Maduro: dark brown.
▸ Ma = Maduro: very dark brown or black (also known as "double Maduro" or "Oscuro.")

Many manufacturers call their wrapper colors "Natural" or "English Market Selection." These colors cover a wide range of browns and we have generally grouped them in the "CC" range. Darker wrappers such as those from the Cameroons show up most often in the "CM" category.

Shape designations are based on our shape chart in section 1.03. Careful readers will note the freedom with which manufacturers attach names of shapes to cigars which do not resemble that shape at all! For easier comparison, all lengths were rounded to the shortest eighth of an inch, although some manufacturers list sizes in 16ths or even 32nds of an inch.

Readers who would like to see their favorite brand listed in the 1999 edition can call or write the compilers as noted after the Table of Contents.

BRANDS WITH ALL-TOBACCO SHAPES

BALMORAL
Machine-made in Duizel, the Netherlands.

Shape	Name	Lgth	Ring	Wrapper
Cigarillo	Shetlands	3⅝	24	CM
Small Panatela	Midlands	4	30	CM
Slim Panatela	Overland	5¼	32	CM

MACHINE-MADE CIGARS: BRAND LISTINGS

This brand was introduced in 1996, offering an all-tobacco cigar with mild-to-medium body and outstanding quality. All of these cigars feature gorgeous Sumatran wrappers, with Java binders and filler blends chosen from premium Brazilian, Javan and Sumatran leaves. The results are outstanding, as is the presentation: an all-cedar box of 10 or 25 cigars or a carton of 10s for the road.

BANCES
Machine-made in Tampa, Florida, USA.

Shape	Name	Lgth	Ring	Wrapper
Robusto	Crowns	5¾	50	Ma
Small Panatela	Demi-Tasse	4	35	CC-Ma
Slim Panatela	Havana Holders	6½	30	CC-Ma
Long Corona	Palmas	6	42	CC-Ma
Grand Corona	No. 3	5¾	46	CC-Ma

This respected brand is also a well-known handmade cigar. The machine-made version offers a Sumatra (natural) or Connecticut (maduro) wrapper, Connecticut binder and a blend of tobaccos from three nations in the filler. Only the Crowns shape uses a homogenized binder. You can find Bances in boxes of 25, except for the Demi-Tasse, offered in 50s.

CANDLELIGHT
Machine-made in Dingelstadt, Germany.

Shape	Name	Lgth	Ring	Wrapper
Cigarillo	Mini Sumatra	2⅞	20	CC
Cigarillo	Mini Brazil	2⅞	20	Ma
Small Panatela	Senorita Sumatra	3¾	30	CC
Small Panatela	Senorita Brazil	3¾	30	Ma
Cigarillo	Panatela Sumatra	5¾	20	CC
Cigarillo	Panatela Brazil	5¾	20	Ma
Small Panatela	Corona Slim Sumatra	4	30	CC
Small Panatela	Corona Slim Brazil	4	30	Ma

MACHINE-MADE CIGARS: BRAND LISTINGS

Short Panatela	Block Corona Sumatra	4¾	38	CC
Short Panatela	Block Corona Brazil	4¾	38	Ma
Petit Corona	Aviso	4	43	CC
Cigarillo	Tip (tipped)	4⅛	25	CC

These small cigars are all-tobacco with a mild taste. The two types are puros; all of the tobacco in the Sumatra-named shapes is from Sumatra, likewise with the Brazilian shapes. Candlelights are offered in tins of 10, or boxes of 25 or 50.

THE CIGAR BARON
Machine-made in the United States.

Shape	Name	Lgth	Ring	Wrapper
Corona Extra	Corona Extra	5¾	45	CC-Ma
Figurado	Perfecto	4¼	43	CC-Ma

These all-tobacco, mild-to-medium bodied cigars feature genuine Connecticut Shade wrappers around a Connecticut Broadleaf binder and Dominican and Honduran fillers. Regularly available in boxes of 50, this brand also offers specially decorated boxes marked "Cigars for Dad" and a colorful holiday box featuring Santa Claus!

CORPS DIPLOMATIQUE
Machine-made in Leuven, Belgium.

Shape	Name	Lgth	Ring	Wrapper
Small Panatela	Deauville	4	34	CC
Small Panatela	Panatela	4⅛	33	CC
Corona	After Dinner	5¼	42	CC
Small Panatela	Gouveneur	4½	33	CC
Slim Panatela	International	5¼	34	CC
Torpedo	Senator	4½	44	CC
Corona	Conference	5¼	42	CC

MACHINE-MADE CIGARS: BRAND LISTINGS

This all-tobacco range of dry-cured cigars offers a mild taste, featuring an Indonesian (Sumatra) wrapper, Java binder and Brazilian and Indonesian filler.

DE OLIFANT
Machine-made in Kampen, the Netherlands.

Shape	Name	Lgth	Ring	Wrapper
Cigarillo	Fantje	3	20	CC
Small Panatela	Knakje	3½	31	CC
Short Panatela	Corona	4½	36	CC
Slim Panatela	Panatela	5	32	CC
Cigarillo	Matelieff	3½	32	CC
Cigarillo	VOC	3½	30	CC

A famous all-tobacco, dry-cured brand in Holland since 1884, De Olifant's line of small cigars comes to the U.S. in 1996. The line offers a full-bodied taste in the smaller sizes and a medium-to-full flavor in the larger shapes. All of these cigars feature Sumatran "sand" wrappers and Javan binders, with filler tobaccos blended from leaves grown in Brazil, Java and Sumatra.

DON ANTONIO
Machine-made in Dingelstadt, Germany.

Shape	Name	Lgth	Ring	Wrapper
Cigarillo	Carmen Sumatra	4½	20	CC
Cigarillo	Carmen Brazil	4½	20	Ma
Cigarillo	El Cerro Sumatra	3½	25	CC
Cigarillo	El Cerro Brazil	3½	25	Ma
Cigarillo	El Lupo Sumatra	3	20	CC
Cigarillo	El Lupo Brazil	3	20	Ma
Slim Panatela	El Gusto Sumatra	6⅛	33	CC
Slim Panatela	El Gusto Brazil	6⅛	33	Ma

Short Panatela	El Toro Sumatra	4⅜	38	CC
Short Panatela	El Toro Brazil	4⅜	38	Ma
Panatela	La Verdad Sumatra	5½	35	CC
Panatela	La Verdad Brazil	5½	35	Ma

This small cigar range was introduced in 1992 and offers either Brazilian or Sumatran wrappers on each shape for a mild-to-medium (Sumatra) or medium-to-full-bodied (Brazil) taste. The binder on all shapes is Indonesian, with filler tobacco from Brazil, the Dominican Republic, Germany, Honduras and Indonesia.

EL CAUTO
Machine-made in Yoe, Pennsylvania, USA.

Shape	Name	Lgth	Ring	Wrapper
Long Corona	Blunt	6	43	CC
Long Corona	Corona Grande	6⅜	44	CC
Grand Corona	Fumas	6⅜	46	CC
Lonsdale	Super Fumas	7	44	CC

This brand includes one all-tobacco style (Corona Grande) and three others which use a sheet binder. El Cautos are offered in either boxes of 50 or bundles of 25.

EL GOZO
Machine-made in Las Palmas, the Canary Islands of Spain.

Shape	Name	Lgth	Ring	Wrapper
Long Corona	Gran Cedro	6	43	CC
Toro	Doble Corona	6¼	49	CC
Robusto	Robusto	5¼	50	CC
Corona	Corona	5¼	42	CC
Small Panatela	Petit Torpedo	4⅛	33	CC

Lonsdales, Coronas Extra and Grand Coronas

Here are examples of three larger-sized cigars: the Lonsdale (named for the Earl of Lonsdale), the Corona Extra and the Grand Corona. The dimensions of these shapes include:

- Lonsdale   6½-7¼ inches long; 40-44 ring.
- Giant Corona   7½ inches and more; 42-45 ring.
- Corona Extra   4½-5½ inches long; 45-47 ring.
- Grand Corona   5⅝-6⅞ inches long; 45-47 ring.

Pictured opposite, from left to right, are:

- **HUGO CASSAR DIAMOND**   *(shape)*
  DOMINICAN MYSTIQUE *Lonsdale*
  (Dominican Republic) 6¾ x 42   Lonsdale

- **CROWN ACHIEVEMENT** *Lonsdale*
  (Honduras)   6½ x 42   Lonsdale

- **ANDUJAR** *Macorix*
  (Dominican Republic) 6¼ x 44   Lonsdale

- **NICOLE MILLER** *Aristocrat*
  (Dominican Republic) 6½ x 46   Grand Corona

- **ROLY** *Corona de Lux*
  (Honduras)   6½ x 46   Grand Corona

- **1861** *Lincoln*
  (Dominican Republic) 6½ x 46   Grand Corona

Cigarillo	Miniatures	3¾	24	CC
Cigarillo	Aromatics	3½	23	CC

This Canary Islands line offers all-tobacco shapes with full body and short filler from the Dominican Republic, Honduras, Indonesia and Germany, offered in boxes of 25. The very small sizes: Petit Torpedo, Miniatures and Aromatics have sheet binders and are offered in boxes of 20, except for the Aromatics, offered in 10s.

EL MACCO
Machine-made in Frankfort, Indiana, USA.

Shape	Name	Lgth	Ring	Wrapper
Corona Extra	Puritano Dark	4¾	45	CM

This brand presents a medium-bodied taste and has a Connecticut leaf wrapper, sheet or Connecticut binder and a blend of Dominican and U.S. tobacco in the filler.

EL VERSO
Machine-made in Frankfort, Indiana, USA.

Shape	Name	Lgth	Ring	Wrapper
Grand Corona	Corona Extra	5¾	47	CM
Corona Extra	Bouquet Dark	4¾	45	CM
Panatela	Commodore	6	36	CM
Corona Extra	Bouquet Light Leaf	4¾	45	CI
Cigarillo	Mellow	4¼	29	CI-CM

The sunny graphics on the El Verso box herald a medium-bodied cigar with a Connecticut wrapper, either a Connecticut or sheet wrapper depending on the model, and American and Dominican filler.

EMANELO
Machine-made in Frankfort, Indiana, USA.

MACHINE-MADE CIGARS: BRAND LISTINGS

Shape	Name	Lgth	Ring	Wrapper
Grand Corona	Gourmet	5¾	47	CC
Long Corona	Executive	6	42	CC
Corona Extra	Premium	5⅛	45	CC
Corona Extra	Classic	4⅝	45	CC

Here's the right cigar for the discerning smoker! Introduced in 1997, this is a mild-to-medium-bodied, all-tobacco blend of aged Connecticut broadleaf wrapper, a broadleaf binder and Connecticut and Pennsylvania filler. A very old brand name, Emanelo was much admired by midwestern smokers in the middle of this century.

EVERMORE
Machine-made in Frankfort, Indiana, USA.

Shape	Name	Lgth	Ring	Wrapper
Corona Extra	Original	4⅝	45	CI-CC-CM
Long Corona	Palma	6	42	CI-CM
Grand Corona	Corona Grande	5¾	47	CI-CM

This is an all-tobacco cigar, with a Connecticut leaf wrapper, Connecticut binder and a blend of American and Dominican tobaccos in the filler.

FARNAM DRIVE
Machine-made in Frankfort, Indiana, USA.

Shape	Name	Lgth	Ring	Wrapper
Corona Extra	Original	5⅛	45	CC-CC-Ma

This is an all-tobacco cigar that offers a medium-bodied taste and uses Connecticut leaves for the wrapper and binder and a blend of American and Dominican tobaccos in the filler.

FIGARO
Machine-made in San Antonio, Texas, USA.

MACHINE-MADE CIGARS: BRAND LISTINGS

Shape	Name	Lgth	Ring	Wrapper
Lonsdale	Figaro	6½	40	CC-Ma

This is a medium-bodied blend of 100% tobacco, which features a Connecticut wrapper and binder and filler tobaccos from the Dominican Republic. It is offered in colorful canisters of 25 each.

GEORGE BURNS VINTAGE
Machine-made in La Romana, Dominican Republic.

Shape	Name		Lgth	Ring	Wrapper
Double Corona	Churchill		7	50	CC
Grand Corona	Double Corona		6½	46	CC
Long Corona	Lonsdale		6	42	CC
Grand Corona	Monarch	*(tubed)*	6½	46	CC

Here is a 1997-introduced tribute to the late George Burns (1896-1996), remembered as a great comedian and as a devoted cigar smoker. These are mild-bodied, all-tobacco cigars, with an Indonesian wrapper, Pennsylvania-grown binder and long and medium filler leaves from the Dominican Republic and Jamaica.

HAVANA BLEND
Machine-made in San Antonio, Texas, USA.

Shape	Name	Lgth	Ring	Wrapper
Short Panatela	Petit Corona	4¾	38	Ma
Cigarillo	Palma Fina	6½	29	Ma
Corona	Coronado	5	43	Ma
Corona	Delicado	5¾	43	Ma
Robusto	Rothschild	5	50	Ma
Lonsdale	Doubloon	6½	42	Ma
Churchill	Churchill	7	47	Ma

MACHINE-MADE CIGARS: BRAND LISTINGS

This is a medium-bodied blend of 100% tobacco, which includes Cuban tobacco from the 1959 crop, as well as Dominican tobacco, in the filler. The wrapper and binder are both Connecticut Broadleaf and the brand is offered in boxes of either 25 or 50 cigars.

DE HEEREN VAN RUYSDAEL
Machine-made in Valkenswaard, the Netherlands.

Shape	Name	Lgth	Ring	Wrapper
Panatela	Invincibles Grandes XO	6⅝	35	CC

This premium brand from Holland uses only the finest tobaccos from Indonesia (wrapper, binder and filler) and Brazil (filler) to create this medium-bodied masterpiece. Each all-cedar box is specially prepared to keep these cigars at their peak, including a special in-the-box humidifier!

IBOLD
Machine-made in Frankfort, Indiana, USA.

Shape	Name	Lgth	Ring	Wrapper
Petit Corona	Blunt	4⅞	44	Cl-CM
Petit Corona	Black Pete	4⅞	44	CM
Robusto	Breva	5⅛	51	Cl-Ma
Cigarillo	Cigarillo	4¼	29	Cl-CM
Panatela	Ideals	5⅞	38	Cl-CM
Short Panatela	Slims	5¼	35	Cl-CM

Manufactured by the National Cigar Corporation, this brand offers a medium-bodied taste thanks to its Connecticut leaf wrapper, sheet or Connecticut binder - depending on the shape - and the filler blend of U.S. and Dominican leaves.

J. CORTES
Machine-made in Moene, Belgium.

Shape	Name	Lgth	Ring	Wrapper
Short Panatela	Casadores	5	38	CC

MACHINE-MADE CIGARS: BRAND LISTINGS

Cigarillo	Classic	4¼	25	CC
Small Panatela	Club	4½	30	CC
Cigarillo	Grand Luxe	4	25	CC
Cigarillo	Havane	3¾	23	CC
Short Panatela	High Class *(tubed)*	5	38	CC
Small Panatela	Milord	4¼	30	CC
Cigarillo	Mini	3⅓	19	CC
Short Panatela	Presidency	4⅛	38	CC
Slim Panatela	Slim Corona	5⅛	34	CC
Slim Panatela	Royal Class *(tubed)*	5¼	30	CC

A European tradition since 1926, J. Cortes is gaining in popularity in the U.S. It is an all-tobacco brand, with Sumatran wrappers, Java binder and blended filler of tobaccos from Brazil and Indonesia. The J. Cortes "blue box" offers a mild taste in boxes of 10, 25 or 50 depending on shape.

JOHN HAY
Machine-made in York, Pennsylvania, USA.

Shape	Name	Lgth	Ring	Wrapper
Robusto	Cadet	5	49	CM
Grand Corona	Diplomat	6	47	CM-Ma

This brand goes back to 1882, when W.W. Stewart actually obtained permission from prominent American statesman John Hay – later Secretary of State – to issue a brand in his honor. The machine-made version is all tobacco, with a Lancaster County, Pennsylvania Broadleaf wrapper, Pennsylvania binder and a medium-filler blend from Connecticut, Maryland and Pennsylvania. This all-American cigar is offered in boxes of 50; be sure to check out the handmade, Dominican-produced version as well. Light one up on the Fourth of July!

JOSE MELENDI
Machine-made in San Antonio, Texas, USA.

MACHINE-MADE CIGARS: BRAND LISTINGS

Shape	Name	Lgth	Ring	Wrapper
Short Panatela	Vega I	5⅜	37	CM
Corona	Vega II	5½	43	CM
Long Corona	Vega III	6	42	CM
Slim Panatela	Vega IV	6½	34	CM
Grand Corona	Vega V	6½	45	CM
Lonsdale	Vega VII	7	45	CM
Slim Panatela	Wild Maduro	6⅞	34	Ma
Robusto	Rothschild Maduro	5	50	Ma

This is a medium-to-full bodied, long-filler blend of 100% tobacco, with a Cameroon wrapper on the Vega series and Connecticut Broadleaf wrappers on the maduro styles. The binder is also Connecticut leaf, with the filler composed of tobaccos from Brazil and the Dominican Republic.

LA EMINENCIA
Machine-made in Tampa, Florida, USA.

Shape	Name	Lgth	Ring	Wrapper
Lonsdale	Churchill Corona	6½	45	CC-Ma
Corona	Brevas	5½	44	CC-Ma
Long Corona	Plazas	6¼	42	CC-Ma
Panatela	Panetelas	6¼	38	CC-Ma

This is a mild-to-medium bodied brand of 100% tobacco, available in two wrapper shades. The wrappers are Ecuadorian-grown, with a Honduran binder and long filler from the Dominican Republic, Honduras and Nicaragua. It is offered is all-cedar boxes of 25.

LA PAZ
Machine-made in Valkenswaard, the Netherlands.

MACHINE-MADE CIGARS: BRAND LISTINGS

Shape	Name		Lgth	Ring	Wrapper
Long Corona	Gran Corona	(tubed)	6	42	CC
Slim Panatela	Wilde Havana		4⅞	33	CC
Cigarillo	Wilde Cigarillos		4⅛	24	CC

The well-known La Paz brand, made of 100% tobacco, dates back to 1814. It is widely appreciated for the "Wilde" series which has an uncut end that provides a rich aroma from the first moment. Both of the Wilde shapes are full-bodied, while the Gran Corona offers a mild taste. The wrappers and binders are all Bezuki leaf from Indonesia, with filler blends of Brazilian and Indonesian tobacco.

LANCER
Machine-made in San Antonio, Texas, USA.

Shape	Name	Lgth	Ring	Wrapper
Small Panatela	Havana Slims	6¼	29	CM

Here is a cigar made of 100% tobacco, including filler tobacco from the 1958 and 1959 Cuban crops. The wrapper and binder are both genuine Connecticut leaf; Lancers are offered in eight-cigar pocket packs.

LE PETIT CHATEAU
Machine-made in Mayaguez, Puerto Rico.

Shape	Name	Lgth	Ring	Wrapper
Small Panatela	Le Petit Chateau	4	32	CC

Here is an all-tobacco, mild-bodied small cigar that utilizes all-Puerto Rican tobacco. It is offered in a box of 50.

LUCKY LADY
Machine-made in Red Lion, Pennsylvania, USA.

Shape	Name		Lgth	Ring	Wrapper
Lonsdale	Corona	(tubed)	6½	43	CM

MACHINE-MADE CIGARS: BRAND LISTINGS

This new, all-tobacco brand for 1997 offers a Connecticut wrapper, imported binder and a blend of imported short-filler tobaccos for an enjoyable mild smoke. Bonus: the wrapper and filler are specially imbued with a rich cherry flavor! Available in single units only.

MUNIEMAKER
Machine-made in McSherrystown, Pennsylvania, USA.

Shape	Name	Lgth	Ring	Wrapper
Corona Extra	Regular	4½	47	Cl-CC-CM
Robusto	Straight	5⅛	48	CC
Grand Corona	Long	6	46	CC
Robusto	Breva 100's	5⅛	48	CC-Ma
Slim Panatela	Panatela 100's	6	33	CC-Ma
Grand Corona	Palma 100's	6	46	CC-Ma
Perfecto	Perfecto 100's	5¼	52	CC-Ma
Corona Extra	Cueto	4⅞	45	Cl-CC
Corona Extra	Bouquet Special (tubed)	5⅛	46	CC-Ma
Corona Extra	Judges Cave	4½	47	Cl-CC-Ma

F.D. Grave began this line in 1884 with the goal of making "the best possible cigars at prices cigar lovers could afford." Now, F.D. Grave & Sons continues this tradition of all-tobacco, medium-to-full-bodied cigars, featuring Connecticut Broadleaf wrappers and binders around a core of U.S. tobaccos in the filler. The Perfecto 100s and Bouquet Specials are boxed in 25s, while all of the other shapes are available in boxes of 50. Handy packs of four and five cigars each are also available of most sizes.

OLD HERMITAGE
Machine-made in Hartford, Connecticut, USA.

Shape	Name	Lgth	Ring	Wrapper
Corona Extra	Golden Perfecto	5½	45	Cl

MACHINE-MADE CIGARS: BRAND LISTINGS

This brand was created in 1908 and is 100% tobacco. The wrapper and binder are Connecticut broadleaf, with the filler incorporating Brazilian, Dominican and U.S. tobaccos. The shape has a perfecto-style tip and is offered in boxes of 50.

PEDRO IGLESIAS
Machine-made in Tampa, Florida, USA.

Shape	Name	Lgth	Ring	Wrapper
Corona Extra	Crowns	5	45	CC-Ma
Long Corona	Regents	6	44	CC-Ma
Lonsdale	Lonsdales	6½	44	CC

This is an all-tobacco brand, featuring a Sumatra wrapper, Connecticut Broadleaf binder and a short-filler blend of tobaccos from three nations. All three shapes are offered in boxes of 50.

PHILLIPS & KING CIGARRENS
Machine-made in Dingelstadt, Germany.

Shape	Name	Lgth	Ring	Wrapper
Small Panatela	No. 1000	4¾	32	CC
Petit Corona	No. 2000	5	40	CC
Corona Extra	No. 3000	4¾	45	CC
Panatela	No. 4000	5½	38	CC

New in the U.S. for 1997, this is a mild, 100% tobacco blend in four popular shapes, each available with a Sumatra-grown wrapper. Look for Cigarrens in boxes of 20, or in easy-to-carry packs of five or 10.

RIVALO
Machine-made in Mayaguez, Puerto Rico.

Shape	Name	Lgth	Ring	Wrapper
Petit Corona	Corona	5	40	CC
Petit Corona	Coronita	5	40	CC

MACHINE-MADE CIGARS: BRAND LISTINGS

Long Corona	Cazadores	6	42	CC
Cigarillo	Sabrosito	4	28	CC
Cigarillo	Criollitos	4	28	CC

These mild and medium-bodied cigars are made in Puerto Rico, with the Cazadores made of 100% tobacco, featuring a Pennsylvania wrapper, Dominican binder and Dominican and Puerto Rico filler tobaccos. The other shapes have a sheet binder; the Sabrositos (chocolate flavored!) and Coronitas have a homogenized wrapper, while the Criollitos (rum-flavored) and Coronas have a Pennsylvania wrapper. The flavored cigars are mild in strength, the other shapes are medium-bodied.

ROSEDALE
Machine-made in Hartford, Connecticut, USA.

Shape	Name	Lgth	Ring	Wrapper
Perfecto	Perfecto	4⅞	46	CM
Corona Extra	Londres	5	46	CM

This brand, made continuously since the 1920s, is a part of the Topper cigar group, made of 100% tobacco. The genuine Connecticut Broadleaf wrapper surrounds a Connecticut binder and filler tobaccos from Brazil, the Dominican Republic and the U.S. Each shape is offered is packs of 5 or boxes of 50.

ROYAL HAWAIIAN
Machine-made in Makawao, Hawaii, USA.

Shape	Name		Lgth	Ring	Wrapper
Lonsdale	Long Corona	(tubed)	6½	43	CM

This is a new, all-tobacco brand in 1997 and offers a mild taste in a remarkable cigar which features the flavor of genuine Kona Coffee from Hawaii. The brand features a Connecticut-grown wrapper, imported binder and a blend of Central American-grown short filler. Royal Hawaiian cigars are offered in three-packs.

MACHINE-MADE CIGARS: BRAND LISTINGS

RUY LOPEZ
Machine-made in Tampa, Florida, USA.

Shape	Name	Lgth	Ring	Wrapper
Panatela	Panetelas	6	38	CC
Grand Corona	Corona Grande	5¾	45	CC
Corona	Vanilla Supreme	6	42	CC

Here is a mild brand, made with 100% tobacco and featuring an Ecuadorian-grown wrapper, Honduran binder and Dominican, Honduran and Nicaraguan tobacco in the filler. Available in bundles of 25, the line also features a flavored shape the Vanilla Supreme.

SCHIMMELPENNICK V.S.O.P.
Machine-made in Wageningen, the Netherlands.

Shape	Name		Lgth	Ring	Wrapper
Petit Corona	Corona		4¼	41	CM
Corona	Grand Corona		5	41	CM
Small Panatela	Senorita		4	31	CM
Petit Corona	Calendula	*(tubed)*	4⅜	40	CM

Created in 1995, here is a fuller-sized Schimmelpennick cigar for those who enjoy the mild taste of this famous brand, founded in 1924. Named for a famous governor of Holland, Rutger Jan Schimmelpennick (1781-1825), these new sizes feature Sumatra sandleaf wrappers and a Java binder, combined with filler tobaccos from Brazil (Bahia type) and Indonesia (Bezuki). In its first year of distribution, it was named the "Cigar of the Year" in Holland and is offered in boxes of 25.

SWISHER SWEETS
Machine-made in Jacksonville, Florida, USA.

Shape	Name	Lgth	Ring	Wrapper
Petit Corona	Blunt	5	42	CC

MACHINE-MADE CIGARS: BRAND LISTINGS

Corona	Kings		5½	42	CC
Petit Corona	Perfecto		5	41	CC
Panatela	Slims		5⅜	36	CC
Cigarillo	Coronella		5	27.5	CC
Small Panatela	Outlaw		4¾	32	CC
Cigarillo	Cigarillo		4⅜	28.5	CC
Cigarillo	Tip Cigarillo	*(tipped)*	4⅞	28	CC
Cigarillo	Wood Tip Cigarillo	*(tipped)*	4⅞	29	CC

Popular? Swisher Sweets are enjoyed everywhere, offering a mild, sweet taste with a manufactured wrapper and binder and a blend of filler tobaccos from four nations. The Outlaw is 100% tobacco and features a Honduran leaf wrapper; the King shape also features a natural leaf wrapper. You can find this brand in thousands of locations, in familiar red five-packs and in boxes of 50.

TAYO
Machine-made in Mayaguez, Puerto Rico.

Shape	Name	Lgth	Ring	Wrapper
Long Corona	Selectos	6	42	CC

These cigars are 100% tobacco, mild in strength and utilize all Puerto Rican leaf for the wrapper, binder and filler. All models are presented in boxes of 5.

TOPPER
Machine-made in McSherrystown, Pennsylvania, USA.

Shape	Name	Lgth	Ring	Wrapper
Long Corona	Grande Corona	6	46	CC
Corona Extra	Breva	5½	45	CI-CC-CM
Perfecto	Old Fashioned	4⅞	44	CI-CC-CM
Corona	Ebony	5½	46	Ma
Petit Corona	Broadleaf	4⅞	44	CM

MACHINE-MADE CIGARS: BRAND LISTINGS

Since 1896, Topper cigars gave offered a mild, flavorful taste with excellent value. Each of these models is made up of 100% tobacco and is offered in handy packs of 4-5 cigars, or in colorful boxes of 50. All feature genuine USA/Connecticut wrappers and binders and short filler from the Dominican Republic and the United States.

TOPSTONE
Machine-made in Tampa, Florida, USA.

Shape	Name	Lgth	Ring	Wrapper
	Connecticut Broadleaf series:			
Long Corona	Supreme	6	42	CC
Corona Extra	Extra Oscuro	5½	46	Ma
Grand Corona	Grande	5¾	46	CC-Ma
Panatela	Panatela	6	39	CC-Ma
Corona Extra	Bouquet	5½	46	CC-Ma
Corona Extra	Oscuro	5½	46	Ma
Churchill	Directors	7¾	46	CC-Ma
	Natural Darks series:			
Churchill	Executives	7¼	47	Ma

These are well-known, 100% tobacco cigars made in Tampa, Florida and featuring dark-cured Connecticut Broadleaf wrapper and binder and a three-nation short filler blend. Each of the shapes is offered in boxes of 50, except for the Directors and Executives, which are available in boxes of 25.

TRAVIS CLUB
Machine-made in San Antonio, Texas, USA.

Shape	Name	Lgth	Ring	Wrapper
Double Corona	Churchill	7	50	CC
Grand Corona	Corona Extra	6¼	46	CC
Toro	Toro	6	50	CC

MACHINE-MADE CIGARS: BRAND LISTINGS

Long Corona	Palma	6	43	CC
Perfecto	Perfecto	5¼	52	CC
Robusto	Robusto	5	50	CC

Here is a beautiful cigar which features all-tobacco, all-long-filler construction and a mild-bodied taste. The elegant wrappers are genuine Connecticut Shade, the binders are also Connecticut-grown and the filler is composed of leaves from the Dominican Republic and Brazil. Travis Club Premium cigars are presented in individual cellophane sleeves inside elegant, varnished wooden cabinets.

VASCO DA GAMA
Machine-made in Bunde, Germany.

Shape	Name	Lgth	Ring	Wrapper
Long Corona	Vasco de Gama	6	42	CC

Named for the famed Portugese explorer who was the first to circle the Cape of Good Hope in 1497. The cigar dates from 1816 (!) and is a mild, 100% tobacco blend of Sumatra-seed Indonesian wrappers, with a German binder and Brazilian and Indonesian filler.

WILLEM II
Machine-made in Valkenswaard, the Netherlands.

Shape	Name		Lgth	Ring	Wrapper
Corona	Optimum	(tubed)	5	41	CC

This is a medium-bodied, all-tobacco cigar which dates back to 1916. It features an Indonesian wrapper and binder and Indonesian and Brazilian filler.

WUHRMANN
Machine-made in Rheinfelden, Switzerland.

Shape	Name	Lgth	Ring	Wrapper
Corona	Bahianos	5¼	44	CM
Lonsdale	Big Ben	7	44	CC

MACHINE-MADE CIGARS: BRAND LISTINGS

Corona	El Prado	5¼	44	CC
Petit Corona	Habana Feu	4	44	CC
Corona Extra	Hand Made Sumatra	5	46	CC
Long Corona	Havana Seed	6	44	CC
Robusto	Impulso	5½	52	CC
Short Panatela	La Coronada	4½	36	CC
Petit Corona	Media Corona	4	44	CC
Robusto	Okay Corona *(tubed)*	5	52	CC
Petit Corona	Rio Santo	4	44	CM
Robusto	San Gonzalo	5	52	CM
Cigarillo	Wuhrillos	4	22	CC

A European favorite since its introduction in 1876, Wuhrmann was introduced to the U.S. market in 1997. These machine-made, mild-to-medium-bodied, all-tobacco cigars feature Brazilian, Sumatra and USA/Connecticut wrappers around Java binders and filler tobaccos from Brazil, the Dominican Republic and Indonesia. Each size is available in boxes of 20, 25, 30 or 50, depending on size.

ZINO
Machine-made in the Netherlands and Switzerland.

Shape	Name	Lgth	Ring	Wrapper
	Made in the Netherlands:			
Cigarillo	Cigarillos Brasil	3½	20	CM
Cigarillo	Panatellas Brasil	5½	22	CM
Cigarillo	Cigarillos Sumatra	3½	20	Co
Cigarillo	Panatellas Sumatra	5½	22	Co
	Made in Switzerland:			
Corona Extra	Grand Classic Brasil	5½	46	CM

MACHINE-MADE CIGARS: BRAND LISTINGS

Slim Panatela	Relax Brasil	5¾	30	CM
Petit Corona	Classic Brasil	4¾	41	CM
Corona Extra	Grand Classic Sumatra	5½	46	Co
Slim Panatela	Relax Sumatra	5¾	30	Co
Petit Corona	Classic Sumatra	4¾	41	Co

Here are beautifully made, mild cigars which feature Brazilian or Sumatran wrappers, Java binders and Brazilian and Indonesian filler tobaccos, offering outstanding quality and value in all-tobacco cigarillos and small cigars.

BRANDS USING HOMOGENIZED TOBACCO LEAF

ANTONIO Y CLEOPATRA
Machine-made in Cayey, Puerto Rico.

Shape	Name	Lgth	Ring	Wrapper
Cigarillo	Grenadier Whiffs	3⅝	23⅔	CM
Corona	Grenadier Tubos	5⅝	42½	CM
Cigarillo	Grenadier Minis	4½	28	DC-CM
Corona	Grenadier Palma Maduro	5⅝	42½	Ma
Slim Panatela	Grenadiers	6¼	33½	DC-CC-CM
Panatela	Grenadier Panatela	5⅝	35½	DC-CC-CM
Corona	Grenadier Coronas	5⅝	42½	DC-CM
Toro	Grenadier Churchills	5¾	50	CM-Ma
Small Panatela	Grenadier Miniatures	4⅝	31	CC
Corona	Grenadier Presidentes	5⅝	42½	CC

This highly popular brand dates back to 1888. Today, it offers a fairly mild taste with Connecticut Broadleaf (for maduro), Connecticut Shade (some shapes) and Javan (most shapes) wrappers, sheet binders and Cuban-seed filler tobaccos.

Coronas Group

Here are examples of the corona-sized cigars, one of the most popular on the market. The corona-related shapes in this group include:

- Petit Corona   4-5 inches long; 40-44 ring.
- Corona   5¼-5¾ inches long; 40-44 ring.
- Long Corona   5⅞-6⅜ inches long; 40-44 ring.

Pictured opposite, from left to right::

- **BELINDA** *Breva Conserva*   *(shape)*
  (Honduras)   5½ x 43   Corona

- **V.S.O.P. VINTAGE RESERVE** *Corona*
  (Dominican Republic) 5½ x 42   Corona

- **NOSTALGIA** *Corona*
  (Honduras)   5¾ x 43   Corona

- **CASA BLANCA** *Corona*
  (Dominican Republic) 5½ x 42   Corona

- **BAHIA** *No. 4*
  (Costa Rica)   5½ x 42   Corona

- **C.A.O.** *Corona*
  (Honduras)   6 x 42   Long Corona

- **FLOR DE LOS REYES** *Extra Corona*
  (Dominican Republic) 6 x 44   Long Corona

MACHINE-MADE CIGARS: BRAND LISTINGS

ARANGO SPORTSMAN
Machine-made in Tampa, Florida, USA.

Shape	Name		Lgth	Ring	Wrapper
Slim Panatela	No. 100		5¾	34	CC-Ma
Lonsdale	No. 200		6¼	42	CC-Ma
Churchill	No. 300		7	46	CC-Ma
Robusto	No. 350		5¾	48	CC-Ma
Churchill	No. 400		7½	48	CC-Ma
Panatela	Tubes	*(tubed)*	6½	36	CC-Ma
Cigarillo	Tens		4½	28	CC

Popular since its introduction in 1984, this is a very mild and aromatic cigar, with a touch of vanilla flavoring. It offers an Ecuadorian wrapper, sheet binder and a filler blend of Dominican and Honduran tobaccos. It is offered in boxes of 25, except for No. 100 and Tens, which come in 50s.

AS YOU LIKE IT
Machine-made in Jacksonville, Florida, USA.

Shape	Name	Lgth	Ring	Wrapper
Long Corona	No. 18	6	41	DC-CC-Ma
Petit Corona	No. 22	4½	41	DC-CC
Long Corona	No. 32	6	43	DC-CC
Slim Panatela	No. 35	5¼	33	CC

This popular brand offers a natural leaf wrapper from Ecuador (candela), Connecticut (natural) or Mexico (maduro), combined with a sheet binder and a four-nation blend of tobaccos for a mild taste, presented in boxes of 50.

BEN BEY
Machine-made in Frankfort, Indiana, USA.

MACHINE-MADE CIGARS: BRAND LISTINGS

Shape	Name		Lgth	Ring	Wrapper
Corona	Crystals	(tubed)	5⅝	44	CC

The Crystals are well named, as they are encased in a glass tube. The blend includes a Connecticut leaf wrapper, sheet binder and U.S. and Dominican tobaccos in the filler. Ben Beys are offered upright in specially-made cedar boxes of 50.

BEN FRANKLIN
Machine-made in Cayey, Puerto Rico

Shape	Name	Lgth	Ring	Wrapper
Petit Corona	Perfectos	4⅞	40	CC
Petit Corona	Blunts	5⅛	40	CC

This venerable brand, named for the Revolutionary Era publisher, statesman and the first Postmaster-General of the United States, features a blend of short-filler tobaccos combined with a homogenized wrapper and binder.

BLACK & MILD
Machine-made in King of Prussia, Pennsylvania, USA.

Shape	Name	Lgth	Ring	Wrapper
Small Panatela	Pipe-Tobacco Cigars (tipped)	5	30	Ma

Love the smell of pipe tobacco? Here's a cigar for you, with a pipe-tobacco filler and a homogenized wrapper and binder, offered in convenient five-packs.

BLACK HAWK
Machine-made in Frankfort, Indiana, USA.

Shape	Name	Lgth	Ring	Wrapper
Corona Extra	Chief	5⅛	45	CM

The Chief has a medium body and uses a Connecticut leaf wrapper, a sheet binder and a blend of Dominican and U.S. tobaccos in the filler

MACHINE-MADE CIGARS: BRAND LISTINGS

BUDD SWEET
Machine-made in Wheeling, West Virginia, USA.

Shape	Name	Lgth	Ring	Wrapper
Petit Corona	Perfecto	5	42½	CC
Slim Panatela	Panatela	5¼	34	CC

The Panatela boasts a genuine Connecticut leaf wrapper, sheet binder and U.S. and Dominican tobaccos in the filler for a medium-bodied taste. The Perfecto has the same binder and filler, but uses a homogenized sheet wrapper.

CARIBBEAN ROUNDS
Machine-made in Yoe, Pennsylvania, USA.

Shape	Name	Lgth	Ring	Wrapper
Lonsdale	Casinos	6½	43	CI-CC-Ma
Short Panatela	Petites	4⅝	36	CC-Ma
Lonsdale	Rounds	7¼	45	CC-Ma
Long Panatela	Royales	6½	36	CC-Ma

Available in fairly large sizes for mass-market cigars, this mild-bodied brand offers a natural leaf wrapper, has a sheet binder and a blend of short-filler tobaccos. Most sizes are offered in wood boxes of 50.

CASINO CLUB
Machine-made in San Antonio, Texas.

Shape	Name	Lgth	Ring	Wrapper
Robusto	Big Casino	5⅛	52	CC
Long Corona	Roulette	6	43	CC
Corona Extra	Keno	4¾	47	CC

Here is a new cigar from the famous Finck Cigar Company of San Antonio, offering a mild smoke. It features an Indonesian wrapper, sheet binder and filler tobaccos from Brazil and Honduras. You can enjoy them in wood boxes of 50!

MACHINE-MADE CIGARS: BRAND LISTINGS

CAZADORES
Machine-made in Jacksonville, Florida, USA.

Shape	Name	Lgth	Ring	Wrapper
Long Corona	No. 16	6	42	CC
Long Corona	No. 26	6	42	Ma
Small Panatela	No. 8	4¼	32	CC

New for 1997 is this mild-tasting, easy-to-draw cigar, available in two-packs or upright boxes of 25. It features a natural leaf wrapper, sheet binder and a blend of cut filler tobaccos. Talk about convenience . . . it comes with a European-style V-cut already made at the top!

CHARLES DENBY
Machine-made in Frankfort, Indiana, USA.

Shape	Name	Lgth	Ring	Wrapper
Corona	Invincible	5½	43	CI

Connecticut wrapper, sheet binders and a blended filler with American and Dominican tobaccos give this brand a medium body.

CHERRY BLEND
Machine-made in King of Prussia, Pennsylvania, USA.

Shape	Name	Lgth	Ring	Wrapper
Small Panatela	Pipe-Tobacco Cigars (tipped)	5	30	Ma

The sweet smell of cherry is the appeal of this pipe-tobacco-filled cigar. Offered in packs of five, it has a homogenized wrapper and binder and a plastic tip for easy smoking.

CIMA
Machine-made in Mayaguez, Puerto Rico.

MACHINE-MADE CIGARS: BRAND LISTINGS

Shape	Name	Lgth	Ring	Wrapper
Long Corona	Embajadores	6	42	CC

These cigars are machine-made with a medium body, featuring a USA/Pennsylvania wrapper and a filler blend of Dominican Republic and Puerto Rican tobaccos, surrounded by a sheet binder.

CUESTA-REY
Machine-made in Tampa, Florida, USA.

Shape	Name	Lgth	Ring	Wrapper
Small Panatela	No. 120	5	31	CC-Ma
Long Corona	Palma Supreme	6¼	42	CC-Ma
Slim Panatela	Caravelle	6¼	34	CC-Ma

A famous brand in cigars for decades, the machine-made version of Cuesta-Rey offers a mild-to-medium body. It features a Connecticut wrapper, homogenized binder and a blend of short filler tobaccos. All sizes are available in ten-packs; the Palma Supreme and Caravelle sizes are offered in boxes of 50.

CYRILLA
Machine-made in Tampa, Florida, USA.

Shape	Name	Lgth	Ring	Wrapper
Long Corona	Nationals	6	42	CC-Ma
Churchill	Kings	7	46	CC-Ma
Churchill	Senators	7½	48	CC-Ma
Panatela	Slims	6½	36	CC-Ma

These are mild cigars, offered in bundles of 25 cigars each. They feature either an Ecuadorian (natural) wrapper or a Connecticut Broadleaf in the maduro shade, a sheet binder and filler tobaccos from the Dominican and Honduras.

DECISION MADURO
Machine-made in Tampa, Florida, USA.

MACHINE-MADE CIGARS: BRAND LISTINGS

Shape	Name	Lgth	Ring	Wrapper
Robusto	No. 250	5½	49	Ma
Grand Corona	No. 350	6¼	45	Ma
Corona	No. 450	5	44	Ma
Short Panatela	No. 550	5⅜	37	Ma

This brand has been around since 1935 and today offers a mild to medium smoke at a great value. The all-maduro series features a Connecticut Broadleaf wrapper, with a sheet binder and filler tobaccos from the Dominican Republic. Each size is available in economical bundles of 20.

DEXTER LONDRES
Machine-made in Jacksonville, Florida, USA.

Shape	Name	Lgth	Ring	Wrapper
Corona	Dexter Londres	5¼	42	CC

This is a mild cigar, with a natural leaf wrapper, sheet binder and a four-nation filler blend. Dexters are available in handy five-packs and in boxes of 50.

DIRECTORS
Machine-made in Jacksonville, Florida, USA.

Shape	Name	Lgth	Ring	Wrapper
Cigarillo	Cigarillo	4⅜	27½	CM
Cigarillo	Coronella	5	27½	CM
Long Corona	Corona	6	42	CM
Short Panatela	Panatela	5⅜	36	CM

This range offers a mild taste, with a Wisconsin sun-grown wrapper, sheet binder and a blend of chopped filler tobaccos.

DON CESAR
Machine-made in Tampa, Florida, USA.

MACHINE-MADE CIGARS: BRAND LISTINGS

Shape	Name	Lgth	Ring	Wrapper
Corona	Palma	5⅝	42	CC

Here is a unique, machine-made cigar made from long-filler tobaccos, rather than the cut filler which is more common. The Sumatran wrapper and sheet binder surrounds filler leaves from the Dominican Republic and Honduras.

DRY SLITZ
Machine-made in Wheeling, West Virginia, USA.

Shape	Name	Lgth	Ring	Wrapper
Slim Panatela	Regular	5½	34	CC

This is a mild-bodied cigar with a homogenized wrapper, sheet binder and U.S. and Dominican tobaccos in the filler. The head of the cigar is finished with a small hole so that you can light it up without cutting!

DUTCH MASTERS
Machine-made in McAdoo, Pennsylvania, USA
and Cayey, Puerto Rico.

Shape	Name	Lgth	Ring	Wrapper
Cigarillo	Cadet Regular	4¾	27½	CC
Cigarillo	Pipearillo	5⅛	27	CM
Petit Corona	Perfecto	4¾	44	CM
Panatela	Panatela	5½	36	CM
Slim Panatela	Elite	6⅛	29½	CM
Corona Extra	Belvedere	4⅞	46½	CM
Corona	President	5⅝	40½	CM
Corona	Corona Deluxe	5¾	43	CM
Corona	Corona Maduro	5¾	43	Ma
Toro	Corona Grande	5¾	50	CM-Ma

	Masters Collection:			
Cigarillo	Cigarillos	4¾	27½	CC
Corona	Palmas	5⅝	42½	CC
Corona	Palmas Maduro	5⅝	42½	Ma
Short Panatela	Panatelas Deluxe	5⅜	35½	CC

Remember the Dutch Masters television commercials of the 1960s, as the actors retired into the brand's trademark portrait at the end? The commercials are history, but the brand continues to do well, offering a mild smoke in both manufactured and natural wrapper styles. All shapes are made in Puerto Rico, except for the Pipearillo. The Corona Deluxe, Elite, Corona Maduro and Corona Grande shapes all feature natural leaf wrappers; all shapes have homogenized binders and a short-filler blend of Cuban-seed tobaccos.

1886

Machine-made in Cayey, Puerto Rico.

Shape	*Name*	*Lgth*	*Ring*	*Wrapper*
Corona	Queens	5⅝	42	CC

This one-shape brand features a Connecticut wrapper, around a sheet binder and a blend of short-filler tobaccos.

El Producto

Machine-made in Cayey, Puerto Rico.

Shape	*Name*	*Lgth*	*Ring*	*Wrapper*
Small Panatela	Little Coronas	4⅝	31	CC
Corona	Blunts	5⅝	40½	CC
Petit Corona	Bouquets	4¾	44	CC
Petit Corona	Panatelas	5½	36	CC
Corona Extra	Puritano Finos	4⅞	46½	CC
Corona	Coronas	5¾	43	CC
Robusto	Favoritas	5	48½	CC

MACHINE-MADE CIGARS: BRAND LISTINGS

Robusto	Escepcionales		5⅛	52½	CC
Corona	Queens	*(tubed)*	5⅝	42	CC

Introduced in 1916, this was the smoke of choice (in the Queens size) for decades for the late comedian George Burns (1896-1996) and it continues to have many contemporary admirers. The many shapes are primarily clothed in manufactured wrappers; the Escepcionales and Queens feature a natural wrapper. All shapes use homogenized binders.

EL TRELLES
Machine-made in Jacksonville, Florida, USA.

Shape	Name	Lgth	Ring	Wrapper
Long Corona	Bankers	6	43	CC
Corona Extra	Blunt Extra	5¼	45	CC
Long Corona	Club House	6	41	Ma
Long Corona	Kings	6	41	CC
Pyramid	Tryangles Deluxe	5¼	45	CC

This is a very mild cigar, with a natural leaf wrapper from Connecticut (natural) or Mexico (maduro), sheet binder and a four-nation filler blend, available in natural and maduro shades. El Trelles cigars are offered in convenient five-packs and by the box (of 50).

EMERSON
Machine-made in Wheeling, West Virginia, USA.

Shape	Name	Lgth	Ring	Wrapper
Petit Corona	Diplomat	4¾	42½	CI

American and Dominican filler tobaccos are at the heart of this one-shape brand. It offers a medium body and has a homogenized wrapper and sheet binder.

FLOR DE BORINQUEN
Machine-made in Mayaguez, Puerto Rico.

MACHINE-MADE CIGARS: BRAND LISTINGS

Shape	Name	Lgth	Ring	Wrapper
Petit Corona	Flor de Borinquen	4¾	42	CC

This Puerto Rican, machine-made cigar offers a medium-bodied flavor based on a USA/Pennsylvania wrapper, sheet binder and blend of Dominican and Puerto Rican filler tobaccos.

FLORIDA QUEEN
Machine-made in Wheeling, West Virginia, USA.

Shape	Name	Lgth	Ring	Wrapper
Petit Corona	Florida Queen	5	42½	CC

Here is a medium-bodied cigar, made up of American and Dominican filler tobaccos, a sheet binder and a genuine Connecticut leaf wrapper.

GARCIA GRANDE
Machine-made in Tampa, Florida, USA.

Shape	Name	Lgth	Ring	Wrapper
Corona	Corona	5½	42	CC-Ma
Toro	Laguitos	5⅝	48	CC-Ma
Long Corona	Pitas	6	43	CC-Ma
Pyramid	Pyramides	5¼	42	CC-Ma
Churchill	Trinidads	7¼	46	CC-Ma

Introduced in 1996, this cigar has a medium body, a Cuban-seed, Honduran-grown wrapper, sheet binder and filler tobaccos from the Dominican Republic, Honduras and Nicaragua. It is an excellent value, offered in bundles.

GARCIA Y VEGA
Machine-made in Dothan, Alabama, USA
and Santiago, Dominican Republic

MACHINE-MADE CIGARS: BRAND LISTINGS

Shape	*Name*	*Lgth*	*Ring*	*Wrapper*
Cigarillo	Cigarillos	4¼	27	DC
Cigarillo	Chicos	4¼	27	CC
Cigarillo	Miniatures	4⅝	29	CC
Cigarillo	Whiffs	3¾	23	CC
Cigarillo	Whiffs Gold	3¾	23	CC
Slim Panatela	Tips *(tipped)*	5¼	30	CC
Slim Panatela	Bravuras	5⅜	34	CC
Slim Panatela	Panatella Deluxe	5⅜	34	DC
Petit Corona	Senators	4½	41	DC
Petit Corona	Barons	4¾	41	CC
Petit Corona	Bouquets	4⅝	45	CC
Short Panatela	Delgado Panatela	5⅜	34	CC
Panatela	Elegantes	6⅜	34	DC
Panatela	Gallantes	6⅜	34	CC
Corona	Presidente	5¾	41	CC
Corona	Napoleons	5¾	41	DC
Corona	English Coronas *(tubed)*	5¼	41	CC
Slim Panatela	Granadas *(tubed)*	6⅜	34	DC
Slim Panatela	Romeros *(tubed)*	6⅜	34	CC
Long Corona	Gran Coronas *(tubed)*	6⅛	41	DC
Long Corona	Gran Premios *(tubed)*	6⅛	41	CC
Slim Panatela	Crystals No. 100 *(tubed)*	6⅜	34	CC
Long Corona	Crystals No. 200 *(tubed)*	6⅛	41	CC
Long Corona	Maduro Crystals *(tubed)*	6⅛	41	Ma
Long Corona	Maduro	6⅛	41	Ma

MACHINE-MADE CIGARS: BRAND LISTINGS

Since 1882, this brand has been a favorite all across the United States, enjoyed more than 300,000 times daily nationwide. The natural leaf wrapper comes from the Cameroon, Connecticut or Mexico and is combined with a sheet binder and a blend of filler tobaccos for the brand's characteristic mild taste. Please note that the Whiffs size offers two flavors: natural and Cavendish. Garcia y Vega cigars are always fresh thanks to in-the-pack pouches or tubes and are offered in packs of 3, 4 or 5 cigars or in boxes of 30, 40 or 50.

GARGOYLE
Machine-made in Frankfort, Indiana, USA.

Shape	Name	Lgth	Ring	Wrapper
Panatela	Lanza	6	38	Cl

The cigar is not as ugly as the brand name might imply! It's actually a medium-bodied smoke with a Connecticut wrapper, sheet binder and a blend of American and Dominican filler.

GOLD & MILD
Machine-made in King of Prussia, Pennsylvania, USA.

Shape	Name	Lgth	Ring	Wrapper
Small Panatela	Pipe-Tobacco Cigars *(tipped)*	5	30	CC

The gentle aroma of pipe & tobacco is the appeal of this brand, which features a plastic tip for easy smoking and a homogenized wrapper and binder. It is offered in convenient five-packs.

GOVERNOR
Machine-made in Tampa, Florida, USA.

Shape	Name	Lgth	Ring	Wrapper
Long Corona	Claro	6	42	DC

Here is a modestly-priced, easy-to-smoke cigar with a natural leaf wrapper, homogenized binder and a three-nation blend of filler tobaccos. It is offered in convenient boxes of 50.

MACHINE-MADE CIGARS: BRAND LISTINGS

HARVESTER
Machine-made in Cayey, Puerto Rico.

Shape	Name	Lgth	Ring	Wrapper
Petit Corona	Perfecto	5	40½	CC
Corona	Record Breaker	5⅝	40½	CC

This brand features a blend of short-filler tobaccos combined with a homogenized wrapper and binder.

HAUPTMANN'S
Machine-made in Frankfort, Indiana, USA.

Shape	Name	Lgth	Ring	Wrapper
Corona Extra	Perfecto	5⅛	45	Cl-CM
Corona	Broadleaf	5¼	43	CM
Corona	Corona	5¼	43	Cl
Panatela	Panatela	5¾	38	Cl-CM

This is a medium-bodied smoke, with a genuine Connecticut leaf wrapper, sheet binder and a blend of Dominican and U.S. tobaccos in the filler.

HAV-A-TAMPA
Machine-made in Tampa, Florida, USA.

Shape	Name		Lgth	Ring	Wrapper
Corona	Blunt		5	43	CC
Small Panatela	Cheroot		4¾	31	CC
Cigarillo	Jewel	(tipped)	5	29	CC
Cigarillo	Jewel Sweet	(tipped)	5	29	CC
Cigarillo	Jewel Classic	(tipped)	5	29	CC
Cigarillo	Jewel Black Gold		5	29	Ma
Cigarillo	Jewel Menthol		5	29	CC

MACHINE-MADE CIGARS: BRAND LISTINGS

Small Panatela	Junior		4½	31	CC
Panatela	Panatela		5½	36	CC
Petit Corona	Perfecto		4¾	43	CC
Petit Corona	Sublime		4¾	43	CC
Cigarillo	Tips Cigarillo	(tipped)	5	28	CC
Cigarillo	Tips	(tipped)	5	28	CC
Cigarillo	Tips Sweet	(tipped)	5	28	CC

This famous brand offers light, mild cigarillos with a manufactured wrapper and binder and a filler blend of Honduran and Dominican tobaccos.

HENRY THE FOURTH
Machine-made in Tampa, Florida, USA.

Shape	Name	Lgth	Ring	Wrapper
Corona	Lydia	5½	43	CM-Ma
Grand Corona	Magnums	5⅝	47	CM-Ma
Long Corona	Mirtas	6	43	CM-Ma
Churchill	Principales	7¾	46	CM-Ma

This brand features a Honduran wrapper, sheet binder and a filler mix of Dominican, Honduran and Nicaraguan tobaccos. Mild to medium in strength, you can find it in bundles of 25 cigars each.

J-R FAMOUS
Machine-made in Tampa, Florida, USA.

Shape	Name	Lgth	Ring	Wrapper
Toro	Churchill	5¾	50	DC-CM-Ma
Panatela	Delicados	6	39	DC-CM-Ma
Long Corona	Plazas	6	42	DC-CM-Ma
Lonsdale	Presidents	7⅛	44	DC-CM-Ma

MACHINE-MADE CIGARS: BRAND LISTINGS

This is a medium-bodied, highly popular cigar with a Honduran wrapper, sheet binder and all-Honduran filler. It is an excellent value and offered in boxes of 50.

KEEP MOVING
Machine-made in Jacksonville, Florida, USA.

Shape	Name	Lgth	Ring	Wrapper
Petit Corona	Goodies	4½	41	CC

This one-size brand has a natural leaf wrapper, sheet binder and blends tobaccos of four nations in the filler. Look for Keep Moving in twin-packs, five-packs and in full boxes of 50.

KING EDWARD
Machine-made in Jacksonville, Florida, USA.

Shape	Name		Lgth	Ring	Wrapper
Corona	Invincible Deluxe		5¾	42	CC
Short Panatela	Panatela Deluxe		5¼	38	CC
Long Corona	Corona Deluxe		6	42	CC
Cigarillo	Cigarillo Deluxe		4¼	28½	CC
Petit Corona	Blunt		5	42	CC
Petit Corona	Imperial		5	40	CC
Panatela	Slim		5⅝	36	CC
Cigarillo	Specials		4⅜	28½	CC
Cigarillo	Tip Cigarillo	(tipped)	4⅞	28	CC
Cigarillo	Wood Tip Cigarillo	(tipped)	5½	29	CC
Cigarillo	Little Cigars		4⅜	29	CC

Britain's King Edward VII (1841-1910) is celebrated as the man who, with four words, revised the Victorian prohibition against tobacco soon after his ascension to the throne in 1901: "Gentlemen, you may smoke." This brand still bears his portrait and is now machine-made with a sheet wrapper and binder and a four-nation filler blend. The Deluxe shapes feature a natural leaf wrapper, while the

MACHINE-MADE CIGARS: BRAND LISTINGS

Wood Tip Cigarillo is available in flavored versions of Sweet Cherry and Sweet Vanilla. Widely available in the U.S. and highly popular in England and 60 other countries, King Edward is offered in five-packs and boxes of 50

LA FENDRICH
Machine-made in Frankfort, Indiana, USA.

Shape	Name	Lgth	Ring	Wrapper
Corona Extra	Favorita	5⅛	45	CI
Small Panatela	Buds	4¼	32	CC

La Fendrich cigars have a medium body, with a Connecticut wrapper, American and Dominican filler tobaccos and a sheet binder.

LORD BEACONSFIELD
Machine-made in Tampa, Florida, USA.

Shape	Name	Lgth	Ring	Wrapper
Churchill	Rounds	7¼	46	DC-CC-Ma
Slim Panatela	Lords	7	34	DC-CC-Ma
Long Corona	Coronas Superba	6¼	42	DC-CC-Ma
Panatela	Lindas	6½	36	DC-CC-Ma
Corona	Cubanola	5½	44	DC-CC-Ma
Churchill	Directors	7¾	46	Ma

This is a veteran brand with a Sumatra wrapper and a three-nation, short filler blend, combined with a sheet binder for a mild taste. It is offered in boxes of 50 except for the Directors, offered in 25s.

LORD CLINTON
Machine-made in Wheeling, West Virginia, USA.

Shape	Name	Lgth	Ring	Wrapper
Slim Panatela	Panatela	5¼	34	CC
Corona	Perfecto	5	42½	CI

MACHINE-MADE CIGARS: BRAND LISTINGS

The Panatela has a genuine Connecticut wrapper, sheet binder and a blend of filler tobaccos from the Dominican Republic and the United States. It has a medium-bodied taste. The Perfecto has the same filler tobaccos, but uses a sheet binder and wrapper.

MARSH
Machine-made in Wheeling, West Virginia, USA.

Shape	Name	Lgth	Ring	Wrapper
Slim Panatela	Mountaineer	5½	34	CC-Ma
Panatela	Virginian	5½	37	CC
Panatela	Pioneer	5½	37	CC
Slim Panatela	Old Reliable	5½	33	Ma
Long Panatela	Deluxe	7	34	Ma
Long Panatela	Deluxe II	7	34	Ma
Long Panatela	Olde Style Stogies	7	34	Ma

This brand began back in 1840 and continues today as a popular mass-market cigar in many parts of the United States. All of the shapes are mild and all use genuine Connecticut-grown leaves for wrappers and sheet binders. Most of the shapes offer a U.S. and Dominican filler blend, except for the Old Reliable, which incorporates fire-cured Kentucky tobacco in its filler. The Deluxe and Old Style Stogies are finished with a pig-tail head. The heads of the Deluxe II shape are pre-drilled with holes to allow instant ignition without cutting.

MIFLIN'S CHOICE
Machine-made in Wheeling, West Virginia, USA.

Shape	Name		Lgth	Ring	Wrapper
Panatela	Panatela	(tubed)	6⅜	32	CM

This small cigar uses a Cameroon wrapper, sheet binder and a blend of Caribbean tobaccos in the filler.

MOCHA LIGHTS
Machine-made in Tampa, Florida, USA.

MACHINE-MADE CIGARS: BRAND LISTINGS

Shape	Name	Lgth	Ring	Wrapper
Grand Corona	Mocha Lights	6⅜	47	CM-Ma

Here is a medium-bodied cigar that features a Honduran-grown leaf wrapper, around a sheet binder and Honduran filler. Available in economical bundles of 20.

MOYA GUSTO
Machine-made in Tampa, Florida, USA.

Shape	Name	Lgth	Ring	Wrapper
Lonsdale	Cazadores	6¼	44	CC-Ma
Corona	Deluxe	5⅜	44	CC-Ma
Lonsdale	Fumas	6¼	44	CC-Ma
Panatela	Panatela	6	34	CC

This brand is full-bodied and features an Indonesian wrapper, sheet binder and filler tobaccos from the Dominican Republic. The Deluxe and Panatela shapes are offered in boxes of 50; the others are packaged in bundles of 25.

MR. B
Machine-made in Tampa, Florida, USA.

Shape	Name	Lgth	Ring	Wrapper
Giant Corona	Mr. B	7½	45	DC-CM-Ma

Here is a medium-bodied, flavorful cigar which features a Honduran wrapper, sheet binder and Honduran filler tobaccos, offered in boxes of 20.

MURIEL
Machine-made in McAdoo, Pennsylvania, USA and Cayey, Puerto Rico.

Shape	Name	Lgth	Ring	Wrapper
Corona Extra	Magnum	4⅝	46½	CC
Small Panatela	Air Tips Regular (tipped)	5	30½	CC

MACHINE-MADE CIGARS: BRAND LISTINGS

Small Panatela	Air Tips Pipe Aroma *(tipped)*	5	30½	CC
Small Panatela	Air Tips Menthol *(tipped)*	5	30½	CC
Small Panatela	Air Tips Sweet *(tipped)*	5	30½	CC
Small Panatela	Coronella	4⅝	31	CC
Small Panatela	Coronella Pipe Aroma	4⅝	31	CC
Small Panatela	Coronella Sweet	4⅝	31	CC
	Muriel Pipe Tobacco Cigars:			
Cigarillo	Black N Cherry	5⅛	27	CM
Cigarillo	Black N Sweet	5⅛	27	CM
	Muriel Sweets Little Cigars:			
Cigarillo	Black & Sweet	3⅞	20	CM
Cigarillo	Sweet & Mild	3⅞	20	CC
Cigarillo	Menthol	3⅞	20	CC

This famous brand features a manufactured wrapper and offer a variety of sizes for every smoker. The Coronella group includes all natural fillers, while the new Pipe Tobacco series includes pipe tobacco filler. All are made in Puerto Rico except for the Sweets, made in Pennsylvania.

NAT CICCO'S
Machine-made in Tampa. Florida, USA and Yoe, Pennsylvania, USA.

Shape	Name	Lgth	Ring	Wrapper
Giant Corona	Churchill Rejects	8	46	DC-CC-Ma
Small Panatela	Jamaican Delights	5	34	CC-Ma
Lonsdale	Jamaican Palmas	6½	43	CC-Ma
Slim Panatela	Jamaican Regales	7⅛	34	CC-Ma
Churchill	Jamaican Rounds	7¼	46	CC-Ma
Long Corona	Plaza	6	42	DC-CC-Ma

Panatela	Rapier	6½	39	DC-CC-Ma
Robusto	Robusto Rejects	5½	49	CC-Ma
	Aromatic and flavored series:			
Panatela	Almond Liquer	6½	39	CC
Panatela	Cuban Cafe	6½	39	CC
Long Corona	Plaza Aromatic	6	42	CC

This series is made primarily in Tampa, except for the Aromatic and Flavored group, made in Pennsylvania. Overall, you can expect a mild taste from the Honduran natural leaf wrappers, homogenized binder and a blend of short-filler tobaccos from three nations. Nat Cicco's shapes are offered in boxes of 50.

NATIONAL CIGAR
Machine-made in Frankfort, Indiana, USA.

Shape	Name	Lgth	Ring	Wrapper
Long Corona	Palma	6	42	CI-CM

Made by the National Cigar Corporation, this medium-bodied blend incorporates a Connecticut wrapper, sheet binder and American and Dominican blended filler

ODIN
Machine-made in Wheeling, West Virginia, USA.

Shape	Name	Lgth	Ring	Wrapper
Petit Corona	Viking	4¾	42½	CC

The Odin Viking offers a medium-bodied taste, with tobaccos from the Dominican Republic and the United States in the filler. The wrapper is homogenized tobacco leaf and a sheet binder is used.

OPTIMO
Machine-made in Jacksonville, Florida, USA.

Shape	Name	Lgth	Ring	Wrapper
Panatela	Diplomat	6⅛	33	DC-CC

MACHINE-MADE CIGARS: BRAND LISTINGS

Long Corona	Admiral	6	41	DC-CC
Corona	Coronas	5¼	42	CC-Ma
Long Corona	Palmas	6	41	Ma
Slim Panatela	Panatela	5¼	33	DC-CC
Petit Corona	Sports	4½	41	DC-CC

This popular brand was, at one time, made of Cuban tobacco, but is today a mass-market favorite. It combines a natural leaf wrapper from Ecuador (candela), Connecticut (natural) or Mexico (maduro), a sheet binder and a four-nation blend in the filler, and is available in twin-packs, five-packs and, of course, full boxes of 50.

PALMA
Machine-made in Yoe, Pennsylvania, USA.

Shape	Name	Lgth	Ring	Wrapper
Lonsdale	Throwouts	6½	43	Cl-CC-Ma

What an undeserving shape name! These are value-priced, machine-made cigars with a natural leaf wrapper, sheet binder and an imported, blended filler. Offered in boxes of 50.

PHILLIES
Machine-made in Selma, Alabama, USA.

Shape	Name	Lgth	Ring	Wrapper
Corona	Perfecto	5¾	43	CC
Long Corona	Titan	6¼	44	CC
Corona	Coronas	5⅝	41	CC
Petit Corona	Blunts	4¾	42	CC
Slim Panatela	Panatella	5½	34	CC
Corona	Sport	5¾	43	CC
Small Panatela	Cheroot	5	32	CC
Slim Panatela	King Cheroot	5½	32	CC

MACHINE-MADE CIGARS: BRAND LISTINGS

Small Panatela	Mexicali Slim		4⅝	32	CC
Petit Corona	Juniors		5	41	CC
Corona	Sweets		5¾	43	CC
Cigarillo	Tips	(tipped)	4½	28	CC
Cigarillo	Tip Sweet	(tipped)	4½	28	CC

This well-known brand is constructed with a sheet wrapper and binder, with the filler blend made from Dominican and Honduran tobaccos, to provide its mild-bodied taste.

POLLACK
Machine-made in Wheeling, West Virginia, USA.

Shape	Name	Lgth	Ring	Wrapper
Slim Panatela	Melo Crown Expert	5½	34	Ma
Slim Panatela	Crown Drum	5½	33	Ma

The Crown Drum offers a mild taste with a Connecticut wrapper, sheet binder and U.S. and Dominican filler tobaccos.

R. G. DUN
Machine-made in Wheeling, West Virginia, USA.

Shape	Name	Lgth	Ring	Wrapper
Petit Corona	Admiral	4¾	42½	CC
Petit Corona	Babies	4⅛	42	CC
Slim Panatela	Youngfellow	5¼	34	CC
Corona	Regal Blunt	5¼	43	CC
Corona	Bouquet	5½	42½	CC
Cigarillo	Cigarillo	4¼	29	Cl

This is a medium-bodied cigar made by M. Marsh & Sons. It offers a Connecticut leaf wrapper, has a sheet binder and a blended filler of American and Dominican tobaccos.

MACHINE-MADE CIGARS: BRAND LISTINGS

RED DOT
Machine-made in Wheeling, West Virginia, USA.

Shape	Name	Lgth	Ring	Wrapper
Slim Panatela	Panatela	5¼	34	CC
Corona	Perfecto	5	42½	CC

This brand offers a medium body, with a Connecticut leaf wrapper, sheet binder and a blend of Domincan and flavored American tobaccos in the filler.

RIGOLETTO
Machine-made in Tampa, Florida, USA.

Shape	Name	Lgth	Ring	Wrapper
Long Corona	Londonaire	6¼	43	CC
Corona Extra	Black Jack	5⅜	46	Ma
Long Corona	Natural Coronas	6	42	CC
Long Corona	Palma Grande	6	41	Cl-CC
Slim Panatela	Natural Panatela	5	33	CC
Small Panatela	Wild Dominicans	4¾	34	CC

This is a mild-to-medium brand produced in Tampa. First introduced in 1905, it features a Connecticut Broadleaf or Shade wrapper, a sheet binder and high-quality filler tobaccos from the Dominican Republic.

ROBERT BURNS
Machine-made in Santiago, Dominican Republic and Dothan, Alabama.

Shape	Name		Lgth	Ring	Wrapper
Corona	Black Watch	*(tubed)*	5⅝	41	CC
Cigarillo	Cigarillo		4½	27	CC

The Black Watch model is made in Santiago, the Dominican Republic, with a Connecticut Shade wrapper, sheet binder and a multi-nation blend of filler tobaccos in three-packs and boxes of 30. The famous Cigarillos are made in Dothan, Alabama with sheet wrappers and binders and blended filler, offered in five-packs and boxes of 50.

ROI-TAN
Machine-made in Cayey, Puerto Rico.

Shape	Name	Lgth	Ring	Wrapper
Petit Corona	Bankers	5	40½	CI
Corona	Blunts	5⅝	40½	CI
Slim Panatela	Falcons	6¼	33½	CI
Panatela	Panatelas	5½	36	CI
Petit Corona	Perfecto Extras	5	40½	CI

Here is a popular old brand which is now using a manufactured wrapper and binder with short filler tobaccos.

SAN FELICE
Machine-made in Wheeling, West Virginia, USA.

Shape	Name	Lgth	Ring	Wrapper
Petit Corona	Original	4¾	42½	CC

This brand has only one shape, but it's a popular corona thanks to its genuine Connecticut wrapper. The filler is a blend of American and Dominican tobaccos, surrounded by a sheet binder.

SIERRA SWEET
Machine-made in Tampa, Florida, USA.

Shape	Name	Lgth	Ring	Wrapper
Panatela	Renos	6¼	36	CC-Ma
Small Panatela	Tahoes	4¾	30	CC-Ma

Here is a vanilla-flavored brand with a natural leaf wrapper, sheet binder and a blend of short-filler tobaccos. You can have your pick in hand carry-cases of five, eight or 10 cigars.

MACHINE-MADE CIGARS: BRAND LISTINGS

'63 AIR-FLO
Machine-made in Wheeling, West Virginia, USA.

Shape	Name	Lgth	Ring	Wrapper
Petit Corona	Londres	5	42½	CC

One of the most unusual names in cigardom adorns this medium-bodied cigar, which has a sheet wrapper and binder and filler tobaccos from the United States and the Dominican Republic.

SWEET-NUT
Machine-made in Tampa, Florida, USA.

Shape	Name	Lgth	Ring	Wrapper
Slim Panatela	Sweet-Nut	5⅜	30	CC

Introduced in 1997, this is a mild, small cigar with features Dominican-grown filler and homogenized tobacco leaf binder and wrapper.

TAMPA CUB
Machine-made in Wheeling, West Virginia, USA.

Shape	Name	Lgth	Ring	Wrapper
Corona	Straights	5	42½	CC

There is only one shape in this brand, but it offers a medium body with American and Dominican filler tobaccos and a manufactured sheet binder and wrapper.

TAMPA NUGGET
Machine-made in Tampa, Florida, USA.

Shape	Name		Lgth	Ring	Wrapper
Petit Corona	Sublime		4¾	43	CC
Petit Corona	Blunt		5	43	CC
Panatela	Panatela		5½	36	CC
Cigarillo	Tip Regular	*(tipped)*	5	28	CC

MACHINE-MADE CIGARS: BRAND LISTINGS

Cigarillo	Tip Sweet	*(tipped)*	5	28	CC
Small Panatela	Juniors		4½	31	CC
Small Panatela	Miniature		4½	31	CC

These "nuggets" incorporate sheet wrappers and binders with a blend of filler tobaccos from the Dominican Republic and Honduras for a mild and flavorful smoke.

TAMPA RESAGOS
Machine-made in Tampa, Florida, USA.

Shape	*Name*	*Lgth*	*Ring*	*Wrapper*
Corona	Regular	5¼	42	CC
Corona	Sweet	5¼	42	CC

These inexpensive cigars offer a mild taste, with homogenized wrappers and binders and filler tobaccos from the Dominican Republic. A favorite since 1951, Tampa Resagos are offered in bags of 20 cigars each.

TAMPA SWEET
Machine-made in Tampa, Florida, USA.

Shape	*Name*		*Lgth*	*Ring*	*Wrapper*
Petit Corona	Perfecto		4¾	43	CC
Small Panatela	Cheroot		4¾	31	CC
Cigarillo	Tip Cigarillo	*(tipped)*	5	28	CC

This three-shape brand features filler tobaccos from Colombia and Italy, surrounded by a homogenized wrapper and binder.

VILLA DE CUBA
Machine-made in Tampa, Florida, USA.

Shape	*Name*	*Lgth*	*Ring*	*Wrapper*
Corona	Brevas	5¾	44	CC-Ma

MACHINE-MADE CIGARS: BRAND LISTINGS

| Long Corona | Majestics | 6⅝ | 43 | CC-Ma |
| Giant Corona | Corona Grande | 7¼ | 45 | CC-Ma |

Choose a Sumatra or Connecticut Broadleaf (maduro) wrapper in this mild-bodied brand. It has a sheet binder and a three-nation blend of filler tobaccos.

VILLAZON DELUXE
Machine-made in Tampa, Florida, USA.

Shape	Name	Lgth	Ring	Wrapper
Giant Corona	Chairman	7¾	43	CM-Ma
Lonsdale	Cetros	7⅛	44	CM-Ma
Lonsdale	Senators	6¾	44	CM-Ma

Here is a veteran brand which features a Sumatra (natural) or Connecticut (maduro) wrapper, sheet binder and a short-filler blend of tobaccos from three nations. It is offered in boxes of 50 except for the Chairman style, offered in 25s.

VILLAZON DELUXE AROMATICS
Machine-made in Tampa, Florida, USA

Shape	Name	Lgth	Ring	Wrapper
Long Corona	Commodores	6	42	DC-CM-Ma
Slim Panatela	Panatella	5¾	34	DC-CM-Ma

Similar to the regular Villazon Deluxe line, this brand is flavored with vanilla and features a Sumatra wrapper to complement the homogenized binder and three-nation filler blend. It is offered in boxes of 50.

WHITE OWL
Machine-made in Dothan, Alabama, USA.

Shape	Name		Lgth	Ring	Wrapper
Cigarillo	Coronetta		4⅝	29	CC
Short Panatela	Demi-Tip	*(tipped)*	5⅛	32	CC

MACHINE-MADE CIGARS: BRAND LISTINGS

Cigarillo	Miniatures	4⅝	29	CC
Cigarillo	Miniatures Sweet	4⅝	29	CC
Slim Panatela	Panatela Deluxe	5¼	34	CC
Corona	Invincible	5⅜	41	CC
Corona	New Yorker	5⅝	41	CC
Slim Panatela	Ranger	6⅜	34	CC
Petit Corona	Sports	4¾	41	CC
	White Owl Select:			
Corona	Imperial	5⅝	41	CC
Petit Corona	Regent	4¾	41	CC
Cigarillo	Squire	4⅝	29	CC
Cigarillo	Darts	3¾	23	CC

This brand started way back in 1887. Today, there are two lines: White Owl and White Owl Select. The regular line includes a sheet wrapper and binder around a five-nation blend of filler tobaccos, while the Select line has a Connecticut Shade wrapper and is offered in packs of four or five cigars. The regular line is offered in twin-packs, five-packs, six-packs or in boxes of 50.

WM. ASCOT
Machine-made in Tampa, Florida, USA.

Shape	Name	Lgth	Ring	Wrapper
Lonsdale	Palma	6¼	42	DC-CC-Ma
Slim Panatela	Panatela	5¾	34	DC-CC-Ma

This is a very mild cigar, featuring an Ecuadorian wraper, sheet binder and Dominican and Honduran filler tobaccos. The Palma is offered in a variety of wrapper shades in boxes of 25 and the Panatela is available in boxes of 50.

WILLIAM PENN
Machine-made in Dothan, Alabama, USA.

MACHINE-MADE CIGARS: BRAND LISTINGS

Shape	Name		Lgth	Ring	Wrapper
Cigarillo	Willow Tips	(tipped)	5	27	CC
Cigarillo	Willow Tips Sweets	(tipped)	5	27	CC
Cigarillo	Braves		4⅝	29	CC
Corona	Perfecto		5⅜	41	CC
Slim Panatela	Panatela		5¼	34	CC

Introduced in 1924, William Penn cigars offer mild taste thanks to a multi-nation blend of filler tobaccos, surrounded by homogenized wrappers and binders. The brand is offered in twin-packs, five-packs and boxes of 50 in the larger sizes.

WINDSOR & MARK IV
Machine-made in Yoe, Pennsylvania, USA.

Shape	Name	Lgth	Ring	Wrapper
Giant Corona	Imperial	8	43	DC
Lonsdale	Maduro	6½	43	Ma
Lonsdale	Magnate	6½	43	DC
Lonsdale	Palma	6½	43	DC
Slim Panatela	Panatela	6½	34	DC
Petit Corona	Sportsmen	5	43	DC

From the respected House of Windsor comes the Windsor & Mark line, which features natural leaf wrappers, sheet binders and a filler blend of imported, short-filler, tobaccos. Most sizes are available in boxes of 50; the Maduro and Magnate sizes are available in boxes of 25.

WOLF BROS.
Machine-made in Yoe, Pennsylvania, USA.

Shape	Name	Lgth	Ring	Wrapper
Cigarillo	Nippers	4	20	CC
Small Panatela	Crookettes	4½	32	CC

MACHINE-MADE CIGARS: BRAND LISTINGS

Perfecto	Rum Crooks	5½	42	CC
Perfecto	Sweet Vanilla Crooks	5½	42	CC

These well-known cigars are also produced by the House of Windsor. Most of these shapes offer an imported leaf wrapper, sheet binder and a blend of imported short filler tobaccos. Please note the well-known flavored rum and vanilla shapes.

X-RATED
Machine-made in Tampa, Florida, USA.

Shape	*Name*	*Lgth*	*Ring*	*Wrapper*
Short Panatela	Honey Pie	5⅜	36	CC

New in 1997, this mild-bodied cigar features filler tobaccos from the Dominican Republic surrounded by homogenized binder and wrapper.

Y.B.
Machine-made in Wheeling, West Virginia, USA.

Shape	*Name*	*Lgth*	*Ring*	*Wrapper*
Petit Corona	Squires	5	42½	CC

This old brand includes only one size, but it offers a medium body thanks to filler tobaccos from the Dominican Republic and the United States and a sheet binder and wrapper.

7.
SMALL CIGARS

This section provides the details on 53 brands of small cigars, generally made by machine for distribution to the widest possible audience in drug stores, supermarkets and, of course, tobacco stores.

For the purposes of this listing, small cigar "brands" are limited to those whose lines are dominated by (i.e., 67 percent or more of the shapes are) cigarillo or cheroot-shaped cigars. In addition, brands in the handmade or mass-market sections that offer the cigarillo shape in their lines include:

Handmade brands (51):

Acapa Sweets	Hamiltons
Andujar	Hamiltons Reserve
Antelo	Hannibal
Belinda	Havana Sunrise
Caoba	Hoyo de Monterrey
Carbonell	Hugo Cassar Private Coll.
Casa de Gonzalez	Iracema
Davidoff	Island Amaretto
Don Antonio	Jimenez
Don Diego	Jose Benito
Don Xavier	José Girbés
El Rey del Mundo	J-R Ultimate
Excalibur	Juan Clemente
Express Imports	La Gloria Cubana
Famous Rum Runner	Macanudo
Fittipaldi	Mendez y Lopez
H. Upmann	Montecruz

SMALL CIGARS: BRAND LISTINGS

Nat Sherman
Old Fashioned
Oscar
Partagas
Pleiades
Pride of Copan
Primo del Rey
Private Stock
Punch

Quirantes
RG Santiago Dominican
Santa Clara 1830
Suerdieck
Te-Amo
12 Stars
West Indies Vanilla
Zino

Mass-market brands (30):
Antonio y Cleopatra
Arango Sportsman
As You Like It
Balmoral
Candlelight
De Olifant
Directors
Don Antonio
Dutch Masters
El Gozo
El Verso
Garcia y Vega
Hav-A-Tampa
Havana Blend
Ibold

J. Cortes
King Edward
La Paz
Muriel
Phillies
R.G. Dun
Rivalo
Robert Burns
Swisher Sweets
Tampa Nugget
Tampa Sweet
White Owl
William Penn
Wolf Bros.
Zino

Each brand listing includes notes on country of manufacture, shapes, names, lengths, ring gauges and wrapper color *as supplied by the manufacturers and/or distributors of these brands.* Ring gauges for some cigarillos were not available.

SMALL CIGARS: BRAND LISTINGS

When comparing and considering cigars listed in this category, it may be worthwhile to remember the standard dimensions of mass-produced cigarettes: almost always 7.9 mm in diameter (20 ring gauge) with lengths of 85 mm (approx. 3¼ inches) or 100 mm (approx. 3⅞ inches).

Please note that while a cigar may be manufactured in one country, it may contain tobaccos from many nations. These cigars utilize short-filler tobaccos unless otherwise noted; a number of brands use homogenized (sheet) leaf for binders and/or filler.

Although manufacturers have recognized more than 70 shades of wrapper color, six major color groupings are used here. Their abbreviations include:

- ▸ DC = Double Claro: green, also known as "AMS."
- ▸ Cl = Claro: a very light tan color.
- ▸ CC = Colorado Claro: a medium brown common to many cigars on this list.
- ▸ Co = Colorado: reddish-brown.
- ▸ CM = Colorado Maduro: dark brown.
- ▸ Ma = Maduro: very dark brown or black (also known as "double Maduro" or "Oscuro.")

Many manufacturers call their wrapper colors "Natural" or "English Market Selection." These colors cover a wide range of browns and we have generally grouped them in the "CC" range. Darker wrappers such as those from Cameroon show up most often in the "CM" category.

SMALL CIGARS: BRAND LISTINGS

Readers who would like to see their favorite brand listed in the 1999 edition can call or write the compilers as noted after the Table of Contents.

AGIO
Machine-made in Geel, Belgium.

Shape	Name	Lgth	Ring	Wrapper
Cigarillo	Biddies Brazil	3¼	20	Ma
Cigarillo	Biddies Sumatra	3¼	20	CC
Cigarillo	Mehari's Sumatra	4	23	CC
Cigarillo	Mehari's Brasil	4	23	Ma
Cigarillo	Mehari's Mild & Light	4	23	CI
Cigarillo	Mehari's Mild & Sweet	4	23	CM
Cigarillo	Mini Mehari's	2⅞	22	CC
Cigarillo	Mini Mehari's Mild & Light	2⅞	22	CI
Cigarillo	Filter Tip *(tipped)*	3	21	CC
Cigarillo	Lights	3	21	CC
Small Panatela	Senoritas Red Label	4	31	CC
Small Panatela	Elegant	4⅛	32	CC

Here is one of the famous brands in cigarillos, offering dry-cured cigarillos and small cigars for almost every taste. Most of the shapes use wrapper leaves from Java; the Mini Mehari's Mild & Light and Mehari's Mild & Light use a Connecticut wrapper; the Mehari's Brasil features a Brazilian-grown wrapper; the Biddies Sumatra, Senoritas Red Label and Elegant have Sumatran wrappers; and the Mehari's wrapper is from the Cameroon. All use a sheet binder and a blend of mild tobaccos in the filler.

AL-CAPONE
Machine-made in Germany.

SMALL CIGARS: BRAND LISTINGS

Shape	Name	Lgth	Ring	Wrapper
Cigarillo	Sweets	3¼		CC
Cigarillo	Pockets	2¾		CC

These cigarillos are made by the famous Dannemann firm and are offered in convenient packs of five (Sweets) and ten (Pockets).

ALTERNATIVOS GOLD & BLACK
Machine-made in Wuustweesel, Belgiuim.

Shape	Name	Lgth	Ring	Wrapper
Cigarillo	Mild	3½	23	CC
Cigarillo	Mild & Light	3½	23	CC

Introduced in 1994, these small cigars offer a blend of Ecuador (wrapper), Java and Malawi tobaccos. The Mild style presents a full flavor, while the Mild & Light style is medium in body.

AVANTI
Machine-made in Scranton, Pennsylvania, USA.

Shape	Name	Lgth	Ring	Wrapper
Cheroot	Avanti	4½	34	Ma
Cheroot	Avanti Continental	5¾	34	Ma
Cheroot	Europa	5¾	34	Ma
Cheroot	Ipenema	5¾	34	Ma
Cheroot	Ramrod Deputy	4½	34	Ma
Cheroot	Ramrod Original	6½	34	Ma
Cheroot	Kentucky Cheroots	5¾	34	Ma

Here is an all-tobacco, dry-cured, medium-bodied line of cigars, famous since their introduction in 1972. The ingredients are simple: fire-cured tobaccos from at least three different crop years of the finest farms in Kentucky and Tennessee, all barn-cured for at least four months. The Avanti and Avanti Continental are flavored with Anisette; the Ramrod Deputy and Ramrod Original are Bourbon flavored.

The Europa, introduced in 1994, uses a Kentucky dark-fired wrapper and binder and a blend of Belgian and Italian dark-fired tobacco for the filler.

BACKWOODS
Machine-made in Cayey, Puerto Rico.

Shape	Name	Lgth	Ring	Wrapper
Cigarillo	Regular	4⅛	27	CC
Cigarillo	Sweet Aromatic	4⅛	27	CC
Cigarillo	Black & Sweet Aromatic	4⅛	27	Ma

This 100% tobacco brand offers a mild taste but a surprise in its unfinished, "open" end. It has a natural or blackened wrapper, no binder and a blend of short-filler tobaccos. It is presented in foil packs of 8.

BETWEEN THE ACTS
Machine-made in Tampa, Florida, USA.

Shape	Name	Lgth	Ring	Wrapper
Cigarillo	Between the Acts	3⅛	20	CC

Between the acts of your favorite show you can enjoy this mild, flavorful smoke, made up of a sheet wrapper and binder and filler tobaccos from Indonesia and the United States. Offered in packs of 20.

BLACKSTONE
Machine-made in Jacksonville, Florida, USA.

Shape	Name	Lgth	Ring	Wrapper
Cigarillo	Mild	4⅞	28	CC
Cigarillo	Sweet Cherry	4⅞	28	CC

This is a new brand for 1997, with a pipe-tobacco filler surrounded by a homogenized wrapper in two easy-to-enjoy flavors.

Cigarillos, Cheroots and Panatelas

Here are examples of the smallest cigars available on the market today:

- Cigarillos and cheroots   6 or less inches long with a ring gauge of 29 or less.

- Panatela group, including
  - . Small Panatela   4-5 inches long; 30-34 ring.
  - . Slim Panatela   5 inches and more; 30-34 ring.
  - . Short Panatela   4-5⅝ inches long; 35-39 ring.
  - . Panatela   5½-6⅞ inches long; 35-39 ring.
  - . Long Panatela   7 inches and more; 35-39 ring.

Pictured opposite, from left to right:

- **CAPTAIN BLACK** *Sweet*   *(shape)*
  (United States)   3⅞ x 20   Little Cigar

- **DAVIDOFF** *Cigarillo*
  (Denmark)   3½ x 20   Cigarillo

- **CHRISTIAN OF DENMARK** *Long Cigarillo*
  (Denmark)   4 x 20   Cigarillo

- **PETRI** *Toscanelli*
  (United States)   4 x 34   Cheroot

- **PARODI** *Kings*
  (United States)   4½ x 34   Cheroot

- **EL REY DEL MUNDO** *Reynitas*
  (Honduras)   5 x 38   Short Panatela

- **DON TOMAS SPECIAL EDITION** *No. 400*
  (Honduras)   7 x 36   Long Panatela

SMALL CIGARS: BRAND LISTINGS

CAPTAIN BLACK LITTLE CIGARS
Machine-made in Tucker, Georgia, USA.

Shape	Name	Lgth	Ring	Wrapper
Cigarillo	Regular	3⅞	20	CC
Cigarillo	Sweets	3⅞	20	CC

Featuring the famous taste of Captain Black pipe tobacco, these little gems offer a mild taste, with a sheet wrapper and a blend of Indonesian, Philippine and United States tobaccos. Available in packs of 20.

CHARLES FAIRMORN
Machine-made in Dingelstadt, Germany.

Shape	Name	Lgth	Ring	Wrapper
Cigarillo	Piper's Mini Vanilla	3	20	CC
Cigarillo	Piper's Mini Cherry	3	20	CM
Cigarillo	Piper's Mini Plum	3	20	Ma
Small Panatela	Piper's Corona Vanilla	4¾	33	CC
Small Panatela	Piper's Corona Cherry	4¾	33	CM
Small Panatela	Piper's Corona Plum	4¾	33	Ma
Cigarillo	Piper's Panatela Vanilla	4½	25	CC
Cigarillo	Piper's Panatela Cherry	4½	25	CM
Cigarillo	Piper's Panatela Plum	4½	25	Ma

This line of cigarillos and small panatelas complements the handmade Charles Fairmorn line. These are all-tobacco, mild cigars available in three flavors and three wrappers: the Vanilla shapes all use Sumatran wrappers, while the Cherry range has Connecticut wrappers and the Plum group uses Brazilian Mata Fina tobacco for its wrappers. All sizes have Javan binders and fillers which are half pipe tobacco and half dry-cured tobacco of several types.

CHRISTIAN OF DENMARK
Machine-made in Denmark.

SMALL CIGARS: BRAND LISTINGS

Shape	*Name*	*Lgth*	*Ring*	*Wrapper*
Cigarillo	Mini Cigarillos	3½	20	CM
Cigarillo	Long Cigarillos	3¾	20	CM
Cigarillo	Light Cigarillos	3½	20	CC

This mild cigarillo is made of dry-cured, 100% tobacco, wrapped in Indonesian leaf (except for the Lights) with Brazilian, Dominican and Indonesian tobacco inside. Christian cigarillos are offered in 20-packs.

DANNEMANN

Machine-made in Germany and Switzerland.

Shape	*Name*	*Lgth*	*Ring*	*Wrapper*
	Made in Germany:			
Cigarillo	Moods	2⅞	20	CC
Cigarillo	Sweets	3⅝	20	CC
Cigarillo	Originale - Brazil	2⅞	20	Ma
Cigarillo	Originale - Sumatra	2⅞	20	CC
Cigarillo	Speciale - Brazil	2⅞	25	Ma
Cigarillo	Speciale - Sumatra	2⅞	25	CC
Cigarillo	Speciale - Lights	2⅞	25	Cl
Cigarillo	Imperial - Brazil	4¼	25	Ma
Cigarillo	Imperial - Sumatra	4¼	25	CC
Cigarillo	Lonja - Brazil	5⅜	25	Ma
Cigarillo	Lonja - Sumatra	5⅜	25	CC
Cigarillo	Menor - Sumatra	3⅞	28	CC
Cigarillo	Pierrot - Brazil	3⅞	28	Ma
	Made in Switzerland:			
Slim Panatela	Lights - Sumatra	6	34	CC
Slim Panatela	Lights - Brazil	6	34	Ma

SMALL CIGARS: BRAND LISTINGS

Corona Extra	Espada - Sumatra	5	45	CC
Corona Extra	Espada - Brazil	5	45	Ma
Cigarillo	Slims - Sumatra	6½	28	CC
Cigarillo	Slims - Brazil	6½	28	Ma

Geraldo Dannemann created this brand in 1873 and today, these famous all-tobacco, dry-cured cigarillos and small cigars feature primarily Sumatran and Brazilian tobaccos and are offered in a dizzying array of packs, tins and boxes of 25 for the small cigars.

DAVIDOFF CIGARILLOS
Machine-made in Denmark and the Netherlands.

Shape	Name	Lgth	Ring	Wrapper
	Made in Ny Kobing, Denmark:			
Cigarillo	Mini Cigarillos	3½	20	CC
Cigarillo	Mini Light	3½	20	Co
Cigarillo	Long Cigarillos	4½	20	CC
	Made in Eersel, the Netherlands:			
Cigarillo	Demi-Tasse	4	22	CC
Cigarillo	Long Panatelas	5½	22	CC

These elegant cigars are all tobacco which use natural leaf and are dry-cured for smoothness. All feature a Sumatra wrapper, Java binder and filler tobaccos from Brazil and Indonesia.

DENOBILI
Machine-made in Scranton, Pennsylvania, USA.

Shape	Name	Lgth	Ring	Wrapper
Cheroot	Popular	3½	34	Ma
Cheroot	Twin Pack	4	34	Ma
Cheroot	Economy	4	34	Ma

SMALL CIGARS: BRAND LISTINGS

Cheroot	Kings	4½	34	Ma
Cheroot	Toscani	6½	34	Ma
Cheroot	Toscani Longs	6½	34	Ma

A wide variety of sizes marks this dry-cured, 100%-tobacco brand, which uses only dark-fired Kentucky and Tennessee tobaccos in its blend. A brand of distinction since 1896, the Denobili range is marked by a mellow, medium-bodied taste.

DUCADOS
Machine-made in Madrid, Spain.

Shape	Name	Lgth	Ring	Wrapper
Cigarillo	Ducados	3	26	CM

These cigarillos are fairly mild, thanks to the Sumatran wrapper. A sheet binder is used, along with a blended filler; Ducados are offered in tins of 10 and and boxes of 50.

DUNHILL SMALL CIGARS
Machine-made in Wageningen, the Netherlands.

Shape	Name	Lgth	Ring	Wrapper
Cigarillo	Miniatures	3¼	26	CC
Cigarillo	Senoritas	3⅞	32	CC
Cigarillo	Panatellas	5½	26	CC

These are elegant cigarillos fully worthy of the revered Dunhill name. Each uses a delicate Sumatra wrapper, Java binder and a combination of Brazilian Bahia and Java fillers to create a mild, flavorful taste. The Senoritas and Pantellas are offered in boxes of five, while the Miniatures are packaged in boxes of 10 cigars each.

DUTCH DELITES
BY VILLIGER
Machine-made in Germany.

SMALL CIGARS: BRAND LISTINGS

Shape	Name	Lgth	Ring	Wrapper
Cigarillo	Light Sumatra	4⅝	20	CC
Cigarillo	Brasil	4⅝	20	CM

The famous Villiger firm offers a choice of wrappers in this cigarillo, available in boxes of 50. The wrappers are from either Sumatra or Brazil, with a sheet binder and a blend of filler tobaccos.

DUTCH TREATS
Machine-made in McAdoo, Pennsylvania, USA.

Shape	Name	Lgth	Ring	Wrapper
Cigarillo	Regular	3⅞	20	CC
Cigarillo	Menthol	3⅞	20	CC
Cigarillo	Pipe Aroma	3⅞	20	CC
Cigarillo	Sweet	3⅞	20	CC
Cigarillo	Ultra Lite	3⅞	20	CC

Here are elegant little cigars, with a homogenized wrapper, no binder and a filler blend of short-filler tobaccos, presented in easy-to-carry packs of 20.

ERIK
Machine-made in Tampa, Florida, USA.

Shape	Name		Lgth	Ring	Wrapper
Cigarillo	Natural	(tipped)	3⅞	21	CM
Cigarillo	Menthol	(tipped)	3⅞	21	CM
Cigarillo	Cherry Flavor	(tipped)	3⅞	21	CM

The familiar Viking-ship logo adorns the ten-pack box of this filter-tipped brand, which features filler tobaccos from the Dominican Republic and the United States with a sheet wrapper and binder.

SMALL CIGARS: BRAND LISTINGS

FLEUR DE SAVANE
Machine-made in France.

Shape	Name	Lgth	Ring	Wrapper
Cigarillo	Petits	3¼	21	CM
Cigarillo	Petits Light	3¼	21	CM
Small Panatela	Wilde Cigares	4¾	31	CM
Cigarillo	Wilde Cigarillos	4	23	CM

New to the United States in 1997, this line features Cameroon wrappers, sheet binders and a blend of Cameroon-grown filler tobaccos. It is offered in packs or 20 or boxes of 50.

FUN LITTLE CIGARS
Machine-made in Wuustweesel, Belgium.

Shape	Name	Lgth	Ring	Wrapper
Cigarillo	Fun	3½	22	CC

Introduced in 1997, this is an all-tobacco cigarillo with an Ecuadorian wrapper and Dominican filler. It is offered in ten-packs.

G.A. ANDRON
Machine-made in Ireland.

Shape	Name	Lgth	Ring	Wrapper
Cigarillo	Brazil Cigarillo	3	23	CM
Cigarillo	Sumatra Cigarillo	3	23	CC

GESTY
Machine-made in Brazil.

Shape	Name	Lgth	Ring	Wrapper
Cigarillo	Muritiba	4¼		Ma
Cigarillo	Mara Longo	5½		Ma

SMALL CIGARS: BRAND LISTINGS

GOLD SEAL
Machine-made in Indonesia.

Shape	Name	Lgth	Ring	Wrapper
Cigarillo	Cigarillos	3⅝	24	CC
Cigarillo	Senoritas	4⅜	28	CC

This is an all-tobacco, dry-cured series, with a Sumatran wrapper, Javan binder and short filler from Brazil and Caribbean nations.

HAV-A-TAMPA LITTLE CIGARS
Machine-made in Tampa, Florida, USA.

Shape	Name	Lgth	Ring	Wrapper
Cigarillo	Naturale	3⅛	20	CC
Cigarillo	Sweet	3⅛	20	CC

This famous brand offers a little cigar with a sheet wrapper and binder and a blend of filler tobaccos from Honduras and the Dominican Republic.

HENRI WINTERMAN
Machine-made in Eersel, the Netherlands.

Shape	Name	Lgth	Ring	Wrapper
Cigarillo	Cafe Creme	2⅞	28	CC
Cigarillo	Cafe Creme Mini Mild	2⅞	28	CC
Cigarillo	Cafe Creme Mini	2⅞	28	CC
Cigarillo	Cafe Creme Plus Mild	2⅞	28	CC
Cigarillo	Cafe Creme Plus	2⅞	28	CC
Cigarillo	Scooters	3½	28	CC-Ma
Cigarillo	Cafe Noir	2⅞	28	Ma
Cigarillo	Cafe Creme Mild	2⅞	28	CC
Cigarillo	Cafe Creme Tips	3⅞	28	CC

SMALL CIGARS: BRAND LISTINGS

Cigarillo	Slim Panatella	6	26	CC
Cigarillo	Senoritas	4	32	CC

Since its introduction in 1963, this is one of the best-known and most appreciated brands in cigarillos and small cigars. These are mild, dry-cured cigars of high quality sold in more than 100 countries worldwide.

INDIANA SLIMS
Machine-made in Germany.

Shape	Name	Lgth	Ring	Wrapper
Cigarillo	Indiana Slims	3¼	26	Ma

Despite the American-sounding name, these rum-dipped cigars are made in Germany, dry-cured and offered in packages of 10 cigars each.

LA CORONA
Machine-made in Cayey, Puerto Rico.

Shape	Name	Lgth	Ring	Wrapper
Cigarillo	Whiffs	3⅝	23⅔	Ma
Cigarillo	Whiffs Light	3⅝	23⅔	Cl

The famous La Corona brand continues with the Whiffs series, with the Light style added in 1995. Both sizes offer a natural Connecticut wrapper and sheet binder to complement the blend of short-filler tobaccos.

MADISON
Machine-made in Tampa, Florida, USA.

Shape	Name	Lgth	Ring	Wrapper
Cigarillo	Madison	3⅛	20	CC

The Madison taste is mild, with a filler blend of Indonesian and United States tobaccos, combined with a sheet wrapper and binder, offered in packs of 20.

SMALL CIGARS: BRAND LISTINGS

MARSH
Machine-made in Wheeling, West Virginia, USA.

Shape	Name	Lgth	Ring	Wrapper
Cigarillo	Rough-Cut	4⅜	28	CM
Cigarillo	Cheroot	4⅜	28	CM

Here is a new for 1997 all-tobacco line which features a Pennsylvania-grown (Amish country!) Broadleaf wrapper and a U.S. and Dominican-grown filler blend. You'll find in special six-packs!

MECCARILLOS
Machine-made in France.

Shape	Name	Lgth	Ring	Wrapper
Cigarillo	Filter Cigarillos	3¼	21	CC

New to the U.S. in 1997, this line features a Sumatra wrapper, sheet binder and a blend of filler tobaccos from Brazil and Indonesia. Offered in packs of 20.

MOCAMBO LITTLE CIGARS
Machine-made in Ireland.

Shape	Name	Lgth	Ring	Wrapper
Cigarillo	Little Cigarillos	3¼	25	CM-Ma
Cigarillo	Wilde Cigarillos	3½	27	CM-Ma
Cigarillo	Senoritas	3½	30	CM-Ma
Short Panatela	Half Corona	3¾	36	CM-Ma
Cigarillo	Wilde Havana	3½	30	CM-Ma

Although the cigars are small, they are of medium body and feature a Sumatra wrapper or maduro wrapper grown in Brazil. They come in packs of 25 or 50.

NOBEL CIGARS
Machine-made in Eersel, the Netherlands.

SMALL CIGARS: BRAND LISTINGS

Shape	Name	Lgth	Ring	Wrapper
Cigarillo	Petit Sumatra	3⅜	20	CC
Cigarillo	Medium Panatela Sumatra	3½	22	CC
Cigarillo	Grand Panatela Sumatra	5½	28	CC
Cigarillo	Petit Corona	3½	32	CC
Cigarillo	Petit Lights	3⅜	20	CC

Introduced in 1898, these elegant cigarillos are dry-cured and made of 100% tobacco, especially Indonesian Sumatran wrappers and Java binders in most sizes.

OMEGA
Machine-made in Tampa, Florida, USA.

Shape	Name		Lgth	Ring	Wrapper
Cigarillo	Omega	*(tipped)*	3⅜	20	CC
Cigarillo	National Slims 100		3⅞	20	CC
Cigarillo	Cherry Flavor Slims 100		3⅞	20	CC
Cigarillo	Menthol Slims 100		3⅞	20	CC

Here's a mild-bodied smoke in a choice of flavors, with a sheet wrapper and binder and a blend of filler tobaccos from Indonesia and the United States.

ORO DE RENITAS
Machine-made in France.

Shape	Name	Lgth	Ring	Wrapper
Cigarillo	Regular	3½	21	CC
Cigarillo	Light	3½	21	CC
Cigarillo	Aromatic	3½	21	CC

Here is a new cigarillo in the U.S. market for 1997, with a Sumatra wrapper, sheet binder and a mix of Brazilian and Indonesian tobaccos in the filler. It is offered in packs of 20.

SMALL CIGARS: BRAND LISTINGS

PANTER
Machine-made in Geel, Belgium.

Shape	Name	Lgth	Ring	Wrapper
Cigarillo	Sprint	2⅞	21	CC
Cigarillo	Small	2⅞	21	CC
Cigarillo	Lights	2⅞	20	CI
Cigarillo	Silhouette	3⅜	20	CC
Cigarillo	Limbo	3⅞	24	CC
Cigarillo	Mignon	3¾	25	CC
Cigarillo	Mignon de Luxe	3⅜	20	CC
Cigarillo	Tango	3⅞	23	CC
Cigarillo	Vitesse	3¾	23	CC
Cigarillo	Mild Panatellas	5¾	21	CC

A famous brand in cigarillos for many years, the Panter is made by the highly-respected Agio Sigarfabrieken in Holland. The Silhouette, Bijou, Limbo and Panatellas shapes are all-tobacco cigars; the other shapes use a sheet binder. Wrappers come from Java (on Sprint, Small, Mignon and the Panatellas), Sumatra (Silhouette, Bijou and Limbo) and Connecticut (Lights). A new shape, the Mignon Deluxe, features an Ecuadorian wrapper.

PARODI
Machine-made in Scranton, Pennsylvania, USA.

Shape	Name	Lgth	Ring	Wrapper
Cheroot	Ammezzati	3½	34	Ma
Cheroot	Twin Pack	4	34	Ma
Cheroot	Bon Gusto	4	34	Ma
Cheroot	Cello	4	34	Ma
Cheroot	Economy	4	34	Ma
Cheroot	Kings	4½	34	Ma

Here are famous dry-cured, 100% tobacco cigars which use only the finest, dark-fired tobaccos from Kentucky and Tennessee. Highly respected since their introduction in 1913, the blend of leaves always includes not less than three different crop years, which contributes to the medium-bodied flavor which Parodi is famous for.

PEDRONI
Machine-made in Switzerland.

Shape	Name	Lgth	Ring	Wrapper
Cheroot	Classico	3⅝	34	Ma
Cheroot	Anisette	3⅝	34	Ma

These small treats feature dry-cured, dark-fired leaves and are all tobacco; Pedronis are offered in twin-packs and five-packs.

PETRI
Machine-made in Scranton, Pennsylvania, USA.

Shape	Name	Lgth	Ring	Wrapper
Cheroot	AA	3½	34	Ma
Cheroot	Squillo	4	34	Ma
Cheroot	Sigaretto	3½	34	Ma
Cheroot	Sigaretto Kings	4	34	Ma
Cheroot	Toscanelli	4	34	Ma
Cheroot	Toscani	6½	34	Ma

Created in 1906, Petri offers all-tobacco, dry-cured cigars with a medium-bodied taste. The wrapper, binder and filler are all dark-fired Kentucky and Tennessee tobaccos from at least three different crop years.

PHILLIES LITTLE CIGARS
Machine-made in Selma, Alabama, USA.

Shape	Name	Lgth	Ring	Wrapper
Cigarillo	Natural	3⅛	20	CC

SMALL CIGARS: BRAND LISTINGS

Cigarillo	Sweet		3⅛	20	CC

Here are little cigars with the mild taste of the famous Phillies line. The filler tobaccos are a combination of chopped Indonesian and United States leaves, surrounded by a sheet wrapper and binder.

PRINCE ALBERT
Machine-made in King of Prussia, Pennsylvania, USA.

Shape	Name	Lgth	Ring	Wrapper
Cigarillo	Soft & Sweet Vanilla *(tipped)*	4⅞	20	CM

These tipped cigars are extremely mild and feature an all-pipe tobacco filler, aimed at providing pipe tobacco taste - and aroma - in cigar form.

RUSTLERS
Machine-made in McAdoo, Pennsylvania, USA.

Shape	Name	Lgth	Ring	Wrapper
Cigarillo	Black 'n Cherry	3⅞	23	CC
Cigarillo	Menthol	3⅞	23	CC
Cigarillo	Sweets	3⅞	23	CC

This is a machine-made little cigar with a filter tip and a manufactured wrapper, offered in three flavored styles in flip-top boxes of seven cigars each.

ST. REGIS
Machine-made in Tampa, Florida, USA.

Shape	Name	Lgth	Ring	Wrapper
Cigarillo	Regular	3⅞	20	CC
Cigarillo	Menthol	3⅞	20	CC
Cigarillo	Pipe Bouquet	3⅞	20	CC

SMALL CIGARS: BRAND LISTINGS

These little cigars have been around since 1951 and offer a mild taste, featuring a blend of U.S. tobaccos in the filler core. Available in packs of 20.

SCHIMMELPENNICK
Machine-made in Wageningen, the Netherlands.

Shape	Name		Lgth	Ring	Wrapper
Small Panatela	Florina		3⅞	32	CC
Short Panatela	Half Corona		3¾	36	CC
Cigarillo	Nostra		2⅞	20	CC
Cigarillo	Media		3	20	CC
Cigarillo	Media Brazil		3	20	Ma
Cigarillo	Mono		3⅜	22	CC
Cigarillo	Mono Brazil		3⅜	22	Ma
Small Panatela	Vada		3⅞	32	CC
Cigarillo	Mini Tips	(tipped)	4	20	CC
Cigarillo	Duet		5⅝	26	CC
Cigarillo	Duet Brazil		5⅝	24	Ma
Cigarillo	Duet Midi		4¾	26	CC
Cigarillo	Duet Mini		2⅞	26	CC
Cigarillo	Duet Plus		3½	26	CC
Cigarillo	Mini Cigar		2¾	20	CC
Cigarillo	Mini Cigar Milds		2¾	20	CC
Cigarillo	Havana Lights		3	20	CC
Cigarillo	Havana Milds		3	20	CC
Cigarillo	Swing		3	20	CC

One of the great names in cigarillos, enjoyed in more than 130 countries. These carefully-blended small cigars utilize tobaccos of a half-dozen nations to achieve their trademark mild-to-medium body and rich flavor. Highlights of the shapes include Indonesian wrappers on the Half Corona, Media, Mini Tip and Mono;

SMALL CIGARS: BRAND LISTINGS

Brazilian and Javan tobaccos in the Florina; a Cameroon wrapper and 12 types of filler tobaccos in the Vada; a combination of Brazilian, Indonesian and Cameroon leaves in the Duet; a Sumatran-seed wrapper grown in Brazil on the Mini, and a Connecticut Shade wrapper on the Mini Mild. The only flavored cigar of the line is the Swing, which offers a surprising taste of mango!

SUERDIECK
Made in Cruz des Almas, Brazil.

Shape	Name	Lgth	Ring	Wrapper
	Handmade, with 100% tobacco:			
Cigarillo	Copacabana	5	29	CC
Cigarillo	Brasilia Petit	3⅛	22	CM
Cigarillo	Beira Mar Finos	5¼	28	CM
	Machine-made, with sheet binders:			
Cigarillo	Palomitas	3½	32	CM
Cigarillo	Reynitas	3⅛	22	CC-CM

The all-tobacco cigarillos are the pride of Brazil, with all home-grown tobaccos used in the blend. The Palomitas shape is available in a classic style plus two flavored styles: cherry and clove.

SUPER VALUE LITTLE CIGARS
Machine-made in McAdoo, Pennsylvania, USA.

Shape	Name	Lgth	Ring	Wrapper
Cigarillo	Cherry	3⅞	20	CC
Cigarillo	Sweet	3⅞	20	CC
Cigarillo	Menthol	3⅞	20	CC
Cigarillo	Ultra Mild	3⅞	20	CC

This brand uses manufactured wrappers and has filter tips. Super Values are offered in packs of 20.

SMALL CIGARS: BRAND LISTINGS

SUPRE SWEETS
*Machine-made in McAdoo, Pennsylvania, USA
and Cayey, Puerto Rico.*

Shape	Name		Lgth	Ring	Wrapper
Cigarillo	Tip Cigarillo	(tipped)	5⅛	27	CM
Cigarillo	Cigarillos		4¾	27½	CM
Petit Corona	Perfectos		4¾	44	CM
Cigarillo	Little Cigars		3⅞	20	CM

The tip Cigarillo and Little Cigars are made in McAdoo, Pennsylvania, while the Perfectos and Cigarillos are produced in Puerto Rico. All styles feature a manufactured wrapper and binder around a short-filler center.

TIJUANA SMALLS
Machine-made in Dothan, Alabama, USA.

Shape	Name		Lgth	Ring	Wrapper
Cigarillo	Aromatic	(tipped)	4¼	21	CC
Cigarillo	Cherry	(tipped)	4¼	21	CC
Cigarillo	Regular	(tipped)	4¼	21	CC

Created in 1968, these mild cigars are tipped and made with sheet wrappers and binders and a blend of filler tobaccos. They are sold only in ten-packs.

TIPARILLO
Machine-made in Dothan, Alabama, USA.

Shape	Name		Lgth	Ring	Wrapper
Cigarillo	Mild Blend	(tipped)	5	27	CC
Cigarillo	Sweet Blend	(tipped)	5	27	CC
Cigarillo	Aromatic	(tipped)	5	27	CC
Cigarillo	Menthol	(tipped)	5	27	CC

SMALL CIGARS: BRAND LISTINGS

These sleek cigars are made with sheet wrapper and binder and a blend of filler tobaccos; all of the sizes feature plastic tips. Tiparillos are offered in five-packs and boxes of 50.

TOBAJARA
Machine-made in Germany.

Shape	Name	Lgth	Ring	Wrapper
Cigarillo	No. 1 Brazil	3¼	20	CM
Cigarillo	No. 2 Brazil	3⅝	26	CM
Cigarillo	Chicos Brazil	5½	28	CM

This is a medium-bodied, dry-cured cigarillo, offered in packs of 20 for the No. 1 and No. 2 models and in five-packs for the Chicos. This brand features a Brazilian wrapper, sheet binder and filler tobacco from Brazil and Indonesia.

TORINO
Machine-made in Scranton, Pennsylvania, USA.

Shape	Name	Lgth	Ring	Wrapper
Cheroot	Twin	4	34	Ma
Cheroot	King	4½	34	Ma

This blend is 100% tobacco, using only dark-fired Kentucky and Tennessee leaves for a medium-bodied taste . . . but flavored with a touch of vanilla!

VICTORIA
Machine-made in Las Palmas, the Canary Islands of Spain.

Shape	Name	Lgth	Ring	Wrapper
Cigarillo	Mini	3¾	23	CC
Cigarillo	Cortados	3½	27	CC
Cigarillo	No. 5	4⅛	26	CC
Small Panatela	No. 10	4	30	CC
Small Panatela	No. 15	4¼	34	CC

SMALL CIGARS: BRAND LISTINGS

Cigarillo	Coronas Reserve	3¼	20	CC
Cigarillo	Helios Capote Mini Club	4	23	CC

This light-bodied smoke features either a Connecticut wrapper (Cortados, Cigarro, No. 15, Coronas Reserve) or a Sheet wrapper (Mini, No. 10, Capote Mini Club), offered in 10-packs (except for the Coronas Reserve, in 20s).

VILLIGER
Machine-made in Germany and Switzerland.

Shape	Name	Lgth	Ring	Wrapper
Cigarillo	Villiger-Kiel Mild *(tipped)*	6⅝	29	CI
Cigarillo	Villiger-Kiel Brasil *(tipped)*	6⅝	29	CM
Cigarillo	Villiger-Kiel Junior Mild *(tipped)*	4½	25	CI
Cigarillo	Villiger-Kiel Junior Brasil *(tipped)*	4½	25	CM
Short Panatela	Villiger Export	4	36	CC
Short Panatela	Villiger Export Kings	5⅛	36	CC
Cigarillo	Villiger Premium No. 3	6⅛	37	CI
Cigarillo	Villiger Premium No. 6	3¾	23	CI
Short Panatela	Villiger Premium No. 7	4	38	CI
Cigarillo	Villiger Premium No. 10	2¾	22	CI
Short Panatela	Jewels	3⅞	38	CC
Panatela	Menorca	6⅛	38	CC
Cigarillo	Rillos *(tipped)*	5	29	CC
Cigarillo	Braniff No. 2	4⅛	20	CI
Cigarillo	Braniff No. 3	4⅛	20	CM
Short Panatela	Braniff No. 8	4	38	CI

SMALL CIGARS: BRAND LISTINGS

| Cigarillo | Braniff Cortos Dark | 3¼ | 20 | CM |
| Cigarillo | Braniff Cortos Filter Light | 3 | 20 | CI |

This famous brand began in 1888 and continues today as one of the world's most respected producers of cigarillos and small cigars. These models range in body from mild-to-medium to medium, using primarily Indonesian and Brazilian wrappers.

WINCHESTER LITTLE CIGARS
Machine-made in the United States.

Shape	*Name*	*Lgth*	*Ring*	*Wrapper*
Cigarillo	100s	3⅞	20	CC
Cigarillo	Light 100s	3⅞	20	CC
Cigarillo	Menthol 100s	3⅞	20	CC
Cigarillo	Sweet 100s	3⅞	20	CC
Cigarillo	Kings	3¼	20	CC
Cigarillo	Menthol Kings	3¼	20	CC

8.
INTERNATIONAL MEASUREMENT TABLE

For readers more conversant with cigar lengths in centimeters and ring gauges (diameter) expressed in millimeters, the following table will allow conversion of imperial measures into their metric equivalents.

Length	
In 1/8ths of an inch	Length in cm
2½	6.35
2⅝	6.68
2¾	6.99
2⅞	7.32
3	7.62
3⅛	7.94
3¼	8.25
3⅜	8.57
3½	8.89
3⅝	9.21
3¾	9.52
3⅞	9.84
4	10.16
4⅛	10.48
4¼	10.79
4⅜	11.11
4½	11.43
4⅝	11.75

Ring Gauge/Diameter	
In 1/64ths of an inch	Diameter in mm
20	7.9
21	8.3
22	8.7
23	9.1
24	9.5
25	9.9
26	10.3
27	10.7
28	11.1
29	11.5
30	11.9
31	12.3
32	12.7
33	13.1
34	13.5
35	13.9
36	14.3
37	14.7

MEASUREMENT CONVERSION TABLE

Length	
In 1/8ths of an inch	Length in cm
4¾	12.06
4⅞	12.38
5	12.70
5⅛	13.02
5¼	13.33
5⅜	13.65
5½	13.97
5⅝	14.29
5¾	14.61
5⅞	14.93
6	15.24
6⅛	15.56
6¼	15.87
6⅜	16.19
6½	16.51
6⅝	16.83
6¾	17.14
6⅞	17.46
7	17.78
7⅛	18.10
7¼	18.41
7⅜	18.73
7½	19.05
7⅝	19.37

Ring Gauge/Diameter	
In 1/64ths of an inch	Diameter in mm
38	15.1
39	15.5
40	15.9
41	16.3
42	16.7
43	17.1
44	17.5
45	17.9
46	18.3
47	18.7
48	19.1
49	19.5
50	19.8
51	20.2
52	20.6
53	21.0
54	21.4
55	21.8
56	22.2
57	22.6
58	23.0
59	23.4
60	23.8
61	24.2

MEASUREMENT CONVERSION TABLE

Length	
In 1/8ths of an inch	Length in cm
7¾	19.68
7⅞	20.00
8	20.32
8⅛	20.64
8¼	20.96
8⅜	21.28
8½	21.59
8⅝	21.92
8¾	22.23
8⅞	22.55
9	22.86
9⅛	23.18
9¼	23.50
9⅜	23.82
9½	24.13
9⅝	24.45
9¾	24.76
9⅞	25.08
10	25.40
11	27.94
12	30.48
13	33.02
14	35.56
15	38.10

Ring Gauge/Diameter	
In 1/64ths of an inch	Diameter in mm
62	24.6
63	25.0
64	25.4
65	25.8
66	26.2

9.
REFERENCES

For more information about cigars, these books make excellent and fun reading:

Andriote, John-Manuel, Falk, Andrew E. and Perez, B. Henry. *The Art of Fine Cigars*. New York: Bulfinch Press, 1996.

Bati, Anwer and Chase, Simon. *The Cigar Companion, A Connoisseur's Guide*. 2nd edition. Philadelphia: Running Press, 1995.

Conrad III, Barnaby. *The Cigar*. San Francisco: Chronicle Books, 1996.

Davidoff, Zino with Gilles Lambert. *The Connoisseur's Book of the Cigar*. Trans. Harold Chester. New York: McGraw-Hill Book Co., 1984.

Dunhill, Alfred. *The Gentle Art of Smoking*. London: Max Reinhardt, Ltd., 1978.

Edmark, Tomima. *Cigar Chic: A Women's Perspective*. Arlington: Summit Publishing Group, 1995.

Garmirian, Paul B.K. *The Gourmet Guide to Cigars*. 3rd edition. McLean: Cedar Publications, 1994.

Hacker, Richard Carleton. *The Ultimate Cigar Book*. 2nd edition. Beverly Hills: Autumngold Publishing, 1996.

REFERENCES

Jeffers, H. Paul and Gordon, Kevin. *The Good Cigar*.
New York: Lyons & Burford, 1996.

Kasper, Rhona. *A Woman's Guide to Cigar Smoking*.
Lawrenceville: Cigar Savvy, Inc., 1996.

LeRoy, Bernard and Szafran, Maurice. *The Illustrated History of Cigars*. Trans. Lexus Translations Ltd. London: Harold Starke Publishers, Ltd., 1993.

Resnick, Jane, *International Connoisseur's Guide to Cigars*.
New York: Black Dog & Leventhal Publishers. 1996.

Rudman, Theo. *Rudman's Complete Pocket Guide to Cigars 1996*. Cape Town: Good Living Publishing, 1996.

Scott, Dale. *How to Select and Enjoy Premium Cigars . . . and Save Money!* 2nd edition. San Diego: Coast Creative Services, 1995.

Sherman, Joel with Robert Ivry. *Nat Sherman's A Passion for Cigars*. Kansas City: Andrews and McMeel, 1996.

Stucklin, Mark. *The Cigar Handbook*. London: Quintet Publishing Limited, 1997.

10.
RING GAUGE GUIDE

Use this handy guide to size up the girth of your cigars. The illustrated ring sizes correspond to the following shapes:

Ring: 32-34   Slim and Small Panatelas
       35-39   Panatelas and Long Panatelas
       40-44   Coronas and Lonsdales
       45-47   Coronas Extra and Grand Coronas
       48-50+   Robustos, Toros, Churchills, Double Coronas and Giants.

RING GAUGE GUIDE

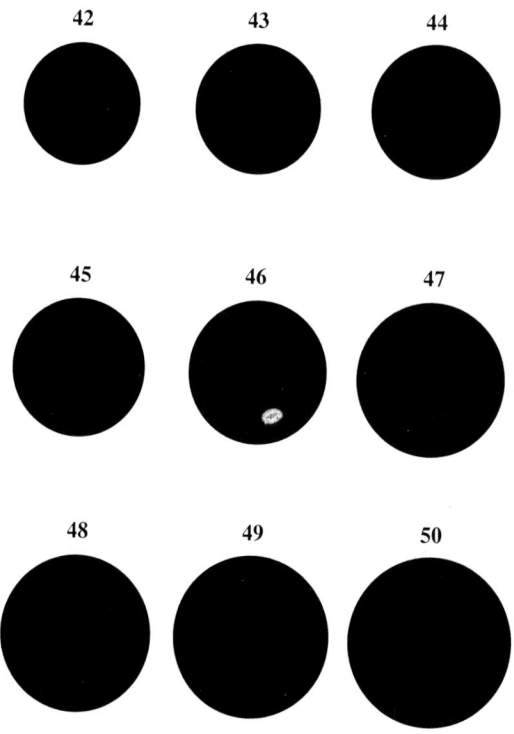

ADDENDUM

Information for these six additional brands of *handmade* cigars was received too late for inclusion in section 3 (index) or section 4 (brand listings). But here they are! Enjoy!

EMPEROR OF THE WORLD
Handmade in Santiago, Dominican Republic.

Wrapper: Ecuador, Indonesia   Binder: Dom. Rep.   Filler: Dom. Rep.

Shape	Name	Lgth	Ring	Wrapper
	Classico series:			
Long Corona	Corona	6	43	CC
Robusto	Robusto	5	50	CC
Double Corona	Churchill	7	50	CC
Giant	Presidente	8	50	CC
	Samatra series, made with medium filler:			
Robusto	Robusto	5	50	CM
Double Corona	Churchill	7½	50	CM

This brand debuted in 1997, offering two distinctive tastes: a mild-to-medium-bodied experience with the Classico line (thanks to its Connecticut-seed wrapper grown in Ecuador) or a medium-to-heavy strength in the Samatra line, which features a Sumatra-grown wrapper. In either case, you can find the Emperor always at rest in all-cedar boxes of 25 (Classico) or bundles of 25 (Samatra).

ESTELA
Handmade in Santiago, Dominican Republic.

Wrapper: Indonesia   Binder: Dom. Rep.   Filler: Dom. Rep.

Shape	Name	Lgth	Ring	Wrapper
Toro	Don Aurelio	6½	50	CM
Churchill	Churchill	6⅞	47	CM
Lonsdale	Lonsdale	6½	42	CM

ADDENDUM

Robusto	Robusto	5½	50	CM

This is a new cigar for 1997, offering a medium-bodied taste under the supervision of brand founder Don Aurelio Estela. It is presented in individual cellophane sleeves inside all-cedar boxes of 25.

HAVANA REPUBLIC
Handmade in Jalapa, Nicaragua.
Wrapper: Ecuador or Indonesia

Binder: Nicaragua   *Filler: Dominican Republic, Nicaragua*

Shape	Name	Lgth	Ring	Wrapper
	Epicurean series:			
Corona	Royal Corona	5½	44	CC
Robusto	Robusto	5	50	CC
Lonsdale	Numero Uno	7	44	CC
Grand Corona	Medal D'Ore	6	46	CC
Giant	Series A	8½	52	CC
Double Corona	Lusitania	7½	52	CC
Churchill	Churchill D'Churchill	7	48	CC
Torpedo	Torpedo	6	52	CC
	Grand Havana series:			
Corona	Royal Corona	5½	44	CM
Robusto	Robusto	5	50	CM
Lonsdale	Numero Uno	7	44	CM
Grand Corona	Medal D'Ore	6	46	CM
Giant	Series A	8½	52	CM
Double Corona	Lusitania	7½	52	CM
Churchill	Churchill D'Churchill	7	48	CM
Torpedo	Torpedo	6	52	CM

ADDENDUM

These two lines, both introduced in 1997, offer a choice of mild or medium-bodied flavor. The Epicurean series features a Connecticut-seed wrapper grown in Ecuador and is quite mild. The Grand Havana series has an Indonesian-grown wrapper and is medium in strength. Both are offered in wood boxes of 25.

J. MANISCALCO COLLECTION
Handmade in Honduras.

Wrapper: Ecuador   *Binder: Honduras*
Filler: Brazil, Dominican Republic, Honduras, Nicaragua

Shape	Name	Lgth	Ring	Wrapper
Pyramid	Pyramid	7	54	CC
Long Corona	Cazadore	6¼	44	CC
Churchill	Churchill	7	48	CC
Robusto	Rothchild	4½	50	CC
Toro	Double Corona	6	50	CC
Giant	Supreme	8½	52	CC

This brand was introduced in 1997 and offers a mild-to-medium-bodied flavor. It is value-priced and is presented in boxes of 25.

SANTIAGO DEL SOL
Handmade in Santiago, Dominican Republic.

Wrapper: Indonesia   *Binder: Dom. Rep.*   *Filler: Dom. Rep.*

Shape	Name	Lgth	Ring	Wrapper
	Premium series:			
Long Corona	Corona	6	44	CM
Robusto	Robusto	5	50	CM
Grand Corona	Gran Corona	6½	46	CM
Churchill	Churchill	7	48	CM
	Flavored series:			
Slim Panatela	Panatela Fina	6	30	CM

Slim Panatela	Panatela	5	34	CM
Panatela	Coronella	5½	38	CM
Petit Corona	Petite Corona	5	42	CM

Introduced in 1996, you can take your choice of a mild-to-medium-bodied line, or a series of flavored shapes featuring the taste of Amaretto, chocolate and vanilla. Either way, you can them in boxes or bundles of 25; the Premium series is also offered in boxes of 10.

VENCEDORA NADAL Y NADAL
Handmade in the Dominican Republic.

Wrapper: Ecuador   *Binder: Dom. Rep.*   *Filler: Dom. Rep.*

Shape	Name	Lgth	Ring	Wrapper
Corona	Coronas	5¾	43	CM
Robusto	Robustos	4¾	52	CM
Toro	Toro	6	50	CM
Long Panatela	Panetelas	7	36	CM
Lonsdale	Numero 1	7	43	CM
Churchill	Churchills	7	48	CM
Double Corona	Presidente	7½	52	CM

Here is a new brand for 1997, offering a medium-bodied flavor and a unique aroma, thanks to its Ecuadorian-grown, Sumatra-seed wrapper. It is presented in boxes of 25.

CRESTON
PRESTIGE CUVEE
ULTRA-PREMIUM HONDURAN CIGARS

Our Hand Made Top Of The line Cigars Are Rated Ultra-Premium

FILLER
100% Selected Honduran from Cuban Seed.

BINDER
100% Honduran from Cuban Seed.

WRAPPER
100% Ecuadorian Shade wrapper form Connecticut seed. The finest & most supple and aromatic wrapper available.

PRE-EMINENT PROVIDER OF PRIVATE LABEL PREMIUM CIGARS & WINES TO THE HOSPITALITY INDUSTRY.

Ultra-Premium Dominican Cigars Also Available

For the selected Tobacconist in your area - **E-Mail- crestoncig@aol.com**

Consider this an Open and Shut Case for Precision.

The first of its kind, the Zino Davidoff w[...]
design and self-sharpening stainless-steel b[...] $12.95 ise,
no imitation cutter even comes close.

Zino
Exclusively by Davidoff